FORMS MANUAL TO ACCOMPANY CASES AND MATERIALS ON
OIL AND GAS LAW
Fifth Edition

By

John S. Lowe
George W. Hutchison Professor of Energy Law
Southern Methodist University

Owen L. Anderson
Eugene Kuntz Chair in Oil, Gas and Natural Resources
The University of Oklahoma

Ernest E. Smith
Rex G. Baker Centennial Chair
in Natural Resources Law
The University of Texas

David E. Pierce
Professor of Law
Washburn University

AMERICAN CASEBOOK SERIES®

THOMSON
™
WEST

D1468423

Mat #40635191

American Casebook Series and West Group are trademarks registered in the U.S. Patent and Trademark Office.

COPYRIGHT © 1986, 1993 WEST PUBLISHING CO.
© West, a Thomson business, 1998, 2004
© 2008 Thomson/West
        610 Opperman Drive
        St. Paul, MN 55123
        1–800–313–9378

Printed in the United States of America

ISBN: 978–0–314–18399–6

 TEXT IS PRINTED ON 10% POST CONSUMER RECYCLED PAPER

Introduction, Disclaimer, and Copyright Warning

This manual is intended as a supplement text for use in teaching a course in oil and gas law. The forms and clauses in this manual are intended for instructional purposes only, may not be suitable for use in actual oil and gas transactions, and should not be used without advice of legal counsel. Furthermore, some forms are protected by copyright law.

When possible, the formatting of the forms in the manual has been altered to provide larger fonts (Times New Roman 12). To partially offset the larger fonts, other formatting changes—particularly paragraph format—have been made. Where possible, line numbers have been added to the forms to facilitate classroom use. In addition, spaces for land descriptions, acknowledgment provisions, and lines for dates and signatures have been omitted on many of the forms.

The authors would like to especially thank Dawn Tomlins, Faculty Support Office Manager, and Peter Kraemer, IT Support Specialist, for their assistance in formatting and preparing the manuscript for camera-ready publication.

TABLE OF CONTENTS

Chapter 1

HISTORY, ACCUMULATION, AND OWNERSHIP

Gas Storage Agreements
§ 284 FERC GAS TARIFF
Original Volume No. 1A
of
HONEOYE STORAGE CORPORATION
Filed With The
Federal Energy Regulatory Commission

Communication Concerning This Tariff
Should Be Addressed To:
* * *

PRELIMINARY STATEMENT

Honeoye Storage Corporation ("HSC" or "Seller"), a New York corporation, owns and operates a natural gas storage facility and related compression equipment and pipelines, collectively known as the Honeoye Storage Project, located in Ontario County, New York. The Honeoye Storage Project receives, injects, stores, withdraws and delivers natural gas transported in interstate commerce subject to jurisdiction of the Federal Energy Regulatory Commission. The facilities are connected to Tennessee Gas Pipeline Company ("Tennessee").

This Original Volume No. 1A of the FERC Gas Tariff of HSC contains the Rates and Charges, Rate Schedules, Forms of Service Agreements and the General Terms and Conditions applicable to open-access storage service and other services performed by HSC.
* * *

SITE MAP

* * *

CURRENTLY EFFECTIVE RATES

FIRM STORAGE SERVICE (FSS)*

RATE

1. Reservation Rate

Deliverability Rate	Reservation Market Negotiable	Based/
Capacity Rate	Reservation Market Negotiable	Based/

2. Injection/Withdrawal Rates

Injection Rate	Market Negotiable	Based/
Overrun Rate	Injection Market Negotiable	Based/
Withdrawal Rate	Market	Based/

| Overrun
Rate | Negotiable
Withdrawal Market
Negotiable | Based/ |

INTERRUPTIBLE STORAGE SERVICE (ISS)*

	RATE
Injection Rate	Market Based/Negotiable
Withdrawal Rate	Market Based/Negotiable
Inventory Rate	Market Based/Negotiable
Late Withdrawal Rate	Market Based/Negotiable
Overrun Storage Commodity Rate	Market Based/Negotiable

FUEL USE - FSS AND ISS

UNITS	RATE
Dth	Fixed

Seller will bill Customer each month for gas lost or unaccounted for in Seller's operations at the rate of one percent (1.0%) of the gas injected on Customer's behalf in the preceding month and at the rate of one percent (1.0%) of the gas withdrawn on Customer's behalf in the preceding month.

*All quantities of natural gas are measured in dekatherms (Dth).

1. AVAILABILITY

This Rate Schedule is available to any person, corporation, partnership or any other party (hereinafter referred to as "Customer") other than Local Distribution Companies that are considered to be affiliates of Seller under Part 161 of the Federal Energy Regulatory Commission's regulations, for the purchase of natural gas storage service from Honeoye Storage Corporation (hereinafter referred to a "Seller"), when:

(a) Seller has determined that it has sufficient available and uncommitted storage capacity or capacity released in accordance with Section 7 of this Rate Schedule FSS to perform service requested by Customer (Seller is not required to provide any requested services for which it does not have such available capacity); and

(b) Customer and Seller have executed a Service Agreement under this Rate Schedule.

2. APPLICABILITY AND CHARACTER OF SERVICE

This Rate Schedule shall apply to all Storage Service which is rendered by Seller for Customer pursuant to an executed Agreement under this Rate Schedule.

Storage Service rendered by Seller under this Rate Schedule shall consist of:

(a) The receipt of Gas on behalf of Customer at the Point of Injection/Withdrawal at daily quantities up to the Maximum Daily Injection Quantity plus Seller's Injection Use;

(b) The Storage of Gas in quantities not to exceed the Maximum Storage Quantity, except as provided for in Section 6 of this Rate Schedule; and

(c) The Tender of Gas for redelivery by Seller to or for the account of Customer at the Point of Injection/Withdrawal at a quantity not to exceed Customer's Working Storage Gas at daily quantities up to the Maximum Daily Withdrawal Quantity reduced by Seller's Withdrawal Use.

(d) The receipt of Gas on behalf of Customer and redelivery of Gas for the account of Customer in excess of its applicable Maximum Daily Injection Quantity and Maximum Daily Withdrawal Quantity on a reasonable efforts basis by Seller when required to allow Customer full utilization of its Maximum Storage Quantity.

(e) Firm Storage Service under this Rate Schedule shall be firm up to the Maximum Storage Quantity and firm up to the Maximum Daily Withdrawal Quantity and Maximum Daily Injection Quantity on any day. The Maximum Storage Quantity, the Maximum Daily Injection Quantity and the Maximum Daily Withdrawal Quantity shall be specified in the executed Agreement. Notwithstanding the foregoing, Seller will use reasonable efforts to permit Customer to inject or withdraw Gas pursuant to Section 6 of this Rate Schedule FSS.

3. GENERAL TERMS AND CONDITIONS

The General Terms and Conditions of this Original Volume No. 1A FERC Gas Tariff are applicable to this Rate Schedule, and are specifically incorporated herein by reference.

4. RATES AND CHARGES

The amounts which shall be paid by Customer to Seller for each Month during the period of service hereunder shall include the sum of the charges due under the subsections of this Section 4 and charges under Section 5 that are applicable to Customer for such Month, computed by use of the applicable rates set forth in this Rate Schedule FSS and in the Customer's Agreement which are effective during such Month or portions thereof. Customer's Agreement will reflect the rates agreed to by Seller and Customer and may or may not include each of the billing components set forth below.

Each total rate computed for a specific transaction shall be rounded to the nearest one tenth of a cent. If, at initiation of service, service is provided for only a portion of a Month, any applicable reservation fee shall be prorated for the number of days that service is provided.

4.1 Unless otherwise agreed to by Seller and Customer, the following Storage Charges will apply:

(a) Reservation Charges:

(1) The FSS Deliverability Reservation Rate shall be paid each Month for each Dekatherm of Customer's Maximum Daily Withdrawal Quantity;

(2) The FSS Capacity Reservation Rate shall be paid each Month for each Dekatherm of Customer's Maximum Storage Quantity.

(3) If, due to Seller's scheduling of necessary maintenance of pipeline facilities, events of force majeure, necessary maintenance of compression facilities and/or facility outages for tie-in of new facilities, Seller fails to Tender for redelivery or accept for storage injection at the Point of Injection/Withdrawal for the account of Customer during any Day the quantity of Gas that Customer has so nominated for such day up to a Customer's Maximum Daily Injection Quantity or Maximum Daily Withdrawal Quantity, as applicable, then subject to the provisions of the General Terms and Conditions, Customer's Monthly bill shall be reduced by an amount equal to the product of

(a):

$$((A \times B)/C + D)/E$$

Where:

A = Deliverability Reservation Rate

B = Maximum Daily Withdrawal Quantity

C = Maximum Storage Quantity

D = Capacity Reservation Rate

E = The Number of Days in the Month

and

(b): the difference between such quantity of Gas nominated for injection or withdrawal up to the Maximum Daily Injection Quantity or Maximum Daily Withdrawal Quantity, as applicable, and the applicable quantity actually injected or withdrawn by Seller for the account of Customer during such Day. Such reductions of Seller's Reservation Charges shall not be applicable if Seller and Customer agree upon and place into effect the makeup of such injection deficiency or withdrawal deficiency under mutually acceptable terms.

(b) Commodity Charge:

The Injection/Withdrawal Rate shall be paid each Month for each Dekatherm of Gas which is delivered by Seller to or for the account of Customer and each Dekatherm of Gas Customer delivers or causes to be delivered at the Point of Injection/Withdrawal during the Month. Such charges shall be applicable both on injection and on withdrawal.

4.2 Overrun Service Charge: An Overrun Service Charge shall be paid for each Dekatherm of service provided on behalf of Customer pursuant to Section 6 of this Rate Schedule. As set forth in the Customer's Agreement, the Overrun Service Charge shall consist of the Overrun Injection Rate for each Dekatherm of Gas the Customer delivers or causes to be delivered at the Point of Injection/Withdrawal in excess of the Customer's Maximum Daily Injection Quantity and the

5

1 Overrun Withdrawal Rate for each Dekatherm of Gas which is delivered to or for the account of
2 the Customer in excess of the Customer's Maximum Daily Withdrawal Quantity.
3 4.3 Seller's Fuel Use Charge: Seller will bill Customer each month for gas lost or unaccounted
4 for in Seller's operations at the rate of (1) one percent (1.0%) of the gas injected on Customer's
5 behalf in the preceding month, and (2) one percent (1.0%) of the gas withdrawn on Customer's
6 behalf in the preceding month.
7 4.4 Regulatory Fees and Charges. Customer shall reimburse Seller for all fees and charges, as
8 required by the Commission or any other regulatory body, that are related to service provided
9 under this Rate Schedule, including, but not limited to, the Commission's Annual Charge
10 Adjustment (ACA).

5. ADDITIONAL CHARGES

12 5.1 Commission and Other Regulatory Fees: Customer shall reimburse Seller for its allocable
13 share of all fees required by the Commission or any other regulatory body which are related to
14 service provided under this Rate Schedule including, but not limited to, filing, reporting and
15 application fees.
16 5.2 Other Charges: Customer shall pay its allocable share of any other charges applicable to
17 service hereunder authorized by the Commission or any other successor agency having
18 jurisdiction.

6. STORAGE OVERRUN SERVICE

20 6.1 Customer may request Seller to inject quantities greater than Customer's Maximum Daily
21 Injection Quantity. If Seller has injection capacity available, Seller shall inject such quantities
22 and Customer shall pay Seller for such injections at the Overrun Injection Charge set forth in
23 Customer's Agreement.
24 6.2 Customer may request Seller to withdraw quantities greater than Customer's Maximum
25 Daily Withdrawal Quantity. If Seller has withdrawal capacity available, Seller shall withdraw
26 such quantities and Customer shall pay Seller for such withdrawals at the Overrun Withdrawal
27 Charge set forth in Customer's Agreement.
28 6.3 Customer may not inject gas into storage pursuant to this rate schedule if the quantity of
29 Customer's Gas in storage equals Customer's Maximum Storage Capacity.
30 6.4 Customer may not withdraw gas from storage in excess of the quantity of Customer's Gas
31 which is actually in storage at any given time.
32 6.5 Seller shall have the right to interrupt all or part of the overrun quantity nominated as the
33 operation of its storage facilities may require pursuant to Section 4 of the General Terms and
34 Conditions of this FERC Gas Tariff in which event Seller shall notify Customer.

7. CAPACITY RELEASE

36 Any Customer or Replacement Customer under Rate Schedule FSS shall be entitled to release all
37 or a portion of its capacity to Seller for resale. Additionally, Customer may release its capacity
38 on a volumetric basis.
39 Any Customer or Replacement Customer releasing capacity will be designated a Releasing
40 Customer. Any person purchasing released capacity shall be designated a Replacement
41 Customer. Any Customer that wants to release capacity must notify Seller that it wants to release
42 capacity and the terms and conditions of such release.
43 7.1(a) PROCEDURE FOR MAKING OFFER TO RELEASE. Releasing Customer shall
44 communicate its release notice through Seller's EBB. The Releasing Customer shall submit the

following information, objectively stated and applicable to all potential Customers on a non-discriminatory basis:

(1) the pricing provisions of the offer to release; any maximum/minimum rates specified by the Releasing Customer should include all demand charges as a total number or as stated separately;

(2) the specific quantity to be released expressed in Dth; the basis for the released quantity should be per day for storage injection/withdrawal, and a per-release quantity for storage capacity and total release period quantity (Releasing Customer in establishing terms for capacity release shall not be limited to the service categories set forth in Section 9; Releasing Customer may release quantities up to the Maximum Daily Injection Quantity, Maximum Daily Withdrawal Quantity, and Maximum Storage Quantity set forth in Releasing Customer's Agreement);

(3) the duration of release or term including any right to recall;

(4) the terms and conditions of any recall rights. Recalls shall not be for less than one (1) Day. Releasing Customer may only recall such released capacity that Replacement Customer has not filled. If releasing customer wishes to recall capacity, it must provide notice to Seller no later than 9:00 a.m. Central Clock Time on the nomination Day. The Releasing Customer shall make such recall by notifying Seller in writing of such recall and by submitting a nomination change to Seller, pursuant to Section 4.1 of the General Terms and conditions of this FERC Gas Tariff;

(5) whether the release is on a permanent or temporary basis;

(6) the length of time the offer to release should be posted for bidding on Seller's EBB;

(7) whether there are any reput rights;

(8) any other conditions or contingencies of the offer to release, including nondiscriminatory provisions necessary to evaluate bids; and the tie breaking criteria, provided, however, that bid evaluations will be limited to highest rate, net revenue and present value;

(9) the legal name of the Replacement Customer that is designated in any Pre-Arranged Release ("Designated Replacement Customer");

(10) the bid evaluation method; and

(11) for volumetric releases, any minimum volumetric commitment.

(b) Seller's creditworthiness standards shall apply to any potential Replacement Customer and Releasing Customer shall not establish its own creditworthiness standards for bidding customer.

(c) Releasing Customer may withdraw any existing offer to release, if a valid and acceptable bid has not been received. Releasing Customer shall be subject to the provisions of Section 8 of this Rate Schedule prior to the commencement of the Agreement with Replacement Customer. Releasing Customer may withdraw its offer to release any time prior to the close of the bidding period via the EBB or Electronic Delivery Mechanism ("EDM") as approved by the Commission, where unanticipated circumstances justify such withdrawal or when no bid has been received which meets the Releasing Customer's minimum conditions. Releasing Customer shall have the option to accept contingent bids which extend beyond the close of the bidding period. Releasing Customer cannot extend the original bid period or the pre-arranged deal Matching Period without posting a new release. Re-release of Released Capacity shall be allowed on the same terms and basis as the primary release (except for volumetric releases which may not be re-released).

(d) CAPACITY RELEASE TIMELINE. The "Capacity Release Timeline" set forth below is applicable to all parties of the Capacity Release process; however it is only applicable if: (1) all information provided by parties to the transaction is valid and Replacement Customer has been determined to be creditworthy before the capacity release bid is tendered and (2) the release contains no special terms or conditions of the release.

(i) SHORT TERM RELEASES (less than 5 months) - the following information is required at time stated on the Day before nominations are due, all listed times are Central Clock Time:

(a) Offers must tendered by 1:00 p.m.

(b) Open season ends 2:00 p.m., evaluation period begins at 2:00 p.m. during which contingency is eliminated, determination of best bid is made, and ties broken;

(c) evaluation period ends at 3:00 p.m.;

(d) match or award is communicated at 3:00 p.m.;

(e) match response by 4:00 p.m.;

(f) award posting by 5:00 p.m.;

(g) contract tendered with contact number by 6:00 p.m.; contract executed, nomination possible for next Day gas flow.

The posting of pre-arranged deals not subject to bid is due by 9:00 a.m. the day of nominations;

(ii) LONG TERM RELEASES (5 months or more) - The Capacity Release Timeline set forth above also applies to long term releases, except that offers of capacity must be posted on the EBB no later than 1:00 p.m. Central Clock Time, four (4) Business Days before capacity is awarded.

(e) COMPETITIVE BIDDING PROCEDURE. Bids may be submitted by potential Replacement Customers via the EBB during the posting period. Seller shall post the terms of each complete bid, but will not post the identity of the bidder. Posted bids will be accessible via EDM. Seller will also require all information set forth in Section 2 of the General Terms and Conditions of this FERC Gas tariff. Upon expiration of the offer, Seller shall remove such offer of release from its EBB.

Potential Replacement Customers may withdraw their posted bids at any time during the bidding period via the EBB or EDM. Bids posted by potential Replacement Customers are binding until written or electronic notice of withdrawal is received by Seller. Potential Replacement Customers cannot withdraw bids after the bidding period ends. Such potential Replacement Customers may not post another bid for the same capacity lower than their previous bid.

(f) PRE-ARRANGED RELEASE

(i) Releasing Customer shall have the right to release capacity to a Pre-Arranged Replacement Customer without posting an offer on the EBB if: (1) the Replacement Customer confirms via the EBB the terms and conditions of the Pre-Arranged Release; and (2) the release is either for a period of one year or more at the maximum rate the Releasing Customer is contractually obligated to pay and meets all other terms and conditions of the release, or the release is less than 31 Days. If Releasing Customer exercises such rights, it must notify Seller prior to the nomination of the released entitlements, and the Replacement Customer shall adhere to the contracting requirements. Seller will post the information on the EBB by 9:00 a.m. Central Clock Time the Day before the release transaction begins. The Replacement Customer shall meet any eligibility requirements under this Section 7.6.

(ii) Matching Rights. A Pre-Arranged Replacement Customer shall have the right of first refusal for a time period as negotiated by the Releasing Customer and the Pre-Arranged Replacement Customer ("Matching Period). If no Matching Period has been negotiated, the Matching Period will be deemed to be one (1) hour following the time the Pre-Arranged Replacement Customer has been notified of the winning bid. In the event a bid is received that more closely meets the criteria specified by the Releasing Customer, Seller shall provide the Pre-Arranged Replacement Customer an opportunity during the Matching Period to match or exceed the bid that more closely meets the criteria specified by the Releasing Customer. No later than 3:00 p.m. Central Clock Time of the Day prior to the Day nominations are due, the Pre-Arranged Replacement Customer shall receive notification on the EBB of the terms and conditions of the prevailing bid and shall have the Matching Period to respond via the EBB. No later than 4:00 p.m. Central Clock Time of the Day prior to the Day nominations are due, the Replacement Customer shall post on the EBB its match response. Absent a response, the capacity shall be awarded to the prevailing bidder no later than 5:00 p.m. Central Clock Time on the Day prior to the Day nominations are due.

(g) Released Capacity will be awarded no later than 5:00 p.m. Central Clock Time of the Day prior to nomination Day. The capacity will be awarded to the Replacement Customer which otherwise satisfies the requirements of this FERC Gas Tariff and also meets all of the conditions of the offer to release capacity. In the case of multiple bid winners, the highest ranking bid will receive the entire maximum amount of capacity bid. The next highest ranking bidder will receive the remainder of the offered capacity provided that the amount remaining is above the bidder's minimum acceptable quantity. Any remaining capacity will be awarded to the next highest bidder under the same provisions as above. This process will repeat until either all of the offered capacity is awarded or the remaining capacity falls below either the Releasing Customer's minimum quantity or all of the remaining bidder's acceptable quantities. Seller shall not be required to contract with parties submitting bids that do not meet the conditions of the offer to release capacity, however, subject to approval of Releasing Customer, Seller may accept bids offering a price or term less than that set forth in the release. Bids will be evaluated by the criteria provided by the Releasing Customer. If no criteria are provided by the Releasing Customer, bids will be accepted in the order of priority based upon the highest economic value offered by the competing bids as defined in Section 10 of the General Terms and Conditions of this FERC Gas Tariff. The ultimate awarding of the capacity will be posted subsequently on Seller's EBB by 5:00 p.m. Central Clock Time on the Day before nomination Day, unless bidder was a contingent bidder and the contingency did not occur. Seller will tender a numbered Agreement to the winning bidder by 10:00 a.m. Central Clock Time on the day nominations are due, and the winning bidder shall enter into an Agreement with Seller pursuant to Section 7.2. Seller is required to meet the Capacity Release Timeline for processing capacity releases only if the Releasing Customer's best bid methodology is either: (1) highest rate, (2) highest net revenue, or (3) greatest net present value. In all cases, Replacement Customers will be subject to all requirements of this Tariff. Storage Service to the Replacement Customer may commence, prior to the posting of the winning bid, if capacity has been awarded and a contract executed.

(h) Recall Reput Rights

(i) A Releasing Customer cannot in any way modify recall rights as specified by a previous Releasing Customer, but may specify its own recall rights, subject to any recall rights specified by a previous Releasing Customer. A potential Replacement Customer is responsible for obtaining from the Releasing Customer with whom it is negotiating for released capacity any information concerning recall rights specified by a previous Releasing Customer. A Releasing Customer specifying recall conditions shall be the only party that can exercise and administer such recall rights. In the event of any conflict, the instructions and communications of the Releasing Customer specifying the recall conditions shall govern. Released capacity can only be recalled for full pipeline days and the party recalling the capacity shall be subject to Seller's nomination procedures in accordance with Section 4 of the General Terms and Conditions of this FERC Gas Tariff. If the release specifies that the Releasing Customer has reput rights and the recall ends prior to the end of the release term at the end of the recall period, capacity shall revert back to the Replacement Customer, if applicable, subject to Seller's nomination procedures.

(ii) Seller shall have no liability to any party in relying on the recall instructions and conditions specified by the Releasing Customer, except to the extent that such party establishes that Seller has incorrectly applied such instructions as a result of the negligent action or willful misconduct of Seller.

7.2 EXECUTION OF SERVICE AGREEMENT. Once the provisions of this Section 7 are satisfied, and as a condition precedent to receiving service pursuant to a capacity release, Replacement Customer shall execute a Service Agreement with Seller.

7.3 BILLING ADJUSTMENT. Releasing Customer shall remain fully obligated under the terms of its Service Agreement with Seller during any capacity release except for usage charges incurred by any Replacement Customer that has purchased capacity released by the Releasing Customer. Seller shall credit the invoice of Releasing Customer each Month for the charges and volumetric rates invoiced, by Seller to Replacement Customer provided, however, that such credit:

(a) shall not include any charges billed to the Replacement Customer under Section 5 of this Rate Schedule or Rate Schedule ISS, and

(b) shall be reduced by the amount of any marketing fee Seller is entitled to collect pursuant to Section 7.4 of this Rate Schedule.

If a Replacement Customer fails to pay all or any part of its charges under the Deliverability Reservation Rate and Capacity Reservation Rate which have been credited to Releasing Customer within fifteen (15) days of the due date, such unpaid amount, with applicable interest accruing from the date Replacement Customer's payment was due, will be charged to the Releasing Customer's next monthly bill and will be due and payable by Releasing Customer, unless Replacement Customer in good faith shall dispute the billed charges in accordance with the provisions set forth in Section 8.2 of the General Terms and Conditions of this FERC Gas Tariff. If such failure to pay continues for thirty (30) days after payment is due, and the Replacement Customer has not disputed billings in accordance with Section 8.2 of the General Terms and Conditions of this FERC Gas Tariff, then Seller may, in addition to any other remedies it may have hereunder, terminate its Agreement with the Replacement Customer, and the Replacement Customer shall be deemed to have consented to abandonment of service under the Agreement. If the Agreement with the Replacement Customer is so terminated and service abandoned, the capacity will revert to the Releasing Customer, and will be governed by the terms and conditions of its existing Agreement with Seller. If Releasing Customer pays delinquent amounts owed by Replacement Customer and Seller subsequently receives payment from Replacement Customer of some or all of such amounts, Seller will credit the amounts received from the Replacement Customer in Seller's next monthly bill to the Releasing Customer.

7.4 MARKETING FEE. Seller may negotiate with Releasing Customer to market all or a portion of the released capacity to potential Replacement Customers who, as a result of such marketing activity, bid for such capacity during the competitive bidding procedure. If Seller, contracts with a Replacement Customer found by Seller, Seller, with the agreement of Releasing Customer, shall be entitled to a marketing fee which will be negotiated between Seller and Releasing

Customer. The basis and method of assessing such fee shall be subject to negotiations between Seller and Releasing Customer. Each Replacement Customer found by Seller, pursuant to Seller's agreement with Releasing Customer concerning a marketing fee, shall submit with its bid a statement attesting to Seller's marketing efforts, which efforts shall consist of more than the simple posting of a notice on Seller's EBB, in connection with such Replacement Customer's decision to purchase released capacity. Such statement shall constitute conclusive evidence of Seller's proactive marketing effort entitling Seller to a marketing fee.

7.5 TERM. Any release under this Section 7 for service under Rate Schedule FSS shall be for a maximum term not longer than the remaining term of the underlying FSS Service Agreement. If capacity is released and the Replacement Customer takes service under Rate Schedule FSS, the minimum term shall be one month.

7.6 RELEASING CUSTOMER'S INJECTION/WITHDRAWAL CHARGES. Releasing Customers' pricing provisions of any offer to release pursuant to Section 7.1 and 7.8 hereof must include Releasing customers' currently effective Injection Rate, Withdrawal Rate, Overrun Injection Rate and Overrun Withdrawal Rate and Fuel Use/Loss Charge.

7.7 VOLUMETRIC RELEASE. Customer may release capacity on a volumetric basis, provided that:

(a) all requirements and conditions of the release be specified by the Releasing Customer in the release notice, including any minimum storage volume requirement, and

(b) the requirements and conditions specified by Releasing Customer must meet all of the requirements and conditions of Seller's Original Volume No. 1A FERC Gas Tariff and,

(c) Seller will bill the Volumetric Rate for Release for volumes actually injected into storage by Seller for the account of Replacement Customer or the minim urn storage volume requirement if actual injected volumes are less than the required minimum storage requirement and,

(d) Replacement Customer shall remain fully responsible for all Usage Charges incurred.

7.8 RELEASES OF 31 DAYS OR LESS OR AT THE MAXIMUM RATE THE RELEASING CUSTOMER IS OBLIGATED TO PAY. Capacity Releases and Pre-Arranged Releases for a period of 31 Days or less, or for any period of one year or more at the maximum rates the Releasing Customer is obligated to pay, need not comply with Section 7.1. Notices of releases shall be posted on Seller's EBB within forty-eight (48) hours after release transaction commences.

7.9 Prior to the commencement of service pursuant to any release request, the Replacement Customer shall submit to Seller, in accordance with Section 2.1 of the General Terms and Conditions of this FERC Gas Tariff, a check in an amount equal to the lesser of $10,000 or the aggregate reservation charges which would be due for two months of released service.

7.9 RELEASES OF 31 DAYS OR LESS AT LESS THE MAXIMUM RATE THE RELEASING CUSTOMER IS OBLIGATED TO PAY. Releases of a period of 31 Days or less at less than the maximum rate the Releasing Customer is obligated to pay may not roll-over, extend, or continue in any way without complying with Section 7.1, and may not be re-released to the same Replacement Customer without being posted for competitive bids until twenty eight (28) Days after the first release period has ended, unless the capacity is being re-released for a term of one year or more at maximum rates.

       8. GAS IN STORAGE AFTER TERMINATION OF AGREEMENT.

If a Customer which has not renewed its FSS Agreement for the next Storage Contract Year fails to withdraw all of its Working Storage Gas by the end of the Storage Contract Year in which such FSS Agreement terminates, then, at Seller's option, and upon forty-eight (48) hours notice, Customer will be deemed to have agreed to the Storage of such remaining Working Storage Gas under Rate Schedule ISS and shall pay a Late Withdrawal Charge of one dollar per Dth per day, or at Seller's option, Seller may retain any remaining quantities of Working Storage Gas free and clear of any adverse claims; provided however, that Seller will notify Customer in writing prior to November 1 of the Contract Year in which the term of its FSS Agreement will expire of the quantity of Storage Volumes being held by Seller for Customer's account and the above options available to Seller in the event Customer fails to withdraw all of its Working Storage Gas by the end of said Storage Year. In the event Seller is unable to withdraw Customer's properly nominated volumes, up to the Customer's Maximum Daily Withdrawal Quantity, on any Day during the last Storage Year prior to the expiration of the Agreement, then the term of the Agreement shall be extended by the number of days Seller is unable to tender quantities of Gas for redelivery.

In the event that a Customer does not renew its FSS agreement and fails to withdraw all of its Working Storage Gas as provided above then the Customer will incur a Late Withdrawal Charge or forfeit remaining quantities of Working Storage Gas. In that event, Seller will credit the Late Withdrawal Charge or the value of the gas retained by Seller to its existing customers in the manner set forth in Section 8.4 of the general terms and conditions of the tariff.

9. DEFINITIONS

9.1 The term "Maximum Daily Injection Quantity" shall mean: the quantity set forth in the Customer's FSS Service Agreement.

9.2 The term "Maximum Daily Withdrawal Quantity" shall mean the quantity set forth in the Customer's FSS Service Agreement:

9.3 The term "Permanent Capacity Release" shall mean the release of capacity by the Customer for the remaining term of its Agreement with Seller. If (i) the terms and conditions of the new Service Agreement with the Replacement Customer are at least as favorable to Seller as the Agreement between Seller and the Releasing Customer, and (ii) the Replacement Customer is at least as creditworthy as the Releasing Customer. Releasing Customer shall not be liable for any charges incurred by the Replacement Customer after the Permanent Capacity Release. Replacement Customer shall be subject to all terms of this FERC Gas Tariff.

9.4 The term "Storage Contract Year" shall mean the period from April 1 of a calendar year through March 31 of the following calendar year.

RATE SCHEDULE ISS
INTERRUPTIBLE STORAGE SERVICE

1. AVAILABILITY

This Rate Schedule is available to any person, corporation, partnership or any other party (hereinafter referred to as "Customer"), other than Local Distribution Companies that are considered to be affiliates of Seller under Part 161 of the Federal Energy Regulatory Commission's regulations for the purchase of natural gas storage service from Honeoye Storage Corporation (hereinafter referred to as "Seller"), when Seller has determined on a non-discriminatory basis, that capacity is available to provide service under the Rate Schedule and when Customer and Seller have executed a Service Agreement under this Rate Schedule.

2. APPLICABILITY AND CHARACTER OF SERVICE

This Rate Schedule shall apply to all Interruptible Storage Service which is rendered by Seller for Customer pursuant to an executed Agreement under this Rate Schedule

(a) Storage Service rendered by Seller under this Rate Schedule shall consist of:

(i) The receipt of Gas on behalf of Customer at the Point of Injection/Withdrawal up to the Maximum Storage Quantity or Customer's Storage Overrun Quantity plus Seller's injection Fuel Use at daily quantities up to the Maximum Daily Injection Quantity plus Seller's Injection Use;

(ii) The Storage of Gas in quantities not to exceed the Maximum Storage Quantity or Customer's Storage Overrun Quantity; and

(iii) The Tender of Gas to or for the account of Customer at the Point of Injection/Withdrawal at a quantity not to exceed Customer's Working Storage Gas or Storage Overrun Quantity reduced by Seller's withdrawal Fuel Use at daily quantities up to the Maximum Daily Withdrawal Quantity reduced by Seller's Withdrawal Use.

(b) Storage Service rendered under this Rate Schedule shall be interruptible, and shall be available only when capacity is not being used for injection, storage and withdrawal of higher priority services. Such interruptible service shall be offered in accordance with the provisions established in the General Terms and Conditions of this Tariff. Seller may, if storage capacity is required by Customers having a higher priority, require Customer to withdraw quantities held in storage by Seller for or on behalf of Customer under Rate Schedule ISS within three (3) days of the date notice is provided to Customer by Seller. Customer indemnifies and holds Seller harmless from and against any and all losses, damages or expenses of any kind which Customer may suffer or be liable for a result of any reduction or interruption in service pursuant to this Rate Schedule.

3. GENERAL TERMS AND CONDITIONS

The General Terms and Conditions of this Original Volume No. 1A FERC Gas Tariff are applicable to this Rate Schedule and are specifically incorporated herein by reference.

4. RATES AND CHARGES

The amounts which shall be paid by Customer to Seller for each Month during the period of service hereunder shall include the sum of the amounts due under the subsections of this Section 4 and charges under Section 5 that are applicable to Customer for such Month, computed by use of the applicable rates set forth in the Customer's Agreement which are effective during such Month or portions thereof. Each total rate computed for a specific transaction shall be rounded to the nearest one tenth of a cent.

4.1 Interruptible Storage Service (ISS) Injection Rate: An injection rate shall be paid for each Dekatherm which is injected for or on behalf of Customer during the month.

4.2 Interruptible Storage Service (ISS) Withdrawal Rate: A withdrawal rate shall be paid for each Dekatherm which is withdrawn for or on behalf of Customer during the month.

4. 3 Interruptible Storage Service (ISS) Inventory Rate: An Inventory Rate shall be paid for each Dekatherm of the Average Monthly Storage Volume which is stored for or on behalf of Customer during the Month.

4.4 Seller's Fuel Use Charge: Seller will bill Customer each month for gas lost or unaccounted for in Seller's operations at the rate of one percent (1%) of (i) the gas injected on Customer's behalf in the preceding month and (ii) one percent (1.0%) of the gas withdrawn on Customer's behalf in the preceding month.

4.5 Regulatory Fees and Charges. Customer shall reimburse Seller for all fees and charges, as required by the Commission or any other regulatory body, that are related to service provided under this rate schedule, including, but not limited to, the Commission's Annual Charge Adjustment (ACA).

4.6 Overrun Storage Commodity Rate: An Overrun Storage Commodity Rate shall be paid for each Dekatherm of service provided on behalf of Customer pursuant to Section 6 of this Rate Schedule. As set forth in the Customer's Agreement, the Overrun Storage Commodity Rate shall consist of the Storage Commodity Rate for each Dekatherm of the Daily Storage Volume which is stored for or on behalf of Customer during the Month greater than the Customer's Maximum Storage Quantity.

5. ADDITIONAL CHARGES

5.1 Commission and other Regulatory Fees: Customer shall reimburse Seller for all fees required by the Commission or any other regulatory body which are related to service provided under this Rate Schedule including, but not limited to, filing, reporting and application fees.

5.2 Other Charges: Customer shall pay any other charges applicable to service hereunder authorized by the Commission or any successor agency having jurisdiction.

6. STORAGE OVERRUN SERVICE

Customer may request Seller to provide storage service under this Rate Schedule for quantities of gas in excess of Customer's Maximum Storage Quantity. Service requested under this section must be nominated separately as "overrun" by Customer. Seller may provide such Overrun Service on an interruptible basis if, in Seller's judgment, it can provide the service without adverse effect on Seller's operations or on Seller's ability to meet higher priority obligations. Customer shall pay the Overrun Storage Commodity Rate pursuant to Section 4.6 of this Rate Schedule ISS for such overrun storage service.

7. LATE WITHDRAWAL RATE

If Customer fails to withdraw all Working Storage Gas quantities held in storage by Seller for or on behalf of Customer by the end of the applicable withdrawal period set forth in Section 2 above, or by the date the ISS Agreement terminates, then Customer shall pay a Late Withdrawal Charge of $1/Dekatherm/day for all customers' gas remaining in inventory or, at Seller's sole option, Seller may retain such remaining quantities of Working Storage Gas free and clear of any adverse claims, unless such failure to withdraw was due to Seller's inability to withdraw the quantities nominated by Customer, in which event such applicable withdrawal period shall be extended by the number of days Seller is unable to tender quantities of Gas for redelivery.

8.TERM

1   The Interruptible agreement shall have a mutually agreeable term which shall not be less than
2   one day.

9. DEFINITIONS

4   9.1 The term "Maximum Daily Injection Quantity" shall be mutually agreed upon and set forth in
5   Customer's ISS Service Agreement.
6   9.2 The term "Maximum Daily Withdrawal Quantity" shall be mutually agreed upon and set
7   forth in Customer's ISS Service Agreement.
8   9.3 The term "Storage Overrun Quantity" shall be mutually agreed upon and set forth in
9   Customer's ISS Service Agreement.
10   Sheet Nos. 28 through 68.

GENERAL TERMS AND CONDITIONS
1. DEFINITIONS

1.1 The term "Agreement" shall mean the Service Agreement executed by the Customer and Seller and any exhibits, attachments and/or amendments thereto.

1.2 The term "Average Monthly Storage Volume" shall mean the sum of Customer's Working Storage Gas at the end of each Day of the Month divided by number of Days in the Month.

1.3 The term "BTU" shall mean one (1) British thermal unit, the amount of heat required to raise the temperature of one (1) pound of water one degree (1) Fahrenheit at sixty degrees (60) Fahrenheit. (BTU is measured on a dry basis at 14.73 psia.)

1.4 The term "Business Day" shall mean every Monday, Tuesday, Wednesday, Thursday or Friday, excluding all federal banking holidays for transactions in the United States.

1.5 The term "Clock Time" shall mean Central Standard Time except for that period when daylight savings is in effect. During this period, Clock Time shall mean Central Daylight Time.

1.6 The term "Commission" and "FERC" shall mean the Federal Energy Regulatory Commission or any successor regulatory authority having jurisdiction.

1.7 The term "Contract Term" shall mean the period beginning on the date storage service under a storage agreement commences and ending on the day the term of the agreement terminates.

1.8 The term " Customer" shall mean any person, corporation, partnership or any other party that executes a valid Service Agreement with Honeoye Storage Corporation for the Storage of Gas, or other services under the terms and conditions of Seller's FERC Gas Tariff Original Volume No.2.

1.9 The term "Day" shall mean a period of consecutive hours, beginning at 9:00 a.m. Clock Time and ending on the following 9:00 a.m. Clock Time as adjusted, when appropriate, for changes from Standard to Daylight Savings Time and vice versa.

1.10 The term "Dekatherm" (Dth) shall mean the quantity of heat energy which is equivalent to one (1) million (1,000,000) BTU; thus the term MDth shall mean one (1) thousand Dth.

1.11 The determination of quantities deemed to be delivered for purposes of use of the term "Each Dekatherm Of Gas Which Is Delivered" shall be the pro rata allocation of the quantities of Gas nominated, after adjustments for Seller's Use and pursuant to Section 4.3 hereof, for injection into storage or for withdrawal from storage.

1.12 The term "EBB" shall mean Honeoye Storage Corporation's electronic bulletin board.

1.13 The term "EDM" shall mean Honeoye Storage Corporation's electronic data mail.

1.14 The term "Equivalent Quantities" shall mean a quantity of Gas containing an amount of Dths equal to the amount of Dths received by Seller for the account of Customer at the Point of Injection /Withdrawal reduced by the Dths removed for Seller's Injection and/or Withdrawal Fuel Use as attributable to the Storage of Customer's Gas.

1.15 The term "Gas" means natural gas in its natural state, produced from wells, including casinghead gas produced with crude oil, natural gas from gas wells, and residue gas resulting from processing both casinghead gas and gas well gas.

1.16 "Gas Industry Standards Board" or "GISB" shall mean that accredited organization established to set standards for certain natural gas industry business practices and procedures.

1.17 "GISB Standards" shall mean the standardized business practices, procedures and criteria which have been adopted and published by the Gas Industry Standards Board and which have been adopted by reference by the Commission.

1.18 The term "Interruptible" shall mean that the storage service is subject to interruption at any time by Seller. An interruptible Customer may be required to withdraw gas from interruptible Storage Capacity or return gas received as Storage Overrun Quantity, should such capacity or gas be required by a firm customer or by another interruptible Customer willing to pay a higher interruptible Storage rate.

1.19 The term "Maximum Storage Quantity" shall mean the greatest number of Dths that Seller is obligated to store on behalf of Customer on any Day excluding Storage Overrun Quantity, if applicable.

1.20 The term "Month" shall mean the period beginning at 9:00 a.m. Central Time on the first Day of a calendar month and ending at the same hour on the first Day of the next succeeding calendar month.

1.21 The term "OBA" shall mean a contract between two parties which specifies the procedures to manage operating variances at an interconnect.

1.22 The term "OFO" shall mean an order issued to deviate conditions which threaten or could threaten the safe operations or system integrity of Seller's system or to maintain operations required to provide efficient and reliable firm service. Whenever Seller experiences these conditions, any pertinent order will be referred to as an OFO.

1.23 The term "Point of Injection/Withdrawal" shall mean the point of interconnection between Seller's Honeoye Storage Project and third party transporter's facilities located in Ontario County, New York or such other location as may be designated by Seller and its Customer.

1.24 The term "Psig" shall mean pounds per square inch gauge.

1.25 The term "Releasing Customer" shall mean any Customer who has agreed to release capacity under Section 7 of Rate Schedule FSS.

1.26 The term "Replacement Customer" shall mean any Customer to which capacity is released under Section 7 of Rate Schedule FSS.

1.27 The term "Seller" shall mean Honeoye Storage Corporation.

1.28 The term "Seller's Injection Use" shall mean the applicable percentage stated in Seller's Rate Schedules multiplied by the quantity of Gas injected into storage for the account of Customer.

1.29 The term "Seller's Use" shall mean the sum of the Seller's Injection Use and the Seller's Withdrawal Use.

1.30 The term "Seller's Withdrawal Use" shall mean the applicable percentage stated in Seller's Rate Schedules multiplied by the quantity of Gas withdrawn from storage for the account of Customer.

1.31 The term "Service Day" shall mean the Day during which Customer receives storage service pursuant to a nomination in accordance with Section 4 of the General Terms and Conditions of this FERC Gas Tariff.

1.32 The term "Storage" or "Storage Service" shall mean the storage of Gas.

1.33 The term "Storage Overrun Quantity" shall mean the number of Dths that Seller provides and stores on behalf of Customer on any day in excess of Customer's Maximum Storage Quantity pursuant to Rate Schedule ISS.

1.34 The terms "Tender," "Tender Gas" and "Tender of Gas" shall mean that the delivering party is able and willing, and offers, to deliver gas to or for the account of the receiving party at the Point of Injection/Withdrawal.

1.35 The term "Transporter" means the Customer's Transporter designated to deliver gas to the Point of Injection/Withdrawal or Customer's Transporter designated to receive gas from the Point of Injection/Withdrawal.

1.36 The term "Usage Charges" shall mean all variable charges associated with the injection/withdrawal of Gas by Seller.

1.37 The term "Wire Transfer" shall mean payments made/effected by wire transfer (Fedwire, CHIPS, or Book Entry), or Automated Clearinghouse, or any other recognized electronic or automated payment mechanism that is agreed upon by Seller in the future.

1.38 The term "Working Storage Gas" shall mean the quantity of Gas held in storage at any given time, by Seller, for the account of Customer.

2. REQUESTS FOR SERVICE

2.1 Requests. To seek to qualify for Storage Service pursuant to Rate Schedules FSS or ISS a potential Customer shall submit a request for such service in writing to the Seller. Seller, as applicable, shall evaluate and respond to such requests as soon as is reasonably possible, and shall begin service as soon as is reasonably possible, after execution of the Agreement or upon the date set forth in the Agreement. Such a request shall be considered acceptable only if the information specified in Section 2.2 below is provided in writing, but Seller may waive all or any portion of such information in individual instances, when the information is already in possession of Seller. Buyer on a non-discriminatory basis may require that each request for service under Rate Schedule FSS by or on behalf of each proposed Customer be accompanied by refundable earnest money in the form of either wire transfer or a check payable to Honeoye Storage Company in the amount of the lesser of ten thousand ($10,000) or the aggregate reservation charges which would be due for two months of service for such requested service, which amount shall be applied, until fully used, against the first amounts due by Customer to Seller as reservation charges; provided, however, that if the request is not accepted by Seller or if service is not otherwise offered, Seller will refund earnest money thirty (30) days after notice to potential Customer that Seller is not accepting offer.

Requests for service shall be sent to:

Honeoye Storage Company

4511 Egypt Road

Canandaigua, NY 14424

Attention: Vice President of Operations

2.2 Form of Request for Storage Service

(a) Each request, to be considered as an acceptable and valid request, must furnish the portion of the information set forth below. The "Honeoye Storage Corporation Service Request Form" is set forth in this FERC Gas Tariff and may be changed from time to time and reissued by Seller.

(b) Requestor's Identification: Name, address, representative, telephone number of party requesting service.

(c) Customer's Identification: (Note: The "Customer" is the party which proposes to execute the Agreement).

(1) Name, address, representative and telephone number of Customer;

(2) A statement of whether Customer is a local distribution company, an intrastate pipeline, an interstate pipeline, marketer/broker, producer, end user or other type of entity (which shall be described);

(3) A statement of whether Customer is acting for itself or as agent for someone else (who must be named); and

(4) A statement of whether Customer is a Replacement Customer and the contract number under which Replacement Customer is requesting service.

(d) Type of Service(s) Category(ies) Requested: Specify which Volume No. 1A Rate Schedule service is desired.

(e) Quantity: (stated in Dekatherms)

(1) Maximum Storage Quantity, which shall not be less than 25,000 Dekatherms, except for volumes under Section 7 of Rate Schedule FSS.

(2) Maximum Daily Withdrawal Quantity, which shall be determined in accordance with Seller's Rate Schedules.

(3) Storage Overrun Quantity, if applicable.

(f) Term of Service:

(1) Date service is requested to commence.

(2) Date service is requested to terminate (Agreements for FSS shall terminate on March 31 and shall be for a minimum length of twelve months, unless otherwise agreed to by Seller).

(g) Point of Injection

(h) Point of Withdrawal

(i) Certified Statement: A certified statement by the Customer that it has, or will have, by the time of execution of an Agreement with Seller, title to, or the legal right to cause to be delivered to Seller, for Storage, the Gas which is to be delivered to Seller and facilities or contractual rights which will cause such Gas to be delivered to and received from Seller.

(j) Credit Evaluation:

(1) Customer should submit year end audited financial statements of Customer (if available) together with the latest quarterly report. If audited financial statements are not available, Customer should furnish unaudited financial statements. In such event, Seller may request additional credit information.

(2) Customer's Affiliates, including parent, subsidiaries of parent and of such subsidiaries, and subsidiaries of Customer.

(3) In the event proceedings have been commenced by or against such Customer for any relief under any bankruptcy or insolvency law, or any law relating to the relief of debtors, readjustment of indebtedness, reorganization, arrangement, composition or extension; or in the event a decree or order of a court having jurisdiction in the premises for the appointment of a receiver or liquidator or trustee or assignee in bankruptcy or insolvency of such Customer, or of a substantial part of its property, or for the winding up or liquidation of its affairs, shall have been entered, or any substantial part of the property of such Customer shall be sequestered or attached and shall not be returned to the possession of such Customer or released from such attachment within thirty (30) Days thereafter; or in the event such Customer shall make a general assignment for the benefit of creditors or shall admit in writing its inability to pay its debts generally as they become due, or in the event that any financial institution has refused to extend credit to Customer within the past year or any rating agency has downgraded the Customer s securities or issued publicly available material giving an opinion that Customer's credit quality or standing has declined, Customer shall be required to fully disclose any and all actions regarding the above described proceedings against Customer or related parties defined in (3) above, in its request for service.

(4) Any other information requested by Seller pursuant to Section 11.5 of the General Terms and Conditions.

2.3 Subsequent Information

(a) If any of the events or actions described in 2.2j(3) above, shall be initiated or imposed during the term of service hereunder, Customer shall provide notification thereof to Seller within two (2) Business Days of any such initiated or imposed event or action. Customer shall also provide, forthwith, such additional Customer credit information as may be reasonably required by Seller, at any time during the term of service hereunder, to determine Customer's creditworthiness.

(b) After receipt of a request for Storage Service hereunder, Seller may require that Customer furnish additional information as a prerequisite to Seller offering to execute an Agreement with Customer. Such information may include proof of Customer's title to the Gas involved and/or its legal right to cause the Gas to be delivered to Seller for Storage and of Customer's contractual and/or physical ability to cause such Gas to be delivered to and received from Seller.

2.4 Request Validity. Customer's request for Storage Service shall be considered null and void if Seller had tendered an Agreement for execution to Customer and Customer fails to execute the Agreement for FSS within thirty (30) Days thereafter or within five (5) days thereafter for ISS. Seller will not execute an Agreement under these Rate Schedules FSS or ISS for which it does not have sufficient available capacity. If sufficient capacity is available, but Customer does not desire to or cannot begin Storage Service within thirty (30) days after the date the request is made pursuant to Section 2.2 of these General Terms and Conditions of this Tariff, or such other period as the parties may agree to in writing, then such request shall be considered null and void.

2.5 Customer's Performance. If a Customer that has executed an Agreement for service under Rate Schedule ISS, on the date service is to commence, fails to nominate, pursuant to Section 4.1 of these General Terms and Conditions, a quantity of Gas for Storage, or, having nominated a quantity of Gas and Seller having scheduled the quantity for Storage, pursuant to Section 4.3 of these General Terms and Conditions, fails to Tender such Gas for Storage on the date it is scheduled, the Seller may terminate Customer's Agreement and the Customer's request for service shall be deemed null and void; provided, however, that the Customer's Agreement shall not be terminated nor shall the Customer's request for service be deemed null and void if the Customer's failure to nominate or tender is caused by an event of force majeure on Seller's system, as defined in Section 9 of these General Terms and Conditions.

2.6 Complaints: In the event that a Customer or potential Customer has a complaint relative to service under this FERC Tariff, the Customer shall:

(a) Provide a description of the complaint, verbally or in writing, including the identification of the storage request (if applicable), and communicate it to:

Honeoye Storage Company
Attn: Vice President of Operations
4511 Egypt Road
Canandaigua, NY 14424
Phone: (585) 229-5161

(b) Within forty-eight (48) hours, or two Business Days, whichever is later from the day of receipt of a complaint, Seller will respond initially to the complaint and Seller shall respond in writing within thirty (30) days advising Customer or potential Customer of the disposition of the complaint.

2.7 Information: Any person may request information on the pricing or other terms of Storage Service and/or capacity availability by contacting Seller at the following:

      Honeoye Storage Company
      Attn: Vice President of Operations
      4511 Egypt Road
      Canandaigua, NY 14424
      (585) 229-5161

2.8 Relationship with Marketing Affiliates:

(a) Seller is affiliated with corporations that engage in marketing or brokering as defined in Part 161 of the Federal Energy Regulatory Commission's regulations. The names and addresses of those marketing affiliates are listed on Seller's EBB. Seller does not share employees or officers with any of its marketing affiliates. Certain directors of Seller are officers or employees of marketing affiliates. These individuals are listed on Seller's EBB.

(b) Seller does not share facilities with any marketing affiliate.

2.9 Electronic Bulletin Board:

(a) Seller will maintain an interactive EBB for the use of its Customers and prospective Customers interested in obtaining information about available storage service. Seller's EBB will provide all information required to be posted thereon under regulations of the FERC, together with such additional information as Seller considers appropriate.

(b) Information posted on Seller's EBB will include the following:

(1) Firm and interruptible storage service currently available from Seller.

(2) Injection and withdrawal capacity currently available.

(3) Firm and recallable capacity released by FSS Customers or Replacement Customers pursuant to Section 4 of the General Terms and Conditions and currently available for allocation.

(4) Firm capacity which is currently available or will become available by reason of the termination of an FSS service agreement

(5) Currently operative offers to purchase capacity tendered pursuant to Section 4 of the General Terms and Conditions.

(c) With respect to each category of information posted on Seller's EBB, Seller shall also include relevant information pertaining to the minimum rate at which capacity is offered to Customers and Replacement Customers, any restrictions, terms, or condition imposed on the reallocation of released capacity by the Customer or Replacement Customer releasing that capacity (including the name of any Replacement Customer designated by the Releasing Customer), and the terms and conditions upon which offers to purchase capacity have been tendered.

3. STORAGE SERVICE

3.1 Treatment of Gas. Seller may subject or permit the subjection of Gas stored hereunder to compression, cooling, cleaning, or other processes to such extent as may be required in Seller's sole opinion.

4. NOMINATIONS, SCHEDULING AND ALLOCATION

4.1

(a) Nominations. Seller will accept nominations for storage service as provided herein. A valid nomination is a data set which contains, at a minimum, the mandatory data elements included in the GISB Standards related to nominations, and any additional Seller-required data elements. All Standard and Intra-Day Nominations for service shall be made via Seller's EDM as approved by the Commission. Seller will accept nominations via mail, fax, courier service or personal delivery. Seller will support the receipt of nominations, via the methods listed above, and EDM in a manner designed to enable Customers to submit nominations seven days a week, twenty-four hours a day.

Each nomination shall indicate whether it is being submitted as a Standard or Intra-Day Nomination. The standard quantity for nominations, for confirmations and scheduling, in the United States, shall be dekatherms per Day.

Customer may use an agent to provide all or a portion of its nomination data, provided that Seller is so advised in advance in writing. A Customer that uses an agent for such nomination purposes shall hold Seller harmless for all actions or inactions of its agent.

(b) Standard Nominations. A "Standard Nomination" is a nomination for storage service for any Day. The Standard Nomination shall include a begin date and end date, which must be within the term of the Customer's service agreement. Each day within a date range nomination is considered an original nomination. Subsequent nominations for one or more days within the range supersede only the days specified. The days outside the range of the subsequent nominations are unaffected. Nominations have a prospective effect only. Seller shall process all new or revised nominations that are submitted by 11:30 a.m. Central Clock Time and received by 11:45 a.m. Central Clock Time on the Day before the applicable Service Day. Customer may nominate zero (0) for a daily quantity, but in the event Customer nominates a daily quantity in excess of zero (0), such daily quantity shall not be less than five-hundred (500) Dth. Customer shall also inform Seller in advance of each Month of the desired order of priority of injections and withdrawals under each Agreement and Seller may rely thereon (or in the absence of such information, upon Seller's judgment) if allocation under such Agreement is required.

(c) Standard Nominations Timetable. The timetable for a Standard Nomination shall be as follows on the Day before a Service Day, Central Clock Time

11:30 a.m. for nominations leaving control of Customer;

11:45 a.m. for receipt of nominations by Seller;

12:00 noon for Seller to send quick response for nominations submitted via EDM;

3:30 p.m. for Seller to receive completed confirmations from connected parties;

4:30 p.m. for Customer and Operators to receive scheduled volume information from Seller.

In addition, at the end of each Day, Seller shall provide Customer the final scheduled quantities for the just completed Day. Seller will send an end of Day Scheduled Quantity document. Recipients of the end of Day Scheduled Quantity document can waive the obligation of Seller to send the Scheduled Quantity document.

Seller, as receiver of nominations, initiates the confirmation process. The party receiving a request for confirmation or an unsolicited confirmation response may waive the obligation of the Seller to send. The sending party will adhere to nomination, confirmation and scheduling deadlines. The party receiving the communication shall have the right to waive any deadline, on a non-discriminatory basis.

(d) Other Nominations. Seller may, at its option, accept nominations which are not timely as described above. In that event, Seller shall not be required to comply with the Standard Nomination timeline set out above.

4.2

(a) Intra-Day Nominations. Any nomination submitted after the standard nomination deadline, by eligible Customers, shall be an "Intra-Day Nomination." An Intra-Day Nomination shall be effective for one (1) Day only. Intra-Day Nominations may be used to nominate new injection or withdrawals. The nomination process set forth in Section 4. l(a) shall apply to the Intra-Day nominations. An Intra-Day quantity shall be a revised daily quantity.

(1) Timetables for Intra-Day Nominations shall be as follows:

(a) Evening Nomination Cycle: shall be as follows on the Day before a Service Day, Central Clock Time:

6:00 p.m. for nominations leaving control of Customer;

6:15 p.m. for receipt of nominations by Seller,

6:30 p.m. for Seller to send quick response for nominations submitted via EDM;

9:00 p.m. for Seller to receive completed confirmations from connected parties;

10:00 p.m. for Customer and operators to receive scheduled volume information from Seller and to provide scheduled quantities to bumped parties (notice to bumped parties).

9:00 a.m. for flow of gas.

(b) Intra-Day 1 Nomination Cycle: shall be as follows on the Service Day, Central Clock Time:

10:00 a.m. for nominations leaving control of Customer;

10:15 a.m. for receipt of nominations by Seller;

10:30 a.m. for Seller to send quick response for nominations submitted via EDM;

1:00 p.m. for Seller to receive completed confirmations from connected parties;

2:00 p.m. for Customer and operators to receive scheduled volume information from Seller and to provide scheduled quantities to bumped parties (notice to bumped parties);

5:00 p.m. for flow of gas.

(c) Intra-Day 2 Nomination Cycle: shall be as follows on the Service Day, Central Clock Time:

5:00 p.m. for nominations leaving control of Customer;

5:15 p.m. for receipt of nominations by Seller;

5:30 p.m. for Seller to send quick response for nominations submitted via EDM;

8:00 p.m. for Seller to receive completed confirmations from connected parties;

9:00 p.m. for Customer and operators to receive scheduled volume information from Seller and to provide notice to bumped parties;

9:00 p.m. for flow of gas.

(d) For purposes of Section 4.2(a)(1)(a), (b), and (c) "provide" shall mean, for transmittals pursuant to GISB Standards 1 .4, receipt at the designated site, and for purposes of other forms of transmittal, it shall mean send or post.

An Intra-Day Nomination is subject to operator's confirmations and Seller's operating conditions. If operator confirmation is not received, the Intra-Day Nomination will not be accepted. Seller will not accept a reduced Intra-Day Nomination for any quantity deemed already delivered based on an average hourly flow.

(b) For purposes of providing notice of any nomination changes to a Customer and/or Customer's agent, Seller shall contact either party by telephone or other instant communication device. With respect to changes initiated by Seller, if a Customer so elects, such Customer may provide a telephone number and Seller will contact Customer at such phone number to alert Customer that a change has been made; provided that where an interruptible Customer's nomination is bumped by a firm Customer's Intra-Day Nomination, Seller shall provide notice of such bump to the interruptible Customer in the same manner that Seller uses to notify Customers of OFOs. .

4.3 Scheduling of Storage and Allocation of Service. For each Day, Seller will schedule injections and withdrawals of Gas, on the basis of: storage nominations made by Customers (which Seller is hereby authorized to rely upon in its scheduling); storage capacity available on

Seller's system in light of nominations and requests; and overall operating conditions from time to time. If, on any Day, Seller determines that the capacity of its system is insufficient to serve all storage nominations scheduled for such Day, or to accept the quantities of Gas tendered, capacity shall be allocated to provide service in the following order:

(a) In scheduling deliveries of firm storage nominations on any Day when capacity is constrained, Seller shall allocate service on a pro rata basis to those Customers nominating volumes on such Day based upon such Customer's contracted daily injection or withdrawal volumes as a fraction of the contracted daily injection or withdrawal volumes of all Customers nominating volumes on such Day.

(b) In scheduling nominated quantities for interruptible Storage Services hereunder, after providing for firm Storage Service, Seller shall utilize the priorities established in Section 10 of these General Terms and Conditions, provided however that no interruptible Customer shall have a claim of priority on any Day to quantities in excess of the lesser of (1) such interruptible Customer's Maximum Daily Injection Quantity or Maximum Daily Withdrawal Quantity as applicable or (2) such interruptible Customer's nomination.

4.4 Delivery of Gas. Seller, subject to the other provisions hereof, shall make daily delivery, to the extent practicable, of Equivalent Quantities of Gas at the Point of Injection/Withdrawal in accordance with Seller's scheduled deliveries.

4.5 Hourly Variation. Injections and withdrawals shall be made at uniform hourly rates to the extent practicable.

4.6 Limitation on obligation. Should the quantities of Gas received from Customer(s) by Seller at the Point of Injection/Withdrawal exceed the Maximum Daily Injection Quantity plus the Seller's Injection Use, Seller shall notify Customer(s) of such fact within a reasonable time after such becomes known, and Customer(s) shall seek to reduce deliveries to Seller forthwith. In the event any such excess delivery would jeopardize the safety of Seller's operations and/or its ability to meet its contract commitments to others, such decisions being solely within the judgment and discretion of Seller, Seller shall have the right to refuse to accept, without any liability to Customer, or any other person, all or such part of said excess delivery as Seller deems necessary, and shall notify Customer accordingly.

4.7 Reduction in Maximum Storage Quantity. In the event that Customer nominates or utilizes less than 50% of its Maximum Storage Quantity under Rate Schedule ISS for a period of one (1) year, Seller may reduce Customer's Maximum Storage Quantity to 125% of the average utilization during such year, which new Maximum Storage Quantity, as applicable, shall be effective on the first Day of the Month following the Month in which Seller gives Customer notice of such reduction.

5. PRESSURE AT POINT OF INJECTION/ WITHDRAWAL

5.1 Pressure at Point of Injection/Withdrawal. Unless otherwise agreed to by the parties as set forth in the Service Agreement, Customer shall cause the Gas to be delivered at the Point of Injection/Withdrawal at a pressure sufficient to allow the Gas to enter Seller's system at the varying pressures that may exist in such system from time to time; provided, however, that such pressure of the Gas delivered or caused to be delivered by Customer shall not exceed the Maximum Allowable Operating Pressure ("MAOP") which Seller specifies for the Point of Injection/Withdrawal. In the event the MAOP of Seller's system, at the Point of Injection/Withdrawal hereunder, is from time to time increased or decreased, then the MAOP of the Gas delivered or caused to be delivered by Customer to Seller at the Point of

1 Injection/Withdrawal shall be correspondingly increased or decreased upon notification by Seller
2 to Customer.
3 Unless otherwise agreed to by the parties as set forth in the Service Agreement, Seller shall
4 Tender the Gas to or for the account of Customer at the Point of Injection/Withdrawal hereunder
5 at such pressure as may be necessary to deliver the natural gas at the prevailing line pressure of
6 Transporter provided that Seller shall not be obligated to deliver gas at pressure in excess of 750
7 pounds per square inch gauge.

8 ## 6. MEASUREMENT AND MEASUREMENT EQUIPMENT

9 6.1 Unit of Volume:
10 (a) The unit of volume for measurement hereunder shall be one thousand cubic foot of gas at a
11 temperature of sixty degrees (60) Fahrenheit and an absolute pressure of fourteen and seventy-
12 three hundredths pounds per square inch, dry, (14.73 psia) having an average Total Heating
13 Value per Cubic Foot of one thousand (1,000) Btus.
14 (b) The Total Heating Value per Cubic Foot of the gas delivered and redelivered hereunder shall
15 be determined by a recording calorimeter of standard manufacture or other method mutually
16 acceptable to both Seller and Transporter, on Customer's behalf, and installed so that it may
17 properly record the gross heat content of the gas at the Point of Injection/Withdrawal. Where a
18 calorimeter is used, the arithmetical average of the hourly gross heat content recording each day
19 shall be deemed to be the heat content of the gas for that day. Such Calorimeter shall be checked
20 at least once each month to assure its proper operation and accuracy. An appropriate certified gas
21 sample of known heat content shall be used to check the calorimeter accuracy.
22 6.2 Computations of volume from Meter Readings and Registrations: The volume of gas
23 delivered or redelivered hereunder shall be determined in the manner specified in AGA Gas
24 Measurement Committee report No. 3 ("AGA report No. 3") published in 1978, as such
25 publication may be revised from time to time, or of other reports and publications which are
26 mutually acceptable to Seller and Transporter, on Customer's behalf.
27 6.3 Flowing Temperature: The flowing temperature of gas delivered and redelivered hereunder
28 shall be determined by means of a standard recording thermometer or other instrument of
29 standard manufacture accepted in the industry. The flowing temperature used in determining the
30 flowing temperature factor for each meter chart shall be the arithmetical average of the
31 temperature shown by the recording instrument during the period of time when gas is passing
32 through the meter.
33 6.4 Specific Gravity: The specific gravity of the gas delivered and redelivered hereunder shall be
34 determined by a recording specific gravity instrument of standard manufacture or other method
35 mutually acceptable to Seller and Transporter, on Customer's behalf, and installed so that it may
36 properly record the specific gravity of the gas at the point of delivery. The arithmetical average
37 of the hourly specific gravity recording each day shall be deemed to be the specific gravity of the
38 gas for that day. Such instrument shall be checked by the use of an Edwards Balance, or by any
39 other method, at intervals mutually agreed to by Seller and Transporter, on Customer's behalf.
40 6.5 Supercompressibility: Adjustment for the effect of supercompressibility for gas delivered and
41 redelivered hereunder shall be made according to the provisions of AGA Report NX-19 as such
42 publication may be revised from time to time, or of other reports and publications which are
43 mutually acceptable to Seller and Transporter, on Customer's behalf, for the average conditions
44 of pressure, flowing temperature and specific gravity at which the gas was measured during the
45 period under consideration and with the proportionate values of carbon dioxide and nitrogen in

the gas delivered and redelivered included in the computation of the applicable supercompressibility factors. Customer shall cause Transporter to exercise due diligence in obtaining initial carbon dioxide and nitrogen fraction values and to obtain subsequent value of these components quarterly or at other intervals mutually agreeable to Seller and Transporter, on Customer's behalf.

6.6 Assumed Atmospheric Pressure: The average absolute atmospheric (barometric) pressure shall be assumed to be fourteen and four-tenths pounds per square inch (14.4 psia) irrespective of actual elevation or location of the point of delivery above sea level or variations in actual barometric pressure from time to time.

6.7 Measuring Equipment: Unless otherwise agreed among Customer, Transporter, and Seller, the gas which Customer delivers or causes Transporter to deliver to Seller for storage hereunder and which Seller redelivers to Transporter for the account of Customer shall be measured by measuring equipment which Customer shall cause Transporter to own, install and operate at the Point of Injection/Withdrawal. Customer shall cause the measuring equipment to be of one-way flow design and of a type and kind generally accepted by the natural gas industry for the measurement of natural gas in accordance with the provisions of this Article hereof at the rates of flow and pressures expected to exist at the Point of Injection/Withdrawal. When orifice meters are used, they shall be of a type specified and recommended in AGA Report No. 3 as such publication may be revised from time to time or of other reports and publications which are mutually agreeable to Seller and Transporter, on Customer's behalf, and the construction and installation shall be in accordance with the recommendations and specifications set forth in said agreed to report.

6.8 Access to Measuring Equipment, Tests and Charts: Unless otherwise agreed among Customer, Transporter, and Seller, Customer shall cause Transporter to provide Seller with access to all measuring equipment at all reasonable hours, but the reading, calibrating and adjusting hereof and the changing of charts or such other measuring equipment shall be done by Transporter on behalf of Customer. Further, Customer shall cause Transporter to provide Seller the right to be present at the time of any installing, testing, reading, cleaning, changing, repairing, inspecting, calibrating or adjusting done in connection with the measuring equipment used in determining the volumes of deliveries and redeliveries hereunder, and to provide Seller with reasonable notice thereof in order that it may be present. The records and charts from such measuring equipment shall remain the property of Transporter but Customer shall cause Transporter to provide, upon request, to Seller such records and charts, or reproductions thereof, together with calculations therefrom for inspection and verification. Original records or charts so submitted will be returned within thirty (30) days after receipt thereof. Additionally, Customer shall cause Transporter to give Seller the option to install at any time and at its own expense, such ancillary materials and equipment which will access measurement data on a real time basis and transmit such data to its operating location.

6.9 Check Measuring Equipment: Unless otherwise agreed among Customer, Transporter, and Seller, Customer shall cause Transporter to allow Seller to install, maintain and operate, at its own expense, such check measuring equipment as it shall desire at the Point of Injection/Withdrawal, and further cause Transporter to provide a suitable site therefore and allow Seller free access to and use of the site; provided that such equipment shall be so installed, maintained and operated as not to interfere with the operation or maintenance of Transporter's measuring equipment at the Point of Injection/Withdrawal. Customer or Transporter shall have free access to the check measuring equipment at all reasonable hours. The reading, calibrating and adjusting thereof and the changing of charts shall be done by Seller , but Customer or Transporter shall be given reasonable notice thereof. Customer shall cause Transporter to allow Seller to remove any of Seller's equipment at any time. It is expressly agreed that Customer or Transporter shall not be responsible or liable for the care or maintenance or for damage, unless due to the negligence of Customer and/or Transporter, to or regarding such check measuring equipment installed by or on behalf of Seller.

6.10 Failure of Measuring Equipment: Seller and Customer agree that if for any reason Transporter's measuring equipment is out of service or out of repair so that the quantity of gas delivered is not correctly indicated by the reading thereof, the gas delivered during the period such measuring equipment is out of service or out of repair shall be estimated and agreed upon on the basis of the best data available, using the first of the following methods which is feasible:

(a) by using the registration of any check meter or meters if installed and accurately registering; or

(b) by using the registration of any storage field meter(s) if installed and accurately registering; or

(c) by correcting the error if the percentage or error is ascertainable by calibration, test or mathematical calculation; or

(d) by estimating the quantity of delivery by deliveries during the preceding periods under similar conditions when the measuring equipment was registering accurately.

6.11 Reasonable care shall be exercised in the installation, maintenance and operation of the measuring equipment so as to avoid any inaccuracy in the determination of the volume of Gas injected and withdrawn. The accuracy of all measuring equipment shall be verified by operator at reasonable intervals, and if requested, in the presence of representatives of the other party, but neither Seller nor Customer shall be required to verify the accuracy of such equipment more frequently than once in any thirty (30) Day period.

If either party at any time desires a special test of any measuring equipment, it will promptly notify the other party and the parties shall then cooperate to secure a prompt verification of the accuracy of such equipment. Transportation and related expenses involved in the testing of meters shall be borne by the party incurring such expenses.

The operator, for purposes of this section, shall be the owner of the equipment referenced herein, or the agent of such owner, or such other person as the parties may agree in writing.

6.12 Correction of Measuring Equipment Errors: unless otherwise agreed among Customer, Transporter, and Seller, Seller and Customer agree that if upon any test, Transporter's measuring equipment is found to be not more than two percent (2.0%) fast or slow, previous readings of such equipment shall be considered correct in computing the deliveries of gas, but such equipment shall be adjusted properly at once to record accurately. Seller and Customer further agree that if upon any test, Transporter's measuring equipment shall be found to be inaccurate by any amount exceeding two percent (2.0%), then any previous readings of such equipment shall be corrected to zero error for any period which is known definitely or agreed upon, but if the period is not known definitely or agreed upon, such correction shall be for a period covering the last half of the time elapsed since the date of the last test.

6.13 The parties agree to preserve for a period of at least three (3) years or such longer period as may be required by public authority, all test data, charts, if any, and other similar records.

6.14 In accordance with the provisions of this Section 6 of the General Terms and Conditions, Seller will use the best information available to close its allocation of quantities for a service Month. For the purposes of this Section , 6, "close" shall mean five (5) Business Days after the applicable service Month. To the extent that adjustments are made after the date of such close, such adjustments ("Prior Period Adjustments" or PPA") shall be treated under this Section 6.14. If the PPA are due to the correction of measurement data or reallocation of volumes, such adjustments should be processed within six (6) Months of the applicable service Month. If the affected party disputes the as-adjusted quantity it is entitled to rebut the basis for the PPA, but only if it does so within three (3) Months of the processing of the as-adjusted quantity. Notwithstanding the above specified deadlines for processing/rebutting PPA, such deadlines shall not apply in the case of deliberate omission or misrepresentation or mutual mistake or fact. Parties' other statutory or contractual rights shall not be diminished by this standard.

6.15 Improvements in Gas Measuring Techniques: If, at any time during the term hereof, a new method or technique is developed with respect to gas measurement or the determination of the factors used in such gas measurement, such new method or technique may be substituted upon mutual agreement of Seller and Transporter on Customer's behalf.

7. QUALITY

7.1 Heat Content. Heat content shall mean the gross heating value per cubic foot of Gas received or delivered hereunder. Such Gas shall have a heat content not less than 967 BTU per cubic foot or more than 1100 BTU when determined on a dry basis. Seller shall have the right to waive such BTU content limits if, in Seller's sole opinion, Seller is able to accept Gas with a BTU content outside such limits without affecting Seller's operations.

For the purpose of calculating injections and withdrawals, the heat content of the Gas so determined at each such point shall be deemed to remain constant at such point until the next determination. The unit of quantity for the purpose of determining total heating value shall be one (1) cubic foot of anhydrous Gas at a temperature of sixty degrees (60) Fahrenheit and an absolute pressure of 14.73 psia, dry.

7.2 Freedom from objectionable Matter. The Gas injected and withdrawn hereunder:

(a) shall be commercially free, at prevailing pressure and temperature in Seller's equipment and facilities, from objectionable odors, dust or other solid or liquid matter which might interfere with its merchantability or cause injury to or interference with proper operation of the lines, regulators, meters and other equipment and facilities of Seller.

(b) shall not contain more than twenty (.20) grains of hydrogen sulfide per one hundred (100) cubic feet of Gas, as determined by methods prescribed in Standards of Gas Service, Circular of the National Bureau of Standards, No. 405, page 134 (1934 edition), and shall be considered free from hydrogen sulfide (H_2S) if a strip, of white filter paper, moistened with a solution containing five percent (5%) by weight of lead acetate, is not distinctly darker than a second paper freshly moistened with the same solution, after the first paper has been exposed to the Gas for one and one-half (1-1/2) minutes in an apparatus of approved form, through which the Gas is flowing at the rate of approximately five (5) cubic feet per hour, the Gas from the jet not impinging directly upon the test paper; or the H_2S content may be determined by an instrument of approved type and by approved methods agreeable to the parties;

(c) shall not contain more than twenty (20) grains of total sulfur (including the sulfur in any hydrogen sulfide and mercaptans) per one hundred (l00) cubic feet of Gas;

1 (d) shall not at any time have an oxygen content in excess of two-tenths of one percent (0.20%)
2 by volume and every reasonable effort to keep the Gas free of oxygen;
3 (e) shall not contain more than four percent (4%) by volume of a combined total of carbon
4 dioxide and nitrogen components; provided, however, that the total carbon dioxide content shall
5 not exceed three (3%) by volume.
6 (f) shall have a temperature of not more than one hundred twenty degrees (120) Fahrenheit;
7 (g) shall have been dehydrated for removal of entrained water present therein in a vapor state,
8 and in no event contain more than seven (7) pounds of entrained water per million cubic feet, at a
9 pressure base of fourteen and seventy three hundredths (14.73) pounds per square inch and a
10 temperature of sixty degrees (60) Fahrenheit as determined by dew-point apparatus approved
11 by the Bureau of Mines or such other apparatus as may be mutually agreed upon.
12 (h) shall not contain polychlorinated biphenyls.
13 In the event Transporter is granted authority by the FERC to change the quality specifications set
14 forth in its transportation tariff in a manner which materially differs from the quality
15 specifications set forth in this tariff, then Seller agrees to waive the affected quality
16 specifications of this tariff and to apply the approved quality specifications of the Transporter's
17 tariff in substitution thereof. Customer shall notify Seller, in writing, within ten (10) days of
18 approval by the FERC of any such changes to Transporters tariff.
19 7.3 Failure to Meet Specifications. Should any Gas Tendered for injection or withdrawal
20 hereunder fail at any time to conform to any of the specifications of this Article, the affected
21 party shall notify the other party of any such failure and the affected party may at its option
22 suspend all or a portion of the receipt of any such Gas, and shall be relieved of obligations
23 hereunder for the duration of such time as the Gas does not meet such specifications.
24 7.4 Notwithstanding anything herein contained to the contrary, if the gas delivered or redelivered
25 hereunder fails at any time to conform to any of the specifications of this Article, including, but
26 not limited to, failure at any time to have a Total Heating Value per Cubic Foot of at least nine
27 hundred and sixty-seven (967) Btus, the party to whom such gas is being delivered or redelivered
28 may notify the other party of such failure and may, at its option, reject further deliveries or
29 redeliveries until the condition is corrected. Customer therefore authorizes Seller to refuse to
30 accept deliveries from Transporter which do not conform to the specifications of this Article
31 unless and until said deliveries are, in Seller's sole opinion, conformed to said standard. After
32 receiving a notice hereunder, the party responsible for such failure shall immediately take all
33 necessary steps to correct the condition and, upon completion thereof, shall resume deliveries
34 and redeliveries in accordance with the terms and conditions of this Agreement. The remedies
35 herein provided are in addition to any and all other remedies to which either party may be
36 entitled.
37 7.5 Commingling. It is recognized that Gas delivered to Seller by Customer will be commingled
38 with other Gas stored hereunder by Seller. Accordingly, the Gas of Customer shall be subject to
39 such changes in heat content as may result from such commingling and Seller shall,
40 notwithstanding any other provision herein, be under no obligation to withdraw for Customer's
41 account, Gas of a heat content identical to that caused to be delivered by Customer to Seller.
42   8. BILLING AND PAYMENT:
43 8.1 Billing. On or before the ninth (9th) Business Day of each Month, Seller shall render, (for
44 purposes of this Section 8 1, "render" shall mean (a) postmarked or (b) time stamped and
45 electronically transmitted via EDM to the designated site, whichever is applicable) an invoice to

Customer setting forth the amount due for such Month under the applicable Rate Schedule(s). Seller's invoice shall be based on actuals (if available) or best available data. Quantities at points where OBA's exist shall be invoiced based on scheduled quantities. Seller may utilize estimates of the quantity of Gas received for injection from or Tendered to or for account of Customer during a Month, in place of actual quantities when actual quantities are not reasonably available; provided that adjustments shall be made in later invoices for differences between such estimated and actual quantities. Such invoice shall include credits for capacity assignment required by Section 7 of Rate Schedule FSS, if any.

When information necessary for invoicing purposes is in the control of Customer, Customer shall furnish such information to Seller on or before the third (3rd) Day of the Month.

Both Seller and Customer have the right to examine at reasonable times, books, records and charts of the other to the extent necessary to verify the accuracy of any invoice, charge or computation made under or pursuant to any of the provisions hereof.

8.2 Payment. Customer shall pay any invoice, on or before the tenth (10th) Day after the date of the invoice. Payments by Customer to Seller shall be made in the form of Wire Transfer directed to a bank account designated by Seller, unless otherwise agreed to by the parties. Customer shall identify the invoice number specified by Seller to which the payment relates. If Customer submits payment different from the invoiced amount, remittance detail must be provided with payment.

If rendition of an invoice by Seller is delayed after the ninth (9th) Business Day of the Month, then the time of payment shall be extended accordingly unless Customer is responsible for such delay. Should Customer fail to pay all of the amount of any invoice as herein provided when such amount is due, interest on the unpaid portion of the invoice shall accrue from the due date until the date of payment at a rate of interest equal to the prime rate plus two percent (2%) charged by FleetBoston, or any such successor bank as may result from a purchase or merger of FleetBoston, to responsible commercial and industrial borrowers, but which in no event shall be higher than the maximum rate permitted by applicable law. If such failure to pay continues, then following thirty (30) Days prior written notice from Seller of its intent to abandon service under the Agreement, Customer shall be deemed to have consented to such abandonment of service, unless within the thirty (30) Day period Customer pays to Seller the entire balance due with interest, and Seller, in addition to any other remedy it may have hereunder, may suspend further injection or withdrawal of Gas for Customer and may enter into Agreements to provide service to others using Customer's capacity and deliverability; provided, however, that if Customer in good faith shall dispute the amount of any such invoice or part thereof and shall pay to Seller such amounts not in dispute, accompanied by documentation supporting the basis for the dispute and, at any time thereafter within thirty (30) Days of a demand made by Seller, shall furnish a good and sufficient surety bond in an amount and with surety satisfactory to Seller or other assurance acceptable to Seller, guaranteeing payment to Seller of the amount ultimately found due upon such invoice after a final determination which may be reached either by agreement or judgment of the courts, as may be the case, then Seller shall not be entitled to suspend further service or to terminate or abandon service under the Agreement unless and until default be made in the conditions of such bond. The foregoing shall be in addition to any other remedies Seller may have, at law or in equity, with respect to Customer s failure to pay the amount of any invoice.

8.3 Adjustment of Invoicing Errors. Subject to the provisions of Section 6 of these General Terms and Conditions, if it shall be found that at any time or times Customer has been overcharged or undercharged and Customer shall have actually paid the invoice containing such charges, then within thirty (30) Days after the final determination thereof, either Seller shall refund the amount of any such overcharge or Customer shall pay the amount of any such undercharge. In the event an error is discovered in the amount invoiced in any invoice rendered by Seller, such error shall be adjusted within thirty (30) Days of the determination thereof, provided that claim therefor shall have been made within thirty (30) Days from the date of discovery of such error, but in any event within six (6) Months from the date of such invoice. The party receiving such request for adjustment shall have three (3) Months to rebut such claim; otherwise the invoice shall be adjusted as requested. The preceding time limits do not apply to deliberate omission or misrepresentation or mutual mistake of fact or government required rate changes. The parties' statutory or contractual rights shall not otherwise be diminished by this Section. If the parties are unable to agree on the adjustment of any claimed error, any resort by either of the parties to legal proceedings shall be commenced within fifteen (15) Months after the supposed cause of action is alleged to have arisen, or shall thereafter be forever barred.

9. FORCE MAJEURE

9.1 Definition. The term "force majeure" as used herein shall mean acts of God, strikes, lockouts, or other industrial disturbances; acts of the public enemy, wars, blockades, insurrections, riots, epidemics, landslides, lightning, earthquakes, fires, storms (including but not limited to tornadoes or tornado warnings), crevasses, floods, washouts; arrests and restraints of the government, either Federal or State, civil or military or civil disturbances. Relative to Seller's service and solely to the operation of its system, force majeure shall also mean shutdowns for purposes of necessary repairs, relocation, or construction of facilities; breakage or accident to machinery, wells or lines of pipe or casings; testing (as required by governmental authority or as deemed necessary by Seller for the safe operation of the underground storage reservoir and facilities required to perform the service hereunder), the necessity of making repairs or alterations to machinery or lines of pipe; failure of wells, surface equipment or pipe lines, well or line freeze ups; accidents, breakdowns, inability to obtain necessary materials, or supplies or permits, or labor or land rights to perform or comply with any obligation or condition of this Agreement; and any other causes, whether of the kind herein enumerated or otherwise which are not reasonably in Seller's control. It is understood and agreed that the settlement of strikes or lockouts or controversies with landowners involving rights of way shall be entirely within Seller's discretion and that the above requirement that any force majeure shall be remedied with all reasonable dispatch shall not require the settlement of strikes or lockouts or controversies with landowners involving rights of way by acceding to the demands of the opposing party when such course is inadvisable in the discretion of Seller.

9.2 Force Majeure. If by reason of force majeure either party hereto is rendered unable, wholly or in part, to carry out its obligations under this Agreement, it is agreed that on such party giving notice in full particulars of such force majeure in writing to the other party within a reasonable time after the occurrence of the cause relied on, the party giving such notice, so far as and to the extent that it is affected by such force majeure, shall not be liable in damages during the continuance of any inability so caused, but for no longer period, and such cause shall so far as possible be remedied with all reasonable dispatch. Seller shall not be liable in damages to

1 Customer other than for acts of gross negligence or willful misconduct and then only where force
2 majeure does not apply.
3 9.3 Limitations. Such force majeure affecting the performance hereunder by either Seller or
4 Customer, however, shall not relieve such party of liability in the event of concurring negligence
5 or a failure to use due diligence to remedy the force majeure situation and to remove the cause in
6 an adequate manner and with all reasonable dispatch, nor shall such causes or contingencies
7 affecting such performance relieve Customer, in whole or in part from its obligations to pay the
8 monthly charges provided for in Section 8 of these General Terms and Conditions.
9   10. PRIORITY OF SERVICE REQUESTS AND SERVICE AGREEMENTS
10 10.1 Open Season.
11 (a) Notice of open season. Prior to or upon the initial availability of FSS and ISS services, Seller
12 shall post notice of the open season on its EBB, at least one (1) day prior to the commencement
13 of the open season. Such notice shall set forth when the open season begins and ends, where
14 interested parties may submit requests for firm or interruptible services, the minimum rates Seller
15 will accept for the available service, and how interested parties may obtain forms for requesting
16 service and additional details about the open season. Upon the termination of FSS and or ISS
17 agreements Seller shall make further postings on its EBB of the available storage services.
18 (b) Duration. The open season shall commence at the time and day specified and for the term
19 indicated in the notice of open season. If, subsequent to an open season any firm capacity
20 remains unsubscribed, Seller shall be permitted to enter into a service agreement with a qualified
21 customer without the need to commence another open season. During this time Seller will accept
22 requests for the service that is available.
23 (c) Execution of agreements. A Customer allocated service in an open season shall be required to
24 execute service agreement(s) for firm service no later than 30 consecutive days following the
25 close of the open season, or forfeit the service that has been allocated to it.
26 10.2 Firm Storage
27 (a) This section sets forth the procedure for allocating firm storage capacity that becomes
28 available other than through Section 10.1, the Right of First Refusal procedure set forth in
29 Section 10.2(b), or the capacity release provisions of Rate Schedule FSS. Firm storage capacity
30 subject to the allocation procedure set forth herein includes any firm storage service that
31 becomes available on Seller's Seller s system, now or in the future, including firm storage
32 service performed under Part 157 for which abandonment authority has been sought or obtained.
33 In the event that firm storage capacity becomes available on Seller's Seller s system, Seller shall
34 post on its EBB all relevant terms and conditions pertaining to such capacity and will solicit bids
35 for at least ten (10) business days. Seller shall evaluate and determine the best bid in a non-
36 discriminatory manner designed to allocate the capacity to the customer who values it the most
37 over the term selected by Seller. Notwithstanding the foregoing, nothing herein shall require
38 Seller to provide service at any rate that does not, in Seller's Seller s sole judgment, yield an
39 acceptable return to Seller. Moreover, Seller shall not be required to enter into Service
40 Agreements with terms of more than one year unless Customer has a long-term debt rating of at
41 least Baa3 according to Moody's Moody s Investor Service or BBB- according to Standard &
42 Poor's Poor s Corporation or unless all obligations to Seller are guaranteed by a person with a
43 long term debt rating equal to or greater than that stated above. Commission's In the event two or
44 more bids with equal economic values are received for combined capacity in excess of the

quantity of available firm capacity, the capacity will be allocated ratably on the basis of the quantities bid.

b) Right of First Refusal:

(i) Contractual Right of First Refusal at End of Contract Term. Seller may discontinue service to Customer at the end of a primary term of an FSS Agreement with a primary term beginning April 1, 2007, unless (i) Seller and Customer mutually agree to a contractual right of first refusal, which shall be negotiated on a not unduly discriminatory basis, and (ii) Customer exercises its contractual right of first refusal for the capacity covered by the FSS Agreement by matching the terms offered to Seller for such capacity by any qualified prospective successor customer during an open season conducted in accordance with the General Terms and Conditions of Seller's currently effective tariff.

(ii) Regulatory Right of First Refusal. A regulatory right of first refusal shall be available on a one-time basis to Customers holding a long term FSS Agreement with a primary term beginning date prior to April 2, 2007. Honeoye may discontinue service to such Customer at the end of such primary term unless Customer exercises its right of first refusal for the capacity covered by such FSS Agreement by matching the terms offered to Seller for such capacity by any qualified prospective successor customer during an open season, conducted in accordance with the General Terms and Conditions of Seller s currently effective tariff.

(iii) A long term FSS Agreement, as that term is used in this Section, is an FSS Agreement having a primary term of two years or more. A prospective successor customer is qualified , within the meaning of this section if such prospective successor customer meets the creditworthiness criteria set forth in the General Terms and Conditions of Seller s currently effective tariff.

(c) Exercise of Right of First Refusal

(i) Not less than three (3) months prior to the termination or expiration of an FSS Agreement subject to a negotiated right of first refusal or, if applicable, the regulatory right of first refusal, an open season will be held for the purpose of awarding the capacity that is to become available upon such FSS Agreement s termination or expiration. This open season will be conducted pursuant to the terms and conditions set forth in the General Terms and Conditions of Seller s currently effective tariff.

(ii) Bids from qualified successor customers who desire, in whole or in part, the capacity to be made available upon the expiration or termination of such FSS Agreement must be received by Seller no later than thirty (30) days after commencement of the open season. Upon expiration of the open season, Seller will select the highest acceptable bid received from a qualified successor customer and, within three (3) Business Days of such selection, communicate the terms of the highest acceptable bid to the current capacity holder, who may elect, within ten (10) Business Days or such greater time as Seller may specify, to execute a renewal FSS Agreement upon the same terms, whether for a part or the entirety of the capacity subject to the current holder s right of first refusal. The current capacity holder s right of first refusal under this Section shall attach irrespective of which party provides written notice of termination of the current capacity holder s existing Service Agreement. In determining which bid for the capacity is the highest, Seller will use the evaluation method specified in the notice of the open season posted on its Internet Web site.

(iii) If the current capacity holder does not elect to match the terms of such highest acceptable bid or the current capacity holder and Seller do not agree on terms or service pursuant to Section

8.3 below, then its FSS Agreement will expire at the conclusion of its term and Seller will be deemed to have all necessary abandonment authorization under the NGA with respect to such service. Seller may enter into a new FSS Agreement with the qualified successor customer who submitted the highest acceptable bid.

(iv) Seller shall retain the right to require a minimum rate, which shall be market-based, for bids during any such open season.

(d) If during the open season, Seller receives no bides or rejects all bids, Seller will post the capacity as unsubscribed capacity and Seller and the current capacity holder may negotiate for continuation of service under mutually satisfactory rates, terms, and conditions. During such negotiations with the current capacity holder, or in the event that the current capacity holder declines to negotiate for continuation or service, Seller may also enter into negotiations with other potential customers for services to commence upon the effective date of the termination of the current capacity holder s FSS Agreement. In no event, however, may the current capacity holder retain capacity subject to the right of first refusal at a rate lower than the highest rate contained in a bid, if any, that has been submitted for such capacity by a qualified prospective successor customer during the open season but rejected pursuant to Section 10.2(c)(ii) of the General Terms and Conditions of Seller s currently effective tariff.

(e) Priority of Firm Storage Under Agreements: All firm Storage Service Agreements under Rate Schedule FSS shall have equal priority as to service, and shall have priority over interruptible Storage Services under Rate Schedule ISS. Service under both FSS and ISS shall have priority over Overrun Service.

10.3 Interruptible and Overrun Storage

(a) Priority of Nominations For Interruptible Service: Seller, in determining the allocation of interruptible service capacity on any Day among Customers which have nominated quantities of service desired on such Day under Rate Schedule ISS, shall be assigned the order of priority of such service on the basis that the highest rate offered for such service shall be accorded the highest priority. If more than one nomination or request for interruptible storage on a Day includes an offer of the same rate, then the order of priority as among such nominations or requests shall be the same, and if the available capacity is insufficient to provide the full level of service proposed in such nominations or requests, the service provided shall be allocated among such Customers pro rata based on the quantities nominated or requested.

(b) A Customer desiring service under Rate Schedule ISS shall submit to Seller, at least one (1) business Day prior to the start of such service, the rate that such Customer is willing to pay for such service . The rate submitted by Customer pursuant to the above provision shall be used to determine priority among nominations on each Day. Once Customer's nomination is accepted, and priority is assigned thereto pursuant to this section, such priority shall not be changed by the execution of new ISS Agreements during the day for service under Rate Schedule ISS.

(c) Notwithstanding the provisions of this Section 10.3, if a Customer under Rate Schedule ISS fails to submit a timely nomination for service for a day, pursuant to these General Terms and Conditions, for such service, then such Customer's priority for such service for that day, shall be changed to a ranking below that of all other Customers who have made timely nominations for service.

10.4 Overrun Service

All requests for overrun Service under Rate Schedules FSS or ISS shall rank in priority below requests for service which are within the Customers' respective Maximum Storage Quantities. If some, but not all, overrun service requests can be satisfied, the service shall be allocated pro rata to the Maximum Storage Quantities of the Customers requesting the overrun service.

10.5 Communications

In offering service from time to time pursuant to this Section 10, to a Customer under an Agreement, Seller may deem any offer made by telephone or other instant communication method to have been refused if acceptance thereof is not communicated to Seller within six (6) normal working hours after such offer, or as otherwise agreed to by the parties.

11. MISCELLANEOUS

11.1 Responsibility for Gas. Upon receipt of Gas to be stored Seller shall be in exclusive control and possession of such Gas, until the Equivalent Quantities of Gas have been delivered for the account of Customer after which Customer shall be in exclusive control and possession of such Gas.

11.2 Warranty. Customer or Replacement Customer warrants for itself, its successors, and assigns, that it has, or will have, at the time of delivery of the Gas for injection hereunder good title to such Gas and/or good right to cause the Gas to be delivered to Seller for Storage. Customer or Replacement Customer warrants for itself, its successors, and assigns, that the Gas it warrants hereunder shall be free and clear of all liens, encumbrances or claims, that it will indemnify and save Seller harmless from all suits, actions, debts, accounts, damages, costs, losses, and expenses arising from or out of adverse claims of any and all persons to said Gas and/or to royalties, taxes, license fees, or charges thereon which are directly applicable to such delivery of Gas and that it will indemnify and save Seller harmless from all taxes or assessments which may be directly levied and assessed upon such delivery and which are by law payable and the obligation of the party making such delivery.

11.3 Waivers. No waiver by either Seller or Customer of any one or more defaults by the other in the performance of any provisions hereunder shall operate or be construed as a waiver of any future default or defaults, whether of a like or a different character. Seller shall retain the right to waive, with respect to Customer, any Section of these General Terms and Conditions and Rate Schedules FSS and ISS, if Seller does so in a non-discriminatory manner.

11.4 Assignments. Any company which shall succeed by purchase, merger or consolidation to the properties, substantially as an entirety, of Customer or of Seller, as the case may be, shall if eligible be entitled to the rights and shall be subject to the obligations of its predecessor in title under the service agreement(s) between Seller and Customer. Either Seller or Customer may assign any of its rights or obligations under its service agreement(s) to a financially responsible corporation with which it is affiliated at the time of such assignment. Furthermore, Seller may, as security for its indebtedness, assign, mortgage or pledge any of its rights or obligations under its service agreement(s), including its rights to receive payments, to any other entity, and Customer will execute any consent agreement with such entity and provide such certificates and other documents as Seller may reasonably request in connection with any such assignment. Customer also may assign or pledge its service agreements under the provisions of any mortgage, deed of trust, indenture or similar instrument which it has executed or may hereafter execute covering substantially all of its properties. Otherwise, except as provided in Section 7 of Rate Schedule FSS, or except as mandated by Section 284.242 of the Regulations of the Commission, neither party shall assign its service agreement(s) or any of its rights thereunder unless it first shall have obtained the consent thereto in writing of the other party.

11.5 Creditworthiness. Seller shall not be required to commence service or, subject to the following provisions, to continue to provide service and may terminate a Agreement with any Customer under Rate Schedule FSS and/or Service Agreements under Rate Schedule ISS, if:

(1) Customer is or has become insolvent;

(2) Customer has applied for bankruptcy under Chapter 11 of the Bankruptcy Code, or a similar state bankruptcy statute;

(3) Customer, when requested by Seller to demonstrate creditworthiness, fails to do so in Seller's reasonable judgment, in light of previous payment experience and changes thereto and the prudent credit analysis of information available; provided, however, that any such Customer that is receiving service shall continue to receive service for a period of fifteen (15) Days after written notice by Seller of any such circumstance, and shall continue thereafter to receive service if, within such fifteen (15) Day notice period, such Customer:

(i) deposits with Seller and maintains, on account, an amount which would be due for three (3) Months service at the full contract quantities set forth in the Service Agreement; or

(ii) furnishes good and sufficient security, which may include an acceptable standby letter of credit, or monthly prepayment agreement or other security as reasonably determined by Seller, of a continuing nature and in an amount equal to such amounts which would be due for service. If such payment on account or payment security is not received within such fifteen (15) Day notice period, Seller may, without waiving any rights or remedies it may have, suspend further service for a period of ten (10) Days. If such payment on account or a payment security is not received within such ten (10) Day suspension period, then Seller shall no longer be obligated to continue to provide service to such Customer.

Seller shall not be required to commence service, or subject to the following provisions, to continue to provide service and may terminate a Service Agreement with any Customer under Rate Schedule FSS having a term of more than one year if Customer, or its guarantor, fails to maintain a long-term debt rating issued by either Moody's Investors Service, or Standard and Poor's Corporation, or Customer's, or its guarantor's, long-term debt rating issued by Moody's Investors Service or Standard and Poor's Corporation falls below a rating of at least Baa3 according to Moody's Investors Service or BBB- according to Standard & Poor's Corporation; provided, however, that any such Customer that is receiving service shall continue to receive service for a period of three (3) Months during which Customer shall have the ability to:

(1) attain minimum long-term debt ratings as described above; or

(2) secure a guarantee by a person with a minimum long-term debt rating as described above, provided further, if Customer should fail to meet the requirements set forth within the three (3) Month period, Seller shall have the right to market the capacity underlying the Service Agreement(s) in question to other customers meeting the requirements as set forth herein.

11.6 Interpretation of Laws. Any Agreement shall be interpreted, performed and enforced in accordance with the laws of the State of New York.

11.7 Regulations. Any Agreement, and all terms and provisions herein, and the respective obligations of the parties thereunder are subject to valid laws, orders, rules and regulations of duly constituted authorities having jurisdiction.

11.8 No Third-Party Beneficiary. It is expressly agreed that there is no Third-Party Beneficiary to any Agreement, and that the provisions of any Agreement and these General Terms and Conditions do not impart enforceable rights in anyone who is not a party or successor or assignee of any party to an Agreement herein.

11.9 Liability. Neither Seller nor Customer shall in any event be liable to the other for incidental, consequential, or indirect damages, whether arising in contract, or tort.

11.10 Counterparts. Any Agreement may be executed in any number of counterparts, each of which shall be deemed an original, but all of which together shall constitute but one and the same instrument.

11.11 Heading. The headings contained in any Agreement are for reference purposes only and shall not affect the meaning or interpretation of any Agreement.

11.11 Compliance with Gas Industry Standards Board. Seller has adopted all of the business practices and electronic communication standards that were incorporated in 18 CFR §284.12(b). Seller specifically incorporates the following practices and standards of Version 1.3 into this Original Volume No. 1A FERC Gas Tariff: Standard Nos. 1.2.8-1.2.12, 1.3.2 (iv), 1.3.15, 1.3.16, 1.3.22-1.3.31, 1.3.32, 1.3.35-1.3.46, 1.4.1-1.4.7, 2.3.1-2.3.6, 2.3.8, 2.3.10-2.3.13, 2.3, 2.3.15-2.3.25, 2.3.27, 2.3.28, 2.3.31, 2.4.1-2.4.6, 3.3.1-3.3.8, 3.3.10-3.3.13, 3.3.16, 3.3.20, 3.3.21, 3.3.22, 3.4.1-3.4.4, 4.1.1-4.1.21, 4.2.1-4.2.8, 4.3.1, 4.3.3, 4.3.5-4.3.35, 5.3.9, 5.3.17, 5.3.18, 5.3.20, 5.3.21, 5.3.30, 5.4.1-5.4.17.

12. FACILITIES:

Unless otherwise agreed to by the parties, Seller shall not be required to own, construct and install any additional facilities to perform the service requested by Customer. In the event Seller agrees to own, construct and install additional facilities to perform the service requested by Customer including, but not limited to, hot tap, processing, measurement, injection/withdrawal wells, gathering system pipe line looping and/or compression facilities, Customer shall reimburse Seller for all Seller's costs associated therewith either on a lump sum or incremental fee basis as agreed to by the parties.

13. ELECTRONIC BULLETIN BOARD

Seller has established an EBB that will be available through subscription, to any existing or potential Customer on Seller's system. The EBB shall contain information relevant to the availability of capacity on Seller's system. The EBB will be provided at Internet "honeoye-gas-storage.com". Access is available to any party upon execution of an EBB Subscription Form; copies of the EBB Subscription Form are available on request by telephoning (585) 229-5161. Seller shall notify Customer of any change to its EBB procedures.

Seller may also charge a fee to users of the EBB to recover variable costs associated with the EBB.

Seller shall maintain daily backups of all storage transactional files and archive them for a period of three (3) years pursuant to Commission regulations, and shall allow any customer access to such historical information, for a reasonable fee, within a reasonable period of any such request.

14. RESPONSIBILITY FOR ASSOCIATED TRANSPORTATION

The transportation of quantities to be stored hereunder to and from the Point of Injection/Withdrawal is solely the Customer's responsibility.

15. TITLE TRANSFERS OF GAS IN STORAGE

15.1 A Customer may sell Working Storage Gas to any other Customer under a Rate Schedule with the same priority, either firm or interruptible, if:

(a) Both purchaser and seller of the Working Storage Gas provides Seller with verification of the transfer in writing; and

(b) The purchase does not cause either Customer to exceed its Maximum Storage Quantity, as specified in the Customers Service Agreement; and

(c) The transfer does not impair Seller's current of future operations or cause Seller to curtail any current or future service to firm Customers or have an adverse financial impact on Seller.

15.2 Seller will recognize the transfer for purposes of computing available Working Storage Gas and applicable Injection and Withdrawal Quantities on a prospective basis within 24 hours after receiving the written verification required by Section 1 15.l(a).

16. OPERATIONAL FLOW ORDER (OFO)

16.1 OFO's Seller's General. Seller, in its discretion, shall have the right to issue OFO s when in its judgment it is necessary to maintain or restore the operational integrity of Seller s storage system. Seller will not be required to issue an OFO:

(a) to redeliver Gas to any Customer that has not nominated and delivered equivalent quantities of gas to Seller s storage system; or

(b) to any other pipeline in order to obtain access to quantities of Gas, except to the extent that such quantities of Gas are being transported by such pipeline for the account of a Customer. Seller shall not be required to respond to any OFO that it receives from an interstate pipeline that is not currently providing equivalent quantities and pressures of Gas to Seller.

16.2 Forms of OFO's. An OFO may:

(a) enable Seller to take or require any other actions as may be deemed necessary by Seller in its judgment in order to maintain the operational integrity of Seller's storage system.

16.3 OFO Operations Conditions. OFO's may be issued in any of the following circumstances:

(a) to alleviate conditions that threaten the operational integrity of Seller's storage system; or

(b) to maintain minimum necessary pressures for storage operations.

The OFO will remain in effect until the operational condition requiring its issuance has been remedied.

16.4 OFO NOTICE, CONTENTS AND PROCEDURES. Seller shall issue an OFO as expeditiously as is reasonably practicable in the circumstances, utilizing electronic communication, (information transmitted via Seller's EBB, electronic delivery mechanism prescribed by GISB or other mutually agreed communication methodologies used to transmit and receive information, including communication by telephone). Seller shall post and provide Customers with updated information concerning the status of operational variables related to the OFO as soon as it is available. Each OFO will contain the following provisions:

(a) time and date of issuance;

(b) time that the OFO is considered to be effective (if no time is specified, the OFO shall be effective immediately);

(c) duration of the OFO (if none is specified, the OFO will be effective until further notice);

(d) the party or parties receiving the OFO;

(e) the quantity of Gas required to remedy the operational condition requiring the issuance of the OFO; and

(f) any other terms Seller may reasonably require to ensure the effectiveness of the OFO.

16.5 Failure to Comply with OFO. If Customer or agent fails to comply with the terms of an OFO, for any reason other than force majeure on an upstream or downstream pipeline, such Customer shall be: (a) liable for any damages including, but not limited to direct, consequential, and exemplary or punitive damages incurred by Seller or any other affected party as a result of such failure. Notwithstanding anything to the contrary in this Section 16.5, if Customer is required to make a nomination pursuant to an OFO, unless critical circumstances dictate otherwise, no damages and/or penalties will be assessed unless Customer is given the opportunity to correct the circumstances giving rise to the OFO.

16.6 Seller's Liability for OFO's. Seller shall not be liable to any person for any costs, damages or other liability associated with the issuance of, or the failure to issue, any OFO's, provided, however, Seller shall be liable for acts of negligence or undue discrimination, such standards to be judged in light of the emergency conditions under which OFO's are issued.

17. SYSTEM INVENTORY MANAGEMENT

In the event that Seller is required to sell natural gas in order to manage its system, Seller may post its need to sell gas on its EBB. Included in such posting shall be:

(a) the quantity of gas to be sold;

(b) any minimum quantity for bidding;

(c) the date and time when all bids shall be due;

(d) the date(s) when such gas shall be sold;

(e) any minimum or maximum daily quantity to be sold;

(f) the point where the gas will be sold; and

(g) the criteria to be used by Seller in evaluating and selecting bids.

18. OFF-SYSTEM PIPELINE CAPACITY

From time to time, Seller may enter into transportation and/or storage agreements with other interstate or intrastate pipeline or storage companies ("off-system pipelines"). In the event that Seller acquires capacity on an off-system pipeline, Seller will use such capacity for operational reasons or to render service for its Customers. In the event that Seller uses off-system pipeline capacity to render service for its Customers, it will only render service to Customers on the acquired capacity pursuant to Seller's FERC Gas Tariff and subject to Seller's approved rates, as such tariff and rates may changes from time to time. For purposes of transactions entered into subject to this Section 18, the "shipper-must-have-title" requirement is waived.

Sheet Nos. 109 through 123

39

HONEOYE STORAGE CORPORATION
SERVICE REQUEST FORM

Send   Honeoye   Storage   Corporation
to: 4511   Egypt   Road
       Canandaigua,   NY   14424
       Date   Received:
       Attention: Vice   President   of   Operations
       Telecopier   No.:   585-229-2015
       Verification: 585-229-5161

NOTE: A check, if required by Section 2.1 of the General Terms and Conditions, must accompany each Storage Service Request to be valid.

INFORMATION REQUIRED FOR VALID STORAGE REQUEST

NOTE: ANY CHANGES IN THE FACTS SET FORTH BELOW, WHETHER BEFORE OR AFTER SERVICE BEGINS, MUST BE PROMPTLY COMMUNICATED TO SELLER IN WRITING.

1.   Requestor: (Do not complete if same as Customer, See No. 3 below) Requestor's Name:_____

2.   Is Requestor affiliated with Seller? YES_____ NO_____
     If yes, type of affiliation and the percentage of ownership between Seller and Requestor
     _____

3.   Customer's Name and Address: (Note: The "Customer" is the party which proposes to execute   the   Storage   Agreement   with   Seller).
     _____
     _____

     Attention:_____   Telephone:_____
     Fax No.:_____   Email address:_____

4.   Is Customer affiliated with Seller? YES_____ NO_____
     If yes, type of affiliation and the percentage of ownership between Seller and Customer
     _____

5.   Customer is a(n): (Check One)
     _____ Local Distribution Company   _____ Producer
     _____ Intrastate Pipeline Company   _____ End-User
     _____ Interstate Pipeline Company   _____ Marketer/Broker
     _____ Other (Describe)_____

6.	Customer is Acting: (Check One)
	_____ for Itself
	_____ as Agent for _____

7.	This request is for: (Check One)
	_____ Firm Storage Service under Rate Schedule FSS
		Requested	Maximum	Daily	Withdrawal	Quantity	(MDWQ)
		_____ dekatherms per day (Dth/d)
	_____ Interruptible Storage Service under Rate Schedule ISS
		Maximum Daily Injection Quantity	$_____ Dth/d
		Maximum Daily Withdrawal Quantity	$_____ Dth/d
		Storage Overrun Quantity	$_____ Dth

8.	Requested Maximum Storage Quantity_____Dth

9.	Point of Injection_____

10.	Point of Withdrawal_____

11.	Term of Service:
	Date service is requested to commence:_____
	Date service is requested to terminate:_____
	(Unless otherwise agreed to by Seller, Agreements for FSS shall commence on April 1 and terminate on March 31 of any following year)

12.	Rate Information:
	Customer will agree to pay for service requested as follows:
	FIRM STORAGE SERVICE (FSS)*

Deliverability Reservation Rate - Monthly	$_____ per Dth/mo
Capacity Reservation Rate- Monthly	$_____ per Dth/mo
Injection Rate	$_____ per Dth
Withdrawal Rate	$_____ per Dth
Overrun Injection Rate (minimum $0.05 per Dth)	$_____ per Dth
Overrun Withdrawal Rate (minimum $0.05 per Dth)	$_____ per Dth

	INTERRUPTIBLE STORAGE SERVICE (ISS)*

Injection Rate	$_____ per Dth
Withdrawal Rate	$_____ per Dth

Inventory Charge	$_____	per Dth/day
Late Withdrawal Rate	$_____	Dth/day
Overrun Storage Commodity Rate	$_____	Dth/day

*All quantities of natural gas are measured in dekatherms (Dth)

13. Certified Statement:
By submitting this request, Customer certifies that customer has or will have by the time of execution of an Agreement with Seller, title to, or the legal right to cause to be delivered to Seller, for Storage, the gas which is to be stored and facilities or contractual rights which will cause such Gas to be delivered to and received from Seller. In the event Customer purchases Storage Overrun Quantity, Customer shall certify that Customer shall have such title to and rights to deliver gas to Seller upon the termination of the Storage Overrun Service in an amount equal to Storage Overrun Service.

14. Credit Evaluation: as required by Section 2.2(j) of the General Terms and Conditions.
THIS STORAGE SERVICE REQUEST IS HEREBY SUBMITTED
This___ day of_____, ____
By_____
Telephone Number ( )_____
Fax Number ( )_____
e-mail address _____

FORM OF FSS SERVICE AGREEMENT

For Use Under Seller's Rate Schedule FSS

THIS AGREEMENT entered into as of the ___ day of _____ , _____, by and between Honeoye Storage Corporation, a New York corporation, hereinafter referred to as "Seller," and_____ , hereinafter referred to as "Customer."

WITNESSETH

WHEREAS, Customer has requested Seller to store Gas on its behalf; and

WHEREAS, Seller has sufficient capacity available to provide the Storage Service for Customer on the terms specified herein;

NOW, THEREFORE, Seller and Customer agree as follows:

ARTICLE I
STORAGE SERVICE

1. Seller's service hereunder shall be subject to receipt of all requisite regulatory authorizations from the Federal Energy Regulatory Commission ("Commission"), or any successor regulatory authority, and any other necessary governmental authorizations, in a manner and form acceptable to Seller.

2. Subject to the terms and provisions of this Agreement, Customer may on any Day cause Gas to be delivered to Seller up to the Maximum Daily Injection Quantity ("MDIQ") plus Seller's Injection Use for Storage of up to the Maximum Storage Quantity ("MSQ") and at Customer's request on any Day Seller agrees to Tender Equivalent Quantities of Gas to or for the account of Customer, on a firm basis, up to the Maximum Daily Withdrawal Quantity ("MDWQ"), reduced by Seller's Withdrawal Use. The MDIQ, MDWQ and MSQ shall be as set forth in Exhibit A to this Agreement.

3. Seller, if requested by Customer, may inject or withdraw from storage daily quantities in excess of the Maximum Daily Injection Quantity ("MDIQ") or Maximum Daily Withdrawal Quantity ("MDWQ") specified in Exhibit A, if it can do so without adverse effect on Seller's operations or its ability to meet its higher priority obligations as specified in paragraph 10 of the General Terms and Conditions of the Part 284 Gas Tariff.

4. Seller shall use reasonable efforts, if requested by Customer, to permit customer to inject or withdraw, quantities of Gas pursuant to Paragraph 3 above up to the Customer's Maximum Storage Quantity reduced by Seller's Injection Use and Withdrawal Use.

ARTICLE II
POINT OF INJECTION/WITHDRAWAL

1. Customer shall deliver or cause to be delivered Gas hereunder at the Point of Injection/ Withdrawal which shall be Honeoye's interconnection with either Tennessee Pipeline Company or New York Sate Gas and Electric Company near Canandaigua, New York.

2. Seller shall Tender to or for the account of Customer, Equivalent Quantities of Gas stored hereunder, at the Point of Injection/Withdrawal.

ARTICLE III
TERM OF AGREEMENT

1. This Agreement shall be effective as of the date first above written and shall remain in effect for a primary term commencing August ___, 2000 and ending March 31, 2001.

ARTICLE IV
RATE SCHEDULE AND CHARGES

1. Each Month, Customer shall pay Seller for the service hereunder, an amount determined in accordance with Seller's Rate Schedule FSS and the applicable provisions of the General Terms and Conditions of Seller's FERC Gas Tariff, Original Volume No. 1A, as filed with the Commission. Such Rate Schedule and General Terms and Conditions are incorporated by reference and made a part hereof. Sections IV & V of Exhibit A hereto sets forth the applicable information as follows, which shall be utilized for transactions hereunder:

(a) Rates and Charges

(b) Additional charges which are applicable.

Exhibit A to this Agreement shall specify the Rates and Charges and Additional charges which are applicable. When the level of any Additional charges is changed pursuant to Commission authorization or direction, Seller may unilaterally effect an amendment to Exhibit A to reflect such change(s) by so specifying in a written communication to Customer.

2. It is further agreed that Seller may seek authorization from the Commission and/or other appropriate body for such changes to any rates, terms and conditions set forth herein, in Rate Schedule FSS or in the General Terms and Conditions of Seller's FERC Gas Tariff, as may be found necessary to assure Seller just and reasonable rates. Nothing herein contained shall be construed to deny Customer any rights it may have under the Natural Gas Act, as amended, including the right to participate fully in rate proceedings by intervention or otherwise to contest Seller's filing in whole or in part.

3. Further Agreement:

(Write None or specify the agreement).

ARTICLE V
NOTICE

1. Except as may be otherwise provided, any notice, request, demand, statement or bill provided for in this Agreement or any notice which a party may desire to give the other shall be in writing and mailed by regular mail, effective as of the postmark date, to the post office address of the party intended to receive the same, as the case may be, as follows:

Seller:

Honeoye Storage Corporation
4511 Egypt Road
Canandaigua, NY 14424

Copy to: Honeoye Storage Corporation
C/O EHA, L.L.C.
55 Union Street, 4th floor
Boston, Massachusetts 02108

Customer: _____
_____
_____
_____

ARTICLE VI
INCORPORATION BY REFERENCE

The provisions of Rate Schedule FSS and the General Terms and Conditions of Seller's FERC Gas Tariff, Original Volume No. 1A, as may be modified or amended from time to time, are specifically incorporated herein by reference and made a part hereof

IN WITNESS WHEREOF, the parties hereto have caused this Agreement to be signed by their respective officers or Representatives hereunto duly authorized.

HONEOYE   STORAGE   CORPORATION

By:
Its:_____   _____

_____
(Customer)
By:
Its:_____   _____

45

EXHIBIT "A"

to
Agreement between
Honeoye Storage Corporation (Seller)
and
_____ (Customer)

Dated_____

I. MAXIMUM STORAGE QUANTITY (MSQ)   _____

       (MDth)

II. MAXIMUM DAILY INJECTION QUANTITY (MDIQ)   _____

       (Dth/d)

III. MAXIMUM DAILY WITHDRAWAL QUANTITY (MDWQ) _____ (Dt/d)

IV. RATES AND CHARGES (monthly)

Deliverability Reservation Rate	$_____	per Dth/mo
Capacity Reservation Rate	$_____	per Dth/mo
Injection Rate	$_____	per Dth
Overrun Injection Rate	$_____	per Dth
Withdrawal Rate	$_____	per Dth
Overrun Withdrawal Rate	$_____	per Dth

V. ADDITIONAL CHARGES - pursuant to Section 5 of Rate Schedule FSS

VI. FSS FUEL USE

NOTES

1.   Honeoye Storage Corporation operates an independent gas storage facility located in Ontario County, NY, about 30 miles south of Rochester. Honeoye began operations in 1975 with a Federal Energy Regulatory Commission (FERC) certificate and 20-year fixed-rate storage contracts with the three major New York City utilities, Con Edison, Brooklyn Union and Long Island Lighting. Storage service was expanded in 1980 when the field pressure was increased, and Boston Gas and Energy North became customers. The contracts became evergreen in 1995 under annual renewal options. Long Island Lighting terminated its contract in 1997 before the merger with Brooklyn Union and was replaced by ProMark Energy and Providence Gas. These older fixed-rate contracts, which are no longer available, are commonly called § 157 FERC contracts.

2.   When Providence and ProMark terminated their contracts, Honeoye sought and received authorization from FERC (Docket Nos CP-93-000, 94-000 and 95-000) to expand the field further by increasing operating pressures. Under FERC authorization issued in 2000, the maximum average reservoir pressure of the field was authorized to be increased from 927 psia to 1100 psia. In 2000 FERC also authorized Honeoye to market both the expanded capacity and the former Providence capacity on an open-access, market-based rate basis, called § 284 FERC contracts. Service is available on either a firm or interruptible basis. Interruptible storage refers to storage that is not guaranteed—that is storage that is available when the reservoir has excess capacity.

3.   Available Firm Storage Capacity can be obtained during an Open Season bidding process, which is posted on Honeoye's website. Firm Storage Capacity, which is not committed as a result of Open Season, is posted as Available Capacity.

Interruptible Storage Service capacity is first offered by postings on Honeoye's website during Open Season. Additional opportunities are also posted as Operationally Available, which allows customers to take advantage of special operating situations or to capitalize on market fluctuations.

4.   The storage field, a Medina age reservoir found at a depth of 2750 feet, covers an area that is about 12 miles east-west and six miles north-south. There are 27 operating wells, 12 observation wells, 19 miles of gathering lines, 2750 hp of compression and a 10.5 mile pipeline running north to the Tennessee Gas and New State Electric and Gas interconnections.

5.   Honeoye's website is: http://www.honeoyestorage.com/

PERMIT TO CONDUCT GEOPHYSICAL OPERATIONS
(Mineral)

Permit #

Project:

Date:

Mineral Owner:
Address:

This Agreement is made and entered into on the date noted below by and between, _____, (Owner) and _____ (Sub-Contractor), on behalf of _____, (Company). Owner hereby grants authority to Company to conduct a geophysical survey on the following described lands wherein Owner owns full or partial interest in the mineral or leasehold estate. This permit is for a 3-D geophysical survey to be conducted on lands including the following described tracts located in _____ County, State of _____. Company and its contractors shall have the right of ingress and egress to and from said lands, solely to the extent necessary to conduct the seismic operations. The geophysical operations will be conducted in accordance with industry standard practices.

The lands described below are located within _____ County, State of _____:

Township_____**, Range**_____**, Section**
       Legal Description

Accepted and agreed to as of the date set forth above

NOTES

1.   The form seeks permission from the owner of a mineral interest to allow a geophysical survey on a tract of land. If mineral ownership is fractionalized, in most jurisdictions only permission from one mineral owner or oil and gas lessee is necessary. Oil and gas lessees frequently do not conduct geophysical tests themselves, but contract with specialized geophysical firms for these services.

2.   Conventional geophysical tests, or surveys, are commonly done in straight lines and may stretch for many miles. So-called 3-D seismic surveys are done in grid lines. 3-D seismic is much more costly to collect and analyze, but it provides more detailed information about the subsurface. To provide as accurate a picture as possible, it may be necessary for the test to cover land in addition to that leased to the company (or companies) requesting the survey.

3.   Consideration for consent to permit seismic testing varies. In some instances a mineral fee owner or company that has an oil and gas lease on land in the path of a proposed seismic survey will condition its consent to testing upon being furnished the data resulting from the test. Most mineral owners expect a cash payment.

PERMIT TO CONDUCT GEOPHYSICAL OPERATIONS
(Surface)

Permit #:

Project:

Date:

Owner:

Address:

Phone:(H)   (W)

_____, as sub-contractor for _____, (hereinafter called "Operator") requests permission to conduct a three-dimensional ("3-D") seismic survey over the following described property located within _____County, State of _____:

[land description]

1) Operator will conduct operations in accordance with good standard practices and in a prudent and workmanlike manner. The undersigned Grantor is either an owner or tenant of the above-described property ("the Grantor"). The intention of this permit is to cover all surface and mineral interests owned by the Grantor within the above described property and within the 3-D seismic survey to be conducted under this permit within _____ and _____ Counties, State of _____, including such lands, rights and interests within the planned survey that may have been inadvertently omitted from the above described property.

2) Grantor hereby agrees to permit personnel and equipment contracted by Operator, its successors and assigns, to enter upon the lands above-described, or any other lands owned by Grantor within the 3-D seismic survey planned hereunder, to conduct geophysical exploration thereon, including 3-D seismic surveys.

3) In consideration for this Permit covering geophysical operations on the lands above described, Operator shall make payment to Grantor of $15.00 per net surface acre owned by Grantor, which is to be covered in the seismic survey. Any other surface acreage owned by the Grantor ultimately included within the 3-D seismic survey to be conducted under this permit discovered or added after the execution of this permit shall be compensated at the same rate of payment as agreed to herein.

4) The amounts paid to Grantor as provided above shall constitute settlement in full of all damages, if any, that may result to Grantor's property as a result of Operator's normal operations. The Operator shall further compensate the Grantor for all damages over and above the usual and ordinary damages that may have occurred as a result of this geophysical survey.

5) Operator agrees to indemnify and hold Grantor harmless from any personal injury or property damage claims that may result from Operator's operations or those of any agents or contractors conducting the subject 3-D seismic survey on the above described property(ies).

6) In the event that Operator does not conduct geophysical operations on the above described propert(y)(ies) as permitted, Operator shall not be obligated to make any payment to Grantor and this permit is null and void.

1   7)   Grantor agrees that if the surface or mineral rights for the above described property(ies) are
2   owned by others, Grantor will advise Operator.
3   8)   Grantor does hereby declare that he/she has the legal authority to sign this permit form and
4   receive payment of permit and damage settlements with respect to the above described
5   property(ies). By accepting payment, Grantor agrees to assume the responsibility for distributing
6   that portion of the proceeds due to the Surface Owner, Surface Tenant or other third parties who
7   claim interests in the property.
8   9)   This permit will be for a term expiring March 31, 2008.
9   10) No fences will be cut or dropped without notifying the owner and making arrangements for
10 its repair/replacement.
11 11) Company will exercise caution and diligent consideration concerning operations when soil
12 conditions are excessively wet.
13 12) Company agrees to not to locate a source point within 300 feet of any house or water well.
14 13) This permit is fully transferable by operator and shall be binding upon and shall inure to the
15 benefit of Owner and operator and their respective licensees, successors, and assigns.
16 14) This permit shall be binding on each Owner executing a counterpart hereof, whether or not
17 executed by any other Owner; this permit shall be effective as of the date of the permit and in the
18 event this permit is executed by more than one (1) owner, it shall be effective as of the date first
19 executed by any owner the ("Effective Date").
20
21   **Surface Restrictions**
22
23 15) See Exhibit "A" attached and made a part hereof.
24
25 [*signatures*]

NOTES

1.   This form seeks permission and a release from liability from the owner of the surface. In most jurisdictions, surface-owner permission is not needed, but industry custom and practice is to obtain permission and to pay a fee to the surface owner for any damage or inconvenience caused by the operations.

2.   This form assumes that the surface owner is the actual occupant of the tract. In fact, the party suffering the damage and inconvenience of a seismic survey may be an agricultural tenant. Unlike oil and gas leases, agricultural leases for farming and grazing are frequently periodic tenancies from year to year and are rarely recorded. A company seeking permission for seismic testing must often rely upon the fee simple owner for information about the existence of such leases and the identity of the surface lessees.

3.   The above form is used for a 3-D seismic survey. Note that payment is based on net surface acreage. In the case of a conventional seismic survey, the amount paid is often based on the length of the survey through the tract (e.g., per rod) or on the number of "shotholes" drilled on the tract. In addition, in the case of conventional or 3-D seismic surveys, additional payments may be made for damages to growing crops.

SWKROA GEOPHYSICAL PERMIT

[name and address of landowner]

Request is hereby respectfully made by _____,
Oil and Gas Lessee, and _____, hereinafter referred to as the "Geophysical Company," to conduct a 3-D 2-D (strike inapplicable portion) seismic survey over and across the following described land situate in _____ County, Kansas, to wit:

In consideration for granting this permission, Geophysical Company agrees that all work performed by it on said land shall be conducted at its own risk and expense.

Geophysical Company further agrees to pay all damages caused by or arising from its operations thereon.

Geophysical Company will further agree to indemnify and hold you harmless from all liability to or claims of others should any such claims result from its operations on your property.

The following conditions shall be complied with while conducting the seismic survey on the above described property:

1. All geophysical work shall be completed by _____, 200__.

2. Entry shall be made only upon verbal contact with and approval by (agricultural tenant) and after securing written permission therefor by the undersigned landowner.

3. All seismic survey work shall be done and all geophones shall be laid in accordance with the attached plat. In the event of a 2-D survey, all geophones shall be laid on or as near the section line as practical.

4. All vehicles used in the survey shall remain in a single track. When necessary to enter upon furrowed irrigated fields, all vehicles shall be made to
run parallel with the irrigation furrows. No vehicles shall be driven on the subject property when the ground is wet or muddy.

5. The following minimum distances shall be maintained by the vibrators in conducting the seismic operations:

Farmstead improvements 1,320 feet

Irrigation and domestic water wells 1,000 feet

Underground concrete irrigation pipe 400 feet

Underground PVC irrigation pipe 200 feet

6. All seismic operations shall be done in such a manner as to cause as little interference with farming operations on said land and cause as little damage to surface and crops as possible.

7. No dynamite charges shall be used without landowner's written permission.

8. All fences and gates shall be left as found. All trash, flagging material and other equipment used in the geophysical work shall be removed upon completion of the seismic survey.

9. Further terms and conditions:

Compensation for such permit shall be at the rate of $_____ per mile, $_____
per acre, $_____ per quarter section (strike inapplicable portion). Such compensation shall be for access to the property and for normal damages associated with seismic operations. Any actual or excess surface and crop damage, potential loss of yield damage caused by breakage of underground irrigation lines, well damage, and damage to farmstead improvements shall be negotiated between the parties.

[signatures]

NOTES

1.   This permit form has been used by members of the Southwest Kansas Royalty Owners Association (SWKROA), a royalty-owner and landowner association. The SWKROA website is: http://www.swkroa.com.

2.   The permit addresses several surface use issues and the payment of compensation for the right to enter the property. You may wish to review this permit after reading the *Hunt Oil Company v. Kerbaugh* case at page 312 of the casebook. The case concerns limitations on a surface owner's ability to insist upon payment and other conditions for the right to conduct seismic operations.

Trespass

   * The tresspass against royalty requires actual damage. Better probability of winning for unleased owner who can show actual damages.

Lease

   * In ownership-in-place states (Texas) a lease likely seen as a fee simple determinable interest (interest in real prty that will automatically terminate upon the happening of a certain described event)

   * NO Theory : lease termin-n by abandonment, cancellation on forfeiture (incorporeal hereditament, profit or license) Lease interest is treated as an interest subject to a condition subsequent (not automat-ly terminate) so failure of production is a failure of a condition that MAY cause a ct. to terminate

Commun. pooling

   * Everybody signs a simple lease that describes all the properties

   * Rule 37 : 467ft from property, 1200 ft from another well
Rule 38 : density : 40 acr oil, 160 acr gas

   * ROC → R.37/38 → Excep-n 37/38 → Volunt. Sub. R. → Century Doct.

pooling Act

   * TMIPA applies to fields disc. after March 8, 61 (after when parties exhaust all means to work out a volun. pooling, state will force), prospectively eliminates forced pool- in old fields

MASTER GEOPHYSICAL

DATA-USE LICENSE

(Multiple Transaction)

Between

_____

("Company")

And

_____

("Contractor")

Dated: _____

(Revised September 2003)

TABLE OF CONTENTS

Master Geophysical Data-Use License
IAGC Model Agreement – 2003 (Sept rev.)

Page 2 of 14

56

This Master Geophysical Data-Use License (the **"License"**) is dated effective this _____ day of _____, _____, between _____, a _____ corporation ("Licensor") and _____, a _____ corporation ("Licensee").

In consideration of the mutual promises contained in this License and other good and valuable consideration, Licensor agrees to grant to Licensee and Licensee agrees to accept a non-exclusive license to use certain Data from time to time upon the terms and conditions set forth in this License. Upon each occasion Licensor licenses specific Data to Licensee, the Parties will execute a supplemental agreement ("Supplement") to this License. The Supplement will be in substantially the form attached to this License as Exhibit A and will identify the specific Data licensed, the consideration to be paid by Licensee, and other particulars concerning the license transaction to which the Parties mutually agree.

1. <u>Definitions</u>: Capitalized terms used in this License have the following meanings:

   1.1 <u>"Acquirer(s)"</u> means Third Parties that acquire, either directly or indirectly, Ownership or Control, whether accomplished by statutory merger, consolidation or share exchange, stock or asset sale or purchase, or any other transaction.

   1.2 <u>"Confidentiality Agreement(s)"</u> means a written agreement between Licensee and a Third Party to maintain the Data and Derivatives in strict confidence as provided herein and not to Show or transfer the Data, Derivatives, or any analyses or interpretations thereof to any Third Party.

   1.3 <u>"Consultant(s)"</u> means Third Parties which are bona fide, recognized consultants in the geophysical industry engaged by Licensee to interpret, reprocess or make other technical studies of the Data for the sole use and benefit of Licensee. Licensee's Consultants may not be Prospective Partners, Partners, Prospective Acquirers or Acquirers, marketers of geophysical data, or otherwise be in the business of exploring for or producing hydrocarbons and may not own an economic interest in any oil and gas lease, production-sharing contract, or other interest within the geological area of the Data being used with the exception of an overriding royalty interest, not to exceed one percent (1%) of the revenues from such geographic area, granted by Licensee via Consultant's compensation package.

   1.4 <u>"Control(s)"</u> means the ability to direct, manage and/or dictate the actions of and/or determine the management of the entity in question whether by the election of members of the Board of Directors or other governing body of such entity, or by having a majority number of members of such governing body or by other means.

1.5 "Data" means geophysical and geological information, regardless of the form or medium on which it is displayed or stored. Data also includes interpretations created by Licensor for license to Third Parties. Specific Data subject to this License is more particularly described in each Supplement.

1.6 "Derivative(s)" means all processed and reprocessed Data regardless of the form or medium on which it is displayed or stored whether produced by Licensee or Third Parties.

1.7 "License" means this agreement as supplemented by each Supplement.

1.8 "Licensee" is defined in the first paragraph of this License.

1.9 "Licensor" is defined in the first paragraph of this License.

1.10 "Licensee Interpretation(s)" means products created by Licensee or its Consultants that are based upon space and time location of the Data and/or Derivatives but do not directly incorporate actual Data or Derivative values or magnitudes.

1.11 "Ownership" or "Owns" means, in the case of a corporation or other entity that issues voting securities, greater than 50% of the outstanding common stock or other voting securities and, in the case of a partnership trust or other entity, greater than 50% of the interest in the profits thereof.

1.12 "Parties" means Licensor and Licensee. "Party" means either Licensor or Licensee.

1.13 "Partner(s)" means Third Parties contractually related to Licensee in Third Party Business Transactions (whether or not such relationships constitute a partnership at law).

1.14 "Processor(s)" means Third Parties which are bona fide recognized contractors that are engaged by Licensee to provide reformatting or reprocessing services for geophysical and geological data for the sole use and benefit of Licensee; provided that such contractors are not, directly or indirectly, related to or in the business of exploring for or producing hydrocarbons.

1.15 "Prospective Acquirer(s)" means any Third Party who is conducting bona fide negotiations in an endeavor to become an Acquirer.

1.16 "Prospective Partner(s)" means any Third Party who is conducting bona fide negotiations in an endeavor to become a Partner.

1.17 "Related Entity or Related Entities" means any entity which, as of the date of this License, is (i) wholly owned by Licensee (Licensee's subsidiary),

Master Geophysical Data-Use License   Page 4 of 14
IAGC Model Agreement – 2003 (Sept rev.)

58

or (ii) wholly owns Licensee (Licensee's parent), or (iii) is a result of an internal reorganization provided such reorganization shall not include entities formed after the date hereof to accomplish a statutory merger, asset sale or purchase, stock sale or purchase or any other transaction with an entity that is not defined as a Related Entity as of the date of this License.

1.18   "Show(n)" means to display or otherwise allow passive viewing, under the direct supervision and control of Licensee, of the Data or Derivatives for short periods of time to a Third Party in secure environments whereby such Third Parties are not able to (i) operate any computer workstation on which the Data or Derivatives are displayed; (ii) make copies, summaries, transcriptions, reproductions or interpretations of any type; (iii) remove copies, summaries or transcriptions of the Data or Derivatives from Licensee's premises; or (iv) otherwise impair the intellectual property value of such Data or Derivatives.

1.19   "Storage Contractor(s)" means Third Parties which are bona fide recognized contractors that are engaged by Licensee to provide central storage facilities and retrieval services and/or electronic databases for geophysical and geological data for the sole use and benefit of Licensee; provided that such contractors are not, directly or indirectly, related to or in the business of exploring for or producing hydrocarbons and are not competitors of Licensor.

1.20   "Supplement(s)" is defined in the second paragraph of this License.

1.21   "Third Party" or "Third Parties" means any corporation, individual, partnership, trust, or other entity not a party to this License (including Prospective Acquirers and Prospective Partners) other than a Related Entity.

1.22   "Third Party Business Transaction(s)" means farmouts, operating agreements, acreage trades, areas of mutual interest, joint development agreements, joint bidding agreements and similar business transactions entered with Third Parties for the joint exploration and/or development of a particular geographical area(s).

2.   Data Ownership/Confidential Treatment:

2.1.   Ownership/Confidentiality   Licensor owns or otherwise has the right to license to others the right to use the Data. Licensor represents, and Licensee acknowledges, that the Data and Derivatives, regardless of the form or the medium on which they are stored, constitute a valuable and highly confidential trade secret that are not generally available and are the sole property and proprietary information of Licensor (and/or those on behalf of which Licensor acts). Title to the Data shall remain in Licensor (and/or those on behalf of which Licensor acts) and Licensee shall acquire, under the terms hereof, only the non-exclusive right to utilize such Data on the terms provided herein. Licensee shall in no event disclose or transfer the Data or any derivation thereof to any individual or entity whatsoever, except as may specifically be provided in this License. Licensor shall have the right at any time to license any part of the Data to persons or entities other than the Licensee at such prices and on such terms as are determined by Licensor.

Except as expressly permitted by this License, Licensee agrees (a) to keep strictly confidential, and shall ensure that its employees and agents keep strictly confidential, the Data and Derivatives and (b) not to Show, allow the use of, or deliver the Data or Derivatives to any other person.

2.2 Original Data-Retention/Licensing/Right to Destroy   It is the intent of Licensor to retain the original Data (such as field tapes and other related information obtained during acquisition); however, Licensee acknowledges that original media may erode, become damaged, and/or contain Data not relevant to the licensed area and in such situations, Licensor may be unable to provide Licensee the portion of the original Data thereby affected. Licensor shall have the sole right to delete or discard the original Data upon making reasonable efforts to notify Licensee of its intention to do so.

Licensee may license such original Data upon payment of an additional license fee.

2.3 Notice of Restricted Use   Licensee may make copies of any Data and Derivatives for the sole purpose of using such copies pursuant to the rights granted herein; provided that all such copies shall have the following Notice printed thereon or attached to it or its container:

NOTICE

"This Data is proprietary to and a trade secret of
_____ ("Licensor"). The use of
this Data and Derivatives is restricted to companies
holding a valid use license from Licensor and is
subject to the confidentiality terms of that license.

This notice shall not be removed, obliterated, concealed or otherwise obscured by Licensee or those to whom the Data or Derivatives is disclosed or transferred, as may be permitted in this License.

3. Disclosure of Data & Derivatives   Licensee shall have the non-exclusive right to use the Data and Derivatives for its internal purposes only. Licensee shall not Show, transfer or otherwise dispose of or allow access to, or use of any or all, of the Data or Derivatives except as specifically provided for in this Article 3. Copies of any Confidentiality Agreements between Licensee and Third Parties as

Master Geophysical Data-Use License   Page 6 of 14
IAGC Model Agreement – 2003 (Sept rev.)

60

required by the terms of this License shall be provided to Licensor upon written request.

3.1 <u>Related Entities</u>   Related Entities shall have the same right of usage of the Data and Derivatives as has Licensee, provided that such Related Entity shall be bound by the terms of this License to the same extent as is Licensee. In the event that any such Related Entity should cease to exist or no longer meet the definition of a Related Entity, all rights of usage by such entity in the Data and Derivatives shall immediately cease and any copies of the Data, Derivatives, or physical manifestations thereof then in the possession of such entity shall immediately be returned to Licensee.

3.2 <u>Government Agencies</u>

3.2.1 Notwithstanding the foregoing, the Data and Derivatives may be disclosed to the extent such disclosure is specifically required by law, governmental or court decree, order rule or regulation, or by any similar legal process. In the event Licensee is required by law, governmental or court decree, order, rule or regulation, or by any similar legal process to disclose any Data or Derivatives, Licensee shall give Licensor prompt notice of such process so that Licensor may seek an appropriate protective order (or other appropriate remedy) with respect to maintaining the confidentiality of the affected Data and Derivatives before disclosure thereof by Licensee. If, in the absence of a protective order, Licensee is nevertheless compelled to disclose Data or Derivatives, Licensee may disclose only that portion of the Data or Derivatives that Licensee is advised by written opinion of counsel is legally required to be disclosed in compliance with the relevant process. In the event of such disclosure, Licensee shall give Licensor written notice of the Data or Derivatives to be disclosed as far in advance of its disclosure as practicable, and upon Licensor's request, Licensee shall use reasonable efforts to obtain assurances that the disclosed Data or Derivatives will be accorded confidential treatment.

3.2.2 Pursuant to regulations (30 CFR Parts 250 and 251) effective January 23, 1998, issued by the Minerals Management Service ("MMS"), an agency of the United States government, Licensor hereby notifies Licensee, and Licensee hereby acknowledges, that by the licensing to Licensee of geological and/or geophysical Data or Derivatives which are subject to the jurisdiction of the MMS, Licensee assumes the obligations under 30 CFR Section 251.11 and/or 251.12, as the case may be, as the same may, from time-to-time, be amended. The provisions of this paragraph do not limit or supersede the provisions of Section 3.2.1 above.

3.3   Outside Service Providers

   3.3.1   Consultants   The Data and Derivatives may be made available to Licensee's Consultant for the sole use and benefit of Licensee provided the Consultant signs a Confidentiality Agreement in advance of the restricted use of the Data or Derivatives. The Data and Derivatives shall remain on the premises of Licensee and all analyses or interpretations thereof by Consultant shall be done on such premises and shall not be removed therefrom without the prior written consent of Licensor. Upon completion of the work for which Consultant has been engaged, the Consultant shall not retain any copies of the Data, Derivatives, or any analyses or interpretations of the Data or Derivatives.

   3.3.2   Processors   The Data may be made available to Licensee's Processors for the purpose of creating Derivatives provided the Processor signs a Confidentiality Agreement in advance of the restricted use of the Data and immediately returns the Data and Derivatives to Licensee upon the completion of the work for which the Processor has been engaged. All Derivatives shall be marked as provided in Section 2.3 above to identify it as containing Data proprietary to Licensor.

   3.3.3   Storage Contractors   The Data and Derivatives may be delivered to the custody of Licensee's Storage Contractor provided the Storage Contractor (i) signs a Confidentiality Agreement prior to the delivery of any Data; (ii) makes such Data and Derivatives available only to Licensee or Licensee's Related Entities as authorized by Licensor as provided herein; and (iii) immediately returns all copies of the Data and Derivatives to Licensee upon completion of the service engagement with Licensee.

3.4   Prospective Acquirers/Prospective Partners   Licensee may Show the Data or Derivatives to Prospective Acquirers or Prospective Partners provided the respective Third Party signs a Confidentiality Agreement in advance of the disclosure of the Data or Derivatives and the Data or Derivatives Shown are limited to such portions of the Data or Derivatives directly pertaining to the prospect(s) under negotiation.

3.5   Partners   Licensee shall not Show or give copies of the Data or Derivatives to any Acquirer of Licensee or any Partner of Licensee without the prior written consent of Licensor.

3.6   Internet Disclosures   Licensee shall not Show Data or Derivatives to Third Parties via the Internet, E-Commerce sites, virtual data rooms, asset divestiture web sites, or any other similar means of virtual access outside of Licensee's premises without the express written consent of Licensor; such consent may be premised upon the payment of a fee to Licensor.

Master Geophysical Data-Use License   Page 8 of 14
IAGC Model Agreement – 2003 (Sept rev.)

62

4.   Taxes:

In the event any sales, gross receipts, value added, use or similar tax is levied or assessed against Licensor as a consequence of the licensing of Data to Licensee hereunder, such taxes shall be for the sole account of Licensee, who shall promptly reimburse Licensor in full for any taxes so paid by Licensor upon receipt by Licensee of Licensor's invoice.

5.   Transfer of License:

Licensee shall not sell, sublicense, assign, or transfer this License to a Third Party, in whole or in part, or transfer its rights or obligations hereunder, except as expressly authorized herein.

   5.1   Acquisitions/Mergers   This License shall automatically terminate at such time a Third Party becomes an Acquirer of Licensee unless Licensor receives payment from either Licensee or the Acquirer in the amount of _____ and the Acquirer signs Licensor's then standard license agreement. Should this License terminate, the provisions of Section 8 regarding the return of Data and Derivatives shall apply.

   5.2   The provisions of this Section 5 shall not apply to situations where the voting securities of Licensee (or any of its parents) are publicly traded and the Ownership of such securities changes over time in the normal course of business *unless*, however, Ownership or Control of Licensee (or any of its parents) becomes, *after the date hereof*, concentrated in one unrelated Third Party or more than one such Third Parties acting together.

6.   WARRANTIES AND DISCLAIMERS:

   6.1   LICENSOR WARRANTS ONLY THAT IT OWNS OR CONTROLS THE OWNERSHIP RIGHTS IN THE DATA AND HAS FULL AUTHORITY AND POWER TO GRANT TO LICENSEE THE USE RIGHTS COVERED BY IN THIS LICENSE. LICENSOR ASSUMES ALL LIABILITIES WHICH MAY ARISE OUT OF ITS ACTIVITIES IN ACQUIRING AND PROCESSING THE DATA, AND AGREES TO INDEMNIFY, DEFEND AND HOLD LICENSEE HARMLESS FROM ANY CLAIMS, ACTIONS, OR DAMAGES, INCLUDING ATTORNEY'S FEES AND EXPENSES, ARISING OUT OF SUCH ACTIVITIES, PROVIDED LICENSEE NOTIFIES LICENSOR PROMPTLY IN WRITING OF ANY SUCH CLAIMS AGAINST IT AND GIVES LICENSOR AUTHORITY, INFORMATION AND ASSISTANCE (AT LICENSOR'S EXPENSE) FOR THE DEFENSE OR ASSISTANCE IN THE DEFENSE OF SUCH PROCEEDINGS.

   6.2   DATA DELIVERED TO LICENSEE HEREUNDER ARE, TO THE BEST OF THE KNOWLEDGE, INFORMATION AND BELIEF OF

Master Geophysical Data-Use License   Page 9 of 14
IAGC Model Agreement – 2003 (Sept rev.)

63

LICENSOR, PREPARED IN ACCORDANCE WITH ACCEPTED PRACTICES OF THE GEOPHYSICAL PROFESSION; HOWEVER, LICENSEE ACKNOWLEDGES IT IS ACCEPTING ALL DATA SUBJECT HERETO "AS IS" AND LICENSOR MAKES NO REPRESENTATION OR WARRANTY, EXPRESS OR IMPLIED, IN RESPECT TO THE QUALITY, ACCURACY OR USEFULNESS OF SUCH DATA OR OTHERWISE AND ANY SUCH IMPLIED WARRANTIES OR REPRESENTATIONS ARE HEREBY EXPRESSLY NEGATED. SUCH DATA ARE DELIVERED HEREUNDER WITH THE EXPLICIT UNDERSTANDING AND AGREEMENT OF LICENSEE THAT ANY ACTION TAKEN OR EXPENDITURES MADE BY LICENSEE AND ITS RELATED ENTITIES AND MEMBERS OF ITS EXPLORATION GROUPS BASED ON ITS OR THEIR EXAMINATION, EVALUATION. INTERPRETATION OR USE OF THE DATA SHALL BE AT ITS OWN RISK AND RESPONSIBILITY AND NEITHER LICENSEE NOR SUCH OTHER PARTIES SHALL HAVE ANY CLAIM AGAINST AND HEREBY RELEASES LICENSOR FROM ANY LIABILITY AS A CONSEQUENCE THEREOF.

6.3 LICENSOR MAKES NO REPRESENTATION THAT OIL AND GAS OR OTHER MINERAL LEASES WILL BE GRANTED OR OTHER EXPLORATION ACTIVITY WILL BE AUTHORIZED FOR AREAS COVERED BY THE DATA BY ANY INDIVIDUAL, CORPORATION, GOVERNMENT ENTITY OR OTHER THIRD PARTY AND ANY IMPLIED WARRANTY OR REPRESENTATION TO THAT EFFECT IS HEREBY EXPRESSLY NEGATED.

6.4 NOTWITHSTANDING ANYTHING TO THE CONTRARY CONTAINED HEREINABOVE, LICENSOR SHALL IN NO EVENT BE LIABLE TO LICENSEE OR ANY OTHER PARTIES FOR PUNITIVE, INDIRECT, INCIDENTAL OR CONSEQUENTIAL DAMAGES RESULTING FROM OR ARISING OUT OF THIS LICENSE OR THE USE BY LICENSEE OR SUCH OTHER PARTIES OF THE DATA, INCLUDING, WITHOUT LIMITATION, LOSS OF PROFIT OR BUSINESS INTERRUPTION, HOWEVER SAME MAY BE CAUSED.

7. Term & Termination:

7.1 Term   Subject to the further provisions hereof, the term of this License shall end ___ (_) years from the date first written above. The term of each Supplement shall end ____ (_) years after the effective date of such Supplement. Notwithstanding the foregoing, the Parties shall continue to be bound by all terms and conditions of this License for the unexpired term of any active Supplement(s).

7.2 Automatic Termination   This License and all Supplement(s) shall automatically terminate should the following occur:

Master Geophysical Data-Use License   Page 10 of 14
IAGC Model Agreement – 2003 (Sept rev.)

64

7.2.1 In accordance with Section 5.1; or

7.2.2 Should Licensee voluntarily file a petition in bankruptcy or assign, voluntarily or involuntarily, its assets for the benefit of its creditors or should proceedings be commenced against or by Licensee under any bankruptcy, insolvency or similar statute; or

7.2.3 Should Licensee commit a material breach of any provision of this License and/or Supplement(s) relating to use, display, Showing, sale, trade, lending, or other disposition of the Data and Derivatives, except as specifically authorized herein.

7.3 Termination Upon Notice   This License and Supplement(s) shall terminate should the following occur:

7.3.1 Should Licensee fail to comply with or breach any other provisions not included in Section 7.2 above and subsequently fails to remedy such breach within thirty (30) days following written notice from Licensor; or

7.3.2 Should Licensee fail to make any payment for use of the Data as set forth in this License or applicable Supplement and subsequently fails to remedy such breach within thirty (30) days following the date of an initial notice from Licensor.

7.4 Waiver   Notwithstanding the foregoing, such terminations may be waived if agreed to in writing by both Parties.

8. Effects of Termination:

8.1 Return of Data   Upon termination of this License or any Supplement, regardless of the cause, Licensee shall within ___ days return and/or destroy all respective Data and Derivatives and shall within the same ___ day period provide written certification that all copies of the Data and Derivatives, and any physical manifestations thereof, subject to this License and/or the affected Supplement, have been returned to Licensor or destroyed, including removal of such Data from Licensee's storage and archival systems, workstations, prospect files, and that Licensee has retained no copies of such Data and Derivatives. For a period of ___ months from the termination of any License or Supplement, Licensor shall have the right to audit Licensee's premises, systems and storage sites to verify that all of the affected Data and Derivatives have been returned or destroyed. The Parties hereby agree that Licensee Interpretations shall not be affected, returned, or destroyed and shall remain the property of Licensee.

8.2 Collection Expenses   If Licensor is required to engage the services of a collection agency or attorney to enforce its rights under this License, including an action for damages, declaratory judgment or injunction,

Licensor shall be entitled to recover, in addition to any other costs and relief that may be granted by the court in any such action, reasonable attorney fees and other costs of collection, as well as court costs and other fees and expenses incurred by reason of such engagement. That recovery shall include court costs and attorney's fees incurred by Licensor during any appeal.

8.3 <u>Cumulative Rights</u> The rights and remedies granted in this License to Licensor in the event of default are cumulative and the exercise of any of those rights and remedies shall be without prejudice to the enforcement of any other right or remedy, including without limitation injunctive relief and specific enforcement, available by law or in equity or authorized by this License.

9. <u>Confidentiality of License Agreement:</u> Licensee agrees that this License and any Supplement and the terms hereof and thereof are confidential and may not be disclosed to any individual or entity without Licensor's prior written consent, except this License and its terms may be disclosed (i) to Licensee's employees as required in the performance of their duties; (ii) to outside auditors, Consultants and counsel to the extent necessary to perform their respective duties to the Licensee; (iii) as required by law or regulatory or judicial order, provided that Licensee provides Licensor with prompt written notice in order that Licensor may seek a protective order or other appropriate remedy and Licensee shall only furnish that portion of the License or Supplement that is legally required and will use its best efforts to obtain reliable assurance that confidential treatment will be accorded such documents; (iv) to Related Entities pursuant to Section 3.1 above; and Licensee may disclose the existence of the License to acknowledge that Licensee holds a valid license to the Data in the geographic area covered by this License hereunder.

10. <u>Notices:</u>

10.1 All notices permitted or required to be given under the terms of this License shall be in writing and shall be deemed effective upon receipt if sent by registered or certified and return receipt requested prepaid post, or by telex, telecopier, facsimile, e-mail or other electronic means (all with receipt confirmation) or by commercial courier/messenger service and addressed to the respective Parties hereto at their respective addresses shown below or at such other address as shall be designated in accordance with this Notice provision.

<u>Licensor</u>   <u>Licensee</u>

10.2 Either Party may change its address for notices purposes at any time upon giving written notice specifying such new address and the effective date of such address change to the other Party, as provided above.

11. <u>Waiver</u>:   The rights of each Party hereto, whether granted by this License or by law or equity, may be exercised, from time to time, singularly or in combination, and the waiver of one or more of such rights shall not be deemed to be a waiver of such right in the future or of any one or more of the other rights which the exercising Party may have.   Any right and any breach of a term, provision or condition of this License by one Party shall not be deemed to have been waived by the other Party hereto, unless such waiver is expressed in writing and signed by an authorized representative of such Party, and the failure of either Party to insist upon the strict performance of any term, provision or condition of this License shall not be construed as a waiver or relinquishment in the future of the same or any other term, provision or condition.

12. <u>Governing Law/Disputes</u>:   All questions arising out of or concerning this License and each Supplement or its validity, interpretation, performance or breach shall be governed and decided by application of the appropriate laws (except for any rule of such laws which would make the law of any other jurisdiction applicable hereto) of the State of _____.   Any dispute between the Parties that cannot be resolved by mutual agreement shall be resolved and decided by the federal or state courts of the State of _____ and the Parties hereto do hereby irrevocably submit themselves to the jurisdiction of such courts for such purposes.

13. <u>Headings</u>:   The headings in this Agreement and any index are for convenience reference only and shall not be used as aids to its interpretation.

14. <u>Entire Agreement</u>:   There are no understandings or agreements relative to this License and each Supplement concluded by the Parties pursuant hereto that are not fully expressed herein.   This License and each Supplement are the entire agreement of the Parties concerning the subject matter hereof, and no modification, amendment or addition to this License or a Supplement may be effected unless in writing which specifically references this License and/or the applicable Supplement and is signed by an authorized representative of each Party.

IN WITNESS WHEREOF, the Parties have caused this License to be executed as of the date first above written.

Licensor: **Licensee:**

By:_____   By:_____

Title: Title:_____

Date:_____   Date:_____

Master Geophysical Data-Use License   Page 13 of 14
IAGC Model Agreement – 2003 (Sept rev.)

67

This Supplemental Agreement No. _____ ("**Supplement**") is dated this _____ day of _____, _____ between _____ ("**Licensor**") and _____ ("**Licensee**") subject to the following:

1.   The License. This Supplement is concluded pursuant to and made a part of that certain Master Geophysical Data-Use License between the Parties hereof dated the _____ day of _____, _____ (the "**License**"), the terms of which are incorporated herein by reference, except as expressly negated or modified below.

2.   The Data. The Data subject hereto is described as:

3.   Compensation.   The compensation to be paid by Licensee to Licensor for the non-exclusive right to use such Data is:

4.   Parameters and Other Technical Matters:

5.   Miscellaneous.

Licensor: **Licensee:**

By:_____   By:_____

Master Geophysical Data-Use License   Page 14 of 14
IAGC Model Agreement – 2003 (Sept rev.)

68

1.   This form is reprinted with permission of the International Association of Geophysical Contractors (IAGC), a trade association that represents geophysical contractors. If you were a prospective licensee, would you try to negotiate any changes in this form?

2.   The IAGC's website is http://www.iagc.org/. This website also contains Statements of Principles for contracting, including negotiating ethics, contract principles for geophysical acquisition services, and for data licensing. For links to these principles, see http://www.iagc.org/en/cms/?122

3.   Geophysical companies often conduct a geophysical survey on a "proprietary" basis for an oil company that will then own the geophysical data. Geophysical companies also conduct geophysical surveys on what is sometimes called a "speculative" basis—meaning that the geophysical company will license the collected data to any party willing to pay a licensing fee. This agreement governs the licensee's rights to examine and analyze the data, while protecting the licensor's ownership interests in further licensing, and limiting the licensor's liability. IAGC has promulgated the following Code of Practice for the use of licensed geophysical data, http://iagc.org/iagcwebdata/public/dlic/cop.pdf :

> Licensed data is the property of the licensing geophysical data owner. This ownership transcends and survives any reprocessing, merging, or enhancement of the data.

> Terms of the data use are bound by a Data License Agreement and Data Licenses are not transferable.

> Data may only be shown to third parties under the terms of the Data License Agreement.

> Partner companies must each hold licenses for data used jointly in multi-company projects.

> Data reviews are for QC and general data assessment, not for obtaining geological or exploration insights without licensing data.

> Any consultants or third parties working with licensed data are bound by the same terms and conditions as licensees.

> Licensed data may not be published in any form without the written permission of the data owner.

Chapter 2

OIL AND GAS CONSERVATION LAW AND REGULATION

RAILROAD COMMISSION OF TEXAS
OIL AND GAS DIVISION

APPLICATION FOR PERMIT TO DRILL, RECOMPLETE OR RE-ENTER

FORM W-1
EFF 10/04

Drilling Permit Fee Based on Depth:	
0'-2000' $200	2001'-4000' $225
4001'-9000' $250	>9000'- $300
Expedited Service Fee ADD $150	
Rule 37/38 Exception Fee ADD $200	

Enter if Assigned:
API No.: 42-

Drilling Permit No.:

Rule 37/38 Case No.:

1. RRC Operator No.:

2. Operator Name (as shown on P-5 Organization Report):

3. Operator Address (include street, city, state, zip):

4. Lease Name:

5. Well No.:

GENERAL INFORMATION

6. Purpose of Filing (Mark ALL appropriate boxes):
- ☐ New Drill
- ☐ Amended
- ☐ Amended as Drilled (BHL) (Also File Form W-1D)
- ☐ Recompletion
- ☐ Reclass
- ☐ Field Transfer
- ☐ Re-enter

7. Wellbore Profile (Mark ALL appropriate boxes):
- ☐ Vertical
- ☐ Horizontal (Also File Form W-1H)
- ☐ Directional (Also File Form W-1D)
- ☐ Sidetrack

8. Total Vertical Depth:

9. Do you have the right to develop minerals under any right of way? ☐ Yes ☐ No

10. Is this well subject to Statewide Rule 36 (hydrogen sulfide area)? ☐ Yes ☐ No

SURFACE LOCATION AND ACREAGE INFORMATION

11. RRC District No:

12. County:

13. Surface Location:
- ☐ Land
- ☐ Bay/estuary
- ☐ Inland waterway
- ☐ Offshore

14. This well is to be located _____ miles in a _____ direction from _____ which is the nearest town in the county.

15. Section:

16. Block:

17. Survey:

18. Abstract No:

19. Distance to nearest lease line:

20. Number of contiguous acres in lease, pooled unit or unitized tract:

21. Lease Perpendiculars: _____ ft. from the _____ line and _____ ft from the _____ line.

22. Survey Perpendiculars: _____ ft from the _____ line and _____ ft from the _____ line.

23. Is this a pooled unit? ☐ Yes ☐ No

24. Unitization Docket No:

25. Are you applying for Substandard Acreage Field? ☐ Yes (attach Form W-1A) ☐ No

FIELD INFORMATION

List all fields of anticipated completion including Wildcat. List one zone per line. Attach an additional Form W-1 if you require more space.

26. RRC District No.	27. Field No:	28. Field Name (exactly as shown in RRC records)	29. Well Type	30. Completion Depth	31. Distance to Nearest Well in this Lease & Reservoir	32. No. of Wells on this Lease in this Reservoir

BOTTOMHOLE LOCATION INFORMATION is required for DIRECTIONAL, HORIZONTAL, AND AMENDED AS DRILLED PERMIT APPLICATIONS – Attach FORM W-1D/FORM W-1H as appropriate

Remarks:

CERTIFICATE: I declare under penalties in Sec. 91.143, Texas Natural Resources Code, that I am authorized to file this application, that this application was prepared by me or under my supervision and direction, and that the data and facts stated therein are true, correct, and complete to the best of my knowledge.

Name of Representative (Print)

Signature

Date (mm/dd/yy)

Telephone (AC and number)

E-mail Address (OPTIONAL – If provided, e-mail address will become part of this public record.)

RRC Use only

72

A.   COMPLIANCE. In order to file a Form W-1 you must have a current P-5 Organization Report and financial assurance (if required) on file with the Commission (RRC) and be in compliance with all RRC rules and orders. DO NOT BEGIN DRILLING OPERATIONS UNTIL YOU HAVE RECEIVED AUTHORIZATION FROM THE RRC. The operator must set and cement sufficient surface casing to protect all usable-quality water strata, as defined by the Texas Commission on Environmental Quality, or its predecessor or successor agencies.

B.   WHERE AND WHAT TO FILE. File with the RRC in Austin the original Form W-1 application package, which consists of the completed Form W-1, fee payment, plat, completed Forms W-1D or W-1H, as necessary, and other documents as required. For fees, make check or money order payable to Railroad Commission of Texas. For information on use of credit cards or pre-paid accounts, contact the RRC. The Rule 37/38 exception fee covers one or more exceptions on the same application; if other than a "new drill," provide the original exception case or docket number. Fees are non-refundable. The RRC may waive fees if an amended application is filed at the request of RRC. Before you may initially file computer-generated paper Forms W-1, the RRC must approve the template. You may also electronically file drilling permit applications. For information, call (512)463-6751 or check the RRC's web site at www.rrc.state.tx.us

C.   PURPOSE OF FILING (Item 6.) *Recompletion* is working over an existing wellbore to complete in a different field/reservoir. *Re-entry* is going back into a wellbore that has been plugged to the surface. *Reclassification* is changing an existing well originally permitted only as injection/disposal or other service well to an oil or gas producing well or changing an existing well in the Panhandle East or West fields from oil to gas or gas to oil production. For anything other than a "New Drill," indicate the API number. If the API number is not known, in "Operator Remarks" area, give the original operator, lease, and well identification and date of original completion or plugging. A materially amended permit requires a new Form W-1 and applicable fees, and usually involves the addition of a field/reservoir or a change in location on a previously permitted well. Include the original drilling permit number when filing an application for an amended permit.

D.   WELLBORE PROFILE (Item 7.) Check "sidetrack" only for recompletions or re-entries, if applicable. File **FORM W-1D**, *Supplemental Directional Well Information*, if the proposed well configuration will be directional with one or more bottomhole locations. File **FORM W-1H**, *Supplemental Horizontal Well Information*, if the proposed well configuration will be horizontal with one or more terminus locations. For these types of completions, several different sets of location data are required. This data may or may not be the same for each field applied for; however, each different proposed bottomhole location or lateral must be associated with at least one field

E.   LOCATION SPACING AND DENSITY. The proposed location must be "regular" in terms of the RRC's spacing (Rule 37 or field rules) and density (Rule 38 or field rules) requirements for each listed field; otherwise, an exception to those requirements must be sought.

    REGULAR locations are in accordance with either (1) statewide spacing minimums – 467' from the nearest lease line and 1,200' from the nearest well (applied for, permitted or completed) on the same lease in the same reservoir and statewide density minimums – 40 acres; (2) spacing and density minimums,(which may vary according to depth) for County Regular Fields (Districts 7B, 9, and McCulloch County), where there are no field rules and the proposed depth is 5,000' or shallower; or (3) spacing and density standards set out in special rules for the field. Field and County Regular rules are available on the Internet at www.rrc.state.tx.us.

    EXCEPTIONS to minimum standard spacing and density requirements may be requested. The application requires additional information on a *certified* plat (see G, below) and a list of names and addresses of all offsetting operators or unleased mineral interest owners of each tract that is contiguous to the drill site tract. Clearly key the list to the plat so that each tract/operator can be readily identified. If you do not have the right to develop the minerals under any right-of-way that crosses or is contiguous to this tract and the well requires a Rule 37 or 38 exception, also list the name and address of the entity that holds that right. If requesting only a lease-line spacing exception, list only the names and addresses of all affected persons for tracts closer to the well than the greater of ½ the prescribed minimum between-well spacing distance or the minimum lease-line spacing distance. If requesting only a between-well spacing exception, list only the names and addresses of all affected persons for each adjacent tract and each tract nearer to the well than the greater of ½ the prescribed minimum between-well spacing distance or the minimum lease-line spacing. *NOTE:* If you penetrate a Rule 37 or 38 field/reservoir not listed on the application, you will not necessarily be allowed to use the existence of this wellbore as justification for an exception to complete this wellbore in such field/reservoir in the future.

F.   ACREAGE – OTHER
    Pooled Units: Multiple tracts may be pooled together to meet minimum drilling unit acreage requirements. Complete and attach Form P-12, *Certificate of Pooling Authority*. On the plat (see G, below) outline pooled unit AND each tract listed on the Form P-12. If pooled or unitized through a hearing and the Docket number is noted in Item 24 of Form W-1, no Form P-12 (Certificate of Pooling Authority) is needed.
    Substandard Acreage: Complete and submit a Form W-1A, *Substandard Acreage Drilling Unit Certification*, with the first and only well on a substandard tract or lease, and when using surplus acreage as a substandard pooled unit.
    Contiguous Acres: Rule 39 requires that all acres in the lease or pooled unit be contiguous. If a Rule 39 exception has already been granted for the subject lease or unit, provide the docket number and issuance date in the box in the upper left-hand corner of the Form W-1.

G.   PLAT. All drilling permit applications must be accompanied by a legible, accurate plat, at a scale of 1" = 1,000' and showing at least the lease or pooled unit line nearest the proposed location AND the nearest section/survey lines. The plat for the initial well on a lease or pooled unit must be of the entire lease or unit (including all tracts being pooled). The plat for subsequent wells on the pooled unit for which a Form P-12 is required must show the entire pooled unit. If necessary, submit the large area plat at a scale of 1" = 2,000' showing the entire lease. Plats for Rule 37 and/or 38 exceptions must also be certified and have offsets keyed to the offset listing (see E, above). The plat must include (1) the surface location of the proposed drilling site (for directional wells, also indicate projected bottomhole location and for horizontal wells also indicate projected penetration points and terminus locations); (2) a line and the distance from the surface location to the nearest point on the lease line or pooled unit line; if there is an unleased interest in a tract of the pooled unit that is nearer than the pooled unit line, use the nearest point on that unleased tract boundary; (3) a perpendicular line from two nearest non-parallel survey/section lines to the proposed surface and the proposed bottomhole or terminus locations and indicate distances. (4) a line from the proposed surface location to the nearest oil or gas well (applied for, permitted, or completed) in the same lease or pooled unit and in the same field (also indicate the distance and the API number of that well); (5) the name, as applicable, of the county, survey, abstract, section, block, lot, subdivision, etc.; (6) a scale bar; and (7) the northerly direction.

H.   INDIVIDUAL ITEMS ON THE FRONT OF FORM W-1:
Item 8. For a recompletion, provide the projected—not measured--true vertical depth. For a plug-back recompletion, give the depth of the plug setting.
Item 10. If the well is subject to Rule 36, you must file a Form H-9 (Certificate of Compliance Statewide Rule 36) with the appropriate RRC district office.
Item 11. Provide RRC District No. associated with the County listed in Item 12.
Item 19. For pooled units, if there is an unleased/non-pooled interest in a tract of the pooled unit that is nearer than the pooled unit line, give the distance to the nearest point on that unleased/non-pooled tract boundary.
Item 26. Provide the RRC District No. associated with the field.
Item 29. Use the following codes for Well Type: O = oil; G = gas; B = oil and gas; I = injection/disposal; R = storage; S = service; V = water supply; C = cathodic protection; T = exploratory test (core, stratigraphic, seismic, sulfur, uranium).
Item 30. Enter the approximate completion depth at which you may complete in each field listed. This depth must be less than or equal to the Total Vertical Depth.
Item 31. Distance to Nearest Well. Required only for wells identified as oil or gas in Item 29 and includes distance to any applied for or permitted location or completed well. This information is necessary for the purpose of ensuring compliance with spacing and density rules.
Item 32. Provide the total combined number of oil and gas wells only (include all applied for or permitted locations and completed wells). Do NOT include injection, disposal or other types of service wells.

1.   All states require a party desirous of drilling a well for oil or gas to obtain a drilling permit. The applicant is typically called the "operator" as in the attached form. The filing of this form allows the conservation agency to determine whether the well will be properly located vis-à-vis neighboring tracts and for the targeted depth and location.

2.   Depending on the state, if the well is a "wildcat," the location rule may be a statewide or district rule and may also vary with the intended depth of the well. Some states have wildcat spacing and density regulations. If the well is a development well, the well must be located in accordance with the applicable well spacing and density rules for the field where the well is located and for the targeted formation.

3.   In many states, the well permit must also be accompanied by a surety bond to assure that the well is properly plugged and abandoned at the end of its economic life. The life of the well will be very short if it is a dry hole. If the well is a producer, it could produce for decades.

Royalty interest is non-possessory (even in Texas)

CASE NO. 9709
ORDER NO. 11423

IN THE MATTER OF A HEARING CALLED ON
A MOTION OF THE COMMISSION TO
CONSIDER THE APPLICATION OF
MARATHON OIL CO. FOR AN ORDER
AMENDING ORDER NO. 11319, THE PROPER
SPACING ORDER FOR THE BAILEY-BAKKEN
POOL, DUNN COUNTY, ND, TO PROVIDE
ADDITIONAL FLEXIBILITY IN LOCATING
THE FIRST WELL ON 1280-ACRE SPACING
UNITS WITHIN THE BAILEY-BAKKEN POOL
WHEN NECESSARY DUE TO SURFACE
TOPOGRAPHY OR OTHER CONDITIONS, OR
GRANTING SUCH OTHER RELIEF AS IS
APPROPRIATE.

ORDER OF THE COMMISSION
THE COMMISSION FINDS:

(1) This cause came on for hearing at 9:00 a.m. on the 17th day of October, 2007.

(2) The witness for Marathon Oil Company (Marathon) provided telephonic testimony in this matter, pursuant to North Dakota Administrative Code (NDAC) Section 43-02-03-88.2. A Telephonic Communication Affidavit was received on October 23, 2007, therefore, such testimony may be considered evidence.

(3) Marathon made application to the Commission for an order amending Order No. 11319, the proper spacing order for the Bailey-Bakken Pool, Dunn County, North Dakota, to provide additional flexibility in locating the first well on 1280-acre spacing units within the Bailey-Bakken Pool when necessary due to surface topography or other conditions, or granting such other relief as is appropriate.

(4) The most recent spacing order for the Bailey-Bakken Pool at the time of this application was Order No. 11319 and it provided for the following in Zone I: All portions of the well bore not isolated by cement of any horizontal well drilled shall be no closer than 500 feet to the boundary of the spacing unit, although the first well drilled shall be no closer than 1320 feet to the east and west boundaries of the spacing unit. A 100-feet tolerance beyond the 1320-feet east and west setback requirement may be allowed by the Director if the necessity therefor can be demonstrated to his satisfaction.

(5) Order No. 11402 entered in Case No. 9690, the most recent spacing order for the Bailey-Bakken Pool, established proper spacing for the development of Zone I in the Bailey-Bakken Pool at up to two horizontal wells per 1280 acres and Zone II at one horizontal well per 640 acres. Case No. 9690 was heard on September 28, 2007 and Order No. 11402 was signed on October 26, 2007.

1   (6) Order No. 11402 provides for the following in Zone I: All portions of the well bore not
2   isolated by cement of any horizontal well drilled shall be no closer than 500 feet to the
3   boundary of the spacing unit, although the first well drilled shall be no closer than 1220 feet to the
4   east and west boundaries of the spacing unit. The Director is hereby authorized to issue an
5   administrative order granting a waiver to the 1220-feet setback requirement for topographic or
6   access reasons, whenever, in his opinion an application for such an order contains sufficient
7   information to determine the necessity therefor. Said waiver cannot exceed the 500-feet setback
8   requirement.
9   (7) Marathon's intent in developing the Bailey-Bakken Pool is to drill up to two single-lateral
10   horizontal wells in each standup spacing unit. The first horizontal well would be drilled from a
11   surface location near the north or south setback requirement on either end of the spacing unit
12   approximately 1320 feet from the east or west spacing unit boundary. The casing would be set
13   horizontally in the Bakken Pool north or south of the surface location at a legal location and the
14   lateral would then be drilled to a bottom hole location near the north or south setback
15   requirement and approximately 1320 feet from the east or west spacing unit boundary. Marathon
16   would then drill a second horizontal well in a similar fashion but not closer than 500 feet from any
17   of the spacing unit boundaries.
18   (8) Marathon presented evidence that in certain areas of the Bailey Field the siting of the surface
19   location can be difficult and limited due to rough topography, waterways, landowner concerns,
20   and regulatory distance requirements combined with the rough topography. In some instances,
21   there may be an existing road which can be utilized thereby improving the economics of drilling a
22   well and decreasing the necessity of building new roads which will minimize surface disturbance and
23   enhance aesthetic values.
24   (9) Requiring all portions of the well bore not isolated by cement of the first horizontal well
25   drilled to be no closer than 1220 feet to the east and west boundaries of the spacing unit,
26   increases the cost and risk associated with setting the production casing at said 1220-feet setback in
27   a well where surface constraints dictate locating it at a less than optimum location. This
28   increased cost and risk is due to the necessity of deviating the normally vertical portion of the
29   well bore and also in encountering potential difficulties in landing the production casing at the
30   aforementioned 1220-feet setback requirement due to increased friction and tortuosity. Deviation
31   of the normally vertical portion of the well bore also results in increased rod wear and less efficient
32   pump setting depth.
33   (10) Flexibility with respect to siting the surface location of wells in the Bailey Field due to
34   surface constraints will increase drilling and production efficiencies allowing the recovery of as
35   much oil and gas as economically possible, will prevent waste and the drilling of unnecessary wells
36   in a manner which will not have a detrimental effect on correlative rights, and will enhance
37   landowner relationships.
38   (11) In order to foster, encourage, and promote the development and production of oil and gas
39   resources, the Director should be granted authority to issue an administrative order, without
40   holding a hearing, allowing the first horizontal well drilled in Zone I in the Bailey-Bakken Pool to
41   be completed open hole between the 500-feet and 1220-feet setback requirements contingent upon
42   the well bore traversing to a point beyond the 1220-feet setback requirement in an
43   expeditious manner. Further deviation from this trajectory should be granted if the necessity
44   therefor can be demonstrated to the Director's satisfaction.
45   (12) Petroleum Development Corporation submitted a letter stating they had received a copy

1   of Marathon's application and, as a working interest owner and operator in the field, they support
2   Marathon's request.
3   (13) There were no objections to this application.
4   (14) Approval of this application will prevent waste, avoid the drilling of unnecessary wells,
5   and protect correlative rights.
6   IT IS THEREFORE ORDERED:
7   (1) The Director is hereby authorized to issue an administrative order granting a waiver allowing
8   the first horizontal well drilled in Zone I in the Bailey-Bakken Pool to be completed open hole
9   between the 500-feet and 1220-feet setback requirements for topographic or access reasons,
10   contingent upon the well bore traversing to a point beyond the 1220-feet setback requirement
11   in an expeditious manner, whenever, in his opinion, the application for such an order contains
12   sufficient information to determine the following:
13   (a) Horizontal drilling technology will be utilized in the Bakken Pool.
14   (b) The proposed production casing setting location is beyond the 500-feet setback requirement.
15   (c) Topography, waterways, regulatory distance requirements combined with the rough
16   topography, road access, or landowner concerns will substantially increase the cost and/or risk in
17   drilling and producing the well.
18   (d) Further deviation from the aforementioned expeditious trajectory may be granted if the
19   necessity therefor can be demonstrated to the Director's satisfaction.
20   (2) Provisions established herein for the Bailey-Bakken Pool are for the exclusive purpose of
21   drilling horizontal wells. Existing and future vertical and directional wells drilled within the area
22   defined in paragraph (3) below shall not be subject to this order.
23   (3) The Bailey Field is hereby redefined as the following described tracts of land in Dunn County,
24   North Dakota:
25
26   TOWNSHIP 147 NORTH, RANGE 95 WEST, 5TH PM ALL OF SECTIONS 26 AND 35,
27
28   TOWNSHIP 146 NORTH, RANGE 95 WEST, 5TH PM
29   ALL OF SECTIONS 1, 2, 3, 10, 11, 12, 13, 14, 23, 24, 26, 27, 34 AND 35,
30
31   TOWNSHIP 146 NORTH, RANGE 94 WEST, 5TH PM
32   ALL OF SECTIONS 1 THROUGH 36, INCLUSIVE,
33
34   TOWNSHIP 146 NORTH, RANGE 93 WEST, 5TH PM
35   ALL OF SECTIONS 3, 4, 5, 6, 7, 8, 9, 10, 15, 16, 17, 18, 19, 20, 21, 22, 27, 28, 29, 30, 31, 32,
36   33 AND 34,
37
38   TOWNSHIP 145 NORTH, RANGE 94 WEST, 5TH PM
39   ALL OF SECTIONS 1, 2, 11, 12, 13, 14, 23, 24, 25, 26, 35 AND 36,
40
41   TOWNSHIP 145 NORTH, RANGE 93 WEST, 5TH PM
42   ALL OF SECTIONS 3, 4, 5, 6, 7, 8, 9, 10, 18, 19, 29, 30, 31 AND 32,
43
44   TOWNSHIP 144 NORTH, RANGE 94 WEST, 5TH PM
45   ALL OF SECTIONS 1, 2, 3, 4, 5, 8, 9, 10, 11 AND 12,

TOWNSHIP 144 NORTH, RANGE 93 WEST, 5TH PM
ALL OF SECTIONS 6 AND 7,

together with those additional sections or governmental lots corresponding thereto as may be proven productive by wells drilled on lands within one mile of the boundaries of the field as set forth above, provided further that such extensions of the field boundaries shall include only sufficient acreage to form a spacing unit for such wells, and any intervening lands.

(4) The Bailey-Bakken Pool is hereby redefined as the following described tracts of land in Dunn County, North Dakota:

ZONE I

TOWNSHIP 147 NORTH, RANGE 95 WEST, 5TH PM
ALL OF SECTIONS 26 AND 35,

TOWNSHIP 146 NORTH, RANGE 95 WEST, 5TH PM
ALL OF SECTIONS 1, 2, 3, 10, 11, 12, 13, 14, 23, 24, 26, 27, 34 AND 35,

TOWNSHIP 146 NORTH, RANGE 94 WEST, 5TH PM
ALL OF SECTIONS 1, 3, 4, 5, 6, 7, 8, 9, 10, 12, 13, 14, 15, 16, 17, 18, 19, 20, 21, 22, 23, 24, 25, 27, 29, 30, 31, 32, 34 AND 36,

TOWNSHIP 146 NORTH, RANGE 93 WEST, 5TH PM
ALL OF SECTIONS 3, 4, 5, 6, 7, 8, 9, 10, 15, 16, 17, 18, 19, 20, 21, 22, 27, 28, 29, 30, 31, 32, 33 AND 34,

TOWNSHIP 145 NORTH, RANGE 94 WEST, 5TH PM
ALL OF SECTIONS 1, 2, 11, 12, 13, 14, 23, 24, 25, 26, 35 AND 36,

TOWNSHIP 145 NORTH, RANGE 93 WEST, 5TH PM
ALL OF SECTIONS 3, 4, 5, 6, 7, 8, 9, 10, 18, 19, 29, 30, 31 AND 32,

TOWNSHIP 144 NORTH, RANGE 94 WEST, 5TH PM
ALL OF SECTIONS 1, 2, 3, 4, 5, 8, 9, 10, 11 AND 12,

TOWNSHIP 144 NORTH, RANGE 93 WEST, 5TH PM
ALL OF SECTIONS 6 AND 7.

ZONE II

TOWNSHIP 146 NORTH, RANGE 94 WEST, 5TH PM ALL OF SECTIONS 2, 11, 26, 28, 33 AND 35,

together with those additional sections or governmental lots corresponding thereto as may be

1 proven productive by wells drilled on lands within one mile of the boundaries of the field as set
2 forth above, provided further that such extensions of the field boundaries shall include only
3 sufficient acreage to form a spacing unit for such wells, and any intervening lands.

4 (5) The Bailey-Bakken Pool is hereby defined as that accumulation of oil and gas found in the
5 interval from 50 feet above the top of the Bakken Formation to 50 feet below the top of the
6 Three Forks Formation within the limits of the field as set forth above.

7 (6) The proper spacing for the development of Zone I in the Bailey-Bakken Pool is hereby set at up
8 to two horizontal wells per 1280 acres.

9 (7) All portions of the well bore not isolated by cement of any horizontal well hereafter drilled
10 in Zone I in the Bailey-Bakken Pool shall be no closer than 500 feet to the boundary of the
11 spacing unit, although the first well drilled shall be no closer than 1220 feet to the east and west
12 boundaries of the spacing unit. Measurement inaccuracies in the directional survey equipment
13 need not be considered except when deemed necessary by the Director. Wells presently
14 permitted to or producing from the pool that do not conform to this spacing pattern shall be
15 considered exceptions.

16 (8) The Director is hereby authorized to issue an administrative order granting a waiver
17 allowing the first horizontal well drilled in Zone I in the Bailey-Bakken Pool to be completed
18 open hole between the 500-feet and 1220-feet setback requirements for topographic or access
19 reasons, contingent upon the well bore traversing to a point beyond the 1220-feet setback
20 requirement in an expeditious manner, whenever, in his opinion, the application for such an
21 order contains sufficient information to determine the following:

22 (a) Horizontal drilling technology will be utilized in the Bakken Pool.

23 (b)The proposed production casing setting location is beyond the 500-feet setback
24 requirement.

25 (c)Topography, waterways, regulatory distance requirements combined with the rough
26 topography, road access, or landowner concerns will substantially increase the cost and/or risk in
27 drilling and producing the well.

28 (d) Further deviation from the aforementioned expeditious trajectory may be granted if the
29 necessity therefor can be demonstrated to the Director's satisfaction.

30 (9) Sections 26 and 35, Township 147 North, Range 95 West; Sections 1 and 12; Sections 2 and
31 11; Sections 3 and 10; Sections 13 and 24; Sections 14 and 23; Sections 26 and 35; Sections
32 27 and 34, Township 146 North, Range 95 West; Sections 1 and 12; Sections 3 and 10; Sections 4
33 and 9; Sections 5 and 8; Sections 6 and 7; Sections 13 and 24; Sections 14 and 23; Sections 15
34 and 22; Sections 16 and 21; Sections 17 and 20; Sections 18 and 19; Sections 25 and 36; Sections
35 27 and 34; Sections 29 and 32; Sections 30 and 31, Township 146 North, Range 94 West; Sections
36 3 and 10; Sections 4 and 9; Sections 5 and 8; Sections 6 and 7; Sections 15 and 22; Sections 17
37 and 20; Sections 18 and 19; Sections 27 and 34; Sections 28 and 33; Sections 29 and 32; Sections
38 30 and 31, Township 146 North, Range 93 West; Sections 1 and 12; Sections 2 and 11; Sections 13
39 and 24; Sections 14 and 23; Sections 25 and 36; Sections 26 and 35, Township 145 North, Range
40 94 West; Sections 3 and 10; Sections 4 and 9; Sections 5 and 8; Sections 6 and 7; Sections 18
41 and 19; Sections 29 and 32; Sections 30 and 31, Township 145 North, Range 93 West; Sections 1
42 and 12; Sections 2 and 11; Sections 3 and 10; Sections 4 and 9; Sections 5 and 8, Township 144
43 North, Range 94 West; and Sections 6 and 7, Township 144 North, Range 93 West, Dunn County,
44 North Dakota, are hereby designated 1280-acrespacing units in Zone I in the Bailey-Bakken
45 Pool.

(10) Sections 16 and 21, Township 146 North, Range 93 West, Dunn County, North Dakota, are hereby designated a 1280-acre spacing unit in Zone I in the Bailey-Bakken Pool. However, a well cannot be permitted on this spacing unit until after March 31, 2008.

(11) Spacing units hereafter created in Zone I in the Bailey-Bakken Pool shall be standup spacing units consisting of two adjacent governmental sections.

(12) Zone I in the Bailey-Bakken Pool shall not be extended except by further order of the Commission after due notice and hearing.

(13) The proper spacing for the development of Zone II in the Bailey-Bakken Pool is hereby set at one horizontal well per 640 acres.

(14) All portions of the well bore not isolated by cement of any horizontal well hereafter drilled in Zone II in the Bailey-Bakken Pool shall be no closer than 500 feet to the boundary of the spacing unit. Measurement inaccuracies in the directional survey equipment need not be considered except when deemed necessary by the Director.

(15) Spacing units hereafter created in Zone II in the Bailey-Bakken Pool shall consist of a governmental section.

(16) The operator of any horizontally drilled well in the Bailey-Bakken Pool shall cause to be made a directional survey of the well bore. The directional survey contractor shall file a certified survey with the Commission within 30 days after completion of the well in accordance with NDAC Section 43-02-03-25. The survey shall be of sufficient quality to enable the Commission to determine the entire completion location of the well and its terminus.

(17) The Director is hereby authorized to exercise continuing jurisdiction to determine whether any well proposed or drilled upon any spacing unit herein established has justified the creation of such unit, to require amendments or modifications to the permit to drill for such well, and to deny a permit to drill in the event a well is proposed to be drilled in a manner inconsistent with the evidence that justified the spacing requirements in the Bailey-Bakken Pool.

(18) The Commission shall have continuing jurisdiction in this matter and specifically reserves the authority, upon its own motion or the motion of any interested party, to: (1) review the spacing requirements for the Bailey-Bakken Pool; (2) determine whether the separate zones of spacing established herein are warranted; and, (3) make such further amendments or modifications to the spacing requirements for the Bailey-Bakken Pool as the Commission deems appropriate.

(19) No well shall be drilled or produced in the Bailey-Bakken Pool, as defined herein, except in conformity with the regulations above without special order of the Commission after due notice and hearing.

(20) The following rules concerning the casing, tubing and equipping of wells shall apply to the subsequent drilling and operation of wells in the Bailey-Bakken Pool:

(a) The surface casing shall consist of new or reconditioned pipe that has been previously tested to 1000 pounds per square inch. The casing shall be set and cemented at a point not less than 50 feet below the base of the Fox Hills Formation. Sufficient cement shall be used to fill the annular space outside the pipe to the surface of the ground, or the bottom of the cellar, and sufficient scratchers and centralizers shall be used to assure a good cement job. Cement shall be allowed to stand a minimum of 12 hours before drilling the plug or initiating tests. The quality of cement shall conform to the standards provided under NDAC Section 43-02-03-21;

(b) The producing or oil string shall consist of new or reconditioned pipe that has been previously tested to 2000 pounds per square inch. Casing shall be set and cemented at a point not higher than the top of the producing formation, or at a point approved by the Director. Sufficient cement shall be used and applied in such a manner as to protect and isolate all formations containing oil and/or gas, protect the pipe through salt sections encountered, and isolate the Dakota-Lakota Series. The cement shall be allowed to stand a minimum of 15 hours before drilling the plug or initiating tests. The quality of cement shall conform to the standards provided under NDAC Section 43-02-03-21. After cementing, the casing shall be tested by application of pump pressure of at least 2000 pounds per square inch. If, at the end of 30 minutes this pressure has dropped 150 pounds per square inch or more, the casing shall be repaired. Thereafter, the casing shall again be tested in the same manner. Further work shall not proceed until a satisfactory test has been obtained;

(c) All well-head fittings and connections shall have a working pressure in excess of that to which they are expected to be subjected; and,

(d) All wells shall be equipped with tubing; a tubing packer must also be utilized in flowing wells unless a waiver is obtained from the Director after demonstrating the casing will not be subjected to excessive pressure or corrosion; all tubing shall be of sufficient internal diameter to allow the passage of a bottom hole pressure gauge for the purpose of obtaining bottom hole pressure measurements.

(21) The gas-oil ratio of all wells not connected to a gas gathering system shall be measured annually during the month of May. The reservoir pressure shall be measured within 45 days in all wells hereinafter completed in the Bailey-Bakken Pool. Drill stem test pressures are acceptable for determining reservoir pressure. Pressure measurements shall be made at or adjusted to a subsea datum of 7900 feet after the well has been shut in for a minimum of 48 hours. All gas-oil ratio and reservoir pressure determinations shall be made by methods approved by the Director and reported to the Director within 15 days following the end of the month in which they are determined. The Director is authorized to waive these requirements if the necessity therefore can be demonstrated to his satisfaction. All additional gas-oil ratio and reservoir pressure determinations conducted on any well, but not specially required herein, shall be reported to the Director within 15 days following the end of the month in which they are determined.

(22) No salt water, drilling mud, crude oil, or waste oil shall be stored in pits in this field, except in an emergency, and approved by the Director.

(23) All wells in the Bailey-Bakken Pool shall be allowed to produce at a maximum efficient rate for a period of 60 days commencing on the first day oil is produced through well-head equipment into tanks from the ultimate producing interval after casing has been run; thereafter, oil production from such wells shall not exceed an average of 100 barrels of oil per day; if and when such wells are connected to a gas gathering and processing facility the foregoing restrictions shall be removed, and the wells shall be allowed to produce at a maximum efficient rate. The Director is authorized to issue an administrative order allowing unrestricted production at a maximum efficient rate for a period not to exceed 120 days, commencing on the first day oil is produced through well-head equipment into tanks from the ultimate producing interval after casing has been run, if the necessity therefor can be demonstrated to his satisfaction.

(24) If the flaring of gas produced with crude oil from the Bailey-Bakken Pool causes, or threatens to cause, degradation of ambient air quality, production from the pool shall be further

1 restricted.

2 (25) This order covers all of the Bailey-Bakken Pool, common source of supply of crude oil and/or

3 natural gas as herein defined, and continues in full force and effect further order of the

4 Commission or until the last well in the pool has been plugged and abandoned.

NOTES

1. The preceding form is a sample spacing order issued by the North Dakota Industrial Commission, the state agency charged with regulating oil and gas. Notice that the North Dakota order is quite specific with respect to the location and shape of spacing units within a field. The only variations allowed by this order relate to the direction of the 320 acre rectangular units, which may be drawn either north-south (vertical or "stand up") or east-west (horizontal or "lay down") within a section. For an example of a field containing both types of units, see the plat accompanying *Larsen v. Oil & Gas Conservation Commission.*

2. Spacing and density rules of the Texas Railroad Commission typically establish the size of drilling units and specify minimum distances between wells on the same lease and between a well and a boundary line, but otherwise leave considerable discretion to the operator in deciding the location and precise shape of units. Spacing orders of most state regulatory agencies are more akin to those of North Dakota than to those of Texas.

3. Many state regulatory agencies give notice of hearings on spacing, well allowables, and requests for exceptions only to parties with a working interest, even though these matters may also affect royalty owners. Some Lessors have attempted to deal with this problem by contractually obligating their lessees to notify them of hearings and requests for agency action. The following clause from a Texas oil and gas lease is an example.

> Lessee agrees to give Lessor reasonable notice of any application that Lessee shall make to the Railroad Commission of the State of Texas or to any other governmental authority for field spacing rules or regulations affecting the leased premises. In the event any hearing for field spacing rules or regulations shall be applied for by any third party or parties and affecting the leased premises, Lessee agrees to promptly notify Lessor of such application.

4. The following form is a compulsory pooling order issued by the North Dakota Industrial Commission. Both the spacing order and pooling order were furnished by Bruce E. Hicks, Assistant Director, Oil and Gas Division, Department of Mineral Resources, North Dakota Industrial Commission. https://www.dmr.nd.gov/oilgas/

CASE NO. 9803
ORDER NO. 11536

IN THE MATTER OF A HEARING CALLED ON
A MOTION OF THE COMMISSION TO
CONSIDER THE APPLICATION OF EOG
RESOURCES, INC. FOR AN ORDER
PURSUANT TO NDAC § 43-02-03-88.1 POOLING
ALL INTERESTS IN A SPACING UNIT FOR THE
RISAN #1-34H, SECTION 34, T.153N., R.90W.,
PARSHALL-BAKKEN POOL, MOUNTRAIL
COUNTY, ND; AUTHORIZING THE
RECOVERY FROM EACH
NONPARTICIPATING OWNER A RISK
PENALTY AS PROVIDED BY NDCC § 38-08-08
AND FOR SUCH OTHER RELIEF AS IS
APPROPRIATE.

ORDER OF THE COMMISSION

THE COMMISSION FINDS:

(1)   This cause came on for hearing at 9:00 a.m. on the 19th day of December, 2007.

(2)   Pursuant to North Dakota Administrative Code Section 43-02-03-88.1, the Director is authorized to sign, on behalf of the Commission, orders relating to, inter alia, pooling under North Dakota Century Code (NDCC) Section 38-08-08.

(3)   The applicant is the owner of an interest in an oil and gas leasehold estate in a spacing unit for the Parshall-Bakken Pool described as all of Section 34, Township 153 North, Range 90 West, Mountrail County, North Dakota.

(4)   Said spacing unit is created in accordance with an order of the Commission and there are separately owned tracts and/or separately owned interests in the spacing unit, and some of the owners thereof have not voluntarily pooled their interests for the development and operation of said spacing unit.

(5)   The Commission makes no findings with regard to the specific acreage or percentage attributed to separately owned tracts or interests.

(6)   NDCC Section 38-08-08 requires the Commission to enter a pooling order upon application when two or more separately owned tracts are embraced within a spacing unit, or there are separately owned interests in all or a part of a spacing unit, in the absence of voluntary pooling. The section further provides that working interest owners in the spacing unit shall pay their share of the reasonable actual cost of drilling and operating the well plus a reasonable charge for supervision. In addition to such costs and charges, nonparticipating lessees may be

required to pay a risk penalty of 200 percent and unleased mineral interest owners may be required to pay a risk penalty of 50 percent of their share of the reasonable actual cost of drilling and completing the well.

(7)   Applicant requests an order of the Commission pooling all interests in the spacing unit, and allowing the recovery of a risk penalty from nonparticipating owners.

(8)   There were no objections to this application.

(9)   This application should be granted in order to prevent waste and protect correlative rights.

IT IS THEREFORE ORDERED:

(1)   All oil and gas interests in a spacing unit for the Parshall-Bakken Pool described as all of Section 34, Township 153 North, Range 90 West, Mountrail County, North Dakota, are hereby pooled for the development and operation of the spacing unit.

(2)   This pooling shall not determine or establish the specific acreage to be attributed to separately owned tracts, or specific interests attributed to separately owned interests.

(3)   The operator of the well for said spacing unit shall conduct operations in a manner so as to protect correlative rights of all interested parties.

(4)   All owners of interests shall recover or receive, without unnecessary expense, their just and equitable share of production from said spacing unit in the proportion as their interests may appear in the spacing unit.

(5)   The working interest owners shall reimburse the operator for their proportionate share of the reasonable actual cost of drilling and operating said well, plus a reasonable charge for supervision.

(6)   In the event of any dispute as to such costs the Commission shall determine the proper cost.

(7)   If a lessee owning an interest in the spacing unit elects not to participate in the risk and cost of drilling a well thereon, the owner paying for the nonparticipating lessee's share of the drilling and operation of a well may recover from the nonparticipating lessee a risk penalty for the risk involved in drilling the well. The risk penalty is 200 percent of the nonparticipating lessee's share of the reasonable actual costs of drilling and completing the well and may be recovered out of, and only out of, production from the pooled spacing unit, as provided by NDCC Section 38-08-10, exclusive of any royalty or overriding royalty.

(8)   If an unleased mineral interest owner in the spacing unit refuses a good-faith attempt to execute a lease and elects not to participate in the risk and cost of drilling a well thereon, the owner paying for the nonparticipating mineral interest owner's share of the drilling and operation of a well may recover from the nonparticipating mineral interest owner a risk penalty for the risk involved in drilling the well. The risk penalty is 50 percent of the nonparticipating mineral interest owner's share of the reasonable actual costs of drilling and completing the well and may be recovered out of, and only out of, production from the pooled spacing unit, as provided by NDCC Section 38-08-10, exclusive of any royalty.

(9)   In the event the size of the spacing unit pooled herein is modified by the Commission, this order shall terminate as of the date of such order.

(10)   This order shall be effective from the date of first operations, and shall remain in full force and effect until further order of the Commission.

Dated this 18th day of January, 2008.

force pooling order

NOTES

1.   This North Dakota compulsory-pooling order illustrates the use of the risk penalty, which is assessed against nonparticipating working-interest owners ("carried" interests). The risk penalties (Order subsection 7 for lessees and Order subsection 8 for owners of unleased mineral interests) are designed to compensate the operator and other participating working-interest owners for essentially assuming the carried parties share of the risk that the well will be a dry hole. If working-interest owners do not elect to participate, they are deemed to be carried, subject to a risk penalty.

2.   Compare these prior two orders with the next two orders issued by the Oklahoma Corporation Commission.

BEFORE THE CORPORATION COMMISSION OF THE STATE OF OKLAHOMA

APPLICANT: WALTER OIL & GAS)
CORPORATION)
)
RELIEF REQUESTED: HORIZONTAL SPACING) CAUSE CD NO. 200704775
)
LEGAL DESCRIPTION: SECTION 10,)
TOWNSHIP 5 SOUTH, RANGE 6 EAST,)
MARSHALL COUNTY, OKLAHOMA.) ORDER NO. _____

INTERIM
ORDER OF THE COMMISSION

This Cause came on for hearing before Michael Porter, Administrative Law Judge for the Corporation Commission of the State of Oklahoma, on the 13th day of August, 2007, at 8:30 a.m., Oklahoma City, Oklahoma, for the purpose of hearing, taking testimony, and reporting findings and recommendations to the Commission.

Eric R. King, Attorney, appeared for the Applicant, Walter Oil & Gas Corporation; and Sally Shipley, Deputy General Counsel for Conservation, filed Notice of Appearance.

The Administrative Law Judge heard the Cause and filed a report, which report has been considered by the Commission and the Commission therefore finds as follows:

FINDINGS

1.   This is an Application by Walter Oil & Gas Corporation for an order establishing 640-acre horizontal drilling and spacing units for the Sycamore, Woodford, Hunton and Viola common sources supply underlying all of Section 10, Township 5 South, Range 6 East, Marshall County, Oklahoma.

2.   Applicant owns existing oil and gas leases in the area or spaced section.

3.   The Commission has jurisdiction over the parties and subject matter herein and to make this Order; that a judicial inquiry was made into the sufficiency of the notice given; that notice has been given in all respects as required by law and by the rules of the Commission; that no protests have been entered to the granting of the application.

4.   Based upon the expert testimony of Applicant, there is underlying all of Section 10, Township 5 South, Range 6 East, Marshall County, Oklahoma, the actual or prospective common sources of supply, named below, which are expected to be encountered and which should be classified with horizontal drilling and spacing units and well location, and established as follows:

In Oklahoma — you can participate (pay own share of completing a well)
- you can grant a lease and receive a bonus and a royalty
- no right to be "carried"

Common Source of Supply	Depth	Unit Size	Classification	Order to be Extended
Sycamore	6,200'	640 horizontal	gas	----
Woodford	6,500'	640 horizontal	gas	----
Hunton	7,100'	640 horizontal	gas	----
Viola	7,800'	640 horizontal	gas	----

The permitted well from its point of entry and along any part of the lateral shall be located no closer than 660 feet from the unit boundaries.

5. From the evidence it appears the Sycamore, Woodford, Hunton and Viola common sources of supply will underlie all of Section 10, Township 5 South, Range 6 East, Marshall County, Oklahoma; that one well will adequately, economically and efficiently drain the recoverable hydrocarbons in the common sources of supply underlying at least 640 acres; and 640-acre horizontal drilling and spacing units, taking into account the development costs and the anticipated recoverable reserves, is the minimum sized unit for the economic and efficient development of said common sources of supply.

7. One well in each drilling and spacing (proration) unit established by this Order is necessary to effectively and efficiently drain the portion of the common sources of supply (reservoir) covered by each such drilling and spacing (proration) unit, there being no existing well within such drilling and spacing (proration) unit, which can effectively and efficiently drain the portion of such common sources of supply (reservoir) covered by such drilling and spacing (proration) unit.

8. In the interest of securing the greatest ultimate recovery from the reservoir, the prevention of waste and the protection of correlative rights, this Application should be granted, and the Commission should establish horizontal drilling and spacing units as set out under "Order" below.

ORDER

IT IS THEREFORE ORDERED by the Corporation Commission of the State of Oklahoma:

1. A horizontal drilling and spacing unit be and the same is hereby established, as follows:

Common Source of Supply	Depth	Unit Size	Classification	Order to be Extended
Sycamore	6,200'	640 horizontal	gas	----
Woodford	6,500'	640 horizontal	gas	----
Hunton	7,100'	640 horizontal	gas	----
Viola	7,800'	640 horizontal	gas	----

underlying all of Section 10, Township 5 South, Range 6 East, Marshall County, Oklahoma.

2. The section shall constitute a single horizontal drilling and spacing unit.

3. Each well hereafter drilled to said common sources of supply on said horizontal drilling and spacing units established hereby from its point of entry and along any part of the lateral shall be located no closer than 660 feet from the unit boundaries.

4. All royalty interests within each horizontal drilling and spacing unit are pooled, and unitized and each royalty owner shall share in the one eighth (1/8) of all production from any well thereon in the proportion that the acreage owned by each such royalty owner bears to the entire acreage in the horizontal drilling and spacing unit.

5. When there are two (2) or more separately owned tracts or undivided interests separately owned within any drilling and spacing unit established hereby, the owners thereof may validly pool their interests and develop the drilling and spacing unit as a unit; that where, however, such owners have not agreed to so pool their interests and to develop the drilling and spacing unit as a unit, their rights and equities shall be pooled and adjudicated as provided in subsection (e), of Title 52, Oklahoma Statutes 87.1 in (1980).

6. No more than one well shall hereafter be produced from the above-mentioned common sources of supply on any horizontal drilling and spacing unit established hereby and the permitted well on any horizontal drilling and spacing unit established hereby shall be drilled only at the location thereon as described above, unless the Commission, prior to the drilling of said well, shall have authorized a well location exception therefor in accordance with Title 52, Oklahoma Statutes, Section 87.1.

7. The permitted well authorized hereby for each drilling and spacing (proration) unit established by this order is necessary to effectively and efficiently drain the portion of the common sources of supply (reservoir) covered by each such drilling and spacing (proration) unit, there being no existing well within any such drilling and spacing (proration) units. This Order shall alter the well spacing rules and requirements previously applicable to the common sources of supply (reservoir) underlying each drilling and spacing (proration) unit established by this Order by superseding the provisions of OCC-OAC 165:10-1-21, General Well Spacing Requirements, to the extent such provisions are inconsistent with this Order.

8. The allowable for the horizontal well drilled on the above-described horizontal well drilling and spacing units shall be determined at the reopening of the hearing in this cause for submission of a directional survey. Said allowable will be effective from the date of first

1 production, even if such production occurs during the drilling and completion state and before
2 this cause is reopened. No underproduction will be accumulated during drilling and testing, and
3 the proposed well will not accrue any overage as long as any production occurring before
4 assignment of an allowable does not exceed the allowable ultimately assigned to the well.
5 9. Pursuant to applicable Corporation Commission rules, a bonus allowable may be
6 established for a horizontally drilled well under the newly established well unit, and the
7 determination and amount of said bonus allowable shall be determined by the applicable
8 Corporation Commission rules upon reopening hereof. No underproduction will be accumulated
9 during drilling and testing, and the proposed well will not accrue any overage as long as any
10 production occurring before assignment of an allowable does not exceed the allowable ultimately
11 assigned to the well.
12 10. Attached hereto and made a part hereof as Exhibit "A" is a plat of the drilling and spacing
13 units established by this Order and the permitted well location therefore.
14 11. **REOPENING**: This cause shall be reopened on the 18th day of August, 2008, for the
15 submission of the downhole survey.
16 12. That this Order shall be effective as of the date of this Order for a period of twelve (12)
17 months from the date of issuance and shall automatically expire at the end of the 12-month
18 period unless: (a) operations for a horizontal well are being conducted, in which case the order
19 shall expire 30 days after completion of operations; (b) a Form 1002A has been filed with the
20 Commission; (c) the order has been previously voided by written request of the Applicant; or (d)
21 a request seeking an extension of time has been submitted. Nevertheless, this order shall expire
22 90 days after the date the last producing well in the unit is plugged and abandoned.

1
2
3
4

4-5S-6E	3-5S-6E	2-5S-6E
9-5S-6E	10-5S-6E the well from its point of entry and along any part of the lateral must be drilled no closer than 660 feet from the unit boundaries	11-5S-6E
16-5S-6E	15-5S-6E	14-5S-6E

5   FORMATIONS SPACED:

6   Sycamore, Woodford, Hunton and Viola

7   UNIT SIZE:

8   640-acre horizontal drilling and spacing unit consisting of all of Section 10, Township 5 South,

9   Range 6 East, Marshall County, Oklahoma

10   WELL PATTERN:

11   Each well hereafter drilled to said common sources of supply on the horizontal drilling and

12   spacing units established hereby from its point of entry and along any part of the lateral must be

13   drilled no closer than 660 feet from the unit boundaries

NOTES

1.   Interim Horizontal Spacing Orders are finalized at the Oklahoma Corporation Commission following completion of the well and the submission to the Commission of a directional survey. Horizontal Spacing can occur concurrently with vertical spacing; however, vertical spacing orders are final from the outset, whereas final horizontal spacing requires a producing horizontal well and the submission of a directional survey. The directional survey must show the point of entry into the common source of supply, the point at which the wellbore turns 90 degrees from the vertical segment to the horizontal segment, the total-depth end point (*i.e.*, end point of horizontal penetration) measured from the 90-degree point, the measured depths of those points, and the distance to the nearest unit boundary from the total-depth end point as well as from the 90-degree point.

2.   In North Dakota, the entire area believed to encompass the reservoir is spaced in two proceedings: an initial "temporary" order, effective for generally 18 months, followed by a "proper" spacing order. The latter order is not called "permanent" because the order may be modified at any time. By contrast, in Oklahoma, a spacing proceeding often encompasses a single spacing unit and generally no more than several units. The reason for this difference is that the Oklahoma Supreme Court has held that a spacing applicant must make a good-faith effort to provide better notice to all interest owners than notice by publication of a spacing proceeding. Harry R. Carlisle Trust v. Cotton Petroleum Corp., 732 P.2d 438 (Okla. 1986). Providing personal service to all interest owners in a large field would be very costly and time consuming. North Dakota still allows service by publication. The Supreme Court of Oklahoma called a spacing proceeding an adjudication. The North Dakota Industrial Commission would argue that spacing is a rulemaking (quasi-legislative) proceeding. Would the classification of spacing, as an adjudication or a rulemaking, make a difference in terms of the manner of notice that must be provided to interested parties?

BEFORE THE CORPORATION COMMISSION OF THE STATE OF OKLAHOMA

APPLICANT: WALTER OIL & GAS CORPORATION)
)
) CAUSE CD NO. 200706888
RELIEF REQUESTED: POOLING)
)
LEGAL DESCRIPTION: SECTION 10,)
TOWNSHIP 5 SOUTH, RANGE 6 EAST,)
MARSHALL COUNTY, OKLAHOMA) ORDER NO. _____

ORDER OF THE COMMISSION

Administrative Law Judge; Date and Place of Hearing:

This Cause came on for hearing before Paul Porter, Administrative Law Judge for the Corporation Commission of the State of Oklahoma, on the 13th day of November, 2007, at 8:30 a.m., Jim Thorpe Building, Oklahoma City, Oklahoma, for the purpose of hearing, taking testimony, and reporting findings and recommendations to the Commission.

Appearances:

Eric R. King, Attorney, appeared for the Applicant, Walter Oil & Gas Corporation; Anne George, Attorney, appeared for Chesapeake Operating, Inc. and Chesapeake Exploration Limited Partnership; and Sally Shipley, Deputy General Counsel for Conservation, filed notice of appearance.

FINDINGS

Relief Requested:

1.   This is an Application by Walter Oil & Gas Corporation for an order pooling the interests and adjudicating the rights and equities of oil and gas owners in the Sycamore, Woodford, Hunton and Viola common sources of supply underlying all of Section 10, Township 5 South, Range 6 East, Marshall County, Oklahoma. The name and address of each party being made a respondent to this application is as shown on Exhibit "A" attached hereto and made a part hereof. If any named natural person is deceased, then the known or unknown heirs, executors, administrators, devisees, trustees and assigns, both immediate and remote, of any such deceased individual are made respondents herein. If any named respondent is a corporation, which does not continue to have legal existence and if any such corporation is dissolved, then the known or unknown successors, trustees and assigns, if any, both immediate and remote, of any such dissolved corporation are made respondents herein. Each of the named entities which is an unincorporated association is made a respondent if it continues to have legal existence and if any such unincorporated association is dissolved or otherwise not in existence, then the known or unknown successors, trustees and assigns, both immediate and remote, of any such dissolved unincorporated association are made a respondent herein. Any party designated as an executor or personal representative is made a respondent if presently acting in such capacity as such executor or personal representative, and if such party is not presently acting in such capacity as executor or personal representative, then the known or unknown successor or successors to such executor or personal representative are made respondents herein.

person, who doesn't want to participate in drilling can be "carried" and pay a risk premium. Statute permits it, but agency doesn't. That's OK.

93

Jurisdiction and Notice:

2.   Applicant is a proper party and that the Commission has jurisdiction over the subject matter herein. Notice of the filing of the application herein and of the time, date and place of the hearing thereon was duly and properly given in all respects as required by law and the rules of the Commission. The Administrative Law Judge has examined the notices by publication, the publishers' affidavits of publication thereof, and the affidavits of mailing. The Administrative Law Judge conducted a judicial and adjudicative inquiry into the sufficiency of the applicant's search to determine the names and whereabouts of the respondents who were served herein by publication, and based on the evidence adduced, the Commission finds that Applicant and the Commission officials have exercised due diligence and have conducted a meaningful search of all reasonably available sources at hand to ascertain the whereabouts of those entitled to notice but who were served solely by publication. The Commission approves the publication service given herein as meeting statutory requirements and the minimum standards of state and federal due process so that notice has been given in all respects as required by law and the rules of the Commission.

3.   The Applicant/Operator has a current plugging agreement and surety or a financial statement on file with the Commission, as required by law and by the rules of the Commission.

Spacing:

4.   Heretofore, the Commission has established a 640-acre drilling and spacing unit for the Sycamore, Woodford, Hunton and Viola common sources of supply by Order No. 543130 underlying all of Section 10, Township 5 South, Range 6 East, Marshall County, Oklahoma.

Heretofore, the Commission has established a horizontal 640-acre drilling and spacing unit for the Sycamore, Woodford, Hunton and Viola common sources of supply by Order No. 543131 underlying all of Section 10, Township 5 South, Range 6 East, Marshall County, Oklahoma.

Granting of Relief and Rationale:

5.   The Applicant is the owner of the right to drill a well to the Sycamore, Woodford, Hunton and Viola common sources of supply underlying all of Section 10, Township 5 South, Range 6 East, Marshall County, Oklahoma, by virtue of valid and subsisting oil and gas leases owned by the Applicant.

6.   Applicant has not agreed with all of the owners subject hereto to pool their interests and to develop said unit as a drilling and spacing unit.

7.   Applicant proposes to drill a drilling and spacing unit well so as to develop each common source of supply, and to avoid the drilling of unnecessary wells and to protect correlative rights, all owners should be required to pool and to develop each common source of supply in the drilling and spacing unit therefore as a drilling and spacing unit, upon the terms and conditions set out in "ORDER" below, all of which are found, after a consideration of the evidence to be supported by substantial evidence, to be just and reasonable and to afford each owner the opportunity to recover or receive, without unnecessary expense, such owner's just and fair share of the production from each drilling and spacing unit well and each common source of supply in the drilling and spacing unit thereof.

8.   In the interest of the prevention of waste and the protection of correlative rights, the Application should be granted, and the rights of all owners pooled and adjudicated.

ORDER

IT IS THEREFORE ORDERED, by the Corporation Commission of Oklahoma as follows:

Well Costs and Considerations Determination; Absorption of Excess Burdens:

1. Applicant proposes to drill a well in Section 10, Township 5 South, Range 6 East, Marshall County, Oklahoma, a drilling and spacing unit for the Sycamore, Woodford, Hunton and Viola common sources of supply, and to develop said unit and said common sources of supply therefor, and the rights and equities of all owners, subject hereto and in said common sources of supply and the drilling and spacing unit therefore are pooled, adjudicated, and determined.

2. That estimated unit well costs are:

Completed as a dry hole - $2,216,200.00

Completed for production - $4,466,200.00

Options:

3. Any owner of the right to drill on said drilling and spacing unit who has not agreed with the Applicant to develop said unit and common sources of supply is accorded the following elections, and each owner, subject hereto, may make any of the elections as to all or any part of the interest of such owner in the unit and must give notices as to which of the elections set forth below such owner accepts.

a.   Participation

Participate in the development of the unit and common sources of supply by agreeing to pay such owner's proportionate part of the actual cost of the well covered hereby and by paying such proportionate part of the estimated completed for production cost thereof, as set out in paragraph 2 above, or securing or furnishing security for such payment satisfactory to the Applicant/Operator; in all events, such owner's cost in said well for which cost participation is elected shall not exceed such owner's proportionate part of the actual or reasonable cost thereof which shall be determined by the Commission in the event there is a dispute as to such costs; the payment of such owner's proportionate part of the estimated completed for production cost of said well, or the securing of costs, of the furnishing of security thereof, as before said, shall be accomplished within 20 days from the date of this Order; such owner's proportionate part of the costs of, and of the production from, such well and unit, to be in proportion to the number of acres such owner has in the unit.

b.   Option of $150.00 per acre with a 1/8th royalty as more fully set out below:

$150.00 per acre cash bonus with the normal 1/8th royalty as defined in 52 O.S., Section 87.1(e), which is a fair, reasonable and equitable bonus to be paid unto each owner who elects not to participate in said development of the unit and common sources of supply by paying such owner's proportionate part of the costs thereof; such cash bonus plus overriding royalty or excess royalty, when paid or tendered as set out in this Order, is satisfaction for all rights and interests of such owner in the unit well except for any normal 1/8th royalty, as defined in 52 O.S., Section 87.1(e) (1971).

c.   Option of $400.00 per acre with a 3/16th royalty as more fully set out below:

$400.00 per acre cash bonus with the normal 1/8th royalty as defined in 52 O.S., Section 87.1(e), and with an additional proportionate share of an undivided 1/16 x 8/8ths of all oil and casinghead gas and 1/16 x 8/8ths of all gas and condensate produced and saved from the unit well, which is a fair, reasonable and equitable bonus to be paid unto each owner who elects not to participate in said development of the unit and common sources of supply by paying such owner's

1 proportionate part of the costs thereof; such cash bonus plus overriding royalty or excess royalty,
2 when paid or tendered as set out in this Order, is satisfaction for all rights and interests of such
3 owner in the unit well except for any normal 1/8th royalty, as defined in 52 O.S., Section 87.1(e)
4 (1971).
5 **d.** **Option of $500.00 per acre with a 1/5th royalty as more fully set out below:**
6 $500.00 per acre cash bonus with the normal 1/8th royalty as defined in 52 O.S., Section 87.1(e),
7 and with an additional proportionate share of an undivided 7.5% x 8/8ths of all oil and
8 casinghead gas and 7.5% x 8/8ths of all gas and condensate produced and saved from the unit
9 well, which is a fair, reasonable and equitable bonus to be paid unto each owner who elects not
10 to participate in said development of the unit and common sources of supply by paying such
11 owner's proportionate part of the costs thereof; such cash bonus plus overriding royalty or excess
12 royalty, when paid or tendered as set out in this Order, is satisfaction for all rights and interests
13 of such owner in the unit well except for any normal 1/8th royalty, as defined in 52 O.S., Section
14 87.1(e) (1971).
15 **e.** **Option of no cash and a 1/4th royalty as more fully set out below:**
16 In addition to the normal 1/8th royalty interest a proportionate share of 1/8 of 8/8ths of all oil and
17 casinghead gas and 1/8 of 8/8ths of all gas and condensate produced and saved from the common
18 sources of supply and the unit well; provided, however, in the event the oil and gas interest of
19 such owner, on the date of this Order is subject to any royalty, overriding royalty, or other
20 payments out of production which create a burden from such interest in excess of the normal
21 1/8th royalty, then such excess shall reduce said 1/8 of 8/8ths of all oil and casinghead gas and
22 1/8 of 8/8ths of all gas and condensate by the amount of any such excess; when paid or tendered,
23 this share of production shall be full satisfaction for all rights and interests of any owner electing
24 under this paragraph in the unit well and in the production therefrom.
25 PROVIDED, further, in the event the oil and gas interest of any owner is subject to any royalty,
26 overriding royalty, or other payments out of production which create a burden on such interest in
27 excess of the burdens set out in paragraph 3b, 3c or 3d above; unless the owner can deliver the
28 net revenue interest of 87.5% for paragraph 3b then the owner cannot elect paragraph 3b; or
29 unless the owner can deliver the net revenue of 81.25% for paragraph 3c then the owner cannot
30 elect paragraph 3b or 3c above; or unless the owner can deliver the net revenue of 80% for
31 paragraph 3d then the owner cannot elect paragraph 3b, 3c or 3d above; and if the owner is
32 unable to deliver at a minimum an 80% net revenue interest, then such owner shall be required to
33 either participate or to accept the additional royalty provided in paragraph 3e above.
34 PROVIDED, however, in the event the oil and gas interest of such owner is subject to any
35 royalty, overriding royalty, or other payments out of production which create a burden on such
36 interest in excess of the normal 1/8th royalty, then such excess shall reduce said 1/16 x 8/8ths of
37 all oil and casinghead gas and 1/16 x 8/8ths of all gas and condensate by the amount of any such
38 excess.
39 PROVIDED, however, in the event the oil and gas interest of such owner is subject to any
40 royalty, overriding royalty, or other payments out of production which create a burden on such
41 interest in excess of the normal 1/8th royalty, then such excess shall reduce said 7.5% x 8/8ths of
42 all oil and casinghead gas and 7.5% x 8/8ths of all gas and condensate by the amount of any such
43 excess.
44 PROVIDED, however, in the event the oil and gas interest of such owner is subject to any
45 royalty, overriding royalty, or other payments out of production which create a burden on such

1 interest in excess of the normal 1/8th royalty, then such excess shall reduce said 1/8 x 8/8ths of
2 all oil and casinghead gas and 1/8 x 8/8ths of all gas and condensate by the amount of any such
3 excess.

Payment of Consideration:

5 4.   To receive the cash bonus plus overriding royalty or excess royalty, as set out in
6 paragraph 3b, 3c, or 3d above, and any cash consideration set out therein, must be paid or
7 tendered, if same can be paid or tendered, by the Operator named herein, within 35 days from the
8 date of this Order.

Escrow Provisions:

10 5.   If any payment of bonuses due and owing under the order by virtue of any election or
11 constructive election made with regard to the proposed initial unit well involved herein cannot be
12 made because the person entitled thereto cannot be located or is unknown, then said bonus shall
13 be deposited (credited) into an escrow account within ninety (90) days after this order as
14 provided in 52 O.S. Section 551 et seq. and OCC-OAC 165:10-25-1 et seq. Any royalty
15 payments or other payments due under this order to any such owner who cannot be located or
16 who is unknown shall also be deposited (credited) into an escrow account established by the
17 holder of such funds as provided in 52 O.S. Section 551 et seq. and OCC-OAC 165:10-25-1 et
18 seq. Such funds shall not be commingled with any funds of the Applicant or Operator. The
19 responsibility for filing reports with the Commission as required under Oklahoma law and the
20 Commission rules, as cited above, as to bonus, royalty or other payments deposited (credited)
21 into any escrow accounts shall be with the holder of such funds. Such funds deposited (credited)
22 in any such escrow accounts shall be held for the exclusive use of, and sole benefit of, the person
23 entitled thereto until such funds can be paid to such owner or until the holder of such funds
24 relinquishes the funds to the Commission as required by law. It shall be the responsibility of the
25 Operator to notify all other holders of this provision and of the Commission rules, cited above,
26 regarding unclaimed monies under pooling orders.
27 If a party who is pooled herein refuses the cash bonus or any other funds due hereunder or if
28 such party's interest, if any, in the units involved in this cause has a defect or cloud in the title
29 thereto or if there is uncertainty as to the interest, if any, of such party or if such party cannot be
30 paid the cash bonus or any other funds due hereunder for any reason other than the reasons set
31 out above, the holder of such cash bonus or other funds may deposit such cash bonus or other
32 funds allegedly due such party in an internal escrow account established in the accounting
33 records of such holder and such cash bonus or other funds shall be credited to such account for
34 the benefit of such party. Any funds deposited (credited) in any escrow account as described
35 above shall be held for the benefit of the party allegedly entitled thereto until such funds can be
36 paid to such party or such party accepts such funds or until such title defect or cloud is cured or
37 removed or the uncertainty as to the interest is removed to the satisfaction of the party
38 responsible or liable for and holding such funds. Said funds shall not be commingled with any
39 funds of the Applicant or Operator.

Elections by Owners; Deemed Election:

41 6.   That each owner of the right to drill in said drilling and spacing unit to said common
42 sources of supply covered hereby, who has not agreed to the development of said unit, other than
43 the Applicant, shall elect which of the alternatives set out in paragraph 3 above such owner
44 accepts, said election to be made to Applicant, in writing, within 15 days from the date of this
45 order; in the event any owner fails to give said notice within the time and in the manner as set out

above which of the alternatives set forth in paragraph 3 above, any such owner accepts, then such owner shall be deemed to have accepted, paragraph 3b above; however, if an owner's interest is burdened with more than the normal 1/8 royalty, then such owner shall be deemed to have accepted paragraph 3c above; however, if an owner's interest is burdened with more than 1/16 x 8/8ths share of production over and above the normal 1/8 royalty, then such owner shall be deemed to have accepted paragraph 3d above; however, if an owner's interest is burdened with more than 7.5% x 8/8ths share of production over and above the normal 1/8 royalty, then such owner shall be deemed to have accepted paragraph 3e above; in the event any owner elects to do other than participate in said well by paying his pro rata share of the costs thereof, or fails to make any election provided above, such owner shall be deemed to have relinquished unto Applicant all of such owner's right, title and interest, or claim in and to the unit, except for any normal 1/8 royalty interest, defined above, or other share in production to which such owner may be entitled by reason of an election hereunder.

Operator's Lien; Deemed Election Upon Failure to Perform:

7.   That Applicant, in addition to any other rights provided herein, shall have a lien, as set out in 52 O.S. Section 87.1(e)(1971), on the interest of any owner, subject to this Order, who has elected to participate in the well covered hereby by paying such owner's proportionate part of the costs thereof; provided, however, that in the event an owner elects to participate in the well by paying his proportionate part of the costs thereof and fails or refuses to pay or to secure the payment of such owner's proportionate part of the completed for production costs as set out in paragraph 2 above, or fails or refuses to pay or make an arrangement with the Applicant for the payment thereof, all within the periods of time as prescribed in this Order, then such owner is deemed to have elected paragraph 3b above; however, if an owner's interest is burdened with more than the normal 1/8 royalty, then such owner shall be deemed to have accepted paragraph 3c above; however, if an owner's interest is burdened with more than 1/16 x 8/8ths share of production over and above the normal 1/8 royalty, then such owner shall be deemed to have accepted paragraph 3d above; however, if an owner's interest is burdened with more than 7.5% x 8/8ths share of production over and above the normal 1/8 royalty, then such owner shall be deemed to have accepted paragraph 3e above. Thereupon, the payment of such cash bonus shall be made by Applicant/Operator within 30 days after the last day on which such defaulting owner, under this Order, should have paid his proportionate part of such costs or should have made satisfactory arrangements for the payment thereof.

Operator Designation:

8.   That: Walter Oil & Gas Corporation
11000 Louisiana, Suite 200
Houston, TX 77002-5299
Attention: Richard Lucas

an owner of the right to drill, is hereby designated as operator of the well, unit and each common source of supply covered hereby; and that all communications and elections to said operator shall be in writing and addressed to it as set out above.

Unit Pooling:

9.   The granting of the relief requested by the Applicant shall include the intent of the Applicant to pool and adjudicate the rights and equities of the owners in the lands described herein as to all those separate common sources of supply set forth on a unit basis and not on a

borehole basis for any well drilled as to any of the respective separate common sources of supply cited herein. That the election not to participate, or the deemed election not to participate, as a cost bearing working interest in the proposed unit well shall operate to foreclose the interests of the respondents as to elections to participate or not, in any subsequent well that may at some indefinite time, if at all, be drilled within the subject lands; and that the initial election made by the respondents herein shall be binding as to the respondents, their assigns, heirs, representatives, agents or estate.

Subsequent Wells and Development:

10. If, subsequent to the drilling of the initial unit well involved herein, Applicant/Operator shall propose another well in the drilling and spacing units and common sources of supply covered hereby under the plan of development established by this order, the Operator named herein shall send written notice of the proposed subsequent well to each party who timely and properly elected to participate, and who perfected their election to so participate, in the development of the separate common sources of supply in the drilling and spacing units involved in this cause under the plan of development. Such written notice is to be delivered by certified mail to the last known address of each respondent or faxed to same and shall contain a brief description of the proposed subsequent well. The notice shall also include the estimated costs of the well as a dry hole and as a producing well. Each party entitled to the above-described written notice shall have 15 days after receipt of such notice or fax to elect, in writing, to the Operator whether or not to continue to participate in the development of the separate common sources of supply in the drilling and spacing units involved in this cause under the plan of development established by this Order as to the proposed subsequent well or in lieu thereof, to elect such parties share of the royalty set forth in paragraph 3b, 3c, or 3d above or to elect such parties' share of the royalty set forth in paragraph 3e above; however, if an owner's interest is burdened with more than the normal 1/8 royalty, then such owner shall be deemed to have accepted paragraph 3c above; however, if an owner's interest is burdened with more than 1/16 x 8/8ths share of production over and above the normal 1/8 royalty, then such owner shall be deemed to have accepted paragraph 3d above; however, if an owner's interest is burdened with more than 7.5% x 8/8ths share of production over and above the normal 1/8 royalty, then such owner shall be deemed to have accepted paragraph 3e above; and such owner shall be deemed to have relinquished unto Operator all of such owner's right, title, interest or claim in and to the unit and common sources of supply involved herein as to such proposed subsequent well and any further subsequent well or wells that may thereafter be proposed and drilled under the plan of development.

In the event any party who is entitled to make a written election as to a subsequent well as provided for herein, shall elect not to participate in further development, or shall fail to timely and properly elect in writing to so participate, or who shall have elected affirmatively in writing not to participate in such subsequent well and further development, then such owner shall be deemed to have relinquished unto Operator all of such owner's right, title, interest or claim in and to the unit and separate common sources of supply involved herein as to such proposed subsequent well and any further subsequent well or wells that may thereafter be proposed and drilled under the plan of development, except for such parties' share of the bonus and royalty set forth in paragraph 3b above; however, if an owner's interest is burdened with more than the normal 1/8 royalty, then such owner shall be deemed to have accepted paragraph 3c; however, if an owner's interest is burdened with more than the 1/16 x 8/8ths share of production over and

1   above the normal 1/8 royalty, then such owner shall be deemed to have accepted paragraph 3d
2   above; however, if an owner's interest is burdened with more than 7.5% x 8/8ths share of
3   production over and above the normal 1/8 royalty, then such owner shall be deemed to have
4   accepted paragraph 3e above.
5   Any party entitled to make a written election as to a subsequent well who elects to
6   continue to participate in the development of the separate common sources of supply in the
7   drilling and spacing units provided for herein under the plan of development established by this
8   Order, shall be deemed to have agreed to pay such party's proportionate part of the actual cost of
9   the subsequent well, and pay such party's proportionate part of the estimated completed for
10   production costs as set forth in the notice within 20 days from receipt thereof, said payment to be
11   made to Walter Oil & Gas Corporation, the Unit Operator, at its then current address. Upon such
12   timely payment, or the furnishing of security satisfactory to the Unit Operator, such party's
13   election to continue to participate in the development of the drilling and spacing unit and
14   common sources of supply as to such subsequent well and future wells shall be perfected. In the
15   event any owner elects as to the proposed subsequent well to continue to participate in the
16   development of the separate common sources of supply under the plan of development
17   established by this Order, but thereafter fails or refuses to pay or secure the payment of such
18   owner's proportionate part of the estimated completed for production costs within the manner
19   and time prescribed herein, then such owner shall be deemed to have withdrawn its election to
20   continue to so participate and such owner, as to the proposed subsequent well and any further
21   subsequent well or wells under the plan of development shall be deemed have elected the bonus
22   and overriding or excess royalty as set forth in paragraph 3b above; however, if an owner's
23   interest is burdened with more than the normal 1/8 royalty, then such owner shall be deemed to
24   have accepted paragraph 3c above; however, if an owner's interest is burdened with more than
25   1/16 x 8/8ths share of production over and above the normal 1/8 royalty, then such owner shall
26   be deemed to have accepted paragraph 3d above; however, if an owner's interest is burdened
27   with more than 7.5% x 8/8ths share of production over and above the normal 1/8 royalty, then
28   such owner shall be deemed to have accepted paragraph 3e above.
29   As to any subsequent well proposed under this paragraph, the Unit Operator shall
30   commence or cause to be commenced, operations for the drilling of the subsequent well within
31   180 days from the date of the written notice proposing the subsequent well, and shall thereafter
32   continue such operations for the drilling of the subsequent well and the well shall be drilled,
33   tested, equipped, and completed with due diligence to completion as a producing well or to
34   plugging same as a dry hole. If operations for the drilling of the proposed subsequent well are
35   not commenced within the above described 180 day period, then the elections of the parties as to
36   the proposed subsequent well shall expire and the parties shall be in the same position relative to
37   each other that they were in immediately prior to the written notice of the subsequent well being
38   transmitted by the Applicant/Operator. In such event all rights acquired from the parties electing
39   not to continue to participate as to the proposed subsequent well in the development of the
40   separate common sources of supply and drilling and spacing units under the plan of development
41   established by this Order, shall be relinquished by Unit Operator and any other acquiring party
42   and such relinquished rights shall revest in the parties who elected not to continue to so
43   participate. Failure to timely commence any subsequent well shall not divest or otherwise affect
44   in any manner the rights and interests of the various parties in any well or wells drilled prior

thereto under the plan of development established by this order and shall not terminate such plan of development.

The term subsequent well for purposes of this paragraph shall not be deemed to include any side-tracking or other operation with respect to the initial unit well, or any subsequent well; and shall not be deemed to be any well that is drilled as a replacement or substitute well for the initial well or any subsequent well covered hereby, by virtue of any mechanical or other problems arising directly in connection with the drilling, completing, equipping or producing of the initial unit well or any subsequent well, and no party subject to this order shall have the right to make any subsequent elections as to any such side-tracking, replacement, or substitute well.

Substitute or Replacement Well:

11. In the event the original unit well is lost due to mechanical problems or for any other reason, operator shall have the right, but not the obligation, to commence the drilling of a substitute or replacement well within a reasonable time, but not to exceed 180 days, after the date the operator gives written notice of abandonment of the first unit well.

In such event, operator shall give written notice, which is to be delivered by certified mail or by fax, of the operator's intent to drill the substitute or replacement well to all owners and respondents subject to this pooling order and who elected to participate and paid their proportionate share of the costs of the first unit. Under these circumstances, no new election is allowed and an owner's original election is not changed.

Commencement of Operations:

12. That operations for the drilling of the unit well covered hereby must be commenced within **180** days from the date of this Order, or this Order shall be of no force and effect, except for the payment of any cash bonus elected or deemed to be elected pursuant to this Order, which cash bonus must be paid; that once operations for the drilling of the unit well have commenced, said operations shall continue and the well shall be drilled, tested, equipped, and completed with due diligence to completion as a producing well or to plugging same as a dry hole. Provided, however, in the event that the proposed well is not drilled to depths sufficient to encounter all of the common sources of supply covered hereby, or is completed in less than all of the common sources of supply encountered, this Order will be operative as to such common sources of supply encountered in the proposed well and thereafter shall continue to be operative with respect to respondents electing or being deemed to have elected not to participate in the drilling of the proposed well as to such of said encountered common sources of supply in which a well drilled with due diligence under this Order is completed as a producing well.

Mailing of this Order:

13. That an affidavit shall be filed with the Secretary of the Commission, within 10 days from the date of this Order, stating that a copy of said Order was mailed within 3 days from the date of this Order to all parties subject hereto, whose addresses are known.

NOTES

1.   Note that under paragraph 2, the Commission has determined that the estimated cost of drilling a dry hole is $2,216,200.00, while the estimated cost of drilling a producing well is $4,466,200.00. A working interest owner who elects to participate in development must pay its proportionate part of the larger sum (or provide some satisfactory security for this amount) within twenty days of the order, and also agree to bear its share "of the actual cost" of the well, which could.

2.   This pooling order pools the respondents interests in prior order. This particular order is very unusual in terms of the elections. Generally, as royalty increases from the statutory 1/8 minimum, the cash bonuses decrease. In the instant case, the testimony revealed the lower values were arms-length transactions between willing buyers and willing sellers that occurred early in the leasing activity. As the area developed and new leases were acquired, the cash bonuses increased so that the 3/16th royalty provided for a $400 per acre bonus while the 1/5th royalty provided for a $500 bonus. These bonuses were the highest prices paid for leases burdened by the respective royalties in arms-length transactions. Note, however, that when the royalty reached 1/4, no cash bonus was offered.

3.   The pooled parties have 15 days to make an election. Notice that the default election would seem to be the poorest election from the standpoint of electing party, but this election reflects the statutory requirements of the Oklahoma pooling statute. Okla. Stat. tit. 52, § 87.1(e). Because some unleased mineral-interest owners are unknown or unlocatable, they will not be given the opportunity to make an actual election. Is it appropriate that they should be deemed to have elected what appears to be the poorest choice?

    Note again that, in the typical pooling order, the election with the 1/8th royalty will carry the highest bonus. In this more common scenario, it would be more difficult for the Commission to decide which election is best for the non-electing party. That decision would depend on the likelihood of successful drilling and on the immediate financial needs of the pooled party.

4.   The prior Oklahoma Spacing and Pooling orders were furnished by Eric R King, Attorney, Gable & Gotwals, Oklahoma City. http://www.gablelaw.com/home.asp

DESIGNATION OF POOLED UNIT AND DECLARATION OF POOLING
(For Oil and/or Gas)

State:
County:
Operator: (Name and Address)
Working Interest Owners: (Names and Addresses)
Effective Date:

Operator and Working Interest Owners, named above, by the terms of the Oil and Gas Leases (the "Leases") described in Exhibit "A" to this Designation, were granted the right and authority to pool and combine the Leases into a pooled unit (the "Unit") and designate the lands covered by and subject to the Leases to be included in a pooled unit for the purpose of drilling a well or wells and producing oil and/or gas.

By the authority granted in the Leases, the following lands that are subject to and included in the Leases are designated as a Unit called the (Name) Unit.

(Description of Lands included in the Unit)

This Designation is executed by the Operator and Working Interest Owners and filed of record in the county where the Leases are located for the purpose of evidencing the election to exercise the pooling authority granted to the lessees in the Leases, to give notice of the Unit being established, and to identify and describe the lands included in the Unit.

This Designation shall be, and the Unit is created, as of the Effective Date stated above. It shall be and remain in effect as long as oil and/or gas is produced from the lands within the Unit, actual drilling or reworking operations are being conducted on the lands within the Unit, delay rentals or shut-in royalties are being paid to maintain the Leases, or the provisions of the Leases are otherwise being complied with to maintain them in full force and effect.

This Designation is signed by Operator and each Working Interest Owner on the date opposite their signature, but shall be effective as of the Effective Date stated above. This Designation may be signed in multiple counterparts, all of which taken together shall be deemed one and the same Designation of Pooled Unit and Declaration of Pooling.

Date: **Operator**

Date: **Working Interest Owners**

[Exhibit "A": Description of Oil and Gas Leases]

pooling

NOTES

1.   Where the operator, perhaps together with other voluntarily participating lessees. hold leases with appropriate pooling clauses, they may declare a pooling. If any lease fails to have an appropriate pooling clause, the lessee might secure the lessor's express consent to form and to pool a unit. This avoids the expense and time of a pooling proceeding. To formalize the pooling, the operator and any other lessees will declare a pooling and perhaps record the declaration. The above form would serve this purpose but would need to be signed by the operator and other lessees and acknowledged so that it could then be recorded. Why might the operator and lessees want to record this declaration?

2.   This form was furnished by Kanes Forms, P.O. Box 53010, Midland, TX 79710, tel. 800-526-3790. http://www.kanesforms.com/new/index.htm

UNIT AGREEMENT

_____ UNIT_____ COUNTY, _____
(This Agreement provides for Phase I and II Tract Participation, based on Calculated Recoverable Reserves)

UNIT AGREEMENT
_____ UNIT
_____ COUNTY, _____

This Unit Agreement (the "Agreement") is entered into as of _____, (the "Effective Date"), by the parties that sign the original of this instrument, a counterpart of it or other instrument agreeing to be bound by its provisions.

In the interest of the public welfare and to promote conversation and increase the ultimate recovery of oil, gas, and associated minerals from the _____ Unit, in _____ County, _____, and to protect the rights of the owners of interest in the lands included in the Unit, it is deemed necessary and desirable to enter into this Agreement, in conformity with (Applicable Statutory reference), to unitize the Oil and Gas Rights in and to the Unitized Formation in order to conduct a secondary recovery, pressure maintenance, or other recovery program as provided for in this Agreement.

In consideration of the premises and of the mutual benefits to be derived, it is agreed as follows:

ARTICLE 1
DEFINITIONS

As used in this Agreement, the following terms shall have the following meaning:

1.1 **Oil and Gas Rights** means the right to explore, develop, and operate lands within the Unit Area for the production of Unitized Substances, or to share in the production so obtained or the proceeds from the production.

1.2 **Outside Substances** means all substances obtained from any source other than the Unitized Formation and which are injected into the Unitized Formation.

1.3 **Royalty Interest** means a right to or interest in any portion of the Unitized Substances or proceeds from it other than a Working Interest.

1.4 **Royalty Owner** means a party who owns a Royalty Interest.

1.5 **Singular and Plural – Gender** means that unless the context otherwise clearly indicates, words used in the singular include the plural, the plural include the singular, and the neuter gender include the masculine and the feminine.

1.6 **Tract** means each parcel of land described as such and given a Tract number in Exhibit "A."

1.7 **Tract Participation** means the percentage shown on Exhibit "A" for allocation Unitized Substances to a Tract under this Agreement.

1.8 **Unit Area** means the lands described by Tracts in Exhibit "A" and shown on Exhibit "B" as to which this Agreement becomes effective or extended, as provided for in this Agreement.

1.9 **Unit Equipment** means all personal property, leases and well equipment, plants, and other facilities and equipment taken over or otherwise acquired for the joint account for use in Unit Operations.

1.10 **Unit Expense** means all cost, expense, or indebtedness incurred by Working Interest Owners or Unit Operator pursuant to this Agreement and the Unit Operating Agreement for or on account of Unit Operations.

1.11 **Unit Operating Agreement** means the agreement entitled "Unit Operating Agreement, _____ Unit, _____ County, _____," of the same effective date of this Agreement, and which is entered into by Working Interest Owners.

1.12 **Unit Operations** means all operations conducted by Working Interest Owners or Unit Operator pursuant to this Agreement and the Unit Operating Agreement for or on account of the development and operation of the Unitized Formation for the production of Unitized Substances.

1.13 **Unit Operator** means the Working Interest Owner designated by Working Interest Owners under the Unit Operating Agreement to develop and operate the Unitized Formation, acting as operator and not as a Working Interest Owner.

1.14 **Unit Participation** of each Working Interest Owner means the sum of the percentages obtained by multiplying the Working Interest of the Working Interest Owner in each Tract by the Tract Participation of that Tract.

1.15 **Unitized Formation** means the subsurface portion of the Unit Area commonly known or described as follows:

That stratigraphic interval between the top of the _____ and a depth of _____ feet below sea level. The top of the _____ is defined as that point located at a depth of _____ feet below the kelly bushing as shown on the _____ log, dated _____, in the _____ Well located _____ feet from the north line and _____ feet from the east line, _____, _____ County, _____.

1.16 **Unitized Substances** means all oil, gas, gaseous substances, sulphur contained in gas, condensate, distillate, and all associated and constituent liquid or liquefiable hydrocarbons within or produced from the Unitized Formation.

1.17 **Working Interest** means an interest in Unitized Substances by virtue of a lease, operating agreement, fee title, or otherwise, including a carried interest, which interest is chargeable with and obligated to pay or bear, either in cash or out of production or otherwise, all or a portion of the cost of drilling, developing, producing, and operating the Unitized Formation. Any interest in Unitized Substances which is a Working Interest as of the date the owner executes or ratifies this Agreement, or which at any later time becomes a Working Interest, shall then be treated as a Working Interest for all purposes of this Agreement.

1.18 **Working Interest Owner** means a party who owns a Working Interest. The owner of Oil and Gas Rights that are free of lease or other instrument conveying the Working Interest to another shall be regarded as a Working Interest Owner to the extent of _____ of that interest in Unitized Substances, and as a Royalty Owner with respect to the remaining _____ interest.

ARTICLE 2
EXHIBITS

2.1   **Exhibits.** Attached to this Agreement are the following Exhibits which are incorporated by reference:

2.1.1   **Exhibit "A,"** which is a schedule that describes each Tract in the Unit Area and shows its Tract Participation.

2.1.2   **Exhibit "B,"** which is a map that shows the boundary lines of the Unit Area and the Tracts in the Unit.

1   **2.1.3**   **Exhibit "B-1,"** which is a map that shows the designated usable wells that
2 have been approved by the Working Interest Owners.
3   **2.2**   **Reference to Exhibits.** When reference is made to an Exhibit, the reference is to
4 the Exhibit as originally attached, or, if revised, to the latest revision.
5   **2.3**   **Exhibits Considered Correct.** An Exhibit shall be considered to be correct until
6 revised as provided for in this Agreement.
7   **2.4**   **Correcting Errors.** The shapes and descriptions of the respective Tracts have
8 been established by using the best information available. If it subsequently appears that any
9 Tract, because of diverse Royalty or Working Interest ownership on the effective date of this
10 Agreement, should be divided into more than one Tract, or that any mechanical miscalculation
11 has been made, Unit Operator, with the approval of Working Interest Owners, may correct the
12 mistake by revising the Exhibits to conform to the facts. The revision shall not include any re-
13 evaluation of engineering or geological interpretations used in determining Tract Participation.
14 Each revision of an Exhibit shall be effective at 7:00 a.m. on the first day of the calendar month
15 next following the filing for record of the revised Exhibit, or on any other date as may be
16 determined by Working Interest Owners and set forth in the revised Exhibit.
17   **2.5**   **Filing Revised Exhibits.** If an exhibit is revised pursuant to this Agreement, Unit
18 Operator shall certify and file the revised Exhibit for record in _____ County, _____.
19
20   **ARTICLE 3**
21   **CREATION AND EFFECT OF UNIT**
22   **3.1**   **Oil and Gas Rights Unitized.** Subject to the provisions of this Agreement, all
23 Oil and Gas Rights of Royalty Owners in and to the lands described in Exhibit "A," and all Oil
24 and Gas Rights of Working Interest Owners in and to those lands, are hereby unitized insofar as
25 the respective Oil and Gas Rights pertain to the Unitized Formation, so that operations may be
26 conducted as if the Unitized Formation had been included in a single lease executed by all
27 Royalty Owners, as lessors, in favor of all Working Interest Owners, as lessees, and as if the
28 lease had been subject to all of the provisions of this Agreement, provided that the terms and
29 conditions are not in conflict with any applicable statute of the State of _____.
30   **3.2**   **Personal Property Excepted.** All lease and well equipment, materials, and other
31 facilities previously or later placed by any of the Working Interest Owners on the lands covered
32 by this Agreement shall be deemed to be and shall remain personal property belonging to and
33 may be removed by the Working Interest Owners. The rights and interests in the personal
34 property, as among Working Interest Owners, are covered by the Unit Operating Agreement.
35   **3.3**   **Amendment of Leases and Other Agreements.** The provisions of the various
36 leases, agreements, division and transfer orders, or other instruments covering the respective
37 Tracts or the production from them are amended to the extent necessary to make them conform
38 to the provisions of this Agreement, but otherwise shall remain in effect, provided that those
39 terms and conditions are not in conflict with any applicable statute of the State of _____.
40   **3.4**   **Continuation of Leases and Term Royalties.** Operations, including drilling
41 operations, conducted with respect to the Unitized Formation on any part of the Unit Area, or
42 production from any part of the Unitized Formation, except for the purpose of determining
43 payments to Royalty Owners, shall be considered as operations on or production from each
44 Tract, and those operations or production shall continue in effect each lease or term royalty

interest as to all lands covered by them just as if the operations had been conducted and a well had been drilled on and was produced from each Tract.

    3.5   **Titles Unaffected by Unitization.** Nothing in this Agreement shall be construed to result in the transfer of title to the Oil and Gas Rights by any party to this Agreement to any other party or to Unit Operator. The intention is to provide for the cooperative development and operation of the Tracts and for the sharing of Unitized Substances as provided in this Agreement.

    3.6   **Injection Rights.** Royalty Owners grant to Working Interest Owners the right to inject into the Unitized Formation any substances in whatever amounts Working Interest Owners deem expedient for Unit Operations including the right to drill and maintain injection wells on the Unit Area and to use producing wells completed in the Unitized Formation, or abandoned oil or gas wells for those purposes.

    3.7   **Development Obligation.** Nothing in this Agreement shall relieve Working Interest Owners from the obligation to reasonably develop, as a whole, the lands and leases committed to and included in the Unit.

ARTICLE 4

PLAN OF OPERATION

    4.1   **Unit Operator.** Working Interest Owners are, as of the Effective Date of this Agreement, entering into the Unit Operating Agreement, designating _____ as the initial Unit Operator. Unit Operator shall have, subject to the terms, provisions, and limitations expressed in the Unit Operating Agreement, the exclusive right to conduct operations. The operations shall conform to the provisions of this Agreement and the Unit Operating Agreement. If there is any conflict between these Agreements, this Agreement shall govern.

    4.2   **Operating Methods.** To the end that the quantity of Unitized Substances ultimately recoverable may be increased and waste prevented, Working Interest Owners shall, with diligence and in accordance with good engineering and production practices, engage in a pressure maintenance or secondary recovery project by means of the injection of gas, water, or other substances, or any combination of two or more of them, into the Unitized Formation.

    4.3   **Change of Operating Methods.** Nothing in this Agreement shall prevent Working Interest Owners from discontinuing or changing in whole or in part any method of operation which, in their opinion, is no longer in accord with good engineering or production practices. Other methods of operation may be conducted or changes may be made by Working Interest Owners from time to time if determined by them to be feasible, necessary, or desirable to increase the ultimate recovery of Unitized Substances.

ARTICLE 5

TRACT PARTICIPATION

    5.1   **Tract Participation.** The participation of each Tract is shown in Exhibit "A" and is split into two periods as follows:

        (1)   Phase I shall be applicable from the Effective Date of this Agreement until 7:00 a.m. on the first day of the calendar month next following the month in which the Unit Area Remaining Primary Reserves are produced. The Unit Area Remaining Primary Reserves as agreed to by the Working Interest Owners are _(#)_ barrels to be produced after _(date)_, from the Tracts included in the original Exhibit "B" dated _____. On the Effective Date, that _(#)_ barrels shall be reduced by the amount of oil produced between _(date)_, and the Effective Date from those Tracts included in the original Exhibit "B" dated _____, and shall be further revised

111

to reflect only those primary reserves remaining at the Effective Date on those Tracts effectively committed to the Unit.

        (2)   Phase II shall be applicable after the termination of Phase I.

The Tract Participation of each Tract was determined as follows:

$$\text{Phase I} = \underline{\quad}\% \times \frac{\text{Tract Remaining Primary Reserves}}{\text{Unit Area Remaining Primary Reserves}} \quad \text{plus}$$

$$\underline{\quad}\% \times \frac{\text{Tract Current Production}}{\text{Unit Area Current Production}}$$

$$\text{Phase II} = \underline{\quad}\% \times \frac{\text{Tract Ultimate Primary}}{\text{Unit Area Ultimate Primary}} \quad \text{plus}$$

$$\underline{\quad}\% \times \frac{\text{Tract Usable Wells}}{\text{Unit Area Usable Wells}}$$

As used in this Article 5, the terms set forth above shall have the following meanings:

        (a)   **Tract Remaining Primary Reserves** means the number of barrels of primary oil for a Tract as agreed upon by the Working Interest Owners.

        (b)   **Unit Area Remaining Primary Reserves** means the summation of the Tract Remaining Primary Reserves of those Tracts effectively committed to this Agreement.

        (c)   **Tract Current Production** means the number of barrels of oil produced from the Unitized Formation from the Tract during the period from __(Date)__, through __(Date)__, and as agreed on by the Working Interest Owners.

        (d)   **Unit Area Current Production** means the summation of the Tract Current Production of those Tracts effectively committed to this Agreement.

        (e)   **Tract Ultimate Primary** means the total cumulative amount of oil from a Tract up to but not including __(Date)__, plus the Tracts Remaining Primary Reserves and as agreed on by the Working Interest Owners.

        (f)   **Unit Area Ultimate Primary** means the summation of Tract Ultimate Primary for those Tracts effectively committed to this Agreement.

        (g)   **Tract Usable Wells** means the number of wells designated by the Working Interest Owners as usable and shown on Exhibit "B-1."

        (h)   **Unit Area Usable Wells** means the summation of the Tract Usable Wells for those Tracts effectively committed to this Agreement.

        5.2   **Relative Tract Participations.** If the Unit Area is enlarged or reduced, the revised Tract Participations of the Tracts remaining in the Unit Area and which were within the Unit Area prior to the enlargement or reduction shall remain in the same ratio one to another.

ARTICLE 6

ALLOCATION OF UNITIZED SUBSTANCES

        6.1   **Allocation to Tracts.** All Unitized Substances produced and saved shall be allocated to the several Tracts in accordance with the respective Tract Participations effective during the period that the Unitized Substances were produced. The amount of Unitized

Substances allocated to each Tract, regardless of whether it is more or less than the actual production of Unitized Substances from the well or wells, if any, on the Tract, shall be deemed for all purposes to have been produced from the Tract.

6.2   Distribution Within Tracts. The Unitized Substances allocated to each Tract shall be distributed among, or accounted for to, the parties entitled to a share in the production from the Tract in the same manner, in the same proportions, and on the same conditions as they would have participated and shared in the production from the Tract, or in the proceeds from production, had this Agreement not been entered into, and with the same legal effect. If any Oil and Gas Rights in a Tract later become divided and owned in severalty as to different parts of the Tract, the owners of the divided interests, in the absence of an agreement providing for a different division, shall share in the Unitized Substances allocated to the Tract, or in the proceeds from production, in proportion to the surface acreage of their respective parts of the Tract.

6.3   Taking Unitized Substances in Kind. The Unitized Substances allocated to each Tract shall be delivered in kind to the respective parties entitled to them by virtue of the ownership of Oil and Gas Rights in the Tract or by purchase from the owners. The parties shall have the right to construct, maintain, and operate within the Unit Area all necessary facilities for that purpose, provided that they are so constructed, maintained, and operated as not to interfere with Unit Operations. Any extra expenditures incurred by Unit Operator by reason of the delivery in kind of any portion of the Unitized Substances shall be borne by the receiving party. If a Royalty Owner has the right to take in kind a share of Unitized Substances and fails to do so, the Working Interest Owner whose Working Interest is subject to that Royalty Interest shall be entitled to take in kind that share of the Unitized Substances.

6.4   Failure to Take in Kind. If any party fails to take in kind or separately dispose of its share of Unitized Substances, Unit Operator shall have the right, but not the obligation, for the time being and subject to revocation at will by the party owning the share, to purchase for its own account or sell to others that share at not less than the market price prevailing in the area and not less than the price Unit Operator receives for its share of Unitized Substances; provided that, all contracts of sale by Unit Operator of any other party's share of Unitized Substances shall only be for a reasonable period of time as are consistent with the minimum needs of the industry under the circumstances, but in no event shall any contract be for a period in excess of one year. The proceeds of the Unitized Substances so disposed of by Unit Operator shall be paid to a payee who shall distribute the proceeds to the parties entitled to them, the payee being the Working Interest Owner of each affected Tract or a party designated by the Working Interest Owners under an agreement between the party and the Working Interest Owners.

6.5   Responsibility for Royalty Settlements. Any party receiving in kind or separately disposing of all or part of the Unitized Substances allocated to any Tract or receiving the proceeds from it shall be responsible for the payment of those proceeds to the persons entitled to them, and shall indemnify all parties to this Agreement, including Unit Operator, against any liability for all royalties, overriding royalties, production payments, and all other payments chargeable against or payable out of those Unitized Substances or the proceeds from them.

6.6   Royalty on Outside Substances. No payments shall be due or payable to Royalty Owners on any Outside Substances.

6.6.1   If gas is the Outside Substance injected, _____ percent (____%) of any gas subsequently produced from the Unitized Formation and sold, or used for other that Unit

Operators, shall be deemed to be the Outside Substance so injected until that total volume equals the total volume of the Outside Substance so injected.

6.6.2 If liquid hydrocarbons are the Outside Substances injected and the Unitized Substances subsequently produced contain those liquid hydrocarbons, as determined by the Working Interest Owners by applicable tests, then commencing on the first day of the calendar month next following such a determination, _____ percent (____%) of all oil produced from the Unitized Formation and sold during any month shall be deemed to be the Outside Substances so injected until the total value equals the total cost of the Outside Substances so injected.

ARTICLE 7

PRODUCTION AS OF THE EFFECTIVE DATE

7.1   **Oil in Lease Tanks.** Unit Operator shall gauge all lease and other tanks within the Unit Area to ascertain the amount of merchantable oil produced from the Unitized Formation in the tanks, about the pipeline connections, as of 7:00 a.m. on the Effective Date of this Agreement. The oil that is a part of the prior allowable of the wells from which it was produced shall remain the property of the parties entitled to it, the same as if the Unit had not been formed. Any of that oil not promptly removed may be sold by the Unit Operator for the account of the parties entitled to it, subject to the payment of all royalties, overriding royalties, production payments, and all other payments under the provisions of the applicable lease or other contracts. The oil that is in excess of any prior allowable of the wells from which it was produced shall be regarded as Unitized Substances produced after the Effective Date of this Agreement.

7.2   **Overproduction.** If, as of the Effective Date of this Agreement, any Tract is overproduced with respect to the allowable of the wells on that Tract and the amount of overproduction has been sold or otherwise disposed of, the overproduction shall be regarded as a part of the Unitized Substances produced after the Effective Date, and shall be charged to the Tract as having been delivered to the parties entitled to Unitized Substances allocated to the Tract.

ARTICLE 8

USE OR LOSS OF UNITIZED SUBSTANCES

8.1   **Use of Unitized Substances.** Working Interest Owners may use as much of the Unitized Substances as they deem necessary for Unit Operations, including but not limited to the injection of them into the Unitized Formation.

8.2   **Royalty Payments.** No royalty, overriding royalty, production, or other payments shall be payable on, or with respect to, Unitized Substances used or consumed in Unit Operations, or which otherwise may be lost or consumed in the production, handling, treating, transportation, or storing of Unitized Substances.

ARTICLE 9

TRACTS TO BE INCLUDED IN UNIT

9.1   **Qualification of Tracts.** On and after the Effective Date and until the enlargement or reduction of this Unit, the Unit Area shall be composed of the Tracts listed in Exhibit "A" that have a usable well, and that corner or have a common boundary (Tracts separated only by a public highway or a railroad right of way shall be considered to have a common boundary), and that otherwise qualify as follows:

9.1.1   Each tract in which Working Interest Owners owning one hundred percent (100%) of the Working Interest have become parties to this Agreement and in which Royalty

Owners owning seventy-five percent (75%) or more of the Royalty Interest have become parties to this Agreement.

9.1.2 Each Tract in which Working Interest Owners owning one hundred percent (100%) of the Working Interest have become parties to this Agreement, and in which Royalty Owners owning less than seventy-five percent (75%) of the Royalty Interest have become parties to this Agreement, and in which the Working Interest Owners in the Tract have executed and delivered an indemnity agreement indemnifying and agreeing to hold harmless the other Working Interest Owners in the Unit Area, their successors and assigns, against a portion of all claims and demands that may be made by non-subscribing owners of Royalty Interest in the Tract on account of the inclusion of the Tract in the Unit Area. The portion of the claims and demands covered by the indemnity shall, as to each Tract, be the fraction in which the numerator is the difference between the percentage of the Royalty Interest signed and seventy-five percent (75%) of the Royalty Interest in the Tract; and the denominator is the difference between the percentage of the Royalty Interest signed and one hundred percent (100%) of the Royalty Interest in the Tract.

9.1.3 Each Tract as to which Working Interest Owners owning less than one hundred percent (100%) of the Working Interest have become parties to this Agreement; and Royalty Owners owning seventy-five percent (75%) or more of the Royalty Interest have become parties to this Agreement, or the indemnity with reference to the claims of non-subscribing owners of Royalty Interest on the Tract is given under the provisions of Section 9.1.2; and as to which (a) the Working Interest Owner who operates the Tract and all of the other Working Interest Owners in the Tract who have become parties to this Agreement have joined in a request for inclusion of the Tract in the Unit Area, and have executed and delivered an indemnity agreement indemnifying and agreement to hold harmless the other Working Interest Owners in the Unit Area, their successors and assigns, against all claims and demands that may be made by the owners of Working Interest in the Tract who are not parties to this Agreement and which arise out of the inclusion of the Tract in the Unit Area; and as to which (b) eight-five percent (85%) of the combined voting interest of the Working Interest Owners in all Tracts that meet the requirements of Sections 9.1.1 and 9.1.2 have voted in favor of the inclusion of the Tract and to accept the indemnity agreement. For the purposes of this Section 9.1.3, the voting interest of each Working Interest Owner shall be equal to the ratio that its Phase II Unit Participation attributable to Tracts that qualify under Section 9.1.1 and 9.1.2 bears to the total Phase II Unit Participation of all Working Interest Owners attributable to all Tracts that qualify under Section 9.1.1 and 9.1.2. On the inclusion of such a Tract in the Unit Area, the Unit Participation that would have been attributed to the non-subscribing owners of the Working Interest in the Tract, had they become parties to this Agreement and the Unit Operating Agreement, shall be attributed to the Working Interest Owners in the Tract who have become parties to such agreements, in proportion to their respective Working Interests in the Tract.

9.1.4 Each Tract, regardless of the percentage of Working Interest or Royalty Interest in it that has been committed to this Agreement, as to which (a) the Working Interest Owner who operates the Tract has become a party to this Agreement, and (b) Working Interest Owners having eighty-five percent (85%) of the combined voting interest of Working Interest Owners in all Tracts that meet the requirements of Section 9.1.1, 9.1.2., or 9.1.3 vote in favor of the inclusion of the Tract. For the purpose of this Section 9.1.4, the voting interest of a Working Interest Owner shall be equal to the ratio that its Phase II Unit Participation attributable to Tracts that qualify under Sections 9.1.1, 9.1.2., or 9.1.3 bears to the total Phase II Unit Participation of all Working Interest Owners attributable to all Tracts that qualify under Section 9.1.1., 9.1.2, or 9.1.3. In the case of the inclusion of a Tract in the Unit Area under the provisions of Section 9.1.4 in which Tract there are non-subscribing owners of Working Interest, the Unit Participation which would have been assigned to the non-subscribing owners of Working Interest, had they signed or ratified this Agreement, shall be allotted to all Working Interest Owners in proportion to their then effective Unit Participation; provided, that the Working Interest Owners shall be fully liable and responsible in the same proportion to the non-subscribing owners of Working Interest in the accounting for production from the Tract and all other matters pertaining to the separate operation of the Tract insofar as the non-subscribing owners are concerned. If a Tract is included in the Unit Area under the provisions of this Section 9.1.4, all Working Interest Owners shall bear, in proportion to their then effective participation, all claims and demands that may be made by the non-subscribing owners of Working Interest or Royalty Interest on account of the inclusion of the Tract in the Unit Area.

9.2 **Subsequent Commitment of Interest to Unit.** After the Effective Date of this Agreement, the commitment of any interest in any Tract within the Unit Area shall be on the terms as may be negotiated by Working Interest Owners and the owner of the interest; provided, however, any formerly committed interest as to which title has failed may be recommitted by the rightful owner on its former basis of participation, as provided in Section 10.1.

9.3 **Revision of Exhibits.** If any of the Tracts described in Exhibit "A" fail to qualify for inclusion in the Unit Area, Unit Operator shall recomputed, using the original basis of computation, the Tract Participation of each of the qualifying Tracts, and shall revise Exhibits "A" and "B" accordingly. The revised Exhibits shall be effective as of the Effective Date of this Agreement.

ARTICLE 10

TITLES

10.1 **Removal of Tract from Unit Area.** If a Tract ceases to have sufficient Working Interest Owns or Royalty Owners committed to this Agreement to meet the conditions of Article 9 because of failure of title of any party, that Tract shall be removed from the Unit Area effective as of the first day of the calendar month in which the failure of title is finally determined; however, the Tract shall not be removed from the Unit Area if, within ninety (90) days of the date of final determination of the failure of title, the Tract requalifies under a Section of Article 9.

10.2 **Revision of Exhibits.** If a Tract is removed from the Unit Area because of the failure of title, Unit Operator, subject to Section 5.2, shall recomputed the Tract Participation of each of the Tracts remaining in the Unit Area and shall revise Exhibits "A" and "B" accordingly. The revised Exhibits shall be effective as of the first day of the calendar month in which the failure of title is finally determined.

10.3 **Working Interest Titles.** If title to a Working Interest fails, the rights and obligations of Working Interest Owners by reason of the failure of title shall be governed by the Unit Operating Agreement.

10.4 **Royalty Owner Titles.** If title to a Royalty Interest fails, but the Tract to which it relates is not removed from the Unit Area, the party whose title failed shall not be entitled to share under the terms of this Agreement with respect to that interest.

10.5   Production Where Title is in Dispute. If the title or right of any party claiming the right to receive in kind all or any portion of the Unitized Substances allocated to a Tract is in dispute, Unit Operator, at the discretion of Working Interest Owner, shall either:

        (a)   require that the party to whom the Unitized Substances are delivered or to whom the proceeds of them are paid, furnish security for the proper accounting to the rightful owner if the title or right of the party fails in whole or in part; or,

        (b)   withhold and market the portion of Unitized Substances with respect to which the title or right is in dispute, and impound the proceeds until the time as the title or right to them is established by a final judgment of a court of competent jurisdiction or otherwise to the satisfaction of Working Interest Owners, at which time the proceeds so impounded shall be paid to the party rightfully entitled to them.

10.6   Payment of Taxes to Protect Title. The owners of (1) the surface rights to lands within the Unit Area, (2) the severed mineral or Royalty Interests in the lands, and (3) the improvements located on the lands not utilized for Unit Operations, shall individually be responsible for the rendition and assessment for ad valorem tax purposes of all that property, and for the payment of the taxes, except as otherwise provided in any contract or agreement between the owners and a Working Interest Owner. If any ad valorem taxes are not paid by the owner responsible for them, when due, Unit Operator may, with approval of Working Interest Owners, at any time prior to tax sale, or expiration of the period of redemption after tax sale, pay the same, redeem the property, and discharge the tax liens as my arise through nonpayment. Any such payment shall be treated as an item of Unit Expense. Unit Operator shall, if possible, withhold from any proceeds derived from the sale of Unitized Substances otherwise due to any delinquent taxpayer or taxpayers an amount sufficient to defray the costs of the payment or redemption, the withholding to be credited to the joint account. The withholding shall be without prejudice to any other remedy, either at law or at equity, which may be available for exercise by the Unit Operator or by the Working Interest Owners.

ARTICLE 11

EASEMENTS OR USE OF SURFACE

11.1   Grant of Easements. The parties to this Agreement, to the extent of their rights and interests, grant to Working Interest Owners the right to use as much of the surface of the land within the Unit Area as may reasonably be necessary for Unit Operations; provided that, nothing in this Agreement shall be construed as leasing or otherwise conveying to Working Interest Owners a site for a water or gas injection, processing or other plant, or camp site.

11.2   Uses of Water. Working Interest Owners shall have free use of water produced from the Unitized Formation.

11.3   Surface Damages. Working Interest Owners shall pay the owner for damages to growing crops, timber, fences, improvements, and structures on the Unit Area that result from Unit Operations.

ARTICLE 12

ENLARGEMENTS OF UNIT AREA

12.1   Enlargements of Unit Area. The Unit Area may be enlarged to include acreage reasonably proved to be productive, on the terms as may be determined by Working Interest Owners, including but not limited to the following:

        12.1.1 The acreage shall qualify under a Section of Article 9.

117

12.1.2 The participation to be allocated to the acreage shall be reasonable, fair, and based on all available information.

12.1.3 There shall be no retroactive allocation or adjustment of Unit Expense or of interests in the Unitized Substances produced, or proceeds from them; however, this limitation shall not prevent an adjustment of investment by reason of the enlargement.

12.2 **Determination of Tract Participation.** Unit Operator, subject to Section 5.2, shall determine the Tract Participation of each Tract within the Unit Area as enlarged, and shall revise Exhibits "A" and "B" accordingly.

12.3 **Effective Date.** The effective date of any enlargement of the Unit Area shall be 7:00 a.m. on the first day of the calendar month following compliance with conditions for enlargement as specified by Working Interest Owners, approval of the enlargement by the appropriate governmental authority, if required, and the filing for record of revised Exhibits "A" and "B" in the records of _____ County, _____.

ARTICLE 13
CHANGE OF TITLE

13.1 **Covenant Running With the Land.** This Agreement shall extend to, be binding on, and inure to the benefit of, the respective heirs, devisees, legal representatives, successors, and assigns of the parties to it, and shall constitute a covenant running with the lands, leases, and interests covered by this Agreement.

13.2 **Notice of Transfer.** Any conveyance of all or any part of any interest owned by any party with respect to any Tract shall be made expressly subject to this Agreement. No change of title shall be binding on the Unit Operator, or on any party to this Agreement other than the party so transferring, until the first day of the calendar month next succeeding the date of receipt by Unit Operator of a photocopy or a certified copy of the recorded instrument evidencing the change in ownership.

13.3 **Waiver of Rights to Partition.** Each party covenants that during the existence of this Agreement, it will not resort to any action to partition the Unit Area or the Unit Equipment, and to that extent waives the benefits of all laws authorizing a partition.

ARTICLE 14
RELATIONSHIP OF PARTIES

14.1 **No Partnership.** The duties, obligations, and liabilities of the parties to this Agreement are intended to be several and not joint or collective. This Agreement is not intended to create, and shall not be construed to create an association or trust, or to impose a partnership duty, obligation, or liability with regard to any one or more of the parties to it. Each p arty to this Agreement shall be individually responsible for its own obligations.

14.2 **No Sharing of Market.** This Agreement is not intended to provide, and shall not be construed to provide, directly or indirectly, for any cooperative refining, joint sale, or marketing of Unitized Substances.

14.3 **Royalty Owners Free of Costs.** The Agreement is not intended to impose, and shall not be construed to impose, upon any Royalty Owner any obligation to pay for Unit Expense unless the Royalty Owner is otherwise so obligated.

14.4 **Information to Royalty Owners.** Each Royalty Owner shall be entitled to all information in the possession of Unit Operator to which the Royalty Owner is entitled by an existing agreement or lease with any Working Interest Owner.

ARTICLE 15
LAWS AND REGULATIONS

15.1 **Laws and Regulations.** This Agreement shall be subject to the conservation laws of the State of _____; to the valid rules, regulations, and orders of _____; and, to all other applicable federal, state, and municipal laws, rules, regulations, and orders.

ARTICLE 16
FORCE MAJEURE

16.1 **Force Majeure.** All obligations imposed by this Agreement on each party, except for the payment of money, shall be suspended while compliance is prevented, in whole or in part, by a strike, fire, war, civil disturbance, act of God; by federal, state, or municipal laws; by any rule, regulation, or order of a governmental agency; by inability to secure materials, or by any other cause or causes beyond the reasonable control of the party. No party shall be required against its will to adjust or settle any labor dispute. Neither this Agreement nor any lease or other instrument subject to it shall be terminated by reason of suspension of Unit Operations due to any one or more of the causes set forth in this Article.

ARTICLE 17
EFFECTIVE DATE

17.1 **Effective Date.** This Agreement shall become binding on each party as of the date the party signs the instrument by which it becomes a party to this Agreement, and, unless sooner terminated as provided in Section 17.2, shall become effective as to qualified Tracts at the time and date as determined by the Working Interest Owners in all the qualified Tracts, and set forth in a certificate filed for record by the Unit Operator in _____ County, _____. The certificate shall not be filed until after the following requirements have been met:

17.1.1 Tracts comprising eighty-five percent (85%) or more of the Phase II Unit Participation in the Unit Area as shown on the Exhibit "B" that have qualified under the provisions of Article 9.

17.1.2 At least one counterpart of this Agreement has been filed for record in _____ County, _____.

17.1.3 This Agreement has been approved by (regulatory agency).

17.2 **Ipso Facto Termination.** If the requirements of Section 17.1 are not accomplished on or before _(Date)_, this Agreement shall ipso facto terminate on that date (the "termination date") and then be of no further effect, unless prior to that time Working Interest Owners owning a combined Unit Participation of at least _____ percent (____%) have become parties to this Agreement, and at least _____ percent (____%) of the committed Working Interest Owners have decided to extend the termination date for a period not to exceed one year. If the termination date is extended and the requirements of Section 17.1 are not accomplished on or before the extended termination date, this Agreement shall ipso facto terminate on the extended termination date and then be of no further effect. For the purpose of this Section, Unit Participation shall be as shown on the original Exhibit _____ attached to the Unit Operating Agreement.

ARTICLE 18
TERM

18.1 **Term.** The term of this Agreement shall be for the time that Unitized Substances are produced in paying quantities and so long thereafter as Unit Operations are conducted without a cessation of more than ninety (90) consecutive days, unless sooner terminated by Working Interest Owners in the manner provided in this Agreement.

18.2   Termination by Working Interest Owners. This Agreement may be terminated by Working Interest Owners having a combined then effective Unit Participation of at least _____ percent (____%) whenever those Working Interest Owners determine that Unit Operations are not longer profitable.

18.3   Effect of Termination.   On termination of this Agreement, the further development and operation of the Unitized Formation as a Unit shall be abandoned, Unit Operations shall cease, and after that time, the parties shall be governed by the provisions of the leases and other instruments affecting the separate Tracts, and Unit Operator shall file a certificate stating that fact and the effective termination date thereof in _____ County, _____.

18.4   Salvaging Equipment On Termination. If not otherwise granted by the leases or other instruments affecting each Tract unitized under this Agreement, Royalty Owners grant Working Interest Owners a period of six (6) months after the date of termination of this Agreement within which to salvage and remove Unit Equipment.

ARTICLE 19
EXECUTION

19.1   Original, Counterpart, or Other Instrument. A person may become a party to this Agreement by signing the original of this Agreement, a counterpart of it, or other instrument agreeing to be bound by the provisions of this Agreement.   The signing of any of these instruments shall have the same effect as if all the parties had signed the same instrument.

19.2   Joinder in Dual Capacity. Execution by any party as either a Working Interest Owner or a Royalty Owner shall commit all interests that may be owned or controlled by that party.

ARTICLE 20
NEW INTEREST

20.1   New Interest.   If any Working Interest Owner shall, after executing this Agreement, create any overriding royalty, production payment, or other similar interest, referred to as "new interest," out of its interest subject to this Agreement, the new interest shall be subject to all the terms and provisions of this Agreement.   In the event the Working Interest Owner owning the interest from which the new interest was created withdraws from this Agreement under the terms of Section 17.1 of the Unit Operating Agreement, or fails to pay any expenses and costs chargeable to it under this Agreement, and the production of the Working Interest Owner is insufficient for that purpose, the owner of the new interest will be liable for the prorata portion of all costs and expenses for which the original Working Interest Owner creating the new interest would have been liable had the same not been transferred.   In this event, the lien provided in Section 21.3 may be enforced against the new interest.   If the owner of the new interest bears a portion of the costs and expenses or is enforced against the new interest, the owner of the new interest will be subrogated to the rights of the Unit operator with respect to the interest primarily chargeable with those costs and expenses.

ARTICLE 21
GENERAL

21.1   Amendments Affecting Working Interest Owners.   Amendments to this Agreement, relating wholly to Working Interest Owners, may be made if signed by all Working Interest Owners.

1   **21.2**   **Action by Working Interest Owners.**   Any action or approval required by
2 Working Interest Owners shall be in accordance with the provisions of the Unit Operating
3 Agreement.
4   **21.3**   **Lien of Unit Operator.**   Unit Operator shall have a lien on the interests of
5 Working Interest Owners in the Unit Area to the extent provided in the Unit Operating
6 Agreement.
7   This Agreement is executed by each party as of the date of the acknowledgment of their
8 signature, to be effective as of the Effective Date.

EXHIBIT "A"
TO UNIT AGREEMENT

TRACTS AND TRACT PARTICIPATION

Participation Tract No.	Tract Name	Land Description	Phase I	Phase II

EXHIBIT "B"
TO UNIT AGREEMENT

(Map of the Boundaries of the Unit
and the Tracts in the Unit)

EXHIBIT "B-1"
TO UNIT AGREEMENT

(Map Designating Useable Wells)

NOTES

1.   The prior form and next form are used to aid in accomplishing the voluntary unitization of substantially developed oil and condensate reservoirs to conduct some form of pressure maintenance, repressuring, water flood, or other form of operation designed to increase ultimate recovery. Both forms must be adapted to conform to the conditions and requirements of particular units and to different state laws.

2.   This form was furnished by Kanes Forms, P.O. Box 53010, Midland, TX 79710, tel. 800-526-3790. The Kanes website is: http://www.kanesforms.com/new/index.htm The form is similar to a form developed in 1970 by the American Petroleum Institute ("API"), a trade organization that represents major oil and gas companies. The API web site is located at http://www.api.org.

UNIT OPERATING AGREEMENT

____UNIT, ____ COUNTY, ____

TABLE OF CONTENTS

126

UNIT OPERATING AGREEMENT
____ UNIT____ COUNTY, ____

      This Unit Operating Agreement (the "Agreement") is dated ____. The Parties to this Agreement are those who have signed the original of it, a counterpart, or other instrument agreeing to become a Party to this Agreement (all collectively called the "Parties").

      The Parties, as Working Interest Owners, have executed an agreement entitled "Unit Agreement," ____Unit, ____County,____(the "Unit Agreement"), which provides for a separate agreement by the Working Interest Owners to provide for Unit Operations as defined in the Unit Agreement.

      In consideration of the mutual agreements provided in this Agreement, the Parties agree as follows:

ARTICLE 1
RATIFICATION OF UNIT AGREEMENT

1.1   CONFIRMATION OF UNIT AGREEMENT. The Unit Agreement is ratified and by reference is made a part of this Agreement.

      The definitions in the Unit Agreement are adopted for all purposes into this Agreement. If there is any conflict between the Unit Agreement and this Agreement, the Unit Agreement shall control.

1.2   AMENDMENT OF JOINT OPERATING CONTRACTS AND OTHER AGREEMENTS. The provisions of existing joint operating contracts and other agreements pertaining to the Unitized Substances, the Unitized Formations or their operations are amended to the extent necessary to make them conform to the provisions of this Agreement. Otherwise, all those contracts and agreements shall remain in effect as between the parties to those contracts and agreements.

ARTICLE 2
EXHIBITS

2.1   EXHIBITS.

    2.1.1 EXHIBITS A, B, C, and D of the Unit Agreement are incorporated into this Agreement by reference.

    2.1.2 EXHIBIT E to this Agreement is a schedule showing the Working Interest of each Working Interest Owner in each Tract in the Unit, the portion of each Working Interest Owner's Unit Participation attributable to each interest, and the Unit Participation of each Working Interest Owner. Unit Participations are those provided in Section _____ of the Unit Agreement, except where a different Tract Participation, Unit Participation, or voting interest is provided for in this Agreement.

    2.1.3 EXHIBIT F attached to this Agreement is the Accounting Procedures applicable to Unit Operations. If there is any conflict between this Agreement and Exhibit F, this Agreement shall control.

    2.1.4 EXHIBIT G to this Agreement is the insurance provisions applicable to Unit Operations.

    2.1.5 EXHIBIT H to this Agreement is the Gas Balancing Agreement.

2.2   REVISION OF EXHIBITS. Whenever Exhibits A and B are revised, Exhibit E shall be revised accordingly and be effective as on the same date as the effective date of the revisions to

Exhibits A and B. Unit Operator shall revise Exhibit E from time to time as necessary to reflect changes in ownership on which Unit Operator has received notice as provided in the Unit Agreement.

2.3 **REFERENCE TO EXHIBITS.** When reference is made to an Exhibit, it is to the exhibit originally attached to the Unit Agreement or this Agreement or, if revised, to the last revision.

ARTICLE 3
SUPERVISION OF OPERATIONS BY WORKING INTEREST OWNERS

3.1 **OVERALL SUPERVISION.** Working Interest Owners shall exercise overall supervision and control of all matters pertaining to Unit Operations pursuant to this Agreement and the Unit Agreement. In the exercise of this authority, each Working Interest Owner shall act solely in its own behalf in the capacity of an individual owner and not on behalf of all the owners as an entirety.

3.2 **SPECIFIC AUTHORITY AND DUTIES.** The matters on which working interest owners shall decide and take action shall include, but not be limited to, the following:

    3.2.1 **Method of Operation.** The method of operation, including the type or types of pressure maintenance, secondary recovery, or other enhanced recovery program to be employed on the Unit.

    3.2.2 **Drilling of Wells.** The drilling of any well for production of Unitized Substances, for use as an injection well, or for other purposes.

    3.2.3 **Well Recompletions and Change of Status.** The recompletion, deepening, abandonment, or change of status of any well, the use of any well for injection, salt water disposal, or other purposes, or the acquisition of wells for Unit Operations.

    3.2.4 **Expenditures.** Any single expenditure in excess of _____ Thousand Dollars ($_____). However, approval by Working Interest Owners of the drilling, reworking, deepening, or plugging back of any well shall include approval of all necessary expenditures required, the completing, testing, and equipping the well, including necessary flow lines, separators, and storage tanks. No separate approval shall be required for any expenditure authorized as part of another expenditure. If Operator prepares an Authority for Expenditure ("AFE") for its own use for any single expenditure costing less than $____, upon request Operator shall furnish the requesting Working Interest Owners with a copy of the AFE.

    3.2.5 **Disposition of Unit Equipment.** The selling or other disposition of any major item of surplus Unit Equipment, if the current price of new similar equipment is _____ Thousand Dollars ($____) or more.

    3.2.6 **Appearance Before a Court or Regulatory Agency.** The designating of a representative to appear before any court or regulatory agency in matters pertaining to Unit Operations. A designation shall not prevent any Working Interest Owner from appearing in person or from designating another representative to appear on the Working Interest Owners behalf, at Working Interest Owner's own expense.

    3.2.7 **Audits.** The auditing of the accounts of Unit Operator pertaining to Unit Operations. Audits shall:

        (a) not be conducted more than once each year except on the resignation or removal of Unit Operator;

(b) be made on the approval of the owner(s) of a majority of the Working Interest other than that of Unit Operator, at the expense of all Working Interest Owners other than Unit Operator, or

(c) be made at the expense of those Working Interest Owners requesting an audit, if owners of less than a majority of Working Interest, other than that of Unit Operator, request an audit; and,

(d) be made only after 30 days written notice to Unit Operator.

3.2.8 **Inventories.** The taking of periodic inventories under the terms of Exhibit F.

3.2.9 **Technical Services.** The authorizing of charges to the joint account of all Working Interest Owners for services by consultants or Unit Operator's technical personnel not covered by the overhead charges provided in Exhibit F.

3.2.10 **Assignments to Committees.** The appointment of committees to study any problems in connection with Unit Operations.

(Sections 3.2.11 through 3.2.15 are to be completed, providing the terms agreed on by parties to this Agreement.)

3.2.11 **The Removal of Unit Operator and The Selection Of A Successor.**

3.2.12 **The Enlargement of the Unit Area.**

3.2.13 **The Adjustment and Readjustment of Investments.**

3.2.14 **The Termination of the Unit Agreement.**

3.2.15 **The Amendment or Modification of Exhibit F.**

ARTICLE 4
EXERCISING SUPERVISION

4.1 **DESIGNATION OF REPRESENTATIVES.** Each Working Interest Owner shall inform Unit Operator in writing of the names and addresses of the representative and alternate authorized to represent and bind the Working Interest Owner concerning Unit Operations. The representative or alternate may be changed from time to time by written notice to Unit Operator.

4.2 **MEETINGS.** All meetings of Working Interest Owners shall be called by Unit Operator on its own motion, or at the request of two or more Working Interest Owners having a total Unit Participation of not less than ____ percent (____%). No less than ____ (____) days advance written notice shall be given before a meeting. An agenda for the meeting must be attached to the notice. Working Interest Owners attending the meeting may amend items included in the agenda and may act upon an amended item or other items presented at the meeting. The representative of Unit Operator will be chairman of each meeting.

4.3 **VOTING PROCEDURE.** Working Interest Owners shall decide all matters coming before them as follows:

4.3.1 **Voting Interest.** Each Working Interest Owner shall have a voting interest equal to its Unit Participation at the time of the vote.

4.3.2 **Vote Required.** Unless otherwise provided in this Agreement or in the Unit Agreement, Working Interest Owners shall determine all matters by the affirmative vote of (three or more) Working Interest Owners having a combined voting interest of at least ____ (____%).

4.3.3 **Vote at Meeting By Nonattending Working Interest Owner.** Any Working Interest Owner who is not represented at a meeting may vote on any agenda item by letter or facsimile addressed to the representative of Unit Operator if the letter or facsimile is received prior to the vote at the meeting.

130

4.3.4 **Poll Votes.** Working Interest Owners may vote on and decide, by letter or facsimile, any matter submitted in writing to Working Interest Owners. If a meeting is not requested, as provided in Section 4.2, within ____ (____) days after a written proposal is sent to Working Interest Owners, the vote taken by letter or facsimile shall become final. Unit Operator will give prompt notice of the results of the voting to all Working Interest Owners.

ARTICLE 5
INDIVIDUAL RIGHTS OF WORKING INTEREST OWNERS

5.1 **RESERVATION OF RIGHTS.** Working Interest Owners severally reserve to themselves all their rights, except as otherwise provided in this Agreement and the Unit Agreement.

5.2 **SPECIFIC RIGHTS.** Each Working Interest Owner shall have, among others, the following specific rights:

5.2.1 **ACCESS TO UNIT AREA.** Access to the Unit Area at all reasonable times to inspect Unit Operations, wells, pertinent records and data.

5.2.2 **Reports.** The right to receive from Unit Operator, on written request, copies of all reports to any governmental agency, reports of oil runs and stocks, inventory reports, gas sales and all other information pertaining to Unit Operations. The cost of gathering and furnishing information not ordinarily furnished by Unit Operator to all Working Interest Owners will be charged to the Working Interest Owner requesting the information.

ARTICLE 6
UNIT OPERATOR

6.1 **UNIT OPERATOR.** ____ is designated Unit Operator.

6.2 **RESIGNATION OR REMOVAL.** Unit Operator may resign at any time. Unit Operator may be removed at any time by the affirmative vote of Working Interest Owners having ____ percent (____%) or more of the voting interest remaining after excluding the voting interest of Unit Operator. A resignation or removal shall not become effective for a period of three months after the resignation or removal, unless the successor Unit Operator takes over Unit Operations before the expiration of that period.

6.3 **SELECTION OF SUCCESSOR.** Upon the resignation or removal of a Unit Operator, a successor Unit Operator shall be selected by Working Interest Owners. If the Unit Operator that is removed fails to vote or votes only to succeed itself, the successor Unit Operator shall be selected by the affirmative vote of Working Interest Owners having ____ percent (____%) or more of the voting interest remaining after excluding the voting interest of the Unit Operator that was removed.

ARTICLE 7
AUTHORITY AND DUTIES OF UNIT OPERATOR

7.1 **EXCLUSIVE RIGHT TO OPERATE UNIT.** Subject to the provisions of this Agreement and to instructions from Working Interest Owners, Unit Operator shall have the exclusive right and be obligated to conduct Unit Operations.

7.2 **WORKMANLIKE CONDUCT.** Unit Operator shall conduct Unit Operations in a good and workmanlike manner as would a prudent operator under the same or similar circumstances. Unit Operator will freely consult with Working Interest Owners and keep them informed of all matters which Unit Operator, in the exercise of its best judgment, considers important. Unit Operator shall not be liable to Working Interest Owners for damages, unless the damages result from Unit Operator's gross negligence or willful misconduct.

7.3 **LIENS AND ENCUMBRANCES.** Unit Operator shall keep the lands and leases in the Unit Area and the Unit Equipment free from all liens and encumbrances occasioned by Unit Operations, except the lien and security interest of Unit Operator and Working Interest Owners granted in this Agreement.

7.4 **EMPLOYEES.** The number of employees used by Unit Operator in conducting Unit Operations, their selection, hours of labor, and compensation shall be determined by Unit Operator. These employees shall be the employees of Unit Operator.

7.5 **RECORDS.** Unit Operator shall keep correct books, accounts, and records of Unit Operations.

7.6 **REPORTS TO WORKING INTEREST OWNERS.** Unit Operator shall furnish Working Interest Owners periodic reports of Unit Operations.

7.7 **REPORTS TO GOVERNMENTAL AUTHORITIES.** Unit Operator shall make all reports to governmental authorities to which there is a duty to report.

7.8 **ENGINEERING AND GEOLOGICAL INFORMATION.** Unit Operator shall furnish to Working Interest Owners, upon written request and at the requesting Working Interest Owner's expense, a copy of all logs and other engineering and geological data pertaining to wells drilled subsequent to the Effective Date of Unit Operations insofar as the information pertains to the Unitized Formation.

7.9 **EXPENDITURES.** Unit Operator is authorized to make single expenditures of not more than _____ Thousand Dollars ($_____) without prior approval of Working Interest Owners. If an emergency occurs, Unit Operator may immediately make or incur expenditures as in its opinion are required to deal with the emergency. Unit Operator shall report to Working Interest Owners, as promptly as possible, the nature of the emergency and the action taken.

7.10 **WELLS DRILLED BY UNIT OPERATOR.** All wells drilled by Unit Operator shall be drilled at the usual rates prevailing in the area of the Unit. Unit Operator may employ its own tools and equipment, but the charges shall not exceed the usual rates prevailing in the area. The work shall be performed by Unit Operator under the same terms and conditions as are usual in the area in contracts of independent contractors doing work of a similar nature.

7.11 **MATHEMATICAL ERRORS.** All parties agree Unit Operator is empowered to correct any mathematical errors that might exist in the exhibits to this Agreement.

7.12 **BORDER AGREEMENTS.** Unit Operator may, after approval by Working Interest Owners, enter into border or lease line agreements with owners of lands adjacent to the Unit Area for the purpose of coordinating operations.

7.13 **INDEMNITIES.** On contracts executed by Unit Operator with an independent contractor covering operations or services to be performed in connection with Unit Operations, Unit Operator shall require any indemnification provision in favor of Unit Operator contained in a contract extend to and inure to the benefit of Working Interest Owners in the same manner as Unit Operator.

ARTICLE 8

TAXES

8.1 **AD VALOREM TAXES.** Beginning with the first calendar year after the Effective Date, Unit Operator shall make and file all necessary ad valorem tax renditions and returns with the proper tax authorities for all property (both real and personal, as permitted by statute or ordinance) of each Working Interest Owner used or held by Unit Operator for Unit Operations. Unit Operator shall settle all resulting assessments. All ad valorem taxes shall be paid by Unit

Operator and charged to the account of all Working Interest Owners. If the interest of a Working Interest Owner is subject to a separately assessed overriding royalty interest, production payment, or other interest of more than a ____ (____) royalty, that Working Interest Owner shall notify Unit Operator of such interest, before the rendition date, and shall be given credit for the reduction in the resulting taxes paid. If the Operator is required to pay ad valorem taxes based in whole or in part upon separate valuations of each party's interest, notwithstanding anything to the contrary, charges to the joint account shall be made and paid by the parties in accordance with the percentages of tax value generated by each party's interest. Any Working Interest Owner dissatisfied with any assessment of its interest in real or personal property shall have the right, at its own expense, to protest an assessment.

8.2   OTHER TAXES. Each Working Interest Owner shall pay or cause to be paid all production, severance, gathering, and other taxes imposed upon or assessed against the production or handling of its share of Unitized Substances.

ARTICLE 9

INSURANCE

9.1   INSURANCE. Unit Operator, with respect to Unit Operations, shall:

    (a)   comply with the Workmen's Compensation Laws of the State of ____;

    (b)   carry Employer's Liability and other insurance required by the laws of the State of ____; and,

    (c)   provide other insurance identified in Exhibit G.

ARTICLE 10

ADJUSTMENT OF INVESTMENTS

10.1   PERSONAL PROPERTY TAKEN OVER. Upon the Effective Date, Working Interest Owners shall deliver to Unit Operator the following:

    10.1.1 Wells. All wells completed in the Unitized Formation ("Unit Wells").

    10.1.2 Wells and Lease Equipment. The casing and tubing in each Unit Well, the wellhead connections, and all other lease and operating equipment used in the operations of Unit Wells which Working Interest Owners determine is necessary or desirable for conducting Unit Operations.

    10.1.3 Records. A copy of all production and well records for the Unit Wells.

10.2   INVENTORY AND EVALUATION OF PERSONAL PROPERTY AND WELL BORES. Working Interest Owners shall, at Unit Expense, inventory and evaluate the personal property taken over by the Unit Operator under Section 10.1.2. The inventory shall include and be limited to those items of equipment considered controllable under Exhibit F except, upon determination of Working Interest Owners, items considered noncontrollable may be included in the inventory to ensure a more equitable adjustment of investment. Casing shall be included in the inventory for record purposes, but shall be excluded from evaluation and investment adjustment.

10.3   WELL BORE ADJUSTMENT. The Working Interest Owners, in adjusting investment, may allocate a reasonable value for each well bore.

10.4   INVESTMENT ADJUSTMENT. On approval of the inventory and evaluation by Working Interest Owners each Working Interest Owner shall be credited with the value of its interest in all personal property taken over under Section 10.1.2, and shall be charged an amount equal to the product of the total value of all personal property taken over under Section 10.1.2 times the Working Interest Owner's Unit Participation. If the charge against any Working

Interest Owner is greater than the amount credited to the Working Interest Owner, the resulting net charge shall be an item of Unit Expense chargeable to the Working Interest Owner. If the credit to any Working Interest Owner is greater than the amount charged against that Working Interest Owner, the resulting net credit shall be paid to the Working Interest Owner by Unit Operator out of funds received by it in settlement of the net charges described above. Each Working Interest Owner shall be charged or credited with the net cash amount necessary to effect the readjustment of the capital investment account.

10.5   GENERAL FACILITIES. The acquisition of any warehouses, warehouse stocks, lease houses, camps, field operating systems, wells (not governed by Section 10.1.1 above) and office buildings necessary for Unit Operations shall be by negotiation by the owners of those facilities and Unit Operator, subject to the approval of Working Interest Owners.

10.6   OWNERSHIP OF PERSONAL PROPERTY AND FACILITIES. Each Working Interest Owner, individually, shall, by virtue of this Agreement, own an undivided interest, equal to its Unit Participation, in all personal property and facilities taken over or otherwise acquired by Unit Operator by the terms of this Agreement.

ARTICLE 11

UNIT EXPENSE

11.1   BASIS OF CHARGE TO WORKING INTEREST OWNERS. Initially, Unit Operator shall pay all Unit Expense. Each Working Interest Owner shall reimburse Unit Operator for its share of Unit Expense. Each Working Interest Owner's share shall be the same as its Unit Participation in effect at the time the expense was incurred, times Unit Expense. All charges, credits, and accounting for Unit Expense shall be made in the manner provided in Exhibit F.

11.2   BUDGETS. Before, or when practical after, the Effective Date, Unit Operator shall prepare a budget of estimated Unit Expense for the remainder of the calendar year, and, on or before the first day of each (month in year) thereafter, shall prepare a budget for the ensuing calendar year. The budget shall set out the estimated Unit Expense by quarterly periods. Budgets shall be estimates only, and shall be adjusted or corrected by Working Interest Owners and Unit Operator whenever an adjustment or correction is proper. A copy of each budget and adjusted budget shall be promptly furnished to each Working Interest Owner.

11.3   ADVANCE BILLINGS. Unit Operator is granted the right, without prejudice to other rights or remedies, to require Working Interest Owners to advance their respective shares of estimated Unit Expense by submitting to Working Interest Owners, on or before the 15th day of any month, an itemized estimate for the succeeding month, with a request for payment in advance. Within 15 days after receipt of the estimate, each Working Interest Owner shall pay to Unit Operator its share of such estimate. Adjustments between estimated and actual Unit Expense shall be made by Unit Operator at the close of each calendar month, and the accounts of Working Interest Owners shall be adjusted accordingly.

11.4   COMMINGLING OF FUNDS. Funds received by Unit Operator under this agreement need not be segregated or maintained by it as a separate fund, but may be commingled with its own funds.

11.5   LIEN AND SECURITY INTEREST. Each Working Interest Owner grants Unit Operator a lien upon its oil and gas rights in each Unit Tract, a security interest in its share of Unitized Substances when extracted and its interest in all Unit Equipment, to secure payment of its share of Unit Expense, with interest at the rate of _____ percent (____%) per annum or the

1 maximum legal interest rate permitted under _____ law, whichever is the lesser. Unit Operator
2 grants a like lien and security interest to Working Interest Owners to secure payment of Unit
3 Operator's proportionate share of Unit Expense. To the extent Unit Operator or Working Interest
4 Owners have a security interest under the Uniform Commercial Code (the "Code") of the State,
5 in which the Unit is located, Unit Operator or Working Interest Owners shall be entitled to
6 exercise the rights and remedies of a secured party under the Code. The bringing of a suit and
7 obtaining a judgment by Unit Operator or Working Interest Owners for the secured indebtedness
8 shall not be deemed an election of remedies or otherwise affect the lien rights or security interest
9 as security for payment. In addition, on default by any Working Interest Owner or the Unit
10 Operator in the payment of its share of Unit Expense, Unit Operator or Working Interest Owner
11 shall have the right, without prejudice to other rights or remedies, to collect from the purchaser
12 of production the proceeds from the sale of the Working Interest Owner's or Unit Operator's
13 share of Unitized Substances until the amount owed by the Working Interest Owner or Unit
14 Operator, plus interest, has been paid. Each purchaser shall be entitled to rely on Unit Operator's
15 or Working Interest Owner's written statement concerning the amount of any default.
16 **11.6   UNPAID UNIT EXPENSE.** If any Working Interest Owner fails to pay its share of Unit
17 Expense within _____ (___) days after rendition of a statement by Unit Operator, each Working
18 Interest Owner agrees, upon request by Unit Operator, to pay its proportionate part of the unpaid
19 share of Unit Expense of the defaulting Working Interest Owner. Working Interest Owners
20 paying the share of Unit Expense of a defaulting Working Interest Owner shall be reimbursed by
21 Unit Operator for the amount paid, plus any interest collected, upon receipt by Unit Operator of
22 any past due amount collected from the defaulting Working Interest Owner. Any Working
23 Interest Owner paying a defaulting Working Interest Owner's share of Unit Expense shall, to
24 obtain reimbursement, be subrogated to the lien and other rights granted to Unit Operator under
25 this Agreement.
26 **11.7   CARVED-OUT INTEREST.** If any Working Interest Owner shall, after executing this
27 Agreement, create an overriding royalty, production payment, net proceeds interest, carried
28 interest, or any other interest out of its Working Interest, the carved-out interest shall be subject
29 to the terms and provisions of this Agreement, specifically including, but without limitation,
30 Section 11.5 entitled "Lien and Security Interest." If the Working Interest Owner creating a
31 carved-out interest: (a) fails to pay any Unit Expense chargeable to that Working Interest Owner
32 under this Agreement, and the production of Unitized Substances accruing to the credit of that
33 Working Interest Owner is insufficient for that purpose; or, (b) withdraws from this Agreement
34 under the terms of Article 17, the carved-out interest shall be chargeable with a pro rata portion
35 of all Unit Expense incurred, the same as though the carved-out interest were a Working Interest,
36 and Unit Operator shall have the right to enforce against the carved-out interest the lien and all
37 other rights granted in Section 11.5 for the purpose of collecting the Unit Expense chargeable to
38 the carved-out interest.
39 **11.8   UNCOMMITTED ROYALTY**. Should an owner of Royalty Interest in any Tract fail
40 to become a party to the Unit Agreement, and, as a result, the actual Royalty Interest payments
41 with respect to the Tract are more or less than the Royalty Interest payments computed on the
42 basis of the Unitized Substances that are allocated to that Tract under the Unit Agreement, the
43 difference shall be borne by or inure to the benefit of Working Interest Owners, in proportion to
44 their respective Unit Participations at the time the Unitized Substances were produced.
45 However, the difference to be borne by or inure to the benefit of Working Interest Owners shall

not exceed an amount computed on the basis of ____ percent (____%) of the difference between the Unitized Substances allocated to the Tract and the Unitized Substances produced from the Tract. These adjustments shall be made by charges and credits to the joint account.

ARTICLE 12
NONUNITIZED FORMATIONS

12.1 RIGHT TO OPERATE. Any Working Interest Owner that now has or later acquires the right to drill for and produce oil, gas, or other minerals, from a formation underlying the Unit Area other than the Unitized Formation, shall have the right to do so despite this Agreement or the Unit Agreement. However, in exercising this right, a Working Interest Owner shall exercise care to prevent unreasonable interference with Unit Operations. No Working Interest Owner shall produce Unitized Substances through any well drilled or operated by it. If any Working Interest Owner drills any well into or through the Unitized Formation, the Unitized Formation shall be protected in a manner satisfactory to Working Interest Owners so that the production of Unitized Substances will not be adversely affected.

12.2 MULTIPLE COMPLETIONS. As of the Effective Date, any well bore in which there is a completion in both the Unitized Formation and any other formation shall be considered a multiple completion. The Working Interest Owners that have contributed the multiple completion reserve and retain the right to use the well bore for operations in any other formation. It shall be the sole responsibility of the owners of the other formation to furnish and install equipment necessary to segregate the production both in the well and on the surface in a manner acceptable to the Working Interest Owners. If there is a conflict of interest between the Working Interest Owners and any other formation owner with respect to a multiple completion, or the operation of the well, the interest of the Working Interest Owners shall prevail.

    12.2.1 Remedial Work. If it becomes necessary to workover, recondition, redrill, or abandon a well in the other formation, the work shall be performed under supervision of Unit Operator by and at the sole risk and expense of the owners of the other formation. If it becomes necessary to perform like work in the Unitized Formation, that work shall be performed by Unit Operator at Unit Expense.

    12.2.2 Liability. The Working Interest Owners shall not be liable or responsible for any damage to or loss of production from the other formation, including the use of the well as an injection well, or for any damage to the well or to the property, equipment, or facilities used in the operation of the well for production unless the damages result from gross negligence or willful misconduct. Likewise, the owners of the other formation shall not be liable or responsible for any damage to or loss of production from the Unitized Formation, including the use of the well as an injection well, or for any damage to the well or to the property, equipment or facilities, unless the damage results from gross negligence or willful misconduct.

    12.2.3 Redrilling. If it becomes necessary and economically feasible to redrill a well in which there is a multiple completion, the costs shall be mutually agreed upon by the Working Interest Owners and the owners in the other formation.

    12.2.4 Division of Expenses. All charges directly attributable to the Unitized Formation in multiple completed wells will be regarded as Unit Expense. All charges directly attributable to another formation in the well will be borne by the owners of the other formation. Those charges that cannot be attributable directly to either the Unitized Formation or the other formation will be regarded as Unit Expense as to one-half and will be borne by the owners of the other formation as to one-half.

ARTICLE 13

TITLES

13.1   WARRANTY AND INDEMNITY. Each Working Interest Owner represents and warrants it is the owner of the Working Interests set opposite its name in Exhibit E, and agrees to indemnify and hold harmless the other Working Interest Owners from any loss due to failure, in whole or part, of its title to its interest, except failure of title arising because of Unit Operations. This indemnity and any liability for breach of warranty shall be limited to an amount equal to the net value received from the sale or receipt of Unitized Substances attributed to the interest to which title failed. Each failure of title will be deemed to be effective, insofar as this Agreement is concerned, as of 7 a.m. on the first day of the calendar month in which the failure is finally determined. There shall be no retroactive adjustment of Unit Expense, retroactive allocation of Unitized Substances or the resulting proceeds, as a result of a title failure.

13.2   FAILURE BECAUSE OF UNIT OPERATIONS. The failure of title to any Working Interest in any Tract because of Unit Operations, including nonproduction from a Tract, shall not change the Unit Participation of the Working Interest Owner whose title failed, in relation to the Unit Participations of the other Working Interest Owners at the time of the title failure.

13.3   TITLE EXAMINATION. Unit Operator is authorized, at any time, to conduct such title examination and title curative work on any interest in any Tract it deems necessary or advisable for purposes of Unit Operations. Each Working Interest Owner who owns any interest in any Tract agrees to cooperate in a title examination and agrees to furnish Unit Operator all records affecting title, including but not limited to title opinions and abstracts of title that may be in a Working Interest Owner's possession or control. All costs and expenses incurred in a title examination and curative work conducted after the Effective Date shall be treated as a Unit Expense.

13.4   WAIVER OF RIGHTS TO PARTITION. Each party agrees, during the existence of this Agreement, it will not resort to any action to partition the Unitized Formation or the Unit Equipment, and to that extent waives the benefit of all laws authorizing a partition.

ARTICLE 14

LIABILITY, CLAIMS, AND SUITS

14.1   INDIVIDUAL LIABILITY. The duties, obligations, and liabilities of Working Interest Owners shall be several and not joint or collective. Nothing in this Agreement shall ever be construed as creating a partnership of any kind, joint venture, association, or trust among Working Interest Owners. Each party shall be individually responsible for its own obligations as provided in this Agreement.

14.2   SETTLEMENTS. Unit Operator may settle any single damage claim or suit involving Unit Operations if the expenditure does not exceed _____ Thousand Dollars ($____) and if the payment is in complete settlement of a claim or suit. If the amount required for settlement exceeds this amount, Working Interest Owners shall assume and take over the further handling of the claim or suit, unless that authority is delegated to Unit Operator. All costs and expense of handling, settling, or otherwise discharging a claim or suit shall be an item of Unit Expense. If a claim is made against any Working Interest Owner or if any Working Interest Owner is sued on account of any matter arising from Unit Operations over which a Working Interest Owner, individually, has no control because of the rights given Working Interest Owners and Unit Operator by this Agreement and the Unit Agreement, the Working Interest Owner shall

137

immediately notify Unit Operator, and the claim or suit shall be treated as any other claim or suit involving unit Operations.

ARTICLE 15
INTERNAL REVENUE PROVISION

15.1 **INTERNAL REVENUE PROVISION.** Despite any provisions in this Agreement that the rights and liabilities of the Parties are several and not joint or collective, or that this Agreement and all operations shall not constitute a partnership, if for federal income tax purposes this Agreement and the operations are regarded as a partnership, each of the parties choose to be excluded from the application of all of the provisions of Subchapter K, Chapter 1, Subtitle A, of the Internal Revenue Code of 1986, as permitted and authorized by Section 761 of the Code and related regulations. Unit Operator is authorized and directed to execute on behalf of each of the parties evidence of this election as may be required by the Secretary of the Treasury of the Unit States or the Federal Internal Revenue Service, including specifically, but not by way of limitation, all of the returns, statements and the data required by Federal Regulations. Should there be any requirement that each Party furnish further evidence of this election, all agree to execute documents and furnish other evidence that may be required by the Federal Internal Revenue Service or as may be necessary to evidence this election. Each Party agrees not to give any notices or take any other action inconsistent with this election. If any present or future income tax laws of the State of ____, or any future income tax laws of the United States, contain provisions similar to those in Subchapter K, Chapter 1, Subtitle A, of the Internal Revenue Code of 1986, as amended, under which an election similar to that provided by Section 761 of Subchapter K of the Code is permitted, each of the Parties agrees to make an election as may be permitted or required by such laws. In making this election, each of the Parties state that the income derived from operations under this Agreement can be adequately determined without the computation of partnership taxable income.

ARTICLE 16
NOTICES

16.1 **NOTICES.** All notices required or permitted in this Agreement shall be in writing and shall be deemed to have been properly served when sent by mail or facsimile to the address of the representative of each Working Interest Owner furnished to Unit Operator as provided in Article 4.

ARTICLE 17
WITHDRAWAL OF WORKING INTEREST OWNER

17.1 **WITHDRAWAL.** Any Working Interest Owner holding any Oil and Gas Rights represented by an oil and gas or oil, gas and mineral lease may be relieved of all obligations and liabilities with respect to the Working Interest under the lease, insofar as that lease is included within a particular Tract, by the assignment or surrender of the lease as provided below. A Working Interest Owner shall give written notice of its desire, to be relieved of the obligations of the Working Interest under a lease, to all other Working Interest Owners in the Tract in which the lease or a portion of the lease is located. Each Working Interest Owner notified shall have the right to receive an assignment of a pro rata interest in the lease or the portion of the lease located within the Tract. If one or more Working Interest Owners exercise the right, by notice in writing to the party desiring to be relieved, the party seeking relief shall assign the lease, or the portion of the lease within the Tract, with special warranty of title, to the party or parties desiring an assignment. If the assignment is in favor of more than one party, the assignment shall be made to them in the proportion that the Working Interest of each in the Tract bears to the total of the Working Interest of all of them in the Tract. The assignment shall include the interest in all Unit wells and Unit Equipment attributable to the leasehold being assigned, but there shall be no payment to the assignor for the assigned interest. After the effective date of the assignment, the assignor shall be relieved of all obligations and liabilities accruing after that date. The assignor shall remain obligated for all amounts that accrued prior to the effective date of the assignment. The assigned Working Interest shall continue to be subject to the provisions of this Agreement and the Unit Agreement. If no Working Interest Owner in the particular Tract chooses to receive an assignment of the lease, or the portion of the lease within the Tract, the Working Interest Owner desiring to be relieved shall surrender (and it shall have the right to surrender) the lease or the portion of the lease within the Tract, by executing and delivering to the lessor, and recording in the appropriate public records a release or surrender of the Working Interest Owner's interest in the lease. The mineral owner or owners whose interests were covered by the lease shall, following the surrender, own the interest in all Unit wells and Unit Equipment that was attributable to the leasehold surrendered. There shall be no payment to the surrendering party. The unleased mineral interest of the owner or owners shall then be treated for all purposes of this Agreement and the Unit Agreement as part Working Interest and part royalty in interest, as provided in Section 1.6 of the Unit Agreement. So treated, the mineral interest shall be subject to the provisions of this Agreement and the Unit Agreement. Upon surrender, the surrendering party shall be relieved of all obligations and liabilities accruing after the effective date of the surrender, but not those previously accrued.

ARTICLE 18
ABANDONMENT OF WELLS

18.1 RIGHTS OF OWNERS. If Working Interest Owners decide to permanently abandon any well within the Unit Area before termination of the Unit Agreement, Unit Operator shall give written notice to the Working Interest Owners of the Tract on which the well is located, and they shall have the option for a period of 60 days after the sending of the notice to notify Unit Operator in writing of their election to take over and own the well. Within 10 days after the Working Interest Owners of the Tract have notified Unit Operator of their election to take over the well, they shall pay Unit Operator, for credit to the Unit joint account, the amount determined by Working Interest Owners to be the net salvage value of the casing and equipment in and on the well. The Working Interest Owners of the Tract, by taking over the well, agree to seal the Unitized Formation, and upon abandonment, to plug the well in compliance with applicable laws and regulations. The Working Interest Owner(s) who takes over the well under this provision shall immediately file the necessary forms with the appropriate state and federal agencies showing the change in the operation of the well.

18.2 PLUGGING. If the Working Interest Owners of a Tract do not choose to take over a well located within the Unit Area that is proposed for abandonment, Unit Operator shall plug and abandon the well in compliance with applicable laws and regulations.

ARTICLE 19
EFFECTIVE DATE AND TERM

19.1 EFFECTIVE DATE. This Agreement shall become effective when the Unit Agreement becomes effective.

19.2 TERM. This Agreement shall continue in effect as long as the Unit Agreement remains in effect, and thereafter until: (a) all Unit wells have been plugged and abandoned or turned over to Working Interest Owners in the manner provided in Article 20; (b) all Unit Equipment and real property acquired for the joint account have been disposed of by Unit Operator in compliance with instructions of Working Interest Owners; and, (c) there has been a final accounting.

ARTICLE 20
ABANDONMENT OF OPERATIONS

20.1   TERMINATION. Upon termination of the Unit Agreement, the following will occur:

        20.1.1   Oil and Gas Rights. Oil and Gas Rights in and to each separate Tract shall no longer be affected by this Agreement. The parties shall be governed by the terms and provisions of the leases, contracts, and other instruments affecting the separate Tracts.

        20.1.2   Right to Operate. Working Interest Owners of any Tract that desire to take over and continue to operate wells located on a Tract may do so by paying Unit Operator, for credit to the Unit joint account, the net salvage value, as determined by Working Interest Owners, of the casing and equipment in and on the wells taken over and by agreeing, upon abandonment, to plug each well in compliance with applicable laws and regulations.

        20.1.3   Salvaging Wells. Unit Operator shall salvage as much of the casing and equipment in or on wells not taken over by Working Interest Owners of separate Tracts as can economically and reasonably be salvaged. Unit Operator shall cause the wells to be plugged and abandoned in compliance with applicable laws and regulations.

        20.1.4   Cost of Abandonment. The cost of abandonment of Unit Operations shall be a Unit Expense.

        20.1.5   Distribution Of Assets. Working Interest Owners shall share in the distribution of Unit Equipment, or the proceeds of the sale of Unit Equipment, in proportion to their Unit Participations.

ARTICLE 21
RIGHTS OF WAY AND EASEMENTS

21.1   ASSIGNMENT TO UNIT OPERATOR. Each Working Interest Owner having rights of way, easements or leasehold interest in surface sites necessary for Unit Operations agrees to assign, to the extent of its right and interest, to Unit Operator for the benefit of the Working Interest Owners, a nonexclusive right and interest in and to those interests. A Working Interest Owner having such an interest shall, within _____ (____) days after the Effective Date execute and deliver to Unit Operator, in recordable form, an assignment of those rights and interests, with copies of the instruments creating the interests and any available maps or plats describing and depicting the effective premises.

21.2   RENTAL PAYMENTS. The owners of the interest agree to make any rental payment or other payments that may become due and avoid termination of an interest for failure to make such payment. Owner shall be obligated to make payments as they come due, including any payments due within _____ (____) days after assignment to Unit Operator. These payments shall be a direct charge under Unit Expense.

21.3   RIGHTS OF UNIT OPERATOR. The interest described in Section 21.1 shall continue in Unit Operator as long as used for Unit Operations. In the event the designated Unit Operator resigns or is removed, it shall assign these rights and interests to the succeeding Unit Operator.

ARTICLE 22

EXECUTION

22.1 ORIGINAL COUNTERPART, OR OTHER INSTRUMENT. An owner of a Working Interest may become a party to this Agreement by signing the original of this instrument, a counterpart, or other instrument agreeing to become a party to this Agreement. The signing of any instrument making an owner of Working Interest a party to this Agreement shall have the same effect as if all Parties had signed the same instrument.

ARTICLE 23

SUCCESSORS AND ASSIGNS

23.1 SUCCESSORS AND ASSIGNS. This Agreement shall extend to, be binding on, and inure to the benefit of the Parties and their respective heirs, devisees, legal representatives, successors, and assigns, and shall constitute a covenant running with the lands, leases, and interests covered by this Agreement.

The Parties have executed this Agreement on the day and dates evidenced by their certificates of acknowledgments of their respective signatures.

EXHIBIT E
TO
UNIT OPERATING AGREEMENT

Name of Working Interest Owner	Tract Number	Tract Participation

EXHIBIT F
TO
UNIT OPERATING AGREEMENT

Accounting Procedure for Unit Operations

Operator shall carry and maintain at all times the following insurance with respect to all operations under this Agreement:

(a)   Insurance that shall comply with the Workmen's Compensation Laws of the State in which operations are conducted under the terms of this Agreement.

(b)   Employers' Liability Insurance with limits of not less than $____ for each occurrence.

(c)   Comprehensive General Liability Insurance with limits of not less than (i) $____ for each occurrence for bodily injury, and (ii) $____ for each occurrence for property damage. This insurance shall include contractual liability, completed operations, explosions, blowout, cratering, and underground resources liability coverage.

(d)   Automobile Liability Insurance, including owned, hired and nonhired vehicles, with the same limits as set forth in subparagraph (c) above.

(e)   Coverages in subparagraphs (c) and (d) above shall include Nonoperators as Additional Insured.

(f)   Excess liability Coverage more than the coverage in subparagraphs (a), (b), (c), (d) and (e) above with a combined single limit for Bodily Injury and Property Damage of not less than $____ for each occurrence. Such liability insurance as is required in this Agreement shall specifically state that the coverage will be deemed to be primary and noncontributing with comparable insurance otherwise available to Nonoperators. The insurance shall contain a provision that it shall not be canceled or subject to material change without at least thirty (30) days prior written notice to Nonoperators.

EXHIBIT H
TO
UNIT OPERATING AGREEMENT

GAS BALANCING AGREEMENT

NOTES

1.   The unit operating agreement is executed at the same time or immediately after a unit agreement has been entered into. It serves basically the same functions as a joint operating agreement, however, a comparison of this form with a JOA will reveal important differences between the two. The JOA is normally used for joint development of a relatively small portion of a reservoir during the primary stages of recovery; whereas the unit operating agreement typically covers the entire reservoir and governs how secondary or enhanced recovery operations are conducted. Unlike the JOA, there are no universally accepted standard forms for unit operating agreements. The Kanes form, reproduced here, may be used as a starting point for further negotiations.

2.   This form was furnished by Kanes Forms, P.O. Box 53010, Midland, TX 79710, tel. 800-526-3790. The Kanes website is: http://www.kanesforms.com/new/index.htm The form is similar to a form developed in 1970 by the American Petroleum Institute ("API"), a trade organization that represents major oil and gas companies. The API web site is located at http://www.api.org.

Chapter 3

THE OIL AND GAS LEASE

A.A.P.L. FORM 675
OIL AND GAS LEASE
TEXAS FORM-SHUT-IN CLAUSE, POOLING CLAUSE

THIS AGREEMENT made and entered into the _____ day of _____, 20_____, by and between _____, Lessor and _____, Lessee. WITNESSETH:

1. Lessor, in consideration of the sum of _____ Dollars ($_____), in hand paid, receipt of which is hereby acknowledged, and the royalties herein provided, does hereby grant, lease and let unto Lessee for the purpose of exploring, prospecting, drilling and mining for and producing oil and gas and all other hydrocarbons, laying pipe lines, building roads, tanks, power stations, telephone lines and other structures thereon to produce, save, take care of, treat, transport and own said products, and housing its employees, and without additional consideration, does hereby authorize Lessee to enter upon the land covered hereby to accomplish said purposes, the following described land in _____ County, Texas, to-wit:

[land description]

This Lease also covers and includes any and all lands owned or claimed by the Lessor adjacent or contiguous to the land described hereinabove, whether the same be in said survey or surveys or in adjacent surveys, although not included within the boundaries of the land described above. For the purpose of calculating rental payments hereinafter provided for the lands covered hereby are estimated to comprise _____ acres, whether it actually comprises more or less.

2. Subject to the other provisions herein contained this Lease shall be for a term of _____ years from this date (called "primary term") and as long thereafter as oil and gas or other hydrocarbons are being produced from said land or land with which said land is pooled hereunder.

3. The royalties to be paid by Lessee are as follows: On oil, one-eighth of that produced and saved from said land, the same to be delivered at the wells or to the credit of Lessor into the pipe line to which the wells may be connected. Lessee shall have the option to purchase any royalty oil in its possession, paying the market price therefore prevailing for the field where produced on the date of purchase. On gas, including casinghead gas, condensate or other gaseous substances, produced from said land and sold or used off the premises or for the extraction of gasoline or other products therefrom, the market value at the well of one-eighth of the gas so sold or used, provided that on gas sold at the wells the royalty shall be one-eighth of the amount realized from such sale. While there is a gas well on this Lease, or on acreage pooled therewith, but gas is not being sold or used Lessee shall pay or tender annually at the end of each yearly period during which such gas is not sold or used, as royalty, an amount equal to the delay rental provided for in paragraph 5 hereof, and while said royalty is so paid or tendered this Lease shall be held as a producing Lease under paragraph 2 hereof. Lessee shall have free use of oil, gas and water from said land, except water from Lessor's wells, for all operations hereunder, and the royalty on oil and gas shall be computed after deducting any so used.

4. Lessee, at its option, is hereby given the right and power to voluntarily pool or combine the acreage covered by this Lease, or any portion thereof, as to the oil and gas, or either of them, with other land, lease or leases in the immediate vicinity thereof to the extent hereinafter stipulated

No same as on p. 359 (e)

1   when in Lessee's judgment it is necessary or advisable to do so in order to properly develop and
2   operate said leased premises in compliance with the Spacing Rules of the Railroad Commission
3   of Texas, or other lawful authorities, or when to do so would, in the judgment of Lessee, promote
4   the conservation of oil and gas from said premises. Units pooled for oil hereunder shall not
5   substantially exceed 80 acres each in area, and units pooled for gas hereunder shall not
6   substantially exceed 640 acres each in area plus a tolerance of ten per-cent thereof in the case of
7   either an oil unit or a gas unit, provided that should governmental authority having jurisdiction
8   prescribe or permit the creation of units larger than those specified, units thereafter created may
9   conform substantially in size with those prescribed by governmental regulations. Lessee under the
10   provisions hereof may pool or combine acreage covered by this Lease, or any portion thereof as
11   above provided for as to oil in any one or more strata and as to gas in any one or more strata. The
12   units formed by pooling as to any stratum or strata need not conform in size or area with the unit or
13   units into which the Lease is pooled or combined as to any other stratum or strata, and oil units
14   need not conform as to area with gas units. The pooling in one or more instances shall not exhaust
15   the rights of Lessee hereunder to pool this Lease, or portions thereof, into other units. Lessee shall
16   file for record in the county records of the county in which the lands are located an instrument
17   identifying and describing the pooled acreage. Lessee may at its election exercise its pooling
18   operation after commencing operations for, or completing an oil or gas well on the leased
19   premises, and the pooled unit may include, but is not required to include, land or leases upon
20   which a well capable of producing oil or gas in paying quantities has theretofore been completed,
21   or upon which operations for drilling of a well for oil or gas have theretofore been commenced.
22   Operations for drilling on or production of oil or gas from any part of the pooled unit composed in
23   whole or in part of the land covered by this Lease, regardless of whether such operations for
24   drilling were commenced or such production was secured before or after the execution of this
25   instrument or the instrument designating the pooled unit, shall be considered as operations for
26   drilling on or production of oil or gas from the land covered by this Lease whether or not the well
27   or wells are actually located on the premises covered by this Lease, and the entire acreage
28   constituting such unit or units, as to oil and gas or either of them as herein provided, shall be
29   treated for all purposes except the payment of royalties on production from the pooled unit as if the
30   same were included in this Lease. For the purpose of computing the royalties to which owners of
31   royalties and payments out of production and each of them shall be entitled upon production of oil
32   and gas, or either of them from the pooled unit, there shall be allocated to the land covered by this
33   Lease and included in said unit a pro rata portion of the oil and gas, or either of them, produced
34   from the pooled unit after deducting that used for operations on the pooled unit. Such allocation
35   shall be on an acreage basis, that is to say, there shall be allocated to the acreage covered by this
36   Lease and included in the pooled unit that pro rata portion of the oil and gas, or either of them,
37   produced from the pooled unit which the number of surface acres covered by this Lease and
38   included in the pooled unit bears to the total number of surface acres included in the pooled unit.
39   Royalties hereunder shall be computed on the portion of such production, whether it be oil or gas
40   or either of them, so allocated to the land covered by this Lease and included in the unit just as
41   though such production were from such land. The production from an oil well will be considered
42   as production from the Lease or oil pooled unit from which it is producing and not as production
43   from a gas pooled unit; and production from a gas well will be considered as production from the
44   Lease or gas pooled unit from which it is producing and not from the oil pooled unit.
45

Pooling clause cont'd

147

5. If operation for drilling are not commenced on said land, or on acreage pooled therewith as above provided for, on or before one year from the date hereof, the Lease shall terminate as to both parties, unless on or before such anniversary date Lessee shall pay or tender to Lessor, or to the credit of Lessor in the _____, Bank at_____, Texas, (which Bank and its successors shall be Lessor's agent and shall continue as the depository for all rentals payable hereunder regardless of changes in ownership of said land or the rentals) the sum of _____ Dollars ($___), herein called rentals, which shall cover the privilege of deferring commencement of drilling operations for a period of twelve (12) months. In like manner and upon like payment or tenders annually the commencement of drilling operations may be further deferred for successive periods of twelve (12) months each during the primary term hereof. The payment or tender of rental under this paragraph and of royalty under paragraph 3 on any gas well from which gas is not being sold or used may be made by check or draft of Lessee mailed or delivered to Lessor, or to said Bank on or before the date of payment. If such Bank, or any successor Bank, should fail, liquidate or be succeeded by another Bank, or for any reason fail or refuse to accept rental, Lessee shall not be held in default for failure to make such payment or tender of rental until thirty (30) days after Lessor shall deliver to Lessee a proper recordable instrument, naming another Bank as Agent to receive such payments or tenders. Cash payment for this Lease is consideration for this Lease according to its terms and shall not be allocated as a mere rental for a period. Lessee may at any time or times execute and deliver to Lessor, or to the depository above named, or place of record a release covering any portion or portions of the above described premises and thereby surrender this Lease as to such portion or portions and be relieved of all obligations as to the acreage surrendered, and thereafter the rentals payable hereunder shall be reduced in the proportion that the acreage covered hereby is reduced by said release or releases.

6. If prior to discovery of oil, gas or other hydrocarbons on this land, or on acreage pooled therewith. Lessee should drill a dry hole or holes thereon, or if after the discovery of oil, gas or other hydrocarbons, the production thereof should cease from any cause, this Lease shall not terminate if Lessee commences additional drilling or re-working operations within sixty (60) days thereafter, or if it be within the primary term, commences or resumes the payment or tender of rentals or commences operations for drilling or re-working on or before the rental paying date next ensuing after the expiration of sixty (60) days from the date of completion of the dry hole, or cessation of production. If at any time subsequent to sixty (60) days prior to the beginning of the last year of the primary term, and prior to the discovery of oil, gas or other hydrocarbons on said land, or on acreage pooled therewith, Lessee should drill a dry hole thereon, no rental payment or operations are necessary in order to keep the Lease in force during the remainder of the primary term. If at the expiration of the primary term, oil, gas or other hydrocarbons are not being produced on said land, or on acreage pooled therewith, but Lessee is then engaged in drilling or re-working operations thereon, or shall have completed a dry hole thereon within sixty (60) days prior to the end of the primary term, the Lease shall remain in force so long as operations are prosecuted with no cessation of more than sixty (60) consecutive days, and if they result in the production of oil, gas or other hydrocarbons, so long thereafter as oil, gas or other hydrocarbons are produced from said land, or acreage pooled therewith. In the event a well or wells producing oil or gas in paying quantities shall be brought in on adjacent land and draining the leased premises, or acreage pooled therewith, Lessee agrees to drill such offset wells as a reasonably prudent operator would drill under the same or similar circumstances.

148

1 7. Lessee shall have the right at any time during or after the expiration of this Lease to remove all
2 property and fixtures placed on the premises by Lessee, including the right to draw and remove all
3 casing. When required by the Lessor, Lessee shall bury all pipelines below ordinary plow depth,
4 and no well shall be drilled within two hundred (200) feet of any residence or barn located on said
5 land as of the date of this Lease without Lessor's consent.
6 8. The rights of each party hereunder may be assigned in whole or in part, and the provisions hereof
7 shall extend to their heirs, successors and assigns, but no change or division in the ownership of
8 the land, rentals or royalties, however accomplished, shall operate to enlarge the obligations, or
9 diminish the rights of Lessee; and no change or division in such ownership shall be binding on
10 Lessee until thirty (30) days after Lessee shall have been furnished with a certified copy of
11 recorded instrument or instruments evidencing such change of ownership. In the event of
12 assignment hereof in whole or in part, liability for breach of any obligation issued hereunder shall
13 rest exclusively upon the owner of this Lease, or portion thereof, who commits such breach. In the
14 event of the death of any person entitled to rentals hereunder, Lessee may pay or tender such
15 rentals to the credit of the deceased or the estate of the deceased, until such time as Lessee has
16 been furnished with the proper evidence of the appointment and qualification of an executor or an
17 administrator of the estate, or if there be none, then until Lessee is furnished satisfactory evidence
18 as to the heirs or devisees of the deceased, and that all debts of the estate have been paid. If at any
19 time two or more persons become entitled to participate in the rental payable hereunder. Lessee
20 may pay or tender such rental jointly to such persons, or to their joint credit in the depository
21 named herein; or, at the Lessee's election, the portion or part of said rental to which each
22 participant is entitled may be paid or tendered to him separately or to his separate credit in said
23 depository; and payment or tender to any participant of his portion of the rentals hereunder shall
24 maintain this Lease as to such participant. In the event of an assignment of this Lease as to a
25 segregated portion of said land, the rentals payable hereunder shall be apportioned as between the
26 several leasehold owners ratably according to the surface area of each, and default in rental
27 payment by one shall not affect the rights of other leasehold owners hereunder. If six or more
28 parties become entitled to royalty payments hereunder, Lessee may withhold payment thereof
29 unless and until furnished with a recordable instrument executed by all such parties designating an
30 agent to receive payment for all.
31 9. The breach by Lessee of any obligations arising hereunder shall not work a forfeiture or
32 termination of this Lease nor cause a termination or reversion of the estate created hereby nor be
33 grounds for cancellation hereof in whole or in part unless Lessor shall notify Lessee in writing of
34 the facts relied upon in claiming a breach hereof, and Lessee, if in default shall have sixty (60)
35 days after receipt of such notice in which to commence the compliance with the obligations
36 imposed by virtue of this instrument, and if Lessee shall fail to do so then Lessor shall have
37 grounds for action in a court of law or such remedy to which he may feel entitled. After the
38 discovery of oil, gas or other hydrocarbons in paying quantities on the lands covered by this
39 Lease, or pooled therewith, Lessee shall reasonably develop the acreage retained hereunder, but in
40 discharging this obligation Lessee shall not be required to drill more than one well per eighty (80)
41 acres of area retained hereunder and capable of producing oil in paying quantities, and one well per
42 six hundred forty (640) acres of the area retained hereunder and capable of producing gas or other
43 hydrocarbons in paying quantities plus a tolerance of ten per-cent in the case of either an oil well
44 or a gas well.
45

Proportionate Reduction Clause

10. Lessor hereby warrants and agrees to defend the title to said lands and agrees also that Lessee at its option may discharge any tax, mortgage or other liens upon said land either in whole or in part, and in the event Lessee does so, it shall be subrogated to such lien with the right to enforce same and apply rentals and royalties accruing hereunder towards satisfying same. Without impairment of Lessee's rights under the warranty in event of failure of title, it is agreed that if Lessor owns an interest in the oil, gas or other hydrocarbons in or under said land, less than the entire fee simple estate then the royalties and rentals to be paid Lessor shall be reduced proportionately. Failure of Lessee to reduce such rental paid hereunder or over-payment of such rental hereunder shall not impair the right of Lessee to reduce royalties payable hereunder.

Force Majeure

11. Should Lessee be prevented from complying with any express or implied covenant of this Lease, from conducting drilling, or reworking operations thereon or from producing oil or gas or other hydrocarbons therefrom by reason of scarcity of, or inability to obtain or to use equipment or material, or by operation of force majeure, or because of any federal or state law or any order, rule or regulation of a governmental authority, then while so prevented, Lessee's obligations to comply with such covenant shall be suspended, and Lessee shall not be liable in damages for failure to comply therewith; and this Lease shall be extended while and so long as Lessee is prevented by any such cause from conducting drilling or reworking operations on, or from producing oil or gas or other hydrocarbons from the leased premises; and the time while Lessee is so prevented shall not be counted against the Lessee, anything in this Lease to the contrary notwithstanding.

IN WITNESS WHEREOF this instrument is executed on the date first above set out.

[*signature of lessors and acknowledgements*]

1.   This form is copyrighted by the American Association of Petroleum Landmen; however, the A.A.P.L. no longer recommends this form for use. Nevertheless, thousands of these forms still hold thousands of acres by production in Texas as do very similar forms in many states. The APPL website is: http://www.landman.org/. A.A.P.L. forms are sold by Kraftbilt Products, Box 800, Tulsa, Oklahoma 74101, 1-800-331-7290, http://www.kraftbilt.com.

2.   A landowner concerned about the structures authorized by the granting clause of this lease might consider adding the following clause, or "rider," to the oil and gas lease:

> Notwithstanding the rights given in Section 1 hereof to lay pipelines, build tanks, power stations and telephone lines on the above lands, it is expressly understood, stipulated and agreed that this Lease does not confer upon Lessee any right or privilege to construct or maintain any lease houses, camps, warehouses, or other like structures on the leased premises; and Lessee shall never construct any such buildings or improvements on the leased premises and shall never use the leased premises for any such purposes; Lessee shall, however, have the right to house employees or consultants of the Lessee, or of any operator, drilling contractor or other contractor of Lessee, in trailer houses and other movable housing located on the leased premises while such personnel are engaged in drilling or reworking operations on the leased premises, and the Lessee or any contractor of Lessee may store material and equipment used or expected to be used in drilling or reworking operations on the leased premises in movable buildings on the leased premises.

The clause set out above was taken from a lease form furnished to the editors by Mr. Dean Patton of the firm of Morrill, Patton & Bauer in Beeville, Texas.

OIL, GAS AND MINERAL LEASE

THIS AGREEMENT made this _____ day of _____

_____ 20____ between, _____

_____ as Lessor (whether one or more),

whose address is _____

_____, and

_____, as

Lessee, WITNESSETH:

1. Lessor in consideration of _____Dollars ($_____) in hand paid, of the
royalties herein provided and of the agreements of Lessee herein contained hereby grants,
leases and lets exclusively to Lessee for the purpose of investigating, exploring,
prospecting, drilling and mining for and producing oil, gas, sulphur, fissionable materials
and all other minerals (whether or not similar to those mentioned), conducting
exploration, geologic and geophysical tests and surveys, injecting gas, water and other
fluids and air into subsurface strata, laying pipelines, establishing and utilizing facilities
for the disposition of salt water, dredging and maintaining canals, building roads, bridges,
tanks, telephone lines, power stations and other structures thereon, and on, over and
across lands owned or claimed by Lessor adjacent and contiguous thereto necessary to
Lessee in operations to produce, save, take care of, treat, transport and own said minerals,
the following described land in _____ County, State of _____,
to wit:

[*land description*]

This lease also covers and includes all land and interest in land owned or claimed by
Lessor adjacent or contiguous to the land particularly described above, whether the same
be in said survey or surveys or in adjacent surveys. For the purpose of calculating rental
payments hereunder, said land is estimated to contain _____acres, whether it
contains more or less.

2. Unless sooner terminated or longer kept in force under other provisions hereof, this
lease shall remain in force for a term of ten (10) years from the date hereof (called
"primary term") and as long thereafter as oil, gas, sulphur, fissionable materials or other
mineral is produced from said land or land pooled therewith.

3. The royalties to be paid by Lessee are: (a) on oil, one-eighth of that produced and
saved from said land, the same to be delivered at the wells or to the credit of Lessor into
the pipeline to which the wells may be connected; Lessee may from time to time
purchase any royalty oil in its possession, paying the market price therefor prevailing for
the field where produced on the date of purchase, and Lessee may sell any royalty oil in
its possession and pay Lessor the price received by Lessee for such oil computed at the
well; (b) on gas, including casinghead gas or other gaseous substance, produced from
said land and sold or used off the premises or for the extraction of gasoline or other

[handwritten margin note: means that after lease signed lessor can't grant a seismic licence to anybody else]

[handwritten margin note: Royalty]

[handwritten note at bottom: other "minerals"]

1   product therefrom, the market value at the well of one-eighth of the gas so sold or used,
2   provided that on gas sold by Lessee the market value shall not exceed the amount
3   received by Lessee for such gas computed at the mouth of the well, and on gas sold at the
4   well the royalty shall be one-eighth of the amount realized by Lessee from such sale; and
5   (c) on fissionable materials and all other minerals mined and marketed, one-tenth either
6   in kind or value at the well or mine, at Lessee's election, except that on sulphur mined or
7   marketed, the royalty shall be Two Dollars ($2.00) per long ton. If the price of any
8   mineral or substance upon which royalty is payable hereunder is regulated by any
9   governmental agency, the market value or market price of such mineral or substance for
10   the purpose of computing royalty hereunder shall not be in excess of the price which
11   Lessee may receive and retain. Lessee shall have free from royalty or other payment the
12   use of water, other than water from Lessor's wells or tanks, and of oil, gas and coal
13   produced from said land in all operations which Lessee may conduct hereunder,
14   including water injection and secondary recovery operations, and the royalty on oil, gas
15   and coal shall be computed after deducting any so used. If Lessee drills a well on land
16   covered by this lease or on land pooled therewith, which well is capable of producing oil
17   or gas but such well is not being produced and this lease is not being maintained
18   otherwise as provided herein, this lease shall not terminate, whether it be during or after
19   the primary term, (unless released by Lessee) and it shall nevertheless be considered that
20   oil and gas is being produced from the land covered by this lease. When the lease is
21   continued in force in this manner, Lessee shall pay or tender as royalty to the parties who
22   at the time of such payment would be entitled to receive royalty hereunder if the well
23   were producing, or deposit to their credit in the depository bank as hereinafter provided a
24   sum equal to 1/12 of the amount of the annual rental payable in lieu of drilling operations
25   during the primary term on the number of acres subject to this lease at the time such
26   payment is made for each calendar month, or portion thereof, thereafter during which
27   said well is situated on said land, or on land pooled therewith, and this lease is not
28   otherwise maintained, or this lease is not released by lessee as to the land on which the
29   horizon, zone or formation in which the well is completed. The first payment of such sum
30   shall be made on or before the first day of the calendar month after expiration of ninety
31   (90) days from the date the lease is not otherwise maintained for all accruals to such date,
32   and thereafter on or before the first day of each third calendar month for all accruals to
33   each such date. Lessee's failure to pay or tender or to properly or timely pay or tender any
34   such sum as royalty shall render Lessee liable for the amount due but it shall not operate
35   to terminate this lease.
36   4. If operations for drilling are not commenced on said land or on land pooled therewith   *Drilling-*
37   on or before one year from the date hereof, this lease shall terminate as to both parties,   *Delay*
38   unless on or before such date Lessee shall pay or tender (or make a bona fide attempt to
39   pay or tender) to Lessor or to the credit of Lessor in _____
40   _____ Bank at _____
41   _____ the sum of _____
42   _____ Dollars ($_____) (herein called
43   "rental") which shall cover the privilege of deferring commencement of drilling
44   operations for a period of twelve (12) months. In like manner and upon like payment or
45   tender annually, the commencement of drilling operations may be further deferred for

successive periods of twelve (12) months each during the primary term. The payment or tender of rental under this paragraph and of royalty under paragraph 3 on any well which is not being produced, hereinafter referred to as "shut-in royalty", may be made by check or draft of Lessee mailed or delivered to the parties entitled thereto or to said bank on or before the date of payment. Such bank and its successors are Lessor's agent and shall continue as depository for all rental and shut-in royalty payable hereunder regardless of changes in ownership of said land, rental or shut-in royalty. If such bank (or any successor bank) should fail, liquidate or be succeeded by another bank or for any reason fail or refuse to accept rental or shut-in royalty, Lessee shall not be held in default for failure to make such payment or tender of rental or shut-in royalty until thirty (30) days after the party or parties entitled thereto shall deliver to Lessee a proper recordable instrument naming another bank as agent to receive such payment or tender. If Lessee shall make a bona fide attempt on or before any payment date to pay or deposit rental to a party or parties entitled thereto, according to Lessee's records, or to a party or parties who, prior to such attempted payment or deposit, have given Lessee notice in accordance with subsequent provisions of this lease of their right to receive rental, and if such payment or deposit shall be ineffective or erroneous in any regard, Lessee shall be unconditionally obligated to pay such party or parties entitled thereto the rental properly payable for the rental period involved, and this lease shall not terminate but shall be maintained in the same manner as if such erroneous or ineffective rental payment or deposit had been properly made, provided that the erroneous or ineffective rental payment or deposit be corrected within thirty (30) days after receipt by Lessee of written notice by such party or parties of such error accompanied by such instruments as are necessary to enable Lessee to make proper payment. Failure to make proper payment or deposit of delay rental as to any interest in said land shall not affect this lease as to any interest therein as to which proper payment or deposit is made. The down cash payment is consideration for this lease according to its terms and shall not be allocated as rental for a period. Lessee may at any time, and from time to time, execute and deliver to Lessor, or to the depository bank, or file for record a release or releases of this lease as to any part or all of said land or of any mineral or subsurface interval or any depths thereunder and thereby be relieved of all obligations as to the released land, mineral, horizon, zone or formation. If this lease is released as to all minerals, horizons, zones and formations under a portion of said land, the delay rental, shut-in royalty and other payments computed in accordance therewith shall thereupon be reduced in the proportion that the acreage released bears to the acreage which was covered by this lease immediately prior to such release.

5. Lessee, at its option, is hereby given the right and power during or after the primary term while this lease is in effect to pool or combine the land covered by this lease, or any portion thereof, as to oil, gas and other minerals, or any of them, with any other land covered by this lease, and/or any other land, lease or leases in the immediate vicinity thereof, when in Lessee's judgment it is necessary or advisable to do so in order properly to explore, or to develop and operate the leased premises in compliance with the spacing rules of the state oil and gas conservation agency, or other lawful authority, or when to do so would, in the judgment of Lessee, promote the conservation of oil, gas or other mineral in and under and that may be produced from the premises. Units pooled for oil

hereunder shall not substantially exceed in area 40 acres each plus a tolerance of 10% thereof, and units pooled for gas hereunder shall not substantially exceed in area 640 acres each plus a tolerance of 10% thereof, provided that should governmental authority having jurisdiction prescribe or permit the creation of units larger than those specified, units thereafter created may conform substantially in size with those prescribed or permitted by governmental regulations. Lessee may pool or combine land covered by this *pooling* lease or any portion thereof, as above provided as to oil in any one or more strata and as to gas in any one or more strata. Units formed by pooling as to any stratum or strata need not conform in size or area with units as to any other stratum or strata, and oil units need not conform as to area with gas units. Pooling in one or more instances shall not exhaust the rights of Lessee to pool this lease or portions thereof into other units. Lessee shall file for record in the appropriate records of any county in which the leased premises are situated an instrument describing and designating the pooled acreage as a pooled unit; the unit shall become effective as provided in said instrument, or if said instrument makes no such provision, it shall become effective upon the date it is filed for record. Each unit shall be effective as to all parties hereto, their heirs, successors and assigns, irrespective of whether or not the unit is likewise effective as to all other owners of surface, mineral, royalty or other rights in land included in such unit. Lessee may at its election exercise its pooling option as to oil, gas and other minerals before or after commencing operations for or completing an oil or gas well or wells or mine for other mineral on the leased premises, and the pooled unit may include, but is not required to include, land or leases upon which a well or mine capable of producing oil, gas or other mineral in paying quantities has theretofore been completed or upon which operations for drilling of a well or mine for oil, gas or other mineral have theretofore been commenced. Operations for drilling on, or production of oil, gas or other mineral from any part of a pooled unit which includes all or a portion of the land covered by this lease, regardless of whether such operations for drilling were commenced or such production was secured before or after the execution of this lease or the instrument designating the pooled unit, shall be considered as operations for drilling on or production of oil, gas or other mineral from land covered by this lease whether or not the well or wells or mine be located on land covered by this lease, and the entire acreage constituting such unit or units, as to oil, gas or other minerals, or any of them, as herein provided, shall be treated for all purposes, except the payment of royalties on production from the pooled unit, as if the same were included in this lease; provided that if after creation of a pooled unit, a well or mine is drilled on the unit area, other than on the land covered hereby and included in the unit, which well is not classified as the type of well for which the unit was created (oil, gas or other mineral as the case may be), such well or mine shall be considered a dry hole for purposes of applying the additional drilling and reworking and resumption of delay rental provisions of Paragraph 6 hereof. If an oil well on an oil unit, which includes all or a portion of the leased premises, is reclassified as a gas well, or if a gas well on a gas unit, which includes all or a portion of the leased premises, is reclassified as an oil well, the date of such reclassification shall be considered as the date of cessation of production for purposes of applying the additional drilling and reworking and resumption of delay rental provisions of Paragraph 6 hereof as to all leases any part of which are included in the unit other than the leased premises on which the well is located. For the purpose of

155

computing royalties to which owners of royalties and payments out of production and each of them shall be entitled on production of oil, gas or other minerals from each pooled unit, there shall be allocated to the land covered by this lease and included in said unit (or to each separate tract within the unit if this lease covers separate tracts within the unit) a pro rata portion of the oil, gas or other minerals produced from the unit after deducting that used for operations on the unit. Such allocation shall be on an acreage basis - that is, there shall be allocated to the acreage covered by this lease and included in the pooled unit (or to each separate tract within the unit if this lease covers separate tracts within the unit) that pro rata portion of the oil, gas or other minerals produced from the unit which the number of surface acres covered by this lease (or in each separate tract) and included in the unit bears to the total number of surface acres included in the unit. As used in this paragraph, the words, "separate tract" mean any tract with royalty ownership differing, now or hereafter, either as to parties or amounts, from that as to any other part of the leased promise. Royalties hereunder shall be computed on the portion of such production, whether it be oil, gas or other minerals, so allocated to the land covered by this lease and included in the unit just as though such production were from such land. Production from an oil well will be considered as production from the lease or oil pooled unit from which it is producing and not as production from a gas pooled unit; and production from a gas well will be considered as production from the lease or gas pooled unit from which it is producing and not from an oil pooled unit. Any pooled unit designated by Lessee in accordance with the terms hereof may be dissolved by Lessee by instrument filed for record in the appropriate records of the county in which the leased premises are situated at any time after completion of a dry hole or cessation of production on said unit.

6. If Lessee shall drill a dry hole or holes on said land, or on acreage pooled therewith, and this lease is not being maintained otherwise as provided herein, or if oil, gas or other mineral is discovered and not produced for any cause, or if the production thereof should cease from any cause, this lease shall not terminate if Lessee commences operations for drilling or reworking within sixty (60) days thereafter and continues drilling or reworking operations on said well or any additional well with no cessation of more than sixty (60) consecutive days, or if it be within the primary term, commences or resumes the payment or tender of rental or commences operations for drilling or reworking on or before the rental paying date next ensuing after the expiration of sixty (60) days from the date of completion of dry hole, or discovery of oil, gas or other mineral, or cessation of production and continues drilling or reworking operations on said well or any additional well with no cessation of more than sixty (60) consecutive days. If at any time subsequent to sixty (60) days prior to the beginning of the last year of the primary term and prior to the discovery of oil, gas or other mineral on said land, or on acreage pooled therewith, Lessee should drill a dry hole thereon, no rental payment or operations are necessary in order to keep this lease in force during the remainder of the primary term. If at the expiration of the primary term, oil, gas or other mineral is not being produced on said land, or on acreage pooled therewith, but Lessee is then engaged in drilling or reworking operations thereon or shall have completed a dry hole thereon within sixty (60) days prior to the end of the primary term, this lease shall remain in force so long as operations on said well or for drilling or reworking of any additional well are prosecuted with no

cessation of more than sixty (60) consecutive days, and if they result in the production of oil, gas or other mineral, so long thereafter as oil, gas or other mineral is produced from said land or acreage pooled therewith. In the event a well or wells producing oil or gas in paying quantities should be brought in by Lessee or any other operator on adjacent land and within three hundred thirty (330) feet of and draining the leased premises, or acreage pooled therewith, Lessee agrees to drill such offset wells as a reasonably prudent operator would drill under the same or similar circumstances.

7. Lessee shall have the right at any time during or after the expiration of this lease to remove all property and fixtures placed by Lessee on said land, including the right to draw and remove all casing. When necessary for utilization of the surface for some intended use by Lessor and upon request of Lessor or when deemed necessary by Lessee for protection of the pipeline, Lessee will bury pipelines below ordinary plow depth, and no well shall be drilled within two hundred (200) feet of any residence or barn now on said land without Lessor's consent.

8. The rights of either party hereunder may be assigned in whole or in part, and the provisions hereof shall extend to their heirs, successors and assigns; but no change or division in ownership of the land, rentals or royalties, however accomplished, shall operate to enlarge the obligations or diminish the rights of Lessee, including, but not limited to, the location and drilling of wells and the measurement of production; and no change or division in such ownership shall be binding on Lessee until forty-five (45) days after Lessee shall have been furnished by registered U.S. mail at Lessee's principal place of business with a certified copy of recorded instrument or instruments evidencing same. In the event of assignment hereof in whole or in part, liability for breach of any obligation hereunder shall rest exclusively upon the owner of this lease or of a portion thereof who commits such breach. In the event of the death of any person entitled to rentals hereunder, Lessee may pay or tender such rentals to the credit of the deceased or the estate of the deceased until such time as Lessee is furnished with proper evidence of the appointment and qualifications of an executor or an administrator of the estate, or if there be none, until Lessee is furnished with evidence satisfactory to it as to the heirs or devisees of the deceased and that all debts of the estate have been paid. If at any time two or more persons be entitled to participate in rental payable hereunder, Lessee may pay or tender said rental jointly to such persons or to their joint credit in the depository bank; or, at Lessee's election, the proportionate part of rental to which each participant is entitled may be paid or tendered to him separately or to his separate credit in said depository; and payment or tender to any participant of his portion of the rental hereunder shall maintain this lease as to such participant. In event of assignment of this lease as to a segregated portion of said land, rental hereunder shall be apportionable as between the several leasehold owners ratably according to the surface area of each, and default in rental payment by one shall not affect the rights of other leasehold owners hereunder. If six or more parties become entitled to royalty hereunder, Lessee may withhold payment thereof unless and until furnished with a recordable instrument executed by all such parties designating an agent to receive payment for all.

9. Breach by Lessee of any obligation hereunder shall not work a forfeiture or termination of this lease nor cause a termination or reversion of the estate created hereby nor be grounds for cancellation hereof in whole or in part. In the event Lessor considers

that operations are not at any time being conducted in compliance with this lease, Lessor shall notify Lessee in writing of the facts relied upon as constituting a breach hereof, and Lessee, if in default, shall have sixty (60) days after receipt of such notice in which to commence compliance with the obligations imposed by this lease. After discovery of oil, gas or other mineral in paying quantities on said premises, Lessee shall develop the acreage retained hereunder as a reasonable prudent operator but in discharging this obligation as to oil and gas it shall in no event be required to drill more than one well per forty (40) acres of the area retained hereunder plus a tolerance of 10% thereof and capable of producing oil in paying quantities and one well per 640 acres plus a tolerance of 10% of 640 acres of the area retained hereunder and capable of producing gas in paying quantities.

10. Lessor hereby warrants and agrees to defend the title to said land and agrees that Lessee at its option may discharge any tax, mortgage or other lien upon said land, either in whole or in part, and if Lessee does so, it shall be subrogated to such lien with right to enforce same and apply rentals and royalties accruing hereunder toward satisfying same. When required by state, federal or other law, Lessee may withhold taxes with respect to rental, royalty and other payments hereunder and remit the amounts withheld to the applicable taxing authority for the credit of Lessor. Without impairment of Lessee's rights under the warranty in event of failure of title, if Lessor owns an interest in the oil, gas or other minerals on, in or under said land less than the entire fee simple estate, whether or not this lease purports to cover the whole or a fractional interest, the royalties, shut-in royalties and rentals to be paid Lessor shall be reduced in the proportion that his interest bears to the whole and undivided fee and in accordance with the nature of the estate of which Lessor is seized. Should any one or more of the parties named above as Lessor fail to execute this lease, it shall nevertheless be binding upon the party or parties executing same. Failure of Lessee to reduce rental paid hereunder shall not impair the right of Lessee to reduce royalties.

11. Should Lessee be prevented from complying with any express or implied covenant of this lease, from conducting drilling or reworking operations thereon or on land pooled therewith or from producing oil, gas or other mineral therefrom or from land pooled therewith by reason of scarcity or of inability to obtain or to use equipment or material, or by operation of force majeure, any federal or state law or any order, rule or regulation of governmental authority, then while so prevented, Lessee's obligation to comply with such covenant shall be suspended, and Lessee shall not be liable in damages for failure to comply therewith; and this lease shall be extended while and so long as Lessee is prevented by any such cause from conducting drilling or reworking operations on or from producing oil, gas or other mineral from the leased premises or land pooled therewith, and the time while Lessee is so prevented shall not be counted against Lessee, anything in this lease to the contrary notwithstanding.

12. Each singular pronoun herein shall include the plural whenever applicable.

IN WITNESS WHEREOF, this instrument is executed on the date first above written.

_____   _____
LESSOR   **LESSOR**
(acknowledgment)

NOTES

1.   The above lease form was developed by a major oil and gas company and various versions of this form are used today by many other companies. Compare this form to the Texas A.A.P.L. 675 form, which precedes it and note the differences. This latter form is designed to avoid many of the possible pitfalls that lessees who choose to use older or less carefully crafted forms may encounter.

2.   Compare the granting clauses in the prior two lease forms with each other and with the following granting clauses. The first is taken from an Appalachian lease form and the second is taken from a California lease form.

> Appalachian Form:
> Lessor, for and in consideration of the sum of _____
> Dollars ($____), the receipt of which is hereby acknowledged, and of the covenants and agreements herein contained, hereby grants, demises, leases and lets exclusively unto Lessee the lands hereafter described for the purposes of prospecting, exploring by geophysical and other methods, drilling, operating for, producing oil or gas, or both, together with the right and easement to construct, operate, repair, maintain and remove pipelines, telephone, power and electric lines, tanks, ponds, roadways, plants, equipment and structures thereon to produce, save, store and take care of such substances, and the exclusive right to inject air, gas, water, brine and other fluids into the subsurface strata and any and all substances, and the exclusive right to inject air, gas, water, brine and other fluids into the subsurface strata and any and all other rights and privileges necessary, incident to, or convenient for the economical operation of the lands, alone or conjointly with neighboring lands for these purposes, said lands being situated in the Borough/Township/Town/District of _____,
> County of _____, State of _____,
> and being bounded now or formerly substantially as follows, to wit:
> On the North by lands of _____
> On the East by lands of_____
> On the South by lands of _____
> On the West by lands of _____
> it being the purpose and intent of Lessor to lease, and Lessor does hereby lease, all strips or parcels of land now owned by Lessor or hereafter acquired which adjoin the lands above described, and all interests in the land above described now owned or hereafter acquired by Lessor. For all purposes of this lease, including determining the amount of delay rentals, royalties and shut-in royalties hereunder, said land shall be deemed to contain_____
> acres, whether it actually contains more or less. For all purposes of this lease, references to oil and gas or either or both of them shall

mean oil, or gas, or both and all substances which are constituents of or produced with oil or gas, whether similar or dissimilar or produced in a gaseous, liquid, or solid state.

California Form:

Lessor, for and in consideration of one dollar and other valuable consideration, receipt and sufficiency of which is hereby acknowledged, and of the royalties and agreements of the Lessee herein provided, hereby grants, lets and leases exclusively unto Lessee the land described and included in paragraph 18 hereof and hereinafter referred to as "said land" for the purposes of exploring and prospecting for (by geological, geophysical, and all other means whether now known or not), drilling for, producing, saving, taking, owning, transporting, storing, handling, treating, and processing oil, gas, all other hydrocarbons, and all other substances produced therewith, collectively hereinafter referred to as "said substances," in, on, under or that may be produced from said land, and hereby grants all rights, privileges and easements useful or convenient for Lessee's operations on said land, on adjacent or contiguous lands, and on other lands in the same vicinity, including, but not limited to, the right to construct, install, maintain, repair, use, replace, and at any time remove therefrom, roads, bridges, pipelines, tanks, pump and power stations, power and communication facilities and lines, facilities for surface and subsurface disposal of produced water and other substances, plants and structures to treat, process, and transport said substances and products manufactured therefrom; and the right to drill wells and use Lessee's existing wells including producing wells to inject gas, water, air or other substances into the subsurface zones.

To what extent, if any, do these granting clauses alter the normal common-law rights of a lessee or mineral owner? In other words, if a severed mineral owner executed any of these leases, which provisions, if any, might not be effective against the rights of the surface owner?

3.   Note that principal lease form continues to use an "unless" type delay rental clause. Why would a Lessee choose to use an "unless" rental clause instead of an "or" type? Compare the delay-rental clauses in the prior two leases with the following clauses. The first is taken from an Appalachian lease form and the second is taken from a California lease form. Note the forfeiture provision in the California form.

Appalachian Form:
Commencing with the first day of the second year of the term hereof, if the Lessee has not theretofore commenced drilling operations on said land, the Lessee shall pay or tender to Lessor annually,   in   advance   as   rental,   the   sum   of
_____Dollars
($_____) per acre per year for so much of said land as may still be held under the lease, until drilling operations

are commenced or this lease is terminated. No implied covenant shall be read into this lease requiring Lessee to drill or to continue drilling on said land, or fixing the measure of diligence therefor. Failure of Lessee to pay the Lessor to delay rental provided for herein shall not cause this lease or any part thereof to terminate, but Lessee shall be obligated to make such payment.

California Form:
The consideration expressed in Paragraph 1 covers all rental for the first _____ year(s) of the primary term. If drilling operations are not commenced on said land on or before one year from the date hereof, then, subject to the provisions of Paragraph 15 hereof, Lessee shall pay or tender to Lessor or to Lessor's credit in the _____ Bank at

_____ (which bank and its successors are Lessor's agents and shall continue as depository for all rentals payable hereunder regardless of changes in the ownership of said land or of the right to receive rentals) the sum of _____ dollars ($____) which shall maintain the lease in force and extend for one additional year the time within which such operations may be commenced. Thereafter, annually and in like manner and upon like payments or tender (all of which are herein called "rentals"), such operations may be deferred for successive periods of one year each during the primary term.

The California lease also contains the following clauses:

If any rental or royalty is not paid when due Lessor shall notify Lessee thereof in writing and this lease shall not terminate unless the Lessee fails to make such payment within fifteen (15) days after receipt of such written notice; provided, however, that if there is a dispute as to the amount due and all undisputed amounts are paid, said 15-day period shall be extended until 5 days after such dispute is settled by final court decree, arbitration or agreement. If Lessee fails to make such payment after receipt of such notice within said period (or such extension thereof), then this lease shall terminate as to the portion or portions thereof as to which Lessee is in default.

Lessee may at any time or times surrender this lease or any zone or portion of either thereof by delivering or mailing a written notice of surrender to Lessor or to the depository bank and upon such delivery or mailing Lessee shall be relieved of all obligations as to the portion surrendered, and thereafter all payments to Lessor provided herein, except royalties on actual production, shall be reduced in the same proportion that the acreage covered hereby is

161

reduced. If Lessee surrenders less than all horizons in any portion of this lease, the rental as to such portion shall not be reduced.

What effect do these clauses have on the delay-rental clause from the California lease?

4.   Compare the shut-in royalty provisions in the prior two lease forms. If a well is capable of production, but is shut in, what saves the lease under each form? Under what circumstances might the following clause save a lease?

> Where gas from a well or wells, capable of producing gas only, is not sold or used for a period of one year, lessee shall pay or tender, as royalty, an amount equal to the delay rental as provided in paragraph (5) hereof, payable annually at the end of each year during which such gas is not sold or used, and while said royalty is so paid or tendered this lease shall be held as a producing property under paragraph numbered two hereof.

This was the shut-in clause in Tucker v. Hugoton Energy Corp., 855 P.2d 929 (Kan. 1983), discussed at page 392 of the casebook.

The following shut-in clause is from an Appalachian oil and gas lease:

> If a well capable of producing gas in paying quantities is completed hereunder and is shut-in for a period of 90 consecutive days, this lease shall not terminate, but Lessee shall be obligated to pay or tender to Lessor as royalty for constructive production, an amount equal to one quarter of the rental specified in Paragraph 4 hereof for each 90-day period that such well is shut in during any calendar year. Such payment or tender shall be made promptly following the end of each such 90-day shut-in period.

Is this an appropriate shut-in clause from the lessee's perspective?

5.   Compare the following force-majeure provision, taken from a California lease, with the force-majeure clause in the prior two lease forms. Which clause offers the best protection for the lessee?

> If Lessee is prevented or hindered from drilling or conducting other operations for the purpose of obtaining or restoring production or from producing said substances by fire, flood, storm, act of God, or any cause beyond Lessee's control (including but not limited to governmental law, order or regulation, labor disputes, war, inability to secure men, materials or transportation, inability to secure a market for gas, or an adverse claim to Lessor's title when Lessor has been notified pursuant to paragraph 14 hereof), then the performance of any such operations of the production of said substances shall be suspended during the period of such prevention or hindrance. If such suspension occurs during the primary term, the payment of delay rental during such

162

suspension shall be excused and the primary term shall be extended for a period of time equal to the period of such suspension and this lease shall remain in full force and effect during such period of suspension and any such extension of the primary term. Lessee may commence or resume the payment or tender of rentals in accordance with paragraph 3 hereof after the period of suspension by paying or tendering within 60 days after the period of suspension the proportionate part of the rental for the rental year remaining after such period of suspension. If such suspension occurs after the primary term, this lease shall remain in full force and effect during such suspension and for a reasonable time thereafter provided that within such time following the period of suspension Lessee diligently commences or resumes operations or the production of said substances. Lessee's obligation to pay royalty on actual production shall never be suspended under this paragraph. Whenever Lessee would otherwise be required to surrender any of said land as an alternative to the performance so suspended, then so long as such performance is suspended by this paragraph Lessee shall not be required to surrender any portion of said land. If the permission or approval of any governmental agency is necessary before drilling operations may be commenced on said land, then if such permission or approval has been applied for at least 30 days prior to the date upon which such operations must be commenced under terms hereof, the obligation to commence such operations shall be suspended until thirty (30) days after the governmental permit is granted or approval given, or if such permit or approval is denied initially, then so long as Lessee in good faith appeals from such denial or conducts further proceedings in an attempt to secure such permit or approval and thirty days thereafter.

6.   Compare the following royalty provisions with the royalty provisions in the prior two lease forms. The first clause is from the Appalachian form and the second is from the California form.

Appalachian Form:
The royalties to be paid by Lessee are: (a) on oil, one-eighth of that produced and saved and delivered at the wells or into the pipeline to which the wells may be connected. Lessee may from time to time purchase any royalty oil in its possession, paying the market price then prevailing for the field where produced, and Lessee may sell any royalty in its possession and pay Lessor the price received by Lessee for such oil computed at the well: (b) on gas, including casinghead gas or other gaseous substance, produced from said land and sold or used beyond the well or for the extraction of gasoline or other product, an amount equal to one-eighth of the net amount realized by Lessee computed at the wellhead from the sale

of such substances. On gas sold at the well, the royalty shall be one-eighth of the amount realized by Lessee from such sale.

California Form:
The term "agreed share" as used herein means _____.
Royalties to be paid by Lessee are: (a) on oil, the value of the agreed share of that produced and saved from said land. It is mutually agreed that the value shall be the price currently offered or paid by Lessee for oil of like gravity and quality in the same field. The volume of oil upon which royalty payments are based may be determined either by metering and sampling or by tank gauges. After such measurement, all or any part of the oil may be transported to locations on said land or other lands and commingled with oil from other lands. Lessor may at any time or times, upon 90 days written notice to Lessee, elect to take Lessor's agreed share of oil in kind, in lieu of such share in value, provided that such election must be for a period of at least one year, and upon such election Lessor's share shall be delivered at the wells into storage furnished by Lessor or to the credit of Lessor into the pipeline to which the wells may be connected. If royalty on oil is payable in cash, Lessee may deduct therefrom the agreed share of the cost of treating unmerchantable oil produced from the leased land to render it merchantable. In the event such oil is treated elsewhere than on the leased land, the Lessor's cash royalty shall also bear the agreed share of the cost of transporting the oil to the treating plant. Nothing herein contained shall be construed as obligating Lessee to treat oil. If Lessor shall elect to receive the royalty on oil in kind, it shall be of the same quality as the oil removed from the leased land for Lessee's own account and if Lessee's own oil shall be treated before such removal, Lessor's oil will be treated therewith before delivery to Lessor, and Lessor, in such event, shall pay a part equal to the agreed share of the cost of treatment; Lessee may deduct from Lessor's royalties a part equal to the agreed share of the cost of disposing of waste water produced with said substances; (b) on gas including casinghead gas and all gaseous substances produced, saved and sold from said land, the agreed share of the net proceeds (which shall be the amount realized from such sale less compressing costs) of the gas so sold; (c) on gas not sold but used off the premises the agreed share of the market value at the well of the gas so used. All or any part of the gas produced from said land may be transported gas and such meter readings together with Lessee's analysis with gas from other lands. Lessee shall meter such transported gas and such meter readings together with Lessee's analysis of gasoline content of gas shall furnish the basis for prorating the amount of gasoline to be credited to said land. Lessee shall not be accountable to Lessor for gas lost or used or consumed in operations hereunder. Lessee may produce gas from said land or from lands with which

said land is pooled or unitized in accordance with any method of ratable taking at any time or from time to time hereafter generally in effect in any pool of which said land or any portion thereof is a part. In the absence of any such method of ratable taking, Lessee shall produce from said land or lands pooled or unitized therewith a fair and equitable proportion of the quantity of gas which markets from lands under lease to it in the pool of which said land is part. Lessee shall be obligated to produce only so much gas as it may be able to market at the well or wells. When there is no market for gas at the wells, Lessee's obligation to produce gas shall be suspended; (d) on gasoline extracted from gas produced on said land, the value of 48% of the agreed share of the gasoline credited to said land by Lessee. It is mutually agreed that the value shall be the price currently offered or paid by Lessee for gasoline of like specifications and quality in the same vicinity; (e) on any other substance, the agreed share of the market value at the well.

For all operations hereunder, Lessee may use, free of royalty, oil, gas or other hydrocarbons and water from said land except water from the Lessor's wells. However, if Lessee shall use in operations hereunder, fuel, power, or other substances not obtained from said land, then Lessee shall be entitled to deduct from the amount of the additional royalty accruing thereby to Lessor the agreed share of the cost of such substituted fuel, power or other substances; provided, no deduction hereunder shall exceed the amount of such additional royalty.

When any of said substances not produced from said land are injected into said land or land pooled or unitized therewith, the initial production thereafter of said substances from any such land shall be free of royalty until the amount of the said substances produced and saved therefrom shall equal that of said substances injected therein.

7.   If you were negotiating a lease on behalf of a Lessor, consider what changes you would make in the prior three lease forms. Rank them in order of priority.

8.   On page 350 of the casebook, footnote 13, a reference is made to the divisibility clause of the Appalachian lease, Paragraph 9. That paragraph provides in relevant part:

> In case lessee assigns this lease, in whole or in part, Lessee shall be relieved of all obligations with respect to the assigned portion or portions arising subsequent to the date of assignment.

BANK DRAFT
First National Bank of Petroleum City

This is not a cash item.
No protest or recall.

Date: _____

PAY TO THE ORDER OF:

_____

_____ dollars

($_____) thirty banking days after sight, pending approval of title.

Memo: _____   By:

(back)

Endorsement: This draft is total consideration for an Oil and Gas lease, dated, _____, from _____, lessee, covering lands in _____ County, State of _____, containing ____ gross acres, Section ____ Township ___ Range ___. Signing bonus.

_____

NOTES

1.   The above form looks much like a check, but it is not. Why not? Commonly called a "sight draft," the draft is payable thirty days after the lessor presents the draft the payor bank, *i.e.*, the First National Bank of Petroleum City, which may be located in another state hundreds of miles away from the lessor. If the lessor presents the draft to his local bank, what will the local bank do?

2.   Suppose the lease described one section of land, consisting of 640 acres. Assuming the lessor owns an undivided five percent interest in the minerals in this land, thirty days after the lessor presents the draft to the payor bank, what amount will the bank pay to the lessor? Why? Hint: consult the granting clause, paragraph 1, and the lesser-interest provision, paragraph 10, in the prior lease.

OIL AND GAS LEASE
(Coalbed Methane)

    This Oil and Gas Lease ("Lease") made this _____ day of _____, 20____, by and between by and between_____having an address at _____, hereinafter collectively called "Lessor" and _____, hereinafter called "Lessee."

    WITNESSETH, That for and in consideration of the premises, and all of the mutual covenants and agreements hereinafter set forth, the Lessor and Lessee agree as follows:

    LEASING CLAUSE: Lessor hereby leases exclusively to Lessee all of the oil and gas including, but not limited to, coalbed methane gas, coalbed gas, coal mine methane, methane gas, gob gas, occluded natural gas in any formation or other naturally occurring gases contained in or associated with any coal seam and all zones in communication therewith along with all hydrocarbon and non-hydrocarbon substances produced in association therewith underlying the land herein leased, together with such exclusive rights as may be necessary or convenient for Lessee, at its election, to explore for, develop, produce, measure, and market production from the Leasehold, and from other lands operated by Lessee, using methods and techniques which are not restricted to current technology, including the right to conduct geophysical and other exploration tests (including core drilling and seismic testing); to drill (either vertically, horizontally or directionally), maintain, operate, cease to operate, treat, vent, dewater, plug, abandon, and remove wells and appurtenant facilities; to stimulate or fracture all coal formations, seams or other strata or formations; to use or install roads, electric power and telephone facilities, and to construct pipelines (to be placed on top of the ground unless required by statute or regulations) with appurtenant facilities, including data acquisition, compression and collection facilities for use in the production and transportation of products from the Leasehold and from neighboring lands across the Leasehold, to establish and utilize facilities for disposition of water, brine or other fluids; and such rights shall survive the term of this Lease for so long thereafter as such operations are continued, to use oil, gas, and non-domestic water sources, free of cost, to store gas of any kind underground, regardless of the source thereof, including the injection of gas therein and removing same therefrom, to protect stored gas, to operate, maintain, repair, and remove materials and equipment.

    The term "gas" as used herein shall include by way of example, helium, carbon dioxide, gaseous sulfur compounds, coalbed methane gas, coalbed gas, methane gas, gob gas, occluded natural gas in any formation or other naturally occurring gases contained in or associated with any coal seam and all zones in communication therewith and any and all other commercial gases, as well as normal hydrocarbon gases.

    DESCRIPTION: The Leasehold covered by this Oil and Gas Lease is located as described in the attached Exhibit A, which is incorporated herein by reference.

    In addition to the land described in Exhibit A, this Lease also covers accretions and any strips or parcels of land which are contiguous or adjacent to the land described in Exhibit A, now or hereafter owned or claimed by Lessor by limitation, prescription, possession or reversion.

    It being the intent of Lessor and Lessee to provide a Leasehold covering all interests held by Lessor, of whatsoever kind and nature in any and all oil and gas being situated in the county of _____ located in the Commonwealth of Kentucky and this Lease shall be construed to encompass any such interests whether the same is specifically described herein or which may have, through inadvertence been omitted from this Lease.

In consideration of the payment of Royalty, as hereinafter described, Lessor agrees to execute at Lessee's request any additional or supplemental instruments for a more complete or accurate description of the lands so covered. For the purpose of determining the amount of any payments based on acreage hereunder, the number of gross acres specified in Exhibit A shall be deemed correct, whether actually more or less.

LEASE TERM: This Lease shall remain in force for a primary term of _____ (____)years from _____, 20___, (the "Primary Term") and for as long thereafter as prescribed payments are made, or for as long thereafter as operations are conducted on any portion of the Leasehold in search of production of oil, gas, or their constituents, or for as long as a well capable of production is located on any portion of the Leasehold, or for as long as extended by other provisions herein, or for as long as any portion of the Leasehold is used for the underground storage of gas or for the protection of stored gas. If after the Primary Term the last producing well on the Leasehold is plugged and abandoned, the Leasehold will remain under lease for an additional period of one (1) year from the date of plugging and abandonment, subject to the payment of Delay Rental. Whenever used in this Lease the word "operations" shall include, but not be limited to, any of the following activities: surveying, staking the location, drilling, testing, stimulating, completing, venting, reworking, recompleting, deepening, dewatering, plugging back or repairing of a well in search for or in an endeavor to obtain production of oil and gas, whether or not in paying quantities.

EXTENSION OF TERM: Lessee may extend the Primary Term for one (1) additional period equal to the Primary Term by paying to Lessor, at any time within the Primary Term, proportionate to Lessor's percentage of ownership an Extension Payment equal in amount to the annual Delay Rental as herein described, or by drilling a well on any portion of the Leasehold which is not capable of commercial production.

ANCILLARY RIGHTS: The rights granted to Lessee hereunder shall include the right of ingress and egress on the Leasehold or lands pooled or unitized therewith, along with such rights as may be necessary or convenient in conducting operations for exploring, developing, producing and marketing oil and gas, including but not limited to geophysical operations, the drilling of wells, and the construction and use of roads, canals, pipelines, tanks, water wells, disposal wells, injection wells, pits, electric and telephone lines, power stations, and other facilities deemed necessary or convenient by Lessee to explore, discover, produce, store, treat and/or transport oil and gas and water produced from the Leasehold or other lands that share central facilities and are jointly operated with the Leasehold for gathering, treating, compression and water disposal. Lessee may use in such operations, free of cost, any oil, gas, water and/or other substances produced on the Leasehold, except water from Lessor's wells or ponds. In exploring, developing, producing or marketing from the Leasehold or lands pooled or unitized therewith, the ancillary rights granted herein shall apply (a) to the entire Leasehold, notwithstanding any partial release or other partial termination of this Lease; and (b) to any other lands in which Lessor now or hereafter has authority to grant such rights in the vicinity of the Leasehold or lands pooled or unitized therewith. Lessee shall have the right at any time to remove its fixtures, equipment and materials, including well casing, from the Leasehold or such other lands during the term of this Lease or within a reasonable time thereafter.

PAYMENT TO LESSOR: Lessee covenants to pay Lessor, proportionate to Lessor's percentage of ownership as follows:

A. DELAY RENTAL: To pay Lessor as Delay Rental for the first lease year at the rate of One Dollar ($1.00) per net mineral acre, due and payable to Lessor within forty-five (45) days from the final execution of this Lease. To pay Lessor as Delay Rental at the rate of One Dollar ($1.00) per net mineral acre per year payable annually in advance, beginning on the first

1 anniversary of this Lease, and continuing thereafter until the commencement of Royalty
2 payments. Upon commencement of oil or gas production, any Delay Rentals shall be credited
3 against production royalties. Delay Rental paid for time beyond the commencement date of
4 Royalty payments shall be credited upon the Royalty payment. Upon conversion to Storage,
5 Delay Rental payment shall be reestablished.
6   B. ROYALTY: It is agreed that the total Royalty that will be paid by Lessee shall be
7 _____ (____%) and that any Royalty conveyance or reservation in Lessor's chain of title
8 shall be subtracted from the _____ (____%) royalty proved herein. To pay Lessor as
9 Royalty, less all taxes, assessments, and adjustments on production from the Leasehold as
10 follows:
11   1. OIL: To deliver to the credit of Lessor a Royalty of the equal _____ (____%)
12 of the sales proceeds actually received by Lessee or, if applicable, its affiliate, for all oil and the
13 constituents sold to an unaffiliated party, less this same percentage share of all Post Production
14 Costs, volume adjustments or assessments of any kind incurred by Lessee, and this same
15 percentage share of all production, severance and ad valorem, excise and privilege taxes now or
16 hereinafter levied or assessed or charged on oil produced from the Leasehold. As used in this
17 provision, Post Production Costs shall mean all costs actually incurred by Lessee, or its affiliate,
18 and all losses of produced volumes whether by use as fuel, line loss, flaring, venting or otherwise
19 from and after the wellhead to the point of sale. These costs include, without limitation, all costs
20 of gathering, marketing, compression, sweetening, processing, trucking, dehydration,
21 transportation, removal of liquid or gaseous substances or impurities from the affected
22 production, and any other treatment or processing now or in the future, whether or not such is
23 specifically herein set forth.
24   2. GAS: To pay Lessor an amount equal to _____ (____%) of the sales proceeds
25 actually received by Lessee or, if applicable, its affiliate, for all gas and the constituents sold to
26 an unaffiliated party, less this same percentage share of all Post Production Costs, volume
27 adjustments or assessments of any kind incurred by Lessee, and this same percentage share of all
28 production, severance, ad valorem, excise and privilege taxes now or hereinafter levied or
29 assessed or charged on gas produced from the Leasehold. As used in this provision, Post
30 Production Costs shall mean all costs actually incurred by Lessee, or its affiliate, and all losses of
31 produced volumes whether by use as fuel, line loss, flaring, venting or otherwise from and after
32 the wellhead to the point of sale. These costs include without limitation, all costs of gathering,
33 marketing, compression, sweetening, processing, trucking, dehydration, transportation, removal
34 of liquid or gaseous substances or impurities from the affected production, and any other
35 treatment or processing now or in the future, whether or not such is specifically herein set forth.
36   Lessee or its affiliate shall have the right to construct, maintain and operate any facilities
37 providing some or all of the services identified as Post Production Costs. If this occurs, the
38 actual costs of such facilities shall be included in the Post Production Costs as a per barrel or per
39 mcf charge, as appropriate, calculated by spreading the construction, maintenance and operating
40 costs for such facilities over the reasonably estimated total production volumes attributable to the
41 well or wells using such facilities.
42   C. DELAY IN MARKETING: In the event that Lessee does not market producible gas,
43 oil, or their constituents from the Leasehold, Lessee shall continue to pay Delay Rental until such
44 time as marketing is established, and such payment shall maintain this Lease in full force and
45 effect to the same extent as payment of Royalty.
46   D. SHUT-IN: In the event that production of oil, gas, or their constituents is interrupted
47 and not marketed for a period of six (6) months, and there is no producing well on the Leasehold,
48 Lessee shall thereafter, as Royalty for constructive production, pay a Shut-In Royalty equal in

frequency and amount to the Delay Rental until such time as production is re-established and said payment shall maintain the Lease in full force and effect to the same extent as payment of Royalty. During Shut-In, Lessee shall have the right to re-work, stimulate, or deepen any well on the Leasehold or drill a new well on the Leasehold in an effort to re-establish production, whether from an original producing formation or from a different formation. In the event that the production from the only producing well on the Leasehold is interrupted for a period of less than six (6) months, this Lease shall remain in full force and effect without payment of Royalty or Shut-In Royalty.

E. DAMAGES: Lessee shall remove unnecessary equipment and materials and grade, reseed, and mulch the drill site area at the completion of all operations, and Lessee agrees to repair any damaged improvements to the land and pay for the loss of crops or marketable timber directly caused by its operations on the Leasehold; provided, however, Lessee shall not be responsible for any damages caused by Lessor or third parties.

F. MANNER OF PAYMENT: Lessee shall make or tender all payments due hereunder by check, payable to Lessor, at Lessor's last known address, and Lessee may withhold any payment without interest pending written notification by Lessor of a change in address. Lessee may defer payment of any sum due Lessor, or to any payee hereunder, until the total sum due to Lessor or to such payee shall equal One Hundred Dollars ($100.00), whereupon such payment shall be made.

G. CHANGES IN LAND OWNERSHIP: Lessee shall not be bound by any change in the ownership of the Leasehold until furnished with such documentation as Lessee may reasonably require. Pending the receipt of documentation, Lessee may elect either to continue to make or withhold payments without interest as if such a change had not occurred.

H. TITLE: In the case of any controversy or dispute regarding title to said Leasehold or any part thereof, or regarding the ownership of sums payable hereunder, Lessee shall have the right to withhold and retain all sums payable hereunder without interest which are subject to said controversy and dispute and then to distribute the same among these lawfully entitled thereto, provided that upon receipt of a bond of indemnity acceptable to Lessee, Lessee may pay all or part of said sums as it may deem advisable and proper.

I. LESSER INTEREST/GREATER INTEREST: If Lessor owns a lesser interest in the oil and gas in said Leasehold than the entire undivided fee simple estate, then the Delay Rental and Royalties hereunder shall be paid to Lessor only in the proportion which Lessor's interest bears to the whole and undivided fee. If the true acreage of the Leasehold shall be found to be less than the number of acres above recited, then Delay Rental hereunder shall be reduced proportionately, and the Lessor releases Lessee from payment of Delay Rental upon any acreage in excess of the true area of said Leasehold. Should the Lessor hereafter acquire any additional right, title or interest in or to the Leasehold, then Lessor's additional interest shall become subject to the provisions hereof, from the date of acquisition to the same extent as if owned by Lessor at the date hereof.

J. LIENS: Lessee may at its option pay and discharge any past due taxes, mortgages, judgments, or other liens and encumbrances on or against any land or interest included in the Leasehold; and Lessee shall be entitled to recover from the debtor, with legal interest and cost, by deduction from any future payments to Lessor or by any other lawful means.

LIMITATION OF FORFEITURE: This Lease shall never be subject to civil action or other proceeding to enforce a claim of forfeiture due to Lessee's alleged failure to perform as specified herein, unless, Lessee has received written notice of Lessor's demand and thereafter fails or refuses to satisfy Lessor's demand within ninety (90) days from receipt of the notice.

1   POOLING/UNITIZATION: Lessor grants Lessee the right to pool, unitize, or combine
2 all or part of the Leasehold with other lands, whether contiguous or not contiguous, leased, or
3 un-leased, whether owned or operated by Lessee or owned or operated by others, at a time before
4 or after drilling to create drilling or production units either by contract right or pursuant to
5 governmental authorization. Lessee is granted the right to change the size, shape and conditions
6 of operations or payment of any unit created. Lessor agrees to accept and receive out of the
7 production or the revenue realized from production of such unit, such proportional share of the
8 Royalty from each unit well as the number of Leasehold acres included in the unit bears to the
9 total number of acres in the unit. Otherwise, the drilling, operations in preparation for drilling,
10 production from, or payment for Royalty, Shut-In Royalty, or Delay In Marketing for a well on
11 such a unit shall have the same effect upon the terms of this Lease as if the well were located on
12 the Leasehold. Lessee has the right, but shall not have any obligation to pool, unitize or combine
13 the Leasehold with other properties.
14   FACILITIES: Lessee shall not drill a well within 200 feet of any occupied dwelling
15 located on the Leasehold without Lessor's written consent, which shall not be unreasonably
16 withheld or delayed. Lessor shall not erect any building or structure, or plant any trees within
17 200 feet of a well or within 25 feet of a pipeline without Lessee's written consent. Lessor shall
18 not improve, modify, degrade or restrict roads and facilities built by Lessee without Lessee's
19 written consent.
20   CONVERSION TO STORAGE: Lessee is hereby granted the right to convert the
21 Leasehold to gas storage. At the time of conversion, Lessee shall pay Lessor's proportionate part
22 for the estimated recoverable gas remaining in the well using methods of calculating gas reserves
23 as are generally accepted by the natural gas industry, and Lessor shall be paid Delay Rental for
24 as long thereafter as the Leasehold is used for gas storage or for protection of gas storage.
25   TITLE AND INTEREST: Lessor agrees to make available to Lessee copies of any of the
26 Lessor's existing title information. Lessor hereby warrants generally and agrees to defend title to
27 the Leasehold against all claims and persons, whomsoever, and covenants that Lessee shall have
28 exclusive, full, free, quiet enjoyment and quiet possession hereunder and shall have the benefit of
29 the doctrine of after acquired title. Should any person having title to the Leasehold fail to
30 execute this Lease, the Lease shall nevertheless be binding upon all persons who do execute it as
31 Lessor.
32   LEASE DEVELOPMENT: There is no covenant to develop the Leasehold within a
33 certain time frame, and there shall be no leasehold forfeiture for implied covenants to develop,
34 produce and market. Provisions herein constitute full compensation for privileges herein
35 granted.
36   ENTIRETY: If the Leasehold is hereafter owned in severalty or in separate tracts the
37 premises, nevertheless, shall be developed and operated as an entirety, and rentals and royalties
38 shall be paid to each separate owner in the proportion that the acreage owned by each separate
39 owner bears to the entire leased acreage.
40   FORCE MAJEURE: In the event Lessee is rendered unable, in whole or part, by a force
41 majeure to carry out its obligations under this Lease, other than to make payments of amounts
42 due hereunder, its obligations so far as they are affected by such force majeure shall be
43 suspended during the continuance of any inability so caused. The term "force majeure" as
44 employed herein shall be acts of God, strikes, lockouts, or other industrial disturbances, acts of
45 the public enemy, wars, blockades, riots, epidemics, lightning, earthquakes, hurricanes, wind and
46 ice storms, explosion, accidents or repairs to machinery or pipes, delays of carriers, inability to
47 obtain permits, inability to obtain materials or rights-of-way on reasonable terms, acts of public
48 authorities, or any other causes, whether or not of the same kind as enumerated herein, not within

the control of the Lessee and which by the exercise of due diligence Lessee is unable to overcome.

ARBITRATION: In the event of a disagreement between Lessor and Lessee concerning this Lease, performance hereunder, or damages caused by Lessee's operations, settlement shall be determined by a panel of three disinterested arbitrators. Lessor and Lessee shall appoint and pay the fee of one each, and the two so appointed shall appoint the third, whose fee shall be borne equally by Lessor and Lessee. The award shall be by unanimous decision of the arbitrators and shall be final.

SURRENDER: Lessee may surrender and cancel this Lease as to all or any part of the Leasehold by recording a Surrender of Lease and if partially surrendered, the Delay Rental provided in the PAYMENTS clause shall be reduced in proportion to the acreage surrendered.

SUCCESSORS: All rights, duties, and liabilities herein benefit and bind Lessor and Lessee and their respective heirs, personal representatives, successors, and assigns.

ENTIRE CONTRACT: The Lease and any Exhibits which may be attached hereto contain the entire agreement between Lessor and Lessee. No oral warranties, representation, or promises have been made or relied upon by either party as an inducement to or modification of this Lease.

DIVISION ORDERS: If the Lessee has requested the Lessor (or any person claiming an interest in any monies due hereunder) to execute its then current division order form which, among other things, sets forth the Lessor's (or such person's) percentage interest in the monies due hereunder, then the Lessee will not be required to pay or tender to Lessor (or such person) Lessor's (or such person's) share of such monies until such division order is executed by Lessor (or such person) and is returned to and received by Lessee.

EXPRESS AND IMPLIED COVENANTS: All expressed or implied covenants of the Lease shall be subject to all Federal and State laws, executive orders, rules or regulations, and this Lease shall not be terminated in whole or in part, nor shall Lessee be held liable in damages, for failure to comply therewith if compliance is prevented by, or if such failure is the result of, any such law, order, rule or regulation.

ASSIGNABILITY: The rights of either party hereunder may be assigned in whole or in part; but no change or division in ownership of the Leasehold, Delay Rentals, Shut-In Royalties, Storage Rentals, or Royalties or in the status of any party, however accomplished, shall operate to enlarge the obligations or diminish the rights of Lessee. No change in such ownership or status shall be binding on Lessee until thirty (30) days after Lessee shall have been furnished by U.S. Mail at Lessee's principal place of business with a certified copy of recorded instrument or instruments evidencing same. In the event of assignment hereof in whole or in part, liability for breach of any obligation hereunder shall rest exclusively upon the owner of this Lease or of a portion thereof who commits such breach. In the event of the death of any person entitled to any sum hereunder, Lessee may pay or tender the same to the credit of the deceased or the estate of the deceased until such time as Lessee is furnished with proper evidence of the appointment and qualification of an executor or administrator of the estate or, if there be none, evidence satisfactory to it as the heirs or devisees of the deceased and that all debts of the estate have been paid. If at any time two or more parties are entitled to or adversely claim any sum payable hereunder, or any part hereof, Lessee may pay or tender the same either jointly to such parties or separately or to each in accordance with his respective ownership thereof. In even of assignment of this Lease as to a segregated portion of the Leasehold the Delay Rentals, Storage Rentals, Shut-In Royalties and Royalties payable hereunder shall be apportionable as between the several leasehold owners ratably according to the surface area of each, and the failure to pay Delay Rentals, Storage Rentals, Shut-In Royalties or Royalties on the one segregated portion of the

Leasehold shall not effect the rights hereunder of the party holding the other segregated portion hereunder. If six or more parties become entitled to royalty hereunder, Lessee may withhold payment unless and until furnished with a recordable instrument executed by all such parties designating an agent to receive payment for all.

PIPELINES: Lessee shall have the exclusive right to lay a pipeline, maintain, operate, repair, replace and remove same over and through the above described lands and maintain, operate, repair, replace and remove a second line of pipe alongside the first line and install drips, dehydration equipment, compressors, and any other equipment necessary and convenient for the purpose of transporting, dehydrating, and compressing gas and/or oil or other products produced from wells on the Leasehold or from wells on adjacent or nearly lands and Lessor covenants that it will not grant similar rights to any person or firm other than Lessee. Lessor agrees that Lessee shall retain all rights set forth in this paragraph regarding pipeline, compressors, dehydration units, and other equipment regardless of whether this Lease is surrendered, terminated, canceled or has lapsed, and any consideration paid to the Lessor during the term of this Lease shall be deemed to be adequate consideration for the retention by Lessee of such rights.

EXCLUSIVE RIGHTS: Lessor further covenants that it will not grant a lease or similar rights for oil or gas covering the Leasehold or any portion thereof to any other person or firm during the term of this Lease or within one (1) year after the termination of this Lease, Lessee being granted an exclusive option for an oil and gas lease covering the described premises for a period of one (1) year after the termination of this Lease, provided that such new lease shall be on such terms and provisions just as favorable to Lessor as those of any bona fide offer which Lessor may receive during said one (1) year and prior to Lessee exercising its option.

COUNTERPARTS: The parties hereto agree that this Lease may be executed in any number of counterparts, each of which shall be an original, but such counterparts shall together constitute but one and the same instrument. Should any one or more of the parties hereinabove named as Lessor fail to execute this Lease, a counterpart or companion lease, it shall nevertheless be binding, effective and enforceable upon all such parties who do execute it as Lessor.

IN WITNESS WHEREOF, this Lease is entered into this the day and year first above written.

NOTES

1.   This form is specially designed for leasing the right to develop coalbed methane. The lease also provides for natural gas storage.

2.   This lease was drafted and furnished by A. George Mason, Jr., Attorney, Lexington, Kentucky. Mr Mason advises that the lease contains the following provisions essential to the development of coalbed methane.

> The right to produce coalbed methane
> The right to stimulate or fracture the coal seam for coalbed methane
> The right to ventilate the coalbed methane without payment of royalties
> The right to produce coalbed methane from the "gob"
> The right to dewater the coal seams
> The right to drill vertical, horizontal, or directional into the coal seams
> The right to escrow funds from the production of coalbed methane
> The right to mine through the coalbed methane well
> The right to conduct operations for coalbed methane

3.   If you were the attorney for a prospective lessor, what changes would you like to make in this form.

LANDOWNERS OIL AND GAS LEASE
(Paid-Up Lease—Barnett Shale)

This Oil and Gas Lease is made on _____ between
_____ (hereafter called Lessor, whether one or more), whose address
is _____, and _____
(hereafter called Lessee), whose address is _____.

1. **Grant.** In consideration of Ten Dollars and other consideration in hand paid, Lessor grants and leases <u>exclusively</u> unto Lessee the following described land (the Land) in _____ County, Texas, for the sole purpose of exploring, drilling, and producing oil and gas, laying pipelines and building roads and tanks thereon to produce, save, treat, process, store, and transport oil and gas and other products manufactured from oil and gas produced from the Land:

[*land description*]

2. **Primary Term.** This Lease is for a term of _____ from this date (called Primary Term) and as long thereafter as oil or gas is produced by Lessee in paying quantities from the Land or land pooled therewith.

3. **Minerals Covered.** This Lease covers only oil and gas. The term "oil and gas" means oil, gas, and other liquid and gaseous hydrocarbons produced through a well bore.

4. **Royalty.**

   (a)   During any period when Lessor is not taking its royalty in kind, Lessee agrees:

   (1)   To deliver free of cost to Lessor at the wells or to the credit of Lessor at the pipeline to which the wells may be connected, _____ percent (the Royalty Fraction) of all oil and other liquid hydrocarbons produced and saved from the Land. At Lessor's option, which may be exercised from time to time, Lessee shall pay to Lessor the same part of the market value at the well of oil and other liquid hydrocarbons of like grade and gravity prevailing on the day the oil and other hydrocarbons are run from the Lease in the general area in which the Land is located.

   (2)   To pay to Lessor:

   (i)   On gas produced from the Land and sold by Lessee or used on or off the Land and to which the following subparagraphs (ii) and (iii) do not apply, the Royalty Fraction of the market value at the point of sale, use, or other disposition.

   (ii)   On gas produced from the Land that is processed in a processing plant in which Lessee or an affiliate of Lessee has a direct or indirect interest, the higher of the Royalty Fraction of the market value of the gas at the inlet to the processing plant, or the Royalty Fraction of the market value of all processed liquids saved from the gas at the plant plus the Royalty Fraction of the market value of all residue gas at the point of sale, use, or other disposition.

   (iii)   On gas produced from the Land that is processed in facilities other than a processing plant in which Lessee or an affiliate of Lessee has a direct or indirect interest, the Royalty Fraction of the market value at the plant of all processed liquids credited to the account of Lessee and attributable to the gas plus the Royalty Fraction of the market value of all residue gas at the point of sale, use, or other disposition.

   (b)   If gas produced from the Land is sold by Lessee pursuant to an arms-length contract with a purchaser that is not an affiliate of Lessee, and for a term no longer than that which is usual and customary in the industry at the time the contract is made, then the market

1   value of the gas sold pursuant to the contract shall be the total proceeds received by Lessee in the
2   sale, subject to the provisions of paragraph 4(c) below.

3   (c)   The market value of gas will be determined at the specified location by reference
4   to the gross heating value (measured in British thermal units) and quality of the gas. The market
5   value used in the calculation of oil and gas royalty will never be less than the total proceeds
6   received by Lessee in connection with the sale, use, or other disposition the oil or gas produced
7   or sold. For purposes of this paragraph, if Lessee receives from a purchaser of oil or gas any
8   reimbursement for all or any part of severance or production taxes, or if Lessee realizes proceeds
9   of production after deduction for any expense of production, gathering, dehydration, separation,
10   compression, transportation, treatment, processing, storage, or marketing, then the
11   reimbursement or the deductions will be added to the total proceeds received by Lessee. Royalty
12   will be payable on oil and gas produced from the Land and consumed by Lessee on the Land for
13   compression, dehydration, fuel, or other use.

14   (d)   Lessor's royalty will never bear, either directly or indirectly, any part of the costs
15   or expenses of production, separation, gathering, dehydration, compression, transportation,
16   trucking, processing, treatment, storage, or marketing of the oil or gas produced from the Land or
17   any part of the costs of construction, operation, or depreciation of any plant or other facilities or
18   equipment used in the handling of oil or gas.

19   (e)   Lessor shall be paid the Royalty Fraction of all payments and other benefits made
20   under any oil or gas sales contract or other arrangement, including take-or-pay payments and
21   payments received in settlement of disputes; provided that if Lessor receives a take-or-pay
22   payment or similar payment for gas that has not been produced, and if the gas is subsequently
23   produced, Lessor will only receive its Royalty Fraction of any payments made for make-up gas
24   taken pursuant to the take or-pay provision or similar provision.

25   (f)   Lessee must disburse or cause to be disbursed to Lessor its royalty on production
26   from a particular well not later than 90 days after completion of the well, in the case of an oil
27   well, or after the pipeline connection, in the case of a gas well. Thereafter, Lessee must disburse
28   or cause to be disbursed to Lessor its royalty on production by the last day of the second month
29   after the month of production. If not paid when due, Lessor's royalty will bear interest at the
30   maximum lawful rate from due date until paid, which amount Lessee agrees to pay. Acceptance
31   by Lessor of royalties that are past due will not act as a waiver or estoppel of its right to receive
32   interest due thereon unless Lessor expressly so provides in writing signed by Lessor. The royalty
33   payment obligations under this Lease shall not be affected by any division order or the
34   provisions of the Section 91.402 of the Texas Natural Resources Code or any similar statute.
35   Should Lessee fail at any time to pay royalty when due, Lessor may give Lessee written notice of
36   the default, and if the default is not cured within 60 days of the notice of the default, Lessor shall
37   have, in addition to all other remedies, the right to terminate this Lease. If Lessor's interest in the
38   Land is subject to a deed of trust or other encumbrance, Lessee may not withhold payment of
39   royalty to Lessor unless there is an assignment of royalty from Lessor to the lien holder, and
40   Lessee is notified by the lien holder that Lessor is in default.

41   (g)   As used in this Lease, "affiliate" means (i) a corporation, joint venture,
42   partnership, or other entity that owns more than ten percent of the outstanding voting interest of
43   Lessee or in which Lessee owns more than ten percent of the outstanding voting interest; or (ii) a
44   corporation, joint venture, partnership, or other entity in which, together with Lessee, more than
45   ten percent of the outstanding voting interests of both Lessee and the other corporation, joint

venture, partnership, or other entity is owned or controlled by the same persons or group of persons.

(h)   The receipt by Lessee from a purchaser or a pipeline company of proceeds of production for distribution to Lessor will not result in Lessee acquiring legal or equitable title to those proceeds, but Lessee will at all time hold the proceeds in trust for the benefit of Lessor. Notwithstanding the insolvency, bankruptcy, or other business failure of a purchaser of production from the Land or pipeline company transporting production from the Land, Lessee will remain liable for payment to Lessor for, and agrees to pay Lessor all royalties due Lessor together with interest if not timely paid.

5.   **Off-Site Drilling.** Lessor grants to Lessee the right to drill wells (Off-Site Wells) to other land not covered by this Lease and not pooled with the Land. No Off-Site Well may be drilled until a horizontal well has been drilled on the Land, or on a pooled unit that includes all of the Land, in a good faith attempt to produce oil or gas from the Barnett Shale formation. No Off-Site Well may be produced from any point less than 600 feet from the boundary of the Land without Lessor's prior written consent. If this Lease terminates as to all or any part of the Land and if Lessee has made a good faith attempt to drill a well on the Land or on a pooled unit that includes all of the Land, the right of Lessee to continue using the drillsite to drill and operate an Off-Site Well or to produce and transport production from an Off-Site Well shall continue for so long as Lessee produces oil or gas from the Off-Site Well or maintains a lease on land from which the Off-Site Well produces, and Lessee shall continue to have the right of ingress and egress to the drillsite for the purpose of using the drillsite in connection with the drilling, operating, producing, and transporting production from the Off-Site Well. Lessee will assign to Lessor an overriding royalty interest equal to _____ percent of all oil, gas, and other liquid and gaseous hydrocarbons produced and saved from each Off-Site Well, to be calculated and paid in accordance with the provisions of paragraph 4 above. Upon commencement of drilling of each Off-Site Well, Lessee shall promptly execute and deliver to Lessor a recordable assignment, in form reasonably acceptable to Lessor, with warranty of title by, through, or under Lessee but not otherwise, conveying the overriding royalty interest due with respect to that well. Operations on or production from an Off-Site Well will not preserve all or any part of this Lease except to the extent specifically set out in this paragraph.

6.   **Shut-in Royalty.** While there is a gas well on this Lease or acreage pooled therewith capable of producing gas in paying quantities, but gas is not being sold, Lessee shall pay or tender in advance an annual shut-in royalty of $_____ for each well from which gas is not being sold. Payment with respect to a well will be due within 60 days after the well is shut-in. While shut-in royalty payments are timely and properly paid, this Lease will be held as a producing lease. The right of Lessee to maintain this Lease in force by payment of shut-in gas royalty is limited to the period of two years that follow the expiration of the Primary Term. The obligation of Lessee to pay shut-in royalty is a condition and not a covenant. The payment or tender of royalty under this paragraph may be made by the check of Lessee mailed or delivered to the parties entitled thereto on or before the due date.

7.   **Drilling Obligations.** On or before _____ from this date, Lessee agrees to commence the actual drilling of a well on the Land and thereafter drill it with reasonable diligence and in a good and workmanlike manner to a depth sufficient to test the Barnett Shale Formation. While drilling the well, if Lessee encounters subsurface conditions that render further drilling impractical, Lessee may commence a substitute well within 30 days after abandoning the

1 well. A substitute well that is drilled to the depth and in the manner required for the first well
2 will satisfy this drilling obligation. If Lessee fails timely to commence the well, or if having
3 commenced the well fails to drill it to the depth and in the manner required, this Lease will
4 terminate.

5 8. **Continuous Development**.

6 (a) If, at the expiration of the Primary Term, oil or gas is not being produced from the
7 Land or on acreage pooled therewith, but Lessee has commenced the drilling of a well on the
8 Land, the Lease will not terminate but will remain in effect for so long thereafter as operations
9 are carried out with due diligence with no cessation of more than 60 days, and if the operations
10 result in the production of oil or gas, the Lease shall remain in force as otherwise provided
11 herein. For the purposes of this Lease, the term operations" means operations for any of the
12 following: drilling, testing, completing, reworking, recompleting, deepening, plugging back, or
13 repairing of a well in search for or in the endeavor to obtain production of oil or gas.

14 (b) After the Primary Term, if this Lease is maintained by production or otherwise, it
15 will remain in force as to all acreage and depths as long as there is no lapse of more than 180
16 days between the completion of one well and the commencement of the actual drilling of another
17 well. If a well has been completed during the Primary Term, the 180 day period for commencing
18 the next well will start at the end of the Primary Term. The commencement of actual drilling
19 means the penetration of the surface with a drilling rig capable of drilling to the anticipated total
20 depth of the well. After a well is commenced, drilling operations must continue with diligence
21 and in a good and workmanlike manner in a good faith effort to reach the anticipated total depth
22 with no cessation of more than 60 consecutive days. A well will be deemed to have been
23 completed on the date of the release of the drilling rig from the drillsite. The permitted time
24 between wells shall be cumulative so that if a well is commenced after the end of the Primary
25 Term but prior to the date it is required to be commenced, the number of days prior to the date on
26 which the well should have been commenced shall be added to the time permitted for the next
27 well.

28 (c) If at any time the maximum time for the commencement of the actual drilling of a
29 well expires without the commencement of the well, or upon the expiration of the Primary Term
30 if the Lease is not maintained by continuous drilling, this Lease will terminate except as to the
31 Retained Tract (defined below) surrounding any well that is then producing in paying quantities
32 or deemed to be producing in paying quantities by virtue of payment of shut-in royalties, and as
33 to each Retained Tract, the Lease will then terminate as to all depths below the stratigraphic
34 equivalent of the base of the deepest producing formation on the Retained Tract and above the
35 top of the stratigraphic equivalent of the shallowest producing formation on the Retained Tract.
36 The Lease will be treated as a separate lease with respect to each Retained Tract and will
37 continue so long as production in paying quantities continues from the tract. If production from a
38 Retained Tract ceases from any cause, this Lease will terminate as to that tract unless Lessee
39 commences operations for drilling or reworking on the tract within 60 days after the cessation of
40 production, in which case the Lease as to that tract will continue in force as long as the
41 operations are prosecuted with no cessation of more than 60 consecutive days, and if they result
42 in production, so long thereafter as there is production from the tract.

43 (d) As used in this Lease, the term "horizontal well" means a well that meets the
44 definition of a "horizontal drainhole well" under Statewide Rule 86 of the Railroad Commission
45 of Texas, and a "vertical well" is a well that is not a horizontal well. The land assigned to a well

for the purposes of this section is referred to as a "Retained Tract." A Retained Tract for a well may not exceed the minimum size required to obtain a drilling permit under the well density rules adopted by the Railroad Commission of Texas for the field, or if there are no field rules that apply, the Retained Tract shall be limited to the smallest size required to obtain a drilling permit under the statewide well density rules of the Railroad Commission of Texas. A Retained Tract for a vertical well producing from the Barnett Shale formation may not exceed 40 acres. If field rules are established later that permit obtaining a drilling permit with less acreage, a Retained Tract for a vertical well may not exceed the minimum size permitted. A Retained Tract for a horizontal well may include the minimum acreage specified above for a vertical well plus the additional acreage listed in the tables in Rule 86 (For Fields with a Density Rule of 40 Acres or Less) and must comply with the requirements of Rule 86 for minimum permitted well density, and if the well is producing from the Barnett Shale formation, the acreage of the Retained Tract shall be assigned as if well density for vertical wells is 40 acres or less. Each Retained Tract for a vertical well must be as nearly in the form of a square as is practical with the well in the center of the square and with the sides of each square running in the cardinal directions. Each Retained Tract for a horizontal well must be in the form of a rectangle with the horizontal drainhole being as nearly as practical along the center line of the long dimension of the rectangle.

(e) Within 60 days after the last to occur of the expiration of the Primary Term or the continuous drilling program, Lessee must file in the county records and furnish to Lessor a document designating each Retained Tract by metes and bounds and the retained depths under the tract, and releasing all other depths and acreage. A gas well that becomes an oil well will hold only the acreage permitted for an oil well, and Lessee must file a redesignation of the Retained Tract in the Real Property Records of the county where the Land is located. If Lessee fails to file timely a document required by this paragraph after Lessor has provided 30 days prior written notice, then Lessor may do so, and the filing will bind Lessee.

9. **Offset Wells**. For purposes of this Lease, an "offsetting well" is a well that is producing oil or gas from adjacent or nearby land and is draining the Land. If an offsetting well is completed, Lessee must, within 60 days after the initial production from the offsetting well, commence operations for the drilling of an offset well on the Land and must diligently pursue those operations to the horizon in which the offsetting well is producing, or at the option of Lessee: (i) execute and deliver to Lessor a release in recordable form of the acreage nearest to the offsetting well; or (ii) pay Lessor a monthly royalty equal to the royalty that would be payable under this Lease if the production from the offsetting well had come from the Land. In the event acreage is released pursuant to (i) above, the release will cover a tract of a size and shape that will permit the drilling of a well to the producing formation and the creation of a proration unit surrounding the well in compliance with the field rules for the field in which the offsetting well is located, but if there are no field rules, in compliance with the statewide rules of the Railroad Commission of Texas. A producing well located within 467 feet of the Land will be conclusively presumed to be draining the Land.

10. **Secondary Recovery.** Lessee will not implement any repressuring, pressure maintenance, recycling, or secondary recovery operations without the prior written consent of Lessor.

11. **Equipment**. While Lessee is not in default under this Lease, and subject to other provisions of this Lease, Lessee will have the right at any time within six months after the expiration of this Lease to remove all personal property placed by Lessee on the Land. If Lessee

1 fails to do so within the permitted period, then at Lessor's option, all or any part of the personal
2 property will become the property of Lessor, and Lessor may require Lessee to remove all
3 property not desired by Lessor. Lessee may not remove any gates or cattle guards installed by it.
4 12. **Surface Use.**
5 (a) Lessee agrees to pay Lessor the reasonable value of the actual damages resulting
6 to the surface of the Land, fences, roads, tanks, structures, improvements, livestock, trees and
7 timber, grass, and crops caused by Lessee's activities hereunder, and to restore the surface of the
8 Land to as near its original condition as may be reasonably done after the completion of each
9 operation. The restoration of the surface shall include removing all gravel, caliche, and fill
10 material and reseeding, resodding, or resprigging as requested by Lessor. Upon Lessor's request,
11 Lessee shall place all removed gravel and caliche upon Lessor's roads in a good and
12 workmanlike manner. Before plugging and abandoning any well on the Land, Lessee must
13 advise Lessor, and upon Lessor's request, must set a plug at the base of the deepest fresh water
14 structure and then deliver the well to Lessor free of cost. The reasonable value for actual
15 damages caused by each of the following activities shall not be less than the stated amounts:
16 $ _____ for each well drilled;
17 $ _____ per foot for pipelines, including flow lines and gathering lines;
18 $ _____ per foot for all roads constructed.
19 THE FOREGOING AMOUNTS SHALL NOT BE CONSIDERED AS COMPLETE
20 PAYMENT FOR DAMAGES THAT ARE IN EXCESS OF THE TYPE NORMALLY
21 ASSOCIATED WITH THE STATED ACTIVITY. FOR PURPOSES OF THIS PARAGRAPH,
22 EACH HORIZONTAL DRAINHOLE WILL BE CONSIDERED A WELL.
23 (b) While drilling or reworking operations are being conducted, Lessee shall
24 construct and maintain a fence around the area of operations and shall take appropriate measures
25 to insure that only authorized persons have access to the drillsite. After the completion of a well,
26 Lessee shall construct and maintain a substantial fence around all tank batteries, separators, and
27 other surface equipment and shall keep all gates locked. Lessee shall keep all surface equipment
28 in a good state of repair and painted as often as is necessary to maintain a good appearance.
29 Lessee shall remove all debris, trash, unused materials, pipe, or equipment from the Land on a
30 continuing basis. Lessee may not construct any buildings or other structures except for temporary
31 mobile buildings utilized during drilling and completion operations. Lessee will use only low
32 profile pumping units on the Land. Lessee shall bury each gathering line, flow line, and pipeline
33 located on the Land so that the top of each line is at least 36 inches below the surface.
34 (c) Lessee may build and use no more than one drillsite for each _____ acres of the
35 Land. A drillsite may not exceed four acres during the drilling of a well and shall be reduced to
36 not more than one acre at all other times. Lessee must obtain Lessor's prior written consent as to
37 the location of drillsites, pits, tank batteries, roads, pipelines, flow lines, and all surface
38 equipment. Roads and pipelines will generally follow the course of roads and fences in order to
39 minimize the impact on the surface of the Land. Lessee recognizes that in some instances this
40 may cause roads or pipelines to be a greater length than necessary for ingress and egress and for
41 transporting oil or gas produced from the Land. No compressors may be located upon the Land
42 without Lessor's prior written consent. Upon the expiration of the Primary Term, or, if this Lease
43 is maintained beyond the Primary Term by continuous drilling, upon the expiration of the
44 continuous drilling period, Lessee shall obtain a survey showing the location of each drillsite,
45 road, and pipeline then located on the Land and shall prepare and deliver to Lessor a release in

181

recordable form, releasing Lessee's right to use any other portion of the surface not designated as a road, drillsite, or pipeline location on the survey.

(d)   Before any drilling equipment is moved to a drillsite, Lessee must build an all-weather, graded, crushed stone road to the drillsite with tinhorns placed where necessary. All roads must meet the approval of Lessor, which approval will not be unreasonably withheld. Lessee shall maintain all roads used by Lessee in a good condition. Lessee agrees to keep the Land clean, to keep equipment painted, to fence all pits until the pits can be filled and leveled by Lessee, to repair all fences damaged by Lessee, and to restore the premises to natural condition insofar as is reasonably possible upon termination of each operation. All salt water produced from the Land must be removed by Lessee from the Land.

(e)   Lessor may construct or install earthen mounds, landscaping, fencing, or use other methods to screen the drillsites and Lessee's equipment from view. In the event Lessor incurs any expense in screening the drillsites or Lessee's equipment from view, Lessee agrees to reimburse Lessor for its out of pocket costs incurred in connection with the screening up to a maximum reimbursement of $_____ per drillsite. If directed by Lessor, Lessee shall plant hedges or provide other landscaping and shall take whatever reasonable measures as may be requested by Lessor to shield all surface equipment from view.

(f)   All pits and cellars must be filled to ten inches above ground level by Lessee within 30 days after completion of each well. If the pits or cellars are too wet to cover within 30 days after completion of a well, Lessee agrees to remove the contents of each from the Land, and to fill the pits as provided above when the ground is dry.

(g)   Water from Lessor's creeks, tanks, or wells may not be used by Lessee, and Lessee may not drill a water well on the Land or construct a pond on the Land without Lessor's prior written consent. If Lessor consents to the drilling of a water well by Lessee, Lessor shall have free use of water produced from the well at all times the well is not being used by Lessee. When the water well is no longer being used by Lessee, or upon termination of this lease, whichever first occurs, it shall tender the well and all related equipment to Lessor, free of cost.

(h)   Lessee may not use sand, gravel, caliche, or any other materials from the Land. Under no circumstances may Lessee, its agents, employees, or contractors bring firearms or dogs or other animals on the Land or hunt or fish on the Land.

13.   **Assignments**. Lessor is granting rights to Lessee that Lessor would not grant to others. Therefore, prior written approval of Lessor is required for any assignment or sublease of this Lease. All assignments and subleases must require the assignee or sublessee to assume all of the obligations imposed upon Lessee by this Lease, but Lessee will remain liable for the lease obligations regardless of any assignment or sublease by it. No assignment or sublease will be effective until a certified copy of the recorded document is furnished to Lessor.

14.   **Force Majeure.** Should Lessee be prevented by reason of Force Majeure from complying with any express or implied covenant of this Lease (other than a requirement to pay money), then while so prevented, that covenant will be suspended; Lessee will not be liable for damages for failure to comply therewith; this Lease will be extended so long as Lessee is prevented from conducting drilling or reworking operations on or from producing oil or gas from the Land; and the time while Lessee is so prevented will not be counted against Lessee. "Force Majeure" means any Act of God, any federal or state law, or any rule or regulation of governmental authority, or other similar cause (other than financial reasons). This paragraph is,

however, in all things subject to the limitations of time during which this Lease may be continued in force by the payment of shut-in gas royalties.

15.   **No Warranties.** Lessor makes no warranty of any kind with respect to title to the Land. By acceptance of this Lease, Lessee acknowledges that it has been given full opportunity to investigate and has conducted sufficient investigation to satisfy itself as to the title to the Land, and Lessee assumes all risk of title failures. If Lessor owns an interest in the Land less than the entire fee simple estate, then the royalties (including shut-in royalties) payable hereunder will be reduced proportionately.

16.   **Curing Defaults.** Should Lessee at any time fail to comply with its obligations hereunder regarding construction, maintenance, or repair within 30 days after written notice from Lessor, Lessor will have the right to do or have done whatever is necessary to fulfill the obligations to its satisfaction, and Lessee shall be liable to Lessor for the reasonable and necessary expenses thus incurred by Lessor, to be paid within ten days after Lessor furnishes to Lessee an itemized written statement of the expenses.

17.   **Notices.** All notices will be deemed given and reports and documents will be deemed delivered if sent by certified letter, return receipt requested, properly addressed and deposited in the United States Postal Service, postage prepaid, to Lessor and Lessee at the addresses shown for each party. Any party may designate a new address by proper notice to the other party or parties.

18.   **Attorney's Fees.** In the event that Lessor is required to employ legal counsel for the enforcement of any provision of this Lease and prevails, Lessor will be entitled to recover from Lessee reasonable attorney's fees and expenses incurred by Lessor.

19.   **Insurance.** At all times while this Lease is in force, Lessee shall acquire and maintain insurance covering all of its activities under this Lease, including any work performed on its behalf by contractors, subcontractors, and others, naming Lessor and related individuals and entities designated by Lessor as additional insureds. The policies shall include coverage for comprehensive general liability, for bodily injury and property damage, blowout and loss of well coverage, and coverage for any damage to the environment, including coverage for the cost of clean up and surface remediation. The coverage shall be in the minimum amount of $5,000,000. Lessee shall furnish an endorsement from the issuing insurance company or companies evidencing the coverage.

20.   Indemnity. LESSEE AGREES TO INDEMNIFY AND HOLD HARMLESS LESSOR, AND LESSOR'S REPRESENTATIVES, SUCCESSORS, AND ASSIGNS AGAINST ALL EXPENSES, CLAIMS, DEMANDS, LIABILITIES, AND CAUSES OF ACTION OF ANY NATURE FOR NUISANCE, FOR INJURY TO OR DEATH OF PERSONS AND FOR LOSS OR DAMAGE TO PROPERTY, OR ANY OF THEM, INCLUDING, WITHOUT LIMITATION, ATTORNEY FEES, EXPERT FEES, AND COURT COSTS, CAUSED BY OR RESULTING FROM LESSEE'S ACTIVITIES ON OR LESSEE'S MARKETING OF PRODUCTION FROM THE LAND OR ANY VIOLATION OF ANY ENVIRONMENTAL REQUIREMENTS BY LESSEE. AS USED IN THIS PARAGRAPH, THE TERM "LESSEE" INCLUDES LESSEE, ITS AGENTS, EMPLOYEES, SERVANTS, CONTRACTORS, AND ANY OTHER PERSON ACTING UNDER ITS DIRECTION AND CONTROL, AND ITS INDEPENDENT CONTRACTORS. LESSEE'S INDEMNITY OBLIGATIONS SURVIVE THE TERMINATION OF THIS LEASE.   LESSEE'S OBLIGATIONS UNDER THIS

1 PARAGRAPH ARE IN NO MANNER LIMITED TO THE AMOUNT OF INSURANCE
2 FURNISHED PURSUANT TO OTHER PROVISIONS OF THIS LEASE.

3 **21.** **Dispute Resolution**. In the event of a dispute under this Lease, the parties agree to
4 attempt to resolve the dispute through good faith mediation to be held in _____ County,
5 Texas.

6 22. **Seismic Activities.** No geophysical activities involving the use of explosives may be
7 conducted by Lessee. Once commenced, those activities must be completed within 30 days. No
8 bulldozers, earth moving, or brush clearing machines may be used in the activities, and surface
9 disturbances will be minimized. At the conclusion of the activities Lessee must restore any
10 surface disturbances and remove any debris. Lessee must strictly comply with all federal, state,
11 and county regulations in conducting the activities.

12 **23.** **Miscellaneous Provisions.**

13 (a) In the event this Lease expires for any reason as to all or any part of the Land,
14 Lessee shall, within 60 days thereafter, furnish Lessor with a written, recordable release covering
15 all of the Land or that portion of the Land to be released.

16 (b) Nothing in this Lease negates the usual implied covenants imposed upon Lessee.

17 (c) Lessee will conduct all of its activities in compliance with the rules of the
18 Railroad Commission of Texas and federal and state environmental laws and regulations. Lessee
19 will give Lessor at least ten days prior notice in writing before conducting drilling, recompletion,
20 or reworking operations on the Land. Upon request by Lessor, Lessee shall furnish to Lessor
21 copies of applications to drill, daily drilling reports, well tests, completion reports, plugging
22 records, gas purchase contracts, and production reports. Lessor has the right, personally or by
23 representative, at Lessor's risk, of access to the derrick floor to observe all operations on all
24 wells drilled on the Land. Lessor will have the right to inspect and take samples of all cores and
25 cuttings and witness the taking of all logs and drill stem tests, and Lessee agrees to furnish
26 Lessor with copies of all logs and surveys taken promptly after taking them. Lessee will divulge
27 to Lessor correct information as requested by Lessor as to each well, the production from the
28 well, and such technical information as Lessee may acquire. Lessor has the right to be present
29 when wells or tanks are gauged and production metered and has the right to examine all run
30 tickets and to have full information as to production and runs and to receive copies of all run
31 tickets upon request.

32 (d) The term "production" and "producing" mean production and producing in paying
33 quantities. No obligation of Lessee to pay money under this Lease will be excused or delayed by
34 reason of Force Majeure. Lessee's obligations to pay money under this Lease are to be
35 performed in _____ County, Texas. Paragraph headings are used in this Lease for
36 convenience only and are not to be considered in the interpretation or construction of this Lease.
37 The execution or ratification by Lessor of any division order, gas contract, or any other
38 document will not alter any provision of this Lease unless the intent to do so is expressly stated
39 in the document. Lessee agrees to furnish to Lessor a copy of each title opinion or report
40 obtained by Lessee that covers all or any part of the Land together with a copy of each title
41 curative document obtained by Lessee.

42 (e) Lessor shall have the right to inspect all records of Lessee relating to this Lease,
43 operations conducted on the Lease, the sale and marketing of production from the Lease, and the
44 payment of royalties, including the right to audit Lessee's books insofar as they relate to the
45 foregoing.

1   (f)   If the Land presently has an agricultural or open space exemption or similar
2   exemption or classification for ad valorem tax purposes, and if this Lease or Lessee's activities
3   cause the imposition of rollback taxes, Lessee agrees to hold Lessor harmless from any and all of
4   the additional taxes.
5   (g)   This Lease is binding upon and for the benefit of Lessor, Lessee, and their
6   respective heirs, personal representatives, successors, and assigns when fully signed and
7   acknowledged by Lessor and Lessee and a copy delivered to Lessor.
8   Executed on the date first written above.
9   LESSOR:
10
11   _____
12
13   LESSEE:
14
15   _____

NOTES

1.   This lease was furnished by the Charles Harris, Harris, Finley & Bogle, P.C., Forth Worth, Texas, http://www.hfblaw.com/main/main.php. This lease is specially designed for use in the Barnett Shale gas play in the Fort Worth area. The setting for this lease play is urban and suburban and much of the rural areas consist of densely settled "ranchettes." Thus, this lease contains a pooling provision, which is not ordinarily found in lessor-oriented lease forms. Why is one included here? Why would a lessor often prefer to omit the pooling clause?

2.   Note that this lease is a "paid-up" lease, *i.e.*, it contains no delay-rental clause. Why would a lessor want to forgo rentals? This lease form does not specify that rentals have been prepaid or that the lessee has no drilling obligation during the primary term. Might this omission resurrect the implied covenant to test, discussed in the casebook at pages 494-95?

3.   Forms similar to this one are often used in Texas by land and mineral owners who are relatively sophisticated when it comes to oil and gas leasing. Similar landowner forms may be encountered in Kansas where the Southwest Kansas Royalty Owners Association, a royalty and mineral owner organization, has been very active in advocating the interests of royalty owners in the Hugoton Field and elsewhere. The association's website is: http://www.swkroa.com/

4.   Other than the owners of large tracts who own all the oil and gas rights, as opposed to owners of only small tracts or small fractional interests, the ability of land and mineral owners to impose lessor-oriented lease forms may be fettered by compulsory pooling practices in many states. Texas has a limited compulsory pooling statute that is seldom used. Kansas has no compulsory pooling statute. But Oklahoma has a compulsory pooling statute that may be used to pool unleased mineral interest owners who drive too hard a bargain. Thus, lessor-oriented leases in use in Oklahoma are not as lessor-oriented as the above Texas form. Nevertheless, a large-tract mineral owner in Texas who drives too hard of a bargain can theoretically be "frozen out" and drained. In other states, lessor-oriented lease forms are occasionally encountered but are not common.

5.   In most states, including Texas, Kansas, and Oklahoma, many mineral owners—particularly those that own only small fractional interests—simply execute the lease that the lessee offers, perhaps bargaining only for a higher lease bonus and higher fractional or percentage royalty share. If you carefully study the royalty provisions in the above form, you will quickly realize that there are more important royalty issues than the stated fraction or percentage.

6.   In *Hitzelberger v. Samedan Oil Corporation*, 948 S.W.2d 497, 504 (Tex.App.—Waco 1997, rev. den.), the court enforced the following lease clause when the lessee breached it during the primary term:

> Within 120 days following the first sale of oil or gas produced from the
> leased premises, settlement shall be made by Lessee or by its agent for

royalties due hereunder with respect to such oil or gas sold off the premises and such royalties shall be paid monthly thereafter without the necessity of Lessor executing a division or transfer order. If said initial royalty payment is not so made under the terms hereof, this lease shall terminate as of 7 A.M. the first day of the month following expiration of said 120-day period. After said initial royalty payment, with respect to oil or gas produced during any month, if royalty is not paid hereunder on or before the last day of the second succeeding month, this lease shall terminate at midnight of such last day.

How does this provision compare with Clause 4(f) in the above lease? Which clause is preferable to a lessor and why?

7.   Why does the landowner form provide for the signature of both the Lessor and the Lessee? Why do lessee-oriented forms usually require only the lessor's signature?

8.   If you were negotiating a lease on behalf of an oil and gas company, consider what changes you would like to make in the above Texas landowner lease form? Then rank them in order of priority. Then consider which, if any, of your desires the lessee's lawyer might accept. What might you do to convince the lessor's lawyer to yield on key issues?

9.   State land departments, such as the Texas General Land Office, bank trust departments that manage large mineral holdings, and timber and railroads companies (or their successors) that hold large mineral acreages also have lessor-oriented lease forms, but the degree of lessor orientation in these leases varies widely. Likewise, federal oil and gas leases, which are supplemented by lengthy regulations, are somewhat lessor-oriented. Federal lease forms are reproduced in Chapter 6.

10.   When landmen take leases on behalf of lessees, they may insist on using the "standard" form that they are accustomed to using or that they were instructed to use. These forms are lessee-oriented; however, a landman desperate for the lease and worried about potential competitors may agree to a lessor-oriented addendum. Accordingly, rather than insist on the use of a lessor-oriented form, savvy lessors might propose a lease addendum, such as the one that follows.

EXHIBIT "A"
Attached to and made a part of that certain Oil and Gas Lease
covering portions of Section _____, Township _____, Range _____
dated _____
by and between, _____ as Lessor,
and _____, as Lessee .

8 The following provisions are part of this Oil and Gas Lease and if there be conflict
9 between these provisions and any of the foregoing provisions, then the following provisions shall
10 apply and take precedence:
11   **COMMENCEMENT:** Commencement of a well according to the terms of this lease
12 will require that a drilling rig capable of drilling to total depth be on location and drilling on or
13 before expiration of the primary term, and that the drilling of said well be continued with due
14 diligence until completion. Construction of a well location without actual drilling as detailed
15 above will not be deemed commencement of a well.
16   **DEPTH CLAUSE:** In the event this lease is extended by commercial production beyond
17 its primary term, then on such date this lease shall terminate as to all rights one hundred feet and
18 more below the stratigraphic equivalent of the deepest producing perforations in the well or wells
19 located on the leased premises, or land unitized therewith. If Lessee is in the process of drilling
20 or completing a well at the end of the primary term of this lease, this clause shall become
21 effective upon conclusion of such operations.
22   **PUGH CLAUSE**: Notwithstanding anything to the contrary in this lease, all portions of
23 this lease not included in a unit created by the Oklahoma Corporation Commission and not
24 producing or upon which drilling operations have not commenced, shall be released at the
25 expiration of the primary term of this lease. Should the unit as established by the Corporation
26 Commission be changed after the expiration of the primary term, all portions of this lease not
27 included in the newly prescribed Corporation Commission unit will be released.
28   **ROYALTY**: Lessee hereby agrees to deliver or cause to be delivered to Lessor, without
29 cost into pipelines, a royalty of three-sixteenths (3/16) part of the oil or gas produced from the
30 leased premises and a three-sixteenths (3/16) part of all casinghead or drip gas or gasoline or
31 other hydrocarbon substances produced from any well or wells on said premises, or in lieu
32 thereof, pay to Lessor without cost into pipelines the gross proceeds thereof, as the Lessor may
33 elect.
34   **NO DEDUCTIONS:** Royalties payable under this lease shall be made without deduction
35 for the cost of producing, gathering, storing, separating, treating, dehydrating, compressing,
36 transporting, marketing and otherwise making the oil, gas and other products produced hereunder
37 ready for sale or use.
38   **PAYMENT IN KIND:** Lessor shall have the option to require that payment of any
39 royalty or other revenues as stipulated in this lease be made in kind, which option shall be
40 exercisable at the discretion of the Lessor from time to time by giving Lessee thirty (30) days
41 written notice.
42   **SEPARATION OF LIQUIDS:** Lessee agrees that before any gas produced from the
43 land hereby leased, containing liquid hydrocarbons, recoverable in commercial quantities by

separator on the lease, is sold, used or processed in a plant, it will be run through an adequate oil and gas separator of conventional type or other equipment at least as efficient.

GROSS VALUE OF PRODUCTION: In the event any gas is processed for the extraction of liquefiable hydrocarbons or other marketable substances, by or for Lessee or Lessee receives any consideration for allowing the gas to be processed, the value of the extracted products and the remaining residue gas attributable thereto shall be considered the gross value of the gas sold for the calculation of royalties due; provided however, for royalty calculations, gross value shall not be less than the value of the gas if such gas had not been processed. Lessee shall also refer to any subsidiary or affiliate of Lessee.

BEST PRICE AVAILABLE: In selling any gas produced from the leased premises, or any lands with which the leased premises may be unitized, the Lessee shall exercise good faith and use due diligence and prudence to market such gas at the best price and upon the most favorable terms that may be obtainable by Lessee at the time or times such gas is contracted for sale, but in no event less than the price obtained by the operator of the well, or the operator's subsidiary, or any of its affiliates.

OTHER CONSIDERATION RECEIVED: Notwithstanding anything to the contrary contained herein, Lessor shall be entitled to receive the stated royalty percentage of all moneys received by Lessee which are in any way related to the interest herein leased, including, but certainly not limited to: take-or-pay settlements; contract negotiation bonuses; contract buy downs;, and contract buy outs. This royalty shall be due within thirty (30) days after Lessee's receipt thereof.

WASTE: Lessee agrees to use diligence to prevent the underground or above ground waste of oil or gas and to avoid the physical waste of gas produced from the leased premises.

LIEN: As part of the consideration for granting this lease, Lessor reserves a lien on the interest conveyed as security payment of royalties due hereunder. Lessee stipulates and agrees that this lien shall continue in effect during the term of the lease and may be enforced and foreclosed by Lessor upon failure by Lessee to pay royalties within ninety (90) days after written notice from Lessor to Lessee that royalty payments due under the lease have not been paid.

CESSATION, DRILLING AND REWORKING: In the event production in paying quantities of oil or gas on the leased premises, after once obtained, shall cease for any cause within sixty (60) days before the expiration of the primary term of this lease or at any time or times thereafter, this lease shall not terminate if the Lessee commences additional drilling or reworking operations within sixty (60) days after such cessation, and this lease shall remain in full force and effect so long as such operations continue in a good faith and workmanlike manner without interruptions totaling more than sixty (60) days during any one such operation; and if such drilling or reworking operations result in the production of oil or gas in paying quantities, this lease shall remain in full force and effect so long as oil or gas is produced in paying quantities or payment of shut-in gas well royalties are made as hereinbefore provided in the lease.

NOTICE OF CESSATION: Lessee shall give Lessor written notice within sixty (60) days after cessation of production.

SHUT-IN ROYALTY: Notwithstanding anything to the contrary herein, it is understood and agreed that this lease may not be maintained in force for any one continuous period of time

1 longer than one (1) year after the expiration of the primary term hereof solely by the provisions
2 of the shut-in royalty clause.
3   **MONITOR DRILLING AND PRODUCTION:** Lessor shall have the right, at Lessor's
4 sole risk and expense, to monitor the re-entry, drilling and production of oil and gas from the
5 leased premises, including without limitation the right to gauge tanks, to inspect gas meters, and
6 to witness meter tests and to install separate meter with which to monitor gas sales. Lessor agrees
7 not to disclose well production and test information to any person other than Lessor's counsel,
8 petroleum engineer, accountant, and support staff without the prior written consent of Lessee.
9   **WELL INFORMATION:** Lessee agrees to furnish Lessor promptly, on request, a true
10 copy of all of the following information pertaining to the leased premises or land unitized
11 therewith, to wit: all gas purchase contracts, and supplemental agreements or amendments
12 thereto which govern the sale of hydrocarbons produced under the terms of this lease; full,
13 complete and correct records showing volumes produced and values received on gross
14 production; gas balancing statements; gas purchaser statements; daily drilling and operations
15 reports; core analysis, drill stem test, well completion, pressure survey and production analysis
16 reports; all well logs of whatever kind; and copies of any filings made to the Oklahoma
17 Corporation Commission.
18   **INDEMNIFICATION:** Lessee agrees to indemnify Lessor against all claims, suits,
19 costs, losses, and expenses that may in any manner result from or arise out of the operations
20 conducted pursuant to this instrument.
21   **ASSIGNMENT:** The rights of Lessor and Lessee hereunder may be assigned in whole or
22 in part. Lessee shall provide Lessor with certified copies of all assignments, mortgages and
23 other encumbrances against the leasehold within thirty (30) days from the making thereof,
24 together with mailing addresses for all assignees. In the event that this lease is assigned in
25 fractional parts to more than one assignee, all assignees shall be jointly and severally liable for
26 the proper payment of royalties and interest set forth herein.
27   **RELEASE:** Upon termination, expiration or surrender of this lease in whole or in part,
28 Lessee shall within thirty (30) days file an appropriate release of lease in the County Records and
29 provide Lessor with a certified copy of same.
30   **WARRANTY:** This lease is expressly made subject to all prior conveyances,
31 requirements, conditions and covenants of record and is without warranty of title.
32   **INTEREST**: Unless stated otherwise herein or if state statutes provide for a shorter
33 period to make proper payments, all payments due to Lessor for royalties herein shall be
34 delivered to him within ninety (90) days after the last day of the month for which said royalties
35 were due. In the event that said payments are not received within that 90 day time period, 12%
36 compounded annual interest, calculated from the last day of the month for which said royalties
37 were due, shall be paid to Lessor by Lessee. At Lessor's option, all payments received shall be
38 applied first to any outstanding interest due on prior late paid royalties, then to any prior
39 outstanding unpaid royalties and then to any current royalties due. No notations on the
40 remittance statements or provisions in any division order shall amend this provision.
41   **FULL PAYMENT:** Lessee or its assigns shall be responsible for the full and proper
42 payment of Lessors' royalty from the date of first production until final depletion. No statute of
43 limitations or other affirmative defense shall be asserted by Lessee or its assigns to prevent the

full and proper payment of Lessors' royalty due herein from the date of first production of any well drilled herein until final depletion of that well.

FORFEITURE: The terms and conditions hereof shall be considered covenants running with the land covered by this lease and shall be binding upon and enure for the benefit of the respective successors and assigns of the parties hereto. If any of the material terms of this lease shall be violated, this lease shall be subject to judicial forfeiture. Provided, however, that forfeiture shall not be the exclusive remedy, but a suit for damages or specific performance, or both, may be instituted. The prevailing party in any action for breach of the provisions of this lease or breach of duties pursuant to this lease shall be entitled to recover reasonable attorney's fees, expert witness fees, litigation expense and court costs.

FAVORED NATION CLAUSE: In the event Lessee pays a bonus amount greater than the amount paid to Lessor, for an oil and gas lease, and/or pooling action, in this section within six (6) months from the date hereof, Lessee agrees to pay the difference between the bonus amount already paid per acre, and the amount per acre of the greater bonus paid, to Lessor.

Lessor:_____

Lessee _____

1.   This lease exhibit was furnished to the editors by the law firm of Burns and Stowers, Norman, Oklahoma. The firm's website is: http://www.burns-stowers.com/location.cfm This exhibit can be adapted for use with virtually any oil and gas lease form. Like all modifications, additions and attachments to a printed form, the appendix should be carefully coordinated with the form to which it is added. Any lease attachment should make clear which controls if there is a discrepancy between language in the attachment and language in the form lease. Obviously, this exhibit is intended to control over the lease form.

2.   The exhibit imposes a flat one-year limit following the expiration of the primary term on the period that the lease can be maintained by payment of shut-in royalties. Compare that provision to the following:

> It is expressly provided that after the expiration of the primary term,
> Lessee shall not have the right to continue this Lease in force by payment
> of shut-in gas rentals for more than 365 total days in the aggregate.

Is the language of either of these clauses adequate to protect a lessor in Oklahoma? In Texas? Would the effectiveness of this language depend on the wording of the shut-in clause in the lease?

3.   Oil and gas terminology is not always used consistently within the industry. For example, the term "Pugh clause" was the name originally given a clause severing pooled acreage from unpooled acreage within an oil and gas lease. The term is used in the Exhibit as the label for a provision that terminates the lease as to all acreage that has not been assigned to a producing well by the end of the primary term. This clause might be more appropriately called a retained-acreage clause, referring to the acreage the lessee retains for each productive well or a continuous-development clause, referring to the need for the lessee to develop the portions of the lease that it wishes to retain. For other examples of continuous-development clauses, see the clauses on page 430 and 431 of the casebook. For a true Pugh clause, see page 430 of the casebook. Conservation practice can also affect the utility of these clauses. For example, in Oklahoma, in the case of a large land holding with 100% of all minerals covered by the lease, the Oklahoma Corporation Commission may not be asked to determine spacing units for a well and no pooling would be necessary. In such a circumstance, which, if any, of the above clause and clauses in the casebook would work as the lessor intends?

4.   In some jurisdictions clauses setting out drilling schedules or requiring offset drilling in stipulated circumstances may be construed as negating implied development or protection covenants. A Lessor wishing to avoid such an interpretation should include express language to that effect. The following language might be set out after a continuous drilling clause:

> The drilling of wells in accordance with the above schedule shall not be
> construed as an agreement or construction on the part of Lessor that such

drilling would constitute reasonable development of the leased premises; but Lessee agrees to drill all such additional well or wells on the leased premises, or such portion or portions thereof as may be in force and effect from time to time, as may be necessary to reasonably develop the same for the production of oil and gas.

RATIFICATION AND RENTAL DIVISION ORDER
(Original Lessor and Lessee/Assignee)

State:

County:

Lessor(s): (Names and Addresses)

Lessee: (Name and Address of Lessee/Assignee)

Effective Date: (This date should be the same date as that of the lease being ratified.)

On (Date of Lease), Lessor, named above, executed and delivered to Lessee, named above, an Oil and Gas Lease (the "Lease") recorded in Volume ____, Page ____ of the ____ Records of the county and state named above, on lands described in the Lease. Reference to the Lease and its recording is made in this Ratification and Rental Division Order for all purposes.

The Lease is owned by Lessee, insofar as the Lease covers the following lands (the "Lands"):

[*description of lands covered by leased acreage owned by lessee/assignee*]

Lessor desires to adopt, ratify, and confirm the Lease insofar as it covers Lessor's rights, title, and interests in the Lands and to set out the division of interest as to any rental payments which may be made pursuant to the terms of the Lease.

For adequate consideration, Lessor adopts, ratifies, and confirms the Lease as of the date of its execution, and recognizes the full validity of the Lease insofar as it affects and pertains to the rights, title, and interests of Lessor in the Lands. Lessor grants, leases, and lets to Lessee all of Lessor's rights, title, and interests in the Lands, subject to and in accordance with the terms and conditions contained in the Lease.

Lessor authorizes Lessee to pay any rentals which may be paid under the terms of the Lease in the following proportions and to the respective depositories which may be specified, or, at Lessee's option, to the depository named in the Lease. Payments, when made in this manner, will fully protect and maintain the Lease as to the mineral interest of Lessor, who only certifies the interest set opposite Lessor's name.

Lessor	Fractional Interest	Amount of Rentals	Name and Address of Depository

The division of ownership set out above is only applicable to the payment of any delay rentals to Lessor, as provided for in the Lease, and does not purport to be applicable to any royalties that may be due under the terms of the Lease.

This Ratification and Rental Division Order is binding on Lessor and Lessor's successors as to the fractional interest in rental payments set out above, but shall not operate to change the depository named in the Lease as to any of Lessor's grantees or assigns. This instrument is binding on each of the undersigned Lessors, if more than one, regardless of whether all parties named in the division of interest set out above execute this Ratification and Rental Division Order.

This Ratification and Rental Division Order is signed by each Lessor as of the date set opposite each Lessor's name, but shall be deemed effective as of the Effective Date stated above.

[*signature and date*]

NOTES

1.   Delay rental division orders are used to avoid disputes over how payments should be divided and to avoid mistakes in payment that may result in total or partial lease termination. They are especially useful if the lessor or lessee has conveyed fractional or divided interest in the leased property. The above form assumes that the original lessee has assigned a portion of the leased premises. As the *Harrison* case (discussed in *Schwartzenberger v. Hunt Trust Estate* at page 341-42 of the casebook) and several of the cases in Chapter 4 illustrate, the size of the interests resulting from conveyances is frequently contested and the special rules of construction applicable to deeds and reservations may be known and understood only by title lawyers.

2.   Most rental division orders contain language whereby the signors ratify the referenced lease.

3.   This form was furnished by Kanes Forms, P.O. Box 53010, Midland, TX 79710, tel. 800-526-3790. http://www.kanesforms.com/new/index.htm

OIL AND GAS DIVISION ORDER

Effective 7:00 a.m. _____

To: Each of the undersigned hereby warrants that he is the Owner of the interest set out opposite his name in the oil and gas (or the proceeds therefrom) produced from the lease or unit known as:

_____ ,

which lease or unit covers and includes the land described as follows:

located in the county or parish of _____, State of _____ , hereinafter referred to as the "Property". You, your successors and assigns are authorized to receive production and measure sales in accordance with the terms hereof and to account to the undersigned Owners for the oil and gas (or the proceeds therefrom) on the basis set forth:

Credit to	Interest	Address	Social Security No.

Oil: You may either purchase the crude oil or other liquid hydrocarbons recovered on the Property (hereinafter called "oil") for your own account or deliver the oil directly to another purchaser and accept payment on behalf of Owner. If you purchase the oil, payments to Owner shall be based on your applicable posted price or, if there is no such posting, it shall be based on the prevailing wellhead market price paid for oil of the same quality on the same date in the same (or nearest) field. If you should deliver the oil to another purchaser rather than purchasing it yourself, payments to Owner shall be subject to the terms of any applicable operating agreement and based on the price received by you, calculated at the wellhead, less a reasonable charge for costs incurred by you in gathering, transporting and treating such oil or otherwise making it merchantable.

Gas: You may either purchase the gas (including casinghead gas) recovered on the Property for your own account, or deliver the gas directly to another purchaser. If you purchase the gas, payments to Owner shall be based on the prevailing wellhead price for gas of the same quality in the same (or nearest) field as provided in comparable gas purchase contracts entered into on the same (or nearest) date as the date on which your purchases commence hereunder. If you deliver the gas to another purchaser rather than purchasing it yourself, payments to Owner shall be subject to the terms of any applicable operating agreement or balancing agreement and based on the price received by you, calculated at the wellhead, less a reasonable charge for costs incurred by you in gathering, transporting, compressing and treating such gas or otherwise making it merchantable.

Settlements: Gas or oil shall become the property of the purchaser at the point it is delivered into the purchaser's pipeline or other facilities. The quantity and quality of oil and gas shall be determined according to standard measuring and testing methods used in the area. Where production is sold, you may rely upon volume computations made by the purchaser or purchasers thereof.

1   Settlements shall be made monthly by check mailed to Owner at the address shown
2 hereon. However, you may withhold payments to Owner until the total amount accrued to
3 Owner's interest is at least $15.00. You may deduct from the amounts due Owner applicable
4 taxes required by law to be deducted and paid by you on his behalf.

5   If all or any part of the Property is now or hereafter included in any unit established by a
6 voluntary agreement or governmental order, settlements hereunder shall be based on the unit
7 production allocated to the Property. If production from the Property is now or hereafter
8 commingled with production from other lands or formations, settlements hereunder shall be
9 based on the commingled production allocated to the Property. In determining such allocations,
10 you may rely on the production data furnished to you by the other parties involved.

11   Settlements with Owner are subject to all present and future federal, state and local laws,
12 regulations and orders. Whenever settlements are to be made on the basis of the price received
13 by you and that price is subject to refund in whole or in part, you may withhold payment for the
14 refundable portion of the price without interest until Owner furnishes you with indemnity
15 satisfactory to you. If the property is a part of a unit, it is understood that you will account or
16 cause others to account to each of the undersigned the amounts due to them respectively for the
17 proceeds derived from the total unit production and each of the undersigned hereby waives any
18 claim or demand therefore as against other owners of interests in such unit, their respective
19 successors and assigns, and the purchasers of all or any portion of the production from such unit.

20   **Evidence of Title:** In the even any dispute or question arises concerning the title of
21 Owner to the Property and/or the oil or gas produced therefrom or the proceeds thereof, you will
22 be furnished evidence of title satisfactory to you upon demand. Until such evidence of title has
23 been furnished and/or such dispute or question of title is corrected or removed to your
24 satisfaction, or until indemnity satisfactory to you has been furnished, you are authorized to
25 withhold the proceeds of such oil or gas received and run, without interest. In the event any
26 action or suit is filed in any court affecting title to the Property or the oil and gas produced from
27 it or the proceeds thereof to which Owner is a party, written notice of the filing of such suit or
28 action shall be immediately furnished to you by the Owner. Owner agrees to indemnify you or
29 any carrier or purchaser designated by you for Owner's proportionate share of any liability, loss,
30 damage and costs (including reasonable attorney's fees) which you or they may incur on account
31 of purchasing, selling or transporting the oil and gas. If you withhold payments pursuant to the
32 provisions hereof, Owner agrees to indemnify you for any taxes (together with all interest and
33 penalties incident thereto) paid by you or assessed against the amounts withheld, and agrees that
34 you may deduct all such taxes, interest and penalties from the amounts paid.

35   **Change of Ownership:** No change of ownership or transfer of interest shall be binding
36 on you until you are furnished at your office or the address shown above a certified copy of the
37 recorded instruments evidencing such transfer and your regular form of transfer order or an
38 amended division order is executed by all parties to such transfer and is returned to you. You
39 shall not be required to recognize such transfer as being effective earlier than 7:00 a.m. of the
40 first day of the calendar month in which said written notice is received by you. You are hereby
41 relieved of responsibility for determining when any interest herein set forth has been increased,
42 decreased, terminated, or transferred and Owner agrees to give written notice to you of any such
43 change and to hold you harmless for all loss or expense that may result from any incorrect
44 payment prior to such written notice.

Miscellaneous: This division order may be executed in counterparts all of which together shall constitute one division order. It shall become valid and binding on each and every Owner when signed by such Owner, regardless of whether or not all owners have signed. Each and every provision hereof shall inure to the benefit of each and every Owner. This division order may be terminated at any time by any Owner as to his interest, but such termination shall not be effective as to such interest until after 7:00 a.m. of the first day of the calendar month following the month in which written notice is received by you and this order shall remain in effect as to all other owners.

Additional Agreements:

[*signatures*]

NOTES

1.   Division orders are often used as oil-sales contracts; note the provisions on the first page of the form. A working-interest owner or a lessor who owns an in-kind oil royalty executes a division order to transfer title to the oil. But the major function of a division order is to protect the purchaser of production or the operator who distributes the sale proceeds from liability for an incorrect accounting or for conversion. The "Evidence of Title" paragraph of the above division order is intended to provide additional protection by giving the person to whom the division order is sent the right to withhold proceeds if there is a dispute over title.

2.   If the person signing the division order later sells or otherwise assigns all or part of the interest, the transferee must comply with the requirements of the Division Order to make the change of ownership binding on the purchaser and to be substituted for the former owner on the purchaser's records. Depending on its own practices, which may vary with the size of the interest, the purchaser of production may recognize the change of ownership without further documentation, may require the transferee to sign a Division Order showing the new ownership, or may require the transferor and transferee to sign a Transfer Order. A Transfer Order is a document that informs the purchaser that an interest in the right to production has been assigned and authorizes the purchaser to make payment to the transferee.

3.   The above division order does more than what is summarized in the prior two notes. Note that it may well substantially alter the manner of payment and amount of royalty payable. Because the division order is not signed for new consideration, most courts have held that the division order is not a contract and thus may be revoked by either party at any time; however, the royalty owner may be estopped from seeking to correct underpayments already made. On the other hand, an increasing number of states have statutes that prohibit a division order from amending the terms of a lease and even prohibit payors from withholding royalty when a lessor fails to execute a division order.

4.   Copies of this form may be obtained from Kraftbilt Products, Box 800, Tulsa, Oklahoma 74101.

TEXAS STATUTORY
OIL DIVISION ORDER

TO: _____ (Payor) Property No. _____

_____ Effective _____

(Date)

The undersigned severally and not jointly certifies it is the legal owner of the interest set out below of all the oil and related liquid hydrocarbons produced from the property described below:

OPERATOR:

Property Name:

County: _____ State: _____

Legal Description: _____

OWNER NO. _____

TAX I.D./SOC. SEC. NO. PAYEE _____

DIVISION OF INTEREST

THIS AGREEMENT DOES NOT AMEND ANY LEASE OR OPERATING AGREEMENT BETWEEN THE INTEREST OWNERS AND THE LESSEE OR OPERATOR OR ANY OTHER CONTRACTS FOR THE PURCHASE OF OIL OR GAS.

The following provisions apply to each interest owner ("owner") who executes this agreement:

TERMS OF SALE: The undersigned will be paid in accordance with the division of interests set out above. The payor shall pay all parties at the price agreed to by the operator for oil to be sold pursuant to this division order. Purchaser shall compute quantity and make corrections for gravity and temperature and make deductions for impurities.

PAYMENT: From the effective date, payment is to be made monthly by payor's check, based on this division of interest, for oil run during the preceding calendar month from the property listed above, less taxes required by law to be deducted and remitted by payor as purchaser. Payments of less than $100 may be accrued before disbursement until the total amount equals $100 or more, or until 12 months' proceeds accumulate, whichever occurs first. However, the payor may hold accumulated proceeds of less than $10 until production ceases or the payor's responsibility for making payment for production ceases, whichever occurs first. Payee agrees to refund to payor any amounts attributable to an interest or part of an interest that payee does not own.

INDEMNITY: The owner agrees to indemnify and hold payor harmless from all liability resulting from payments made to the owner in accordance with such division of interest, including but not limited to attorney fees or judgments in connection with any suit that affects the owner's interest to which payor is made a party.

DISPUTE; WITHHOLDING OF FUNDS: If a suit is filed that affects the interest of the owner, written notice shall be given to payor by the owner together with a copy of the complaint or petition filed. In the event of a claim or dispute that affects title to the division of interest credited herein, payor is authorized to withhold payments accruing to such interest, without interest unless otherwise required by applicable statute, until the claim or dispute is settled.

TERMINATION: Termination of this agreement is effective on the first day of the month that begins after the 30th day after the date written notice of termination is received by either party.

NOTICES: The owner agrees to notify payor in writing of any change in the division of interest, including changes of interest contingent on payment of money or expiration of time.

No change of interest is binding on payor until the recorded copy of the instrument of change or documents satisfactorily evidencing such change are furnished to payor at the time the change occurs. Any change of interest shall be made effective on the first day of the month following receipt of such notice by payor.

Any correspondence regarding this agreement shall be furnished to the addresses listed unless otherwise advised by either party.

In addition to the legal rights provided by the terms and provisions of this division order, an owner may have certain statutory rights under the laws of this state.

	Signature of	Social Security/	
Witness	Interest Owner	Tax I.D. No.	Address
_____	_____	_____	_____
_____	_____	_____	_____
_____	_____	_____	_____

Failure to furnish your Social Security/Tax I.D. number will result in withholding tax in accordance with federal law, and any tax withheld will not be refundable by payor.

[*signatures*]

1.   Unlike the preceding form, which applies to both oil and gas, the Texas statutory model division order form, codified at Tex. Nat. Res. Code Ann. § 91.402(d), is limited to oil. There is no equivalent statutory form for gas production. Oil division-order forms serve the important purpose of a "contract of sale" for the Lessor's share of production where royalty oil is reserved "in kind." Gas royalty clauses seldom reserve gas in kind; however, one common form of gas royalty clause provides that the lessee is to deliver the Lessor's share of gas "to the credit of the Lessor, free of cost in the pipeline." While not a pure in-kind provision, this clause suggests the need for a "bill of sale."

2.   Unlike Texas, other state statutes more commonly provide that a Lessor does not have to execute a division order to obtain royalty, and a number of states have no division-order legislation. The Texas statute entitles the payor of oil or gas royalty to require a signed division order as a condition to payment of royalty if the contents of the division order are limited to those set forth in the statute. The statute provides that a division order "does not amend any lease or operating agreement between the interest owner and the lessee or operator or any other contracts for the purchase of oil or gas." Tex. Nat. Res. Code Ann. § 91.402(c)(2). Moreover, "[t]he execution of division order between a royalty owner and lessee or between a royalty owner and a party other than lessee shall not change or relieve the lessee's specific, expressed or implied obligations under an oil and lease, including any obligation to market production as a reasonably prudent lessee." *Id.* at § 91.402(h). The statute also invalidates a division order provision between a payee and a lessee to the extent that the division order contradicts a lease provision. *Id.* Nevertheless, division orders are "binding for the time and to the extent that they have been acted on and made the basis for settlement and payments." *Id.* at § 91.402(g). Either party may terminate a division order upon 30 days notice. *Id.* Does this "binding" clause limit the effect of *Gavenda v. Strata Energy, Inc.,* 705 S. W.2d 690 (Tex. 1986) (excerpted in the Casebook at page 514)? The Texas statute also contains the following provision:

> A division order may be used to clarify royalty settlement terms in the oil and gas lease. With respect to oil and/or gas sold in the field where produced or at a gathering point in the immediate vicinity, the terms "market value," "market price," "prevailing price in the field," or other such language, when used as a basis of valuation in the oil and gas lease, shall be defined as the amount realized at the mouth of the well by the seller of such production in an arm's length transaction.

Id. at § 91.402(i). In view of the provision that a division order may not amend a lease, what does "clarify" mean? What effects, if any, does defining "market value" and "market price" have on the *Vela* rule, which distinguishes leases that provide for "market-value" or "market-price" royalty from leases that provide for "proceeds" royalty. What effect, if any, does this statutory provision have on a lease that provides for royalty on "market value" or "market price" or on a lease that expressly moves the royalty-valuation point downstream of the mouth of the well?

DIVISION ORDER

Property No.:   **Date Prepared:**
Property Name: **Prepared By:**
Operator: **Telephone Number:**
County and State: **Effective Date:**

Property Description:

Production	Oil : _____	Gas: _____	Other : _____

Owner No.:
Owner Name:
Owner Address:

Lease No.	Tract No.	Interest Calculation	Decimal Interest	Type

Total Decimal:

THE UNDERSIGNED CERTIFIES THE OWNERSHIP OF THEIR DECIMAL INTEREST IN PRODUCTION OR PROCEEDS AS DESCRIBED ABOVE PAYABLE BY _____ (PAYOR).

PAYOR SHALL BE NOTIFIED IN WRITING, OF ANY CHANGE IN OWNERSHIP, DECIMAL INTEREST, OR PAYMENT ADDRESS. ALL SUCH CHANGES SHALL BE EFFECTIVE THE FIRST DAY OF THE MONTH FOLLOWING RECEIPT OF SUCH NOTICE.

Payor is authorized to withhold payment pending resolution of a title dispute or adverse claim asserted regarding the interest in production claimed herein by the undersigned. The undersigned agrees to indemnify and reimburse Payor any amount attributable to an interest to which the undersigned is not entitled.

Payor may accrue proceeds until the total amount equals $100, or pay June 30 of each year, whichever occurs first, or as required by applicable state statute.

This Division Order does not amend any lease or operating agreement between the undersigned and the lessee or operator or any other contracts for the purchase of oil or gas.

In addition to terms and conditions of this Division Order, the undersigned and Payor may have certain statutory rights under the laws of the state in which the property is located.

Special Clauses:

Owner(s)   Signature(s):   _____

_____

Owner(s) Social Security
Or Tax I. D. Number   _____   **Address:**

_____

_____

Phone Number: _____

Federal Law requires you to furnish your Social Security or Taxpayer Identification Number. Failure to comply will result in a significant tax withholding as required by the IRS and will not be refundable by Payor.

1.   This "bare-bones" division order form is a "model" form drafted through the joint efforts of the National Association of Division Order Analysts, http://www.nadoa.org./, an oil company trade and educational organization, and the National Royalty Owners Association (NARO), http://www.naro-us.org/, a royalty owner trade and educational organization.

2.   The form is designed for general use throughout the country, and its purpose was to minimize the controversy that surrounds the use of division order forms that attempt to do more than determine the proper allocation of interests. Do you see any potential problem with using this form? What if the underlying lease provided for oil royalty to be paid in kind? Although designed for general use throughout the country, including Texas, the NADOA form does not contain all of the provisions that a payor can demand in Texas under Tex. Nat. Res. Code § 91.402(c).

Chapter 4

TITLES AND CONVEYANCES:
INTERESTS IN OIL AND GAS

Warranty Deed

(reserving oil, gas, and minerals)

State:
County:
Grantors: (Names and Addresses and marital status)
Grantees: (Name and Address)
Effective Date:

For adequate consideration, the receipt of which is acknowledged, Grantors hereby grant, bargain, sell, convey, transfer, assign, and deliver unto Grantees, their heirs, successors, and assigns, all of following described lands:

This Deed is subject to Grantors' reservation of all oil, gas, and minerals in and under the lands described, together with the right of ingress and egress and any rights of any lessee of an oil, gas, and mineral lease or leases on the lands that are the subject of this Deed, to the extent such lease or leases are valid, in force and effect; it is not Grantors intent to revive, renew, or extend any lease that has expired by its own terms.

Grantors agree to execute such further assurances or documents that may be requested or required by Grantees to allow Grantee full use and enjoyment of the lands described and rights conveyed to Grantees, and give full notice and effect to the terms of this Deed.

Each Grantor herein for himself and his heirs, executors, and administrators warrants and agrees to defend all titled granted unto Grantees, their heirs, successors and assigns against ever person lawfully claiming the described lands or any part thereof.

This deed is signed by each Grantor as of the date of acknowledgment of their signature but shall be deemed effective, for all purposes, as of the Effective Date stated above.

Grantors:

[*signatures and acknowledgments*]

NOTES

1.   This form was adapted from a form furnished by Kanes Forms, P.O. Box 53010, Midland, TX 79710, tel. 800-526-3790. http://www.kanesforms.com/new/index.htm

2.   Acknowledgment provisions have been omitted from the deeds in this manual. The form of acknowledgment would vary, depending upon state law and may further vary if the property was the homestead of the grantors.

Mineral Deed (Texas)

THE STATE OF TEXAS

County of _____

Know All Men by These Presents: That _____ of _____ County, State of Texas, hereinafter called grantor (whether one or more and referred to in the singular number and masculine gender), for and in consideration of the sum of _____ Dollars ($_____), paid by _____ hereinafter called grantee, the receipt of which is hereby acknowledged, has granted, sold and conveyed and by these presents does grant, sell and convey unto said grantee an undivided _____ interest in and to all of the oil, gas and other minerals of every kind and character in, on or under that certain tract or parcel of land situated in the County of , State of Texas, and described as follows:

[land description]

In addition to the lands above specifically described by metes and bounds the parties hereto intend this deed to cover and include and the same is hereby made to cover and include not only the above described land, but also any and all other land and interest in land owned or claimed by the Grantor in said surveyor surveys in which the above described land is located or in adjoining surveys and adjoining the above described land. Should the foregoing particular description for any reason prove incorrect or inadequate to cover the land intended to be conveyed as above specified grantor agrees to execute such instrument or instruments that may be necessary to correct such particular description.

To have and to hold the said undivided interest in all of the said oil, gas and other minerals in, on and under said land, together with all and singular the rights and appurtenances thereto in any wise belonging, with the right of ingress and egress and possession at all times for the purpose of mining, drilling and operating for said minerals and the maintenance of facilities and means necessary or convenient for producing, treating and transporting such minerals, and for housing and boarding employees, unto said grantee, his heirs and assigns forever; and grantor herein for himself and his heirs, executors and administrators hereby agrees to warrant and forever defend all and singular the said interest in said minerals, unto the said grantee, his heirs, successors and assigns against every person whomsoever lawfully claiming or to claim the same or any part thereof.

This conveyance is made subject to any valid and subsisting oil, gas or other mineral lease or leases on said land, including also any mineral lease, if any, heretofore made or being contemporaneously made from-grantor to-grantee: but, for the same consideration hereinabove mentioned, grantor has sold, transferred, assigned and conveyed and by these presents does sell, transfer, assign and convey unto grantee, his heirs, successors and assigns, the same undivided interest (as the undivided interest hereinabove conveyed in the oil, gas and other minerals in said land) in all the rights, rentals, royalties and other benefits accruing or to accrue under said lease

1 or leases from the above described land; to have and to hold unto grantee, his heirs, successors
2 and assigns.
3
4   Grantee, at his option, may discharge in whole or in part any tax, mortgage or other lien
5 upon said land, and in the event grantee does so he shall be subrogated to such lien with the right
6 to enforce the same. Should all or any part of the royalties and/or delay rentals to which Grantee
7 is entitled hereunder be applied by any lessee, pipe line company, or any other person for the
8 purpose of discharging in whole or in part any tax, mortgage or other lien upon said land, then,
9 and in that event, Grantee shall be subrogated to such lien with the right to enforce the same; and
10 an equal amount of all remaining royalties and/or delay rentals due or that may become due
11 Grantors after the execution and delivery hereof is hereby assigned and transferred to Grantee.
12
13 Witness the signature of the grantor this _____ day of _____ A.D., 19____.
14
15 _____
16
17 [*signatures and acknowledgments*]

NOTES

1.   This form is from 6 West's Texas Forms: Minerals, Oil and Gas § 1.3 (Richard Hemingway ed. 1991). The form is typical of mineral deed forms used in Texas.

2.   The sentence following the land description is commonly called a "Mother Hubbard" or "cover-all" clause. This type of clause is used less frequently in mineral deeds than in oil and gas leases, although the need is equally great in both cases. It is included to make sure that the instrument covers small adjacent strips of land that are owned by the grantor but that lie outside the area specifically described. Land underlying a road easement and land acquired by adverse possession after a fence has been relocated are examples of tracts that would be covered by the Mother Hubbard clause but might not be included in the land description.

3.   Note that the reference to "any valid and subsisting" oil and gas lease makes this grant subject to all outstanding oil and gas leases, whether or not recorded.

Mineral Deed (Oklahoma)

KNOW ALL MEN BY THESE PRESENTS THAT _____ of
_____ hereinafter called Grantor, (whether one or more) for
and in consideration of the sum of _____ Dollars, ($_____)
cash in hand paid and other good and valuable considerations, the receipt of which is hereby
acknowledged, do(es) hereby grant, bargain, sell, convey, transfer, assign and deliver unto
_____ of _____, hereinafter called Grantee,
(whether one or more) an undivided _____ interest in and to all of the oil, gas
and other minerals in and under and that may be produced from the following described lands
situated in _____ County, State of _____, to-wit:

[land description]

containing _____ acres, more or less, together with the right of ingress and egress at all
times for the purpose of mining, drilling, exploring, operating and developing said lands for oil,
gas, and other minerals, and storing, handling, transporting and marketing the same therefrom
with the right to remove from said land all of Grantee's property and improvements.

This sale is made subject to any rights now existing to any lessee or assigns under any
valid and subsisting oil and gas lease of record heretofore executed, it being understood and
agreed that said Grantee shall have, receive, and enjoy the herein granted undivided interest in
and to all bonuses, rents, royalties and other benefits which may accrue under the terms of said
lease insofar as it covers the above described land from and after the date hereof, precisely as if
the Grantee herein had been at the date of the making of said lease the owner of a similar
undivided interest in and to the lands described and Grantee one of the lessors therein.

Grantor agrees to execute such further assurances as may be requisite for the full and
complete enjoyment of the rights herein granted and likewise agrees that Grantee herein shall
have the right at any time to redeem for said Grantor by payment, any mortgage, taxes, or other
liens on the above described land, upon default in payment by the Grantor, and be subrogated to
the rights of the holder thereof.

TO HAVE AND TO HOLD The above described property and easement with all and
singular the rights, privileges, and appurtenances thereunto or in any wise belonging to said
Grantee herein, _____ heirs, successors, personal representatives,
administrators, executors, and assigns forever, and Grantor does hereby warrant said title to
Grantee _____ heirs, executors, administrators, personal
representatives, successors and assigns forever, and does hereby agree to defend all and singular
the said property unto the said Grantee herein _____ heirs, successors,
executors, personal representatives, and assigns against all and every person or persons
whomsoever lawfully claiming or to claim the same, or any part thereof.

[date, signatures, and acknowledgment]

NOTES

1.   This form of deed is frequently used in Kansas, Oklahoma, and many states in the Rocky Mountain region.

2.   The complete form may be obtained from Burkhart Printing and Stationery Co., 4317 South Sheridan Road, Tulsa, Oklahoma 74145.

Conveyance of Terminable Nonparticipating Royalty Interest

KNOW ALL MEN BY THESE PRESENTS: That _____,
hereinafter called "Grantors" for good and valuable consideration in hand paid, the receipt and
sufficiency of which Grantors hereby acknowledge, do hereby grant, bargain, sell, convey,
transfer, assign, and deliver   unto   _____, hereinafter   called
"Grantee," or the term hereinafter specified, an undivided _____ interest in any
and all Royalty (as hereinafter defined) on oil gas, casinghead gas, distillate, condensate, and any
and all other hydrocarbon or nonhydrocarbon substances, Whether similar or dissimilar, which
may be produced or extracted and saved from the following described land situated in
_____ County, Oklahoma:

[land description]

or from lands pooled or unitized with any portion thereof, or from lands located within any
governmental drilling and spacing unit which includes any portion thereof, together with the
right of ingress and egress to the surface thereof for the purpose of taking and receiving the
herein granted interest in production.

"Royalty," as used herein, shall mean: (1) Any interest in production or the proceeds
therefrom reserved by or granted to Grantors, their successors or assigns, in connection with any
present or future lease for the production or extraction of substances from said lands, including,
but not limited to, whether similar or dissimilar, any royalty, excess royalty, overriding royalty,
net profits interest, or production payment: (2) any payment so granted or reserved to be paid in
lieu of production, including, but not limited to, whether similar or dissimilar, any shut-in well
payments or minimum royalty: (3) in the event of the development of any portion of the above
described land by Grantors, their successors or assigns, for the production or extraction of any
substances, the same interest in production, proceeds, or payment to which Grantee would have
been entitled if Grantors, as of the date of commencement of development, had executed a lease
providing for a royalty equivalent to that set forth in the succeeding paragraph. As to production
or extraction of substances from lands pooled or unitized with the above described land or from
lands located within any governmental drilling and spacing unit which includes any portion
thereof, "Royalty" shall include only that portion of said production, proceeds or payments
attributable to the above described land's interest in said production unit. "Royalty" shall not
include any cash bonus received by Grantor at the time of executing any future oil, gas, or
mineral lease, or any rental paid for the privilege of deferring commencement of development
under any existing or future lease.

Grantors, their successors and assigns, reserve the exclusive right to execute leases for
the production or extraction of substances from the above described land; provided that no lease
or contract for the development of said land shall provide for a royalty less than that customarily
then being received by lessors in the area, and in no event less than one-eighth (1/8) of all
substances produced and extracted, delivered free and clear of all cost and expense except a
proportionate part of taxes on production; and provided further than Grantors, their successors
and assigns in exercising said leasing power, shall be deemed to owe a fiduciary duty to Grantee.

1   TO HAVE AND TO HOLD unto Grantee, his successors and assigns, **[forever]** *OR* **[for**
2 **a term of years from the date hereof, and as long thereafter as oil, gas, or other minerals is**
3 **being produced from, or a shut-in well is located on, or operations are being conducted on,**
4 **the above described land, or from lands pooled or unitized with any portion thereof, or**
5 **from lands located within any governmental drilling and spacing unit which includes any**
6 **portion thereof]**; and Grantors do hereby warrant title to the herein granted interest to Grantee,
7 his successors and assigns, and do hereby agree to defend all and singular such interest unto
8 Grantee, his successors or assigns, against any person whomsoever claiming or to claim the same
9 or any part thereof; and Grantors, on behalf of themselves, their successors and assigns, do
10 hereby agree to execute such further assurances as may be requisite for the full and complete
11 enjoyment of the herein granted interest.
12
13   [*date, signatures, and acknowledgments*]

NOTES

1.   The habendum clause contains alternative forms of language that can be used, depending upon whether the parties intend to grant a perpetual or a terminable royalty.

2.   Note that this form attempts to avoid many of the problems raised by the Problem on page 542 of the casebook.

Royalty Reservation Clauses

[the following language follows the land description]

Save and Except and Reserved in favor of the undersigned Grantor, his heirs, successors, and assigns, out of the _____ acres of land, more or less, a part of the _____ Survey, Abstract No. _____, in _____ County, Texas, and described in the deed dated _____, recorded in Volume _____, page _____, of the Deed Records of _____ County, Texas, an undivided _____ (_____) of Royalty (being equal to not less than an undivided _____ (_____) of all the oil, gas and/or other minerals in, to and under or that may be produced from said acres aforesaid, to be paid or delivered to said Grantor, his heirs, successors, an assigns, as his own property, free of cost Forever; together with the right of ingress and egress at all times for the purpose of storing, treating, marketing and removing the same therefrom.

Said interest hereby reserved is a Non-Participating Royalty and Grantor shall not participate in the Bonuses paid for any oil, gas or other mineral lease covering said land, nor shall he participate in the money Rentals which may be paid to extend the time within which a well may be begun under the terms of any lease covering said land. It shall not be necessary for the undersigned Grantor, his successors and assigns, to join in the execution of any lease covering said Royalty interest herein reserved, and the Grantee herein, his heirs and assigns, shall have the right to lease said land for oil, gas and other minerals, provided, however, that all such leases shall provide for Royalty of not less than one-eighth ($^1/_8$):

(a)   On oil, gas and other minerals, liquid or solid;
(b)   Of the net proceeds from the sale of liquid hydrocarbons such as gasoline, butane, propane or from the sale of any other manufactured or processed by-products extracted or recovered from said natural gas or casinghead gas;
(c)   Of the net proceeds derived from the sale of all residue gas or its by-products.

In the event oil, gas or other minerals are produced from said land, then said Grantor, or his heirs and assigns, shall receive not less than _____ (_____) portion (being equal to _____ (_____) of the customary one-eighth ($^1/_8$) Royalty) of the entire gross production and/or such net proceeds as hereinabove provided as its own property to be paid or delivered to said Grantor free of all cost from royalty oil, gas and/or other minerals, by-products manufactured or processed therefrom.

Nothing herein contained shall grant the Grantee, or his assigns, the right to pool the royalty interest hereinabove reserved in favor of Grantor.

1.   This form can be used by a grantor who wishes to retain a non-participating royalty in the land conveyed. Language describing the retained interest both as a fraction "of Royalty" and a fraction of production is typical of instruments that presuppose a traditional one-eighth landowner's royalty.

2.   If the blanks on line 9 were filled in "one-half" and "1/2," how should the blanks that follow be completed?

3.   This form is taken from 6 West's Texas Forms: Minerals, Oil and Gas section 2.6 (Richard Hemingway ed. 1991).

remainderman signs it, life tenant signs lease

Ratification of Oil and Gas Lease

KNOW ALL MEN BY THESE PRESENTS:

THAT, in consideration on ONE DOLLAR ($1.00) and other valuable considerations paid to _____ hereinafter designated as party of the first part, (whether one or more), and _____ _life tenant_ hereinafter designated as party of the second part, (whether one or more), said party of the first part does hereby adopt, ratify and confirm the certain oil and gas mining lease dated _____, 19___, between _____ as lessor, and _____ as lessee, covering the following described lands in _____ County, State of _____, to-wit:

which lease is recorded in Book _____ at Page _____ of the records of _____ County, State of _____.

AND, for said consideration, said party of the first part does hereby grant, demise, lease and let the above described lands for the purposes stated in said lease and does further covenant _remainderman_ and agree that said lease shall be held to cover all of the right, title and interest of said party of the first part in and to said lands with the same force and effect as if party of the first part had joined in the execution thereof.

IT IS FURTHER agreed that all delay rentals due or to become due under the terms of said oil and gas mining lease shall be paid to _____ _____ or deposited to their credit in the depository bank, as provided for in said lease.

THIS AGREEMENT shall bind the parties hereto, their heirs, successors and assigns, and first party does hereby waive and relinquish all dower and homestead rights existing under and by virtue of the laws of the State in which the land is situated.

WITNESS the execution hereof this _____ day of _____, 19___.

[_signatures and acknowledgments_]

NOTES

1. Ratification forms, usually containing present words of grant, are used routinely as curative devices in the oil and gas industry. Thus, a cotenant, who has not executed an oil and gas lease or the Owner of a nonparticipating royalty whose interest would not otherwise be bound by the exercise of the pooling power in the lease, may be asked to sign such a form. Ratification agreements may be used solely to obtain a person's assent to a lease or incorporated within a delay-rental or production division order.

2. The complete form may be obtained from Burkhart Printing and Stationery Co., 4317 Sheridan Road, Tulsa, Oklahoma 74145.

- Rentals go to L/T (income)
- Bonus + royalty → to R (corpus), but are invested during the life tenant's life and L/T receives income
- Exceptions: Open mine & uniform principal and income act

where property is being developed for minerals or is under lease for min. dev-nt when life estate is created, then all benefits → to L/T

Oil and Gas Top Leasing Clauses

[The following clauses are taken from a top lease form.]

(handwritten margin note: avoid rap by granting a contingent interest that will vest or be destroyed within the rap period)

2. This lease is subject to an existing oil and gas lease of record in the above specified County in Book ___ at Page ___ and shall become effective upon the expiration of such lease (such date herein called "Effective Date" and all references herein to "anniversary date" shall be considered a reference to an anniversary of the Effective Date); provided that if such existing oil and gas lease has not expired prior to _1_ years after its primary term, this lease shall automatically terminate. This lease is also subject to an unrecorded Supplemental Agreement between the parties hereto dated as of the date first above written which affects the provisions of this lease. Subject to the other provisions herein contained, this lease shall be for a primary term of ten years from the Effective Date and for as long thereafter as oil or gas is produced from the above described land or from land pooled with all or any part thereof.

* * *

15. In the event that Lessor, during the primary term of this lease, receives a bona fide offer which Lessor is willing to accept from any party offering to purchase from Lessor a lease covering any or all of the substances covered by this lease and covering all or a portion of the land described herein, with the lease becoming effective upon expiration of this lease. Lessor hereby agrees to notify Lessee in writing of said offer immediately, including in the notice the name and address of the offeror, the price offered and all other pertinent terms and conditions of the offer. Lessee, for a period of fifteen days after the receipt of the notice, shall have the prior and preferred right and option to purchase the lease or part thereof or interest therein, covered by the offer at the price and according to the terms and conditions specified in the offer. All offers made up to and including the last day of the primary term of this lease shall be subject to the terms and conditions of this Section. Should Lessee elect to purchase the lease pursuant to the terms hereof, it shall so notify Lessor in writing by mail or telegram prior to expiration of said 15-day period. Lessee shall promptly thereafter furnish to Lessor the new lease for execution on behalf of Lessor(s) along with Lessee's sight draft payable to Lessor in payment of the specified amount as consideration for the new lease, such draft being subject only to approval of title according to the terms thereof. Upon receipt thereof, Lessor(s) shall promptly execute said lease and return same along with the endorsed draft to Lessee's representative or through Lessor(s) bank of record for payment.

(handwritten: Top lease)

NOTES

1.   This form illustrates a common drafting technique utilized to avoid the perpetuities problem posed by *Peveto v. Starkey*, 645 S.W.2d 770 (Tex. 1982), discussed at page 701 of the casebook. However, bear in mind that a typical drafting technique or form is "good" only if it expresses the intentions and serves the purposes of the parties.

2.   Clause 2, above, provides for automatic termination if the bottom lease has not expired within "__ years" of the primary term of the existing ("bottom") lease. How many years should be inserted so that the lease will be sure to vest, if at all, within the period of the rule against perpetuities?

3.   A different technique for avoiding the perpetuities problem is to include language such as the following:

> Lessor agrees not to execute any instrument extending or renewing the present existing lease. This lease is granted on Lessor's reversionary interest in said premises and is hereby vested in interest, but is subject to an existing Oil and Gas lease by _____ , as Lessor, and _____ , as Lessee dated _____ , recorded in Book _____ Page _____ . The interest covered herein shall vest in possession upon the termination of said lease.

[handwritten margin note: avoid rap by granting an already vested interest (Oklahoma)]

Under this language the lease immediately vests a legal interest in the lessee with the right to possession postponed until the termination of the bottom lease. Does this avoid the rule against perpetuities?

[handwritten: Top lease]

Chapter 5

CONTRACTS AND TRANSFERS
BY THE LESSEE

MASTER LAND SERVICES CONTRACT

This Master Land Services Contract (the "Contract") is made and entered into effective this day of _____, 2000, between _____, whose address is _____, ("Company"), and _____, whose address is _____, ("Contractor").

In consideration of the mutual covenants and agreements, and subject to the terms and conditions contained in this Contract, Company and Contractor agree as follows:

ARTICLE I.   SERVICES PROVIDED BY CONTRACTOR

A.   Contractor shall provide on a non-exclusive basis such land related services as Company may request from time to time and Contractor agrees to perform such services. Those services shall generally relate to services and duties that are customarily a part of the oil and gas or mineral land function.

B.   The specific services to be provided in connection with any particular project shall be specified in a written Work Order in substantially the form of the attached Exhibit "A" (the "Work Order"). In the event of a conflict between this Contract and any term of the Work Order, the specific terms of the Work Order shall control with respect to the services relating to the relevant project. In all other respects, and in the absence of a Work Order, the terms and provisions of this Contract shall control the relationship between Company and Contractor

C.   All work and services provided by Contractor pursuant to this Contract shall be performed according to the specifications of Company, in a good and workman-like manner, with diligence and in accordance with good industry practices and procedures. Company shall exercise no control over Contractor's (i) employees, servants, agents representatives, or subcontractors, (ii) the employees, servants, agents or representatives of its subcontractors, or (iii) the methods or means employed by Contractor or its subcontractors in the performance of such work or services, Company being solely interested in the attainment of the desired results.

D.   Neither party may assign, or transfer this Contract, or any part thereof, without the advance written consent of the other. Any permitted assignee, transferee, delegatee or sub-contractor that performs any part of the services or other matters contracted for herein shall be bound by all of the terms and covenants of this Contract. Notwithstanding the foregoing, Company expressly agrees that Contractor (__) may, (__) may not, utilize or employ sub-brokers in performance of such services under this Contract as Contractor sees fit, which sub-brokers shall for all purposes hereunder be deemed to be subcontractors or employees, as the case may be, of Contractor. Company shall never have any duty or liability to such sub-contractors, including without limitation the obligation to pay to a subcontractor any fees, charges, per diem or expenses incurred in performance of this Contract. Contractor shall at all times be primarily liable to its subcontractors and agrees to defend, indemnify and hold harmless Company in connection herewith. Contractor agrees that it shall at all times be responsible for the performance of this Contract and for the performance of its subcontractors and delegatees.

1

ARTICLE II. RELATIONSHIP OF COMPANY AND CONTRACTOR

A.   This Contract does not create an employer-employee relationship between Company and Contractor. Contractor shall at all times act as an independent contractor in furnishing all services under this Contract.

B.   Contractor, its employees, servants, agents, representatives or subcontractors shall not be entitled to any pension, health insurance, profit sharing or other benefits that Company provides for its employees.

C.   In the event that a services provided by Contractor include the acquisition of oil, gas or mineral leases, minerals, royalties, rights-of-way, seismic permits, options to acquire any of the foregoing, or interests in other real or personal property for the account of Company, Contractor shall act as agent on behalf of Company within the authority and for the purposes specified in the relevant Work Order, but shall have no authority to bind Company in any other manner or for any other purpose, or to enter into any contract or agreement on behalf of Company. Notwithstanding the foregoing, Company shall approve in advance the form of all oil and gas leases, seismic permits, options, and similar agreements to acquire real property interests.

D.   Company shall not be required to pay or withhold from any sums due to Contractor under this Contract any payroll taxes, self-employment taxes, contributions for unemployment insurance, old age and survivor's insurance or annuities, or worker's compensation insurance which are based in whole or in part upon wages, salaries or other compensation paid to Contractor or its employees. Contractor shall be solely liable for the payment of such sums, if any, which may be due in connection with work performed pursuant to this Contract and shall defend, indemnify and hold harmless Company therefrom. Company agrees each year to timely furnish to Contractor a completed Internal Revenue Service Form 1099.

E.   Except as provided in Article IV.C. below, nothing herein contained shall be deemed to prevent either party from engaging in other activities for profit, either in the oil and gas business or otherwise, or, separately or collectively with one or more of the other parties in the future. Except as expressly prohibited in this Contract, the parties recognize Contractor's right to compete and/or to work for others.

ARTICLE III. TERM AND TERMINATION

A.   This Contract shall continue in full force and effect until terminated as herein provided.

B.   Either party may cancel this Contract without cause at any time by giving the other party thirty (30) days written notice.

C.   Any Work Order, and additional or further services provided in connection therewith, may be canceled by Company without cause at any time upon forty eight (48) hours advance notice, which notice shall be promptly confirmed in writing, or by Contractor in the same manner upon ten (10) days advance notice.

D.   Either party may immediately terminate this Contract or cancel any Work Order for good cause, which shall include (i) material breach of the terms hereof, (ii) conduct by one party exposing the

2

other to potential liability to a third party for tort or contract damages, or (iii) occurrence of either an event or events reasonably beyond the control of the terminating party or the discovery of information not reasonably known at the time of this Contract or commencement of any Work Order, either of which renders continuation commercially unreasonable.

E.   Termination of this Contract or cancellation of any Work Order shall not extinguish or diminish those rights and obligations of either Company or Contractor that may have accrued prior thereto.

ARTICLE IV. CONFIDENTIALITY, NON-DISCLOSURE AND CONFLICT OF INTEREST

A.   Unless otherwise designated by Company, all work-related information, title information, areas of interest, maps, letters, memoranda, and other information provided by Company, and all other materials, plans, and negotiations with third parties concerning the services requested of Contractor under any Work Order are proprietary to Company and shall be held strictly confidential by Contractor, its employees and permitted subcontractors during the period that such Work Order is effective and for twelve (12) months thereafter. Contractor shall take all reasonable steps to identify all such confidential information to its employees and permitted subcontractors, and to ensure that those parties observe the provisions of this paragraph. All maps, reports and other work product produced by Contractor in the performance of this Contract shall be the exclusive property of Company, and shall be delivered to Company at its request within a reasonable time upon completion of services pursuant to the applicable Work Order.

B.   During the period that any Work Order is in effect, and for twelve months (12) thereafter, Contractor shall not negotiate for nor purchase oil, gas or mineral leases, royalties, fee or mineral interests, options for any of the foregoing, or seismic permits, nor perform for third parties any services which are the subject matter of this Contract, in the geographic area covered by the Work Order without Company's written consent.

C.   Contractor and Company agree that no employee of Company has a direct or indirect financial interest in Contractor's business. Company, its employees, directors or officers, may not request and shall not receive from Contractor any commissions, gifts or compensation of any type or value above that normally encountered in usual and customary business practices and exceeding either (i) those permitted under Company policy or (ii) what is permitted by applicable law.

ARTICLE V. MISCELLANEOUS

A.   All funds advanced by Company to Contractor for use on Company's behalf in connection with this Contract (the "Trust funds") shall be held by Contractor as Trustee for the benefit of Company and shall be disbursed by Contractor only in the manner and amounts approved by Company. All Trust funds shall be deposited in a federally insured bank or savings account separate and apart from Contractor's own funds, which account shall clearly be identified on the bank's records as a trust account. Company shall have the right, at any time, to withdraw or demand repayment of all or any part of the Trust funds that have not been previously authorized for disbursement. Upon such demand, Contractor shall immediately pay to Company all of said Trust funds. All earned interest attributable to the Trust funds, if any, shall belong to Company. In the event of Contractor's death or incapacity, all remaining Trust funds shall be returned to Company immediately upon Company's request, and the bank or savings institution

shall be authorized to pay such funds directly to Company upon presentation of an original counterpart of this Contract and evidence of the correct amount of such funds. Upon either

3

authorized disbursement of all Trust funds, or return to Company of all remaining Trust funds on hand, the trust established by this paragraph shall terminate. Contractor shall account to Company in writing on a monthly basis for all Trust funds. The Trust funds shall never be a part of Contractor's estate.

B. Company shall have the right at any time within two (2) years after making any payment hereunder to audit any and all records, books and invoices related thereto. This right survives the termination of this Agreement. Company's failure to timely exercise its audit rights shall in no event constitute a waiver of any of Company's rights under this Contract, or otherwise.

C. Contractor agrees to pay all claims for labor, material, services and supplies necessary to accomplish the work or service to be performed by Contractor, and Contractor agrees to allow no lien or charge to be fixed upon any lease or other property of Company.

D. Unless otherwise agreed, Contractor shall invoice Company no less often than monthly, nor more frequently than biweekly for fees and expenses incurred in accordance with the terms of this Contract. Company shall pay contractor's invoices within twenty (20) days of receipt of invoice by Company. Contractor's invoices which are not paid timely as provided herein shall bear interest monthly at the rate of 1 ½%, or the highest rate permitted by law, whichever is lower, until paid.

E. Contractor shall be solely responsible for all its own insurance and shall at all times maintain such types and amounts of insurance, including without limitation, automobile, general liability and worker's compensation insurance, as may be reasonably required by Company. Contractor shall furnish to Company proof of required insurance upon request.

F. Contractor and Company each agree to defend, indemnify and hold harmless the other from any claims, losses, damages, attorneys fees, court costs, or reasonable expenses of litigation, arising out of the indemnifying party's performance or non-performance of services, duties or obligations in connection with this contract. This indemnity provision is limited to the extent necessary to comply with any applicable state or federal law, and this provision is deemed to be amended to comply therewith. The limit of the indemnity provided herein shall not exceed the maximum lawful amount permitted by the laws of the applicable jurisdiction.

G. This Contract shall be governed by the laws of the State of _____, without reference to conflict of law rules or principles. All services provided pursuant to this Contract shall be performed in accordance with applicable laws, rules and regulations.

H. This Contract, and any related Work Order, constitutes the entire agreement of the parties. If any part of this Contract shall be unenforceable for any reason, the remaining parts of the Contract shall nevertheless be binding upon and inure to the benefit of the parties.

I. The failure of either Company or Contractor to exercise any of its rights under this Contract shall not constitute a waiver of such rights with respect to any future occurrence or breach of this Contract.

J. All notices required or permitted in connection with this Contract shall be delivered in the manner provided herein to the parties' address above. Notices required to be in writing may be delivered by U.S. first class mail, properly addressed and with all postage paid, by courier, or by

4

facsimile transmission. Unless otherwise specified herein, all notices shall be effective when received. Any party may change their address for notices in writing to the other party.

K.   Contractor agrees that all of its services provided hereunder for the account of Company shall be conducted ethically in accordance with the Standards of Practice published by the American Association of Professional Landmen.

ARTICLE VI. <u>EXECUTION</u>

This Contract may be executed in any number of counterparts or duplicate originals, but shall not be binding upon any party hereto unless and until executed and accepted by all parties. When properly executed and accepted, this Contract shall be binding upon and inure to the benefit of Contractor and Company, their respective heirs, successors and assigns.

COMPANY   **CONTRACTOR**

By:_____   By:_____

   (Printed name)   (Printed name)

   (Capacity)   (Capacity)

Telephone: Telephone:
Fax: Fax:

5

230

WORK ORDER

Master Land Services Contract No.: _____   Date: _____

COMPANY: _____

CONTRACTOR: _____

Geographic Area where work is to be performed (if applicable):

    State: _____

    County: _____

    (__) Plat Attached, and/or (__) Description as follows:

GENERAL DESCRIPTION OF SERVICES TO BE PERFORMED, SPECIAL INSTRUCTIONS and LIMITATIONS on AUTHORITY:

FEES CHARGEABLE BY CONTRACTOR:

6

NOTES

1.   This form was furnished by the American Association of Professional Landmen. The A.A.P.L. website is: http://www.landman.org/ . The form is intended for use when an oil company wishes to engage land services from an independent landman, who will provide services as an independent contractor.

2.   Oil companies engage the services of independent landmen for a variety of reasons. In periods of boom, an oil company may need additional help. But even in periods of bust, an oil company may prefer to hire independent landmen to check title and to secure leases on behalf of the company. The land services company may take the leases in its name and then assign them as a group to the oil company client when the acquisition process is complete. This helps maintain confidentiality regarding the actual party in interest. In addition, the oil company may find that outsourcing these types of tasks is more cost effective.

2.   Independent landmen are usually compensated for their work—perhaps on a day-rate or hourly basis, plus travel expenses. In addition, when the lease acreage is assigned to the oil company, the land services company or senior landmen working on the project may retain an overriding royalty.

3.   Landmen must be trained to perform simple title examinations to determine mineral ownership within the "prospect" area and further trained in the art of acquiring leases from mineral owners. They also perform routine "curative" work to address any minor deficiencies in the title chain. While many landmen have law degrees and most have college degrees, some landmen learn this trade with on-the-job training.

ROCKY MOUNTAIN MINERAL LAW FOUNDATION

Form 7

Confidentiality and Nondisclosure Agreement

1996

CONFIDENTIALITY AND NONDISCLOSURE AGREEMENT

This Confidentiality and Nondisclosure Agreement (this "Agreement"), dated as of _____, _____ , is between _____ ("Provider"), and _____ ("Recipient").

Recipient desires to obtain certain Confidential Information (as defined below) relating to Provider and its business for the limited purposes described in the Schedule hereto (the "Purposes"). Provider has agreed to make the Confidential Information available to Recipient upon the terms and conditions set forth herein.

In consideration of the mutual promises set forth herein, and other good and valuable consideration, the receipt and sufficiency of which are hereby acknowledged, Provider and Recipient agree as follows:

1. **Confidential Information.** Provider will disclose and make available to Recipient certain Confidential Information for Recipient's use in connection with the Purposes. The term "Confidential Information" as used in this Agreement shall mean all information, data, knowledge, and know-how (in whatever form and however communicated) relating, directly or indirectly, to Provider (or to its affiliates or to its or their businesses, operations, properties, products, markets, or financial positions) that is delivered or disclosed by Provider or any of its officers, directors, partners, members, employees, agents, affiliates, or shareholders to Recipient in writing, electronically, verbally, or through visual means, or which Recipient learns or obtains aurally, through observation or through analyses, interpretations, compilations, studies, or evaluations of such information, data, knowledge, or know-how. The term "Confidential Information" shall not include information, data, knowledge, and know-how, as shown by written records, that (a) is in Recipient's possession prior to disclosure to Recipient, (b) is in the public domain prior to disclosure to Recipient, or (c) lawfully enters the public domain through no violation of this Agreement after disclosure to Recipient; however, such term shall include all analyses, interpretations, compilations, studies, and evaluations of such information, data, knowledge, and know-how generated or prepared by or on behalf of Provider or Recipient. The term "document," as used in this Agreement, shall include, without limitation, any writing, instrument, agreement, letter, memorandum, chart, graph, blueprint, photograph, financial statement, or data, telex, facsimile, cable, tape, disk, or other electronic, digital, magnetic, laser, or other recording or image in whatever form or medium.

2. **Use of Confidential Information.** Recipient agrees to use the Confidential Information solely for the Purposes and for no other purpose.

3. **Disclosure of Confidential Information.** Recipient agrees to keep the Confidential Information confidential and not to disclose the Confidential Information to any person or entity other than (a) such of Recipient's officers, directors, partners, members, employees, attorneys, accountants, or financial advisors who have a bona fide need to have access to such Confidential Information in order for Recipient to carry out the Purposes and who have agreed in writing supplied to, and enforceable by, Provider to be likewise bound by the provisions of this Agreement, and (b) such other persons as Provider hereafter agrees in writing may receive such Confidential Information (which agreement may be withheld for any reason or for no reason). Recipient shall be responsible and liable for any use or disclosure of the Confidential Information by such parties in violation of this Agreement. Nothing contained herein shall be deemed to prevent disclosure of any of the Confidential Information if, in the written opinion of Recipient's legal counsel, such disclosure is legally required to be made in a judicial, administrative, or governmental proceeding pursuant to a valid subpoena or other applicable order; provided, however, Recipient shall give Provider at least ten days prior written notice (unless less time is permitted by the applicable proceeding) before disclosing any of the Confidential Information in any such proceeding and, in making such disclosure, Recipient shall disclose only that portion thereof required to be disclosed and shall take all reasonable efforts to preserve the confidentiality thereof, including obtaining protective orders and supporting Provider in intervention.

-1-

4. **Representations and Warranties.** Provider represents and warrants to Recipient that it has full right, power, and authority to disclose or make available the Confidential Information to Recipient as provided for in this Agreement without the violation of any contractual, legal, or other obligation to any entity or person. Provider specifically disclaims and makes no representation or warranty, expressed or implied, as to the accuracy, completeness, usefulness, or reliability of the Confidential Information or any portion thereof, and Recipient shall use the Confidential Information at its own risk.

5. **Copies of Documents.** Recipient agrees not to make or reproduce any copies of any document (or any portion thereof) which is part of the Confidential Information, except to deliver copies of such documents to the persons described in paragraph 3 of this Agreement.

6. **Return of Documents.** Recipient agrees to return to Provider, within ____ business days after a written request by Provider, all documents (including all copies thereof) which have been delivered or disclosed to Recipient, or which Recipient has obtained, as part of the Confidential Information, and to destroy, and certify to Provider in writing that Recipient has destroyed, all other related documents, including, without limitation, all documents prepared by Recipient or others utilizing or relating to any portion of the Confidential Information.

7. **Legal Remedies.** Recipient agrees that if this Agreement is breached, or if a breach hereof is threatened, the remedy at law may be inadequate, and therefore, without limiting any other remedy available at law or in equity, an injunction, restraining order, specific performance, and other forms of equitable relief or money damages or any combination thereof shall be available to Provider. The successful party in any action or proceeding brought to enforce this Agreement shall be entitled to recover the costs, expenses, and fees incurred in any such action or proceeding, including, without limitation, attorneys' fees and expenses.

8. **Nondisclosure of this Agreement.** Neither Recipient nor Provider shall, directly or indirectly, disclose to any third party the terms and conditions of this Agreement or the transactions that are the subject of this Agreement, without the other party's prior written consent. Nothing contained herein shall be deemed to prevent disclosure of any of the terms and conditions of this Agreement or the transactions that are the subject of this Agreement (a) to the extent necessary to enforce this Agreement, or (b) if, in the written opinion of the party's legal counsel, such disclosure is legally required to be made in a judicial, administrative, or governmental proceeding pursuant to a valid subpoena or other applicable order; provided, however, such party shall give the other party at least ten days prior written notice (unless less time is permitted by the applicable proceeding) before disclosing any of the terms and conditions of this Agreement or the transactions that are the subject of this Agreement in any such proceeding and, in making such disclosure, the party shall disclose only that portion thereof required to be disclosed and shall take all reasonable efforts to preserve the confidentiality thereof, including obtaining protective orders and supporting the other party in intervention.

9. **No Unauthorized Contact.** Unless otherwise authorized, Recipient will not contact any of Provider's officers, directors, partners, members, employees, agents, affiliates, or shareholders for the purpose of obtaining information in connection with the Purposes.

10. **Severability.** If any provision of this Agreement is invalid or unenforceable in any jurisdiction, such provision shall be fully severable from this Agreement and the other provisions hereof shall remain in full force and effect in such jurisdiction and the remaining provisions hereof shall be liberally construed to carry out the provisions and intent hereof. The invalidity or unenforceability of any provision of this Agreement in any jurisdiction shall not affect the validity or enforceability of such provision in any other jurisdiction, nor shall the invalidity or unenforceability of any provision of this Agreement with respect to any person or entity affect the validity or enforceability of such provision with respect to any other person or entity.

-2-

235

11. Governing Law. THIS AGREEMENT SHALL BE GOVERNED BY AND CONSTRUED IN ACCORDANCE WITH THE LAWS OF THE STATE OF _____ WITHOUT GIVING EFFECT TO THE CONFLICT OF LAWS PROVISIONS THEREOF. THE PARTIES CONSENT TO THE EXCLUSIVE JURISDICTION AND VENUE IN ANY COURT OF COMPETENT JURISDICTION IN SUCH STATE AND IN THE UNITED STATES DISTRICT COURT FOR SUCH STATE, AND TO SERVICE OF PROCESS UNDER THE STATUTES OF SUCH STATE.

12. Additional Provisions. The additional provisions, if any, set forth on the Schedule hereto are hereby incorporated into this Agreement and form a part hereof.

13. Notices. All notices and other communications required under this Agreement to be in writing shall be addressed to the parties at the addresses or facsimile numbers set forth below each party's signature, or to such other addresses or facsimile numbers of which a party may from time to time notify the other party pursuant hereto. Such notices and communications shall be deemed given upon the earlier of (a) actual receipt, (b) five business days after being mailed by registered or certified mail, return receipt requested with postage prepaid, (c) when sent by facsimile with receipt confirmed by telephone, or (d) one business day after being deposited with a recognized overnight courier service with charges prepaid.

14. Assignment and Transfer. Recipient may not assign, pledge, or otherwise transfer its rights or delegate its duties or obligations under this Agreement without the prior written consent of Provider. Provider may assign or otherwise transfer its rights and delegate its duties or obligations under this Agreement without the consent of Recipient in connection with a sale or other transfer of all or substantially all of its assets, or the sale or other transfer of its assets relating to the Confidential Information. In addition, Provider may grant a security interest in this Agreement without the consent of Recipient in connection with granting liens on or security interests in all or substantially all of its assets or the assets relating to the Confidential Information, and this Agreement may be assigned upon foreclosure of such a security interest or transfer in lieu thereof without the consent of Recipient.

15. Entire Agreement. This Agreement constitutes the entire understanding between the parties with respect to the subject matter thereof and supersedes all negotiations, prior discussions, or prior agreements and understandings relating to such subject matter. Neither this Agreement nor the parties' performance hereunder shall be deemed to create any special relationship or obligations between the parties other than those expressly set forth herein, and no implied covenants shall apply to this Agreement other than those of good faith and fair dealing. All duties, obligations, rights, powers, and remedies provided for herein are cumulative, and not exclusive, of any and all duties, obligations, rights, powers, and remedies existing at law or in equity, and Provider shall, in addition to the duties, obligations, rights, powers, and remedies herein conferred, be entitled to avail itself of all such other duties, obligations, rights, powers, and remedies as may now or hereafter exist, including, without limitation, the Uniform Trade Secrets Act and similar statutes and rules of law pertaining to trade secrets and confidential and proprietary information. Neither Provider nor Recipient shall have any obligation or duty to pursue any further agreement or understanding, or to proceed with respect to any additional transaction relating to the Purposes, until a definitive agreement relating thereto has been duly authorized, executed, and delivered by the parties.

16. Miscellaneous. This Agreement may not be altered or amended, nor may any rights hereunder be waived, except by an instrument in writing and executed by the party or parties to be charged with such amendment or waiver. No waiver of any term, provision, or condition of this Agreement shall be deemed to be, or construed as, a further or continuing waiver of any such term, provision, or condition, or as a waiver of any other term, provision, or condition hereof. To the extent the parties have deemed necessary, they have consulted with their legal, tax, financial, and accounting advisors with respect to the subject matter of this Agreement. Pronouns in masculine, feminine, and neuter gender shall be construed to include any other gender. Words in the

-3-

1 singular form shall be construed to include the plural, and words in the plural form shall be construed to include
2 the singular, unless the context otherwise requires. The headings used in this Agreement are inserted for
3 convenience only and shall be disregarded in construing this Agreement. This Agreement shall be binding upon
4 the parties hereto and, except as otherwise prohibited, their respective successors and assigns. Except for
5 Recipient and Provider, and their permitted successors and assigns, nothing in this Agreement, express or implied,
6 is intended to confer upon any other entity or person any benefits, rights, or remedies. This Agreement may be
7 executed in counterparts and shall become operative when each party has executed and delivered at least one
8 counterpart. This Agreement may be delivered by facsimile or similar transmission, and a facsimile or similar
9 transmission evidencing execution shall be effective as a valid and binding agreement between the parties for all
10 purposes.

11

12   This Agreement has been executed on the dates set forth below to be effective as of the date first set forth
13 above.

14
15
16 **PROVIDER:**   **RECIPIENT:**
17
18 _____   _____
19
20
21 By: _____   By: _____
22
23 Name: _____   Name: _____
24
25 Title: _____   Title: _____
26
27 Address: _____   Address: _____
28
29 _____   _____
30
31 _____   _____
32
33 _____   _____
34
35 Telephone: _____   Telephone: _____
36
37 Facsimile: _____   Facsimile: _____
38
39 Date: _____   Date: _____
40
41
42
43
44
45
46
47
48
49
50

-4-

1	**SCHEDULE**
2	
3	
4	
5	**PURPOSES:**
6	
7	
8	
9	
10	
11	
12	
13	
14	
15	
16	
17	
18	
19	
20	
21	**ADDITIONAL PROVISIONS:**
22	
23	
24	
25	
26	
27	
28	
29	
30	
31	
32	
33	
34	
35	
36	
37	
38	
39	
40	
41	
42	
43	
44	
45	
46	
47	
48	
49	
50	

-5-

NOTES

1.   When oil companies do business with each other regarding prospects, one of the first agreements customarily signed is a confidentiality agreement. Confidentiality agreements have two somewhat conflicting purposes. First, a confidentiality agreement protects the disclosing party from having its proprietary information disseminated to competitors without its consent. Second, a confidentiality agreement protects the receiving party from liability at law or equity for improper use of the proprietary information. In general, improper use means any use that is beyond the scope of use reasonably expected by the disclosing party.

2.   The prior form has been developed by the Rocky Mountain Mineral Law Foundation for use by in the mining and oil and gas sectors. The Foundation is administered by a board of trustees composed of representatives of state bar associations, mining and landsmen groups, and universities from across the western United States and Canada. In addition to sponsoring annual institutes and special institutes addressing oil and gas, mining, water, environmental, and public lands topics, the Foundation publishes a variety of documents and books, including the American Law of Mining and the Law of Federal Oil and Gas Leases, that are of special aid to practitioners and academics. Copies of the model form gas balancing agreement, and other Foundation publications, can be obtained from the Rocky Mountain Mineral Law Foundation, 7039 East 18th Avenue, Denver, Colorado 80220, (303) 321-8100, http://www.rmmlf.org.

ASSIGNMENT OF OIL AND GAS LEASES

STATE OF
COUNTY OF

    Reference is made to the following oil and gas leases:

(1) Oil   and   Gas   Lease   from _____   to
    _____ , dated _____ and recorded in
    Volume _____, Page ___, Deed Records of _____ County, Texas, BUT
    ONLY insofar as this lease covers the following lands and ONLY as to the
    depths from _____ to _____:
        (Description)
(2) * * *

(3) * * *

    * * *

These leases, insofar as they cover the above-described lands and depths, will be
referred to as the "Subject Leases".
    For the sum of One Hundred Dollars ($100.00) and other valuable and
adequate   consideration,   the   receipt   of   which   is   hereby   acknowledged,
_____(which will be referred to as "Assignor") hereby assigns, sells, and
conveys to _____" (address) _____(which will be referred to as
"Assignee"), 100% of the working interest in the Subject Leases, and all rights
thereunder, together with a like interest in all leasehold equipment and personal
property located on the above-described lands and used in connection with the
Subject Leases.
    ASSIGNOR RESERVES, however, and there is not hereby conveyed, an
overriding royalty interest equal to 25% of 8/8 of the oil, gas and, if applicable, other
minerals produced and saved from the Subject Leases, to be borne in its entirety by
the interest herein conveyed. Said overriding royalty interest shall bear and absorb the
burden of all royalty interests, overriding royalty interests, production payments and
any other burdens on production which currently exist of record against the Subject
Leases. The reserved overriding royalty interest shall be free of all costs and expenses
of exploration, development and operation of the Subject Leases and of any and all
other costs, except it proportionate share of taxes. Said overriding royalty interest
shall apply to any renewals or extensions of the Subject Leases which may be taken
by Assignees or its successors or assigns within one year from termination of the
relevant Subject Lease. If any of the Subject Leases cover less than the full interest in
the lands described therein and covered by this Assignment, then said overriding
royalty interest shall be proportionately reduced as to the relevant Subject Lease.
Assignee is hereby given the right and power, without further approval from

Assignor, to pool said overriding royalty interest in the same manner and to the same extent as is provided in the relevant Subject Lease for the pooling of its Lessor's interest.

ASSIGNOR FURTHER RESERVES all lands, depths and interests not herein specifically assigned, together with such rights of ingress and egress over, on and through the lands covered by the Subject Leases as may be necessary or useful in the exploration, development and operation of the lands, depths, and interest so reserved.

This Assignment is made subject to the terms of the following instruments insofar as the same are valid, subsisting and binding on Assignor as of this date:

(a) _____

(b)_____

(c) _____

* * *

Reference herein to any instrument shall not be interpreted as a ratification or confirmation thereof.

Assignor specifically warrants and agrees to defend the title to the Subject Leases against the claim and demands of all persons claiming the same or any part thereof by, through or under Assignor, but not otherwise. Assignor warrants that all rental and royalty payments that have become due under the terms of the Subject Leases have been paid in a timely manner, that the Subject Leases are free and clear of all liens and encumbrances, and that there are no facts in existence as of this date which might give rise to liens or privileges against the Subject Leases in favor of third parties. ASSIGNOR EXPRESSLY DISCLAIMS AND NEGATES AS TO PERSONAL PROPERTY AND FIXTURES: (a) ANY IMPLIED OR EXPRESS WARRANTY OF' MERCHANTABILITY; (b) ANY IMPLIED OR EXPRESS WARRANTY OF FITNESS FOR A PARTICULAR PURPOSE; AND (c) ANY IMPLIED OR EXPRESS WARRANTY OF CONFORMITY TO MODELS OR SAMPLES OF MATERIALS.

This Assignment shall be binding upon and shall inure to the benefit of Assignor and Assignee and their respective heirs, successors and assigns.

This Assignment may be executed in any number of counterparts with each having the force and effect of an original.

[date, signatures, and acknowledgments]

NOTES

1.   Transfers of oil and gas interests rarely contain general warranties. In some instances, warranties are specifically negated by statements that the transfer is made without express or implied warranty of any kind. Alternatively, a transfer or assignment may contain a limited warranty in which the transferor warrants against claims arising "by, through or under" the transferor, but not otherwise. The above form contains a limited warranty of title and a warranty that all delay rentals and shut-in royalties are current and that the assigned leases are free of any liens or encumbrances.

2.   The interests and instruments to which the assignment is subject are of special importance to an assignee. These might include prior transfers of overriding royalties, farmout agreements, and gas purchase contracts dedicating well production.

PURCHASE AND SALE AGREEMENT
(Of Oil and Gas Properties and Related Assets)

Section

PURCHASE AND SALE AGREEMENT
(of Oil and Gas Properties and Related Assets)

_____, as "Seller," and _____, as "Buyer," are entering into this Purchase and Sale Agreement (the "Agreement"), as evidence of Seller's agreement to sell, and Buyer's agreement to buy the properties described in and subject to this Agreement.

In consideration of the mutual covenants, conditions, and considerations provided below, Buyer and Seller agree as follows:

1.   The Properties. Seller shall assign and convey to Buyer all of Seller's interest in and to the following, all of which are collectively referred to in this Agreement as (the "Properties"):

a.   All of Seller's rights, title and interests (of whatever kind or character, whether legal or equitable, and whether vested or contingent) in and to the oil, gas and other minerals in and under and that may be produced from the lands described in Exhibit "A" including, without limitation, interests in oil, gas and/or mineral leases covering any part of the lands, overriding royalty interests, production payments, and net profits interests in any part of the lands or leases, fee royalty interests, fee mineral interests, and other interests in oil, gas and other minerals in any part of the lands, whether the lands are described in any of the descriptions set out in Exhibit "A" or by reference to another instrument for description, even though the Seller's interests may be incorrectly described in, or omitted from, Exhibit "A";

b.   All right, title, and interests of Seller in all presently existing and valid oil, gas and/or mineral unitization, pooling, and/or communitization agreements, declarations, and/or orders and the properties covered or included in the units (including, without limitation, units formed under orders, rules, regulations, or other official acts of any federal, state or other authority having jurisdiction, voluntary unitization agreements, designations, and/or declarations, and any "working interest units" (created under operating agreements or otherwise) which relate to any of the Properties described in subparagraph a. above;

c.   All rights, title and interests of Seller in all presently existing and valid production sales (and sales related) contracts, operating agreements, and other agreements and contracts which relate to any of the Properties described in subparagraphs a. and b. above, or which relate to the exploration, development, operation, or maintenance of the Properties or the treatment, storage, transportation, or marketing of production from or allocated to the Properties; and,

d.   All rights, title and interests of Seller in and to all materials, supplies, machinery, equipment, improvements, and other personal property and fixtures (including, but not limited to the Properties, all wells, wellhead equipment, pumping units, flow lines, tanks, buildings, injection facilities, salt water disposal facilities, compression facilities, gathering systems, and other equipment), all easements, rights-of-way, surface leases, and other surface rights, all permits and licenses, and all other appurtenances, used or held for use in connection with or related to the exploration, development, operation, or maintenance of any of the Properties described in subparagraphs a. and b. above, or the treatment, storage, transportation, or marketing of production from or allocated to the Properties.

2.   Purchase Price. Buyer shall pay to Seller at Closing, to an account designated by Seller, in cash or immediately available funds, the sum of $____ (the "Purchase Price"), subject to the adjustment provided for below.

1   **3.   Closing.** The sale and purchase of the Properties (the "Closing") shall be on ____ (the
2   "Closing Date") at Seller's offices in ____ , or such other place as Buyer and Seller shall
3   mutually agree. At Closing Seller shall deliver to Buyer executed assignments and instruments
4   of conveyance of the Properties in form similar to those attached as Exhibit "B" and Buyer shall
5   deliver to Seller the Purchase Price provided in Section 2.
6   **4.   Effective Date, Proration of Production and Expenses.** The conveyance by Seller
7   shall be effective as of 7 a.m. local time, where the Properties are located, on ____ (the
8   "Effective Date").   All production from the Properties and all proceeds from the sale of
9   production prior to the Effective Date shall be the property of Seller. Seller shall be responsible
10   for payment of all expenses attributable to the Properties prior to the Effective Date. Buyer shall
11   be responsible for payment of all expenses attributable to the Properties after the Effective Date.
12   An accounting for net proceeds from production less applicable expenses will be made according
13   to a Settlement Agreement in form and substance similar to the Agreement in Exhibit "C."
14   **5.   Taxes.** Seller shall be responsible for all taxes relating to the Properties prior to the
15   Effective Date. Buyer shall be responsible for all taxes (exclusive of federal, state or local
16   income taxes due by Seller) relating to the Property from and after the Effective Date.
17   **6.   Indemnity.** Seller shall indemnify and hold Buyer, its directors, officers, employees, and
18   agents harmless from and against any and all liability, liens, demands, judgments, suits, and
19   claims of any kind or character arising out of, in connection with, or resulting from Seller's
20   ownership of the Properties, for all periods prior to the Effective Date. Seller shall remain
21   responsible for all claims relating to the drilling, operating, production, and sale of hydrocarbons
22   from the Properties and the proper accounting and payment to parties for their interests and any
23   retroactive payments, refunds, or penalties to any party or entity, insofar as any claims relate to
24   periods of time prior to the Effective Date.
25   Buyer shall indemnify and hold Seller harmless from and against any and all liability,
26   liens, demands, judgments, suits, and claims of any kind or character arising out of, in
27   connection with, or resulting from Buyer's ownership of the Properties, for periods from and
28   after the Effective Date. Buyer shall be responsible for all claims relating to the drilling,
29   operating, production, and sale of hydrocarbons from the Properties and the proper accounting
30   and payment to parties for their interests, and any retroactive payments, refunds, or penalties to
31   any party or entity as such claims relate to periods from and after the Effective Date.
32   Buyer and Seller shall have the right to participate in the defense of any suit in which one
33   of them may be a party without relieving the other party of the obligation to defend the suit.
34   **7.   Representations and Warranties of Seller.** Seller represents and warrants to Buyer as
35   follows:
36   **7.1.   Organization.** Seller is a corporation duly organized, validly existing, and in
37   good standing under the laws of the State of ____. Seller is qualified to do business in and is in
38   good standing under the laws of each state in which the Properties are located.
39   **7.2.   Authority and Conflicts.** Seller has full corporate power and authority to carry
40   on its business as presently conducted, to enter into this Agreement, and to perform its
41   obligations under this Agreement. The execution and delivery of this Agreement by Seller does
42   not, and the consummation of the transactions contemplated by this Agreement shall not: (a)
43   violate, conflict with, or require the consent of any person or entity under any provision of
44   Seller's Articles of Incorporation or bylaws or other governing documents; (b) conflict with,

result in a breach of, constitute a default (or an event that with the lapse of time or notice or both would constitute a default) or require any consent, authorization, or approval under any agreement or instrument to which Seller is a party or to which any of the Properties or Seller is bound, except as disclosed in Exhibit "A"; (c) violate any provision of or require any consent, authorization, or approval under any judgment, decree, judicial or administrative order, award, writ, injunction, statute, rule, or regulation applicable to Seller; or, (d) result in the creation of any lien, charge, or encumbrance on any of the Properties.

7.3. **Authorization.** The execution and delivery of this Agreement has been, and the performance of this Agreement and the transactions contemplated by this Agreement shall be at the time required to be performed, duly and validly authorized by all requisite corporate action on the part of Seller.

7.4. **Enforceability.** This Agreement has been duly executed and delivered on behalf of Seller and constitutes the legal and binding obligation of Seller enforceable in accordance with its terms, except as enforceability may be limited by applicable bankruptcy, reorganization, or moratorium statues, equitable principles, or other similar laws affecting the rights of creditors generally ("Equitable Limitations"). At Closing, all documents and instruments required to be executed and delivered by Seller shall be duly executed and delivered and shall constitute legal, valid, enforceable, and binding obligations of Seller, except as enforceability may be limited by Equitable Limitations.

7.5. **Title.**

7.5.1. Seller has Marketable title to the Property. For the purposes of this Agreement, "Marketable Title" means such title that will enable Buyer, as Seller's successor in title, to receive from each of the Properties at least the "Net Revenue Interest" for the wells identified on Exhibit "A" associated with each of the Properties, without reduction, suspension, or termination throughout the productive life of the wells, except for any reduction, suspension, or termination: (a) caused by Buyer, any of its affiliates successors in title or assigns; (b) caused by orders of the appropriate regulatory agency having jurisdiction over a Property that are promulgated after the Effective Date and that concern pooling, unitization, communitization, or spacing matters affecting a Property; (c) caused by any contract described in Exhibit "A" containing a sliding-scale royalty clause or other similar clause with respect to a production burden associated with a particular Property; or, (d) otherwise set out in Exhibit "A." "Marketable Title" also means title that will obligate Buyer, as Seller's successor in title, to bear no greater "Working Interest" than the Working Interest for each of the wells identified on Exhibit "A" as being associated with each of the Properties, without increase throughout the productive life of the wells, except for any increase: (a) caused by Buyer, any of its affiliates, successors in title or assigns; (b) that also results in the Net Revenue Interest associated with the well being proportionately increased; (c) caused by contribution requirements provided for under provisions similar to those contained in Article ____ of the A.A.P.L. Form 610-____ Model Form Operating Agreement; (d) caused by orders of the appropriate regulatory agency having jurisdiction over a Property that are promulgated after the Effective Date and that concern pooling, unitization, communitization, or spacing matters affecting a particular Property; or, (e) otherwise set forth in Exhibit "A." "Marketable Title" means the Properties are free and clear of all encumbrances, liens, claims, easements, rights, agreements, instruments, obligations, burdens, or defects (collectively the "Liens"), except for Permitted Encumbrances.

7.5.2. For the purposes of this Agreement, "Permitted Encumbrances" means: (a) liens for taxes not yet delinquent; (b) lessor's royalties, overriding royalties, reversionary interests, and similar burdens that do not operate to reduce the Net Revenue Interest of Seller in any of the Properties to less than the amount set forth on Exhibit "A"; (c) the consents and rights described in Exhibit "A" insofar as such contracts and agreements do not operate to increase the Working Interest of Seller or decrease the Net Revenue Interest of Seller, as set forth on Exhibit "A," for any of the Properties.

7.5.3. Seller has good and defensible title, subject to the Permitted Encumbrances, to all of the Properties.

7.6. **Contracts.** Exhibit "A" contains a complete list of all contracts, agreements, undertakings (whether written or oral), and instruments that are not described in any other Exhibit to this Agreement that constitute a part of the Properties or by which the Properties are bound or subject.

7.7. **Litigation and Claims.** Except as is set forth on Exhibit "D," no claim, demand, filing, cause of action, administrative proceeding, lawsuit, or other litigation is pending, or to the best knowledge of Seller, threatened, that could now or later adversely affect the ownership or operation of any of the Properties, other than proceedings relating to the industry generally and to which Seller is not a named party. No written or oral notice from any governmental agency or any other person has been received by Seller: (a) claiming any violation or repudiation of all or any part of the Properties or any violation of any law or any environmental, conservation or other ordinance, code, rule or regulation; or, (b) require or calling attention to the need for any work, repairs, construction, alterations, or installations on or in connection with the Properties, with which Seller has not complied.

7.8. **Approvals and Preferential Rights.** Exhibit "E" contains a complete and accurate schedule of all approvals required to be obtained by Seller for the assignment of the Properties to Buyer, and all preferential purchase rights that affect the Properties.

7.9. **Compliance with Law and Permits.** The Properties have been operated in compliance with the provision and requirements of the applicable oil and gas leases, and all laws, orders, regulations, rules, and ordinances issued or promulgated by all governmental authorities having jurisdiction with respect to the Properties. All necessary governmental certificates, consents, permits, licenses, or other authorizations with regard to the ownership or operation of the Properties have been obtained and no violations exist or have been recorded in respect of such licenses, permits or authorizations. None of the documents and materials filed with or furnished to any governmental authority with respect to the Properties contains any untrue statement of a material fact or omits any statement of a material fact necessary to make the statement not misleading.

7.10. **Status of Contracts.** All of the Contracts and other obligations of Seller relating to the Properties are in full force and effect. Seller has no knowledge of any other party being in breach of or default of the Contracts, to the extent any breach or default has an adverse impact on any of the Properties. To Seller's knowledge, no other party has given or threatened to give notice of any default, inquired into any possible default, or taken action to alter, terminate, rescind, or procure a judicial reformation of any Contract. Seller does not anticipate any other party to a Contract will be in breach of, default under, or repudiate any of its obligations of a

Contract, to the extent such breach, default, or repudiation will have an adverse impact on any of the Properties.

7.11. <u>Production Burdens, Taxes, Expenses and Revenues</u>. All rentals, royalties, excess royalty, overriding royalty interests, and other payments due under or with respect to the Properties have been properly and timely paid. All ad valorem, property, production, severance, and other taxes based on or measured by the ownership of the Properties or the production from the Properties have been properly and timely paid. All expenses payable under the terms of the Contracts identified in Exhibit "A" have been properly and timely paid except for expenses currently paid, prior to delinquency, in the ordinary course of business. All proceeds from the sale of production are being properly and timely paid to Seller by the purchasers of production, without suspense.

7.12. <u>Pricing</u>. The prices being received for production do not violate any contract, law or regulation. Where applicable, all of the wells and production from the wells have been properly classified under appropriate governmental regulations.

7.13. <u>Production Balances</u>. Except as described in Schedule 7.13., none of the purchasers under any production sales contracts are entitled to "makeup" or otherwise receive deliveries of oil or gas at any time after the Effective Date without paying, at such time, the full contract price for oil or gas. No person is entitled to receive any portion of the interest of Seller in any oil or gas, or to receive cash or other payments to "balance" any disproportionate allocation of oil or gas under any operating agreement, gas balancing and storage agreement, gas processing or dehydration agreement, or other similar agreements.

7.14. <u>Adverse Changes</u>. Since __(Date)__ the Properties, viewed as a whole, have not experienced any material reduction in the rate of production, other than changes in the ordinary course of operations, changes that result from depletion in the ordinary course of operations, and changes that result from variances in markets for oil and gas production. None of the Properties have suffered any material destruction, damage or loss.

7.15. <u>WELL STATUS</u>. THERE ARE NO WELLS LOCATED ON THE PROPERTIES THAT: (A) SELLER IS CURRENTLY OBLIGATED BY LAW OR CONTRACT TO PLUG AND ABANDON; (B) SELLER WILL NOT BE OBLIGATED BY LAW OR CONTRACT TO PLUG OR ABANDON WITH THE LAPSE OF TIME OR NOTICE OR BOTH BECAUSE THE WELL IS NOT CURRENTLY CAPABLE OF PRODUCING IN COMMERCIAL QUANTITIES; (C) ARE SUBJECT TO EXCEPTIONS TO A REQUIREMENT TO PLUG AND ABANDON ISSUED BY A REGULATORY AUTHORITY HAVING JURISDICTION OVER THE PROPERTIES; OR, (D) TO THE BEST KNOWLEDGE OF SELLER, HAVE BEEN PLUGGED AND ABANDONED BUT HAVE NOT BEEN PLUGGED IN ACCORDANCE WITH ALL APPLICABLE REQUIREMENTS OF EACH REGULATORY AUTHORITY HAVING JURISDICTION OVER THE PROPERTIES.

7.16. <u>Equipment</u>. The equipment constituting a part of the Properties is in good repair, working order, and operating condition, and is adequate for the operation of the Properties.

7.17. <u>Current Commitments</u>. Exhibit "F" contains a true and complete list of: (a) all authorities for expenditure ("AFEs") and other oral or written commitments to drill or rework wells on the Properties or for capital expenditures pursuant to any Contracts, that have been proposed by any person on or after the Effective Date, whether or not accepted by Seller or any other person; and, (b) all AFEs and oral or written commitments to drill or rework wells or for

1 other capital expenditures pursuant to any Contracts, for which all of the activities anticipated in
2 AFEs or commitments have not been completed by the date of this Agreement.
3   **7.18. Accuracy of Representation.** No representation or warranty by Seller in this
4 Agreement or any agreement or document delivered by Seller pursuant to this Agreement
5 contains an untrue statement of a material fact or omits to state a material fact necessary to make
6 the statements contained in any representation or warranty, in light of the circumstances under
7 which it was made, not misleading. There is no fact known to Seller that materially and
8 adversely affects, or may materially and adversely affect the operation, prospects or condition of
9 any portion of the Properties that has not been identified in this Agreement.
10 **8.**   **Representations by Buyer.** Buyer represents to Seller that the following statements are
11 true and correct:
12   **8.1.**   **Organization.** Buyer is a ____ corporation duly organized, in good standing, and
13 qualified to carry on its business in each state in which the Properties are located, and has the
14 power and authority to carry on its business as presently conducted, to own and hold the
15 Properties, and to perform all obligations required by this Agreement.
16   **8.2.**   **Authority.** Pursuant to its bylaws and certificate of incorporation, Buyer has the
17 power and authority to acquire, own, and hold the Properties and to perform the obligations
18 required by this Agreement.
19 **9.**   **Title and Other Examinations and Curative.**
20   **9.1.**   Prior to Closing, Buyer shall examine title to the Properties at its own expense.
21 However, Seller shall make available to Buyer all of Seller's title opinions, certificates of title,
22 abstracts of title, title data, records and files relating to the Properties (including without
23 limitation all well files and well logs) and information relating to the Properties as soon as
24 possible after the execution of this Agreement. Seller will, at Seller's expense, use Seller's best
25 efforts to promptly cure all title defects discovered by Buyer and obtain all consents and waivers
26 of preferential or other rights to purchase from third parties and governmental authorities as in
27 the opinion of Buyer may be desirable or necessary to the conveyance, assignment, and transfer
28 to Buyer of the Properties. In the event title to the Properties is not satisfactory, or if the
29 Properties are otherwise not as represented, Buyer may, at its option, either terminate this
30 Agreement at any time on or before Closing, or reduce the Purchase Price by an amount
31 agreeable to both parties. Seller shall promptly furnish Buyer a copy of all gas contracts, gas
32 transportation and treating agreements, operating agreements and all amendments to each, and
33 provide a schedule showing the status of any gas balancing, take or pay, or other similar
34 arrangements.
35   **9.2.**   If Buyer's review and appraisal of the data, Contracts and agreements reflects
36 such data, Contracts, or agreements are materially different, and that such difference results in a
37 material difference in the value of the Properties, from those assumed by Buyer at the time of its
38 (Date) offer, Buyer shall have the option to either terminate this Agreement without penalty or
39 request renegotiations of the Purchase Price to reflect the adverse changes. Except for title
40 matters, Buyer must exercise this option, if applicable, on or before (Date), or any material
41 differences shall be deemed waived, but without prejudice to Buyer's other rights under this
42 Agreement.
43 **10.**   **Conditions.** The consummation of the sale and purchase contemplated by this
44 Agreement will be subject to the following conditions:

10.1. The representations and warranties by seller set forth in Section 7 shall be true and correct in all material respects as of the date when made and as of the date of closing.

10.2. There shall have been no material adverse change in the condition of the Properties except depletion through normal production within authorized allowables and rates of production, depreciation of equipment through ordinary wear and tear, and other transactions permitted under this Agreement or approved in writing by Buyer between the date of this Agreement and Closing.

10.3. All requirements made by Buyer with regard to title to the Properties shall have been fully satisfied or waived by Buyer. All consents, approvals and authorizations of assignments, and waivers of preferential rights to purchase required by Buyer shall have been submitted to and approved by Buyer.

10.4. Seller and Buyer understand and agree that if: (1) title to the Properties is not satisfactory to Buyer; (2) Seller's actual interests in the Properties is different than as represented by Seller and the difference causes a diminution in Seller's net revenue interest of more than ____% of that which Seller represents to own; (3) contracts, claims or litigation to which Buyer takes exception are material; or, (4) Seller fails to comply with any of the conditions set forth in this Agreement; Buyer may, at its option, either terminate this Agreement at any time on or before Closing, or reduce the Purchase Price by an amount agreeable to both parties. However, any reduction in Seller's net revenue interests below that which is represented in Exhibit "A" shall result in an automatic reduction in the Purchase Price commensurate with the reduction in such net revenue interest.

10.5. The parties shall have performed or complied with all agreements and covenants required by this Agreement of which performance or compliance is required prior to or at Closing.

10.6. All legal matters in connection with and the consummation of the transactions contemplated by this Agreement shall be approved by counsel for Buyer and there shall have been furnished by Seller such records and information as Buyer's counsel may reasonably request for that purpose.

10.7. Notwithstanding anything to the contrary in this Agreement, at Buyer's option, Buyer shall have the unilateral right to terminate this Agreement not later than (Date) if Buyer determines it does not have the rights to obtain and maintain the rights to be Operator of the Properties pursuant to existing Operating Agreements at Closing. Operations shall be transferred from Seller to Buyer at Closing.

11. Transfer, Documentary Taxes, Commissions, and Brokerage Fees. Seller shall pay and bear all documentary or transfer taxes resulting from this transaction. No commission or brokerage fees will be paid by Buyer in connection with this transaction. Seller will indemnify and hold Buyer harmless from any claims of brokers or finders acting, or claiming to have acted, on behalf of Seller.

12. Further Assurances, Intent. It is Seller's intent to convey to Buyer all of Seller's interests, legal, beneficial, or equitable in the Properties. Seller agrees to execute and deliver to Buyer all instruments, conveyances, and other documents and to do such other acts not inconsistent with this Agreement as may be necessary or advisable to carry out Seller's intent.

13.   **Notices.** At notices and communications required or permitted under this Agreement shall be in writing, delivered to or sent by U.S. Mail or Express Delivery, postage prepaid, or by prepaid telegram, or facsimile addressed as follows:

Seller:

Buyer:

14.   **Parties in Interest.** This Agreement shall inure to the benefit of and be binding upon Seller and Buyer and their respective successors and assigns. However, no assignment by any party shall relieve any party of any duties or obligations under this Agreement.

15.   **Complete Agreement.** This Agreement constitutes the complete agreement between the parties regarding the purchase and sale of the Properties. Where applicable, all of the terms of this Agreement shall survive the Closing.

16.   **Survival.** All representatives and warranties in this Agreement shall be deemed conditions to the Closing. The representatives and warranties recited in Section 7. shall not survive the Closing except for: (Identify those Representations and Warranties that will Survive Closing.) All other terms of Agreement shall survive the Closing, including, but not limited to, the indemnification and hold harmless provisions contained in Section 6.

17.   **Termination.** Should either party terminate this Agreement pursuant to a right granted in this Agreement to do so, the termination shall be without liability to the other party, and the non-terminating party shall have no liability to the terminating party.

Seller

Buyer

* * *

EXHIBIT "A"

1.   Description of Properties. [A description of oil and gas leases, lands covered by oil and gas leases and the Seller's Working (cost bearing) and Net Revenue (income) Interest in each of the identified Properties. (Section 1.)]

2.   [Contracts, agreements, and instruments to which Seller is a party and which the Properties are bound or subject to. (Sections 1.c., 7.2. and 7.6.)]

EXHIBIT "B"

[Form of Instruments of Conveyance to be Delivered at Closing (Section 3.; e.g., Assignment, Bill of Sale, Deed, etc.)]

* * *

EXHIBIT "C"
SETTLEMENT AGREEMENT
(Section 4)

5   This Settlement Agreement (the "Agreement"), is dated ____ , but effective ____ , and is
6   between ____ , Seller, and ____ , Buyer. Buyer and Seller are sometimes individually referred to
7   as a "Party" or collectively as the "Parties."

8   By Assignment, Bill of Sale and Conveyance (the "Assignment"), dated to be effective
9   ____ , at 7 a.m. (the "Effective Date"), the time to be determined for each locality described on
10 Exhibit "A" to the Assignment being the time observed in each locality, Seller conveyed and
11 assigned to Buyer certain oil and gas interests and rights (the "Interests") in "Properties," all as
12 more specifically described in the Assignment, which Assignment is incorporated into this
13 Agreement by reference.

14   This Closing Agreement sets forth certain rights and defines certain obligations and
15 duties of the Parties with respect to the Interests and Properties. Its execution is provided for in
16 the Purchase and Sale Agreement dated ____ between Seller and Buyer.

17   In consideration of the covenants and promises contained in this Agreement, and other
18 good and valuable consideration, the receipt and sufficiency of which are acknowledged, the
19 Parties agree as follows:

20 1.   Base Purchase Price. The purchase price for the Interests is $____ (the "Base Purchase
21 Price"), which shall be adjusted, as provided for in paragraph 2. below, to arrive at the Final
22 Purchase Price.

23 2.   Final Purchase Price. In arriving at the Final Purchase Price the Base Purchase Price
24 shall be adjusted as follows:

25   a.   The Base Purchase Price shall be adjusted upward by the following: (1) the value
26 of all merchantable, allowable oil in storage above the pipeline connection at the Effective Date
27 which is credited to the Interests, the value to be determined based on the market price in effect
28 as of the Effective Date, less applicable taxes; (2) the amount of all actual direct operating
29 expenditure (including royalties and production taxes paid with respect to the Interests and
30 excluding any expenses not covered by the reimbursement provisions of applicable operating
31 agreements), or in the absence of such agreements, those expenses normally charged by the
32 Operator and paid by Seller in connection with the operation of the Interests from the Effective
33 Date to the date of this Agreement; and, (3) any other amounts agreed upon by Seller and Buyer,
34 including any gas imbalances at the current applicable contractual market price (or at current
35 spot market price if no contract is in effect).

36   b.   The Base Purchase Price shall be adjusted downward by the following: (1) the
37 proceeds received by Seller from and after the Effective Date to the date of this Agreement
38 attributable to the Interests and which are attributable to production during the period of time
39 between the Effective Date and the date of this Agreement; and, (2) any other amounts agreed
40 upon by Seller and Buyer, including any gas imbalances at the current applicable contractual
41 market price (or at current spot market price if no contract is in effect).

42   The Base Purchase Price, as adjusted by the provisions of 2.a. and 2.b. above is referred
43 to as the "Final Purchase Price."

3. Preliminary Amount. Because certain of the adjustments and payments provided for in paragraph 2. cannot be determined as of the date of this Agreement, Seller and Buyer have agreed upon an estimate, through (Date), of the Final Purchase Price (the "Preliminary Amount") which is to be delivered by Buyer to Seller concurrent with the execution and delivery of this Agreement. The Preliminary Amount and the values used to determine such amount are set out in the "Preliminary Settlement Statement" attached to this Agreement. As soon as practicable after the date of this Agreement, but no later than ____ days following the Closing Date provided for in the Purchase and Sale Agreement between the Parties, Seller shall prepare (in accordance with this Agreement and generally accepted accounting principles), and submit to Buyer a statement (the "Final Settlement Statement") setting forth each adjustment or payment which was not finally determined as of the date of this Agreement, showing the values used to determine such adjustments. Should the Final Settlement Statement not be submitted to Buyer on or before ____ days following Closing, the amount owed the Buyer, if any, per the Final Settlement Statement, shall bear interest from the ____ day to the date of receipt of the Final Settlement Statement by Buyer at the prime rate of interest as used by ____ Bank. As soon as practicable after receipt of the Final Settlement Statement, Buyer shall deliver to Seller a written report containing any changes which Buyer proposes be made to the Final Settlement Statement. Seller and Buyer shall undertake to agree with respect to the amounts due pursuant to the post-closing adjustment no later than ____ (____) days after the Closing Date. The date upon which the agreement is reached, or upon which the Final Purchase Price is otherwise established, shall be called the "Settlement Date." Should agreement to the amount due to Seller, if any, not be agreed to, as a result of Buyer's delay, no later than ____ (____) days after the Closing Date, the amount owed to Seller shall bear interest from the ____ day to the Settlement Date at the prime rate of interest as used by ____ Bank. In the event that (a) the Final Purchase Price is more than the Preliminary Amount, Buyer shall pay to Seller the amount of the difference or, (b) the Final Purchase Price is less than the Preliminary Amount, Seller shall pay to Buyer the amount of the difference. The payment shall be made within ____ days of the Settlement Date.

4. Information. Seller agrees to deliver or make available to Buyer all title information, agreements, records, production and operation information and other information and documents pertaining to the Interests which Buyer reasonably requests, which Seller has not previously provided to Buyer, and which Seller is not contractually prohibited from providing.

5. Possession. Seller has delivered to Buyer the Assignment and exclusive possession of the Interests and Properties.

6. Indemnification.

a. Seller agrees to indemnify, save, and hold Buyer harmless against all claims, costs, expenses, and liabilities with respect to the Interests which relate to times prior to the Effective Date, but not including those incurred by Buyer with respect to the purchase of the Interests by Buyer or the negotiations leading to such purchase, and not including those relating to the title, quality, and quantity of oil, gas, and mineral reserves.

b. Buyer agrees to indemnify, save, and hold Seller harmless against all claims, costs, expenses, and liabilities with respect to the Interests which relate to times after the Effective Date, but not including those incurred by Seller with respect to the sale of the Interests by Seller or the negotiations leading to such sale, and not including those which result from the negligence or willful misconduct of Seller or Seller's employees or agents with respect to the operation or maintenance of the Interests).

      c.   Seller agrees Buyer shall be entitled to receive all proceeds, including proceeds from production of oil and gas attributable to the Interests, after the Effective Date.

      d.   Buyer agrees Seller shall be entitled to receive all proceeds including proceeds from production of oil and gas attributable to the Interests, before the Effective Date.

7.   Files. Seller shall deliver to Buyer, within (Period of Time) after Closing, all property, lease and well files related to the Interests and Properties; provided, however, Buyer agrees to allow Seller access to those files at all reasonable business hours for inspection and copying if Seller, in Seller's sole opinion, require the files to defend any judicial or administrative action brought by any individual or governmental agency against Seller.

8.   Transfer/Division Orders. Buyer recognizes and understands that Buyer is responsible for obtaining transfer/division orders from all purchasers of production from the Interests. Seller agrees to execute all orders or other forms of directions for payment necessary to effect payment to Buyer from and after the Effective Date.

9.   Buyer shall pay any sales and/or use taxes occasioned by the sale of the Interests.

This Agreement shall be binding on and inure to the benefit of the Parties and there respective successors and assigns.

EXECUTED and dated _____ .

Seller

Buyer

* * *

EXHIBIT "D"

[Schedule of Claims, Demands, Filings, Causes of Action, Administrative Proceedings, Lawsuits, Litigation (Section 7.7.)]

EXHIBIT "E"

[Schedule of all Approvals Required to be Obtained by Seller, and Preferential Purchase Rights Affecting the Properties (Section 7.8.).]

SCHEDULE 7.13
(Schedule of Imbalances)

* * *

EXHIBIT "F"

[Schedule of all authorities for expenditures ("AFEs"), other commitments to drill/rework wells, or commitments to capital expenditures. (Section 7.17.)]

1.   This form was furnished by Kanes Forms, P.O. Box 53010, Midland, TX 79710, tel. 800-526-3790. http://www.kanesforms.com/new/index.htm

2.   Some oil and gas companies specialize in exploration only. Others, with sufficient working capital, concentrate on developing discoveries made by an exploration company. Still others may simply take over fully developed fields to secure production and reserves. Some companies have special expertise in enhanced recovery. Salvage operators, with low overhead, may buy up properties near the end of their productive lives. Thus, during the life of a producing oil and gas field, properties may be bought and sold several times.

3.   This form is a simple purchase-and-sale agreement for producing properties. These agreements are often much longer and more complex. In some, the seller may retain an overriding royalty, back-in rights, and promises by the buyer to develop the property up to specified level. Thus, these agreements are frequently highly customized to particular purposes. This form is included here to give you an introduction into the types of provisions that would be commonly included in most purchase-and-sale agreements.

4.   Illustrating the need to customize purchase and sale agreements, in an actual sale in 2008, Sellers assigned an undivided 75% undivided net-revenue interest in leases covering approximately 150,000 gross acres in Texas. The parties further agreed to share on a 75%-25% basis any additional leases acquired within a designated area of mutual interest (AMI). The sale included five productive wells that had been drilled to prove up the prospect. Buyer paid several million dollars cash and, within 30 months of closing, agreed to shoot several hundred square miles of 3-D seismic and to share the resulting data with Seller and agreed to drill 15 wells. The agreement specified that Sellers were to be "carried" as to their retained 25% working interest in these 15 wells but become "at risk" working-interest owners in any subsequent wells. If Buyer failed to drill all 15 wells, then the following forfeiture provision applied:

> If all fifteen wells are not spud within this 30-month period, Buyer shall forfeit an undivided percentage of its non-developed acreage in the Leases, which shall be calculated by multiplying the total non-developed net acreage Buyer owns in the lands covered by the Leases by a fraction, the denominator of which is 15 and the numerator of which is the positive difference between 15 and the number of wells spud within the first 30 months of this Agreement. For example, if Buyer spuds only 10 wells in the first 30 months, then Buyer shall forfeit an undivided 33.3% (15 minus 10 divided by 15) interest in that portion of the lands covered by the Leases that are not then part of a pro-ration unit in which operations are not then underway. For purposes of this Agreement, a "spud well" shall mean a well drilled or actually being drilled.

FARMOUT AGREEMENT
(Providing for Multiple Wells with Dry Hole Earning an Assignment)

FARMOR: (Name and Address)
FARMEE: (Name and Address)
NAME OF AREA/PROSPECT:

This Farmout Agreement (the "Agreement") is between Farmor, and Farmee, and shall be effective as of the date it is executed by Farmee as provided in Section 9.

1.   EXHIBITS.

The following exhibits, if checked, are attached and shall be considered part of this Agreement:

[ ]   **Exhibit A:**   General Terms and Conditions which shall apply to this Agreement unless they are in conflict with the terms and conditions provided in the body of this Agreement.

[ ]   **Exhibit B-1**: Descriptions of lands covered by this Agreement ("Farmout Lands").

[ ]   **Exhibit B-2**: Lease Schedule describing the oil and gas leases subject to this Agreement.

[ ]   **Exhibit C:**   Accounting Procedures, used in calculating payout of the Earning Well provided in Section 2.

[ ]   **Exhibit D**:   Tax Partnership Agreement.

[ ]   **Exhibit E**:   Operating Agreement.

[ ]   **Exhibit F**:   Geological Requirements.

[ ]   **Exhibit G**:   (Other Exhibits)

2.   INITIAL EARNING WELL.

2.1   Well Specifications.   Farmee shall drill a well, (the "Initial Earning Well"), strictly in compliance with the following well specifications:

(a)   Location: (Describe Location)

(b)   Spudding Deadline: (Specify Date)

(c)   Required Depth: (Specify Depth)

(d)   Completion/Plugging Deadline: (State Date)

2.2   Earned Assignment.   As soon as practicable after Farmor is satisfied Farmee has complied with all of its obligations under this Agreement with regard to the Initial Earning Well, including the specifications provided in Section 2.1, Farmor shall deliver to Farmee the following (check applicable alternatives):

[ ]   **Producing Well**.   If the Initial Earning Well is completed as a producer of oil and/or gas in paying quantities, Farmor shall deliver (check one or both):

[ ]   A drill site acreage assignment as described in Section 2.3.

[ ]   An additional acreage assignment as described in Section 2.4.

[ ]   **Dry Hole**.   If the Initial Earning Well is plugged and abandoned as a dry hole, Farmor shall deliver the dry hole assignment described in Section 2.5.

2.3   Drill Site Acreage Assignment.   If a drill site acreage assignment is earned, such assignment shall cover

1		[ ]	all	[ ]	an undivided ____ %

of Farmor's rights, title and interests in the Farmout Lands, subject to the reserved overriding royalty interest described in Section 4, and subject to the following area and/or depth limitations (check appropriate limitations):

Area   [ ]   Limited to the "drilling unit" for the Initial Earning Well as defined in paragraph 3.2 of Exhibit A; or,

           [ ]   Limited to the following area: (Describe Area)

Depth   [ ]   Limited to the interval between the surface of the ground and 100 feet below the stratigraphic equivalent of the total depth drilled in the Initial Earning Well; or,

           [ ]   Limited to the following interval: (Describe Interval)

    2.4   **Additional Acreage Assignment**. If an outside acreage assignment is earned under Section 2.2, the assignment shall cover

           [ ]   all   [ ]   an undivided ____ %

of Farmor's rights, title and interests in the Farmout Lands not covered by the drill site acreage assignment provided for in Section 2.3, subject to the following area and/or depth limitations (check appropriate limitations):

Area   [ ]   No area limitation.

           [ ]   Limited to the following area: (Describe Area)

Depth   [ ]   Limited to the interval between the surface of the ground and 100 feet below the stratigraphic equivalent of the total depth drilled in the Initial Earning Well; or,

           [ ]   Limited to the following interval: (Describe Interval)

    2.5   **Dry Hole Assignment**. If a dry hole assignment is earned under Section 2.2, such assignment shall cover

           [ ]   all   [ ]   an undivided ____ %

of Farmor's rights, title and interests in the farmout lands, subject to the following area and/or depth limitations (check appropriate limitations):

Area   [ ]   Limited to the "drilling unit" for the Initial Earning Well as defined in paragraph 3.2 of Exhibit A; or,

           [ ]   Limited to the following area: (Describe Area)

Depth   [ ]   Limited to the interval between the surface of the ground and 100 feet below the stratigraphic equivalent of the total depth drilled in the Initial Earning Well; or,

           [ ]   Limited to the following interval: (Describe Interval)

3.   ADDITIONAL EARNING WELLS.

    3.1   **Farmor's Option**. If the Initial Earning Well is completed as a producer of oil and/or gas in paying quantities, or as a dry hole, but Farmee does not earn all of the Farmout Lands, Farmee shall have the additional right, but not the obligation, to (check appropriate alternative):

           [ ]   Drill one Additional Earning Well.

           [ ]   Drill one or more Additional Earning Wells as a continuous optional drilling program.

    3.2   **Well Specifications**. Farmee shall drill each Additional Earning Well strictly in

accordance with the following well specifications:
                    (a)   Location: (Describe Location)
                    (b)   Spudding Deadline: (Specify Date)
                    (c)   Required Depth: (Specify Depth)
                    (d)   Completion/Plugging Deadline: (State Date)
          3.3   Earned Assignments. As soon as practicable after Farmor is satisfied that Farmee has complied with all of its obligations under this Agreement with regard to an Additional Earning Well, including well specifications provided in Section 3.2, Farmor shall deliver to Farmee the following (check applicable alternatives):
                    [ ]   **Producing Well**. If an Additional Earning Well is completed as a
          producer of oil and/or gas in paying quantities, Farmor shall deliver (check one or both assignments):
                              [ ]   A drill site acreage assignment as described in Section 3.4.
                              [ ]   An outside acreage assignment as described in Section 3.5.
                    [ ]   **Dry Hole**. If an Additional Earning Well is plugged and
          abandoned as a dry hole, Farmor shall deliver the dry hole assignment described in Section 3.6.
          3.4   Drill Site Acreage Assignment. If a drill site acreage assignment is earned under Section 3.3, such assignment shall cover
                    [ ]   all   [ ]   an undivided ____%
of Farmor's rights, title and interests in the Farmout Lands, subject to the reserved overriding royalty interest described in Section 4, and subject to the following area and/or depth limitations (check appropriate limitations):
Area   [ ]   Limited to the "drilling unit" for the Additional Earning Well as
                              defined in paragraph 3.2 of Exhibit A; or,
                    [ ]   Limited to the following area: (Describe Area)
Depth   [ ]   Limited to the interval between the surface of the ground and 100 feet
                              below the stratigraphic equivalent of the total depth drilled in the
                              Additional Earning Well; or,
                    [ ]   Limited to the following interval: (Describe Interval)
          3.5   Additional Acreage Assignment. If an outside acreage assignment is earned under Section 3.3, the assignment shall cover
                    [ ]   all   [ ]   an undivided ____%
of Farmor's rights, title and interests in the Farmout Lands not covered by the drill site acreage assignment described in Section 3.4, subject to the following area and/or depth limitations (check appropriate limitations):
Area   [ ]   No area limitation.
                    [ ]   Limited to the following area: (Describe Area)
Depth   [ ]   Limited to the interval between the surface of the ground and 100 feet
                              below the stratigraphic equivalent of the total depth drilled in the
                              Additional Earning Well; or,
                    [ ]   Limited to the following interval: (Describe Interval)
          3.6   Dry Hole Assignment. If a dry hole assignment is earned under Section 3.3, such assignment shall cover

1	[ ]	all	[ ]	an undivided ____ %	

of Farmor's rights, title and interests in the Farmout Lands, subject to the following area and/or depth limitations (check appropriate limitations):

Area   [ ]   Limited to the "drilling unit" for the Additional Earning Well as defined in paragraph 3.2 of Exhibit A; or,

             [ ]   Limited to the following area: _(Describe Area)

Depth   [ ]   Limited to the interval between the surface of the ground and 100 feet below the stratigraphic equivalent of the total depth drilled in the Additional Earning Well; or,

             [ ]   Limited to the following interval: (Describe Interval)

4.   **RESERVED OVERRIDING ROYALTY INTEREST.**

      4.1   **Reservation**. In each Drill Site Acreage Assignment by Farmor, Farmor shall reserve an overriding royalty interest in production from the appropriate Earning Well equal to (check appropriate alternative):

             [ ]   ____ % of production if the Earning Well is an oil well, and ____ % of production if the Earning Well is a gas well, reduced in proportion to the assigned interest and calculated in accordance with paragraph 4.1 of Exhibit A; or,

             [ ]   the amount by which ____ % of production, reduced in proportion to the assigned interest, exceeds the sum of all royalties, overriding royalties and other payments out of production which burden the assigned interest at the time the Drill Site Acreage Assignment is made.

      4.2   **Conversion**. Check appropriate alternative:

             [ ]   Upon "payout" of each Earning Well, as defined in paragraph 4.3 of Exhibit A, Farmor's reserved overriding royalty interest shall be convertible, at Farmor's election, to an undivided working interest equal to ____ % of the working interest covered by the appropriate Drill Site Acreage Assignment; or,

             [ ]   Farmor's reserved overriding royalty interest shall not be convertible to a working interest.

5.   **OPERATING AGREEMENT.**

      If an Operating Agreement is attached as Exhibit E to this Agreement, it shall be executed at the time this Agreement is executed and shall become effective if and when Farmor and Farmee become co-owners of working interest in any of the Farmout Lands. The Operating Agreement shall govern all operations on jointly owned Farmout Lands, but shall be subject to this Agreement. If there is any conflict between the Farmout Agreement and this Agreement, this Agreement shall govern.

6.   **DELAY RENTALS.**

      Until a lease(s) included in the Farmout Lands is assigned in whole or in part to Farmee, by the terms of this Agreement, Farmor shall be responsible for paying any and all delay rentals required to maintain the lease(s) in effect and, within 30 days after receipt of an invoice from Farmor, Farmee shall promptly reimburse Farmor for ____ % of the delay rentals paid by Farmor. If Farmee fails to pay Farmor, the balance of any unpaid delay rental invoice shall bear interest monthly at the rate of ____ % per annum, or the maximum contract rate permitted by the applicable usury laws in the state in which the Farmout Lands are located, whichever is the lesser, plus attorney's fees, court costs, and any other costs in connection with the collection of the unpaid balance. After the lease(s) has been assigned in whole or in part to Farmee, the responsibility for making delay rental payments shall belong to

    [ ]   Farmor   [ ] Farmee

subject to _____% reimbursement by the other party upon receipt of an invoice as described above. The party responsible for paying rentals shall not be liable to the other party for any loss resulting from a good faith effort to make such payments.

7.   NOTICES AND WELL INFORMATION.

    7.1   General. All well data, information and notices to be given to Farmor or Farmee as provided in this Farmout Agreement shall be given as follows:

Farmor: (Name and Address)   Farmee: (Name and Address)

Farmor or Farmee may change their address at any time by furnishing a written notice of change of address to the other party.

8.   AGREEMENTS AFFECTING FARMOUT LANDS.

    8.1   Farmee Bound. Except as may be otherwise provided Farmee shall be bound by any agreement, which affects the Farmout Lands at the time of assignment to Farmee. Farmor shall not be liable for its good faith failure to disclose the existence or effect of any such agreement to Farmee, either in this Agreement or otherwise.

    8.2   Other Agreements. Subject to the disclaimer of liability contained in Section 8.1, Farmor believes, in good faith, that the only other agreements affecting any interest to be assigned to Farmee are the oil and gas leases described in Exhibit B and the following agreements:

(Description of Other Agreements. If there are no Other Agreements, State "None.")

9.   EXECUTION. Duplicate originals of this Agreement are being executed. This Agreement shall be null and void, at Farmor's option, if one of the duplicate originals of this Agreement is not executed by Farmee and returned to Farmor within _____ days after the date shown below Farmor's signature.

FARMOR   **FARMEE**

By: By:
Title: Title:
Date: Date:

* * *

1. Titles and Access to Farmout Lands.

1.1 **Title Information**. On written request by Farmee, Farmor shall make available to Farmee copies of all title opinions, abstracts of title, and other title information in Farmor's possession with respect to the Farmout Lands. Providing such items shall not be construed as a warranty or representation by Farmor of title or ownership. Any curative work or additional title examination required by Farmee shall be conducted by Farmee at its sole cost and risk. On request, Farmee shall provide Farmor with a copy of all curative work, title information, and title opinions resulting from any additional title examinations conducted by Farmee.

1.2 **Access by Farmee and Farmor**. To the extent Farmor can authorize it, Farmee and its contractors and subcontractors shall be entitled to exercise all of Farmor's rights of ingress and egress pertaining to the Farmout Lands for the purpose of conducting operations. Farmor shall advise Farmee of any unusual limitations or restrictions on ingress or egress, known to Farmor, and Farmee and its contractors and subcontractors shall comply with such limitations or restrictions. During Farmee's operations Farmor and Farmor's representatives shall have access at all times to the well-site, including the derrick floor, for the purpose of observation. All information requested by Farmor concerning operations shall be promptly furnished by Farmee.

2. Conduct of Operations.

2.1 **Cost and Risk**. All operations conducted by Farmee shall be at Farmee's sole cost and risk, and subject to the indemnity provisions of paragraph 5.2 below.

2.2 **Performance Standards**. All of Farmee's operations shall be conducted in a diligent and workmanlike manner, and in accordance with all applicable federal, state and local laws, regulations, and orders. Whether or not the Earning Well must be completed as a producer of oil and/or gas in order to earn an assignment, Farmee shall use its best efforts, in accordance with good oil and gas practice, to complete the well as a producer of oil and/or gas in paying quantities. Farmee shall conduct such coring, logging, testing, fracing, and acidizing operations as Farmor may reasonably request or as a prudent operator would conduct under the same or similar circumstances. If the well cannot reasonably be completed as a producer of oil and/or gas, Farmee shall promptly plug the well and perform all necessary surface restoration work. Time is of the essence in Farmee's performance of all undertakings provided for in the Agreement.

2.3 **Federal Contract Requirements**. If applicable, Farmee agrees to comply with the requirements of all applicable Executive Orders governing Federal contractors, as well as all related rules, regulations and orders, and any amendments or additions of or to those rules and orders. Farmee additionally agrees to supply Farmor all certificates required pursuant to any applicable rules, regulations, and orders.

2.4 **Lease Obligations**. Except as otherwise provided in the body of the Farmout Agreement, Farmee shall at its sole cost, risk, and expense comply with all of the express and implied covenants and other obligations of the oil and gas leases covering the Farmout Lands, including the payment of royalties, shut-in royalties, and delay rentals, and the cost of any renewals or extensions of the leases.

2.5 Well Information. During Farmee's operations, Farmee shall promptly furnish Farmor the following information pertaining to the Earning Well and any other well drilled by Farmee:

(a) Written notice of the exact time and date on which the well is spudded.

(b) A daily drilling report showing all formations encountered and the depths at which those formations were encountered during the immediately preceding day, and the well operations conducted during the immediately preceding day.

(c) Written reports on all cuttings and cores taken in the well, along with representative samples of the cuttings and cores, if requested by Farmor.

(d) Reasonable advance notice of any production tests, pressure tests, cores, and logs to be run in the well so that Farmor may witness the operations. Written report of such operations, when they are completed, shall be furnished to Farmor.

(e) Copies of all reports and other forms filed with any federal, state, or local governmental authority concerning the well.

(f) A complete copy of the driller's log and a complete copy of all electrical logs, on a scale of not less than 2 inches per 100 feet, from the bottom of the surface casing to the total depth of the well.

(g) Copies of all fluid analyses and other reports or information obtained with respect to the well.

(h) Any other information specifically required by Farmor as part of this Farmout Agreement.

2.6 Confidentiality. Without Farmor's prior written consent, Farmee shall not divulge information obtained from Farmee's operations under the terms of this Agreement to any party other than Farmor, any party owning an interest in the well, and the appropriate governmental authority.

2.7 Substitute Wells. If Farmee has failed to earn an assignment under the terms of this Agreement, either (i) because the original Earning Well failed to reach the required depth as a result of mechanical problems or impenetrable strata or other conditions in the hole which make further drilling impracticable, under generally accepted oil field practices; or (ii) because the original Earning Well was drilled to the required depth but it is not capable of producing in paying quantities, Farmee shall have the option, but not the obligation, to drill one or more substitute wells subject to the following provisions:

(a) Farmee shall give Farmor written notice describing the status of the well and stating whether or not Farmee elects to drill a substitute well. This notice shall be given while the drilling rig or completion unit is on the well, or within 10 days after its release. Failure to timely make such an election shall be deemed to be an election by Farmee not to drill a substitute well.

(b) If Farmee elects to drill a substitute well, Farmor shall advise Farmee within 10 days after receipt of Farmee's notice, or within 72 hours if the rig is on location, to either plug the original well or turn it over to Farmor as provided in paragraph 2.8 below, and to proceed with the substitute well as provided in paragraph 2.7(d) below.

(c) If Farmee elects not to drill a substitute well, or if Farmee has waived its right to do so as provided in paragraph 2.7(a) above, Farmor shall advise Farmee within 10 days after receipt of Farmee's notice, or within 72 hours if the rig is on location, whether or not Farmor elects to take over the well as provided in paragraph 2.8 below. If Farmor elects not to take over the well or fails to make an election, Farmee shall promptly plug and abandon the well and restore the surface. In either event, Farmee shall have no right to drill a substitute well in order to earn an assignment.

(d)   Any substitute well drilled by Farmee shall be spudded within 30 days after Farmee's election to drill it, at a mutually acceptable location, and the well shall be drilled, tested, and completed or plugged and abandoned in accordance with all of the requirements specified for the original Earning Well, and with the same consequences. The substitute well shall be considered as the Earning Well for all purposes of this Agreement.

2.8   Takeover by Farmor. If Farmor elects to take over a well, the effective date of the takeover shall be 72 hours after the date of Farmor's election to do so or when Farmor takes actual custody of the well, whichever is earlier. If Farmor elects to takeover a well it shall own Farmee's interest in the well and the related equipment, along with any and all interest Farmee owns (or has a right to earn under other contracts or agreements) in the drilling unit for the well taken over, excluding any other producing wells and related equipment in the drilling unit, and excluding any depth intervals or formations which would not have been earned under this Agreement. As soon as practicable after Farmor takes over the well, Farmee shall make an assignment to Farmor, as may be necessary to evidence the foregoing, at which time Farmor shall reimburse Farmee for the estimated salvage value of Farmee's salvable equipment in and on the well, less estimated salvage costs. Farmee shall have no further rights or obligations under this Agreement, except Farmee shall be liable for all actions which occurred prior to the effective date of the takeover.

2.9   Additional Wells After Earning Well. For the purpose of this paragraph, the term "Earned Acreage" means that portion of the Farmout Lands, if any, in which Farmee has earned all of Farmor's interest, subject to an overriding royalty interest retained by Farmor in production from the Earning Well. The term "Additional Well" means each additional well Farmee drills or participates in drilling on Earned Acreage or on the Earning Well's drilling unit after completion of the Earning Well. As to each such Additional Well the following provisions shall apply:

(a)   If Farmor's overriding royalty interest in the Earning Well is not convertible at payout to a working interest as described in paragraph 4.3 below, or if the overriding royalty interest was convertible but Farmor elected at payout not to convert, that overriding royalty interest shall apply, without conversion rights, to the Additional Well in the same manner as that interest applies to the Earning Well.

(b)   If Farmor's overriding royalty interest in the Earning Well is convertible to a working interest as described in paragraph 4.3 below, but the Earning Well has not yet reached payout, Farmee shall notify Farmor in writing of its intention to drill or participate in drilling the Additional Well at least 60 days before such drilling commences. Within 45 days after receipt of such notice, Farmor shall advise Farmee in writing of Farmor's election either: (i) to have its overriding royalty interest, with conversion rights at payout, apply to the Additional Well in the same manner (but with separate payout accounts) as the interest applies to the Earning Well; or, (ii) to participate as a working interest owner in the Additional Well from the commencement of operations.

Farmor's election and the resulting consequences (including the calculation of payout) shall apply separately to each Additional Well. If Farmor elects to participate in the Additional Well as a working interest owner, Farmee shall promptly reassign to Farmor all of the interest Farmor would otherwise have been entitled to receive upon payout of the Earning Well, except: (i) Farmee's interest in the Earning Well itself and all equipment attributable to that well; (ii) Farmee's interest in any previously drilled Additional Well (and equipment attributable to that well) in which Farmor elected an overriding royalty with conversion rights, but which has not yet reached payout; and, (iii) Farmee's interests in any previously drilled Additional Well (and related equipment) in which Farmor elected an overriding royalty with conversion rights, and which has reached payout, but Farmor has not converted its overriding royalty interest to a working interest. Reassignments by Farmee shall be free and clear of all royalties, overriding royalties, and other payments out of production, and all claims, liabilities, and other encumbrances except those in existence as of the effective date of this Agreement. If Farmor elects to participate in the Additional Well as a working interest owner, as between Farmor and Farmee, all operations shall be governed by the Operating Agreement provided for in the body of this Agreement.

3. Earned Assignment.

3.1 Scope of Assignment. Any assignment of interest earned by Farmee shall be subject to all of the provisions of the Agreement and all its Exhibits, whether or not any of the provisions are recited in the assignment. Farmor shall retain all rights and interests not expressly assigned to Farmee. Farmor expressly retains the right to use all or any part of the assigned Farmout Lands to explore, develop, and operate the Farmout Lands and other lands not assigned to Farmee. The assignments shall be without warranty of title, express or implied, but the assigned interest shall be free and clear of all royalties, overriding royalties and other such payments out of production, except those in existence as of the effective date of the Agreement, and any overriding royalty to be reserved by Farmor.

3.2 Drilling Unit. Whenever an assignment relates to the "drilling unit" for the Earning Well, the term "drilling unit" is deemed to mean the area within the surface boundaries of the drilling unit, spacing unit or proration unit, as the case may be, established or prescribed as of the date of the Agreement by field rules or special order of the appropriate regulatory authority for the objective reservoir to be tested or the reservoir in which the Earning Well is completed, if other than the objective reservoir. In the absence of field rules or special order, the drilling unit shall be 160 acres if the Earning Well is completed as a gas well, and 40 acres if the Earning Well is completed as an oil well, or is not completed as a producer of either oil or gas in paying quantities. However, if the Earning Well is completed as a producer in a reservoir for which a larger unit is subsequently established by field rules or special order within 120 days after completion, the larger unit shall be considered the drilling unit for the Earning Well and any previous assignment earned by Farmee shall be supplemented accordingly. For the purpose of this Farmout Agreement, the meanings of the terms "oil well" and "gas well" shall be as defined by law or by the appropriate regulatory authority. In the absence of such definitions, an oil well shall be a well with an initial gas-oil ratio of less than 100,000 cubic feet per barrel, and a gas well shall be a well with an initial gas-oil ratio of 100,000 cubic feet or more per barrel, based on a 24-hour production test conducted by Farmee, and witnessed by Farmor, under normal producing conditions and using standard lease separator facilities or equivalent testing equipment.

3.3 **Default by Farmee**. If Farmee fails to spud the Earning Well within the deadline established in this Agreement, this Farmout Agreement shall automatically terminate without notice, effective as of the date of the deadline. If Farmee defaults in the timely and proper performance of any other obligation, Farmor shall have the right to terminate this Agreement by giving notice of termination to Farmee. Upon termination, Farmee shall have no further rights except rights already earned, and, in addition to any other available legal or equitable remedies, Farmor may elect to take over, pursuant to paragraph 2.8 above, any well which has not yet satisfied the earning requirements of this Agreement.

4. **Reserved Overriding Royalty Interest**.

4.1 **Calculation and Payment**. Any overriding royalty interest reserved by Farmor in an assignment of interest to Farmee shall be based on the volume of oil, gas, and other minerals produced and saved from the Earning Well, reduced in proportion to the interest assigned. At Farmor's option, exercised by written notice to Farmee, the overriding royalty interest shall be delivered in kind into Farmor's tanks or pipeline as produced, or paid monthly on the basis of the gross value of production during the preceding calendar month. For the purpose of this Farmout Agreement, "gross value" means the gross proceeds actually received by Farmee in an arm's length sale of production, or, in the absence of an arm's length sale, the prevailing market value of the production of the wellhead when produced. The overriding royalty interest shall be in addition to any other royalty, overriding royalty interest, and payment out of production and free and clear of all costs except applicable production or severance taxes and federal excise taxes.

4.2 **Monthly Statements**. If Farmor is granted the right to convert its overriding royalty interest to a working interest, each overriding royalty interest payment by Farmee shall be accompanied by a statement showing cumulatively, and for the month covered by the statement, the following information in form and substance acceptable to Farmor:

(a) The Farmee's costs, which are the costs incurred by Farmee in drilling, testing, reworking, completing, equipping, and operating the Earning Well as calculated in accordance with the accounting procedures provided for in "Exhibit C" to the Agreement, insofar as those costs are attributable to the interest assigned to Farmee under this Agreement.

(b) The Farmee's revenue, which is the gross value of production as defined in paragraph 4.1 above, less: (i) applicable production or severance taxes and any federal excise taxes; (ii) all royalties, overriding royalties, and other payments out of production which, as of the effective date of this Agreement, burden the interest assigned to Farmee; and, (iii) the overriding royalty interest reserved by Farmor. Where Farmor has taken its overriding royalty interest in kind, the calculation of farmout revenue shall be made as though the overriding royalty interest had been paid on the basis of the gross value of production, as defined above.

4.3 **Conversion of Overriding Royalty Interest**. If and when the Farmee's revenue equals the Farmee's costs, as shown by Farmee's monthly statements, the Earning Well shall be considered as having achieved "payout" status. If Farmor is granted the right to convert its reserved overriding royalty interest to a working interest, the Farmor may exercise that right by written notice to Farmee within 60 days after receipt of Farmee's written advice to Farmor stating that payout status has been achieved, accompanied by Farmee's monthly statements supporting that advice. Within that 60 day period Farmee shall provide Farmor all pertinent well production history and most recent test data, if any, and Farmor shall have the right to exercise its conversion privilege within 30 days after its receipt of all that data. Upon receipt of Farmor's conversion notice, Farmee shall promptly reassign to Farmor the working interest Farmor is entitled to receive, including an equivalent interest in the Earning Well and the equipment and all subsequent production effective as of 7:00 a.m. of the day following the date of payout. Farmor's overriding royalty shall be deemed to be extinguished. The reassignment of Farmor's working interest shall be without warranty of title, express or implied, free and clear of all royalties, overriding royalties, and other payments out of production, and all claims, liabilities and other encumbrances except those in existence as of the effective date of this Agreement. This conversion of overriding royalty interest option shall apply in like manner to any other well drilled on the Farmout Lands by Farmee in which Farmor has reserved a conversion option.

 4.4 Audits. Upon written notice to Farmee, Farmor may, during normal business hours, audit Farmee's books and records relating to overriding royalty payments and/or the calculation of payout. Such audit rights may be exercised at any time while overriding royalties are payable and for a period of 24 months after payout status has been achieved, despite an earlier termination of this Farmout Agreement.

5. Liability and Insurance.

 5.1 Relationship of Parties. In performing its obligations, Farmee shall be an independent contractor and not the agent of Farmor. Nothing in this Agreement shall be construed as creating a partnership or otherwise establishing joint or collective liability. The relationship of the parties for federal and state income tax purposes shall be as set forth in Exhibit D to this Agreement (Tax Partnership Agreement). If no Exhibit D is attached to this Agreement, the relationship of the parties for federal and state income tax purposes shall be as set forth in paragraph 11.2 below, and shall be effective from and after the effective date of this Agreement.

 5.2 Farmee's Indemnity. Farmee shall indemnify and hold harmless Farmor and its employees and agents from all claims, demands, losses, and liabilities of every kind and character arising out of Farmee's performance or failure to perform under this Agreement, or the acts of or failure to act by Farmee's employees, agents, contractors and/or subcontractors.

 5.3 Required Insurance Coverage. At all times while Farmee has the right to earn an assignment of interest or is conducting operations on the Farmout Lands, Farmee shall maintain, at its sole cost, the following insurance coverage for its operations:

  (a) Worker's Compensation Insurance and Employer's Liability Insurance with such limits as are specified by law in the jurisdiction in which the Farmout Lands are located.

  (b) Comprehensive General Public Liability Insurance, including Contractual Liability coverage, with a combined single limit of $____ for bodily injury and property damage.

  (c) Automobile Liability Insurance with the same limits as prescribed above for Comprehensive General Public Liability Insurance.

 5.4 Proof of Coverage. Prior to the commencement of operations, Farmee shall furnish Farmor one or more certificates signed by the insurance carrier or carriers showing, to Farmor's satisfaction, that the required insurance coverage is in force and stating that the coverage shall not be canceled or materially altered without at least 10 days advance written notice to Farmor. A cancellation or material alteration, if not accompanied by new insurance coverage satisfactory to Farmor, shall constitute a default by Farmee under paragraph 3.3 above. Each certificate shall also contain a waiver by the insurance carrier of any right to be subrogated to the rights of any claimant against Farmor or Farmor's employees and agents, except that the carrier shall be subrogated to the rights of Farmee against Farmor with respect to any risk expressly assumed by Farmor.

6. Option to Purchase or Process Production.

6.1 Oil Production. Farmor shall have a continuing option to purchase Farmee's share of oil and liquid hydrocarbons produced and saved from the Farmout Lands through standard lease separator facilities, to the extent the production is attributable to the interest assigned to Farmee. The option may be exercised by Farmor at any time and from time to time while production continues, by giving written notice to Farmee not less than 30 days before the date on which Farmor's purchases are to commence. The price paid by Farmor for the production shall be equal to the prevailing wellhead market price then being paid in the same field for production of the same or similar grade and gravity, or if there is no prevailing price being paid in the same field, the prevailing price being paid in the nearest field. Farmor may terminate its purchases by giving written notice to Farmee not less than 30 days before the date of termination.

6.2 Gas Production. Farmor shall have the option to purchase Farmee's share of gas, including casinghead gas, produced and saved from the Farmout Lands through standard lease separator facilities, to the extent the production is attributable to the interest assigned to Farmee. When Farmee's gas becomes available for purchase initially, and at any time thereafter, Farmee shall advise Farmor in writing and Farmor shall have 60 days thereafter to give Farmee written notice of Farmor's election to purchase the gas at the prevailing wellhead market price paid for gas of the same or similar quantity and quality in the same field (or if there is no price then prevailing in the same field, then in the nearest field in which there is a prevailing price) pursuant to comparable purchase contracts entered into on the same or nearest preceding date as the date of Farmor's election to purchase gas.

6.3 Gas Processing. If Farmor does not elect to purchase Farmee's share of gas under paragraph 6.2 above, Farmor shall nevertheless have a continuing option to process Farmee's share of gas, including casinghead gas, produced and saved through standard lease separator facilities, to the extent the gas is attributable to the interest assigned to Farmee, all in accordance with the following provisions:

(a) Farmor may exercise its option at any time, before or after commencement of gas production, by giving written notice to Farmee not less than 60 days before Farmor's processing is to begin. Any agreement made by Farmee for the sale of its gas shall be made expressly subject to Farmor's processing option, whether or not exercised by Farmor.

(b) If Farmor exercises its processing option, Farmor shall have the right to remove any or all commercially liquefiable hydrocarbons from the gas before or after delivery to Farmee's gas purchaser, and to redeliver the residue gas to Farmee or its gas purchaser at the tailgate of the gas processing plant.

(c) Farmor shall own all liquefiable hydrocarbons removed from the gas in processing and shall bear all of the costs and risks thereof, but Farmor shall reimburse Farmee, or its gas purchaser, for the BTU reduction caused by such processing, using either of the following reimbursement methods, from time to time, at Farmor's sole discretion:

267

       (i)   The reimbursement shall be a cash payment equal to the BTU reduction caused by processing, times the net price per BTU which Farmee would have received for the gas under its gas sales contract if no such processing had occurred; or,

       (ii)   The reimbursement shall be a volume of residue gas having a total BTU content equal to the BTU reduction caused by processing, delivered in kind to Farmee, or its gas purchaser at the tailgate of the plant.

    (d)   Farmor's processing of gas and any in-kind reimbursement for the processing shall not reduce the BTU content of gas delivered to Farmee or its gas purchaser below 950 BTU's per standard cubic foot, nor shall the pressure of such gas be reduced by more than 50 pounds between the point it is delivered to Farmor for processing and the point it is redelivered to Farmee or its gas purchaser.

7.   **Assignments, Encumbrances and Restrictions**.

This Agreement shall be binding on the respective heirs, successors, and assigns of Farmor and Farmee. Farmor may freely assign or encumber its interest at any time, but Farmee shall not assign or encumber its interest without the prior written consent of Farmor, which consent shall not be unreasonably withheld. Any attempt by Farmee to assign or encumber its interest without Farmor's prior written consent shall constitute a default under paragraph 3.3 above. When an assignment or encumbrance is made, Farmee shall promptly furnish a copy to Farmor. Any rights of reverter and the rights to reassignment retained by Farmor shall be superior to all liens, encumbrances, debts, judgments, claims, overriding royalty interests, and production payment burdens and other obligations created or incurred by Farmee and asserted against any oil and gas lease that is the subject of this Agreement. Any interest in any oil and gas lease included in the Farmout Lands reverting to Farmor or reassigned to Farmor shall be free and clear of all such liens, encumbrances, debts, judgments, claims, overriding royalty interests, and production payment burdens and other obligations. Farmee agrees not to use, for any promotion purposes or for the purpose of selling stock in any organization, and not to advertise in any manner, Farmee's relationship with Farmor arising out of this Agreement.

8.   **Reassignment Rights of Farmor**.

    8.1   **Termination or Cancellation of Leases**. If at any time after an interest in any oil and gas lease is assigned to Farmee, and Farmee elects to surrender its interest in the lease, or allow the lease to expire by its terms, or subjects the lease to possible cancellation for failure to comply with any express or implied covenant, Farmee shall notify Farmor in writing at least 60 days before the intended date of surrender or expiration, or as soon as practicable in the event of possible cancellation, and Farmor shall then have 30 days to notify Farmee in writing of Farmor's election to reacquire such interest. If Farmor elects to reacquire the interest, Farmee shall promptly assign it to Farmor free and clear of all royalties, overriding royalties interests, and other payments out of production and any other lease burden, except those in existence as of the effective date of this Agreement and except those to which Farmor has consented. Upon such assignment, Farmor shall reimburse Farmee for Farmee's share of the estimated salvage value of any salvable equipment in and on any wells covered by the assignment, less estimated salvage costs. Farmor's failure to notify Farmee in writing shall be deemed an election to not reacquire the interest.

1   **8.2**   **Abandonment of Wells**. Farmee shall not plug and abandon any Earning Well or
2 Additional Well drilled without giving Farmor written notice at least 30 days before the intended
3 plugging date. Farmor shall then have 15 days to notify Farmee in writing of Farmor's election
4 to take over the well. Upon giving that notice, Farmor shall own Farmee's interest in the well
5 and the related equipment, along with any and all interest Farmee owns (or has a right to earn
6 under other contracts or agreements) in the drilling unit for the well taken over, excluding any
7 other producing wells and related equipment in the drilling unit, and excluding any depth
8 intervals or formations which would not have been earned under this Agreement. As soon as
9 practicable after that time, Farmee shall make such assignment to Farmor as may be necessary to
10 evidence the foregoing. At that time, Farmor shall reimburse Farmee for the estimated salvage
11 value of Farmee's salvable equipment in and on the well, less estimated salvage costs. Farmee
12 shall have no further rights or obligations under this Agreement, except Farmee shall be liable
13 for all actions which occurred prior to the effective date of the takeover. Farmor's failure to
14 notify Farmee in writing shall be deemed an election by Farmor to not take over the well.
15   If Farmor's election to take over results in a diversity of ownership giving rise to a
16 commingling of production with uncommon ownership, in Farmee's storage tanks, Farmor shall
17 be responsible for and shall bear all cost of setting and connecting tanks and pipelines for
18 production from the well taken over by Farmor.
19 **9.**   **Renewals and Extensions**.
20   If any oil and gas lease included in the Farmout Lands is extended or renewed in whole
21 or in part by either party or their agents, during the term of the Agreement, this Agreement shall
22 apply to such extension or renewal to the same extent as it would have applied to the original
23 lease. For this purpose, any new lease covering an interest originally included in the Farmout
24 Lands and acquired within 90 days after the termination of the original lease shall be considered
25 an extension or renewal.
26 **10.**   **Term of Farmout Agreement**.
27   The Farmout Agreement shall be in effect until such time as: (i) Farmee's rights to earn
28 an assignment of interest have expired without Farmee having earned an assignment; (ii) Farmee
29 has earned an assignment of interest and neither Farmee nor Farmor have any further rights or
30 obligations under the Agreement; or, (iii) this Agreement terminates pursuant to paragraph 3.3
31 above as a consequence of Farmee's default.
32 **11.**   **Miscellaneous**.
33   **11.1** **Taxes**. Farmee shall pay when due all taxes, including, but not limited to, federal
34 excise taxes, and state and local ad valorem, occupation, severance, excise, privilege or
35 regulatory taxes, now or hereafter lawfully assessed against Farmee's interest in the Farmout
36 Lands or the production attributable to Farmee's interest.
37   **11.2** **Income Tax Provisions**. If this Agreement is or may be construed as creating a
38 partnership for federal or state income tax purposes, then, unless the parties expressly provide for
39 a tax partnership in this Agreement and Exhibit D to this Agreement, Farmee is authorized and
40 directed to execute and file on behalf of all parties an election to be excluded from application of
41 the provisions of Subchapter K, Chapter 1, Subtitle A of the current United States Internal
42 Revenue Code, and any amendments, or to be excluded from application of any comparable
43 provisions of state law. Each party agrees to furnish such additional evidence of that election as
44 may be necessary or proper.

11.3 Payments by Farmor. Farmor shall have the right to pay rentals, royalties, or other payments which may become due under any oil and gas lease included in the Farmout Lands, and Farmee agrees to reimburse Farmor for the full amount of those payments which Farmor is not obligated to bear. Farmee shall pay interest on paid sums effective as of the date of the payment by Farmor at the interest rate provided in the body of this Agreement.

11.4 Division of Proceeds. To make proper division of the proceeds from the sale of oil and gas production from the Farmout Lands, Farmor shall have the right, but not the obligation, to collect such proceeds. After deducting the overriding royalty or working interest to which it is entitled, Farmor shall pay to Farmee its portion of the proceeds thus collected.

11.5 Furnishing Data. Each party has the affirmative duty to timely supply adequate data to the other party when such data is necessary to comply with Federal, State or local reporting requirements.

* * *

EXHIBIT B-1
TO FARMOUT AGREEMENT

DESCRIPTION OF FARMOUT LANDS

The Farmout Lands covered by the Farmout Agreement and in which Farmee shall have the right to earn an Assignment under the terms of the Farmout Agreement are described as follows (check appropriate limitations):

Area: [ ]   All lands covered by the oil and gas leases described on Exhibit B-2.

            [ ]   Limited to the following area: (Describe area)

Depth: [ ]   All depths.

            [ ]   Limited to the following interval: (Describe depth)

* * *

EXHIBIT B-2
TO FARMOUT AGREEMENT
LEASE SCHEDULE

Lease No:

County:

State:

Lessor:

Lessee:

Lands Covered:

Recording Information:

1 **Lease No:**
2 **County:**
3 **State:**
4 **Lessor:**
5 **Lessee:**
6 **Lands Covered:**
7 **Recording Information:**
8
9
10
11 **Lease No:**
12 **County:**
13 **State:**
14 **Lessor:**
15 **Lessee:**
16 **Lands Covered:**
17 **Recording Information:**
18
19 * * *
20 **EXHIBIT C**
21 **TO FARMOUT AGREEMENT**
22 **ACCOUNTING PROCEDURES**
23
24 The Accounting Procedure used in calculating payout of an Earning Well under the
25 Farmout Agreement shall be the same Accounting Procedure attached as Exhibit "C" to the
26 Operating Agreement, which is attached as Exhibit "E" to this Farmout Agreement.
27 * * *
28
29 **EXHIBIT D**
30 **TO FARMOUT AGREEMENT**
31 **TAX PARTNERSHIP AGREEMENT**
32
33 * * *
34 **EXHIBIT E**
35 **TO FARMOUT AGREEMENT**
36 **OPERATING AGREEMENT**
37
38 * * *
39 **EXHIBIT F**
40 **TO FARMOUT AGREEMENT**
41 **GEOLOGICAL REQUIREMENTS**

NOTES

1.   This form was furnished by Kanes Forms, P.O. Box 53010, Midland, TX 79710, tel. 800-526-3790. http://www.kanesforms.com/new/index.htm. Farmout agreements may be "drill to earn" or "produce to earn," and they may "option to drill" or "obligation to drill." What does the above form provide?

2.   A form used in assigning acreage earned by the farmee may be attached to the agreement as an exhibit. One matter of concern to the farmee is whether it retains earned acreage for the entire life of the underlying lease or whether its rights terminate upon the occurrence of specified events, such as cessation of production. One assignment form frequently used in farmouts contains the following clause:

> At the time any well located on the Assigned Premises ceases production, this agreement shall automatically terminate as to such well and the acreage attributable thereto unless Grantor commences additional drilling or reworking operations within sixty (60) days of cessation of production. If such operations are continuously prosecuted with no cessation of over thirty (30) consecutive days and result in the restoration of production in paying quantities, then this agreement shall remain in effect so long as oil or gas are produced from the Assigned Premises in paying quantities. If such operations are not continuously prosecuted or production in paying quantities is not restored, this agreement shall automatically terminate as to such well and the acreage attributable thereto and Grantee agrees to make, execute and deliver to Grantor within sixty (60) days of such termination an instrument in recordable form, at no cost to Grantor, reassigning to Grantor all rights so forfeited.

This clause appears to require actual production from a well. Payment of shut-in royalty on a gas well would apparently not maintain the assignee's rights to the well or the acreage attributed to it.

3.   Article 5.3 of the General Terms and Conditions requires the farmee to obtain the types of insurance set out in that provision. Frequently, insurance matters are specified in a separate exhibit and will frequently require more insurance coverage, including worker's compensation insurance, employer's liability insurance, commercial general liability insurance, automobile liability insurance, excess liability insurance in umbrella form, control of well insurance, and perhaps pollution insurance. The insurance provisions in the farmout agreement will usually provide that the insurers waive subrogation in favor of the farmee and may even provide that the farmor be named an "additional insured" under the farmee's policies.

* * *

OPERATING AGREEMENT
DATED
_____, 19__,

OPERATOR:
CONTRACT AREA:
COUNTY OR PARISH:
STATE OF

* * *

* * *

TABLE OF CONTENTS

11   * * *

OPERATING AGREEMENT

12
13   THIS AGREEMENT, entered into by and between _____, hereinafter designated and
14 referred to as "Operator," and the signatory party or parties other than Operator, sometimes
15 hereinafter referred to individually as "Non–Operator," and collectively as "Non–Operators."
16   WITNESSETH:
17   WHEREAS, the parties to this agreement are owners of Oil and Gas Leases and/or Oil
18 and Gas Interests in the land identified in Exhibit "A," and the parties hereto have reached an
19 agreement to explore and develop these Leases and/or Oil and Gas Interests for the production of
20 Oil and Gas to the extent and as hereinafter provided,
21   NOW, THEREFORE, it is agreed as follows:
22

ARTICLE I.
DEFINITIONS

23
24
25   As used in this agreement, the following words and terms shall have the meanings here
26 ascribed to them:
27   A. The term "AFE" shall mean an Authority for Expenditure prepared by a party to this
28 agreement for the purpose of estimating the costs to be incurred in conducting an operation
29 hereunder.
30   B. The term "Completion" or "Complete" shall mean a single operation intended to
31 complete a well as a producer of Oil and Gas in one or more Zones, including, but not limited to,
32 the setting of production casing, perforating, well stimulation and production testing conducted
33 in such operation.
34   C. The term "Contract Area" shall mean all of the lands, Oil and Gas Leases and/or Oil
35 and Gas Interests intended to be developed and operated for Oil and Gas purposes under this
36 agreement. Such lands, Oil and Gas Leases and Oil and Gas Interests are described in Exhibit
37 "A."
38   D. The term "Deepen" shall mean a single operation whereby a well is drilled to an
39 objective Zone below the deepest Zone in which the well was previously drilled, or below the
40 deepest Zone proposed in the associated AFE, whichever is the lesser.
41   E. The terms "Drilling Party" and "Consenting Party" shall mean a party who agrees to
42 join in and pay its share of the cost of any operation conducted under the provisions of this
43 agreement.
44   F. The term "Drilling Unit" shall mean the area fixed for the drilling of one well by order
45 or rule of any state or federal body having authority. If a Drilling Unit is not fixed by any such

rule or order, a Drilling Unit shall be the drilling unit as established by the pattern of drilling in the Contract Area unless fixed by express agreement of the Drilling Parties.

G. The term "Drillsite" shall mean the Oil and Gas Lease or Oil and Gas Interest on which a proposed well is to be located.

H. The term "Initial Well" shall mean the well required to be drilled by the parties hereto as provided in Article VI.A.

I. The term "Non-Consent Well" shall mean a well in which less than all parties have conducted an operation as provided in Article VI.B.2.

J. The terms "Non-Drilling Party" and "Non-Consenting Party" shall mean a party who elects not to participate in a proposed operation.

K. The term "Oil and Gas" shall mean oil, gas, casinghead gas, gas condensate, and/or all other liquid or gaseous hydrocarbons and other marketable substances produced therewith, unless an intent to limit the inclusiveness of this term is specifically stated.

L. The term "Oil and Gas Interests" or "Interests" shall mean unleased fee and mineral interests in Oil and Gas in tracts of land lying within the Contract Area which are owned by parties to this agreement.

M. The terms "Oil and Gas Lease," "Lease" and "Leasehold" shall mean the oil and gas leases or interests therein covering tracts of land lying within the Contract Area which are owned by the parties to this agreement.

N. The term "Plug Back" shall mean a single operation whereby a deeper Zone is abandoned in order to attempt a Completion in a shallower Zone.

O. The term "Recompletion" or "Recomplete" shall mean an operation whereby a Completion in one Zone is abandoned in order to attempt a Completion in a different Zone within the existing wellbore.

P. The term "Rework" shall mean an operation conducted in the wellbore of a well after it is Completed to secure, restore, or improve production in a Zone which is currently open to production in the wellbore. Such operations include, but are not limited to, well stimulation operations but exclude any routine repair or maintenance work or drilling, Sidetracking, Deepening, Completing, Recompleting, or Plugging Back of a well.

Q. The term "Sidetrack" shall mean the directional control and intentional deviation of a well from vertical so as to change the bottom hole location unless done to straighten the hole or to drill around junk in the hole to overcome other mechanical difficulties.

R. The term "Zone" shall mean a stratum of earth containing or thought to contain a common accumulation of Oil and Gas separately producible from any other common accumulation of Oil and Gas.

Unless the context otherwise clearly indicates, words used in the singular include the plural, the word "person" includes natural and artificial persons, the plural includes the singular, and any gender includes the masculine, feminine, and neuter.

ARTICLE II.
EXHIBITS

The following exhibits, as indicated below and attached hereto, are incorporated in and made a part hereof:

_____ A. Exhibit "A," shall include the following information:

(1) Description of lands subject to this agreement,

(2) Restrictions, if any, as to depths, formations, or substances,

(3) Parties to agreement with addresses and telephone numbers for notice purposes,

(4) Percentages or fractional interests of parties to this agreement,

(5) Oil and Gas Leases and/or Oil and Gas Interests subject to this agreement,

(6) Burdens on production.

_____ B. Exhibit "B," Form of Lease.

_____ C. Exhibit "C," Accounting Procedure.

_____ D. Exhibit "D," Insurance.

_____ E. Exhibit "E," Gas Balancing Agreement.

_____ F. Exhibit "F," Non–Discrimination and Certification of Non–Segregated Facilities.

_____ G. Exhibit "G," Tax Partnership.

_____ H. Other: _____

If any provision of any exhibit, except Exhibits "E," "F" and "G," is inconsistent with any provision contained in the body of this agreement, the provisions in the body of this agreement shall prevail.

ARTICLE III.
INTERESTS OF PARTIES

A. Oil and Gas Interests:

If any party owns an Oil and Gas Interest in the Contract Area, that Interest shall be treated for all purposes of this agreement and during the term hereof as if it were covered by the form of Oil and Gas Lease attached hereto as Exhibit "B," and the owner thereof shall be deemed to own both royalty interest in such lease and the interest of the lessee thereunder.

B. Interests of Parties in Costs and Production:

Unless changed by other provisions, all costs and liabilities incurred in operations under this agreement shall be borne and paid, and all equipment and materials acquired in operations on the Contract Area shall be owned, by the parties as their interests are set forth in Exhibit "A." In the same manner, the parties shall also own all production of Oil and Gas from the Contract Area subject, however, to the payment of royalties and other burdens on production as described hereafter.

Regardless of which party has contributed any Oil and Gas Lease or Oil and Gas Interest on which royalty or other burdens may be payable and except as otherwise expressly provided in this agreement, each party shall pay or deliver, or cause to be paid or delivered, all burdens on its share of the production from the Contract Area up to, but not in excess of, _____ and shall indemnify, defend and hold the other parties free from any liability therefor. Except as otherwise expressly provided in this agreement, if any party has contributed hereto any Lease or Interest which is burdened with any royalty, overriding royalty, production payment or other burden on production in excess of the amounts stipulated above, such party so burdened shall assume and alone bear all such excess obligations and shall indemnify, defend and hold the other parties hereto harmless from any and all claims attributable to such excess burden. However, so long as the Drilling Unit for the productive Zone(s) is identical with the Contract Area, each party shall pay or deliver, or cause to be paid or delivered, all burdens on production from the Contract Area due under the terms of the Oil and Gas Lease(s) which such party has contributed to this agreement, and shall indemnify, defend and hold the other parties free from any liability therefor.

No party shall ever be responsible, on a price basis higher than the price received by such party, to any other party's lessor or royalty owner, and if such other party's lessor or royalty owner should demand and receive settlement on a higher price basis, the party contributing the affected Lease shall bear the additional royalty burden attributable to such higher price.

Nothing contained in this Article III.B. shall be deemed an assignment or cross-assignment of interests covered hereby, and in the event two or more parties contribute to this agreement jointly owned Leases, the parties' undivided interests in said Leaseholds shall be deemed separate leasehold interests for the purposes of this agreement.

C. Subsequently Created Interests:

If any party has contributed hereto a Lease or Interest that is burdened with an assignment of production given as security for the payment of money, or if, after the date of this agreement, any party creates an overriding royalty, production payment, net profits interest, assignment of production or other burden payable out of production attributable to its working interest hereunder, such burden shall be deemed a "Subsequently Created Interest." Further, if any party has contributed hereto a Lease or Interest burdened with an overriding royalty, production payment, net profits interest, or other burden payable out of production created prior to the date of this agreement, and such burden is not shown on Exhibit "A," such burden also shall be deemed a Subsequently Created Interest to the extent such burden causes the burdens on such party's Lease or Interest to exceed the amount stipulated in Article III.B. above.

The party whose interest is burdened with the Subsequently Created Interest (the "Burdened Party") shall assume and alone bear, pay and discharge the Subsequently Created Interest and shall indemnify, defend and hold harmless the other parties from and against any liability therefor. Further, if the Burdened Party fails to pay, when due, its share of expenses chargeable hereunder, all provisions of Article VII.B. shall be enforceable against the Subsequently Created Interest in the same manner as they are enforceable against the working interest of the Burdened Party. If the Burdened Party is required under this agreement to assign or relinquish to any other party, or parties, all or a portion of its working interest and/or the production attributable thereto, said other party, or parties, shall receive said assignment and/or production free and clear of said Subsequently Created Interest, and the Burdened Party shall indemnify, defend and hold harmless said other party, or parties, from any and all claims and demands for payment asserted by owners of the Subsequently Created Interest.

ARTICLE IV.
TITLES

A. Title Examination:

Title examination shall be made on the Drillsite of any proposed well prior to commencement of drilling operations and, if a majority in interest of the Drilling Parties so request or Operator so elects, title examination shall be made on the entire Drilling Unit, or maximum anticipated Drilling Unit, of the well. The opinion will include the ownership of the working interest, minerals, royalty, overriding royalty and production payments under the applicable Leases. Each party contributing Leases and/or Oil and Gas Interests to be included in the Drillsite or Drilling Unit, if appropriate, shall furnish to Operator all abstracts (including

278

federal lease status reports), title opinions, title papers and curative material in its possession free of charge. All such information not in the possession of or made available to Operator by the parties, but necessary for the examination of the title, shall be obtained by Operator. Operator shall cause title to be examined by attorneys on its staff or by outside attorneys. Copies of all title opinions shall be furnished to each Drilling Party. Costs incurred by Operator in procuring abstracts, fees paid outside attorneys for title examination (including preliminary, supplemental, shut-in royalty opinions and division order title opinions) and other direct charges as provided in Exhibit "C" shall be borne by the Drilling Parties in the proportion that the interest of each Drilling Party bears to the total interest of all Drilling Parties as such interests appear in Exhibit "A." Operator shall make no charge for services rendered by its staff attorneys or other personnel in the performance of the above functions.

Each party shall be responsible for securing curative matter and pooling amendments or agreements required in connection with Leases or Oil and Gas Interests contributed by such party. Operator shall be responsible for the preparation and recording of pooling designations or declarations and communitization agreements as well as the conduct of hearings before governmental agencies for the securing of spacing or pooling orders or any other orders necessary or appropriate to the conduct of operations hereunder. This shall not prevent any party from appearing on its own behalf at such hearings. Costs incurred by Operator, including fees paid to outside attorneys, which are associated with hearings before governmental agencies, and which costs are necessary and proper for the activities contemplated under this agreement, shall be direct charges to the joint account and shall not be covered by the administrative overhead charges as provided in Exhibit "C" Operator shall make no charge for services rendered by its staff attorneys or other personnel in the performance of the above functions.

No well shall be drilled on the Contract Area until after (1) the title to the Drillsite or Drilling Unit, if appropriate, has been examined as above provided, and (2) the title has been approved by the examining attorney or title has been accepted by all of the Drilling Parties in such well.

B. Loss or Failure of Title:

1. _Failure of Title:_ Should any Oil and Gas Interest or Oil and Gas Lease be lost through failure of title, which results in a reduction of interest from that shown on Exhibit "A," the party credited with contributing the affected Lease or Interest (including, if applicable, a successor in interest to such party) shall have ninety (90) days from final determination of title failure to acquire a new lease or other instrument curing the entirety of the title failure, which acquisition will not be subject to Article VIII.B., and failing to do so, this agreement, nevertheless, shall continue in force as to all remaining Oil and Gas Leases and Interests; and,

(a) The party credited with contributing the Oil and Gas Lease or Interest affected by the title failure (including, if applicable, a successor in interest to such party) shall bear alone the entire loss and it shall not be entitled to recover from Operator or the other parties any development or operating costs which it may have previously paid or incurred, but there shall be no additional liability on its part to the other parties hereto by reason of such title failure;

(b) There shall be no retroactive adjustment of expenses incurred or revenues received from the operation of the Lease or Interest which has failed, but the interests of the parties contained on Exhibit "A" shall be revised on an acreage basis, as of the time it is determined finally that title failure has occurred, so that the interest of the party whose Lease or Interest is affected by the title failure will thereafter be reduced in the Contract Area by the amount of the Lease or Interest failed;

(c) If the proportionate interest of the other parties hereto in any producing well previously drilled on the Contract Area is increased by reason of the title failure, the party who bore the costs incurred in connection with such well attributable to the Lease or Interest which has failed shall receive the proceeds attributable to the increase in such interest (less costs and burdens attributable thereto) until it has been reimbursed for unrecovered costs paid by it in connection with such well attributable to such failed Lease or Interest;

(d) Should any person not a party to this agreement, who is determined to be the owner of any Lease or Interest which has failed, pay in any manner any part of the cost of operation, development, or equipment, such amount shall be paid to the party or parties who bore the costs which are so refunded;

(e) Any liability to account to a person not a party to this agreement for prior production of Oil and Gas which arises by reason of title failure shall be borne severally by each party (including a predecessor to a current party) who received production for which such accounting is required based on the amount of such production received, and each such party shall severally indemnify, defend and hold harmless all other parties hereto for any such liability to account;

(f) No charge shall be made to the joint account for legal expenses, fees or salaries in connection with the defense of the Lease or Interest claimed to have failed, but if the party contributing such Lease or Interest hereto elects to defend its title it shall bear all expenses in connection therewith; and

(g) If any party is given credit on Exhibit "A" to a Lease or Interest which is limited solely to ownership of an interest in the wellbore of any well or wells and the production therefrom, such party's absence of interest in the remainder of the Contract Area shall be considered a Failure of Title as to such remaining Contract Area unless that absence of interest is reflected on Exhibit "A."

2. Loss by Non-Payment or Erroneous Payment of Amount Due: If, through mistake or oversight, any rental, shut-in well payment, minimum royalty or royalty payment, or other payment necessary to maintain all or a portion of an Oil and Gas Lease or Interest is not paid or is erroneously paid, and as a result a Lease or Interest terminates, there shall be no monetary liability against the party who failed to make such payment. Unless the party who failed to make the required payment secures a new Lease or Interest covering the same interest within ninety (90) days from the discovery of the failure to make proper payment, which acquisition will not be subject to Article VIII.B., the interests of the parties reflected on Exhibit "A" shall be revised on an acreage basis, effective as of the date of termination of the Lease or Interest involved, and the party who failed to make proper payment will no longer be credited with an interest in the Contract Area on account of ownership of the Lease or Interest which has terminated. If the party who failed to make the required payment shall not have been fully reimbursed, at the time of the loss, from the proceeds of the sale of Oil and Gas attributable to the lost Lease or Interest, calculated on an acreage basis, for the development and operating costs previously paid on account of such Lease or Interest, it shall be reimbursed for unrecovered actual costs previously

paid by it (but not for its share of the cost of any dry hole previously drilled or wells previously abandoned) from so much of the following as is necessary to effect reimbursement:

(a) Proceeds of Oil and Gas produced prior to termination of the Lease or Interest, less operating expenses and lease burdens chargeable hereunder to the person who failed to make payment, previously accrued to the credit of the lost Lease or Interest, on an acreage basis, up to the amount of unrecovered costs;

(b) Proceeds of Oil and Gas, less operating expenses and lease burdens chargeable hereunder to the person who failed to make payment, up to the amount of unrecovered costs attributable to that portion of Oil and Gas thereafter produced and marketed (excluding production from any wells thereafter drilled) which, in the absence of such Lease or Interest termination, would be attributable to the lost Lease or Interest on an acreage basis and which as a result of such Lease or Interest termination is credited to other parties, the proceeds of said portion of the Oil and Gas to be contributed by the other parties in proportion to their respective interests reflected on Exhibit "A"; and,

(c) Any monies, up to the amount of unrecovered costs, that may be paid by any party who is, or becomes, the owner of the Lease or Interest lost, for the privilege of participating in the Contract Area or becoming a party to this agreement.

3. Other Losses: All losses of Leases or Interests committed to this agreement, other than those set forth in Articles IV.B.1. and IV.B.2. above, shall be joint losses and shall be borne by all parties in proportion to their interests shown on Exhibit "A." This shall include but not be limited to the loss of any Lease or Interest through failure to develop or because express or implied covenants have not been performed (other than performance which requires only the payment of money), and the loss of any Lease by expiration at the end of its primary term if it is not renewed or extended. There shall be no readjustment of interests in the remaining portion of the Contract Area on account of any joint loss.

4. Curing Title: In the event of a Failure of Title under Article IV.B.1. or a loss of title under Article IV.B.2. above, any Lease or Interest acquired by any party hereto (other than the party whose interest has failed or was lost) during the ninety (90) day period provided by Article IV.B.1. and Article IV.B.2. above covering all or a portion of the interest that has failed or was lost shall be offered at cost to the party whose interest has failed or was lost, and the provisions of Article VIII.B. shall not apply to such acquisition.

ARTICLE V.
OPERATOR
A. Designation and Responsibilities of Operator:

_____ shall be the Operator of the Contract Area, and shall conduct and direct and have full control of all operations on the Contract Area as permitted and required by, and within the limits of this agreement. In its performance of services hereunder for the Non–Operators, Operator shall be an independent contractor not subject to the control or direction of the Non–Operators except as to the type of operation to be undertaken in accordance with the election procedures contained in this agreement. Operator shall not be deemed, or hold itself out as, the agent of the Non–Operators with authority to bind them to any obligation or liability assumed or incurred by Operator as to any third party. Operator shall conduct its activities under this agreement as a reasonable prudent operator, in a good and workmanlike manner, with due

281

1 diligence and dispatch, in accordance with good oilfield practice, and in compliance with
2 applicable law and regulation, but in no event shall it have any liability as Operator to the other
3 parties for losses sustained or liabilities incurred except such as may result from gross negligence
4 or willful misconduct.[2]

B. Resignation or Removal of Operator and Selection of Successor:

6   1. <u>Resignation or Removal of Operator:</u> Operator may resign at any time by giving
7 written notice thereof to Non-Operators. If Operator terminates its legal existence, no longer
8 owns an interest hereunder in the Contract Area, or is no longer capable of serving as Operator,
9 Operator shall be deemed to have resigned without any action by Non-Operators, except the
10 selection of a successor. Operator may be removed only for good cause by the affirmative vote
11 of Non-Operators owning a majority interest based on ownership as shown on Exhibit "A"
12 remaining after excluding the voting interest of Operator; such vote shall not be deemed
13 effective until a written notice has been delivered to the Operator by a Non-Operator detailing
14 the alleged default and Operator has failed to cure the default within thirty (30) days from its
15 receipt of the notice or, if the default concerns an operation then being conducted, within
16 forty-eight (48) hours of its receipt of the notice. For purposes hereof, "good cause" shall mean
17 not only gross negligence or willful misconduct but also the material breach of or inability to
18 meet the standards of operation contained in Article V.A. or material failure or inability to
19 perform its obligations under this agreement.

20   Subject to Article VII.D.1., such resignation or removal shall not become effective until
21 7:00 o'clock A.M. on the first day of the calendar month following the expiration of ninety (90)
22 days after the giving of notice of resignation by Operator or action by the Non-Operators to
23 remove Operator, unless a successor Operator has been selected and assumes the duties of
24 Operator at an earlier date. Operator, after effective date of resignation or removal, shall be
25 bound by the terms hereof as a Non-Operator. A change of a corporate name or structure of
26 Operator or transfer of Operator's interest to any single subsidiary, parent or successor
27 corporation shall not be the basis for removal of Operator.

28   2. <u>Selection of Successor Operator:</u> Upon the resignation or removal of Operator under
29 any provision of this agreement, a successor Operator shall be selected by the parties. The
30 successor Operator shall be selected from the parties owning an interest in the Contract Area at
31 the time such successor Operator is selected. The successor Operator shall be selected by the
32 affirmative vote of two (2) or more parties owning a majority interest based on ownership as
33 shown on Exhibit "A"; provided, however, if an Operator which has been removed or is deemed
34 to have resigned fails to vote or votes only to succeed itself, the successor Operator shall be
35 selected by the affirmative vote of the party or parties owning a majority interest based on
36 ownership as shown on Exhibit "A" remaining after excluding the voting interest of the Operator
37 that was removed or resigned. The former Operator shall promptly deliver to the successor
38 Operator all records and data relating to the operations conducted by the former Operator to the
39 extent such records and data are not already in the possession of the successor operator. Any
40 cost of obtaining or copying the former Operator's records and data shall be charged to the joint
41 account.

42   3. <u>Effect of Bankruptcy:</u> If Operator becomes insolvent, bankrupt or is placed in
43 receivership, it shall be deemed to have resigned without any action by Non-Operators, except
44 the selection of a successor. If a petition for relief under the federal bankruptcy laws is filed by

or against Operator, and the removal of Operator is prevented by the federal bankruptcy court, all Non-Operators and Operator shall comprise an interim operating committee to serve until Operator has elected to reject or assume this agreement pursuant to the Bankruptcy Code, and an election to reject this agreement by Operator as a debtor in possession, or by a trustee in bankruptcy, shall be deemed a resignation as Operator without any action by Non-Operators, except the selection of a successor. During the period of time the operating committee controls operations, all actions shall require the approval of two (2) or more parties owning a majority interest based on ownership as shown on Exhibit "A." In the event there are only two (2) parties to this agreement, during the period of time the operating committee controls operations, a third party acceptable to Operator, Non-Operator and the federal bankruptcy court shall be selected as a member of the operating committee, and all actions shall require the approval of two (2) members of the operating committee without regard for their interest in the Contract Area based on Exhibit "A."

C. Employees and Contractors:

The number of employees or contractors used by Operator in conducting operations hereunder, their selection, and the hours of labor and the compensation for services performed shall be determined by Operator, and all such employees or contractors shall be the employees or contractors of Operator.

D. Rights and Duties of Operator:

1. Competitive Rates and Use of Affiliates: All wells drilled on the Contract Area shall be drilled on a competitive contract basis at the usual rates prevailing in the area. If it so desires, Operator may employ its own tools and equipment in the drilling of wells, but its charges therefor shall not exceed the prevailing rates in the area and the rate of such charges shall be agreed upon by the parties in writing before drilling operations are commenced, and such work shall be performed by Operator under the same terms and conditions as are customary and usual in the area in contracts of independent contractors who are doing work of a similar nature. All work performed or materials supplied by affiliates or related parties of Operator shall be performed or supplied at competitive rates, pursuant to written agreement, and in accordance with customs and standards prevailing in the industry.

2. Discharge of Joint Account Obligations: Except as herein otherwise specifically provided, Operator shall promptly pay and discharge expenses incurred in the development and operation of the Contract Area pursuant to this agreement and shall charge each of the parties hereto with their respective proportionate shares upon the expense basis provided in Exhibit "C." Operator shall keep an accurate record of the joint account hereunder, showing expenses incurred and charges and credits made and received.

3. Protection from Liens: Operator shall pay, or cause to be paid, as and when they become due and payable, all accounts of contractors and suppliers and wages and salaries for services rendered or performed, and for materials supplied on, to or in respect of the Contract Area or any operations for the joint account thereof, and shall keep the Contract Area free from liens and encumbrances resulting therefrom except for those resulting from a bona fide dispute as to services rendered or materials supplied.

4. Custody of Funds: Operator shall hold for the account of the Non-Operators any funds of the Non-Operators advanced or paid to the Operator, either for the conduct of operations hereunder or as a result of the sale of production from the Contract Area, and such funds shall

remain the funds of the Non-Operators on whose account they are advanced or paid until used for their intended purpose or otherwise delivered to the Non-Operators or applied toward the payment of debts as provided in Article VII.B. Nothing in this paragraph shall be construed to establish a fiduciary relationship between Operator and Non-Operators for any purpose other than to account for Non-Operator funds as herein specifically provided. Nothing in this paragraph shall require the maintenance by Operator of separate accounts for the funds of Non-Operators unless the parties otherwise specifically agree.

5. <u>Access to Contract Area and Records:</u> Operator shall, except as otherwise provided herein, permit each Non-Operator or its duly authorized representative, at the Non-Operator's sole risk and cost, full and free access at all reasonable times to all operations of every kind and character being conducted for the joint account on the Contract Area and to the records of operations conducted thereon or production therefrom, including Operator's books and records relating thereto. Such access rights shall not be exercised in a manner interfering with Operator's conduct of an operation hereunder and shall not obligate Operator to furnish any geologic or geophysical data of an interpretive nature unless the cost of preparation of such interpretive data was charged to the joint account. Operator will furnish to each Non-Operator upon request copies of any and all reports and information obtained by Operator in connection with production and related items, including, without limitation, meter and chart reports, production purchaser statements, run tickets and monthly gauge reports, but excluding purchase contracts and pricing information to the extent not applicable to the production of the Non-Operator seeking the information. Any audit of Operator's records relating to amounts expended and the appropriateness of such expenditures shall be conducted in accordance with the audit protocol specified in Exhibit "C."

6. <u>Filing and Furnishing Governmental Reports:</u> Operator will file, and upon written request promptly furnish copies to each requesting Non-Operator not in default of its payment obligations, all operational notices, reports or applications required to be filed by local, State, Federal or Indian agencies or authorities having jurisdiction over operations hereunder. Each Non-Operator shall provide to Operator on a timely basis all information necessary to Operator to make such filings.

7. <u>Drilling and Testing Operations:</u> The following provisions shall apply to each well drilled hereunder, including but not limited to the Initial Well:

(a) Operator will promptly advise Non-Operators of the date on which the well is spudded, or the date on which drilling operations are commenced.

(b) Operator will send to Non-Operators such reports, test results and notices regarding the progress of operations on the well as the Non-Operators shall reasonably request, including, but not limited to, daily drilling reports, completion reports, and well logs.

(c) Operator shall adequately test all Zones encountered which may reasonably be expected to be capable of producing Oil and Gas in paying quantities as a result of examination of the electric log or any other logs or cores or tests conducted hereunder.

8. <u>Cost Estimates.</u> Upon request of any Consenting Party, Operator shall furnish estimates of current and cumulative costs incurred for the joint account at reasonable intervals during the conduct of any operation pursuant to this agreement. Operator shall not be held liable for errors in such estimates so long as the estimates are made in good faith.

1 9. Insurance: At all times while operations are conducted hereunder, Operator shall
2 comply with the workers compensation law of the state where the operations are being
3 conducted; provided, however, that Operator may be a self-insurer for liability under said
4 compensation laws in which event the only charge that shall be made to the joint account shall be
5 as provided in Exhibit "C." Operator shall also carry or provide insurance for the benefit of the
6 joint account of the parties as outlined in Exhibit "D" attached hereto and made a part hereof.
7 Operator shall require all contractors engaged in work on or for the Contract Area to comply
8 with the workers compensation law of the state where the operations are being conducted and to
9 maintain such other insurance as Operator may require.
10   In the event automobile liability insurance is specified in said Exhibit "D," or
11 subsequently receives the approval of the parties, no direct charge shall be made by Operator for
12 premiums paid for such insurance for Operator's automotive equipment.
13
14   **ARTICLE VI.**
15   **DRILLING AND DEVELOPMENT**
16 **A. Initial Well:**
17   On or before the _____ day of _____, 19__, Operator shall commence the drilling of
18 the Initial Well at the following location:
19
20 and shall thereafter continue the drilling of the well with due diligence to
21
22 The drilling of the Initial Well and the participation therein by all parties is obligatory, subject to
23 Article VI.C.1. as to participation in Completion operations and Article VI.F. as to termination of
24 operations and Article XI as to occurrence of force majeure.
25 **B. Subsequent Operations:**
26   1. Proposed Operations: If any party hereto should desire to drill any well on the
27 Contract Area other than the Initial Well, or if any party should desire to Rework, Sidetrack,
28 Deepen, Recomplete or Plug Back a dry hole or a well no longer capable of producing in paying
29 quantities in which such party has not otherwise relinquished its interest in the proposed
30 objective Zone under this agreement, the party desiring to drill, Rework, Sidetrack, Deepen,
31 Recomplete or Plug Back such a well shall give written notice of the proposed operation to the
32 parties who have not otherwise relinquished their interest in such objective Zone under this
33 agreement and to all other parties in the case of a proposal for Sidetracking or Deepening,
34 specifying the work to be performed, the location, proposed depth, objective Zone and the
35 estimated cost of the operation. The parties to whom such a notice is delivered shall have thirty
36 (30) days after receipt of the notice within which to notify the party proposing to do the work
37 whether they elect to participate in the cost of the proposed operation. If a drilling rig is on
38 location, notice of a proposal to Rework, Sidetrack, Recomplete, Plug Back or Deepen may be
39 given by telephone and the response period shall be limited to forty-eight (48) hours, exclusive
40 of Saturday, Sunday and legal holidays. Failure of a party to whom such notice is delivered to
41 reply within the period above fixed shall constitute an election by that party not to participate in
42 the cost of the proposed operation. Any proposal by a party to conduct an operation conflicting
43 with the operation initially proposed shall be delivered to all parties within the time and in the
44 manner provided in Article VI.B.6.

If all parties to whom such notice is delivered elect to participate in such a proposed operation, the parties shall be contractually committed to participate therein provided such operations are commenced within the time period hereafter set forth, and Operator shall, no later than ninety (90) days after expiration of the notice period of thirty (30) days (or as promptly as practicable after the expiration of the forty-eight (48) hour period when a drilling rig is on location, as the case may be), actually commence the proposed operation and thereafter complete it with due diligence at the risk and expense of the parties participating therein; provided, however, said commencement date may be extended upon written notice of same by Operator to the other parties, for a period of up to thirty (30) additional days if, in the sole opinion of Operator, such additional time is reasonably necessary to obtain permits from governmental authorities, surface rights (including rights-of-way) or appropriate drilling equipment, or to complete title examination or curative matter required for title approval or acceptance. If the actual operation has not been commenced within the time provided (including any extension thereof as specifically permitted herein or in the force majeure provisions of Article XI) and if any party hereto still desires to conduct said operation, written notice proposing same must be resubmitted to the other parties in accordance herewith as if no prior proposal had been made. Those parties that did not participate in the drilling of a well for which a proposal to Deepen or Sidetrack is made hereunder shall, if such parties desire to participate in the proposed Deepening or Sidetracking operation, reimburse the Drilling Parties in accordance with Article VI.B.4. in the event of a Deepening operation and in accordance with Article VI.B.5. in the event of a Sidetracking operation.

2. Operations by Less Than All Parties:

(a) Determination of Participation. If any party to whom such notice is delivered as provided in Article VI.B.1. or VI.C.1. (Option No. 2) elects not to participate in the proposed operation, then, in order to be entitled to the benefits of this Article, the party or parties giving the notice and such other parties as shall elect to participate in the operation shall, no later than ninety (90) days after the expiration of the notice period of thirty (30) days (or as promptly as practicable after the expiration of the forty-eight (48) hour period when a drilling rig is on location, as the case may be) actually commence the proposed operation and complete it with due diligence. Operator shall perform all work for the account of the Consenting Parties; provided, however, if no drilling rig or other equipment is on location, and if Operator is a Non-Consenting Party, the Consenting Parties shall either: (i) request Operator to perform the work required by such proposed operation for the account of the Consenting Parties, or (ii) designate one of the Consenting Parties as Operator to perform such work. The rights and duties granted to and imposed upon the Operator under this agreement are granted to and imposed upon the party designated as Operator for an operation in which the original Operator is a Non-Consenting Party. Consenting Parties, when conducting operations on the Contract Area pursuant to this Article VI.B.2., shall comply with all terms and conditions of this agreement.

If less than all parties approve any proposed operation, the proposing party, immediately after the expiration of the applicable notice period, shall advise all Parties of the total interest of the parties approving such operation and its recommendation as to whether the Consenting Parties should proceed with the operation as proposed. Each

286

Consenting Party, within forty-eight (48) hours (exclusive of Saturday, Sunday and legal holidays) after delivery of such notice, shall advise the proposing party of its desire to (i) limit participation to such party's interest as shown on Exhibit "A" or (ii) carry only its proportionate part (determined by dividing such party's interest in the Contract Area by the interests of all Consenting Parties in the Contract Area) of Non-Consenting Parties' interests, or (iii) carry its proportionate part (determined as provided in (ii)) of Non-Consenting Parties' interests together with all or a portion of its proportionate part of any Non-Consenting Parties' interests that any Consenting Party did not elect to take. Any interest of Non-Consenting Parties that is not carried by a Consenting Party shall be deemed to be carried by the party proposing the operation if such party does not withdraw its proposal. Failure to advise the proposing party within the time required shall be deemed an election under (i). In the event a drilling rig is on location, notice may be given by telephone, and the time permitted for such a response shall not exceed a total of forty-eight (48) hours (exclusive of Saturday, Sunday and legal holidays). The proposing party, at its election, may withdraw such proposal if there is less than 100% participation and shall notify all parties of such decision within ten (10) days, or within twenty-four (24) hours if a drilling rig is on location, following expiration of the applicable response period. If 100% subscription to the proposed operation is obtained, the proposing party shall promptly notify the Consenting Parties of their proportionate interests in the operation and the party serving as Operator shall commence such operation within the period provided in Article VI.B.1., subject to the same extension right as provided therein.

(b) Relinquishment of Interest for Non-Participation. The entire cost and risk of conducting such operations shall be borne by the Consenting Parties in the proportions they have elected to bear same under the terms of the preceding paragraph. Consenting Parties shall keep the leasehold estates involved in such operations free and clear of all liens and encumbrances of every kind created by or arising from the operations of the Consenting Parties. If such an operation results in a dry hole, then subject to Articles VI.B.6. and VI.E.3., the Consenting Parties shall plug and abandon the well and restore the surface location at their sole cost, risk and expense; provided, however, that those Non-Consenting Parties that participated in the drilling, Deepening or Sidetracking of the well shall remain liable for, and shall pay, their proportionate shares of the cost of plugging and abandoning the well and restoring the surface location insofar only as those costs were not increased by the subsequent operations of the Consenting Parties. If any well drilled, Reworked, Sidetracked, Deepened, Recompleted or Plugged Back under the provisions of this Article results in a well capable of producing Oil and/or Gas in paying quantities, the Consenting Parties shall Complete and equip the well to produce at their sole cost and risk, and the well shall then be turned over to Operator (if the Operator did not conduct the operation) and shall be operated by it at the expense and for the account of the Consenting Parties. Upon commencement of operations for the drilling, Reworking, Sidetracking, Recompleting, Deepening or Plugging Back of any such well by Consenting Parties in accordance with the provisions of this Article, each Non-Consenting Party shall be deemed to have relinquished to Consenting Parties, and the Consenting Parties shall own and be entitled to receive, in proportion to their respective interests, all of such Non–Consenting Party's interest in the well and share of production therefrom or, in the case of a Reworking, Sidetracking, Deepening, Recompleting or Plugging Back, or a Completion pursuant to Article VI.C.1. Option No. 2, all of such Non–Consenting Party's interest in the production obtained from the operation in which the Non–Consenting Party did not elect to participate. Such relinquishment shall be effective until the proceeds of the sale of such share, calculated at the well, or market value thereof if such share is not sold (after deducting applicable ad valorem, production, severance, and excise taxes, royalty, overriding royalty and other interests not excepted by Article III.C. payable out of or measured by the production from such well accruing with respect to such interest until it reverts), shall equal the total of the following:

    (i) _____% of each such Non–Consenting Party's share of the cost of any newly acquired surface equipment beyond the wellhead connections (including but not limited to stock tanks, separators, treaters, pumping equipment and piping), plus 100% of each such Non–Consenting Party's share of the cost of operation of the well commencing with first production and continuing until each such Non–Consenting Party's relinquished interest shall revert to it under other provisions of this Article, it being agreed that each Non–Consenting Party's share of such costs and equipment will be that interest which would have been chargeable to such Non–Consenting Party had it participated in the well from the beginning of the operations; and

    (ii) _____% of (a) that portion of the costs and expenses of drilling, Reworking, Sidetracking, Deepening, Plugging Back, testing, Completing, and Recompleting, after deducting any cash contributions received under Article VIII.C., and of (b) that portion of the cost of newly acquired equipment in the well (to and including the wellhead connections), which would have been chargeable to such Non–Consenting Party if it had participated therein.

Notwithstanding anything to the contrary in this Article VI.B., if the well does not reach the deepest objective Zone described in the notice proposing the well for reasons other than the encountering of granite or practically impenetrable substance or other condition in the hole rendering further operations impracticable, Operator shall give notice thereof to each Non–Consenting Party who submitted or voted for an alternative proposal under Article VI.B.6. to drill the well to a shallower Zone than the deepest objective Zone proposed in the notice under which the well was drilled, and each such Non–Consenting Party shall have the option to participate in the initial proposed Completion of the well by paying its share of the cost of drilling the well to its actual depth, calculated in the manner provided in Article VI.B.4.(a). If any such Non–Consenting Party does not elect to participate in the first Completion proposed for such well, the relinquishment provisions of this Article VI.B.2.(b) shall apply to such party's interest.

(c) Reworking, Recompleting or Plugging Back. An election not to participate in the drilling, Sidetracking or Deepening of a well shall be deemed an election not to participate in any Reworking or Plugging Back operation proposed in such a well, or portion thereof, to which the initial non-consent election applied that is conducted at any time prior to full recovery by the Consenting Parties of the Non-Consenting Party's recoupment amount. Similarly, an election not to participate in the Completing or Recompleting of a well shall be deemed an election not to participate in any Reworking operation proposed in such a well, or portion thereof, to which the initial non-consent election applied that is conducted at any time prior to full recovery by the Consenting Parties of the Non-Consenting Party's recoupment amount. Any such Reworking, Recompleting or Plugging Back operation conducted during the recoupment period shall be deemed part of the cost of operation of said well and there shall be added to the sums to be recouped by the Consenting Parties __% of that portion of the costs of the Reworking, Recompleting or Plugging Back operation which would have been chargeable to such Non-Consenting Party had it participated therein. If such a Reworking, Recompleting or Plugging Back operation is proposed during such recoupment period, the provisions of this Article VI.B. shall be applicable as between said Consenting Parties in said well.

(d) Recoupment Matters. During the period of time Consenting Parties are entitled to receive Non-Consenting Party's share of production, or the proceeds therefrom, Consenting Parties shall be responsible for the payment of all ad valorem, production, severance, excise, gathering and other taxes, and all royalty, overriding royalty and other burdens applicable to Non-Consenting Party's share of production not excepted by Article III.C.

In the case of any Reworking, Sidetracking, Plugging Back, Recompleting or Deepening operation, the Consenting Parties shall be permitted to use, free of cost, all casing, tubing and other equipment in the well, but the ownership of all such equipment shall remain unchanged; and upon abandonment of a well after such Reworking, Sidetracking, Plugging Back, Recompleting or Deepening, the Consenting Parties shall account for all such equipment to the owners thereof, with each party receiving its proportionate part in kind or in value, less cost of salvage.

Within ninety (90) days after the completion of any operation under this Article, the party conducting the operations for the Consenting Parties shall furnish each Non-Consenting Party with an inventory of the equipment in and connected to the well, and an itemized statement of the cost of drilling, Sidetracking, Deepening, Plugging Back, testing, Completing, Recompleting, and equipping the well for production; or, at its option, the operating party, in lieu of an itemized statement of such costs of operation, may submit a detailed statement of monthly billings. Each month thereafter, during the time the Consenting Parties are being reimbursed as provided above, the party conducting the operations for the Consenting Parties shall furnish the Non-Consenting Parties with an itemized statement of all costs and liabilities incurred in the operation of the well, together with a statement of the quantity of Oil and Gas produced from it and the amount of proceeds realized from the sale of the well's working interest production during the preceding month. In determining the quantity of Oil and Gas produced during any month, Consenting Parties shall use industry accepted methods such as but not limited to metering or periodic well tests. Any amount realized from the sale or other disposition of equipment newly acquired in connection with any such operation which would have been owned by a Non-Consenting Party had it participated therein shall be credited against the total unreturned costs of the work done and of the equipment purchased in determining when the interest of such Non–Consenting Party shall revert to it as above provided; and if there is a credit balance, it shall be paid to such Non–Consenting Party.

If and when the Consenting Parties recover from a Non–Consenting Party's relinquished interest the amounts provided for above, the relinquished interests of such Non–Consenting Party shall automatically revert to it as of 7:00 a.m. on the day following the day on which such recoupment occurs, and, from and after such reversion, such Non–Consenting Party shall own the same interest in such well, the material and equipment in or pertaining thereto, and the production therefrom as such Non–Consenting Party would have been entitled to had it participated in the drilling, Sidetracking, Reworking, Deepening, Recompleting or Plugging Back of said well. Thereafter, such Non–Consenting Party shall be charged with and shall pay its proportionate part of the further costs of the operation of said well in accordance with the terms of this agreement and Exhibit "C" attached hereto.

3. <u>Stand–By Costs:</u> When a well which has been drilled or Deepened has reached its authorized depth and all tests have been completed and the results thereof furnished to the parties, or when operations on the well have been otherwise terminated pursuant to Article VI.F., stand-by costs incurred pending response to a party's notice proposing a Reworking, Sidetracking, Deepening, Recompleting, Plugging Back or Completing operation in such a well (including the period required under Article VI.B.6. to resolve competing proposals) shall be charged and borne as part of the drilling or Deepening operation just completed. Stand-by costs subsequent to all parties responding, or expiration of the response time permitted, whichever first occurs, and prior to agreement as to the participating interests of all Consenting Parties pursuant to the terms of the second grammatical paragraph of Article VI.B.2.(a), shall be charged to and borne as part of the proposed operation, but if the proposal is subsequently withdrawn because of insufficient participation, such stand-by costs shall be allocated between the Consenting Parties in the proportion each Consenting Party's interest as shown on Exhibit "A" bears to the total interest as shown on Exhibit "A" of all Consenting Parties.

In the event that notice for a Sidetracking operation is given while the drilling rig to be utilized is on location, any party may request and receive up to five (5) additional days after expiration of the forty-eight hour response period specified in Article VI.B.1. within which to respond by paying for all stand-by costs and other costs incurred during such extended response period; Operator may require such party to pay the estimated stand-by time in advance as a condition to extending the response period. If more than one party elects to take such additional time to respond to the notice, standby costs shall be allocated between the parties taking additional time to respond on a day-to-day basis in the proportion each electing party's interest as shown on Exhibit "A" bears to the total interest as shown on Exhibit "A" of all the electing parties.

4. <u>Deepening:</u> If less than all the parties elect to participate in a drilling, Sidetracking, or Deepening operation proposed pursuant to Article VI.B.1., the interest relinquished by the Non–Consenting Parties to the Consenting Parties under Article VI.B.2. shall relate only and be limited to the lesser of (i) the total depth actually drilled or (ii) the objective depth or Zone of which the parties were given notice under Article VI.B.1. ("Initial Objective"). Such well shall

not be Deepened beyond the Initial Objective without first complying with this Article to afford the Non-Consenting Parties the opportunity to participate in the Deepening operation.

In the event any Consenting Party desires to drill or Deepen a Non-Consent Well to a depth below the Initial Objective, such party shall give notice thereof, complying with the requirements of Article VI.B.1., to all parties (including Non-Consenting Parties). Thereupon, Articles VI.B.1. and 2. shall apply and all parties receiving such notice shall have the right to participate or not participate in the Deepening of such well pursuant to said Articles VI.B.1. and 2. If a Deepening operation is approved pursuant to such provisions, and if any Non-Consenting Party elects to participate in the Deepening operation, such Non-Consenting party shall pay or make reimbursement (as the case may be) of the following costs and expenses:

(a) If the proposal to Deepen is made prior to the Completion of such well as a well capable of producing in paying quantities, such Non-Consenting Party shall pay (or reimburse Consenting Parties for, as the case may be) that share of costs and expenses incurred in connection with the drilling of said well from the surface to the Initial Objective which Non-Consenting Party would have paid had such Non-Consenting Party agreed to participate therein, plus the Non-Consenting Party's share of the cost of Deepening and of participating in any further operations on the well in accordance with the other provisions of this Agreement; provided, however, all costs for testing and Completion or attempted Completion of the well incurred by Consenting Parties prior to the point of actual operations to Deepen beyond the Initial Objective shall be for the sole account of Consenting Parties.

(b) If the proposal is made for a Non-Consent Well that has been previously Completed as a well capable of producing in paying quantities, but is no longer capable of producing in paying quantities, such Non-Consenting Party shall pay (or reimburse Consenting Parties for, as the case may be) its proportionate share of all costs of drilling, Completing, and equipping said well from the surface to the Initial Objective, calculated in the manner provided in paragraph (a) above, less those costs recouped by the Consenting Parties from the sale of production from the well. The Non-Consenting Party shall also pay its proportionate share of all costs of re-entering said well. The Non-Consenting Parties' proportionate part (based on the percentage of such well Non-Consenting Party would have owned had it previously participated in such Non-Consent Well) of the costs of salvable materials and equipment remaining in the hole and salvable surface equipment used in connection with such well shall be determined in accordance with Exhibit "C." If the Consenting Parties have recouped the cost of drilling, Completing, and equipping the well at the time such Deepening operation is conducted, then a Non-Consenting Party may participate in the Deepening of the well with no payment for costs incurred prior to re-entering the well for Deepening.

The foregoing shall not imply a right of any Consenting Party to propose any Deepening for a Non-Consent Well prior to the drilling of such well to its Initial Objective without the consent of the other Consenting Parties as provided in Article VI.F.

5. Sidetracking: Any party having the right to participate in a proposed Sidetracking operation that does not own an interest in the affected wellbore at the time of the notice shall, upon electing to participate, tender to the wellbore owners its proportionate share (equal to its

interest in the Sidetracking operation) of the value of that portion of the existing wellbore to be utilized as follows:

(a) If the proposal is for Sidetracking an existing dry hole, reimbursement shall be on the basis of the actual costs incurred in the initial drilling of the well down to the depth at which the Sidetracking operation is initiated.

(b) If the proposal is for Sidetracking a well which has previously produced, reimbursement shall be on the basis of such party's proportionate share of drilling and equipping costs incurred in the initial drilling of the well down to the depth at which the Sidetracking operation is conducted, calculated in the manner described in Article VI.B.4(b) above. Such party's proportionate share of the cost of the well's salvable materials and equipment down to the depth at which the Sidetracking operation is initiated shall be determined in accordance with the provisions of Exhibit "C."

6. Order of Preference of Operations. Except as otherwise specifically provided in this agreement, if any party desires to propose the conduct of an operation that conflicts with a proposal that has been made by a party under this Article VI, such party shall have fifteen (15) days from delivery of the initial proposal, in the case of a proposal to drill a well or to perform an operation on a well where no drilling rig is on location, or twenty-four (24) hours, exclusive of Saturday, Sunday and legal holidays, from delivery of the initial proposal, if a drilling rig is on location for the well on which such operation is to be conducted, to deliver to all parties entitled to participate in the proposed operation such party's alternative proposal, such alternate proposal to contain the same information required to be included in the initial proposal. Each party receiving such proposals shall elect by delivery of notice to Operator within five (5) days after expiration of the proposal period, or within twenty-four (24) hours (exclusive of Saturday, Sunday and legal holidays) if a drilling rig is on location for the well that is the subject of the proposals, to participate in one of the competing proposals. Any party not electing within the time required shall be deemed not to have voted. The proposal receiving the vote of parties owning the largest aggregate percentage interest of the parties voting shall have priority over all other competing proposals; in the case of a tie vote, the initial proposal shall prevail. Operator shall deliver notice of such result to all parties entitled to participate in the operation within five (5) days after expiration of the election period (or within twenty-four (24) hours, exclusive of Saturday, Sunday and legal holidays, if a drilling rig is on location). Each party shall then have two (2) days (or twenty-four (24) hours if a rig is on location) from receipt of such notice to elect by delivery of notice to Operator to participate in such operation or to relinquish interest in the affected well pursuant to the provisions of Article VI.B.2.; failure by a party to deliver notice within such period shall be deemed an election *not* to participate in the prevailing proposal.

7. Conformity to Spacing Pattern. Notwithstanding the provisions of this Article VI.B.2., it is agreed that no wells shall be proposed to be drilled to or Completed in or produced from a Zone from which a well located elsewhere on the Contract Area is producing, unless such well conforms to the then-existing well spacing pattern for such Zone.

8. Paying Wells. No party shall conduct any Reworking, Deepening, Plugging Back, Completion, Recompletion, or Sidetracking operation under this agreement with respect to any well then capable of producing in paying quantities except with the consent of all parties that have not relinquished interests in the well at the time of such operation.

C. Completion of Wells; Reworking and Plugging Back:

1   1. <u>Completion:</u> Without the consent of all parties, no well shall be drilled, Deepened or
2 Sidetracked, except any well drilled, Deepened or Sidetracked pursuant to the provisions of
3 Article VI.B.2. of this agreement. Consent to the drilling, Deepening or Sidetracking shall
4 include:
5   ☐ **Option No. 1:** All necessary expenditures for the drilling, Deepening or Sidetracking,
6   testing, Completing and equipping of the well, including necessary tankage and/or
7   surface facilities.
8   ☐ **Option No. 2:** All necessary expenditures for the drilling, Deepening or Sidetracking
9   and testing of the well. When such well has reached its authorized depth, and all logs,
10   cores and other tests have been completed, and the results thereof furnished to the parties,
11   Operator shall give immediate notice to the Non-Operators having the right to participate
12   in a Completion attempt whether or not Operator recommends attempting to Complete
13   the well, together with Operator's AFE for Completion costs if not previously provided.
14   The parties receiving such notice shall have forty-eight (48) hours (exclusive of Saturday,
15   Sunday and legal holidays) in which to elect by delivery of notice to Operator to
16   participate in a recommended Completion attempt or to make a Completion proposal with
17   an accompanying AFE. Operator shall deliver any such Completion proposal, or any
18   Completion proposal conflicting with Operator's proposal, to the other parties entitled to
19   participate in such Completion in accordance with the procedures specified in Article
20   VI.B.6. Election to participate in a Completion attempt shall include consent to all
21   necessary expenditures for the Completing and equipping of such well, including
22   necessary tankage and/or surface facilities but excluding any stimulation operation not
23   contained on the Completion AFE. Failure of any party receiving such notice to reply
24   within the period above fixed shall constitute an election by that party *not* to participate
25   in the cost of the Completion attempt; provided, that Article VI.B.6. shall control in the
26   case of conflicting Completion proposals. If one or more, but less than all of the parties,
27   elect to attempt a Completion, the provisions of Article VI.B.2. hereof (the phrase
28   "Reworking, Sidetracking, Deepening, Recompleting or Plugging Back" as contained in
29   Article VI.B.2. shall be deemed to include "Completing") shall apply to the operations
30   thereafter conducted by less than all parties; provided, however, that Article VI.B.2. shall
31   apply separately to each separate Completion or Recompletion attempt undertaken
32   hereunder, and an election to become a Non-Consenting Party as to one Completion or
33   Recompletion attempt shall not prevent a party from becoming a Consenting Party in
34   subsequent Completion or Recompletion attempts regardless whether the Consenting
35   Parties as to earlier Completions or Recompletions have recouped their costs pursuant to
36   Article VI.B.2.; provided further, that any recoupment of costs by a Consenting Party
37   shall be made solely from the production attributable to the Zone in which the
38   Completion attempt is made. Election by a previous Non-Consenting Party to participate
39   in a subsequent Completion or Recompletion attempt shall require such party to pay its
40   proportionate share of the cost of salvable materials and equipment installed in the well
41   pursuant to the previous Completion or Recompletion attempt, insofar and only insofar as
42   such materials and equipment benefit the Zone in which such party participates in a
43   Completion attempt.

2. <u>Rework, Recomplete or Plug Back:</u> No well shall be Reworked, Recompleted or Plugged Back except a well Reworked, Recompleted, or Plugged Back pursuant to the provisions of Article VI.B.2. of this agreement. Consent to the Reworking, Recompleting or Plugging Back of a well shall include all necessary expenditures in conducting such operations and Completing and equipping of said well, including necessary tankage and/or surface facilities.

D. Other Operations:

Operator shall not undertake any single project reasonably estimated to require an expenditure in excess of _____ Dollars ($_____) except in connection with the drilling, Sidetracking, Reworking, Deepening, Completing, Recompleting or Plugging Back of a well that has been previously authorized by or pursuant to this agreement; provided, however, that, in case of explosion, fire, flood or other sudden emergency, whether of the same or different nature, Operator may take such steps and incur such expenses as in its opinion are required to deal with the emergency to safeguard life and property but Operator, as promptly as possible, shall report the emergency to the other parties. If Operator prepares an AFE for its own use, Operator shall furnish any Non-Operator so requesting an information copy thereof for any single project costing in excess of _____ Dollars ($_____). Any party who has not relinquished its interest in a well shall have the right to propose that Operator perform repair work or undertake the installation of artificial lift equipment or ancillary production facilities such as salt water disposal wells or to conduct additional work with respect to a well drilled hereunder or other similar project (but not including the installation of gathering lines or other transportation or marketing facilities, the installation of which shall be governed by separate agreement between the parties) reasonably estimated to require an expenditure in excess of the amount first set forth above in this Article VI.D. (except in connection with an operation required to be proposed under Articles VI.B.1. or VI.C.1. Option No. 2, which shall be governed exclusively by those Articles). Operator shall deliver such proposal to all parties entitled to participate therein. If within thirty (30) days thereof Operator secures the written consent of any party or parties owning at least _____% of the interests of the parties entitled to participate in such operation, each party having the right to participate in such project shall be bound by the terms of such proposal and shall be obligated to pay its proportionate share of the costs of the proposed project as if it had consented to such project pursuant to the terms of the proposal.

E. Abandonment of Wells:

1. <u>Abandonment of Dry Holes:</u> Except for any well drilled or Deepened pursuant to Article VI.B.2., any well which has been drilled or Deepened under the terms of this agreement and is proposed to be completed as a dry hole shall not be plugged and abandoned without the consent of all parties. Should Operator, after diligent effort, be unable to contact any party, or should any party fail to reply within forty-eight (48) hours (exclusive of Saturday, Sunday and legal holidays) after delivery of notice of the proposal to plug and abandon such well, such party shall be deemed to have consented to the proposed abandonment. All such wells shall be plugged and abandoned in accordance with applicable regulations and at the cost, risk and expense of the parties who participated in the cost of drilling or Deepening such well. Any party who objects to plugging and abandoning such well by notice delivered to Operator within forty-eight (48) hours (exclusive of Saturday, Sunday and legal holidays) after delivery of notice of the proposed plugging shall take over the well as of the end of such forty-eight (48) hour notice period and conduct further operations in search of Oil and/or Gas subject to the provisions

294

of Article VI.B.; failure of such party to provide proof reasonably satisfactory to Operator of its financial capability to conduct such operations or to take over the well within such period or thereafter to conduct operations on such well or plug and abandon such well shall entitle Operator to retain or take possession of the well and plug and abandon the well. The party taking over the well shall indemnify Operator (if Operator is an abandoning party) and the other abandoning parties against liability for any further operations conducted on such well except for the costs of plugging and abandoning the well and restoring the surface, for which the abandoning parties shall remain proportionately liable.

2. Abandonment of Wells That Have Produced: Except for any well in which a Non-Consent operation has been conducted hereunder for which the Consenting Parties have not been fully reimbursed as herein provided, any well which has been completed as a producer shall not be plugged and abandoned without the consent of all parties. If all parties consent to such abandonment, the well shall be plugged and abandoned in accordance with applicable regulations and at the cost, risk and expense of all the parties hereto. Failure of a party to reply within sixty (60) days of delivery of notice of proposed abandonment shall be deemed an election to consent to the proposal. If, within sixty (60) days after delivery of notice of the proposed abandonment of any well, all parties do not agree to the abandonment of such well, those wishing to continue its operation from the Zone then open to production shall be obligated to take over the well as of the expiration of the applicable notice period and shall indemnify Operator (if Operator is an abandoning party) and the other abandoning parties against liability for any further operations on the well conducted by such parties. Failure of such party or parties to provide proof reasonably satisfactory to Operator of their financial capability to conduct such operations or to take over the well within the required period or thereafter to conduct operations on such well shall entitle Operator to retain or take possession of such well and plug and abandon the well.

Parties taking over a well as provided herein shall tender to each of the other parties its proportionate share of the value of the well's salvable material and equipment, determined in accordance with the provisions of Exhibit "C," less the estimated cost of salvaging and the estimated cost of plugging and abandoning and restoring the surface; provided, however, that in the event the estimated plugging and abandoning and surface restoration costs and the estimated cost of salvaging are higher than the value of the well's salvable material and equipment, each of the abandoning parties shall tender to the parties continuing operations their proportionate shares of the estimated excess cost. Each abandoning party shall assign to the non-abandoning parties, without warranty, express or implied, as to title or as to quantity, or fitness for use of the equipment and material, all of its interest in the wellbore of the well and related equipment, together with its interest in the Leasehold insofar and only insofar as such Leasehold covers the right to obtain production from that wellbore in the Zone then open to production. If the interest of the abandoning party is or includes an Oil and Gas Interest, such party shall execute and deliver to the non-abandoning party or parties an oil and gas lease, limited to the wellbore and the Zone then open to production, for a term of one (1) year and so long thereafter as Oil and/or Gas is produced from the Zone covered thereby, such lease to be on the form attached as Exhibit "B." The assignments or leases so limited shall encompass the Drilling Unit upon which the well is located. The payments by, and the assignments or leases to, the assignees shall be in a ratio based upon the relationship of their respective percentage of participation in the Contract Area to

1 the aggregate of the percentages of participation in the Contract Area of all assignees. There
2 shall be no readjustment of interests in the remaining portions of the Contract Area.
3   Thereafter, abandoning parties shall have no further responsibility, liability, or interest in
4 the operation of or production from the well in the Zone then open other than the royalties
5 retained in any lease made under the terms of this Article. Upon request, Operator shall continue
6 to operate the assigned well for the account of the non-abandoning parties at the rates and
7 charges contemplated by this agreement, plus any additional cost and charges which may arise as
8 the result of the separate ownership of the assigned well. Upon proposed abandonment of the
9 producing Zone assigned or leased, the assignor or lessor shall then have the option to repurchase
10 its prior interest in the well (using the same valuation formula) and participate in further
11 operations therein subject to the provisions hereof.
12   3. <u>Abandonment of Non-Consent Operations:</u> The provisions of Article VI.E.1. or
13 VI.E.2. above shall be applicable as between Consenting Parties in the event of the proposed
14 abandonment of any well excepted from said Articles; provided, however, no well shall be
15 permanently plugged and abandoned unless and until all parties having the right to conduct
16 further operations therein have been notified of the proposed abandonment and afforded the
17 opportunity to elect to take over the well in accordance with the provisions of this Article VI.E.;
18 and provided further, that Non-Consenting Parties who own an interest in a portion of the well
19 shall pay their proportionate shares of abandonment and surface restoration costs for such well as
20 provided in Article VI.B.2.(b).
21 **F. Termination of Operations:**
22   Upon the commencement of an operation for the drilling, Reworking, Sidetracking,
23 Plugging Back, Deepening, testing, Completion or plugging of a well, including but not limited
24 to the Initial Well, such operation shall not be terminated without consent of parties bearing
25 _____% of the costs of such operation; provided, however, that in the event granite or other
26 practically impenetrable substance or condition in the hole is encountered which renders further
27 operations impractical, Operator may discontinue operations and give notice of such condition in
28 the manner provided in Article VI.B.1., and the provisions of Article VI.B. or VI.E. shall
29 thereafter apply to such operation, as appropriate.
30 **G. Taking Production in Kind:**
31   ☐ **Option No. 1: Gas Balancing Agreement Attached**
32   Each party shall take in kind or separately dispose of its proportionate share of all
33 Oil and Gas produced from the Contract Area, exclusive of production which may be
34 used in development and producing operations and in preparing and treating Oil and Gas
35 for marketing purposes and production unavoidably lost. Any extra expenditure incurred
36 in the taking in kind or separate disposition by any party of its proportionate share of the
37 production shall be borne by such party. Any party taking its share of production in kind
38 shall be required to pay for only its proportionate share of such part of Operator's surface
39 facilities which it uses.
40   Each party shall execute such division orders and contracts as may be necessary
41 for the sale of its interest in production from the Contract Area, and, except as provided
42 in Article VII.B., shall be entitled to receive payment directly from the purchaser thereof
43 for its share of all production.

If any party fails to make the arrangements necessary to take in kind or separately dispose of its proportionate share of the Oil produced from the Contract Area, Operator shall have the right, subject to the revocation at will by the party owning it, but not the obligation, to purchase such Oil or sell it to others at any time and from time to time, for the account of the non-taking party. Any such purchase or sale by Operator may be terminated by Operator upon at least ten (10) days written notice to the owner of said production and shall be subject always to the right of the owner of the production upon at least ten (10) days written notice to Operator to exercise at any time its right to take in kind, or separately dispose of, its share of all Oil not previously delivered to a purchaser. Any purchase or sale by Operator of any other party's share of Oil shall be only for such reasonable periods of time as are consistent with the minimum needs of the industry under the particular circumstances, but in no event for a period in excess of one (1) year.

Any such sale by Operator shall be in a manner commercially reasonable under the circumstances but Operator shall have no duty to share any existing market or to obtain a price equal to that received under any existing market. The sale or delivery by Operator of a non-taking party's share of Oil under the terms of any existing contract of Operator shall not give the non-taking party any interest in or make the non-taking party a party to said contract. No purchase shall be made by Operator without first giving the non-taking party at least ten (10) days written notice of such intended purchase and the price to be paid or the pricing basis to be used.

All parties shall give timely written notice to Operator of their Gas marketing arrangements for the following month, excluding price, and shall notify Operator immediately in the event of a change in such arrangements. Operator shall maintain records of all marketing arrangements, and of volumes actually sold or transported, which records shall be made available to Non–Operators upon reasonable request:

In the event one or more parties' separate disposition of its share of the Gas causes split-stream deliveries to separate pipelines and/or deliveries which on a day-to-day basis for any reason are not exactly equal to a party's respective proportionate share of total Gas sales to be allocated to it, the balancing or accounting between the parties shall be in accordance with any Gas balancing agreement between the parties hereto, whether such an agreement is attached as Exhibit "E" or is a separate agreement. Operator shall give notice to all parties of the first sales of Gas from any well under this agreement.

☐ **Option No. 2: No Gas Balancing Agreement:**

Each party shall take in kind or separately dispose of its proportionate share of all Oil and Gas produced from the Contract Area, exclusive of production which may be used in development and producing operations and in preparing and treating Oil and Gas for marketing purposes and production unavoidably lost. Any extra expenditure incurred in the taking in kind or separate disposition by any party of its proportionate share of the production shall be borne by such party. Any party taking its share of production in kind shall be required to pay for only its proportionate share of such part of Operator's surface facilities which it uses.

Each party shall execute such division orders and contracts as may be necessary for the sale of its interest in production from the Contract Area, and, except as provided in Article VII.B., shall be entitled to receive payment directly from the purchaser thereof for its share of all production.

If any party fails to make the arrangements necessary to take in kind or separately dispose of its proportionate share of the Oil and/or Gas produced from the Contract Area, Operator shall have the right, subject to the revocation at will by the party owning it, but not the obligation, to purchase such Oil and/or Gas or sell it to others at any time and from time to time, for the account of the non-taking party. Any such purchase or sale by Operator may be terminated by Operator upon at least ten (10) days written notice to the owner of said production and shall be subject always to the right of the owner of the production upon at least ten (10) days written notice to Operator to exercise its right to take in kind, or separately dispose of, its share of all Oil and/or Gas not previously delivered to a purchaser; provided, however, that the effective date of any such revocation may be deferred at Operator's election for a period not to exceed ninety (90) days if Operator has committed such production to a purchase contract having a term extending beyond such ten (10) -day period. Any purchase or sale by Operator of any other party's share of Oil and/or Gas shall be only for such reasonable periods of time as are consistent with the minimum needs of the industry under the particular circumstances, but in no event for a period in excess of one (1) year.

Any such sale by Operator shall be in a manner commercially reasonable under the circumstances, but Operator shall have no duty to share any existing market or transportation arrangement or to obtain a price or transportation fee equal to that received under any existing market or transportation arrangement. The sale or delivery by Operator of a non-taking party's share of production under the terms of any existing contract of Operator shall not give the non-taking party any interest in or make the non-taking party a party to said contract. No purchase of Oil and Gas and no sale of Gas shall be made by Operator without first giving the non-taking party ten days written notice of such intended purchase or sale and the price to be paid or the pricing basis to be used. Operator shall give notice to all parties of the first sale of Gas from any well under this Agreement.

All parties shall give timely written notice to Operator of their Gas marketing arrangements for the following month, excluding price, and shall notify Operator immediately in the event of a change in such arrangements. Operator shall maintain records of all marketing arrangements, and of volumes actually sold or transported, which records shall be made available to Non-Operators upon reasonable request.

ARTICLE VII.
EXPENDITURES AND LIABILITY OF PARTIES
A. Liability of Parties:

The liability of the parties shall be several, not joint or collective. Each party shall be responsible only for its obligations, and shall be liable only for its proportionate share of the costs of developing and operating the Contract Area. Accordingly, the liens granted among the parties in Article VII.B. are given to secure only the debts of each severally, and no party shall have any liability to third parties hereunder to satisfy the default of any other party in the payment of any expense or obligation hereunder. It is not the intention of the parties to create,

1 nor shall this agreement be construed as creating, a mining or other partnership, joint venture,
2 agency relationship or association, or to render the parties liable as partners, co-venturers, or
3 principals. In their relations with each other under this agreement, the parties shall not be
4 considered fiduciaries or to have established a confidential relationship but rather shall be free to
5 act on an arm's-length basis in accordance with their own respective self-interest, subject,
6 however, to the obligation of the parties to act in good faith in their dealings with each other with
7 respect to activities hereunder.

B. Liens and Security Interests:

9 Each party grants to the other parties hereto a lien upon any interest it now owns or
10 hereafter acquires in Oil and Gas Leases and Oil and Gas Interests in the Contract Area, and a
11 security interest and/or purchase money security interest in any interest it now owns or hereafter
12 acquires in the personal property and fixtures on or used or obtained for use in connection
13 therewith, to secure performance of all of its obligations under this agreement including but not
14 limited to payment of expense, interest and fees, the proper disbursement of all monies paid
15 hereunder, the assignment or relinquishment of interest in Oil and Gas Leases as required
16 hereunder, and the proper performance of operations hereunder. Such lien and security interest
17 granted by each party hereto shall include such party's leasehold interests, working interests,
18 operating rights, and royalty and overriding royalty interests in the Contract Area now owned or
19 hereafter acquired and in lands pooled or unitized therewith or otherwise becoming subject to
20 this agreement, the Oil and Gas when extracted therefrom and equipment situated thereon or
21 used or obtained for use in connection therewith (including, without limitation, all wells, tools,
22 and tubular goods), and accounts (including, without limitation, accounts arising from gas
23 imbalances or from the sale of Oil and/or Gas at the wellhead), contract rights, inventory and
24 general intangibles relating thereto or arising therefrom, and all proceeds and products of the
25 foregoing.

26 To perfect the lien and security agreement provided herein, each party hereto shall
27 execute and acknowledge the recording supplement and/or any financing statement prepared and
28 submitted by any party hereto in conjunction herewith or at any time following execution hereof,
29 and Operator is authorized to file this agreement or the recording supplement executed herewith
30 as a lien or mortgage in the applicable real estate records and as a financing statement with the
31 proper officer under the Uniform Commercial Code in the state in which the Contract Area is
32 situated and such other states as Operator shall deem appropriate to perfect the security interest
33 granted hereunder. Any party may file this agreement, the recording supplement executed
34 herewith, or such other documents as it deems necessary as a lien or mortgage in the applicable
35 real estate records and/or a financing statement with the proper officer under the Uniform
36 Commercial Code.

37 Each party represents and warrants to the other parties hereto that the lien and security
38 interest granted by such party to the other parties shall be a first and prior lien, and each party
39 hereby agrees to maintain the priority of said lien and security interest against all persons
40 acquiring an interest in Oil and Gas Leases and Interests covered by this agreement by, through
41 or under such party. All parties acquiring an interest in Oil and Gas Leases and Oil and Gas
42 Interests covered by this agreement, whether by assignment, merger, mortgage, operation of law,
43 or otherwise, shall be deemed to have taken subject to the lien and security interest granted by

299

this Article VII.B. as to all obligations attributable to such interest hereunder whether or not such obligations arise before or after such interest is acquired.

To the extent that parties have a security interest under the Uniform Commercial Code of the state in which the Contract Area is situated, they shall be entitled to exercise the rights and remedies of a secured party under the Code. The bringing of a suit and the obtaining of judgment by a party for the secured indebtedness shall not be deemed an election of remedies or otherwise affect the lien rights or security interest as security for the payment thereof. In addition, upon default by any party in the payment of its share of expenses, interests or fees, or upon the improper use of funds by the Operator, the other parties shall have the right, without prejudice to other rights or remedies, to collect from the purchaser the proceeds from the sale of such defaulting party's share of Oil and Gas until the amount owed by such party, plus interest as provided in "Exhibit C," has been received, and shall have the right to offset the amount owed against the proceeds from the sale of such defaulting party's share of Oil and Gas. All purchasers of production may rely on a notification of default from the non-defaulting party or parties stating the amount due as a result of the default, and all parties waive any recourse available against purchasers for releasing production proceeds as provided in this paragraph.

If any party fails to pay its share of cost within one hundred twenty (120) days after rendition of a statement therefor by Operator, the non-defaulting parties, including Operator, shall, upon request by Operator, pay the unpaid amount in the proportion that the interest of each such party bears to the interest of all such parties. The amount paid by each party so paying its share of the unpaid amount shall be secured by the liens and security rights described in Article VII.B., and each paying party may independently pursue any remedy available hereunder or otherwise.

If any party does not perform all of its obligations hereunder, and the failure to perform subjects such party to foreclosure or execution proceedings pursuant to the provisions of this agreement, to the extent allowed by governing law, the defaulting party waives any available right of redemption from and after the date of judgment, any required valuation or appraisement of the mortgaged or secured property prior to sale, any available right to stay execution or to require a marshalling of assets and any required bond in the event a receiver is appointed. In addition, to the extent permitted by applicable law, each party hereby grants to the other parties a power of sale as to any property that is subject to the lien and security rights granted hereunder, such power to be exercised in the manner provided by applicable law or otherwise in a commercially reasonable manner and upon reasonable notice.

Each party agrees that the other parties shall be entitled to utilize the provisions of Oil and Gas lien law or other lien law of any state in which the Contract Area is situated to enforce the obligations of each party hereunder. Without limiting the generality of the foregoing, to the extent permitted by applicable law, Non–Operators agree that Operator may invoke or utilize the mechanics' or materialmen's lien law of the state in which the Contract Area is situated in order to secure the payment to Operator of any sum due hereunder for services performed or materials supplied by Operator.

C. Advances:

Operator, at its election, shall have the right from time to time to demand and receive from one or more of the other parties payment in advance of their respective shares of the estimated amount of the expense to be incurred in operations hereunder during the next succeeding month, which right may be exercised only by submission to each such party of an itemized statement of such estimated expense, together with an invoice for its share thereof. Each such statement and invoice for the payment in advance of estimated expense shall be submitted on or before the 20th day of the next preceding month. Each party shall pay to Operator its proportionate share of such estimate within fifteen (15) days after such estimate and invoice is received. If any party fails to pay its share of said estimate within said time, the amount due shall bear interest as provided in Exhibit "C" until paid. Proper adjustment shall be made monthly between advances and actual expense to the end that each party shall bear and pay its proportionate share of actual expenses incurred, and no more.

D. Defaults and Remedies:

If any party fails to discharge any financial obligation under this agreement, including without limitation the failure to make any advance under the preceding Article VII.C. or any other provision of this agreement, within the period required for such payment hereunder, then in addition to the remedies provided in Article VII.B. or elsewhere in this agreement, the remedies specified below shall be applicable. For purposes of this Article VII.D., all notices and elections shall be delivered only by Operator, except that Operator shall deliver any such notice and election requested by a non-defaulting Non–Operator, and when Operator is the party in default, the applicable notices and elections can be delivered by any Non–Operator. Election of any one or more of the following remedies shall not preclude the subsequent use of any other remedy specified below or otherwise available to a non-defaulting party.

1. Suspension of Rights: Any party may deliver to the party in default a Notice of Default, which shall specify the default, specify the action to be taken to cure the default, and specify that failure to take such action will result in the exercise of one or more of the remedies provided in this Article. If the default is not cured within thirty (30) days of the delivery of such Notice of Default, all of the rights of the defaulting party granted by this agreement may upon notice be suspended until the default is cured, without prejudice to the right of the non-defaulting party or parties to continue to enforce the obligations of the defaulting party previously accrued or thereafter accruing under this agreement. If Operator is the party in default, the Non–Operators shall have in addition the right, by vote of Non–Operators owning a majority in interest in the Contract Area after excluding the voting interest of Operator, to appoint a new Operator effective immediately. The rights of a defaulting party that may be suspended hereunder at the election of the non-defaulting parties shall include, without limitation, the right to receive information as to any operation conducted hereunder during the period of such default, the right to elect to participate in an operation proposed under Article VI.B. of this agreement, the right to participate in an operation being conducted under this agreement even if the party has previously elected to participate in such operation, and the right to receive proceeds of production from any well subject to this agreement.

2. Suit for Damages: Non-defaulting parties or Operator for the benefit of non-defaulting parties may sue (at joint account expense) to collect the amounts in default, plus interest accruing on the amounts recovered from the date of default until the date of collection at the rate specified in Exhibit "C" attached hereto. Nothing herein shall prevent any party from suing any defaulting party to collect consequential damages accruing to such party as a result of the default.

3. Deemed Non–Consent: The non-defaulting party may deliver a written Notice of Non–Consent Election to the defaulting party at any time after the expiration of the thirty-day

cure period following delivery of the Notice of Default, in which event if the billing is for the drilling of a new well or the Plugging Back, Sidetracking, Reworking or Deepening of a well which is to be or has been plugged as a dry hole, or for the Completion or Recompletion of any well, the defaulting party will be conclusively deemed to have elected not to participate in the operation and to be a Non–Consenting Party with respect thereto under Article VI.B. or VI.C., as the case may be, to the extent of the costs unpaid by such party, notwithstanding any election to participate theretofore made. If election is made to proceed under this provision, then the non-defaulting parties may not elect to sue for the unpaid amount pursuant to Article VII.D.2.

Until the delivery of such Notice of Non–Consent Election to the defaulting party, such party shall have the right to cure its default by paying its unpaid share of costs plus interest at the rate set forth in Exhibit "C," provided, however, such payment shall not prejudice the rights of the non-defaulting parties to pursue remedies for damages incurred by the non-defaulting parties as a result of the default. Any interest relinquished pursuant to this Article VII.D.3. shall be offered to the non-defaulting parties in proportion to their interests, and the non-defaulting parties electing to participate in the ownership of such interest shall be required to contribute their shares of the defaulted amount upon their election to participate therein.

4. Advance Payment: If a default is not cured within thirty (30) days of the delivery of a Notice of Default, Operator, or Non–Operators if Operator is the defaulting party, may thereafter require advance payment from the defaulting party of such defaulting party's anticipated share of any item of expense for which Operator, or Non–Operators, as the case may be, would be entitled to reimbursement under any provision of this agreement, whether or not such expense was the subject of the previous default. Such right includes, but is not limited to, the right to require advance payment for the estimated costs of drilling a well or Completion of a well as to which an election to participate in drilling or Completion has been made. If the defaulting party fails to pay the required advance payment, the non-defaulting parties may pursue any of the remedies provided in this Article VII.D. or any other default remedy provided elsewhere in this agreement. Any excess of funds advanced remaining when the operation is completed and all costs have been paid shall be promptly returned to the advancing party.

5. Costs and Attorneys' Fees. In the event any party is required to bring legal proceedings to enforce any financial obligation of a party hereunder, the prevailing party in such action shall be entitled to recover all court costs, costs of collection, and a reasonable attorney's fee, which the lien provided for herein shall also secure.

E. Rentals, Shut-in Well Payments and Minimum Royalties:

Rentals, shut-in well payments and minimum royalties which may be required under the terms of any lease shall be paid by the party or parties who subjected such lease to this agreement at its or their expense. In the event two or more parties own and have contributed interests in the same lease to this agreement, such parties may designate one of such parties to make said payments for and on behalf of all such parties. Any party may request, and shall be entitled to receive, proper evidence of all such payments. In the event of failure to make proper payment of any rental, shut-in well payment or minimum royalty through mistake or oversight where such payment is required to continue the lease in force, any loss which results from such non-payment shall be borne in accordance with the provisions of Article IV.B.2.

Operator shall notify Non–Operators of the anticipated completion of a shut-in well, or the shutting in or return to production of a producing well, at least five (5) days (excluding

Saturday, Sunday and legal holidays) prior to taking such action, or at the earliest opportunity permitted by circumstances, but assumes no liability for failure to do so. In the event of failure by Operator to so notify Non-Operators, the loss of any lease contributed hereto by Non-Operators for failure to make timely payments of any shut-in well payment shall be borne jointly by the parties hereto under the provisions of Article IV.B.3.

F. Taxes:

Beginning with the first calendar year after the effective date hereof, Operator shall render for ad valorem taxation all property subject to this agreement which by law should be rendered for such taxes, and it shall pay all such taxes assessed thereon before they become delinquent. Prior to the rendition date, each Non-Operator shall furnish Operator information as to burdens (to include, but not be limited to, royalties, overriding royalties and production payments) on Leases and Oil and Gas Interests contributed by such Non-Operator. If the assessed valuation of any Lease is reduced by reason of its being subject to outstanding excess royalties, overriding royalties or production payments, the reduction in ad valorem taxes resulting therefrom shall inure to the benefit of the owner or owners of such Lease, and Operator shall adjust the charge to such owner or owners so as to reflect the benefit of such reduction. If the ad valorem taxes are based in whole or in part upon separate valuations of each party's working interest, then notwithstanding anything to the contrary herein, charges to the joint account shall be made and paid by the parties hereto in accordance with the tax value generated by each party's working interest. Operator shall bill the other parties for their proportionate shares of all tax payments in the manner provided in Exhibit "C."

If Operator considers any tax assessment improper, Operator may, at its discretion, protest within the time and manner prescribed by law, and prosecute the protest to a final determination, unless all parties agree to abandon the protest prior to final determination. During the pendency of administrative or judicial proceedings, Operator may elect to pay, under protest, all such taxes and any interest and penalty. When any such protested assessment shall have been finally determined, Operator shall pay the tax for the joint account, together with any interest and penalty accrued, and the total cost shall then be assessed against the parties, and be paid by them, as provided in Exhibit "C."

Each party shall pay or cause to be paid all production, severance, excise, gathering and other taxes imposed upon or with respect to the production or handling of such party's share of Oil and Gas produced under the terms of this agreement.

ARTICLE VIII.
ACQUISITION, MAINTENANCE OR TRANSFER OF INTEREST

A. Surrender of Leases:

The Leases covered by this agreement, insofar as they embrace acreage in the Contract Area, shall not be surrendered in whole or in part unless all parties consent thereto.

However, should any party desire to surrender its interest in any Lease or in any portion thereof, such party shall give written notice of the proposed surrender to all parties, and the parties to whom such notice is delivered shall have thirty (30) days after delivery of the notice within which to notify the party proposing the surrender whether they elect to consent thereto. Failure of a party to whom such notice is delivered to reply within said 30-day period shall constitute a consent to the surrender of the Leases described in the notice. If all parties do not agree or consent thereto, the party desiring to surrender shall assign, without express or implied warranty of title, all of its interest in such Lease, or portion thereof, and any well, material and equipment which may be located thereon and any rights in production thereafter secured, to the parties not consenting to such surrender. If the interest of the assigning party is or includes an Oil and Gas Interest, the assigning party shall execute and deliver to the party or parties not consenting to such surrender an oil and gas lease covering such Oil and Gas Interest for a term of one (1) year and so long thereafter as Oil and/or Gas is produced from the land covered thereby, such lease to be on the form attached hereto as Exhibit "B." Upon such assignment or lease, the assigning party shall be relieved from all obligations thereafter accruing, but not theretofore accrued, with respect to the interest assigned or leased and the operation of any well attributable thereto, and the assigning party shall have no further interest in the assigned or leased premises and its equipment and production other than the royalties retained in any lease made under the terms of this Article. The party assignee or lessee shall pay to the party assignor or lessor the reasonable salvage value of the latter's interest in any well's salvable materials and equipment attributable to the assigned or leased acreage. The value of all salvable materials and equipment shall be determined in accordance with the provisions of Exhibit "C," less the estimated cost of salvaging and the estimated cost of plugging and abandoning and restoring the surface. If such value is less than such costs, then the party assignor or lessor shall pay to the party assignee or lessee the amount of such deficit. If the assignment or lease is in favor of more than one party, the interest shall be shared by such parties in the proportions that the interest of each bears to the total interest of all such parties. If the interest of the parties to whom the assignment is to be made varies according to depth, then the interest assigned shall similarly reflect such variances.

Any assignment, lease or surrender made under this provision shall not reduce or change the assignor's, lessor's or surrendering party's interest as it was immediately before the assignment, lease or surrender in the balance of the Contract Area; and the acreage assigned, leased or surrendered, and subsequent operations thereon, shall not thereafter be subject to the terms and provisions of this agreement but shall be deemed subject to an Operating Agreement in the form of this agreement.

B. Renewal or Extension of Leases:

If any party secures a renewal or replacement of an Oil and Gas Lease or Interest subject to this agreement, then all other parties shall be notified promptly upon such acquisition or, in the case of a replacement Lease taken before expiration of an existing Lease, promptly upon expiration of the existing Lease. The parties notified shall have the right for a period of thirty (30) days following delivery of such notice in which to elect to participate in the ownership of the renewal or replacement Lease, insofar as such Lease affects lands within the Contract Area, by paying to the party who acquired it their proportionate shares of the acquisition cost allocated to that part of such Lease within the Contract Area, which shall be in proportion to the interests held at that time by the parties in the Contract Area. Each party who participates in the purchase of a renewal or replacement Lease shall be given an assignment of its proportionate interest therein by the acquiring party.

If some, but less than all, of the parties elect to participate in the purchase of a renewal or replacement Lease, it shall be owned by the parties who elect to participate therein, in a ratio based upon the relationship of their respective percentage of participation in the Contract Area to the aggregate of the percentages of participation in the Contract Area of all parties participating in the purchase of such renewal or replacement Lease. The acquisition of a renewal or replacement Lease by any or all of the parties hereto shall not cause a readjustment of the interests of the parties stated in Exhibit "A," but any renewal or replacement Lease in which less than all parties elect to participate shall not be subject to this agreement but shall be deemed subject to a separate Operating Agreement in the form of this agreement.

If the interests of the parties in the Contract Area vary according to depth, then their right to participate proportionately in renewal or replacement Leases and their right to receive an assignment of interest shall also reflect such depth variances.

The provisions of this Article shall apply to renewal or replacement Leases whether they are for the entire interest covered by the expiring Lease or cover only a portion of its area or an interest therein. Any renewal or replacement Lease taken before the expiration of its predecessor Lease, or taken or contracted for or becoming effective within six (6) months after the expiration of the existing Lease, shall be subject to this provision so long as this agreement is in effect at the time of such acquisition or at the time the renewal or replacement Lease becomes effective, but any Lease taken or contracted for more than six (6) months after the expiration of an existing Lease shall not be deemed a renewal or replacement Lease and shall not be subject to the provisions of this agreement.

The provisions in this Article shall also be applicable to extensions of Oil and Gas Leases.

C. Acreage or Cash Contributions:

While this agreement is in force, if any party contracts for a contribution of cash towards the drilling of a well or any other operation on the Contract Area, such contribution shall be paid to the party who conducted the drilling or other operation and shall be applied by it against the cost of such drilling or other operation. If the contribution be in the form of acreage, the party to whom the contribution is made shall promptly tender an assignment of the acreage, without warranty of title, to the Drilling Parties in the proportions said Drilling Parties shared the cost of drilling the well. Such acreage shall become a separate Contract Area and, to the extent possible, be governed by provisions identical to this agreement. Each party shall promptly notify all other parties of any acreage or cash contributions it may obtain in support of any well or any other operation on the Contract Area. The above provisions shall also be applicable to optional rights to earn acreage outside the Contract Area which are in support of wells drilled inside the Contract Area.

If any party contracts for any consideration relating to disposition of such party's share of substances produced hereunder, such consideration shall not be deemed a contribution as contemplated in this Article VIII.C.

D. Assignment; Maintenance of Uniform Interest:

For the purpose of maintaining uniformity of ownership in the Contract Area in the Oil and Gas Leases, Oil and Gas Interests, wells, equipment and production covered by this agreement no party shall sell, encumber, transfer or make other disposition of its interest in the Oil and Gas Leases and Oil and Gas Interests embraced within the Contract Area or in wells, equipment and production unless such disposition covers either:

1. the entire interest of the party in all Oil and Gas Leases, Oil and Gas Interests, wells, equipment and production; or

1   2. an equal undivided percent of the party's present interest in all Oil and Gas
2   Leases, Oil and Gas Interests, wells, equipment and production in the Contract Area.
3   Every sale, encumbrance, transfer or other disposition made by any party shall be made
4 expressly subject to this agreement and shall be made without prejudice to the right of the other
5 parties, and any transferee of an ownership interest in any Oil and Gas Lease or Interest shall be
6 deemed a party to this agreement as to the interest conveyed from and after the effective date of
7 the transfer of ownership; provided, however, that the other parties shall not be required to
8 recognize any such sale, encumbrance, transfer or other disposition for any purpose hereunder
9 until thirty (30) days after they have received a copy of the instrument of transfer or other
10 satisfactory evidence thereof in writing from the transferor or transferee. No assignment or other
11 disposition of interest by a party shall relieve such party of obligations previously incurred by
12 such party hereunder with respect to the interest transferred, including without limitation the
13 obligation of a party to pay all costs attributable to an operation conducted hereunder in which
14 such party has agreed to participate prior to making such assignment, and the lien and security
15 interest granted by Article VII.B. shall continue to burden the interest transferred to secure
16 payment of any such obligations.
17
18   If, at any time the interest of any party is divided among and owned by four or more
19 co-owners, Operator, at its discretion, may require such co-owners to appoint a single trustee or
20 agent with full authority to receive notices, approve expenditures, receive billings for and
21 approve and pay such party's share of the joint expenses, and to deal generally with, and with
22 power to bind, the co-owners of such party's interest within the scope of the operations embraced
23 in this agreement; however, all such co-owners shall have the right to enter into and execute all
24 contracts or agreements for the disposition of their respective shares of the Oil and Gas produced
25 from the Contract Area and they shall have the right to receive, separately, payment of the sale
26 proceeds thereof.
27 **E. Waiver of Rights to Partition:**
28   If permitted by the laws of the state or states in which the property covered hereby is
29 located, each party hereto owning an undivided interest in the Contract Area waives any and all
30 rights it may have to partition and have set aside to it in severalty its undivided interest therein.
31 **F. Preferential Right to Purchase:**
32 ☐ **(Optional; Check if applicable.)**
33   Should any party desire to sell all or any part of its interests under this agreement, or its
34 rights and interests in the Contract Area, it shall promptly give written notice to the other parties,
35 with full information concerning its proposed disposition, which shall include the name and
36 address of the prospective transferee (who must be ready, willing and able to purchase), the
37 purchase price, a legal description sufficient to identify the property, and all other terms of the
38 offer. The other parties shall then have an optional prior right, for a period of ten (10) days after
39 the notice is delivered, to purchase for the stated consideration on the same terms and conditions
40 the interest which the other party proposes to sell; and, if this optional right is exercised, the
41 purchasing parties shall share the purchased interest in the proportions that the interest of each
42 bears to the total interest of all purchasing parties. However, there shall be no preferential right
43 to purchase in those cases where any party wishes to mortgage its interests, or to transfer title to
44 its interests to its mortgagee in lieu of or pursuant to foreclosure of a mortgage of its interests, or

1   to dispose of its interests by merger, reorganization, consolidation, or by sale of all or
2   substantially all of its Oil and Gas assets to any party, or by transfer of its interests to a
3   subsidiary or parent company or to a subsidiary of a parent company, or to any company in
4   which such party owns a majority of the stock.
5

6   **ARTICLE IX.**
7   **INTERNAL REVENUE CODE ELECTION**
8   If, for federal income tax purposes, this agreement and the operations hereunder are
9   regarded as a partnership, and if the parties have not otherwise agreed to form a tax partnership
10   pursuant to Exhibit "G" or other agreement between them, each party thereby affected elects to
11   be excluded from the application of all of the provisions of Subchapter "K," Chapter 1, Subtitle
12   "A," of the Internal Revenue Code of 1986, as amended ("Code"), as permitted and authorized
13   by Section 761 of the Code and the regulations promulgated thereunder. Operator is authorized
14   and directed to execute on behalf of each party hereby affected such evidence of this election as
15   may be required by the Secretary of the Treasury of the United States or the Federal Internal
16   Revenue Service, including specifically, but not by way of limitation, all of the returns,
17   statements, and the data required by Treasury Regulations § 1.761. Should there be any
18   requirement that each party hereby affected give further evidence of this election, each such
19   party shall execute such documents and furnish such other evidence as may be required by the
20   Federal Internal Revenue Service or as may be necessary to evidence this election. No such
21   party shall give any notices or take any other action inconsistent with the election made hereby.
22   If any present or future income tax laws of the state or states in which the Contract Area is
23   located or any future income tax laws of the United States contain provisions similar to those in
24   Subchapter "K," Chapter 1, Subtitle "A," of the Code, under which an election similar to that
25   provided by Section 761 of the Code is permitted, each party hereby affected shall make such
26   election as may be permitted or required by such laws. In making the foregoing election, each
27   such party states that the income derived by such party from operations hereunder can be
28   adequately determined without the computation of partnership taxable income.
29

30   **ARTICLE X.**
31   **CLAIMS AND LAWSUITS**
32   Operator may settle any single uninsured third party damage claim or suit arising from
33   operations hereunder if the expenditure does not exceed _____ Dollars ($_____) and if the
34   payment is in complete settlement of such claim or suit. If the amount required for settlement
35   exceeds the above amount, the parties hereto shall assume and take over the further handling of
36   the claim or suit, unless such authority is delegated to Operator. All costs and expenses of
37   handling, settling, or otherwise discharging such claim or suit shall be at the joint expense of the
38   parties participating in the operation from which the claim or suit arises. If a claim is made
39   against any party or if any party is sued on account of any matter arising from operations
40   hereunder over which such individual has no control because of the rights given Operator by this
41   agreement, such party shall immediately notify all other parties, and the claim or suit shall be
42   treated as any other claim or suit involving operations hereunder.
43

44   **ARTICLE XI.**

FORCE MAJEURE

If any party is rendered unable, wholly or in part, by force majeure to carry out its obligations under this agreement, other than the obligation to indemnify or make money payments or furnish security, that party shall give to all other parties prompt written notice of the force majeure with reasonably full particulars concerning it; thereupon, the obligations of the party giving the notice, so far as they are affected by the force majeure, shall be suspended during, but no longer than, the continuance of the force majeure. The term "force majeure," as here employed, shall mean an act of God, strike, lockout, or other industrial disturbance, act of the public enemy, war, blockade, public riot, lightning, fire, storm, flood or other act of nature, explosion, governmental action, governmental delay, restraint or inaction, unavailability of equipment, and any other cause, whether of the kind specifically enumerated above or otherwise, which is not reasonably within the control of the party claiming suspension.

The affected party shall use all reasonable diligence to remove the force majeure situation as quickly as practicable. The requirement that any force majeure shall be remedied with all reasonable dispatch shall not require the settlement of strikes, lockouts, or other labor difficulty by the party involved, contrary to its wishes; how all such difficulties shall be handled shall be entirely within the discretion of the party concerned.

ARTICLE XII.
NOTICES

All notices authorized or required between the parties by any of the provisions of this agreement, unless otherwise specifically provided, shall be in writing and delivered in person or by United States mail, courier service, telegram, telex, telecopier or any other form of facsimile, postage or charges prepaid, and addressed to such parties at the addresses listed on Exhibit "A." All telephone or oral notices permitted by this agreement shall be confirmed immediately thereafter by written notice. The originating notice given under any provision hereof shall be deemed delivered only when received by the party to whom such notice is directed, and the time for such party to deliver any notice in response thereto shall run from the date the originating notice is received. "Receipt" for purposes of this agreement with respect to written notice delivered hereunder shall be actual delivery of the notice to the address of the party to be notified specified in accordance with this agreement, or to the telecopy, facsimile or telex machine of such party. The second or any responsive notice shall be deemed delivered when deposited in the United States mail or at the office of the courier or telegraph service, or upon transmittal by telex, telecopy or facsimile, or when personally delivered to the party to be notified, provided, that when response is required within 24 or 48 hours, such response shall be given orally or by telephone, telex, telecopy or other facsimile within such period. Each party shall have the right to change its address at any time, and from time to time, by giving written notice thereof to all other parties. If a party is not available to receive notice orally or by telephone when a party attempts to deliver a notice required to be delivered within 24 or 48 hours, the notice may be delivered in writing by any other method specified herein and shall be deemed delivered in the same manner provided above for any responsive notice.

ARTICLE XIII.
TERM OF AGREEMENT

308

This agreement shall remain in full force and effect as to the Oil and Gas Leases and/or Oil and Gas Interests subject hereto for the period of time selected below; provided, however, no party hereto shall ever be construed as having any right, title or interest in or to any Lease or Oil and Gas Interest contributed by any other party beyond the term of this agreement.

☐ **Option No. 1**: So long as any of the Oil and Gas Leases subject to this agreement remain or are continued in force as to any part of the Contract Area, whether by production, extension, renewal or otherwise.

☐ **Option No. 2**: In the event the well described in Article VI.A., or any subsequent well drilled under any provision of this agreement, results in the Completion of a well as a well capable of production of Oil and/or Gas in paying quantities, this agreement shall continue in force so long as any such well is capable of production, and for an additional period of _____ days thereafter; provided, however, if, prior to the expiration of such additional period, one or more of the parties hereto are engaged in drilling, Reworking, Deepening, Sidetracking, Plugging Back, testing or attempting to Complete or Re-complete a well or wells hereunder, this agreement shall continue in force until such operations have been completed and if production results therefrom, this agreement shall continue in force as provided herein. In the event the well described in Article VI.A., or any subsequent well drilled hereunder, results in a dry hole, and no other well is capable of producing Oil and/or Gas from the Contract Area, this agreement shall terminate unless drilling, Deepening, Sidetracking, Completing, Re-completing, Plugging Back or Reworking operations are commenced within _____ days from the date of abandonment of said well. "Abandonment" for such purposes shall mean either (i) a decision by all parties not to conduct any further operations on the well or (ii) the elapse of 180 days from the conduct of any operations on the well, whichever first occurs.

The termination of this agreement shall not relieve any party hereto from any expense, liability or other obligation or any remedy therefor which has accrued or attached prior to the date of such termination.

Upon termination of this agreement and the satisfaction of all obligations hereunder, in the event a memorandum of this Operating Agreement has been filed of record, Operator is authorized to file of record in all necessary recording offices a notice of termination, and each party hereto agrees to execute such a notice of termination as to Operator's interest, upon request of Operator, if Operator has satisfied all its financial obligations.

ARTICLE XIV.
COMPLIANCE WITH LAWS AND REGULATIONS

A. Laws, Regulations and Orders:

This agreement shall be subject to the applicable laws of the state in which the Contract Area is located, to the valid rules, regulations, and orders of any duly constituted regulatory body of said state; and to all other applicable federal, state, and local laws, ordinances, rules, regulations and orders.

B. Governing Law:

This agreement and all matters pertaining hereto, including but not limited to matters of performance, nonperformance, breach, remedies, procedures, rights, duties, and interpretation or construction, shall be governed and determined by the law of the state in which the Contract

1 Area is located. If the Contract Area is in two or more states, the law of the state of _____
2 shall govern.

3 **C. Regulatory Agencies:**

4   Nothing herein contained shall grant, or be construed to grant, Operator the right or
5 authority to waive or release any rights, privileges, or obligations which Non–Operators may
6 have under federal or state laws or under rules, regulations or orders promulgated under such
7 laws in reference to oil, gas and mineral operations, including the location, operation, or
8 production of wells, on tracts offsetting or adjacent to the Contract Area.

9   With respect to the operations hereunder, Non–Operators agree to release Operator from
10 any and all losses, damages, injuries, claims and causes of action arising out of, incident to or
11 resulting directly or indirectly from Operator's interpretation or application of rules, rulings,
12 regulations or orders of the Department of Energy or Federal Energy Regulatory Commission or
13 predecessor or successor agencies to the extent such interpretation or application was made in
14 good faith and does not constitute gross negligence.[1] Each Non–Operator further agrees to
15 reimburse Operator for such Non–Operator's share of production or any refund, fine, levy or
16 other governmental sanction that Operator may be required to pay as a result of such an incorrect
17 interpretation or application, together with interest and penalties thereon owing by Operator as a
18 result of such incorrect interpretation or application.
19

20   **ARTICLE XV.**
21   **MISCELLANEOUS**

22 **A. Execution:**

23   This agreement shall be binding upon each Non–Operator when this agreement or a
24 counterpart thereof has been executed by such Non–Operator and Operator notwithstanding that
25 this agreement is not then or thereafter executed by all of the parties to which it is tendered or
26 which are listed on Exhibit "A" as owning an interest in the Contract Area or which own, in fact,
27 an interest in the Contract Area. Operator may, however, by written notice to all Non–Operators
28 who have become bound by this agreement as aforesaid, given at any time prior to the actual
29 spud date of the Initial Well but in no event later than five days prior to the date specified in
30 Article VI.A. for commencement of the Initial Well, terminate this agreement if Operator in its
31 sole discretion determines that there is insufficient participation to justify commencement of
32 drilling operations. In the event of such a termination by Operator, all further obligations of the
33 parties hereunder shall cease as of such termination. In the event any Non–Operator has
34 advanced or prepaid any share of drilling or other costs hereunder, all sums so advanced shall be
35 returned to such Non–Operator without interest. In the event Operator proceeds with drilling
36 operations for the Initial Well without the execution hereof by all persons listed on Exhibit "A"
37 as having a current working interest in such well, Operator shall indemnify Non–Operators with
38 respect to all costs incurred for the Initial Well which would have been charged to such person
39 under this agreement if such person had executed the same and Operator shall receive all
40 revenues which would have been received by such person under this agreement if such person
41 had executed the same.

42 **B. Successors and Assigns:**

This agreement shall be binding upon and shall inure to the benefit of the parties hereto and their respective heirs, devisees, legal representatives, successors and assigns, and the terms hereof shall be deemed to run with the Leases or Interests included within the Contract Area.

C. Counterparts:

This instrument may be executed in any number of counterparts, each of which shall be considered an original for all purposes.

D. Severability:

For the purposes of assuming or rejecting this agreement as an executory contract pursuant to federal bankruptcy laws, this agreement shall not be severable, but rather must be assumed or rejected in its entirety, and the failure of any party to this agreement to comply with all of its financial obligations provided herein shall be a material default.

ARTICLE XVI.
OTHER PROVISIONS

IN WITNESS WHEREOF, this agreement shall be effective as of the _____ day of _____, 19___.

[signatures of operator and nonoperators and acknowledgements]

NOTES

1.   The American Association of Professional Landmen has created four model form operating agreements that have been widely used by the industry for onshore oil and gas operations. The most current version is the 1989 form reproduced in this Manual. Prior versions include a 1956 form, sometimes referred to as the "ROSS-Martin" form, and the A.A.P.L. Form 610-1977, and A.A.P.L. Form 610-1982 forms. The A.A.P.L. holds the Copyright on all of its forms, which can be obtained from Kraftbilt Products, Box 800, Tulsa, Oklahoma 74101, 1-800-331-7290, http://www.kraftbill.com. Kraftbilt also distributes other A.A.P.L. products.

2.   The A.A.P.L. model operating agreements must be modified for horizontal wells. Definitions for "Deepen," "Drillsite," and "Plug Back" are customarily changed, and new defined terms, including "Lateral," "Horizontal Well," "Multi-Lateral Well," and "Total Depth," are usually added. The initial well, under Article VI.A., is usually described in terms of its surface location and lateral direction and length. The so-called "casing-point election," under Article VI.C.1.(Option No. 2), is not well suited to a horizontal well. Special provisions govern the order and priority of subsequent operations and the sidetracking provisions of Article VI.B.5. are not applicable to operations in the lateral portion of a well.

3.   Article II of the Model Form Operating Agreement contemplates the attachment of over a number of exhibits to the agreement. Some of these, such as Exhibit F, Non-Discrimination and Certification of Non-Segregated Facilities, will normally consist of unchanging boiler-plate provisions; whereas others, such as Exhibit A, must be drafted specially for each separate operating agreement. Of special importance to the investor, especially the investor with little or no prior experience in the oil business, is Exhibit C, Accounting Procedure.

c o p a s

Exhibit " "
ACCOUNTING PROCEDURE
JOINT OPERATIONS

1   Attached to and made part of _____
2   _____
3   _____
4   _____
5
6   I. GENERAL PROVISIONS
7
8   IF THE PARTIES FAIL TO SELECT EITHER ONE OF COMPETING "ALTERNATIVE" PROVISIONS, OR SELECT ALL THE
9   COMPETING "ALTERNATIVE" PROVISIONS, ALTERNATIVE 1 IN EACH SUCH INSTANCE SHALL BE DEEMED TO HAVE
10   BEEN ADOPTED BY THE PARTIES AS A RESULT OF ANY SUCH OMISSION OR DUPLICATE NOTATION.
11
12   IN THE EVENT THAT ANY "OPTIONAL" PROVISION OF THIS ACCOUNTING PROCEDURE IS NOT ADOPTED BY THE
13   PARTIES TO THE AGREEMENT BY A TYPED, PRINTED OR HANDWRITTEN INDICATION, SUCH PROVISION SHALL NOT
14   FORM A PART OF THIS ACCOUNTING PROCEDURE, AND NO INFERENCE SHALL BE MADE CONCERNING THE INTENT
15   OF THE PARTIES IN SUCH EVENT.
16
17   1.   DEFINITIONS
18
19   All terms used in this Accounting Procedure shall have the following meaning, unless otherwise expressly defined in the Agreement:
20
21   "Affiliate" means for a person, another person that controls, is controlled by, or is under common control with that person. In this
22   definition, (a) control means the ownership by one person, directly or indirectly, of more than fifty percent (50%) of the voting securities
23   of a corporation or, for other persons, the equivalent ownership interest (such as partnership interests), and (b) "person" means an
24   individual, corporation, partnership, trust, estate, unincorporated organization, association, or other legal entity.
25
26   "Agreement" means the operating agreement, farmout agreement, or other contract between the Parties to which this Accounting
27   Procedure is attached.
28
29   "Controllable Material" means Material that, at the time of acquisition or disposition by the Joint Account, as applicable, is so classified
30   in the Material Classification Manual most recently recommended by the Council of Petroleum Accountants Societies (COPAS).
31
32   "Equalized Freight" means the procedure of charging transportation cost to the Joint Account based upon the distance from the nearest
33   Railway Receiving Point to the property.
34
35   "Excluded Amount" means a specified excluded trucking amount most recently recommended by COPAS.
36
37   "Field Office" means a structure, or portion of a structure, whether a temporary or permanent installation, the primary function of which is
38   to directly serve daily operation and maintenance activities of the Joint Property and which serves as a staging area for directly chargeable
39   field personnel.
40
41   "First Level Supervision" means those employees whose primary function in Joint Operations is the direct oversight of the Operator's
42   field employees and/or contract labor directly employed On-site in a field operating capacity. First Level Supervision functions may
43   include, but are not limited to:
44
45   • Responsibility for field employees and contract labor engaged in activities that can include field operations, maintenance,
46   construction, well remedial work, equipment movement and drilling
47   • Responsibility for day-to-day direct oversight of rig operations
48   • Responsibility for day-to-day direct oversight of construction operations
49   • Coordination of job priorities and approval of work procedures
50   • Responsibility for optimal resource utilization (equipment, Materials, personnel)
51   • Responsibility for meeting production and field operating expense targets
52   • Representation of the Parties in local matters involving community, vendors, regulatory agents and landowners, as an incidental
53   part of the supervisor's operating responsibilities
54   • Responsibility for all emergency responses with field staff
55   • Responsibility for implementing safety and environmental practices
56   • Responsibility for field adherence to company policy
57   • Responsibility for employment decisions and performance appraisals for field personnel
58   • Oversight of sub-groups for field functions such as electrical, safety, environmental, telecommunications, which may have group
59   or team leaders.
60
61   "Joint Account" means the account showing the charges paid and credits received in the conduct of the Joint Operations that are to be
62   shared by the Parties, but does not include proceeds attributable to hydrocarbons and by-products produced under the Agreement.
63
64   "Joint Operations" means all operations necessary or proper for the exploration, appraisal, development, production, protection,
65   maintenance, repair, abandonment, and restoration of the Joint Property.
66

1

1   "**Joint Property**" means the real and personal property subject to the Agreement.

3   "**Laws**" means any laws, rules, regulations, decrees, and orders of the United States of America or any state thereof and all other governmental bodies, agencies, and other authorities having jurisdiction over or affecting the provisions contained in or the transactions contemplated by the Agreement or the Parties and their operations, whether such laws now exist or are hereafter amended, enacted, promulgated or issued.

8   "**Material**" means personal property, equipment, supplies, or consumables acquired or held for use by the Joint Property.

10   "**Non-Operators**" means the Parties to the Agreement other than the Operator.

12   "**Offshore Facilities**" means platforms, surface and subsea development and production systems, and other support systems such as oil and gas handling facilities, living quarters, offices, shops, cranes, electrical supply equipment and systems, fuel and water storage and piping, heliport, marine docking installations, communication facilities, navigation aids, and other similar facilities necessary in the conduct of offshore operations, all of which are located offshore.

17   "**Off-site**" means any location that is not considered On-site as defined in this Accounting Procedure.

19   "**On-site**" means on the Joint Property when in direct conduct of Joint Operations. The term "On-site" shall also include that portion of Offshore Facilities, Shore Base Facilities, fabrication yards, and staging areas from which Joint Operations are conducted, or other facilities that directly control equipment on the Joint Property, regardless of whether such facilities are owned by the Joint Account.

23   "**Operator**" means the Party designated pursuant to the Agreement to conduct the Joint Operations.

25   "**Parties**" means legal entities signatory to the Agreement or their successors and assigns. Parties shall be referred to individually as "Party."

28   "**Participating Interest**" means the percentage of the costs and risks of conducting an operation under the Agreement that a Party agrees, or is otherwise obligated, to pay and bear.

31   "**Participating Party**" means a Party that approves a proposed operation or otherwise agrees, or becomes liable, to pay and bear a share of the costs and risks of conducting an operation under the Agreement.

34   "**Personal Expenses**" means reimbursed costs for travel and temporary living expenses.

36   "**Railway Receiving Point**" means the railhead nearest the Joint Property for which freight rates are published, even though an actual railhead may not exist.

39   "**Shore Base Facilities**" means onshore support facilities that during Joint Operations provide such services to the Joint Property as a receiving and transshipment point for Materials; debarkation point for drilling and production personnel and services; communication, scheduling and dispatching center; and other associated functions serving the Joint Property.

43   "**Supply Store**" means a recognized source or common stock point for a given Material item.

45   "**Technical Services**" means services providing specific engineering, geoscience, or other professional skills, such as those performed by engineers, geologists, geophysicists, and technicians, required to handle specific operating conditions and problems for the benefit of Joint Operations; provided, however, Technical Services shall not include those functions specifically identified as overhead under the second paragraph of the introduction of Section III (*Overhead*). Technical Services may be provided by the Operator, Operator's Affiliate, Non-Operator, Non-Operator Affiliates, and/or third parties.

51   2.   **STATEMENTS AND BILLINGS**

53   The Operator shall bill Non-Operators on or before the last day of the month for their proportionate share of the Joint Account for the preceding month. Such bills shall be accompanied by statements that identify the AFE (authority for expenditure), lease or facility, and all charges and credits summarized by appropriate categories of investment and expense. Controllable Material shall be separately identified and fully described in detail, or at the Operator's option, Controllable Material may be summarized by major Material classifications. Intangible drilling costs, audit adjustments, and unusual charges and credits shall be separately and clearly identified.

59   The Operator may make available to Non-Operators any statements and bills required under Section 1.2 and/or Section 1.3.A (*Advances and Payments by the Parties*) via email, electronic data interchange, internet websites or other equivalent electronic media in lieu of paper copies. The Operator shall provide the Non-Operators instructions and any necessary information to access and receive the statements and bills within the timeframes specified herein. A statement or billing shall be deemed as delivered twenty-four (24) hours (exclusive of weekends and holidays) after the Operator notifies the Non-Operator that the statement or billing is available on the website and/or sent via email or electronic data interchange transmission. Each Non-Operator individually shall elect to receive statements and billings electronically, if available from the Operator, or request paper copies. Such election may be changed upon thirty (30) days prior written notice to the Operator.

3. ADVANCES AND PAYMENTS BY THE PARTIES

A. Unless otherwise provided for in the Agreement, the Operator may require the Non-Operators to advance their share of the estimated cash outlay for the succeeding month's operations within fifteen (15) days after receipt of the advance request or by the first day of the month for which the advance is required, whichever is later. The Operator shall adjust each monthly billing to reflect advances received from the Non-Operators for such month. If a refund is due, the Operator shall apply the amount to be refunded to the subsequent month's billing or advance, unless the Non-Operator sends the Operator a written request for a cash refund. The Operator shall remit the refund to the Non-Operator within fifteen (15) days of receipt of such written request.

B. Except as provided below, each Party shall pay its proportionate share of all bills in full within fifteen (15) days of receipt date. If payment is not made within such time, the unpaid balance shall bear interest compounded monthly at the prime rate published by the *Wall Street Journal* on the first day of each month the payment is delinquent, plus three percent (3%), per annum, or the maximum contract rate permitted by the applicable usury Laws governing the Joint Property, whichever is the lesser, plus attorney's fees, court costs, and other costs in connection with the collection of unpaid amounts. If the *Wall Street Journal* ceases to be published or discontinues publishing a prime rate, the unpaid balance shall bear interest compounded monthly at the prime rate published by the Federal Reserve plus three percent (3%), per annum. Interest shall begin accruing on the first day of the month in which the payment was due. Payment shall not be reduced or delayed as a result of inquiries or anticipated credits unless the Operator has agreed. Notwithstanding the foregoing, the Non-Operator may reduce payment, provided it furnishes documentation and explanation to the Operator at the time payment is made, to the extent such reduction is caused by:

    (1) being billed at an incorrect working interest or Participating Interest that is higher than such Non-Operator's actual working interest or Participating Interest, as applicable; or

    (2) being billed for a project or AFE requiring approval of the Parties under the Agreement that the Non-Operator has not approved or is not otherwise obligated to pay under the Agreement; or

    (3) being billed for a property in which the Non-Operator no longer owns a working interest, provided the Non-Operator has furnished the Operator a copy of the recorded assignment or letter in-lieu. Notwithstanding the foregoing, the Non-Operator shall remain responsible for paying bills attributable to the interest it sold or transferred for any bills rendered during the thirty (30) day period following the Operator's receipt of such written notice; or

    (4) charges outside the adjustment period, as provided in Section I.4 (*Adjustments*).

4. ADJUSTMENTS

A. Payment of any such bills shall not prejudice the right of any Party to protest or question the correctness thereof; however, all bills and statements, including payout statements, rendered during any calendar year shall conclusively be presumed to be true and correct, with respect only to expenditures, after twenty-four (24) months following the end of any such calendar year, unless within said period a Party takes specific detailed written exception thereto making a claim for adjustment. The Operator shall provide a response to all written exceptions, whether or not contained in an audit report, within the time periods prescribed in Section I.5 (*Expenditure Audits*).

B. All adjustments initiated by the Operator, except those described in items (1) through (4) of this Section I.4.B, are limited to the twenty-four (24) month period following the end of the calendar year in which the original charge appeared or should have appeared on the Operator's Joint Account statement or payout statement. Adjustments that may be made beyond the twenty-four (24) month period are limited to adjustments resulting from the following:

    (1) a physical inventory of Controllable Material as provided for in Section V (*Inventories of Controllable Material*), or

    (2) an offsetting entry (whether in whole or in part) that is the direct result of a specific joint interest audit exception granted by the Operator relating to another property, or

    (3) a government/regulatory audit, or

    (4) a working interest ownership or Participating Interest adjustment.

5. EXPENDITURE AUDITS

A. A Non-Operator, upon written notice to the Operator and all other Non-Operators, shall have the right to audit the Operator's accounts and records relating to the Joint Account within the twenty-four (24) month period following the end of such calendar year in which such bill was rendered; however, conducting an audit shall not extend the time for the taking of written exception to and the adjustment of accounts as provided for in Section I.4 (*Adjustments*). Any Party that is subject to payout accounting under the Agreement shall have the right to audit the accounts and records of the Party responsible for preparing the payout statements, or of the Party furnishing information to the Party responsible for preparing payout statements. Audits of payout accounts may include the volumes of hydrocarbons produced and saved and proceeds received for such hydrocarbons as they pertain to payout accounting required under the Agreement. Unless otherwise provided in the Agreement, audits of a payout account shall be conducted within the twenty-four (24) month period following the end of the calendar year in which the payout statement was rendered.

Where there are two or more Non-Operators, the Non-Operators shall make every reasonable effort to conduct a joint audit in a manner that will result in a minimum of inconvenience to the Operator. The Operator shall bear no portion of the Non-Operators' audit cost incurred under this paragraph unless agreed to by the Operator. The audits shall not be conducted more than once each year without prior approval of the Operator, except upon the resignation or removal of the Operator, and shall be made at the expense of

3

those Non-Operators approving such audit.

The Non-Operator leading the audit (hereinafter "lead audit company") shall issue the audit report within ninety (90) days after completion of the audit testing and analysis; however, the ninety (90) day time period shall not extend the twenty-four (24) month requirement for taking specific detailed written exception as required in Section I.4.A (*Adjustments*) above. All claims shall be supported with sufficient documentation.

A timely filed written exception or audit report containing written exceptions (hereinafter "written exceptions") shall, with respect to the claims made therein, preclude the Operator from asserting a statute of limitations defense against such claims, and the Operator hereby waives its right to assert any statute of limitations defense against such claims for so long as any Non-Operator continues to comply with the deadlines for resolving exceptions provided in this Accounting Procedure. If the Non-Operators fail to comply with the additional deadlines in Section I.5.B or I.5.C, the Operator's waiver of its rights to assert a statute of limitations defense against the claims brought by the Non-Operators shall lapse, and such claims shall then be subject to the applicable statute of limitations, provided that such waiver shall not lapse in the event that the Operator has failed to comply with the deadlines in Section I.5.B or I.5.C.

B. The Operator shall provide a written response to all exceptions in an audit report within one hundred eighty (180) days after Operator receives such report. Denied exceptions should be accompanied by a substantive response. If the Operator fails to provide substantive response to an exception within this one hundred eighty (180) day period, the Operator will owe interest on that exception or portion thereof, if ultimately granted, from the date it received the audit report. Interest shall be calculated using the rate set forth in Section I.3.B (*Advances and Payments by the Parties*).

C. The lead audit company shall reply to the Operator's response to an audit report within ninety (90) days of receipt, and the Operator shall reply to the lead audit company's follow-up response within ninety (90) days of receipt; provided, however, each Non-Operator shall have the right to represent itself if it disagrees with the lead audit company's position or believes the lead audit company is not adequately fulfilling its duties. Unless otherwise provided for in Section I.5.E, if the Operator fails to provide substantive response to an exception within this ninety (90) day period, the Operator will owe interest on that exception or portion thereof, if ultimately granted, from the date it received the audit report. Interest shall be calculated using the rate set forth in Section I.3.B (*Advances and Payments by the Parties*).

D. If any Party fails to meet the deadlines in Sections I.5.B or I.5.C or if any audit issues are outstanding fifteen (15) months after Operator receives the audit report, the Operator or any Non-Operator participating in the audit has the right to call a resolution meeting, as set forth in this Section I.5.D or it may invoke the dispute resolution procedures included in the Agreement, if applicable. The meeting will require one month's written notice to the Operator and all Non-Operators participating in the audit. The meeting shall be held at the Operator's office or mutually agreed location, and shall be attended by representatives of the Parties with authority to resolve such outstanding issues. Any Party who fails to attend the resolution meeting shall be bound by any resolution reached at the meeting. The lead audit company will make good faith efforts to coordinate the response and positions of the Non-Operator participants throughout the resolution process; however, each Non-Operator shall have the right to represent itself. Attendees will make good faith efforts to resolve outstanding issues, and each Party will be required to present substantive information supporting its position. A resolution meeting may be held as often as agreed to by the Parties. Issues unresolved at one meeting may be discussed at subsequent meetings until each such issue is resolved.

If the Agreement contains no dispute resolution procedures and the audit issues cannot be resolved by negotiation, the dispute shall be submitted to mediation. In such event, promptly following one Party's written request for mediation, the Parties to the dispute shall choose a mutually acceptable mediator and share the costs of mediation services equally. The Parties shall each have present at the mediation at least one individual who has the authority to settle the dispute. The Parties shall make reasonable efforts to ensure that the mediation commences within sixty (60) days of the date of the mediation request. Notwithstanding the above, any Party may file a lawsuit or complaint (1) if the Parties are unable after reasonable efforts, to commence mediation within sixty (60) days of the date of the mediation request, (2) for statute of limitations reasons, or (3) to seek a preliminary injunction or other provisional judicial relief, if in its sole judgment an injunction or other provisional relief is necessary to avoid irreparable damage or to preserve the status quo. Despite such action, the Parties shall continue to try to resolve the dispute by mediation.

E. ☐ (*Optional Provision – Forfeiture Penalties*)
If the Non-Operators fail to meet the deadline in Section I.5.C, any unresolved exceptions that were not addressed by the Non-Operators within one (1) year following receipt of the last substantive response of the Operator shall be deemed to have been withdrawn by the Non-Operators. If the Operator fails to meet the deadlines in Section I.5.B or I.5.C, any unresolved exceptions that were not addressed by the Operator within one (1) year following receipt of the audit report or receipt of the last substantive response of the Non-Operators, whichever is later, shall be deemed to have been granted by the Operator and adjustments shall be made, without interest, to the Joint Account.

6. **APPROVAL BY PARTIES**

A. GENERAL MATTERS

Where an approval or other agreement of the Parties or Non-Operators is expressly required under other Sections of this Accounting Procedure and if the Agreement to which this Accounting Procedure is attached contains no contrary provisions in regard thereto, the

4

c o p a s

Operator shall notify all Non-Operators of the Operator's proposal and the agreement or approval of a majority in interest of the Non-Operators shall be controlling on all Non-Operators.

This Section I.6.A applies to specific situations of limited duration where a Party proposes to change the accounting for charges from that prescribed in this Accounting Procedure. This provision does not apply to amendments to this Accounting Procedure, which are covered by Section I.6.B.

B.   AMENDMENTS

If the Agreement to which this Accounting Procedure is attached contains no contrary provisions in regard thereto, this Accounting Procedure can be amended by an affirmative vote of _____ (_____) or more Parties, one of which is the Operator, having a combined working interest of at least _____ percent (_____%), which approval shall be binding on all Parties, provided, however, approval of at least one (1) Non-Operator shall be required.

C.   AFFILIATES

For the purpose of administering the voting procedures of Sections I.6.A and I.6.B, if Parties to this Agreement are Affiliates of each other, then such Affiliates shall be combined and treated as a single Party having the combined working interest or Participating Interest of such Affiliates.

For the purposes of administering the voting procedures in Section I.6.A, if a Non-Operator is an Affiliate of the Operator, votes under Section I.6.A shall require the majority in interest of the Non-Operator(s) after excluding the interest of the Operator's Affiliate.

II. DIRECT CHARGES

The Operator shall charge the Joint Account with the following items:

1.   **RENTALS AND ROYALTIES**

Lease rentals and royalties paid by the Operator, on behalf of all Parties, for the Joint Operations.

2.   **LABOR**

A.   Salaries and wages, including incentive compensation programs as set forth in COPAS MFI-37 ("Chargeability of Incentive Compensation Programs"), for:

(1)   Operator's field employees directly employed On-site in the conduct of Joint Operations,

(2)   Operator's employees directly employed on Shore Base Facilities, Offshore Facilities, or other facilities serving the Joint Property if such costs are not charged under Section II.6 (*Equipment and Facilities Furnished by Operator*) or are not a function covered under Section III (*Overhead*),

(3)   Operator's employees providing First Level Supervision,

(4)   Operator's employees providing On-site Technical Services for the Joint Property if such charges are excluded from the overhead rates in Section III (*Overhead*),

(5)   Operator's employees providing Off-site Technical Services for the Joint Property if such charges are excluded from the overhead rates in Section III (*Overhead*).

Charges for the Operator's employees identified in Section II.2.A may be made based on the employee's actual salaries and wages, or in lieu thereof, a day rate representing the Operator's average salaries and wages of the employee's specific job category.

Charges for personnel chargeable under this Section II.2.A who are foreign nationals shall not exceed comparable compensation paid to an equivalent U.S. employee pursuant to this Section II.2, unless otherwise approved by the Parties pursuant to Section I.6.A (*General Matters*).

B.   Operator's cost of holiday, vacation, sickness, and disability benefits, and other customary allowances paid to employees whose salaries and wages are chargeable to the Joint Account under Section II.2.A, excluding severance payments or other termination allowances. Such costs under this Section II.2.B may be charged on a "when and as-paid basis" or by "percentage assessment" on the amount of salaries and wages chargeable to the Joint Account under Section II.2.A. If percentage assessment is used, the rate shall be based on the Operator's cost experience.

C.   Expenditures or contributions made pursuant to assessments imposed by governmental authority that are applicable to costs chargeable to the Joint Account under Sections II.2.A and B.

5

D. Personal Expenses of personnel whose salaries and wages are chargeable to the Joint Account under Section II.2.A when the expenses are incurred in connection with directly chargeable activities.

E. Reasonable relocation costs incurred in transferring to the Joint Property personnel whose salaries and wages are chargeable to the Joint Account under Section II.2.A. Notwithstanding the foregoing, relocation costs that result from reorganization or merger of a Party, or that are for the primary benefit of the Operator, shall not be chargeable to the Joint Account. Extraordinary relocation costs, such as those incurred as a result of transfers from remote locations, such as Alaska or overseas, shall not be charged to the Joint Account unless approved by the Parties pursuant to Section I.6.A (*General Matters*).

F. Training costs as specified in COPAS MFI-35 ("Charging of Training Costs to the Joint Account") for personnel whose salaries and wages are chargeable under Section II.2.A. This training charge shall include the wages, salaries, training course cost, and Personal Expenses incurred during the training session. The training cost shall be charged or allocated to the property or properties directly benefiting from the training. The cost of the training course shall not exceed prevailing commercial rates, where such rates are available.

G. Operator's current cost of established plans for employee benefits, as described in COPAS MFI-27 ("Employee Benefits Chargeable to Joint Operations and Subject to Percentage Limitation"), applicable to the Operator's labor costs chargeable to the Joint Account under Sections II.2.A and B based on the Operator's actual cost not to exceed the employee benefits limitation percentage most recently recommended by COPAS.

H. Award payments to employees, in accordance with COPAS MFI-49 ("Awards to Employees and Contractors") for personnel whose salaries and wages are chargeable under Section II.2.A.

3. MATERIAL

Material purchased or furnished by the Operator for use on the Joint Property in the conduct of Joint Operations as provided under Section IV (Material *Purchases, Transfers, and Dispositions*). Only such Material shall be purchased for or transferred to the Joint Property as may be required for immediate use or is reasonably practical and consistent with efficient and economical operations. The accumulation of surplus stocks shall be avoided.

4. TRANSPORTATION

A. Transportation of the Operator's, Operator's Affiliate's, or contractor's personnel necessary for Joint Operations.

B. Transportation of Material between the Joint Property and another property, or from the Operator's warehouse or other storage point to the Joint Property, shall be charged to the receiving property using one of the methods listed below. Transportation of Material from the Joint Property to the Operator's warehouse or other storage point shall be paid for by the Joint Property using one of the methods listed below:

(1) If the actual trucking charge is less than or equal to the Excluded Amount the Operator may charge actual trucking cost or a theoretical charge from the Railway Receiving Point to the Joint Property. The basis for the theoretical charge is the per hundred weight charge plus fuel surcharges from the Railway Receiving Point to the Joint Property. The Operator shall consistently apply the selected alternative.

(2) If the actual trucking charge is greater than the Excluded Amount, the Operator shall charge Equalized Freight. Accessorial charges such as loading and unloading costs, split pick-up costs, detention, call out charges, and permit fees shall be charged directly to the Joint Property and shall not be included when calculating the Equalized Freight.

5. SERVICES

The cost of contract services, equipment, and utilities used in the conduct of Joint Operations, except for contract services, equipment, and utilities covered by Section III (*Overhead*), or Section II.7 (*Affiliates*), or excluded under Section II.9 (*Legal Expense*). Awards paid to contractors shall be chargeable pursuant to COPAS MFI-49 ("Awards to Employees and Contractors").

The costs of third party Technical Services are chargeable to the extent excluded from the overhead rates under Section III (*Overhead*).

6. EQUIPMENT AND FACILITIES FURNISHED BY OPERATOR

In the absence of a separately negotiated agreement, equipment and facilities furnished by the Operator will be charged as follows:

A. The Operator shall charge the Joint Account for use of Operator-owned equipment and facilities, including but not limited to production facilities, Shore Base Facilities, Offshore Facilities, and Field Offices, at rates commensurate with the costs of ownership and operation. The cost of Field Offices shall be chargeable to the extent the Field Offices provide direct service to personnel who are chargeable pursuant to Section II.2.A (*Labor*). Such rates may include labor, maintenance, repairs, other operating expense, insurance, taxes, depreciation using straight line depreciation method, and interest on gross investment less accumulated depreciation not to exceed _____ percent (_____%) per annum; provided, however, depreciation shall not be charged when the equipment and facilities investment have been fully depreciated. The rate may include an element of the estimated cost for abandonment, reclamation, and dismantlement. Such rates shall not exceed the average commercial rates currently prevailing in the immediate area of the Joint Property.

B. In lieu of charges in Section II.6.A above, the Operator may elect to use average commercial rates prevailing in the immediate area of the Joint Property, less twenty percent (20%). If equipment and facilities are charged under this Section II.6.B, the Operator shall adequately document and support commercial rates and shall periodically review and update the rate and the supporting documentation. For automotive equipment, the Operator may elect to use rates published by the Petroleum Motor Transport Association (PMTA) or such other organization recognized by COPAS as the official source of rates.

7. AFFILIATES

A. Charges for an Affiliate's goods and/or services used in operations requiring an AFE or other authorization from the Non-Operators may be made without the approval of the Parties provided (i) the Affiliate is identified and the Affiliate goods and services are specifically detailed in the approved AFE or other authorization, and (ii) the total costs for such Affiliate's goods and services billed to such individual project do not exceed $_____ If the total costs for an Affiliate's goods and services charged to such individual project are not specifically detailed in the approved AFE or authorization or exceed such amount, charges for such Affiliate shall require approval of the Parties, pursuant to Section I.6.A (*General Matters*).

B. For an Affiliate's goods and/or services used in operations not requiring an AFE or other authorization from the Non-Operators, charges for such Affiliate's goods and services shall require approval of the Parties, pursuant to Section I.6.A (*General Matters*), if the charges exceed $_____ in a given calendar year.

C. The cost of the Affiliate's goods or services shall not exceed average commercial rates prevailing in the area of the Joint Property, unless the Operator obtains the Non-Operators' approval of such rates. The Operator shall adequately document and support commercial rates and shall periodically review and update the rate and the supporting documentation; provided, however, documentation of commercial rates shall not be required if the Operator obtains Non-Operator approval of its Affiliate's rates or charges prior to billing Non-Operators for such Affiliate's goods and services. Notwithstanding the foregoing, direct charges for Affiliate-owned communication facilities or systems shall be made pursuant to Section II.12 (*Communications*).

If the Parties fail to designate an amount in Sections II.7.A or II.7.B, in each instance the amount deemed adopted by the Parties as a result of such omission shall be the amount established as the Operator's expenditure limitation in the Agreement. If the Agreement does not contain an Operator's expenditure limitation, the amount deemed adopted by the Parties as a result of such omission shall be zero dollars ($ 0.00).

8. DAMAGES AND LOSSES TO JOINT PROPERTY

All costs or expenses necessary for the repair or replacement of Joint Property resulting from damages or losses incurred, except to the extent such damages or losses result from a Party's or Parties' gross negligence or willful misconduct, in which case such Party or Parties shall be solely liable.

The Operator shall furnish the Non-Operator written notice of damages or losses incurred as soon as practicable after a report has been received by the Operator.

9. LEGAL EXPENSE

Recording fees and costs of handling, settling, or otherwise discharging litigation, claims, and liens incurred in or resulting from operations under the Agreement, or necessary to protect or recover the Joint Property, to the extent permitted under the Agreement. Costs of the Operator's or Affiliate's legal staff or outside attorneys, including fees and expenses, are not chargeable unless approved by the Parties pursuant to Section I.6.A (*General Matters*) or otherwise provided for in the Agreement.

Notwithstanding the foregoing paragraph, costs for procuring abstracts, fees paid to outside attorneys for title examinations (including preliminary, supplemental, shut-in royalty opinions, division order title opinions), and curative work shall be chargeable to the extent permitted as a direct charge in the Agreement.

10. TAXES AND PERMITS

All taxes and permitting fees of every kind and nature, assessed or levied upon or in connection with the Joint Property, or the production therefrom, and which have been paid by the Operator for the benefit of the Parties, including penalties and interest, except to the extent the penalties and interest result from the Operator's gross negligence or willful misconduct.

If ad valorem taxes paid by the Operator are based in whole or in part upon separate valuations of each Party's working interest, then notwithstanding any contrary provisions, the charges to the Parties will be made in accordance with the tax value generated by each Party's working interest.

7

c o p a s

1   Costs of tax consultants or advisors, the Operator's employees, or Operator's Affiliate employees in matters regarding ad valorem or other
2   tax matters, are not permitted as direct charges unless approved by the Parties pursuant to Section I.6.A (*General Matters*).

4   Charges to the Joint Account resulting from sales/use tax audits, including extrapolated amounts and penalties and interest, are permitted,
5   provided the Non-Operator shall be allowed to review the invoices and other underlying source documents which served as the basis for
6   tax charges and to determine that the correct amount of taxes were charged to the Joint Account. If the Non-Operator is not permitted to
7   review such documentation, the sales/use tax amount shall not be directly charged unless the Operator can conclusively document the
8   amount owed by the Joint Account.

11. INSURANCE

12   Net premiums paid for insurance required to be carried for Joint Operations for the protection of the Parties. If Joint Operations are
13   conducted at locations where the Operator acts as self-insurer in regard to its worker's compensation and employer's liability insurance
14   obligation, the Operator shall charge the Joint Account manual rates for the risk assumed in its self-insurance program as regulated by the
15   jurisdiction governing the Joint Property. In the case of offshore operations in federal waters, the manual rates of the adjacent state shall be
16   used for personnel performing work On-site, and such rates shall be adjusted for offshore operations by the U.S. Longshoreman and
17   Harbor Workers (USL&H) or Jones Act surcharge, as appropriate.

12. COMMUNICATIONS

21   Costs of acquiring, leasing, installing, operating, repairing, and maintaining communication facilities or systems, including satellite, radio
22   and microwave facilities, between the Joint Property and the Operator's office(s) directly responsible for field operations in accordance
23   with the provisions of COPAS MFI-44 ("Field Computer and Communication Systems"). If the communications facilities or systems
24   serving the Joint Property are Operator-owned, charges to the Joint Account shall be made as provided in Section II.6 (*Equipment and
25   Facilities Furnished by Operator*). If the communication facilities or systems serving the Joint Property are owned by the Operator's
26   Affiliate, charges to the Joint Account shall not exceed average commercial rates prevailing in the area of the Joint Property. The Operator
27   shall adequately document and support commercial rates and shall periodically review and update the rate and the supporting
28   documentation.

13. ECOLOGICAL, ENVIRONMENTAL, AND SAFETY

32   Costs incurred for Technical Services and drafting to comply with ecological, environmental and safety Laws or standards recommended by
33   Occupational Safety and Health Administration (OSHA) or other regulatory authorities. All other labor and functions incurred for
34   ecological, environmental and safety matters, including management, administration, and permitting, shall be covered by Sections II.2
35   (*Labor*), II.5 (*Services*), or Section III (*Overhead*), as applicable.

37   Costs to provide or have available pollution containment and removal equipment plus actual costs of control and cleanup and resulting
38   responsibilities of oil and other spills as well as discharges from permitted outfalls as required by applicable Laws, or other pollution
39   containment and removal equipment deemed appropriate by the Operator for prudent operations, are directly chargeable.

14. ABANDONMENT AND RECLAMATION

43   Costs incurred for abandonment and reclamation of the Joint Property, including costs required by lease agreements or by Laws.

15. OTHER EXPENDITURES

47   Any other expenditure not covered or dealt with in the foregoing provisions of this Section II (*Direct Charges*), or in Section III
48   (*Overhead*) and which is of direct benefit to the Joint Property and is incurred by the Operator in the necessary and proper conduct of the
49   Joint Operations. Charges made under this Section II.15 shall require approval of the Parties, pursuant to Section I.6.A (*General Matters*).

III. OVERHEAD

As compensation for costs not specifically identified as chargeable to the Joint Account pursuant to Section II (*Direct Charges*), the Operator
shall charge the Joint Account in accordance with this Section III.

Functions included in the overhead rates regardless of whether performed by the Operator, Operator's Affiliates or third parties and regardless
of location, shall include, but not be limited to, costs and expenses of:

- warehousing, other than for warehouses that are jointly owned under this Agreement
- design and drafting (except when allowed as a direct charge under Sections II.13, III.1.A(ii), and III.2, Option B)
- inventory costs not chargeable under Section V (*Inventories of Controllable Material*)
- procurement
- administration
- accounting and auditing
- gas dispatching and gas chart integration

8

c o p a s

- human resources
- management
- supervision not directly charged under Section II.2 (*Labor*)
- legal services not directly chargeable under Section II.9 (*Legal Expense*)
- taxation, other than those costs identified as directly chargeable under Section II.10 (*Taxes and Permits*)
- preparation and monitoring of permits and certifications; preparing regulatory reports; appearances before or meetings with governmental agencies or other authorities having jurisdiction over the Joint Property, other than On-site inspections; reviewing, interpreting, or submitting comments on or lobbying with respect to Laws or proposed Laws.

Overhead charges shall include the salaries or wages plus applicable payroll burdens, benefits, and Personal Expenses of personnel performing overhead functions, as well as office and other related expenses of overhead functions.

1. **OVERHEAD—DRILLING AND PRODUCING OPERATIONS**

   As compensation for costs incurred but not chargeable under Section II (*Direct Charges*) and not covered by other provisions of this Section III, the Operator shall charge on either:

   ☐ (Alternative 1) Fixed Rate Basis, Section III.1.B.
   ☐ (Alternative 2) Percentage Basis, Section III.1.C.

   A. **TECHNICAL SERVICES**

      (i) Except as otherwise provided in Section II.13 (*Ecological Environmental, and Safety*) and Section III.2 (*Overhead – Major Construction and Catastrophe*), or by approval of the Parties pursuant to Section I.6.A (*General Matters*), the salaries, wages, related payroll burdens and benefits, and Personal Expenses for On-site Technical Services, including third party Technical Services:

         ☐ (Alternative 1 – Direct) shall be charged <u>direct</u> to the Joint Account.

         ☐ (Alternative 2 – Overhead) shall be covered by the <u>overhead</u> rates.

      (ii) Except as otherwise provided in Section II.13 (*Ecological, Environmental, and Safety*) and Section III.2 (*Overhead – Major Construction and Catastrophe*), or by approval of the Parties pursuant to Section I.6.A (*General Matters*), the salaries, wages, related payroll burdens and benefits, and Personal Expenses for Off-site Technical Services, including third party Technical Services:

         ☐ (Alternative 1 – All Overhead) shall be covered by the <u>overhead</u> rates.

         ☐ (Alternative 2 – All Direct) shall be charged <u>direct</u> to the Joint Account.

         ☐ (Alternative 3 – Drilling Direct) shall be charged <u>direct</u> to the Joint Account, <u>only</u> to the extent such Technical Services are directly attributable to drilling, redrilling, deepening, or sidetracking operations, through completion, temporary abandonment, or abandonment if a dry hole. Off-site Technical Services for all other operations, including workover, recompletion, abandonment of producing wells, and the construction or expansion of fixed assets not covered by Section III.2 (*Overhead - Major Construction and Catastrophe*) shall be covered by the overhead rates.

   Notwithstanding anything to the contrary in this Section III, Technical Services provided by Operator's Affiliates are subject to limitations set forth in Section II.7 (*Affiliates*). Charges for Technical personnel performing non-technical work shall not be governed by this Section III.1.A, but instead governed by other provisions of this Accounting Procedure relating to the type of work being performed.

   B. **OVERHEAD—FIXED RATE BASIS**

      (1) The Operator shall charge the Joint Account at the following rates per well per month:

         Drilling Well Rate per month $_____ (prorated for less than a full month)

         Producing Well Rate per month $_____

      (2) Application of Overhead—Drilling Well Rate shall be as follows:

         (a) Charges for onshore drilling wells shall begin on the spud date and terminate on the date the drilling and/or completion equipment used on the well is released, whichever occurs later. Charges for offshore and inland waters drilling wells shall begin on the date the drilling or completion equipment arrives on location and terminate on the date the drilling or completion equipment moves off location, or is released, whichever occurs first. No charge shall be made during suspension of drilling and/or completion operations for fifteen (15) or more consecutive calendar days.

9

(b) Charges for any well undergoing any type of workover, recompletion, and/or abandonment for a period of five (5) or more consecutive work–days shall be made at the Drilling Well Rate. Such charges shall be applied for the period from date operations, with rig or other units used in operations, commence through date of rig or other unit release, except that no charges shall be made during suspension of operations for fifteen (15) or more consecutive calendar days.

(3) Application of Overhead—Producing Well Rate shall be as follows:

(a) An active well that is produced, injected into for recovery or disposal, or used to obtain water supply to support operations for any portion of the month shall be considered as a one-well charge for the entire month.

(b) Each active completion in a multi-completed well shall be considered as a one-well charge provided each completion is considered a separate well by the governing regulatory authority.

(c) A one-well charge shall be made for the month in which plugging and abandonment operations are completed on any well, unless the Drilling Well Rate applies, as provided in Sections III.1.B.(2)(a) or (b). This one-well charge shall be made whether or not the well has produced.

(d) An active gas well shut in because of overproduction or failure of a purchaser, processor, or transporter to take production shall be considered as a one-well charge provided the gas well is directly connected to a permanent sales outlet.

(e) Any well not meeting the criteria set forth in Sections III.1.B.(3) (a), (b), (c), or (d) shall not qualify for a producing overhead charge.

(4) The well rates shall be adjusted on the first day of April each year following the effective date of the Agreement; provided, however, if this Accounting Procedure is attached to or otherwise governing the payout accounting under a farmout agreement, the rates shall be adjusted on the first day of April each year following the effective date of such farmout agreement. The adjustment shall be computed by applying the adjustment factor most recently published by COPAS. The adjusted rates shall be the initial or amended rates agreed to by the Parties increased or decreased by the adjustment factor described herein, for each year from the effective date of such rates, in accordance with COPAS MFI-47 ("Adjustment of Overhead Rates").

C. OVERHEAD—PERCENTAGE BASIS

(1) Operator shall charge the Joint Account at the following rates:

(a) Development Rate _____ percent (_____) % of the cost of development of the Joint Property, exclusive of costs provided under Section II.9 (*Legal Expense*) and all Material salvage credits.

(b) Operating Rate _____ percent (_____%) of the cost of operating the Joint Property, exclusive of costs provided under Sections II.1 (*Rentals and Royalties*) and II.9 (*Legal Expense*); all Material salvage credits; the value of substances purchased for enhanced recovery; all property and ad valorem taxes, and any other taxes and assessments that are levied, assessed, and paid upon the mineral interest in and to the Joint Property.

(2) Application of Overhead—Percentage Basis shall be as follows:

(a) The Development Rate shall be applied to all costs in connection with:

    [i] drilling, redrilling, sidetracking, or deepening of a well
    [ii] a well undergoing plugback or workover operations for a period of five (5) or more consecutive work–days
    [iii] preliminary expenditures necessary in preparation for drilling
    [iv] expenditures incurred in abandoning when the well is not completed as a producer
    [v] construction or installation of fixed assets, the expansion of fixed assets and any other project clearly discernible as a fixed asset, other than Major Construction or Catastrophe as defined in Section III.2 (*Overhead-Major Construction and Catastrophe*).

(b) The Operating Rate shall be applied to all other costs in connection with Joint Operations, except those subject to Section III.2 (*Overhead-Major Construction and Catastrophe*).

2. OVERHEAD—MAJOR CONSTRUCTION AND CATASTROPHE

To compensate the Operator for overhead costs incurred in connection with a Major Construction project or Catastrophe, the Operator shall either negotiate a rate prior to the beginning of the project, or shall charge the Joint Account for overhead based on the following rates for any Major Construction project in excess of the Operator's expenditure limit under the Agreement, or for any Catastrophe regardless of the amount. If the Agreement to which this Accounting Procedure is attached does not contain an expenditure limit, Major Construction Overhead shall be assessed for any single Major Construction project costing in excess of $100,000 gross.

10

Major Construction shall mean the construction and installation of fixed assets, the expansion of fixed assets, and any other project clearly discernible as a fixed asset required for the development and operation of the Joint Property, or in the dismantlement, abandonment, removal, and restoration of platforms, production equipment, and other operating facilities.

Catastrophe is defined as a sudden calamitous event bringing damage, loss, or destruction to property or the environment, such as an oil spill, blowout, explosion, fire, storm, hurricane, or other disaster. The overhead rate shall be applied to those costs necessary to restore the Joint Property to the equivalent condition that existed prior to the event.

A. If the Operator absorbs the engineering, design and drafting costs related to the project:

    (1) _____% of total costs if such costs are less than $100,000; plus

    (2) _____% of total costs in excess of $100,000 but less than $1,000,000; plus

    (3) _____% of total costs in excess of $1,000,000.

B. If the Operator charges engineering, design and drafting costs related to the project directly to the Joint Account:

    (1) _____% of total costs if such costs are less than $100,000; plus

    (2) _____% of total costs in excess of $100,000 but less than $1,000,000; plus

    (3) _____% of total costs in excess of $1,000,000.

Total cost shall mean the gross cost of any one project. For the purpose of this paragraph, the component parts of a single Major Construction project shall not be treated separately, and the cost of drilling and workover wells and purchasing and installing pumping units and downhole artificial lift equipment shall be excluded. For Catastrophes, the rates shall be applied to all costs associated with each single occurrence or event.

On each project, the Operator shall advise the Non-Operator(s) in advance which of the above options shall apply.

For the purposes of calculating Catastrophe Overhead, the cost of drilling relief wells, substitute wells, or conducting other well operations directly resulting from the catastrophic event shall be included. Expenditures to which these rates apply shall not be reduced by salvage or insurance recoveries. Expenditures that qualify for Major Construction or Catastrophe Overhead shall not qualify for overhead under any other overhead provisions.

In the event of any conflict between the provisions of this Section III.2 and the provisions of Sections II.2 (*Labor*), II.5 (*Services*), or II.7 (*Affiliates*), the provisions of this Section III.2 shall govern.

3. **AMENDMENT OF OVERHEAD RATES**

The overhead rates provided for in this Section III may be amended from time to time if, in practice, the rates are found to be insufficient or excessive, in accordance with the provisions of Section I.6.B (*Amendments*).

IV. MATERIAL PURCHASES, TRANSFERS, AND DISPOSITIONS

The Operator is responsible for Joint Account Material and shall make proper and timely charges and credits for direct purchases, transfers, and dispositions. The Operator shall provide all Material for use in the conduct of Joint Operations; however, Material may be supplied by the Non-Operators, at the Operator's option. Material furnished by any Party shall be furnished without any express or implied warranties as to quality, fitness for use, or any other matter.

1. **DIRECT PURCHASES**

Direct purchases shall be charged to the Joint Account at the price paid by the Operator after deduction of all discounts received. The Operator shall make good faith efforts to take discounts offered by suppliers, but shall not be liable for failure to take discounts except to the extent such failure was the result of the Operator's gross negligence or willful misconduct. A direct purchase shall be deemed to occur when an agreement is made between an Operator and a third party for the acquisition of Material for a specific well site or location. Material provided by the Operator under "vendor stocking programs," where the initial use is for a Joint Property and title of the Material does not pass from the manufacturer, distributor, or agent until usage, is considered a direct purchase. If Material is found to be defective or is returned to the manufacturer, distributor, or agent for any other reason, credit shall be passed to the Joint Account within sixty (60) days after the Operator has received adjustment from the manufacturer, distributor, or agent.

11

2.   TRANSFERS

A transfer is determined to occur when the Operator (i) furnishes Material from a storage facility or from another operated property, (ii) has assumed liability for the storage costs and changes in value, and (iii) has previously secured and held title to the transferred Material. Similarly, the removal of Material from the Joint Property to a storage facility or to another operated property is also considered a transfer; provided, however, Material that is moved from the Joint Property to a storage location for safe-keeping pending disposition may remain charged to the Joint Account and is not considered a transfer. Material shall be disposed of in accordance with Section IV.3 (*Disposition of Surplus*) and the Agreement to which this Accounting Procedure is attached.

A.   PRICING

The value of Material transferred to/from the Joint Property should generally reflect the market value on the date of physical transfer. Regardless of the pricing method used, the Operator shall make available to the Non-Operators sufficient documentation to verify the Material valuation. When higher than specification grade or size tubulars are used in the conduct of Joint Operations, the Operator shall charge the Joint Account at the equivalent price for well design specification tubulars, unless such higher specification grade or sized tubulars are approved by the Parties pursuant to Section I.6.A (*General Matters*). Transfers of new Material will be priced using one of the following pricing methods; provided, however, the Operator shall use consistent pricing methods, and not alternate between methods for the purpose of choosing the method most favorable to the Operator for a specific transfer:

(1)   Using published prices in effect on date of movement as adjusted by the appropriate COPAS Historical Price Multiplier (HPM) or prices provided by the COPAS Computerized Equipment Pricing System (CEPS).

   (a)   For oil country tubulars and line pipe, the published price shall be based upon eastern mill carload base prices (Houston, Texas, for special end) adjusted as of date of movement, plus transportation cost as defined in Section IV.2.B (*Freight*).

   (b)   For other Material, the published price shall be the published list price in effect at date of movement, as listed by a Supply Store nearest the Joint Property where like Material is normally available, or point of manufacture plus transportation costs as defined in Section IV.2.B (*Freight*).

(2)   Based on a price quotation from a vendor that reflects a current realistic acquisition cost.

(3)   Based on the amount paid by the Operator for like Material in the vicinity of the Joint Property within the previous twelve (12) months from the date of physical transfer.

(4)   As agreed to by the Participating Parties for Material being transferred to the Joint Property, and by the Parties owning the Material for Material being transferred from the Joint Property.

B.   FREIGHT

Transportation costs shall be added to the Material transfer price using the method prescribed by the COPAS Computerized Equipment Pricing System (CEPS). If not using CEPS, transportation costs shall be calculated as follows:

(1)   Transportation costs for oil country tubulars and line pipe shall be calculated using the distance from eastern mill to the Railway Receiving Point based on the carload weight basis as recommended by the COPAS MFI-38 ("Material Pricing Manual") and other COPAS MFIs in effect at the time of the transfer.

(2)   Transportation costs for special mill items shall be calculated from that mill's shipping point to the Railway Receiving Point. For transportation costs from other than eastern mills, the 30,000-pound interstate truck rate shall be used. Transportation costs for macaroni tubing shall be calculated based on the interstate truck rate per weight of tubing transferred to the Railway Receiving Point.

(3)   Transportation costs for special end tubular goods shall be calculated using the interstate truck rate from Houston, Texas, to the Railway Receiving Point.

(4)   Transportation costs for Material other than that described in Sections IV.2.B.(1) through (3), shall be calculated from the Supply Store or point of manufacture, whichever is appropriate, to the Railway Receiving Point

Regardless of whether using CEPS or manually calculating transportation costs, transportation costs from the Railway Receiving Point to the Joint Property are in addition to the foregoing, and may be charged to the Joint Account based on actual costs incurred. All transportation costs are subject to Equalized Freight as provided in Section II.4 (*Transportation*) of this Accounting Procedure.

C.   TAXES

Sales and use taxes shall be added to the Material transfer price using either the method contained in the COPAS Computerized Equipment Pricing System (CEPS) or the applicable tax rate in effect for the Joint Property at the time and place of transfer. In either case, the Joint Account shall be charged or credited at the rate that would have governed had the Material been a direct purchase.

D. CONDITION

    (1) Condition "A" – New and unused Material in sound and serviceable condition shall be charged at one hundred percent (100%) of the price as determined in Sections IV.2.A (*Pricing*), IV.2.B (*Freight*), and IV.2.C (*Taxes*). Material transferred from the Joint Property that was not placed in service shall be credited as charged without gain or loss; provided, however, any unused Material that was charged to the Joint Account through a direct purchase will be credited to the Joint Account at the original cost paid less restocking fees charged by the vendor. New and unused Material transferred from the Joint Property may be credited at a price other than the price originally charged to the Joint Account provided such price is approved by the Parties owning such Matters, pursuant to Section I.6.A (*General Matters*). All refurbishing costs required or necessary to return the Material to original condition or to correct handling, transportation, or other damages will be borne by the divesting property. The Joint Account is responsible for Material preparation, handling, and transportation costs for new and unused Material charged to the Joint Property either through a direct purchase or transfer. Any preparation costs incurred, including any internal or external coating and wrapping, will be credited on new Material provided these services were not repeated for such Material for the receiving property.

    (2) Condition "B" – Used Material in sound and serviceable condition and suitable for reuse without reconditioning shall be priced by multiplying the price determined in Sections IV.2.A (*Pricing*), IV.2.B (*Freight*), and IV.2.C (*Taxes*) by seventy-five percent (75%).

    Except as provided in Section IV.2.D(3), all reconditioning costs required to return the Material to Condition "B" or to correct handling, transportation or other damages will be borne by the divesting property.

    If the Material was originally charged to the Joint Account as used Material and placed in service for the Joint Property, the Material will be credited at the price determined in Sections IV.2.A (*Pricing*), IV.2.B (*Freight*), and IV.2.C (*Taxes*) multiplied by sixty-five percent (65%).

    Unless otherwise agreed to by the Parties that paid for such Material, used Material transferred from the Joint Property that was not placed in service on the property shall be credited as charged without gain or loss.

    (3) Condition "C" – Material that is not in sound and serviceable condition and not suitable for its original function until after reconditioning shall be priced by multiplying the price determined in Sections IV.2.A (*Pricing*), IV.2.B (*Freight*), and IV.2.C (*Taxes*) by fifty percent (50%).

    The cost of reconditioning may be charged to the receiving property to the extent Condition "C" value, plus cost of reconditioning, does not exceed Condition "B" value.

    (4) Condition "D" – Material that (i) is no longer suitable for its original purpose but useable for some other purpose, (ii) is obsolete, or (iii) does not meet original specifications but still has value and can be used in other applications as a substitute for items with different specifications, is considered Condition "D" Material. Casing, tubing, or drill pipe used as line pipe shall be priced as Grade A and B seamless line pipe of comparable size and weight. Used casing, tubing, or drill pipe utilized as line pipe shall be priced at used line pipe prices. Casing, tubing, or drill pipe used as higher pressure service lines than standard line pipe, e.g., power oil lines, shall be priced under normal pricing procedures for casing, tubing, or drill pipe. Upset tubular goods shall be priced on a non-upset basis. For other items, the price used should result in the Joint Account being charged or credited with the value of the service rendered or use of the Material, or as agreed to by the Parties pursuant to Section I.6.A (*General Matters*).

    (5) Condition "E" – Junk shall be priced at prevailing scrap value prices.

E. OTHER PRICING PROVISIONS

    (1) Preparation Costs

    Subject to Section II (*Direct Charges*) and Section III (*Overhead*) of this Accounting Procedure, costs incurred by the Operator in making Material serviceable including inspection, third party surveillance services, and other similar services will be charged to the Joint Account at prices which reflect the Operator's actual costs of the services. Documentation must be provided to the Non-Operators upon request to support the cost of service. New coating and/or wrapping shall be considered a component of the Materials and priced in accordance with Sections IV.1 (*Direct Purchases*) or IV.2.A (*Pricing*), as applicable. No charges or credits shall be made for used coating or wrapping. Charges and credits for inspections shall be made in accordance with COPAS MFI-38 ("Material Pricing Manual").

    (2) Loading and Unloading Costs

    Loading and unloading costs related to the movement of the Material to the Joint Property shall be charged in accordance with the methods specified in COPAS MFI-38 ("Material Pricing Manual").

13

3. **DISPOSITION OF SURPLUS**

Surplus Material is that Material, whether new or used, that is no longer required for Joint Operations. The Operator may purchase, but shall be under no obligation to purchase, the interest of the Non-Operators in surplus Material.

Dispositions for the purpose of this procedure are considered to be the relinquishment of title of the Material from the Joint Property to either a third party, a Non-Operator, or to the Operator. To avoid the accumulation of surplus Material, the Operator should make good faith efforts to dispose of surplus within twelve (12) months through buy/sale agreements, trade, sale to a third party, division in kind, or other dispositions as agreed to by the Parties.

Disposal of surplus Materials shall be made in accordance with the terms of the Agreement to which this Accounting Procedure is attached. If the Agreement contains no provisions governing disposal of surplus Material, the following terms shall apply:

- The Operator may, through a sale to an unrelated third party or entity, dispose of surplus Material having a gross sale value that is less than or equal to the Operator's expenditure limit as set forth in the Agreement to which this Accounting Procedure is attached without the prior approval of the Parties owning such Material.

- If the gross sale value exceeds the Agreement expenditure limit, the disposal must be agreed to by the Parties owning such Material.

- Operator may purchase surplus Condition "A" or "B" Material without approval of the Parties owning such Material, based on the pricing methods set forth in Section IV.2 (*Transfers*).

- Operator may purchase Condition "C" Material without prior approval of the Parties owning such Material if the value of the Materials, based on the pricing methods set forth in Section IV.2 (*Transfers*), is less than or equal to the Operator's expenditure limitation set forth in the Agreement. The Operator shall provide documentation supporting the classification of the Material as Condition C.

- Operator may dispose of Condition "D" or "E" Material under procedures normally utilized by Operator without prior approval of the Parties owning such Material.

4. **SPECIAL PRICING PROVISIONS**

A. **PREMIUM PRICING**

Whenever Material is available only at inflated prices due to national emergencies, strikes, government imposed foreign trade restrictions, or other unusual causes over which the Operator has no control, for direct purchase the Operator may charge the Joint Account for the required Material at the Operator's actual cost incurred in providing such Material, making it suitable for use, and moving it to the Joint Property. Material transferred or disposed of during premium pricing situations shall be valued in accordance with Section IV.2 (*Transfers*) or Section IV.3 (*Disposition of Surplus*), as applicable.

B. **SHOP-MADE ITEMS**

Items fabricated by the Operator's employees, or by contract laborers under the direction of the Operator, shall be priced using the value of the Material used to construct the item plus the cost of labor to fabricate the item. If the Material is from the Operator's scrap or junk account, the Material shall be priced at either twenty-five percent (25%) of the current price as determined in Section IV.2.A (*Pricing*) or scrap value, whichever is higher. In no event shall the amount charged exceed the value of the item commensurate with its use.

C. **MILL REJECTS**

Mill rejects purchased as "limited service" casing or tubing shall be priced at eighty percent (80%) of K-55/J-55 price as determined in Section IV.2 (*Transfers*). Line pipe converted to casing or tubing with casing or tubing couplings attached shall be priced as K-55/J-55 casing or tubing at the nearest size and weight.

V. INVENTORIES OF CONTROLLABLE MATERIAL

The Operator shall maintain records of Controllable Material charged to the Joint Account, with sufficient detail to perform physical inventories.

Adjustments to the Joint Account by the Operator resulting from a physical inventory of Controllable Material shall be made within twelve (12) months following the taking of the inventory or receipt of Non-Operator inventory report. Charges and credits for overages or shortages will be valued for the Joint Account in accordance with Section IV.2 (*Transfers*) and shall be based on the Condition "B" prices in effect on the date of physical inventory unless the inventorying Parties can provide sufficient evidence another Material condition applies.

14

c o p a s

1. **DIRECTED INVENTORIES**

Physical inventories shall be performed by the Operator upon written request of a majority in working interests of the Non-Operators (hereinafter, "directed inventory"); provided, however, the Operator shall not be required to perform directed inventories more frequently than once every five (5) years. Directed inventories shall be commenced within one hundred eighty (180) days after the Operator receives written notice that a majority in interest of the Non-Operators has requested the inventory. All Parties shall be governed by the results of any directed inventory.

Expenses of directed inventories will be borne by the Joint Account; provided, however, costs associated with any post-report follow-up work in settling the inventory will be absorbed by the Party incurring such costs. The Operator is expected to exercise judgment in keeping expenses within reasonable limits. Any anticipated disproportionate or extraordinary costs should be discussed and agreed upon prior to commencement of the inventory. Expenses of directed inventories may include the following:

A. A per diem rate for each inventory person, representative of actual salaries, wages, and payroll burdens and benefits of the personnel performing the inventory or a rate agreed to by the Parties pursuant to Section I.6.A (*General Matters*). The per diem rate shall also be applied to a reasonable number of days for pre-inventory work and report preparation.

B. Actual transportation costs and Personal Expenses for the inventory team.

C. Reasonable charges for report preparation and distribution to the Non-Operators.

2. **NON-DIRECTED INVENTORIES**

A. OPERATOR INVENTORIES

Physical inventories that are not requested by the Non-Operators may be performed by the Operator, at the Operator's discretion. The expenses of conducting such Operator-initiated inventories shall not be charged to the Joint Account.

B. NON-OPERATOR INVENTORIES

Subject to the terms of the Agreement to which this Accounting Procedure is attached, the Non-Operators may conduct a physical inventory at reasonable times at their sole cost and risk after giving the Operator at least ninety (90) days prior written notice. The Non-Operator inventory report shall be furnished to the Operator in writing within ninety (90) days of completing the inventory fieldwork.

C. SPECIAL INVENTORIES

The expense of conducting inventories other than those described in Sections V.1 (*Directed Inventories*), V.2.A (*Operator Inventories*), or V.2.B (*Non-Operator Inventories*), shall be charged to the Party requesting such inventory; provided, however, inventories required due to a change of Operator shall be charged to the Joint Account in the same manner as described in Section V.1 (*Directed Inventories*).

15

NOTES

1.   Of special importance to the parties is Article III, which provides for the operator's overhead charges. Monthly overhead may be charged either as a fixed rate for each well, with the rate differing according to whether the well is being drilled or produced, or a percentage basis of actual costs of development and operation. Section 2 of Article III addresses overhead incurred by the operator in constructing and installing fixed assets and in providing for catastrophic occurrences.

2.   As with the A.A.P.L.'s Model Form Operating Agreement, the COPAS Accounting Procedure has been published in several revised editions. The 2005 form is the COPAS' most recent version.

3.   This form is recommended for use by the Council of Petroleum Accountants Societies (COPAS), which holds the copyright on the form. The form, which is frequently referred to by the acronym, COPAS, can be obtained from Kraftbilt Products, Box 800, Tulsa, Oklahoma 74101,1-800-331-7290, http://www.kraftbilt.com. Kraftbilt also distributes other COPAS products, including the COPAS Guide Manuals and Bulletins.

COST ESTIMATE AND AUTHORIZATION FOR EXPENDITURE
FOR:_____ (Name of Well and/or Operation)_____

No.:_____   Date:_____
Lease and Well No:_____Field:_____
Location:_____
_____County:_____State:_____
Required Spud Date:_____ Depth:_____
Classification: ____Exploration   ____Development   ____Oil ____Gas

	TANGIBLES	ESTIMATED COSTS			
	Lease & Well Equip.	Drilling	Completion	Total	Remarks
1.	Surface Csg & Conductor				
2.	Salt String				
3.	Prod Csg & Liner				
4.	Tubin				
5.	Life Equipment				
6.	Wellhead Equipment				
7.	Flow Lines				
8.	Process & Storage Equip.				
	Total Lease & Well Equip	$	$	$	
	INTANGIBLES				
1.a	Footage ft. @ $				
.b	Mobilization				
.c	Daywk. days@ $___ /day				
.d	Service Rig Completion				
.e	Water				
.f	Mud & Chemicals				
.g	Mud Logging Trailer Rental				
2.	Supervision (Overhead)				
.a	Engineer				
.b	Geologists				
3.a	Cement Surface				
.b	Cement Salt String				
.c	Cement Prod Csg				
.d	Float Equipment				
.e	Welding				

4.a	Logging				
.b	Perforating				
5.a	Acidizing Services				
.b	Fracture Treating				
6.a	Survey				
.b	Location				
7.	Roustabouts				
8.	Rental Tools				
9.	Miscellaneous				
	Total Intangibles	$	$	$	
	Contingencies 7.5% of T&I				
	Total Well Estimated Cost	$	$	$	

Prepared by:_____   Accepted by:_____

Approved by:_____   Title:_____

Lease Operator's Name:_____   Firm:_____

Date:_____   Date:_____

NOTES

1.   Whenever an operator does not own the full working interest in a well or occasionally when an operator is seeking a letter contribution from a non-owner, the operator customarily sends out an Authorization for Expenditure (AFE). Joint-operating agreements customarily require them.

2.   By signing an AFE, a working-interest owner agrees to the expenditure and agrees to pay its share of costs. Some AFEs are "information only," indicating that the parties have already committed to the expenditure. In this circumstance, the AFE advises that the expenditure is about to made and serves as a request for funds.

EXHIBIT

GAS BALANCING AGREEMENT

Attached to and made a part of that certain Operating Agreement dated _____ by and between _____ Operator, and _____, non-Operator(s).

1. Ownership of Gas Production

(a) It is the intent of the parties that each party shall have the right to take in kind and separately dispose of its proportionate share of gas (including casinghead gas) produced from each formation in each well located on acreage ("Contract Area") covered by the Operating Agreement to which this Exhibit is attached ("Operating Agreement").

(b) Operator shall control the gas production and be responsible for administering the provisions of this Agreement and shall make reasonable efforts to deliver or cause to be delivered gas to the parties' gas purchasers as may be required in order to balance the accounts of the parties in accordance with the provisions herein contained. For purposes of this Agreement, Operator shall maintain production accounts of the parties based upon the number of MMBtu's actually contained in the gas produced from a particular formation in a well and delivered at the outlet of lease equipment for each party's account regardless of whether sales of such gas are made on a wet or dry basis. All references in this Agreement to quantity or volume shall refer to the number of MMBtu's contained in the gas stream. Toward this end, Operator shall periodically determine or cause to be determined the Btu content of gas produced from each formation in each well on a consistent basis and under standard conditions pursuant to any method customarily used in the industry.

2. Balancing of Production Accounts

(a) Any time a party, or such party's purchaser, is not taking or marketing its full share of gas produced from a particular formation in a well ("non-marketing" party), the remaining parties ("marketing" parties) shall have the right, but not the obligation, to produce, take, sell and deliver for such marketing parties accounts, in addition to the full share of gas to which the marketing parties are otherwise entitled, all or any portion of the gas attributable to a non-marketing party. (Gas attributable to a non-marketing party taken by a marketing party, is referred to in this Agreement as "overproduction"). If there is more than one marketing party taking gas attributable to a non-marketing party, each marketing party shall be entitled to take a non-marketing party's gas in the ratio that such marketing party's interest in production bears to the total interest in production of all marketing parties.

(b) A party that has not taken its proportionate share of gas produced from any formation in a well ("Underproduced Party") shall be credited with gas in storage equal to its share of gas produced but not taken, less its share of gas used in lease operations, vented or lost ("underproduction"). Such Underproduced Party, upon giving timely written notice to Operator, shall be entitled, on a monthly basis beginning the month following receipt of notice, to produce, take, sell and deliver, in addition to the full share of gas to which such party is otherwise entitled, a quantity of gas ("make-up gas") equal to fifty percent (50%) of the total share of gas

332

attributable to all parties having cumulative overproduction (individually called "Overproduced Party"). Such make-up gas shall be credited against such Underproduced Party's accrued underproduction in order of accrual. Notwithstanding the foregoing and subject to subsection (e) below: (i) an Overproduced Party shall never be obligated to reduce its takes to less than fifty percent (50%) of the quantity to which such party is otherwise entitled and (ii) an Underproduced Party shall never be allowed to make up underproduction during the months of December, January, February and March.

(c) If there is more than one Underproduced Party desiring make-up gas, each such Underproduced Party shall be entitled to make-up gas in the ratio that such party's interest in production bears to the total interest in production of all parties then desiring make-up gas. Any portion of the make-up gas to which an Underproduced Party is entitled and which is not taken by such Underproduced Party may be taken by any other Underproduced Party(ies).

(d) If there is more than one Overproduced Party required to furnish make-up gas, each such Overproduced Party shall furnish make-up gas in the ratio that such party's interest in production bears to the total interest in production of all parties then required to furnish make-up gas. Except as provided in (e) below, each Overproduced Party in any formation in a well shall be entitled, on a monthly basis, to take its full share of gas less its share of the make-up gas then being produced from the particular formation in the well in which it is overproduced.

(e) If Operator in good faith believes that an Overproduced Party has recovered one hundred percent (100%) of such Overproduced Party's share of the recoverable reserves from a particular formation in a well, such Overproduced Party, upon being notified in writing of such fact by Operator, shall cease taking gas from such formation in such well and the remaining parties shall be entitled to take one hundred percent (100%) of such production until the accounts of the parties are balanced. Thereafter, such Overproduced Party shall again have the right to take its share of the remaining production, if any, in accordance with the provisions herein contained. Notwithstanding anything to the contrary herein, after an Overproduced Party has recovered one hundred percent (100%) of its full share of the recoverable reserves as so determined by Operator from a particular formation in a well, such Overproduced Party may continue to produce if such continued production is (i) necessary for lease maintenance purposes or (ii) permitted by a majority of interest of the parties who have not produced one hundred percent (100%) of their recoverable reserves from such formation in such well after written ballot conducted by Operator.

3. Cash Balancing Upon Depletion

(a) If gas production from a particular formation in a well ceases and no attempt is made to restore production (or substitute therefor) within sixty (60) days, Operator shall distribute, within ninety (90) days of the date the well last produced gas from such formation, a statement of net unrecouped underproduction and overproduction and the months and years in which such unrecouped production accrued ("final accounting").

(b) Within thirty (30) days of receipt of such final accounting, each Overproduced Party shall remit to Operator for disbursement to the Underproduced Parties, a sum of money (which sum shall not include interest) equal to the amount actually received or constructively received under subparagraph (e) below, by Overproduced Party for sales during the month(s) of overproduction, calculated in order of accrual but less applicable taxes, royalties and reasonable costs of marketing and transporting such gas actually paid by such Overproduced Party. Such remittance shall be based on number of MMBtu's of overproduction and shall be accompanied by a statement showing volumes and prices for each month with accrued unrecouped overproduction.

(c) Within thirty (30) days of receipt of any such remittance by Operator from an Overproduced Party, Operator shall disburse such funds to the Underproduced Party(ies) in accordance with the final accounting Operator assumes no liability with respect to any such payment (unless such payment is attributable to Operator's overproduction), it being the intent of the parties that each Overproduced Party shall be solely responsible for reimbursing each Underproduced Party for such Underproduced Party's respective share of overproduction taken by such Overproduced Party in accordance with the provisions herein contained. If any party fails to pay any sum due under the terms hereof after demand therefor by the Operator, the Operator may turn responsibility for the collection of such sum to the party or parties to whom it is owed, and Operator shall have no further responsibility for collection.

(d) In determining the amount of overproduction for which settlement is due, production taken during any month by an Underproduced Party in excess of such Underproduced Party's share shall be treated as make-up and shall be applied to reduce prior deficits in the order of accrual of such deficits.

(e) An Overproduced Party that took gas in kind for its own use, sold gas to an affiliate, or otherwise disposed of gas in other than a cash sale shall pay for such gas at market value at the time it was produced, even if the Overproduced Party sold such gas to an affiliate at a price greater or lesser than market value.

(f) If refunds are later required by any governmental authority, each party shall be accountable for its respective share of such refunds as finally balanced hereunder.

4. Deliverability Tests

At the request of any party, Operator may produce the entire well stream for a deliverability test not to exceed seventy-two (72) hours in duration (or such longer period of time as may be mutually agreed upon by the parties) if required under such requesting party's gas sales or transportation contract.

5. Nominations

Each party shall, on a monthly basis, give Operator sufficient time and data either to nominate such party's respective share of gas to the transporting pipeline(s) or, if Operator is not nominating such party's gas, to inform Operator of the manner in which to dispatch such party's gas. Except as and to the extent caused by Operator's gross negligence or willful misconduct, Operator shall not be responsible for any fees and/or penalties associated with imbalances charged by any pipeline to any Underproduced or Overproduced Party(ies).[1]

6. Statements

On or before the twenty-fifth (25th) day of the month following the month of production, each party taking gas shall furnish or cause to be furnished to Operator a statement of gas taken expressed in terms of MMBtu's. If actual volume information sufficient to prepare such statement is not made available to the taking party in sufficient time to prepare it, such taking party shall nevertheless furnish a statement of its good faith estimate of volumes taken. Within twenty (20) days of the receipt of any such statements, Operator shall furnish to each party a statement of the gas balance among the parties, including the total quantity of gas produced from each formation in each well, the portion thereof used in operations, vented or lost, and the total quantity delivered for each party's account. Any error or discrepancy in Operator's monthly statement shall be promptly reported to Operator and Operator shall make a proper adjustment thereof within thirty (30) days after final determination of the correct quantities involved; provided, however, that if no errors or discrepancies are reported to Operator within two (2) years from the date of any statement, such statement shall be conclusively deemed to be correct. Additionally, within thirty (30) days from the end of each calendar year, non-operators shall furnish to Operator, for the sole purpose of establishing records sufficient to verify cash balancing values, a statement reflecting amounts actually received or constructively received under paragraph 3(e), on a monthly basis for the calendar year preceding the immediately concluded calendar year. Operator shall not allow a party to produce gas for its account during any month when such party is delinquent in so furnishing the monthly or annual statements.

7. Payment of Taxes

Each party taking gas shall pay or cause to be paid any and all production, severance, utility, sales, excise, or other taxes due on such gas.

8. Operating Expenses

The operating expenses are to be borne as provided in the Operating Agreement, regardless of whether all parties are selling or using gas or whether the sales and use of each are in proportion to their respective interests in such gas.

9. Overproducing Allowable

Each party shall give Operator sufficient time and data to enable Operator to make appropriate nominations, forecasts and/or filings with the regulatory bodies having jurisdiction to establish allowables. Each party shall at all times regulate its takes and deliveries from the Contract Area so that the well(s) covered hereby shall not be curtailed and/or shut-in for overproducing the allowable production assigned thereto by the regulatory body having jurisdiction.

10. Payment of Leasehold Burdens

At all times while gas is produced from the Contract Area, each party agrees to make appropriate settlement of all royalties, overriding royalties and other payments out of or in lieu of production for which such party is responsible just as if such party were taking or delivering to a purchaser such party's full share, and such party's full share only, of such gas production exclusive of gas used in operations, vented or lost, and each party agrees to indemnify and hold each other party harmless from and all claims relating thereto.

11. Application of Agreement

The provisions of this Agreement shall be separately applicable and shall constitute a separate agreement with respect to gas produced from each formation in each well located on the Contract Area.

12. Term

This Agreement shall terminate when gas production under the Operating Agreement permanently ceases and the accounts of the parties are finally settled in accordance with the provisions herein contained.

13. Operator's Liability

Except as otherwise provided herein, Operator is authorized to administer the provisions of this Agreement, but shall have no liability to the other parties for losses sustained or liability incurred which arise out of or in connection with the performance of Operator's duties hereunder except such as may result from Operator's gross negligence or willful misconduct.[1]

14. Audits

Any Underproduced Party shall have the right for a period of two (2) years after receipt of payment pursuant to a final accounting and after giving written notice to all parties, to audit an Overproduced Party's accounts and records relating to such payment. Any Overproduced Party shall have the right for a period of two (2) years after tender of payment for unrecouped volumes and upon giving written notice to all parties, to audit an Underproduced Party's records as to volumes. The party conducting such audit shall bear its costs of the audit. Additionally, Operator shall have the right for a period of two (2) years after receipt of an annual statement from a non-operator under paragraph 6 after giving written notice to the affected non-operator, to audit such non-operators accounts and records relating to such payment. Costs of such audit shall be borne by the joint account.

15. Successors and Assigns

The terms, covenants, and conditions of this Agreement shall be binding upon and shall inure to the benefit of the parties and to their respective successors and assigns, and may be assigned in whole or in part from time to time, provided, however, that (a) any such assignment shall be made subject to this Agreement and as among the parties shall not be valid without the express written acceptance of the terms of this Agreement by the Assignee, (b) the Assignee shall acquire such interest subject to any overproduction and/or underproduction imbalances existing at such time as well as any cash balancing obligation created thereby and (c) no such assignment shall relieve the Assignor from any obligation to the other parties with respect to any overproduction taken by Assignor prior to such assignment.

16. Liquefiable Hydrocarbons Not Covered Under Agreement

The parties shall share proportionately in and own all liquid hydrocarbons recovered with the gas by lease equipment in accordance with their respective interests.

17. Conflict

If there is a conflict between the terms of this Agreement and the terms of any gas sales contract covering the Contract Area entered into by any party, the terms of this Agreement shall govern.

18. Arbitration

Any controversy or claim arising out of or relating to this Agreement, or the breach thereof, shall be settled by binding arbitration in accordance with the Commercial Arbitration Rules of the American Arbitration Association, and judgment upon the award may be entered in any Court having jurisdiction thereof. The arbitrator shall not award punitive damages in settlement of any controversy or claim.[2]

19. Operator's Fees

Operator shall charge the Joint Account $_____ per formation in each well per month for each month during which Operator maintains accounts hereunder for such well in a formation.

ADDITIONAL PROVISIONS

336

NOTES

1.　The gas balancing agreement is an optional attachment to the joint operating agreement. Article VI.G. of the JOA refers to this document as governing the parties' rights when a party's separate sales or deliveries are not proportionate to that party's share of the gas. Note that the gas balancing form itself contains a series of optional provisions that the parties may choose to incorporate or not in their agreement.

2.　The model form gas balancing agreement was drafted under the aegis of the Rocky Mountain Mineral Law Foundation, which holds the copyright. The Foundation is administered by a board of trustees composed of representatives of state bar associations, mining and landsmen groups, and universities from across the western United States and Canada. In addition to sponsoring annual institutes and special institutes addressing oil and gas, mining, water, environmental, and public lands topics, the Foundation publishes a variety of documents and books, including the American Law of Mining and the Law of Federal Oil and Gas Leases, that are of special aid to practitioners and academics. Copies of the model form gas balancing agreement, and other Foundation publications, can be obtained from the Rocky Mountain Mineral Law Foundation, 7039 East 18th Avenue, Denver, Colorado 80220, (303) 321-8100, http://www.rmmlf.org.

Revised April, 2003

INTERNATIONAL ASSOCIATION OF DRILLING CONTRACTORS
DRILLING BID PROPOSAL
AND
DAYWORK DRILLING CONTRACT - U.S.

TO: _____

_____

Please submit bid on this drilling contract form for performing the work outlined below, upon the terms and for the consideration set forth, with the understanding that

if the bid is accepted by _____

this instrument will constitute a Contract between us. Your bid should be mailed or delivered not later than _____ P.M. on _____, 20_____

to the following address: _____

_____

THIS CONTRACT CONTAINS PROVISIONS RELATING TO INDEMNITY, RELEASE OF LIABILITY, AND ALLOCATION OF RISK - SEE PARAGRAPHS 4.9, 6.3(c), 10, 12, AND 14

This Contract is made and entered into on the date hereinafter set forth by and between the parties herein designated as "Operator" and "Contractor".

OPERATOR: _____

Address: _____

_____

CONTRACTOR: _____

Address: _____

_____

IN CONSIDERATION of the mutual promises, conditions and agreements herein contained and the specifications and special provisions set forth in Exhibit "A" and Exhibit "B" attached hereto and made a part hereof (the "Contract"), Operator engages Contractor as an independent contractor to drill the hereinafter designated well or wells in search of oil or gas on a Daywork Basis.

For purposes hereof, the term "Daywork" or "Daywork Basis" means Contractor shall furnish equipment, labor, and perform services as herein provided, for a specified sum per day under the direction, supervision and control of Operator (inclusive of any employee, agent, consultant or subcontractor engaged by Operator to direct drilling operations). **When operating on a Daywork Basis, Contractor shall be fully paid at the applicable rates of payment and assumes only the obligations and liabilities stated herein. Except for such obligations and liabilities specifically assumed by Contractor, Operator shall be solely responsible and assumes liability for all consequences of operations by both parties while on a Daywork Basis, including results and all other risks or liabilities incurred in or incident to such operations.**

1. **LOCATION OF WELL:**
   Well Name
   and Number: _____

   Parish/
   County: _____ State: _____ Field Name: _____

   Well location and
   land description: _____

   _____

   1.1 Additional Well Locations or Areas: _____

   _____

   Locations described above are for well and Contract identification only and Contractor assumes no liability whatsoever for a proper survey or location stake on Operator's lease.

2. **COMMENCEMENT DATE:**
   Contractor agrees to use reasonable efforts to commence operations for the drilling of the well by the _____ day of _____

   20_____, or _____

3. **DEPTH:**
   3.1 **Well Depth:** The well(s) shall be drilled to a depth of approximately _____ feet, or to the _____

   formation, whichever is deeper, but the Contractor shall not be required hereunder to drill said well(s) below a maximum depth of _____ feet, unless Contractor and Operator mutually agree to drill to a greater depth.

4. **DAYWORK RATES:**
   Contractor shall be paid at the following rates for the work performed hereunder.

   4.1 **Mobilization:** Operator shall pay Contractor a mobilization fee of $_____ or a mobilization rate of $_____

   per day. This sum shall be due and payable in full at the time the rig is rigged up or positioned at the well site ready to spud. Mobilization shall include:

   _____

   _____

   4.2 **Demobilization:** Operator shall pay Contractor a demobilization fee of $_____ or a demobilization rate during tear down of

   $_____ per day, provided however that no demobilization fee shall be payable if the Contract is terminated due to the total loss or destruction of the rig. Demobilization shall include: _____

   _____

   4.3 **Moving Rate:** During the time the rig is in transit to or from a drill site, or between drill sites, commencing on _____, Operator shall

   pay Contractor a sum of $_____ per twenty-four (24) hour day.

   4.4 **Operating Rate:** For work performed per twenty-four (24) hour day with _____ man crew the operating rate shall be:

Depth Intervals			
From	To	Without Drill Pipe	With Drill Pipe
_____	_____	$_____ per day	$_____ per day
_____	_____	$_____ per day	$_____ per day
_____	_____	$_____ per day	$_____ per day

Using Operator's drill pipe $_____ per day.

The rate will begin when the drilling unit is rigged up at the drilling location, or positioned over the location during marine work, and ready to commence operations; and will cease when the rig is ready to be moved off the location.

If under the above column "With Drill Pipe" no rates are specified, the rate per twenty-four hour day when drill pipe is in use shall be the applicable rate specified in the column "Without Drill Pipe" plus compensation for any drill pipe actually used at the rates specified below, computed on the basis of the maximum drill pipe in use at any time during each twenty-four hour day.

DRILL PIPE RATES PER 24-HOUR DAY

Straight Hole	Size	Grade	Directional or Uncontrollable Deviated Hole	Size	Grade
$_____$ per ft.	_____	_____	$_____$ per ft.	_____	_____
$_____$ per ft.	_____	_____	$_____$ per ft.	_____	_____
$_____$ per ft.	_____	_____	$_____$ per ft.	_____	_____

Directional or uncontrolled deviated hole will be deemed to exist when deviation exceeds _____ degrees or when the change of angle exceeds_____ degrees per one hundred feet.

Drill pipe shall be considered in use not only when in actual use but also while it is being picked up or laid down. When drill pipe is standing in the derrick, it shall not be considered in use, provided, however, that if Contractor furnishes special strings of drill pipe, drill collars, and handling tools as provided for in Exhibit "A", the same shall be considered in use at all times when on location or until released by Operator. In no event shall fractions of an hour be considered in computing the amount of time drill pipe is in use but such time shall be computed to the nearest hour, with thirty minutes or more being considered a full hour and less than thirty minutes not to be counted.

4.5 Repair Time: In the event it is necessary to shut down Contractor's rig for repairs, excluding routine rig servicing, Contractor shall be allowed compensation at the applicable rate for such shut down time up to a maximum of _____ hours for any one rig repair job, but not to exceed _____ hours of such compensation for any calendar month. Thereafter, Contractor shall be compensated at a rate of $_____ per twenty-four (24) hour day. Routine rig servicing shall include, but not be limited to, cutting and slipping drilling line, changing pump or swivel expendables, testing BOP equipment, lubricating rig, and__

4.6 Standby Time Rate: $_____ per twenty-four (24) hour day. Standby time shall be defined to include time when the rig is shut down although in readiness to begin or resume operations but Contractor is waiting on orders of Operator or on materials, services or other items to be furnished by Operator.

4.7 Drilling Fluid Rates: When drilling fluids of a type and characteristic that increases Contractor's cost of performance hereunder, including, but not limited to, oil-based mud or potassium chloride, are in use Operator shall pay Contractor in addition to the operating rate specified above:
(a) $_____ per man per day for Contractor's rig-site personnel;
(b) $_____ per day additional operating rate; and
(c) Cost of all labor, material and services plus _____ hours operating rate to clean rig and related equipment.

4.8 Force Majeure Rate: $_____ per twenty-four (24) hour day for any continuous period that normal operations are suspended or cannot be carried on due to conditions of Force Majeure as defined in Paragraph 17 hereof. It is, however, understood that subject to Subparagraph 6.3 below, Operator can release the rig in accordance with Operator's right to direct stoppage of the work, effective when conditions will permit the rig to be moved from the location.

4.9 Reimbursable Costs: Operator shall reimburse Contractor for the costs of material, equipment, work or services which are to be furnished by Operator as provided for herein but which for convenience are actually furnished by Contractor at Operator's request, plus _____ percent for such cost of handling. *When, at Operator's request and with Contractor's agreement, the Contractor furnishes or subcontracts for certain items or services which Operator is required herein to provide, for purposes of the indemnity and release provisions of this Contract said items or services shall be deemed to be Operator furnished items or services. Any subcontractors so hired shall be deemed to be Operator's contractor, and Operator shall not be relieved of any of its liabilities in connection therewith.*

4.10 Revision in Rates: The rates and/or payments herein set forth due to Contractor from Operator shall be revised to reflect the change in costs if the costs of any of the items hereinafter listed shall vary by more than _____ percent from the costs thereof on the date of this Contract or by the same percent after the date of any revision pursuant to this Subparagraph:
(a) Labor costs, including all benefits, of Contractor's personnel;
(b) Contractor's cost of insurance premiums;
(c) Contractor's cost of fuel, including all taxes and fees; the cost per gallon/MCF being $_____;
(d) Contractor's cost of catering, when applicable;
(e) If Operator requires Contractor to increase or decrease the number of Contractor's personnel;
(f) Contractor's cost of spare parts and supplies with the understanding that such spare parts and supplies constitute _____ percent of the operating rate and that the parties shall use the U.S. Bureau of Labor Statistics Oil Field and Gas Field Drilling Machinery Producer Price Index (Series ID WPU119102) to determine to what extent a price variance has occurred in said spare parts and supplies;
(g) If there is any change in legislation or regulations in the area in which Contractor is working or other unforeseen, unusual event that alters Contractor's financial burden.

5. TIME OF PAYMENT:
Payment is due by Operator to Contractor as follows:

5.1 Payment for mobilization, drilling and other work performed at applicable rates, and all other applicable charges shall be due, upon presentation of invoice therefor, upon completion of mobilization, demobilization, rig release or at the end of the month in which such work was performed or other charges are incurred, whichever shall first occur. All invoices may be mailed to Operator at the address hereinabove shown, unless Operator does hereby designate that such invoices shall be mailed as follows: _____

5.2 Disputed Invoices and Late Payment: Operator shall pay all invoices within _____ days after receipt except that if Operator disputes an invoice or any part thereof, Operator shall, within fifteen days after receipt of the invoice, notify Contractor of the item disputed, specifying the reason therefor, and payment of the disputed item may be withheld until settlement of the dispute, but timely payment shall be made of any undisputed portion. Any sums (including amounts ultimately paid with respect to a disputed invoice) not paid within the above specified days shall bear interest at the rate of _____ percent or the maximum legal rate, whichever is less, per month from the due date until paid. If Operator does not pay undisputed items within the above stated time, Contractor may suspend operations or terminate this Contract as specified under Subparagraph 6.3.

6. TERM:

6.1 Duration of Contract: This Contract shall remain in full force and effect until drilling operations are completed on the well or wells specified in Paragraph 1 above, or for a term of _____, commencing on the date specified in Paragraph 2 above.

6.2 Extension of Term: Operator may extend the term of this Contract for _____ well(s) or for a period of _____ by giving notice to Contractor at least _____ days prior to completion of the well then being drilled or by_____

6.3 Early Termination:
(a) **By Either Party:** Upon giving of written notice, either party may terminate this Contract when total loss or destruction of the rig, or a major breakdown with indefinite repair time necessitate stopping operations hereunder.
(b) **By Operator:** Notwithstanding the provisions of Paragraph 3 with respect to the depth to be drilled, Operator shall have the right to direct the stoppage of the work to be performed by Contractor hereunder at any time prior to reaching the specified depth, and even though Contractor has made no default hereunder. In such event Operator shall reimburse Contractor as set forth in Subparagraph 6.4 hereof.
(c) **By Contractor:** Notwithstanding the provisions of Paragraph 3 with respect to the depth to be drilled, in the event Operator shall become insolvent, or be adjudicated a bankrupt, or file, by way of petition or answer, a debtor's petition or other pleading seeking adjustment of Operator's debts, under any bankruptcy or debtor's relief laws now or hereafter prevailing, or if any such be filed against Operator, or in case a receiver be appointed of Operator or Operator's property, or any part thereof, or Operator's affairs be placed in the hands of a Creditor's Committee, or, following three business days prior written notice to Operator if Operator does not pay Contractor within the time specified in Subparagraph 5.2 all undisputed items due and owing, Contractor may, at its option, (1) elect to terminate further performance of any work under this Contract and Contractor's right to compensation shall be as set forth in Subparagraph 6.4 hereof or (2) suspend operations until payment is made by Operator in which event the standby time rate contained in Subparagraph 4.6 shall apply until payment is made by Operator and operations are resumed. *In addition to Contractor's rights to suspend operations or terminate performance under this Paragraph, Operator hereby expressly agrees to protect, defend and indemnify Contractor from and against any claims, demands and causes of action, including all costs of defense, in favor of Operator, Operator's co-venturers, co-lessees and joint owners, or any other parties arising out of any drilling commitments or obligations contained in any lease, farmout agreement or other agreement, which may be affected by such suspension of operations or termination of performance hereunder.*

6.4   Early Termination Compensation:

(a) **Prior to Commencement:** In the event Operator terminates this Contract prior to commencement of operations hereunder, Operator shall pay Contractor as liquidated damages and not as a penalty a sum equal to the standby time rate (Subparagraph 4.6) for a period of _____ days or a lump sum of $_____.

(b) **Prior to Spudding:** If such termination occurs after commencement of operations but prior to the spudding of the well, Operator shall pay to Contractor the sum of the following: (1) all expenses reasonably and necessarily incurred and to be incurred by Contractor by reason of the Contract and by reason of the premature termination of the work, including the expense of drilling or other crew members and supervision directly assigned to the rig; (2) ten percent (10%) of the amount of such reimbursable expenses; and (3) a sum calculated at the standby time rate for all time from the date upon which Contractor commences any operations hereunder down to such date subsequent to the date of termination as will afford Contractor reasonable time to dismantle its rig and equipment provided, however, if this Contract is for a term of more than one well or for a period of time, Operator shall pay Contractor, in addition to the above, the Force Majeure Rate less any unnecessary labor, from that date subsequent to termination upon which Contractor completes dismantling its rig and equipment until the end of the term or _____

_____

_____ .

(c) **Subsequent to Spudding:** If such termination occurs after the spudding of the well, Operator shall pay Contractor (1) the amount for all applicable rates and all other charges and reimbursements due to Contractor; but in no event shall such sum, exclusive of reimbursements due, be less than would have been earned for _____ days at the applicable rate "Without Drill Pipe" and the actual amount due for drill pipe used in accordance with the above rates; or (2) at the election of Contractor and in lieu of the foregoing, Operator shall pay Contractor for all expenses reasonably and necessarily incurred and to be incurred by reason of this Contract and by reason of such premature termination plus a lump sum of $_____ provided, however, if this Contract is for a term of more than one well or for a period of time, Operator shall pay Contractor, in addition to the above, the Force Majeure Rate less any unnecessary labor from the date of termination until the end of the term or _____

_____

_____ .

7.   CASING PROGRAM:

Operator shall have the right to designate the points at which casing will be set and the manner of setting, cementing and testing. Operator may modify the casing program, however, any such modification which materially increases Contractor's hazards or costs can only be made by mutual consent of Operator and Contractor and upon agreement as to the additional compensation to be paid Contractor as a result thereof.

8.   DRILLING METHODS AND PRACTICES:

8.1   Contractor shall maintain well control equipment in good condition at all times and shall use all reasonable means to prevent and control fires and blowouts and to protect the hole.

8.2   Subject to the terms hereof, and at Operator's cost, at all times during the drilling of the well, Operator shall have the right to control the mud program, and the drilling fluid must be of a type and have characteristics and be maintained by Contractor in accordance with the specifications shown in Exhibit "A".

8.3   Each party hereto agrees to comply with all laws, rules, and regulations of any federal, state or local governmental authority which are now or may become applicable to that party's operations covered by or arising out of the performance of this Contract. When required by law, the terms of Exhibit "B" shall apply to this Contract. In the event any provision of this Contract is inconsistent with or contrary to any applicable federal, state or local law, rule or regulation, said provision shall be deemed to be modified to the extent required to comply with said law, rule or regulation, and as so modified said provision and this Contract shall continue in full force and effect.

8.4   Contractor shall keep and furnish to Operator an accurate record of the work performed and formations drilled on the IADC-API Daily Drilling Report Form or other form acceptable to Operator. A legible copy of said form shall be furnished by Contractor to Operator.

8.5   If requested by Operator, Contractor shall furnish Operator with a copy of delivery tickets covering any material or supplies provided by Operator and received by Contractor.

9.   INGRESS, EGRESS, AND LOCATION:

Operator hereby assigns to Contractor all necessary rights of ingress and egress with respect to the tract on which the well is to be located for the performance by Contractor of all work contemplated by this Contract. Should Contractor be denied free access to the location for any reason not reasonably within Contractor's control, any time lost by Contractor as a result of such denial shall be paid for at the standby time rate. Operator agrees at all times to maintain the road and location in such a condition that will allow free access and movement to and from the drilling site in an ordinarily equipped highway type vehicle. If Contractor is required to use bulldozers, tractors, four-wheel drive vehicles, or any other specialized transportation equipment for the movement of necessary personnel, machinery, or equipment over access roads or on the drilling location, Operator shall furnish the same at its expense and without cost to Contractor. The actual cost of repairs to any transportation equipment furnished by Contractor or its personnel damaged as a result of improperly maintained access roads or location will be charged to Operator. Operator shall reimburse Contractor for all amounts reasonably expended by Contractor for repairs and/or reinforcement of roads, bridges and related or similar facilities (public and private) required as a direct result of a rig move pursuant to performance hereunder. Operator shall be responsible for any costs associated with leveling the rig because of location settling.

10. SOUND LOCATION:

Operator shall prepare a sound location adequate in size and capable of properly supporting the drilling rig, and shall be responsible for a casing and cementing program adequate to prevent soil and subsoil wash out. It is recognized that Operator has superior knowledge of the location and access routes to the location, and must advise Contractor of any subsurface conditions, or obstructions (including, but not limited to, mines, caverns, sink holes, streams, pipelines, power lines and communication lines) which Contractor might encounter while en route to the location or during operations hereunder. *In the event subsurface conditions cause a cratering or shifting of the location surface, or if seabed conditions prove unsatisfactory to properly support the rig during marine operations hereunder, and loss or damage to the rig or its associated equipment results therefrom, Operator shall, without regard to other provisions of this Contract, including Subparagraph 14.1 hereof, reimburse Contractor for all such loss or damage including removal of debris and payment of Force Majeure Rate during repair and/or demobilization if applicable.*

11. EQUIPMENT CAPACITY:

Operations shall not be attempted under any conditions which exceed the capacity of the equipment specified to be used hereunder or where canal or water depths are in excess of _____ feet. Without prejudice to the provisions of Paragraph 14 hereunder, Contractor shall have the right to make the final decision as to when an operation or attempted operation would exceed the capacity of specified equipment.

12. TERMINATION OF LOCATION LIABILITY:

When Contractor has concluded operations at the well location, Operator shall thereafter be liable for damage to property, personal injury or death of any person which occurs as a result of conditions of the location and Contractor shall be relieved of such liability; provided, however, if Contractor shall subsequently reenter upon the location for any reason, including removal of the rig, any term of the Contract relating to such reentry activity shall become applicable during such period.

13. INSURANCE:

During the life of this Contract, Contractor shall at Contractor's expense maintain, with an insurance company or companies authorized to do business in the state where the work is to be performed or through a self-insurance program, insurance coverages of the kind and in the amounts set forth in Exhibit "A", insuring the liabilities specifically assumed by Contractor in Paragraph 14 of this Contract. Contractor shall procure from the company or companies writing said insurance a certificate or certificates that said insurance is in full force and effect and that the same shall not be canceled or materially changed without ten (10) days prior written notice to Operator. For liabilities assumed hereunder by Contractor, its insurance shall be endorsed to provide that the underwriters waive their right of subrogation against Operator. Operator will, as well, cause its insurer to waive subrogation against Contractor for liability it assumes and shall maintain, at Operator's expense, or shall self insure, insurance coverage as set forth in Exhibit "A" of the same kind and in the same amount as is required of Contractor, insuring the liabilities specifically assumed by Operator in Paragraph 14 of this Contract. Operator shall procure from the company or companies writing said insurance a certificate or certificates that said insurance is in full force and effect and that the same shall not be canceled or materially changed without ten (10) days prior written notice to Contractor. Operator and Contractor shall cause their respective underwriters to name the other additionally insured but only to the extent of the indemnification obligations assumed herein.

14. RESPONSIBILITY FOR LOSS OR DAMAGE, INDEMNITY, RELEASE OF LIABILITY AND ALLOCATION OF RISK:

14.1 Contractor's Surface Equipment: Contractor shall assume liability at all times for damage to or destruction of Contractor's surface equipment, regardless of when or how such damage or destruction occurs, and Contractor shall release Operator of any liability for any such loss, except loss or damage under the provisions of Paragraph 10 or Subparagraph 14.3.

14.2 Contractor's In-Hole Equipment: Operator shall assume liability at all times for damage to or destruction of Contractor's in-hole equipment, including, but not limited to, drill pipe, drill collars, and tool joints, and Operator shall reimburse Contractor for the value of any such loss or damage; the value to be determined by agreement between Contractor and Operator as current repair costs or _____ percent of current new replacement cost of such equipment delivered to the well site.

14.3 Contractor's Equipment - Environmental Loss or Damage: Notwithstanding the provisions of Subparagraph 14.1 above, Operator shall assume liability at all times for damage to or destruction of Contractor's equipment resulting from the presence of H_2S, CO_2 or other corrosive elements that enter the drilling fluids from subsurface formations or the use of corrosive, destructive or abrasive additives in the drilling fluids.

14.4 Operator's Equipment: Operator shall assume liability at all times for damage to or destruction of Operator's or its co-venturers', co-lessees' or joint owners' equipment, including, but not limited to, casing, tubing, well head equipment, and platform if applicable, regardless of when or how such damage or destruction occurs, and Operator shall release Contractor of any liability for any such loss or damage.

14.5 The Hole: In the event the hole should be lost or damaged, Operator shall be solely responsible for such damage to or loss of the hole, including the casing therein. Operator shall release Contractor and its suppliers, contractors and subcontractors of any tier of any liability for damage to or loss of the hole, and shall protect, defend and indemnify Contractor and its suppliers, contractors and subcontractors of any tier from and against any and all claims, liability, and expense relating to such damage to or loss of the hole.

14.6 Underground Damage: Operator shall release Contractor and its suppliers, contractors and subcontractors of any tier of any liability for, and shall protect, defend and indemnify Contractor and its suppliers, contractors and subcontractors of any tier from and against any and all claims, liability, and expense resulting from operations under this Contract on account of injury to, destruction of, or loss or impairment of any property right in or to oil, gas, or other mineral substance or water, if at the time of the act or omission causing such injury, destruction, loss, or impairment, said substance had not been reduced to physical possession above the surface of the earth, and for any loss or damage to any formation, strata, or reservoir beneath the surface of the earth.

14.7 Inspection of Materials Furnished by Operator: Contractor agrees to visually inspect all materials furnished by Operator before using same and to notify Operator of any apparent defects therein. Contractor shall not be liable for any loss or damage resulting from the use of materials furnished by Operator, and Operator shall release Contractor from, and shall protect, defend and indemnify Contractor from and against, any such liability.

14.8 Contractor's Indemnification of Operator: Contractor shall release Operator of any liability for, and shall protect, defend and indemnify Operator from and against all claims, demands, and causes of action of every kind and character, without limit and without regard to the cause or causes thereof or the negligence of any party or parties, arising in connection herewith in favor of Contractor's employees or Contractor's subcontractors of any tier (inclusive of any agent or consultant engaged by Contractor) or their employees, or Contractor's invitees, on account of bodily injury, death or damage to property. Contractor's indemnity under this Paragraph shall be without regard to and without any right to contribution from any insurance maintained by Operator pursuant to Paragraph 13. If it is judicially determined that the monetary limits of insurance required hereunder or of the indemnities voluntarily assumed under Subparagraph 14.8 (which Contractor and Operator hereby agree will be supported either by available liability insurance, under which the insurer has no right of subrogation against the indemnitees, or voluntarily self-insured, in part or whole) exceed the maximum limits permitted under applicable law, it is agreed that said insurance requirements or indemnities shall automatically be amended to conform to the maximum monetary limits permitted under such law.

14.9 Operator's Indemnification of Contractor: Operator shall release Contractor of any liability for, and shall protect, defend and indemnify Contractor from and against all claims, demands, and causes of action of every kind and character, without limit and without regard to the cause or causes thereof or the negligence of any party or parties, arising in connection herewith in favor of Operator's employees or Operator's contractors of any tier (inclusive of any agent, consultant or consultant engaged by Operator) or their employees, or Operator's invitees, other than those parties identified in Subparagraph 14.8 on account of bodily injury, death or damage to property. Operator's indemnity under this Paragraph shall be without regard to and without any right to contribution from any insurance maintained by Contractor pursuant to Paragraph 13. If it is judicially determined that the monetary limits of insurance required hereunder or of the indemnities voluntarily assumed under Subparagraph 14.9 (which Contractor and Operator hereby agree will be supported either by available liability insurance, under which the insurer has no right of subrogation against the indemnitees, or voluntarily self-insured, in part or whole) exceed the maximum limits permitted under applicable law, it is agreed that said insurance requirements or indemnities shall automatically be amended to conform to the maximum monetary limits permitted under such law.

14.10 Liability for Wild Well: Operator shall be liable for the cost of regaining control of any wild well, as well as for cost of removal of any debris and cost of property remediation and restoration, and Operator shall release, protect, defend and indemnify Contractor and its suppliers, contractors and subcontractors of any tier from and against any liability for such cost.

14.11 Pollution or Contamination: Notwithstanding anything to the contrary contained herein, except the provisions of Paragraphs 10 and 12, it is understood and agreed by and between Contractor and Operator that the responsibility for pollution or contamination shall be as follows:

(a) Contractor shall assume all responsibility for, including control and removal of, and shall protect, defend and indemnify Operator from and against all claims, demands and causes of action of every kind and character arising from pollution or contamination, which originates above the surface of the land or water from spills of fuels, lubricants, motor oils, pipe dope, paints, solvents, ballast, bilge and garbage, except unavoidable pollution from reserve pits, wholly in Contractor's possession and control and directly associated with Contractor's equipment and facilities.

(b) Operator shall assume all responsibility for, including control and removal of, and shall protect, defend and indemnify Contractor and its suppliers, contractors and subcontractors of any tier from and against all claims, demands, and causes of action of every kind and character arising directly or indirectly from all other pollution or contamination which may occur during the conduct of operations hereunder, including, but not limited to, that which may result from fire, blowout, cratering, seepage or any other uncontrolled flow of oil, gas, water or other substance, as well as the use or disposition of all drilling fluids, including, but not limited to, oil emulsion, oil base or chemically treated drilling fluids, contaminated cuttings or cavings, lost circulation and fish recovery materials and fluids. Operator shall release Contractor and its suppliers, contractors and subcontractors of any tier of any liability for the foregoing.

(c) In the event a third party commits an act or omission which results in pollution or contamination for which either Contractor or Operator, for whom such party is performing work, is held to be legally liable, the responsibility therefor shall be considered, as between Contractor and Operator, to be the same as if the party for whom the work was performed had performed the same and all of the obligations respecting protection, defense, indemnity and limitation of responsibility and liability, as set forth in (a) and (b) above, shall be specifically applied.

14.12 Consequential Damages: Subject to and without affecting the provisions of this Contract regarding the payment rights and obligations of the parties or the risk of loss, release and indemnity rights and obligations of the parties, each party shall at all times be responsible for and hold harmless and indemnify the other party from and against its own special, indirect or consequential damages, and the parties agree that special, indirect or consequential damages shall be deemed to include, without limitation, the following: loss of profit or revenue; costs and expenses resulting from business interruptions; loss of or delay in production; loss of or damage to the leasehold; loss of or delay in drilling or operating rights; cost of or loss of use of property, equipment, materials and services, including without limitation those provided by contractors or subcontractors of every tier or by third parties. Operator shall at all times be responsible for and hold harmless and indemnify Contractor and its suppliers, contractors and subcontractors of any tier from and against all claims, demands and causes of action of every kind and character in connection with such special, indirect or consequential damages suffered by Operator's co-owners, co-venturers, co-lessees, farmors, farmees, partners and joint owners.

14.13 Indemnity Obligation: Except as otherwise expressly limited in this Contract, it is the intent of parties hereto that all releases, indemnity obligations and/or liabilities assumed by such parties under terms of this Contract, including, without limitation, Subparagraphs 4.9 and 6.3(c), Paragraphs 10 and 12, and Subparagraphs 14.1 through 14.12 hereof, be without limit and without regard to the cause or causes thereof, including but not limited to pre-existing conditions, defect or ruin of premises or equipment, strict liability, regulatory or statutory liability, products liability, breach of representation or warranty (express or implied), breach of duty (whether statutory, contractual or otherwise), any theory of tort, breach of contract, fault, the negligence of any degree or character (regardless of whether such negligence is sole, joint or concurrent, active, passive or gross) of any party or parties, including the party seeking the benefit of the release, indemnity or assumption of liability, or any other theory of legal liability. The indemnities and releases and assumptions of liability extended by the parties hereto under the provisions of Subparagraphs 4.9 and 6.3 and Paragraphs 10, 12, and 14 shall inure to the benefit of such parties, their co-venturers, co-lessees, joint owners, their parent, holding and affiliated companies and the officers, directors, stockholders, partners, managers, representatives, employees, consultants, agents, servants and insurers of each. Except as otherwise provided herein, such indemnification and assumptions of liability shall not be deemed to create any rights to indemnification in any person or entity not a party to this Contract, either as a third party beneficiary or by reason of any agreement of indemnity between one of the parties hereto and another person or entity not a party to this Contract.

15. AUDIT:

    If any payment provided for hereunder is made on the basis of Contractor's costs, Operator shall have the right to audit Contractor's books and records relating to such costs. Contractor agrees to maintain such books and records for a period of two (2) years from the date such costs were incurred and to make such books and records available to Operator at any reasonable time or times within the period.

16. NO WAIVER EXCEPT IN WRITING:

    It is fully understood and agreed that none of the requirements of this Contract shall be considered as waived by either party unless the same is done in writing, and then only by the persons executing this Contract, or other duly authorized agent or representative of the party.

17. FORCE MAJEURE:

    Except as provided in this Paragraph 17 and without prejudice to the risk of loss, release and indemnity obligations under this Contract, each party to this Contract shall be excused from complying with the terms of this Contract, except for the payment of monies when due, if and for so long as such compliance is hindered or prevented by a Force Majeure Event. As used in this Contract, "Force Majeure Event" includes: acts of God, action of the elements, wars (declared or undeclared), insurrection, revolution, rebellions or civil strife, piracy, civil war or hostile action, terrorist acts, riots, strikes, differences with workmen, acts of public enemies, federal or state laws, rules, regulations, dispositions or orders of any governmental authorities having jurisdiction in the premises or of any other group, organization or informal association (whether or not formally recognized as a government), inability to procure material, equipment, fuel or necessary labor in the open market, acute and unusual labor or material, equipment or fuel shortages, or any other causes (except financial) beyond the control of either party. Neither Operator nor Contractor shall be required against its will to adjust any labor or similar disputes except in accordance with applicable law. In the event that either party hereto is rendered unable, wholly or in part, by any of these causes to carry out its obligation under this Contract, it is agreed that such party shall give notice and details of Force Majeure in writing to the other party as promptly as possible after its occurrence. In such cases, the obligations of the party giving the notice shall be suspended during the continuance of any inability so caused except that Operator shall be obligated to pay to Contractor the Force Majeure Rate provided for in Subparagraph 4.8 above.

18. GOVERNING LAW:

    This Contract shall be construed, governed, interpreted, enforced and litigated, and the relations between the parties determined in accordance with the laws of _____.

19. INFORMATION CONFIDENTIAL:

    Upon written request by Operator, information obtained by Contractor in the conduct of drilling operations on this well, including, but not limited to, depth, formations penetrated, the results of coring, testing and surveying, shall be considered confidential and shall not be divulged by Contractor or its employees, to any person, firm, or corporation other than Operator's designated representatives.

20. SUBCONTRACTS:

    Either party may employ other contractors to perform any of the operations or services to be provided or performed by it according to Exhibit "A".

21. ATTORNEY'S FEE:

    If this Contract is placed in the hands of an attorney for collection of any sums due hereunder, or suit is brought on same, or sums due hereunder are collected through bankruptcy or arbitration proceedings, then the prevailing party shall be entitled to recover reasonable attorney's fees and costs.

22. CLAIMS AND LIENS:

    Contractor agrees to pay all valid claims for labor, material, services, and supplies to be furnished by Contractor hereunder, and agrees to allow no lien by such third parties to be fixed upon the lease, the well, or other property of the Operator or the land upon which said well is located.

23. ASSIGNMENT:

    Neither party may assign this Contract without the prior written consent of the other, and prompt notice of any such intent to assign shall be given to the other party. In the event of such assignment, the assigning party shall remain liable to the other party as a guarantor of the performance by the assignee of the terms of this Contract. If any assignment is made that materially alters Contractor's financial burden, Contractor's compensation shall be adjusted to give effect to any increase or decrease in Contractor's operating costs.

24. NOTICES AND PLACE OF PAYMENT:

    Notices, reports, and other communications required or permitted by this Contract to be given or sent by one party to the other shall be delivered by hand, mailed, digitally transmitted or telecopied to the address hereinabove shown. All sums payable hereunder to Contractor shall be payable at its address hereinabove shown unless otherwise specified herein.

25. CONTINUING OBLIGATIONS:

    Notwithstanding the termination of this Contract, the parties shall continue to be bound by the provisions of this Contract that reasonably require some action or forbearance after such termination.

26. ENTIRE AGREEMENT:

    This Contract constitutes the full understanding of the parties, and a complete and exclusive statement of the terms of their agreement, and shall exclusively control and govern all work performed hereunder. All representations, offers, and undertakings of the parties made prior to the effective date hereof, whether oral or in writing, are merged herein, and no other contracts, agreements or work orders, executed prior to the execution of this Contract, shall in any way modify, amend, alter or change any of the terms or conditions set out herein.

27. SPECIAL PROVISIONS:

27. SPECIAL PROVISIONS (Continued):

28. ACCEPTANCE OF CONTRACT:

The foregoing Contract, including the provisions relating to indemnity, release of liability and allocation of risk of Subparagraphs 4.9 and 6.3(c), Paragraphs 10 and 12, and Subparagraphs 14.1 through 14.12, is acknowledged, agreed to and accepted by Operator this _____ day of _____, 20_____.

OPERATOR _____

By _____

Title _____

The foregoing Contract, including the provisions relating to indemnity, release of liability and allocation of risk of Subparagraphs 4.9 and 6.3(c), Paragraphs 10 and 12, and Subparagraphs 14.1 through 14.12, is acknowledged, agreed to and accepted by Contractor this _____ day of _____, 20_____, which is the effective date of this Contract, subject to rig availability, and subject to all of its terms and provisions, with the understanding that unless said Contract is thus executed by Operator within _____ days of the above date, Contractor shall be in no manner bound by its signature thereto.

CONTRACTOR _____

By _____

Title _____

Revised April, 2003

EXHIBIT "A"

To Daywork Contract dated _____, 20_____

Operator _____   Contractor _____

_____

Well Name and Number_____

SPECIFICATIONS AND SPECIAL PROVISIONS

1. CASING PROGRAM (See Paragraph 7)

	Hole Size	Casing Size	Weight	Grade	Approximate Setting Depth	Wait on Cement Time
Conductor	_____ in.	_____ in.	_____ lbs/ft.	_____	_____ ft.	_____ hrs
Surface	_____ in.	_____ in.	_____ lbs/ft.	_____	_____ ft.	_____ hrs
Protection	_____ in.	_____ in.	_____ lbs/ft.	_____	_____ ft.	_____ hrs
	_____ in.	_____ in.	_____ lbs/ft.	_____	_____ ft.	_____ hrs
Production	_____ in.	_____ in.	_____ lbs/ft.	_____	_____ ft.	_____ hrs
Liner	_____ in.	_____ in.	_____ lbs/ft.	_____	_____ ft.	_____ hrs
_____	_____ in.	_____ in.	_____ lbs/ft.	_____	_____ ft.	_____ hrs

2. MUD CONTROL PROGRAM (See Subparagraph 8.2)

Depth Interval (ft) From	To	Type Mud	Weight (lbs./gal.)	Viscosity (Secs)	Water Loss (cc)
_____	_____	_____	_____	_____	_____
_____	_____	_____	_____	_____	_____
_____	_____	_____	_____	_____	_____
_____	_____	_____	_____	_____	_____
_____	_____	_____	_____	_____	_____
_____	_____	_____	_____	_____	_____
_____	_____	_____	_____	_____	_____

Other mud specifications: _____
_____
_____
_____
_____
_____
_____
_____

3. INSURANCE (See Paragraph 13)

3.1 Adequate Workers' Compensation Insurance complying with State Laws applicable or Employers' Liability Insurance with limits of $_____ covering all of Contractor's employees working under this Contract.

3.2 Commercial (or Comprehensive) General Liability Insurance, including contractual obligations as respects this Contract and proper coverage for all other obligations assumed in this Contract. The limit shall be $_____ combined single limit per occurrence for Bodily Injury and Property Damage.

3.3 Automobile Public Liability Insurance with limits of $_____ for the death or injury of each person and $_____ for each accident; and Automobile Public Liability Property Damage Insurance with limits of $_____ for each accident.

3.4 In the event operations are over water, Contractor shall carry in addition to the Statutory Workers' Compensation Insurance, endorsements covering liability under the Longshoremen's & Harbor Workers' Compensation Act and Maritime liability including maintenance and cure with limits of $_____ for each death or injury to one person and $_____ for any one accident.

3.5 Other Insurance: _____
_____
_____
_____

4. EQUIPMENT, MATERIALS AND SERVICES TO BE FURNISHED BY CONTRACTOR:

The machinery, equipment, tools, materials, supplies, instruments, services and labor hereinafter listed, including any transportation required for such items, shall be provided at the well location at the expense of Contractor unless otherwise noted by this Contract.

4.1 Drilling Rig:

Complete drilling rig, designated by Contractor as its Rig No. _____, the major items of equipment being:

Drawworks: Make and Model _____

Engines: Make, Model, and H.P. _____

No. on Rig _____

Pumps: No. 1 Make, Size, and Power _____

No. 2 Make, Size, and Power _____

Mud Mixing Pump: Make, Size, and Power _____

Boilers: Number, Make, H.P. and W.P. _____

Derrick or Mast: Make, Size, and Capacity _____
_____

Substructure: Size and Capacity _____

Rotary Drive: Type _____

Drill Pipe: Size _____ in. _____ ft.; Size _____ in. _____ ft.

Drill Collars: Number and Size _____

Blowout Preventers: _____

Size	Series or Test Pr.	Make & Model	Number
_____	_____	_____	_____
_____	_____	_____	_____
_____	_____	_____	_____
_____	_____	_____	_____

B.O.P. Closing Unit: _____

B.O.P. Accumulator: _____

4.2 Derrick timbers.

4.3 Normal strings of drill pipe and drill collars specified above.

4.4 Conventional drift indicator.

4.5 Circulating mud pits.

4.6 Necessary pipe racks and rigging up material.

4.7 Normal storage for mud and chemicals.

4.8 Shale Shaker.

4.9 _____

4.10 _____

4.11 _____

4.12 _____

4.13 _____

4.14 _____

4.15 _____

4.16 _____

4.17 _____

4.18 _____

4.19 _____

4.20 _____

5. EQUIPMENT, MATERIALS AND SERVICES TO BE FURNISHED BY OPERATOR:

The machinery, equipment, tools, materials, supplies, instruments, services and labor hereinafter listed, including any transportation required for such items, shall be provided at the well location at the expense of Operator unless otherwise noted by this Contract.

5.1 Furnish and maintain adequate roadway and/or canal to location, right-of-way, including rights-of-way for fuel and water lines, river crossings, highway crossings, gates and cattle guards.

5.2 Stake location, clear and grade location, and provide turnaround, including surfacing when necessary.

5.3 Test tanks with pipe and fittings.

5.4 Mud storage tanks with pipe and fittings.

5.5 Separator with pipe and fittings.

5.6 Labor and materials to connect and disconnect mud tank, test tank, and mud gas separator.

5.7 Labor to disconnect and clean test tanks and mud gas separator.

5.8 Drilling mud, chemicals, lost circulation materials and other additives.

5.9 Pipe and connections for oil circulating lines.

5.10 Labor to lay, bury and recover oil circulating lines.

5.11 Drilling bits, reamers, reamer cutters, stabilizers and special tools.

5.12 Contract fishing tool services and tool rental.

5.13 Wire line core bits or heads, core barrels and wire line core catchers if required.

5.14 Conventional core bits, core catchers and core barrels.

5.15 Diamond core barrel with head.

5.16 Cement and cementing service.

5.17 Electrical wireline logging services.

5.18 Directional, caliper, or other special services.

5.19 Gun or jet perforating services.

5.20 Explosives and shooting devices.

5.21 Formation testing, hydraulic fracturing, acidizing and other related services.

5.22 Equipment for drill stem testing.

5.23 Mud logging services.

5.24 Sidewall coring service.

5.25 Welding service for welding bottom joints of casing, guide shoe, float shoe, float collar and in connection with installing of well head equipment if required.

5.26 Casing, tubing, liners, screen, float collars, guide and float shoes and associated equipment.

5.27 Casing scratchers and centralizers.

5.28 Well head connections and all equipment to be installed in or on well or on the premises for use in connection with testing, completion and operation of well.

5.29 Special or added storage for mud and chemicals.

5.30 Casinghead, API series, to conform to that shown for the blowout preventers specified in Subparagraph 4.1 above.

5.31 Blowout preventer testing packoff and testing services.

5.32 Replacement of BOP rubbers, elements and seals, if required, after initial test.

5.33 Casing Thread Protectors and Casing Lubricants.

5.34 H_2S training and equipment as necessary or as required by law.

5.35 Site septic systems.

5.36 _____

5.37 _____

5.38 _____

5.39 _____

5.40 _____

5.41 _____

5.42 _____

5.43 _____

5.44 _____

5.45 _____

5.46 _____

5.47 _____

5.48 _____

5.49 _____

5.50 _____

6. EQUIPMENT, MATERIALS AND SERVICES TO BE FURNISHED BY DESIGNATED PARTY:

The machinery, equipment, tools, materials, supplies, instruments, services, and labor listed as the following numbered items, including any transportation required

(U.S. Daywork Contract - Exhibit "A" - Page 2)
Copyright © 2003 International Association of Drilling Contractors

for such items unless otherwise specified, shall be provided at the well location and at the expense of the party hereto as designated by an X mark in the appropriate column.

	Item	To Be Provided By and At The Expense Of	
		Operator	Contractor
6.1	Cellar		
6.2	Ditches and sumps		
6.3	Fuel (located at _____)		
6.4	Fuel Lines (length _____)		
6.5	Water at source, including required permits		
6.6	Water well, including required permits		
6.7	Water lines, including required permits		
6.8	Water storage tanks _____ capacity		
6.9	Potable water		
6.10	Labor to operate water well or water pump		
6.11	Maintenance of water well, if required		
6.12	Water Pump		
6.13	Fuel for water pump		
6.14	Mats for engines and boilers, or motors and mud pumps		
6.15	Transportation of Contractor's property:		
	Move in		
	Move out		
6.16	Materials for "boxing in" rig and derrick		
6.17	Special strings of drill pipe and drill collars as follows:		
6.18	Kelly joints, subs, elevators, tongs, slips and BOP rams for use with special drill pipe		
6.19	Drill pipe protectors for Kelly joint and each joint of drill pipe running inside of Surface Casing as required, for use with normal strings of drill pipe		
6.20	Drill pipe protectors for Kelly joint and drill pipe running inside of Protection Casing		
6.21	Rate of penetration recording device		
6.22	Extra labor for running and cementing casing (Casing crews)		
6.23	Casing tools		
6.24	Power casing tongs		
6.25	Laydown and pickup machine		
6.26	Tubing tools		
6.27	Power tubing tong		
6.28	Crew Boats, Number _____		
6.29	Service Barge		
6.30	Service Tug Boat		
6.31	Rat Hole		
6.32	Mouse Hole		
6.33	Reserve Pits		
6.34	Upper Kelly Cock		
6.35	Lower Kelly Valve		
6.36	Drill Pipe Safety Valve		
6.37	Inside Blowout Preventer		
6.38	Drilling hole for or driving for conductor pipe		
6.39	Charges, cost of bonds for public roads		
6.40	Portable Toilet		
6.41	Trash Receptacle		
6.42	Linear Motion Shale Shaker		
6.43	Shale Shaker Screens		
6.44	Mud Cleaner		
6.45	Mud/Gas Separator		
6.46	Desander		
6.47	Desilter		
6.48	Degasser		
6.49	Centrifuge		
6.50	Rotating Head		
6.51	Rotating Head Rubbers		
6.52	Hydraulic Adjustable Choke		
6.53	Pit Volume Totalizer		
6.54	Communications, type _____		
6.55	Forklift, capacity _____		
6.56	Corrosion Inhibitor for protecting drill string		
6.57	_____		
6.58	_____		
6.59	_____		
6.60	_____		

7. OTHER PROVISIONS:

EXHIBIT "B"

(See Subparagraph 8.3)

The following clauses, when required by law, are incorporated in the Contract by reference as if fully set out.

(1) The Equal Opportunity Clause prescribed in 41 CFR 60-1.4.

(2) The Affirmative Action Clause prescribed in 41 CFR 60-250.4 regarding veterans and veterans of the Vietnam era.

(3) The Affirmative Action Clause for handicapped workers prescribed in 41 CFR 60-741.4.

(4) The Certification of Compliance With Environmental Laws prescribed in 40 CFR 15.20.

NOTES

1.   This copyrighted form was developed by the International Association of Drilling Contractors (IADC), a drilling contractor trade association, and is reprinted here with permission. The IADC has a series of drilling agreement forms, including a footage contract, a turnkey contract, a series of offshore contracts, and an international daywork contract. The IADC website is: http://fwww.iadc.org/.

2.   IADC forms are more drilling-contractor oriented than forms prepared by oil and gas operators. Nevertheless, IADC forms are widely used throughout the United States. Review the preamble, paragraphs 10, 14, and 17, and contractor's acceptance under paragraph 28 of the IADC daywork form. Would you be comfortable counseling an operator to sign this contract?

2.   The footage contract differs from a daywork contract regarding the primary method of payment. Under a footage contract, the drilling contractor is paid for each foot of hole drilled, while under a daywork contract, the drilling contractor is paid for each day of operations—generally regardless of progress. Under a turnkey contract, the drilling contractor is paid a set sum of money for the drilling of a well, but completion is generally separately addressed because these costs can be saved if the well is dry. A daywork contract is the most drilling-contractor oriented form of drilling agreement. A turnkey contract is the most operator-oriented form of drilling agreement, with the footage contract falling in between.

3.   Both footage and turnkey contracts contain provisions providing that work will proceed on a daywork basis in specified circumstances. In general, under the IADC footage and turnkey forms, drilling will proceed on a daywork basis if an event occurs that substantially increases the risk of loss of the well or the time of drilling.

4.   From a lawyer's perspective, the most important provisions of a drilling contract are the indemnity and risk-of-loss provisions. Carefully read paragraph 14 of the IADC daywork contract. Paragraphs 14.8 and 14.9 illustrate what are commonly called "knock-for-knock" indemnity provisions. Many of the other provisions of paragraph 14 address special circumstances or exceptions (often called "carve outs") to paragraph 14.8. Under paragraphs 14.8 and 14.9, the operator and drilling contractor indemnify each other for harm to their respective employees and equipment, regardless of negligence. Why would the parties choose to do this?

5.   Under the IADC daywork form, the operator further indemnifies contractor against harm to the equipment and employees of operator's other contractors. The drilling contractor does likewise regarding its subcontractors' equipment and employees. Not all contracts contain indemnity provisions that are this broad. Most operators would prefer that the drilling contractor (and all other contractors) indemnify the operator and the operator's other contractors, but operator would prefer to indemnify the drilling contractor (and its other contractors) only for harm to its own equipment and employees. Do you see why? Consider *Foreman v. Exxon Corp.*, 770 F.2d 490 (5th Cir. La. 1985).

Base Contract for Sale and Purchase of Natural Gas

This Base Contract is entered into as of the following date: _____

The parties to this Base Contract are the following:

PARTY A [INSERT COUNTERPARTY LEGAL ENTITY NAME]	PARTY NAME	PARTY B [INSERT COUNTERPARTY LEGAL ENTITY NAME]
	ADDRESS	
www._____	**BUSINESS WEBSITE**	www._____
	CONTRACT NUMBER	
	D-U-N-S® NUMBER	
☐ US FEDERAL: ☐ OTHER:	**TAX ID NUMBERS**	☐ US FEDERAL: ☐ OTHER:
	JURISDICTION OF ORGANIZATION	
☐ Corporation ☐ LLC ☐ Limited Partnership ☐ Partnership ☐ LLP ☐ Other: _____	**COMPANY TYPE**	☐ Corporation ☐ LLC ☐ Limited Partnership ☐ Partnership ☐ LLP ☐ Other: _____
	GUARANTOR (IF APPLICABLE)	

CONTACT INFORMATION

ATTN: _____ TEL#: _____ FAX#: _____ EMAIL: _____	• COMMERCIAL	ATTN: _____ TEL#: _____ FAX#: _____ EMAIL: _____
ATTN: _____ TEL#: _____ FAX#: _____ EMAIL: _____	• SCHEDULING	ATTN: _____ TEL#: _____ FAX#: _____ EMAIL: _____
ATTN: _____ TEL#: _____ FAX#: _____ EMAIL: _____	• CONTRACT AND LEGAL NOTICES	ATTN: _____ TEL#: _____ FAX#: _____ EMAIL: _____
ATTN: _____ TEL#: _____ FAX#: _____ EMAIL: _____	• CREDIT	ATTN: _____ TEL#: _____ FAX#: _____ EMAIL: _____
ATTN: _____ TEL#: _____ FAX#: _____ EMAIL: _____	• TRANSACTION CONFIRMATIONS	ATTN: _____ TEL#: _____ FAX#: _____ EMAIL: _____

ACCOUNTING INFORMATION

ATTN: _____ TEL#: _____ FAX#: _____ EMAIL: _____	• INVOICES • PAYMENTS • SETTLEMENTS	ATTN: _____ TEL#: _____ FAX#: _____ EMAIL: _____
BANK: _____ ABA: _____ ACCT: _____ OTHER DETAILS: _____	WIRE TRANSFER NUMBERS (IF APPLICABLE)	BANK: _____ ABA: _____ ACCT: _____ OTHER DETAILS: _____
BANK: _____ ABA: _____ ACCT: _____ OTHER DETAILS: _____	ACH NUMBERS (IF APPLICABLE)	BANK: _____ ABA: _____ ACCT: _____ OTHER DETAILS: _____
ATTN: _____ ADDRESS: _____	CHECKS (IF APPLICABLE)	ATTN: _____ ADDRESS: _____

NAESB Standard 6.3.1
September 5, 2006

Base Contract for Sale and Purchase of Natural Gas

(Continued)

This Base Contract incorporates by reference for all purposes the General Terms and Conditions for Sale and Purchase of Natural Gas published by the North American Energy Standards Board. The parties hereby agree to the following provisions offered in said General Terms and Conditions. In the event the parties fail to check a box, the specified default provision shall apply. <u>Select the appropriate box(es) from each section:</u>

Section 1.2 Transaction Procedure	☐ Oral (default) OR ☐ Written
Section 2.7 Confirm Deadline	☐ 2 Business Days after receipt (default) OR ☐ _____ Business Days after receipt
Section 2.8 Confirming Party	☐ Seller (default) OR ☐ Buyer ☐ _____
Section 3.2 Performance Obligation	☐ Cover Standard (default) OR ☐ Spot Price Standard
Note: The following Spot Price Publication applies to both of the immediately preceding.	
Section 2.31 Spot Price Publication	☐ Gas Daily Midpoint (default) OR ☐ _____
Section 6 Taxes	☐ Buyer Pays At and After Delivery Point (default) OR ☐ Seller Pays Before and At Delivery Point
Section 7.2 Payment Date	☐ 25th Day of Month following Month of delivery (default) OR ☐ _____ Day of Month following Month of delivery
Section 7.2 Method of Payment	☐ Wire transfer (default) ☐ Automated Clearinghouse Credit (ACH) ☐ Check
Section 7.7 Netting	☐ Netting applies (default) OR ☐ Netting does not apply

Section 10.2 Additional Events of Default	No Additional Events of Default (default) ☐ Indebtedness Cross Default Party A: _____ Party B: _____ Transactional Cross Default <u>Specified Transactions:</u> _____ _____
Section 10.3.1 Early Termination Damages	☐ Early Termination Damages Apply (default) OR ☐ Early Termination Damages Do Not Apply
Section 10.3.2 Other Agreement Setoffs	Other Agreement Setoffs Apply (default) ☐ Bilateral (default) ☐ Triangular OR Other Agreement Setoffs Do Not Apply
Section 15.5 Choice Of Law	_____
Section 15.10 Confidentiality	Confidentiality applies (default) OR Confidentiality does not apply

Special Provisions Number of sheets attached: _____
Addendum(s): _____

IN WITNESS WHEREOF, the parties hereto have executed this Base Contract in duplicate.

[INSERT COUNTERPARTY LEGAL ENTITY NAME]	*PARTY NAME*	[INSERT COUNTERPARTY LEGAL ENTITY NAME]
By: _____	*SIGNATURE*	By: _____
[Insert Name]	*PRINTED NAME*	[Insert Name]
[Insert Title]	*TITLE*	[Insert Title]

NAESB Standard 6.3.1
September 5, 2006

SECTION 1. PURPOSE AND PROCEDURES

1.1. These General Terms and Conditions are intended to facilitate purchase and sale transactions of Gas on a Firm or Interruptible basis. "Buyer" refers to the party receiving Gas and "Seller" refers to the party delivering Gas. The entire agreement between the parties shall be the Contract as defined in Section 2.9.

The parties have selected either the "Oral Transaction Procedure" or the "Written Transaction Procedure" as indicated on the Base Contract.

Oral Transaction Procedure:

1.2. The parties will use the following Transaction Confirmation procedure. Any Gas purchase and sale transaction may be effectuated in an EDI transmission or telephone conversation with the offer and acceptance constituting the agreement of the parties. The parties shall be legally bound from the time they so agree to transaction terms and may each rely thereon. Any such transaction shall be considered a "writing" and to have been "signed". Notwithstanding the foregoing sentence, the parties agree that Confirming Party shall, and the other party may, confirm a telephonic transaction by sending the other party a Transaction Confirmation by facsimile, EDI or mutually agreeable electronic means within three Business Days of a transaction covered by this Section 1.2 (Oral Transaction Procedure) provided that the failure to send a Transaction Confirmation shall not invalidate the oral agreement of the parties. Confirming Party adopts its confirming letterhead, or the like, as its signature on any Transaction Confirmation as the identification and authentication of Confirming Party. If the Transaction Confirmation contains any provisions other than those relating to the commercial terms of the transaction (i.e., price, quantity, performance obligation, delivery point, period of delivery and/or transportation conditions), which modify or supplement the Base Contract or General Terms and Conditions of this Contract (e.g., arbitration or additional representations and warranties), such provisions shall not be deemed to be accepted pursuant to Section 1.3 but must be expressly agreed to by both parties; provided that the foregoing shall not invalidate any transaction agreed to by the parties.

Written Transaction Procedure:

1.2. The parties will use the following Transaction Confirmation procedure. Should the parties come to an agreement regarding a Gas purchase and sale transaction for a particular Delivery Period, the Confirming Party shall, and the other party may, record that agreement on a Transaction Confirmation and communicate such Transaction Confirmation by facsimile, EDI or mutually agreeable electronic means, to the other party by the close of the Business Day following the date of agreement. The parties acknowledge that their agreement will not be binding until the exchange of nonconflicting Transaction Confirmations or the passage of the Confirm Deadline without objection from the receiving party, as provided in Section 1.3.

1.3. If a sending party's Transaction Confirmation is materially different from the receiving party's understanding of the agreement referred to in Section 1.2, such receiving party shall notify the sending party via facsimile, EDI or mutually agreeable electronic means by the Confirm Deadline, unless such receiving party has previously sent a Transaction Confirmation to the sending party. The failure of the receiving party to so notify the sending party in writing by the Confirm Deadline constitutes the receiving party's agreement to the terms of the transaction described in the sending party's Transaction Confirmation. If there are any material differences between timely sent Transaction Confirmations governing the same transaction, then neither Transaction Confirmation shall be binding until or unless such differences are resolved including the use of any evidence that clearly resolves the differences in the Transaction Confirmations. In the event of a conflict among the terms of (i) a binding Transaction Confirmation pursuant to Section 1.2, (ii) the oral agreement of the parties which may be evidenced by a recorded conversation, where the parties have selected the Oral Transaction Procedure of the Base Contract, (iii) the Base Contract, and (iv) these General Terms and Conditions, the terms of the documents shall govern in the priority listed in this sentence.

1.4. The parties agree that each party may electronically record all telephone conversations with respect to this Contract between their respective employees, without any special or further notice to the other party. Each party shall obtain any necessary consent of its agents and employees to such recording. Where the parties have selected the Oral Transaction Procedure in Section 1.2 of the Base Contract, the parties agree not to contest the validity or enforceability of telephonic recordings entered into in accordance with the requirements of this Base Contract.

SECTION 2. DEFINITIONS

The terms set forth below shall have the meaning ascribed to them below. Other terms are also defined elsewhere in the Contract and shall have the meanings ascribed to them herein.

2.1. "Additional Event of Default" shall mean Transactional Cross Default or Indebtedness Cross Default, each as and if selected by the parties pursuant to the Base Contract.

2.2. "Affiliate" shall mean, in relation to any person, any entity controlled, directly or indirectly, by the person, any entity that controls, directly or indirectly, the person or any entity directly or indirectly under common control with the person. For this purpose, "control" of any entity or person means ownership of at least 50 percent of the voting power of the entity or person.

NAESB Standard 6.3.1
September 5, 2006

2.3.   "Alternative Damages" shall mean such damages, expressed in dollars or dollars per MMBtu, as the parties shall agree upon in the Transaction Confirmation, in the event either Seller or Buyer fails to perform a Firm obligation to deliver Gas in the case of Seller or to receive Gas in the case of Buyer.

2.4.   "Base Contract" shall mean a contract executed by the parties that incorporates these General Terms and Conditions by reference; that specifies the agreed selections of provisions contained herein; and that sets forth other information required herein and any Special Provisions and addendum(s) as identified on page one.

2.5.   "British thermal unit" or "Btu" shall mean the International BTU, which is also called the Btu (IT).

2.6.   "Business Day(s)" shall mean Monday through Friday, excluding Federal Banking Holidays for transactions in the U.S.

2.7.   "Confirm Deadline" shall mean 5:00 p.m. in the receiving party's time zone on the second Business Day following the Day a Transaction Confirmation is received or, if applicable, on the Business Day agreed to by the parties in the Base Contract; provided, if the Transaction Confirmation is time stamped after 5:00 p.m. in the receiving party's time zone, it shall be deemed received at the opening of the next Business Day.

2.8.   "Confirming Party" shall mean the party designated in the Base Contract to prepare and forward Transaction Confirmations to the other party.

2.9.   "Contract" shall mean the legally-binding relationship established by (i) the Base Contract, (ii) any and all binding Transaction Confirmations and (iii) where the parties have selected the Oral Transaction Procedure in Section 1.2 of the Base Contract, any and all transactions that the parties have entered into through an EDI transmission or by telephone, but that have not been confirmed in a binding Transaction Confirmation, all of which shall form a single integrated agreement between the parties.

2.10.   "Contract Price" shall mean the amount expressed in U.S. Dollars per MMBtu to be paid by Buyer to Seller for the purchase of Gas as agreed to by the parties in a transaction.

2.11.   "Contract Quantity" shall mean the quantity of Gas to be delivered and taken as agreed to by the parties in a transaction.

2.12.   "Cover Standard", as referred to in Section 3.2, shall mean that if there is an unexcused failure to take or deliver any quantity of Gas pursuant to this Contract, then the performing party shall use commercially reasonable efforts to (i) if Buyer is the performing party, obtain Gas, (or an alternate fuel if elected by Buyer and replacement Gas is not available), or (ii) if Seller is the performing party, sell Gas, in either case, at a price reasonable for the delivery or production area, as applicable, consistent with: the amount of notice provided by the nonperforming party; the immediacy of the Buyer's Gas consumption needs or Seller's Gas sales requirements, as applicable; the quantities involved; and the anticipated length of failure by the nonperforming party.

2.13.   "Credit Support Obligation(s)" shall mean any obligation(s) to provide or establish credit support for, or on behalf of, a party to this Contract such as cash, an irrevocable standby letter of credit, a margin agreement, a prepayment, a security interest in an asset, guaranty, or other good and sufficient security of a continuing nature.

2.14.   "Day" shall mean a period of 24 consecutive hours, coextensive with a "day" as defined by the Receiving Transporter in a particular transaction.

2.15.   "Delivery Period" shall be the period during which deliveries are to be made as agreed to by the parties in a transaction.

2.16.   "Delivery Point(s)" shall mean such point(s) as are agreed to by the parties in a transaction.

2.17.   "EDI" shall mean an electronic data interchange pursuant to an agreement entered into by the parties, specifically relating to the communication of Transaction Confirmations under this Contract.

2.18.   "EFP" shall mean the purchase, sale or exchange of natural Gas as the "physical" side of an exchange for physical transaction involving gas futures contracts. EFP shall incorporate the meaning and remedies of "Firm", provided that a party's excuse for nonperformance of its obligations to deliver or receive Gas will be governed by the rules of the relevant futures exchange regulated under the Commodity Exchange Act.

2.19.   "Firm" shall mean that either party may interrupt its performance without liability only to the extent that such performance is prevented for reasons of Force Majeure; provided, however, that during Force Majeure interruptions, the party invoking Force Majeure may be responsible for any Imbalance Charges as set forth in Section 4.3 related to its interruption after the nomination is made to the Transporter and until the change in deliveries and/or receipts is confirmed by the Transporter.

2.20.   "Gas" shall mean any mixture of hydrocarbons and noncombustible gases in a gaseous state consisting primarily of methane.

2.21.   "Guarantor" shall mean any entity that has provided a guaranty of the obligations of a party hereunder.

2.22.   "Imbalance Charges" shall mean any fees, penalties, costs or charges (in cash or in kind) assessed by a Transporter for failure to satisfy the Transporter's balance and/or nomination requirements.

2.23.   "Indebtedness Cross Default" shall mean if selected on the Base Contract by the parties with respect to a party, that it or its Guarantor, if any, experiences a default, or similar condition or event however therein defined, under one or more agreements or instruments, individually or collectively, relating to indebtedness (such indebtedness to include any obligation whether present or future, contingent or otherwise, as principal or surety or otherwise) for the payment or repayment of borrowed money in an aggregate amount greater than the threshold specified in the Base Contract with respect to such party or its Guarantor, if any, which results in such indebtedness becoming immediately due and payable.

2.24.   "Interruptible" shall mean that either party may interrupt its performance at any time for any reason, whether or not caused by an event of Force Majeure, with no liability, except such interrupting party may be responsible for any Imbalance Charges as set forth in Section 4.3 related to its interruption after the nomination is made to the Transporter and until the change in deliveries and/or receipts is confirmed by Transporter.

2.25.   "MMBtu" shall mean one million British thermal units, which is equivalent to one dekatherm.

2.26.   "Month" shall mean the period beginning on the first Day the calendar month and ending immediately prior to the commencement of the first Day of the next calendar month.

2.27.   "Payment Date" shall mean a date, as indicated on the Base Contract, on or before which payment is due Seller for Gas received by Buyer in the previous Month.

2.28.   "Receiving Transporter" shall mean the Transporter receiving Gas at a Delivery Point, or absent such receiving Transporter, the Transporter delivering Gas at a Delivery Point.

2.29.   "Scheduled Gas" shall mean the quantity of Gas confirmed by Transporter(s) for movement, transportation or management.

2.30.   "Specified Transaction(s)" shall mean any other transaction or agreement between the parties for the purchase, sale or exchange of physical Gas, and any other transaction or agreement identified as a Specified Transaction under the Base Contract.

2.31.   "Spot Price " as referred to in Section 3.2 shall mean the price listed in the publication indicated on the Base Contract, under the listing applicable to the geographic location closest in proximity to the Delivery Point(s) for the relevant Day; provided, if there is no single price published for such location for such Day, but there is published a range of prices, then the Spot Price shall be the average of such high and low prices. If no price or range of prices is published for such Day, then the Spot Price shall be the average of the following: (i) the price (determined as stated above) for the first Day for which a price or range of prices is published that next precedes the relevant Day; and (ii) the price (determined as stated above) for the first Day for which a price or range of prices is published that next follows the relevant Day.

2.32.   "Transaction Confirmation" shall mean a document, similar to the form of Exhibit A, setting forth the terms of a transaction formed pursuant to Section 1 for a particular Delivery Period.

2.33.   "Transactional Cross Default" shall mean if selected on the Base Contract by the parties with respect to a party, that it shall be in default, however therein defined, under any Specified Transaction.

2.34.   "Termination Option" shall mean the option of either party to terminate a transaction in the event that the other party fails to perform a Firm obligation to deliver Gas in the case of Seller or to receive Gas in the case of Buyer for a designated number of days during a period as specified on the applicable Transaction Confirmation.

2.35.   "Transporter(s)" shall mean all Gas gathering or pipeline companies, or local distribution companies, acting in the capacity of a transporter, transporting Gas for Seller or Buyer upstream or downstream, respectively, of the Delivery Point pursuant to a particular transaction.

SECTION 3.   PERFORMANCE OBLIGATION

3.1.   Seller agrees to sell and deliver, and Buyer agrees to receive and purchase, the Contract Quantity for a particular transaction in accordance with the terms of the Contract. Sales and purchases will be on a Firm or Interruptible basis, as agreed to by the parties in a transaction.

The parties have selected either the "Cover Standard" or the "Spot Price Standard" as indicated on the Base Contract.
Cover Standard:
3.2.   The sole and exclusive remedy of the parties in the event of a breach of a Firm obligation to deliver or receive Gas shall be recovery of the following: (i) in the event of a breach by Seller on any Day(s), payment by Seller to Buyer in an amount equal to the positive difference, if any, between the purchase price paid by Buyer utilizing the Cover Standard and the Contract Price, adjusted for commercially reasonable differences in transportation costs to or from the Delivery Point(s), multiplied by the difference between the Contract Quantity and the quantity actually delivered by Seller for such Day(s) excluding any quantity for which no replacement is available; or (ii) in the event of a breach by Buyer on any Day(s), payment by Buyer to Seller in the amount equal to the positive difference, if any, between the Contract Price and the price received by Seller utilizing the Cover Standard for the resale of such Gas, adjusted for commercially reasonable differences in transportation costs to or from the Delivery Point(s), multiplied by the difference between the Contract Quantity and the quantity actually taken by Buyer for such Day(s) excluding any quantity for which no sale is available; and (iii) in the event that Buyer has used commercially reasonable efforts to replace the Gas or Seller has used commercially reasonable efforts to sell the Gas to a third party, and no such replacement or sale is available for all or any portion of the Contract Quantity of Gas, then in addition to (i) or (ii) above, as applicable, the sole and exclusive remedy of the performing party with respect to the Gas not replaced or sold shall be an amount equal to any unfavorable difference between the Contract Price and the Spot Price, adjusted for such transportation to the applicable Delivery Point, multiplied by the quantity of such Gas not replaced or sold. Imbalance Charges shall not be recovered under this Section 3.2, but Seller and/or Buyer shall be responsible for Imbalance Charges, if any, as provided in Section 4.3. The amount of such unfavorable difference shall be payable five Business Days after presentation of the performing party's invoice, which shall set forth the basis upon which such amount was calculated.

NAESB Standard 6.3.1
September 5, 2006

Spot Price Standard:

3.2.   The sole and exclusive remedy of the parties in the event of a breach of a Firm obligation to deliver or receive Gas shall be recovery of the following: (i) in the event of a breach by Seller on any Day(s), payment by Seller to Buyer in an amount equal to the difference between the Contract Quantity and the actual quantity delivered by Seller and received by Buyer for such Day(s), multiplied by the positive difference, if any, obtained by subtracting the Contract Price from the Spot Price; or (ii) in the event of a breach by Buyer on any Day(s), payment by Buyer to Seller in an amount equal to the difference between the Contract Quantity and the actual quantity delivered by Seller and received by Buyer for such Day(s), multiplied by the positive difference, if any, obtained by subtracting the applicable Spot Price from the Contract Price. Imbalance Charges shall not be recovered under this Section 3.2, but Seller and/or Buyer shall be responsible for Imbalance Charges, if any, as provided in Section 4.3. The amount of such unfavorable difference shall be payable five Business Days after presentation of the performing party's invoice, which shall set forth the basis upon which such amount was calculated.

3.3.   Notwithstanding Section 3.2, the parties may agree to Alternative Damages in a Transaction Confirmation executed in writing by both parties.

3.4.   In addition to Sections 3.2 and 3.3, the parties may provide for a Termination Option in a Transaction Confirmation executed in writing by both parties. The Transaction Confirmation containing the Termination Option will designate the length of nonperformance triggering the Termination Option and the procedures for exercise thereof, how damages for nonperformance will be compensated, and how liquidation costs will be calculated.

SECTION 4.   TRANSPORTATION, NOMINATIONS, AND IMBALANCES

4.1.   Seller shall have the sole responsibility for transporting the Gas to the Delivery Point(s). Buyer shall have the sole responsibility for transporting the Gas from the Delivery Point(s).

4.2.   The parties shall coordinate their nomination activities, giving sufficient time to meet the deadlines of the affected Transporter(s). Each party shall give the other party timely prior Notice, sufficient to meet the requirements of all Transporter(s) involved in the transaction, of the quantities of Gas to be delivered and purchased each Day. Should either party become aware that actual deliveries at the Delivery Point(s) are greater or lesser than the Scheduled Gas, such party shall promptly notify the other party.

4.3.   The parties shall use commercially reasonable efforts to avoid imposition of any Imbalance Charges. If Buyer or Seller receives an invoice from a Transporter that includes Imbalance Charges, the parties shall determine the validity as well as the cause of such Imbalance Charges. If the Imbalance Charges were incurred as a result of Buyer's receipt of quantities of Gas greater than or less than the Scheduled Gas, then Buyer shall pay for such Imbalance Charges or reimburse Seller for such Imbalance Charges paid by Seller. If the Imbalance Charges were incurred as a result of Seller's delivery of quantities of Gas greater than or less than the Scheduled Gas, then Seller shall pay for such Imbalance Charges or reimburse Buyer for such Imbalance Charges paid by Buyer.

SECTION 5.   QUALITY AND MEASUREMENT

All Gas delivered by Seller shall meet the pressure, quality and heat content requirements of the Receiving Transporter. The unit of quantity measurement for purposes of this Contract shall be one MMBtu dry. Measurement of Gas quantities hereunder shall be in accordance with the established procedures of the Receiving Transporter.

SECTION 6.   TAXES

The parties have selected either "Buyer Pays At and After Delivery Point" or "Seller Pays Before and At Delivery Point" as indicated on the Base Contract.

Buyer Pays At and After Delivery Point:

Seller shall pay or cause to be paid all taxes, fees, levies, penalties, licenses or charges imposed by any government authority ("Taxes") on or with respect to the Gas prior to the Delivery Point(s). Buyer shall pay or cause to be paid all Taxes on or with respect to the Gas at the Delivery Point(s) and all Taxes after the Delivery Point(s). If a party is required to remit or pay Taxes that are the other party's responsibility hereunder, the party responsible for such Taxes shall promptly reimburse the other party for such Taxes. Any party entitled to an exemption from any such Taxes or charges shall furnish the other party any necessary documentation thereof.

Seller Pays Before and At Delivery Point:

Seller shall pay or cause to be paid all taxes, fees, levies, penalties, licenses or charges imposed by any government authority ("Taxes") on or with respect to the Gas prior to the Delivery Point(s) and all Taxes at the Delivery Point(s). Buyer shall pay or cause to be paid all Taxes on or with respect to the Gas after the Delivery Point(s). If a party is required to remit or pay Taxes that are the other party's responsibility hereunder, the party responsible for such Taxes shall promptly reimburse the other party for such Taxes. Any party entitled to an exemption from any such Taxes or charges shall furnish the other party any necessary documentation thereof.

SECTION 7.   BILLING, PAYMENT, AND AUDIT

7.1.   Seller shall invoice Buyer for Gas delivered and received in the preceding Month and for any other applicable charges, providing supporting documentation acceptable in industry practice to support the amount charged. If the actual quantity delivered is not known by the billing date, billing will be prepared based on the quantity of Scheduled Gas. The invoiced quantity will then be adjusted to the actual quantity on the following Month's billing or as soon thereafter as actual delivery information is available.

NAESB Standard 6.3.1
September 5, 2006

7.2.   Buyer shall remit the amount due under Section 7.1 in the manner specified in the Base Contract, in immediately available funds, on or before the later of the Payment Date or 10 Days after receipt of the invoice by Buyer; provided that if the Payment Date is not a Business Day, payment is due on the next Business Day following that date. In the event any payments are due Buyer hereunder, payment to Buyer shall be made in accordance with this Section 7.2.

7.3.   In the event payments become due pursuant to Sections 3.2 or 3.3, the performing party may submit an invoice to the nonperforming party for an accelerated payment setting forth the basis upon which the invoiced amount was calculated. Payment from the nonperforming party will be due five Business Days after receipt of invoice.

7.4.   If the invoiced party, in good faith, disputes the amount of any such invoice or any part thereof, such invoiced party will pay such amount as it concedes to be correct; provided, however, if the invoiced party disputes the amount due, it must provide supporting documentation acceptable in industry practice to support the amount paid or disputed without undue delay. In the event the parties are unable to resolve such dispute, either party may pursue any remedy available at law or in equity to enforce its rights pursuant to this Section.

7.5.   If the invoiced party fails to remit the full amount payable when due, interest on the unpaid portion shall accrue from the date due until the date of payment at a rate equal to the lower of (i) the then-effective prime rate of interest published under "Money Rates" by The Wall Street Journal, plus two percent per annum; or (ii) the maximum applicable lawful interest rate.

7.6.   A party shall have the right, at its own expense, upon reasonable Notice and at reasonable times, to examine and audit and to obtain copies of the relevant portion of the books, records, and telephone recordings of the other party only to the extent reasonably necessary to verify the accuracy of any statement, charge, payment, or computation made under the Contract. This right to examine, audit, and to obtain copies shall not be available with respect to proprietary information not directly relevant to transactions under this Contract. All invoices and billings shall be conclusively presumed final and accurate and all associated claims for under- or overpayments shall be deemed waived unless such invoices or billings are objected to in writing, with adequate explanation and/or documentation, within two years after the Month of Gas delivery. All retroactive adjustments under Section 7 shall be paid in full by the party owing payment within 30 Days of Notice and substantiation of such inaccuracy.

7.7.   Unless the parties have elected on the Base Contract not to make this Section 7.7 applicable to this Contract, the parties shall net all undisputed amounts due and owing, and/or past due, arising under the Contract such that the party owing the greater amount shall make a single payment of the net amount to the other party in accordance with Section 7; provided that no payment required to be made pursuant to the terms of any Credit Support Obligation or pursuant to Section 7.3 shall be subject to netting under this Section. If the parties have executed a separate netting agreement, the terms and conditions therein shall prevail to the extent inconsistent herewith.

SECTION 8.   TITLE, WARRANTY, AND INDEMNITY

8.1.   Unless otherwise specifically agreed, title to the Gas shall pass from Seller to Buyer at the Delivery Point(s). Seller shall have responsibility for and assume any liability with respect to the Gas prior to its delivery to Buyer at the specified Delivery Point(s). Buyer shall have responsibility for and assume any liability with respect to said Gas after its delivery to Buyer at the Delivery Point(s).

8.2.   Seller warrants that it will have the right to convey and will transfer good and merchantable title to all Gas sold hereunder and delivered by it to Buyer, free and clear of all liens, encumbrances, and claims. EXCEPT AS PROVIDED IN THIS SECTION 8.2 AND IN SECTION 15.8, ALL OTHER WARRANTIES, EXPRESS OR IMPLIED, INCLUDING ANY WARRANTY OF MERCHANTABILITY OR OF FITNESS FOR ANY PARTICULAR PURPOSE, ARE DISCLAIMED.

8.3.   Seller agrees to indemnify Buyer and save it harmless from all losses, liabilities or claims including reasonable attorneys' fees and costs of court ("Claims"), from any and all persons, arising from or out of claims of title, personal injury (including death) or property damage from said Gas or other charges thereon which attach before title passes to Buyer. Buyer agrees to indemnify Seller and save it harmless from all Claims, from any and all persons, arising from or out of claims regarding payment, personal injury (including death) or property damage from said Gas or other charges thereon which attach after title passes to Buyer.

8.4.   The parties agree that the delivery of and the transfer of title to all Gas under this Contract shall take place within the Customs Territory of the United States (as defined in general note 2 of the Harmonized Tariff Schedule of the United States 19 U.S.C. §1202, General Notes, page 3); provided, however, that in the event Seller took title to the Gas outside the Customs Territory of the United States, Seller represents and warrants that it is the importer of record for all Gas entered and delivered into the United States, and shall be responsible for entry and entry summary filings as well as the payment of duties, taxes and fees, if any, and all applicable record keeping requirements.

8.5.   Notwithstanding the other provisions of this Section 8, as between Seller and Buyer, Seller will be liable for all Claims to the extent that such arise from the failure of Gas delivered by Seller to meet the quality requirements of Section 5.

SECTION 9.   NOTICES

9.1.   All Transaction Confirmations, invoices, payment instructions, and other communications made pursuant to the Base Contract ("Notices") shall be made to the addresses specified in writing by the respective parties from time to time.

9.2.   All Notices required hereunder shall be in writing and may be sent by facsimile or mutually acceptable electronic means, a nationally recognized overnight courier service, first class mail or hand delivered.

9.3.   Notice shall be given when received on a Business Day by the addressee. In the absence of proof of the actual receipt date, the following presumptions will apply. Notices sent by facsimile shall be deemed to have been received upon the sending party's receipt of its facsimile machine's confirmation of successful transmission. If the day on which such facsimile is received is

NAESB Standard 6.3.1
September 5, 2006

not a Business Day or is after five p.m. on a Business Day, then such facsimile shall be deemed to have been received on the next following Business Day. Notice by overnight mail or courier shall be deemed to have been received on the next Business Day after it was sent or such earlier time as is confirmed by the receiving party. Notice via first class mail shall be considered delivered five Business Days after mailing.

9.4.   The party receiving a commercially acceptable Notice of change in payment instructions or other payment information shall not be obligated to implement such change until ten Business Days after receipt of such Notice.

SECTION 10.   FINANCIAL RESPONSIBILITY

10.1.   If either party ("X") has reasonable grounds for insecurity regarding the performance of any obligation under this Contract (whether or not then due) by the other party ("Y") (including, without limitation, the occurrence of a material change in the creditworthiness of Y or its Guarantor, if applicable), X may demand Adequate Assurance of Performance. "Adequate Assurance of Performance" shall mean sufficient security in the form, amount, for a term, and from an issuer, all as reasonably acceptable to X, including, but not limited to cash, a standby irrevocable letter of credit, a prepayment, a security interest in an asset or guaranty. Y hereby grants to X a continuing first priority security interest in, lien on, and right of setoff against all Adequate Assurance of Performance in the form of cash transferred by Y to X pursuant to this Section 10.1. Upon the return by X to Y of such Adequate Assurance of Performance, the security interest and lien granted hereunder on that Adequate Assurance of Performance shall be released automatically and, to the extent possible, without any further action by either party.

10.2.   In the event (each an "Event of Default") either party (the "Defaulting Party") or its Guarantor shall: (i) make an assignment or any general arrangement for the benefit of creditors; (ii) file a petition or otherwise commence, authorize, or acquiesce in the commencement of a proceeding or case under any bankruptcy or similar law for the protection of creditors or have such petition filed or proceeding commenced against it; (iii) otherwise become bankrupt or insolvent (however evidenced); (iv) be unable to pay its debts as they fall due; (v) have a receiver, provisional liquidator, conservator, custodian, trustee or other similar official appointed with respect to it or substantially all of its assets; (vi) fail to perform any obligation to the other party with respect to any Credit Support Obligations relating to the Contract; (vii) fail to give Adequate Assurance of Performance under Section 10.1 within 48 hours but at least one Business Day of a written request by the other party; (viii) not have paid any amount due the other party hereunder on or before the second Business Day following written Notice that such payment is due; or ix) be the affected party with respect to any Additional Event of Default; then the other party (the "Non-Defaulting Party") shall have the right, at its sole election, to immediately withhold and/or suspend deliveries or payments upon Notice and/or to terminate and liquidate the transactions under the Contract, in the manner provided in Section 10.3, in addition to any and all other remedies available hereunder.

10.3.   If an Event of Default has occurred and is continuing, the Non-Defaulting Party shall have the right, by Notice to the Defaulting Party, to designate a Day, no earlier than the Day such Notice is given and no later than 20 Days after such Notice is given, as an early termination date (the "Early Termination Date") for the liquidation and termination pursuant to Section 10.3.1 of all transactions under the Contract, each a "Terminated Transaction". On the Early Termination Date, all transactions will terminate, other than those transactions, if any, that may not be liquidated and terminated under applicable law ("Excluded Transactions"), which Excluded Transactions must be liquidated and terminated as soon thereafter as is legally permissible, and upon termination shall be a Terminated Transaction and be valued consistent with Section 10.3.1 below. With respect to each Excluded Transaction, its actual termination date shall be the Early Termination Date for purposes of Section 10.3.1.

The parties have selected either "Early Termination Damages Apply" or "Early Termination Damages Do Not Apply" as indicated on the Base Contract.

Early Termination Damages Apply:

10.3.1.   As of the Early Termination Date, the Non-Defaulting Party shall determine, in good faith and in a commercially reasonable manner, (i) the amount owed (whether or not then due) by each party with respect to all Gas delivered and received between the parties under Terminated Transactions and Excluded Transactions on and before the Early Termination Date and all other applicable charges relating to such deliveries and receipts (including without limitation any amounts owed under Section 3.2), for which payment has not yet been made by the party that owes such payment under this Contract and (ii) the Market Value, as defined below, of each Terminated Transaction. The Non-Defaulting Party shall (x) liquidate and accelerate each Terminated Transaction at its Market Value, so that each amount equal to the difference between such Market Value and the Contract Value, as defined below, of such Terminated Transaction(s) shall be due to the Buyer under the Terminated Transaction(s) if such Market Value exceeds the Contract Value and to the Seller if the opposite is the case; and (y) where appropriate, discount each amount then due under clause (x) above to present value in a commercially reasonable manner as of the Early Termination Date (to take account of the period between the date of liquidation and the date on which such amount would have otherwise been due pursuant to the relevant Terminated Transactions).

For purposes of this Section 10.3.1, "Contract Value" means the amount of Gas remaining to be delivered or purchased under a transaction multiplied by the Contract Price, and "Market Value" means the amount of Gas remaining to be delivered or purchased under a transaction multiplied by the market price for a similar transaction at the Delivery Point determined by the Non-Defaulting Party in a commercially reasonable manner. To ascertain the Market Value, the Non-Defaulting Party may consider, among other valuations, any or all of the settlement prices of NYMEX Gas futures contracts, quotations from leading dealers in energy swap contracts or physical gas trading markets, similar sales or purchases and any other bona fide third-party offers, all adjusted for the length of the term and differences in transportation costs. A party shall not be required to enter into a replacement transaction(s) in order to determine the Market Value. Any extension(s) of the term of a transaction to which parties are not bound as of the Early Termination Date (including but not limited to "evergreen provisions") shall not be considered in determining Contract Values and

---

Market Values. For the avoidance of doubt, any option pursuant to which one party has the right to extend the term of a transaction shall be considered in determining Contract Values and Market Values. The rate of interest used in calculating net present value shall be determined by the Non-Defaulting Party in a commercially reasonable manner.

Early Termination Damages Do Not Apply:

10.3.1.   As of the Early Termination Date, the Non-Defaulting Party shall determine, in good faith and in a commercially reasonable manner, the amount owed (whether or not then due) by each party with respect to all Gas delivered and received between the parties under Terminated Transactions and Excluded Transactions on and before the Early Termination Date and all other applicable charges relating to such deliveries and receipts (including without limitation any amounts owed under Section 3.2), for which payment has not yet been made by the party that owes such payment under this Contract.

The parties have selected either "Other Agreement Setoffs Apply" or "Other Agreement Setoffs Do Not Apply" as indicated on the Base Contract.

Other Agreement Setoffs Apply:

Bilateral Setoff Option:

10.3.2.   The Non-Defaulting Party shall net or aggregate, as appropriate, any and all amounts owing between the parties under Section 10.3.1, so that all such amounts are netted or aggregated to a single liquidated amount payable by one party to the other (the "Net Settlement Amount"). At its sole option and without prior Notice to the Defaulting Party, the Non-Defaulting Party is hereby authorized to setoff any Net Settlement Amount against (i) any margin or other collateral held by a party in connection with any Credit Support Obligation relating to the Contract; and (ii) any amount(s) (including any excess cash margin or excess cash collateral) owed or held by the party that is entitled to the Net Settlement Amount under any other agreement or arrangement between the parties.

Triangular Setoff Option:

10.3.2.   The Non-Defaulting Party shall net or aggregate, as appropriate, any and all amounts owing between the parties under Section 10.3.1, so that all such amounts are netted or aggregated to a single liquidated amount payable by one party to the other (the "Net Settlement Amount"). At its sole option, and without prior Notice to the Defaulting Party, the Non-Defaulting Party is hereby authorized to setoff (i) any Net Settlement Amount against any margin or other collateral held by a party in connection with any Credit Support Obligation relating to the Contract; (ii) any Net Settlement Amount against any amount(s) (including any excess cash margin or excess cash collateral) owed by or to a party under any other agreement or arrangement between the parties; (iii) any Net Settlement Amount owed to the Non-Defaulting Party against any amount(s) (including any excess cash margin or excess cash collateral) owed by the Non-Defaulting Party or its Affiliates to the Defaulting Party under any other agreement or arrangement; (iv) any Net Settlement Amount owed to the Defaulting Party against any amount(s) (including any excess cash margin or excess cash collateral) owed by the Defaulting Party to the Non-Defaulting Party or its Affiliates under any other agreement or arrangement; and/or (v) any Net Settlement Amount owed to the Defaulting Party against any amount(s) (including any excess cash margin or excess cash collateral) owed by the Defaulting Party or its Affiliates to the Non-Defaulting Party under any other agreement or arrangement.

Other Agreement Setoffs Do Not Apply:

10.3.2.   The Non-Defaulting Party shall net or aggregate, as appropriate, any and all amounts owing between the parties under Section 10.3.1, so that all such amounts are netted or aggregated to a single liquidated amount payable by one party to the other (the "Net Settlement Amount"). At its sole option and without prior Notice to the Defaulting Party, the Non-Defaulting Party may setoff any Net Settlement Amount against any margin or other collateral held by a party in connection with any Credit Support Obligation relating to the Contract.

10.3.3.   If any obligation that is to be included in any netting, aggregation or setoff pursuant to Section 10.3.2 is unascertained, the Non-Defaulting Party may in good faith estimate that obligation and net, aggregate or setoff, as applicable, in respect of the estimate, subject to the Non-Defaulting Party accounting to the Defaulting Party when the obligation is ascertained. Any amount not then due which is included in any netting, aggregation or setoff pursuant to Section 10.3.2 shall be discounted to net present value in a commercially reasonable manner determined by the Non-Defaulting Party.

10.4.   As soon as practicable after a liquidation, Notice shall be given by the Non-Defaulting Party to the Defaulting Party of the Net Settlement Amount, and whether the Net Settlement Amount is due to or due from the Non-Defaulting Party. The Notice shall include a written statement explaining in reasonable detail the calculation of the Net Settlement Amount, provided that failure to give such Notice shall not affect the validity or enforceability of the liquidation or give rise to any claim by the Defaulting Party against the Non-Defaulting Party. The Net Settlement Amount as well as any setoffs applied against such amount pursuant to Section 10.3.2, shall be paid by the close of business on the second Business Day following such Notice, which date shall not be earlier than the Early Termination Date. Interest on any unpaid portion of the Net Settlement Amount as adjusted by setoffs, shall accrue from the date due until the date of payment at a rate equal to the lower of (i) the then-effective prime rate of interest published under "Money Rates" by The Wall Street Journal, plus two percent per annum; or (ii) the maximum applicable lawful interest rate.

10.5.   The parties agree that the transactions hereunder constitute a "forward contract" within the meaning of the United States Bankruptcy Code and that Buyer and Seller are each "forward contract merchants" within the meaning of the United States Bankruptcy Code.

10.6.   The Non-Defaulting Party's remedies under this Section 10 are the sole and exclusive remedies of the Non-Defaulting Party with respect to the occurrence of any Early Termination Date. Each party reserves to itself all other rights, setoffs, counterclaims and other defenses that it is or may be entitled to arising from the Contract.

357

10.7.   With respect to this Section 10, if the parties have executed a separate netting agreement with close-out netting provisions, the terms and conditions therein shall prevail to the extent inconsistent herewith.

SECTION 11.   FORCE MAJEURE

11.1.   Except with regard to a party's obligation to make payment(s) due under Section 7, Section 10.4, and Imbalance Charges under Section 4, neither party shall be liable to the other for failure to perform a Firm obligation, to the extent such failure was caused by Force Majeure. The term "Force Majeure" as employed herein means any cause not reasonably within the control of the party claiming suspension, as further defined in Section 11.2.

11.2.   Force Majeure shall include, but not be limited to, the following: (i) physical events such as acts of God, landslides, lightning, earthquakes, fires, storms or storm warnings, such as hurricanes, which result in evacuation of the affected area, floods, washouts, explosions, breakage or accident or necessity of repairs to machinery or equipment or lines of pipe; (ii) weather related events affecting an entire geographic region, such as low temperatures which cause freezing or failure of wells or lines of pipe; (iii) interruption and/or curtailment of Firm transportation and/or storage by Transporters; (iv) acts of others such as strikes, lockouts or other industrial disturbances, riots, sabotage, insurrections or wars, or acts of terror, and (v) governmental actions such as necessity for compliance with any court order, law, statute, ordinance, regulation, or policy having the effect of law promulgated by a governmental authority having jurisdiction. Seller and Buyer shall make reasonable efforts to avoid the adverse impacts of a Force Majeure and to resolve the event or occurrence once it has occurred in order to resume performance.

11.3.   Neither party shall be entitled to the benefit of the provisions of Force Majeure to the extent performance is affected by any or all of the following circumstances: (i) the curtailment of interruptible or secondary Firm transportation unless primary, in-path, Firm transportation is also curtailed; (ii) the party claiming excuse failed to remedy the condition and to resume the performance of such covenants or obligations with reasonable dispatch; or (iii) economic hardship, to include, without limitation, Seller's ability to sell Gas at a higher or more advantageous price than the Contract Price, Buyer's ability to purchase Gas at a lower or more advantageous price than the Contract Price, or a regulatory agency disallowing, in whole or in part, the pass through of costs resulting from this Contract; (iv) the loss of Buyer's market(s) or Buyer's inability to use or resell Gas purchased hereunder, except, in either case, as provided in Section 11.2; or (v) the loss or failure of Seller's gas supply or depletion of reserves, except, in either case, as provided in Section 11.2. The party claiming Force Majeure shall not be excused from its responsibility for Imbalance Charges.

11.4.   Notwithstanding anything to the contrary herein, the parties agree that the settlement of strikes, lockouts or other industrial disturbances shall be within the sole discretion of the party experiencing such disturbance.

11.5.   The party whose performance is prevented by Force Majeure must provide Notice to the other party. Initial Notice may be given orally; however, written Notice with reasonably full particulars of the event or occurrence is required as soon as reasonably possible. Upon providing written Notice of Force Majeure to the other party, the affected party will be relieved of its obligation, from the onset of the Force Majeure event, to make or accept delivery of Gas, as applicable, to the extent and for the duration of Force Majeure, and neither party shall be deemed to have failed in such obligations to the other during such occurrence or event.

11.6.   Notwithstanding Sections 11.2 and 11.3, the parties may agree to alternative Force Majeure provisions in a Transaction Confirmation executed in writing by both parties.

SECTION 12.   TERM

This Contract may be terminated on 30 Day's written Notice, but shall remain in effect until the expiration of the latest Delivery Period of any transaction(s). The rights of either party pursuant to Section 7.6, Section 10, Section 13, the obligations to make payment hereunder, and the obligation of either party to indemnify the other, pursuant hereto shall survive the termination of the Base Contract or any transaction.

SECTION 13.   LIMITATIONS

FOR BREACH OF ANY PROVISION FOR WHICH AN EXPRESS REMEDY OR MEASURE OF DAMAGES IS PROVIDED, SUCH EXPRESS REMEDY OR MEASURE OF DAMAGES SHALL BE THE SOLE AND EXCLUSIVE REMEDY. A PARTY'S LIABILITY HEREUNDER SHALL BE LIMITED AS SET FORTH IN SUCH PROVISION, AND ALL OTHER REMEDIES OR DAMAGES AT LAW OR IN EQUITY ARE WAIVED. IF NO REMEDY OR MEASURE OF DAMAGES IS EXPRESSLY PROVIDED HEREIN OR IN A TRANSACTION, A PARTY'S LIABILITY SHALL BE LIMITED TO DIRECT ACTUAL DAMAGES ONLY. SUCH DIRECT ACTUAL DAMAGES SHALL BE THE SOLE AND EXCLUSIVE REMEDY, AND ALL OTHER REMEDIES OR DAMAGES AT LAW OR IN EQUITY ARE WAIVED. UNLESS EXPRESSLY HEREIN PROVIDED, NEITHER PARTY SHALL BE LIABLE FOR CONSEQUENTIAL, INCIDENTAL, PUNITIVE, EXEMPLARY OR INDIRECT DAMAGES, LOST PROFITS OR OTHER BUSINESS INTERRUPTION DAMAGES, BY STATUTE, IN TORT OR CONTRACT, UNDER ANY INDEMNITY PROVISION OR OTHERWISE. IT IS THE INTENT OF THE PARTIES THAT THE LIMITATIONS HEREIN IMPOSED ON REMEDIES AND THE MEASURE OF DAMAGES BE WITHOUT REGARD TO THE CAUSE OR CAUSES RELATED THERETO, INCLUDING THE NEGLIGENCE OF ANY PARTY, WHETHER SUCH NEGLIGENCE BE SOLE, JOINT OR CONCURRENT, OR ACTIVE OR PASSIVE. TO THE EXTENT ANY DAMAGES REQUIRED TO BE PAID HEREUNDER ARE LIQUIDATED, THE PARTIES ACKNOWLEDGE THAT THE DAMAGES ARE DIFFICULT OR IMPOSSIBLE TO DETERMINE, OR OTHERWISE OBTAINING AN ADEQUATE REMEDY IS INCONVENIENT AND THE DAMAGES CALCULATED HEREUNDER CONSTITUTE A REASONABLE APPROXIMATION OF THE HARM OR LOSS.

SECTION 14. MARKET DISRUPTION

If a Market Disruption Event has occurred then the parties shall negotiate in good faith to agree on a replacement price for the Floating Price (or on a method for determining a replacement price for the Floating Price) for the affected Day, and if the parties have not so agreed on or before the second Business Day following the affected Day then the replacement price for the Floating Price shall be determined within the next two following Business Days with each party obtaining, in good faith and from non-affiliated market participants in the relevant market, two quotes for prices of Gas for the affected Day of a similar quality and quantity in the geographical location closest in proximity to the Delivery Point and averaging the four quotes. If either party fails to provide two quotes then the average of the other party's two quotes shall determine the replacement price for the Floating Price. "Floating Price" means the price or a factor of the price agreed to in the transaction as being based upon a specified index. "Market Disruption Event" means, with respect to an index specified for a transaction, any of the following events: (a) the failure of the index to announce or publish information necessary for determining the Floating Price; (b) the failure of trading to commence or the permanent discontinuation or material suspension of trading on the exchange or market acting as the index; (c) the temporary or permanent discontinuance or unavailability of the index; (d) the temporary or permanent closing of any exchange acting as the index; or (e) both parties agree that a material change in the formula for or the method of determining the Floating Price has occurred. For the purposes of the calculation of a replacement price for the Floating Price, all numbers shall be rounded to three decimal places. If the fourth decimal number is five or greater, then the third decimal number shall be increased by one and if the fourth decimal number is less than five, then the third decimal number shall remain unchanged.

SECTION 15. MISCELLANEOUS

15.1. This Contract shall be binding upon and inure to the benefit of the successors, assigns, personal representatives, and heirs of the respective parties hereto, and the covenants, conditions, rights and obligations of this Contract shall run for the full term of this Contract. No assignment of this Contract, in whole or in part, will be made without the prior written consent of the non-assigning party (and shall not relieve the assigning party from liability hereunder), which consent will not be unreasonably withheld or delayed; provided, either party may (i) transfer, sell, pledge, encumber, or assign this Contract or the accounts, revenues, or proceeds hereof in connection with any financing or other financial arrangements, or (ii) transfer its interest to any parent or Affiliate by assignment, merger or otherwise without the prior approval of the other party. Upon any such assignment, transfer and assumption, the transferor shall remain principally liable for and shall not be relieved of or discharged from any obligations hereunder.

15.2. If any provision in this Contract is determined to be invalid, void or unenforceable by any court having jurisdiction, such determination shall not invalidate, void, or make unenforceable any other provision, agreement or covenant of this Contract.

15.3. No waiver of any breach of this Contract shall be held to be a waiver of any other or subsequent breach.

15.4. This Contract sets forth all understandings between the parties respecting each transaction subject hereto, and any prior contracts, understandings and representations, whether oral or written, relating to such transactions are merged into and superseded by this Contract and any effective transaction(s). This Contract may be amended only by a writing executed by both parties.

15.5. The interpretation and performance of this Contract shall be governed by the laws of the jurisdiction as indicated on the Base Contract, excluding, however, any conflict of laws rule which would apply the law of another jurisdiction.

15.6. This Contract and all provisions herein will be subject to all applicable and valid statutes, rules, orders and regulations of any governmental authority having jurisdiction over the parties, their facilities, or Gas supply, this Contract or transaction or any provisions thereof.

15.7. There is no third party beneficiary to this Contract.

15.8. Each party to this Contract represents and warrants that it has full and complete authority to enter into and perform this Contract. Each person who executes this Contract on behalf of either party represents and warrants that it has full and complete authority to do so and that such party will be bound thereby.

15.9. The headings and subheadings contained in this Contract are used solely for convenience and do not constitute a part of this Contract between the parties and shall not be used to construe or interpret the provisions of this Contract.

15.10. Unless the parties have elected on the Base Contract not to make this Section 15.10 applicable to this Contract, neither party shall disclose directly or indirectly without the prior written consent of the other party the terms of any transaction to a third party (other than the employees, lenders, royalty owners, counsel, accountants and other agents of the party, or prospective purchasers of all or substantially all of a party's assets or of any rights under this Contract, provided such persons shall have agreed to keep such terms confidential) except (i) in order to comply with any applicable law, order, regulation, or exchange rule, (ii) to the extent necessary for the enforcement of this Contract , (iii) to the extent necessary to implement any transaction, (iv) to the extent necessary to comply with a regulatory agency's reporting requirements including but not limited to gas cost recovery proceedings; or (v) to the extent such information is delivered to such third party for the sole purpose of calculating a published index. Each party shall notify the other party of any proceeding of which it is aware which may result in disclosure of the terms of any transaction (other than as permitted hereunder) and use reasonable efforts to prevent or limit the disclosure. The existence of this Contract is not subject to this confidentiality obligation. Subject to Section 13, the parties shall be entitled to all remedies available at law or in equity to enforce, or seek relief in connection with this confidentiality obligation. The terms of any transaction hereunder shall be kept confidential by the parties hereto for one year from the expiration of the transaction.

In the event that disclosure is required by a governmental body or applicable law, the party subject to such requirement may disclose the material terms of this Contract to the extent so required, but shall promptly notify the other party, prior to disclosure,

Copyright © 2006 North American Energy Standards Board, Inc.
All Rights Reserved
Page 11 of 13

NAESB Standard 6.3.1
September 5, 2006

359

and shall cooperate (consistent with the disclosing party's legal obligations) with the other party's efforts to obtain protective orders or similar restraints with respect to such disclosure at the expense of the other party.

15.11. The parties may agree to dispute resolution procedures in Special Provisions attached to the Base Contract or in a Transaction Confirmation executed in writing by both parties

15.12. Any original executed Base Contract, Transaction Confirmation or other related document may be digitally copied, photocopied, or stored on computer tapes and disks (the "Imaged Agreement"). The Imaged Agreement, if introduced as evidence on paper, the Transaction Confirmation, if introduced as evidence in automated facsimile form, the recording, if introduced as evidence in its original form, and all computer records of the foregoing, if introduced as evidence in printed format, in any judicial, arbitration, mediation or administrative proceedings will be admissible as between the parties to the same extent and under the same conditions as other business records originated and maintained in documentary form. Neither Party shall object to the admissibility of the recording, the Transaction Confirmation, or the Imaged Agreement on the basis that such were not originated or maintained in documentary form. However, nothing herein shall be construed as a waiver of any other objection to the admissibility of such evidence.

Copyright © 2006 North American Energy Standards Board, Inc.
All Rights Reserved
Page 12 of 13

NAESB Standard 6.3.1
September 5, 2006

360

| Letterhead/Logo | Date: _____, _____ |
| | Transaction Confirmation #: _____ |

This Transaction Confirmation is subject to the Base Contract between Seller and Buyer dated _____. The terms of this Transaction Confirmation are binding unless disputed in writing within 2 Business Days of receipt unless otherwise specified in the Base Contract.

SELLER:

_____
_____
_____
Attn: _____
Phone: _____
Fax: _____
Base Contract No. _____
Transporter: _____
Transporter Contract Number: _____

BUYER:

_____
_____
_____
Attn: _____
Phone: _____
Fax: _____
Base Contract No. _____
Transporter: _____
Transporter Contract Number: _____

Contract Price: $_____/MMBtu or _____

Delivery Period: Begin: _____, ____   End: _____, ____

Performance Obligation and Contract Quantity: (Select One)

Firm (Fixed Quantity):

_____ MMBtus/day

      EFP

Firm (Variable Quantity):

_____ MMBtus/day Minimum
_____ MMBtus/day Maximum
subject to Section 4.2. at election of
Buyer or   Seller

Interruptible:

Up to _____ MMBtus/day

Delivery Point(s): _____
(If a pooling point is used, list a specific geographic and pipeline location):

Special Conditions:

Seller: _____

By: _____

Title: _____

Date: _____

Buyer: _____

By: _____

Title: _____

Date: _____

NOTES

1.   This copyrighted form is furnished by the North American Energy Standards Board (NAESB), 1301 Fannin, Suite 2350, Houston, TX 77002, http://www.naesb.org. This form is reprinted with the permission of the NAESB and is intended for illustrative purposes only. This form establishes "Base Contract" terms that will govern gas transactions between the parties and may be used for both short- and long-term contracts. However, the specific details of each individual gas transaction will be evidenced by the "EXHIBIT A" titled "Transaction Confirmation for Immediate Delivery." The "Base Contract" incorporating the "General Terms and Conditions" will be negotiated once and put into place. The "EXHIBIT A" will then be used to establish the price and delivery requirements of specific gas volumes for each transaction under the "Base Contract." This avoids the need to renegotiate the details contained in the "Base Contract."

2.   Term contracts, which completely dominated the gas market in previous decades, are still used, but are likely to be for much shorter periods than in earlier years. Before 1980 such contracts were frequently for 20 years or for the life of the well. Today the period will probably range from one to five years.

3.   Typical features of earlier gas contracts that frequently led to disputes included provisions dedicating production from specified wells or fields to the contract and take-or-pay clauses. The dedication provision effectively prevented the producer from selling gas to anyone but the pipeline purchaser. However, during times of falling prices or oversupply the pipeline frequently found it economically impractical to connect to new wells in the field dedicated to contract performance, thereby making it impossible for the seller to market production from new wells. Even more litigation was generated by take-or-pay clauses, which required the purchaser to take a specified quantity of gas or pay for it even if not taken. Such clauses varied significantly in complexity. The following is an example of a relatively simple take-or-pay clause.

Subject to all the other provisions of this Contract, Seller agrees to sell and deliver and Pipeline agrees to purchase and receive, or pay for if made available hereunder but not taken, a daily contract quantity of gas, averaged over each accounting period (contract quantity) during the term hereof, equal to seventy-five percent (75 %) of the maximum quantity of gas the Seller's well/s can deliver to Pipeline.

GAS PURCHASE & PROCESSING CONTRACT
Between _____ as Seller
And DCP MIDSTREAM, LP as Buyer
Dated _____, 200_

* * *

* * *

GAS PURCHASE CONTRACT

This Contract is entered as of _____ __, 20__, between _____ ("Seller") and **DCP MIDSTREAM, LP** ("Buyer").

For and in consideration of the mutual covenants contained herein, the parties agree as follows:

    1.   **COMMITMENT.**   Seller will sell and deliver and Buyer will purchase and receive gas produced from all wells now or later located on all oil and gas interests now or later owned or controlled by Seller on or allocated to the following lands in _____ County, [State]:

                             See Exhibit B.

Definitions and General Terms and Conditions included in this Contract are attached as Exhibit A. All Exhibits referenced herein are attached and incorporated by reference.

    2.   **DELIVERY POINTS.** The Delivery Points for gas to be delivered by Seller to Buyer for existing sources of production will be at the inlets of Buyer's Facilities at a mutually agreeable site at or near Seller's sources of production. The Delivery Points for future sources of production committed under this Contract will be established under Section B.2 of Exhibit A. Title to the gas and all its components shall pass to and vest in Buyer at the Delivery Points without regard to the purposes for which Buyer may later use or sell the gas or its components.

    3.   **DELIVERY PRESSURE.** Seller will deliver the gas at the Delivery Points at a pressure sufficient to enable it to enter Buyer's Facilities against the working pressure at reasonably uniform rates of delivery, not to exceed the maximum allowable operating pressure established by Buyer or pressures that prevent others from producing ratably. Buyer in its discretion may require that Seller install and operate a pressure relief or reduction device upstream of any Delivery Point set at the pressure designated by Buyer to limit the pressure at which Seller delivers gas, where Seller's deliveries might interfere with ratable deliveries from others, or to enhance safety.

    4.   **QUANTITY.** (a)   Seller shall deliver and Buyer shall purchase and take Seller's gas subject to the operating conditions and capacity of Buyer's Facilities and resale markets. Although there is no specific purchase quantity, Buyer will use commercially reasonable efforts to market gas for resale and operate its facilities in an effort to maintain consistent takes of all available quantities. If Buyer takes less than the full quantities available, Buyer will use commercially reasonable efforts to purchase gas from the lands covered by this Contract ratably with its purchases of similar gas in each common gathering system or area within its capabilities using existing facilities, in compliance with Buyer's existing contracts and with applicable laws and regulations, including ratable purchases from Buyer's Affiliates.

    (b)   Seller may dispose of any gas not taken by Buyer for any reason, including events of Force Majeure, subject to Buyer's right to resume purchases at any subsequent time. If Buyer does not take gas for ____ consecutive Days and Seller secures a different temporary market, Buyer may resume purchases only upon ____ Days' advance written notice as of the beginning of a month unless otherwise agreed.

(c)   Seller will use commercially reasonable efforts to deliver gas meeting the quality requirements of Section F of Exhibit A and to avoid delivery of Inferior Liquids as defined in Section A of Exhibit A. If the gas at any Delivery Point becomes insufficient in volume, quality, or pressure, Buyer may cease gas takes from the Delivery Point as long as the condition exists. If Buyer ceases taking gas under this Section for ___ consecutive Days for reasons other than quality [Exhibit A Section F] or Force Majeure [Exhibit A Section H], Seller may terminate this Contract with respect to the affected Delivery Points as to the then productive zones upon ____ Days' advance written notice to Buyer; provided that during the notice period Buyer may resume consistent takes and purchases, and thereby avoid Contract termination under Seller's notice.

5.   PRICE.

5.1   Consideration.   As full consideration for the gas and all its components delivered to Buyer each Month, Buyer shall pay Seller (a) ___% of the net value under Section 5.2 for Residue Gas attributable to Seller's gas, and (b) ___% of the net value under Section 5.3 below for any recovered NGLs attributable to Seller's gas. No separate payment or value calculation is to be made under this Contract for helium, sulfur, CO_2, other non-hydrocarbons, or for Inferior Liquids.

5.2   Residue Gas Resale Proceeds.   (a)   The Residue Gas value will be the weighted average of the prices per MMBtu received by Buyer f.o.b. Buyer's Facilities for Residue Gas sold during the Month. The particular resales and sites where resales are made for purposes of weighted average resale price calculations will be established from time to time in good faith by Buyer. The prices received f.o.b. Buyer's Facilities shall be the amounts per MMBtu actually received by Buyer, including any allowances, adjustments, and payments received by Buyer attributable to the gathering and resale of gas sold from Buyer's Facilities, and any reimbursement for severance or similar taxes on production. However, all costs, adjustments, and charges incurred by Buyer or its Affiliates for and value added by handling, transportation, storage, and resale of gas downstream from Buyer's Facilities will be deducted or excluded from resale prices. Some of the downstream items to be deducted are transportation and storage costs, transport fuel charges, and sales and excise taxes levied on Buyer's resales. If Buyer installs or operates additional facilities downstream from Buyer's Facilities to provide additional access to resale markets or to meet the specifications of Buyer's resale purchasers or transporters, Buyer may deduct the reasonable cost (including return on and of investment) of installation and operation of those added facilities.

(b)   Buyer shall have the right in its sole discretion to negotiate and renegotiate gas sales contracts from time to time as market conditions change. Buyer shall not be obligated to make payment to Seller based on any price that Buyer for any reason does not receive or retain. Should Buyer make payment to Seller based on a price that Buyer does not receive or retain, the price shall be reduced accordingly, and Seller will refund to Buyer or Buyer may at its option recoup any previous excess payment against subsequent payments.

5.3   NGL Value.   The net value of any recovered NGLs attributable to Seller will be determined by multiplying the quantity of each NGL component attributable to Seller's gas by the average price per gallon for each NGL component f.o.b. Buyer's Facilities. "Average price" as to each NGL component means the simple average of the midpoint of the daily high/low spot price for (i) ethane in E-P mix, (ii) Non-TET propane, (iii) Non-TET isobutane, (iv) Non-TET normal butane, and (v) Non-TET natural gasoline (pentanes and heavier) during the month as reported for Mont Belvieu, Texas by the *Oil Price Information Service* (or in its absence, a comparable successor publication designated by Buyer) less a transportation, fractionation, and storage ("TF&S") fee of $0.0_____ per gallon. As of January 1 of each calendar year beginning with ____, Buyer will adjust the TF&S fee upward or downward as follows, but it will never be less than the initial fee. Buyer will adjust (i) __% of the TF&S fee by an amount equal to the annual percentage of change in the preliminary estimate of the implicit price deflator, seasonally adjusted, for the gross domestic product ("GDP") as computed and

1 most recently published by the U.S. Department of Commerce, rounded to the nearest 100th cent, or in
2 its absence, a similar successor adjustment factor designated by Buyer, and (ii) __% of the TF&S fee by
3 the percentage difference between the yearly average of the previous year's monthly Index Prices
4 defined in Section 5.2 above and those for the second previous year.

5   **5.4**   **Low Volume Delivery Points.** The price for gas delivered at any metered Delivery
6 Points at which the volume delivered to Buyer has been less than _____ Mcf per month for ____
7 consecutive months will be reduced to _____ of that computed under Sections 5.1, 5.2, and 5.3
8 effective the first Day of the month following the _____ month period. The price for gas from the
9 affected Delivery Points will remain so reduced until the quantity delivered from the Delivery Point is
10 again at least ____ Mcf per month for _____ consecutive months effective as of the first Day of the
11 following month.

12   **5.5**   **Allocation of Residue Gas and NGLs.** Buyer will determine the Residue Gas and
13 NGLs attributable to Seller on a proportional basis by component using the following definitions and
14 procedures. Additional definitions are in Section A of Exhibit A. From time to time Buyer may make
15 changes and adjustments in its allocation methods to improve accuracy or efficiency.

16   **(a)**   **NGLs Allocable to Seller.** The quantity of each NGL component allocable to
17 Seller's gas will be determined by multiplying the total quantity of each NGL component
18 recovered at the plant or plants by a fraction. The numerator will be the gallons of that NGL
19 component contained in the gas delivered by Seller, determined by chromatographic analysis or
20 other accepted method in the industry, and the denominator will be the total gallons of that
21 component contained in all gas delivered to Buyer from sources connected to Buyer's Facilities.
22 Sub-area breakdowns may be used as stated in (b)(ii) below.

23   **(b)**   **Residue Gas Allocable to Seller.**
24   (i)   The MMBtus of "Residue Gas allocable to Seller" will be determined by
25 multiplying the MMBtus of "Residue Gas available for sale" from Buyer's Facilities by a
26 fraction. The numerator will be the "theoretical MMBtus of Residue Gas remaining from
27 Seller's gas" delivered by Seller, and the denominator will be the total of the theoretical MMBtus
28 of Residue Gas remaining from all gas delivered to Buyer from the common sources connected
29 to Buyer's Facilities. "Residue Gas available for sale" means all remaining Residue Gas
30 available from Buyer's Facilities, net of Residue Gas used for the operation of Buyer's Facilities.
31 "Theoretical MMBtus of Residue Gas remaining from Seller's gas" means the sum of the
32 MMBtus of methane and heavier hydrocarbons contained in Seller's gas, determined by
33 chromatographic analysis or other accepted method in the industry, less the MMBtus of
34 recovered NGLs attributable to Seller's gas.

35   (ii)   Buyer may apply the allocation principles of this Section repeatedly to sub-areas
36 or separately measured systems to improve accuracy. For example, Buyer may allocate plant
37 NGL and Residue Gas volumes to field gathering system boosters, then use the same principles
38 to allocate those results further to sources behind those boosters. For any gas delivered initially
39 into a high-pressure gathering system, unless sub-area allocations to low pressure sources or
40 other methods are used, Seller's theoretical MMBtus of Residue Gas remaining will be adjusted
41 upward by four percent (4%) to recognize the fuel economies realized by Buyer's avoidance of
42 compression for these high pressure deliveries.

43   (iii)   The parties desire that Buyer have adequate incentives to take actions that
44 increase efficiency and decrease fuel consumption. Therefore, if Buyer makes material capital
45 investments to develop fuel conservation projects, including without limitation waste heat
46 recovery, more efficient compression, or other expenditures that result in reduction of fuel
47 consumption, Buyer may retain the benefits of each project during an agreed payout period of

three (3) years after project startup; then the benefits of the project will be shared by the parties in the percentages stated in Section 5.1. During the agreed payout period, Buyer will allocate residue gas and NGLs by deducting from the available quantities the difference between the average monthly fuel consumption for the 12 month period prior to project startup and the reduced computed fuel consumption after project startup. At the end of the agreed payout period, Buyer shall resume payments based on actual fuel consumed except to the extent other fuel reduction projects are in payout periods.

6.   **TERM.**   This Contract shall be in force for a primary term through _____, 200_, and from year to year thereafter until canceled by either party as of the end of the primary term or as of any anniversary thereafter by giving the other party at least ____ Days' but no more than ____ Days' advance written notice of termination.

7.   **ADDRESSES AND NOTICES.** Either party may give notices to the other party by first class mail postage prepaid, by overnight delivery service, or by facsimile with receipt confirmed at the following addresses or other addresses furnished by a party by written notice. Unless Seller objects in writing, Buyer may also use Seller's current address for payments. Any telephone numbers below are solely for information and are not for Contract notices. The parties opt out of electronic delivery of notices and amendments under this Contract, except that notices and hand-signed amendments may be delivered by facsimile with receipt confirmed as stated above.

Notices to Seller - Correspondence   [Seller]
Attn: Gas Contract Administration
[address]
Phone: (__) _____
Fax: (__) _____

Notices to Seller – Payments: Bank: _____
Acct. #: _____
ABA/ACH: _____

Notices to Buyer – Billings & Statements: DCP Midstream, LP
Attn: Revenue Accounting
[address]
Phone: (__) _____
Fax: (__) _____

Buyer - Correspondence   DCP Midstream, LP
Attn: Contract Administration
[address]
Phone: (__) _____
Fax: (__) _____

8.   **TERMINATION OF PRIOR CONTRACTS AND RELEASE.**

8.1   **Termination and Release.**   This Contract terminates and supersedes any prior contracts for the sale or handling of gas between the parties or their predecessors in interest that apply or applied to any gas produced from any sources covered by this Contract effective as of its date. In negotiating the terms of this Contract, the parties have compromised and settled any and all price, fee, payment, and other disputes relating to or under the superseded contract(s). In consideration of the covenants contained herein, each party hereby releases the other party, its Affiliates, and its predecessors in interest under the prior contracts from any causes of action, claims, and liabilities (i) that they failed to pay the full prices or fees under the prior contracts, including interest, (ii) that they failed to perform any other obligation under the prior contracts, and (iii) arising from their relationship as parties to the prior contracts.

8.2 **Exceptions.** This termination and release does not include, and the parties expressly retain, the right to receive payments under the prior contract(s) for current gas production for which payment is not yet due and for which a party has not yet made payment in the ordinary course of business. This mutual release also does not include matters relating to title to gas and gas processing rights, Seller's obligations for payment of third parties and severance taxes, related interest and penalties, or gas imbalances under prior gathering or take in kind agreements.

The parties have signed this Contract by their duly authorized representatives as of the date first set forth above.

[date and signatures]
* * *

EXHIBIT A to GAS PURCHASE AND PROCESSING CONTRACT
Between _____ as Seller and
DCP MIDSTREAM, LP as Buyer
Dated as of _____, 20__

GENERAL TERMS & CONDITIONS
A. DEFINITIONS

Except where the context indicates a different meaning or intent, and whether or not capitalized, the following terms will have meanings as follows:

a.   Affiliate – a company (i) in which a party owns directly or indirectly 50% or more of the issued and outstanding voting stock or other equity interests; (ii) which owns directly or indirectly 50% or more of the issued and outstanding voting stock or equity interests of the party; and (iii) in which a company described in (ii) owns, directly or indirectly, 50% or more of the issued and outstanding voting stock or other equity interests.

b.   Btu – British thermal unit. MMBtu – one million Btus.

c.   Buyer's Facilities – the gas delivered by Seller will be gathered in gathering systems and may be redelivered to a gas processing plant or plants for the removal of NGLs together with gas produced from other properties. The gathering systems and plant or plants, or successor facilities, are "Buyer's Facilities" whether owned by buyer, an Affiliate of Buyer, or an unaffiliated third party. No facilities downstream of the processing plant or plants other than short connecting lines to transmission lines are included in "Buyer's Facilities."

d.   Day – a period of 24 consecutive hours beginning and ending at _____ local time, or other 24 hour period designated by Buyer and a downstream pipeline.

e.   Delivery Points – whether one or more, see Sections 2, B.1 and B.2.

f.   Force Majeure – see Section H.2 below.

g.   Gas or gas – all natural gas that arrives at the surface in the gaseous phase, including all hydrocarbon and non-hydrocarbon components, casinghead gas produced from oil wells, gas well gas, and stock tank vapors.

h.   GPM – NGL gallons per Mcf.

i.   Inferior Liquids – Mixed crude oil, slop oil, salt water, nuisance liquids, and other liquids recovered by Buyer in its gathering system or at plant inlet receivers. Revenues from Inferior Liquids, drips, and other gathering system liquids will be retained by Buyer to defray costs of treating and handling; Buyer will not allocate or pay for those liquids.

j. Mcf – 1,000 cubic feet of gas at standard base conditions of 60°F and _____ psia.

k. MMcf – 1,000 Mcf.

l. Month or month – a calendar month beginning on the first Day of a Month.

m. NGL or NGLs – natural gas liquids, or ethane and heavier liquefiable hydrocarbons separated from gas and any incidental methane in NGL after processing.

n. psi – pounds per square inch; psia – psi absolute; psig – psi gauge.

o. Residue Gas – merchantable hydrocarbon gas available for sale from Buyer's Facilities remaining after processing, and hydrocarbon gas resold by Buyer without first being processed.

p. TET – price quotes for NGL on the Texas Eastern Products Pipeline Company, LLC system.

q. TF&S – NGL transportation, fractionation, and storage, see Section 5.3.

B. DELIVERY DATE; COMPRESSION

B.1 **Connected Sources Delivery Date.** As to committed sources of production already connected to Buyer's Facilities, deliveries under this Contract will commence as of _____, 200__.

B.2 **Additional Sources.** As to sources not yet connected, Seller will commence and complete with due diligence the construction of the facilities necessary to enable Seller to deliver the committed gas at the Delivery Points and Buyer will cause prompt commencement and complete with due diligence the construction of the facilities necessary and economically feasible to enable Buyer or its gas gathering contractor to receive deliveries of gas at the Delivery Points. If Buyer determines it is not profitable to construct the facilities, Seller will have the option to construct facilities necessary to deliver gas into Buyer's then existing facilities. If neither Buyer nor Seller elect to construct the necessary facilities, either party may cancel this Contract as to the affected gas upon ____ Days advance written notice to the other.

B.3 **Delivery Rates.** Under normal conditions, Seller and Buyer will deliver and receive gas at reasonably uniform rates of delivery. Seller will have agents or employees available at all reasonable times to receive advice and directions from Buyer for changes in the rates of delivery of gas as required from time to time.

B.4 **Options to Compress.** If Seller's wells become incapable of delivering gas into Buyer's Facilities, neither party will be obligated to compress, but either party will have the option to do so. If neither party elects to compress within a reasonable time after the need for compression appears, Buyer upon written request of Seller will either arrange promptly to provide compression or as Seller's sole remedy, release the affected gas sources as to the then-producing formations from commitment under this Contract. If Buyer provides additional compression, the price to be paid by Buyer for Seller's gas shall be reduced by a reasonable compression fee that allows recovery of the related fuel and provides Buyer a reasonable return on investment.

C. RESERVATIONS OF SELLER

C.1 **Reservations.** Seller reserves the following rights with respect to its interests in the oil and gas properties committed by Seller to Buyer under this Contract together with sufficient gas to satisfy those rights:

a. To operate Seller's oil and gas properties free from control by Buyer as Seller in Seller's sole discretion deems advisable, including without limitation the right, but never the obligation, to drill new wells, to repair and rework old wells, renew or extend, in whole or in part, any oil and gas lease covering any of the oil and gas properties, and to abandon any well or surrender any oil and gas lease, in whole or in part, when no longer deemed by Seller to be capable of producing gas in paying quantities under normal methods of operation.

b. To use gas for developing and operating Seller's oil and gas properties committed under this Contract and to fulfill obligations to Seller's lessors for those properties.

1   c.   To pool, combine, and unitize any of Seller's oil and gas properties with other properties in the
2 same field, and to alter pooling, combinations, or units; this Contract will then cover Seller's allocated
3 interest in unitized production insofar as that interest is attributable to the oil and gas properties
4 committed under this Contract, and the description of the property committed will be considered to have
5 been amended accordingly.
6 **C.2**   **Exception.** Notwithstanding Section C.1, Seller will not engage in any operation, including
7 without limitation reinjection, recycling, or curtailment, that would materially reduce the amount of gas
8 available for sale to Buyer except upon ____ Days advance written notice to Buyer, or as much advance
9 notice as is feasible under the circumstances. If Seller ceases or materially curtails deliveries to Buyer
10 under this Section C, the Contract term will be extended by the duration of the interruptions and
11 curtailments. Buyer will own and be entitled to collect and pay Seller for any NGLs that condense or
12 are manufactured from gas during any of Seller's operations, excluding crude oil and distillate recovered
13 from gas by conventional type mechanical separation equipment and not delivered to Buyer.
14   **D. METERING AND MEASUREMENT**
15 **D.1**   **Buyer to Install Meters.** Buyer will own, maintain, and operate orifice meters or other
16 measuring devices of standard make at or near the Delivery Points. Except as otherwise specifically
17 provided to the contrary in this Section D, orifice meters or other measurement devices will be installed
18 and volumes computed in accordance with accepted industry practice. Buyer may re-use metering
19 equipment not meeting current standards but meeting 1985 or later published standards for gas sources
20 not expected to deliver in excess of 100 Mcf per Day. A party providing compression facilities will also
21 provide sufficient pulsation dampening equipment to prevent pulsation from affecting measurement at
22 the Delivery Points. Electronic recording devices may be used. Seller will have access to Buyer's
23 metering equipment at reasonable hours, but only Buyer will calibrate, adjust, operate, and maintain it.
24 **D.2**   **Unit of Volume.** The unit of volume will be one cubic foot of gas at a base temperature of
25 60 |F and at a pressure base of ____ psia. Computations of volumes will follow industry accepted
26 practice.
27 **D.3**   **Pressure, Temperature.** Buyer may measure the atmospheric pressure or may assume the
28 atmospheric pressure to be ____ psia. Buyer may determine the gas temperature by using a recording
29 thermometer; otherwise, the temperature will be assumed to be 60□F.
30 **D.4**   **Check Meters.** Seller may install, maintain, and operate in accordance with accepted industry
31 practice at its own expense pressure regulators and check measuring equipment of standard make using
32 separate taps. Check meters shall not interfere with operation of Buyer's equipment. Buyer will have
33 access to Seller's check measuring equipment at all reasonable hours, but only Seller will calibrate,
34 adjust, operate, and maintain it.
35 **D.5**   **Meter Tests.** At least annually, Buyer will verify the accuracy of Buyer's measuring equipment,
36 and Seller or its lease operator will verify the accuracy of any check measuring equipment. If Seller's
37 lease operator or Buyer notifies the other that it desires a special test of any measuring equipment, they
38 will cooperate to secure a prompt verification of the accuracy of the equipment. If either at any time
39 observes a variation between the delivery meter and the check meter, it will promptly notify the other,
40 and both will then cooperate to secure an immediate verification of the accuracy of the equipment. Only
41 if so requested in advance by Seller in writing, Buyer will give Seller's lease operator reasonable
42 advance notice of the time of all special tests and calibrations of meters and of sampling for
43 determinations of gas composition and quality, so that the lease operator may have representatives
44 present to witness tests and sampling or make joint tests and obtain samples with its own equipment.
45 Seller will give or cause its lease operator to give reasonable advance notice to Buyer of the time of tests
46 and calibrations of any check meters and of any sampling by Seller for determination of gas composition
47 and quality.

D.6   **Correction of Errors.** If at any time any of the measuring or testing equipment is found to be out of service or registering inaccurately in any percentage, it will be adjusted promptly to read accurately within the limits prescribed by the manufacturer. If any measuring equipment is found to be inaccurate or out of service by an amount exceeding the greater of (i) 2.0 percent at a recording corresponding to the average hourly rate of flow for the period since the last test, or (ii) 100 Mcf per month, previous readings will be corrected to zero error for any known or agreed period. The volume of gas delivered during that period will be estimated by the first feasible of the following methods:

    (i)   Using the data recorded by any check measuring equipment if registering accurately;

    (ii) Correcting the error if the percentage of error is ascertainable by calibration, test, or mathematical calculation; or

    (iii) Using deliveries under similar conditions during a period when the equipment was registering accurately.

No adjustment will be made for inaccuracies unless they exceed the greater of (i) 2.0 percent of affected volumes, or (ii) 100 Mcf per month.

D.7   **Meter Records.** The parties will preserve for a period of at least two years all test data, charts and similar measurement records. The parties will raise metering questions as soon as practicable after the time of production. No party will have any obligation to preserve metering records for more than two years except to the extent that a metering question has been raised in writing and remains unresolved.

E.   DETERMINATION OF GAS COMPOSITION, GRAVITY, AND HEATING VALUE

At least annually, Buyer will obtain a representative sample of Seller's gas delivered at each Delivery Point; Buyer may use spot sampling, continuous samplers or on-line chromatography. By chromatography or other accepted method in the industry, Buyer will determine the composition, gravity, and gross heating value of the hydrocarbon components of Seller's gas in Btu per cubic foot on a dry basis at standard conditions, then adjust the result for the water vapor content of the gas (by either the volume or Btu content method) using an industry accepted practice. No heating value will be credited for Btus in H_2S or other non-hydrocarbon components. The first determination of Btu content for Seller's deliveries will be made within a reasonable time after deliveries of gas begin. If a continuous sampler or on-line chromatography is used, the determinations will apply to the gas delivered while the sampler was installed. If not, the determination will apply until the first Day of the month following the next determination.

F. QUALITY OF GAS

F.1   **Quality Specifications.** The gas shall be merchantable natural gas, at all times complying with the following quality requirements. The gas shall be commercially free of crude oil, water in the liquid phase, brine, air, dust, gums, gum-forming constituents, bacteria, and other objectionable liquids and solids, and not contain more than:

a.   _____ grain of H_2S per 100 cubic feet.

b.   _____ grains of total sulfur nor more than _____ grain of mercaptan per 100 cubic feet.

c.   _____ mole percent of carbon dioxide.

d.   _____ mole percent of nitrogen.

e.   _____ parts per million by volume of oxygen, and not have been subjected to any treatment or process that permits or causes the admission of oxygen, that dilutes the gas, or otherwise causes it to fail to meet these quality specifications.

f.   _____ mole percent of combined carbon dioxide, nitrogen, and oxygen.

The gas shall:

1   g.   Not exceed 120 |F in temperature at the Delivery Point.

2   h.   Have a total heating value of at least _____ Btus per cubic foot.

3   j.   If a third party pipeline receiving the gas delivered has more stringent quality specifications than

4 those stated above, Seller's gas shall conform to the more stringent pipeline quality standard.

5 **F.2**   **Quality Tests.**   Buyer will make determinations of conformity of the gas with the above

6 specifications using procedures generally accepted in the gas industry as often as Buyer reasonably

7 deems necessary. If in the lease operator's judgment the result of any test or determination is inaccurate,

8 Buyer upon request will again conduct the questioned test or determination. The costs of the additional

9 test or determination will be borne by Seller unless it shows the original test or determination to have

10 been materially inaccurate.

11 **F.3**   **Separation Equipment.**   Seller will employ only conventional mechanical separation equipment

12 at all production sites covered by this Contract. Low temperature, absorption, and similar separation

13 facilities are not considered conventional mechanical separation equipment. Except for liquids removed

14 through operation of conventional mechanical separators and except for removal of substances as

15 required to enable Seller to comply with this Section F, Seller will remove no components of the gas

16 prior to delivery to Buyer.

17 **F.4**   **Rights as to Off Specification Gas.**

18 (a)   If any of the gas delivered by Seller fails to meet the quality specifications stated in this Section,

19 Buyer may at its option accept delivery of and pay for the gas or discontinue or curtail taking of gas at

20 any Delivery Point whenever its quality does not conform to the quality specifications. If Buyer accepts

21 delivery of off specification gas from Seller or incurs costs relating to inferior gas quality in its gathering

22 system, Buyer may deduct from the proceeds otherwise payable a reasonable fee for monitoring the gas

23 quality and treating and handling the gas. Buyer typically adjusts gas quality deduction levels annually,

24 but may do so more often if needed.

25 (b)   If Buyer is declining to take off quality gas, Seller may by written notice to Buyer request a

26 release of the affected gas from commitment under this Contract. In response, Buyer will within ____

27 Days either (i) waive its right to refuse to take the affected off quality gas (subject to its right to charge

28 treating fees under this Section F) and again take gas from the affected sources, or (ii) release the

29 affected gas from commitment under this Contract.

30   **G.   BILLING AND PAYMENT**

31 **G.1**   **Statement and Payment Date.**   Buyer will render to Seller on or before the last Day of each

32 month a statement showing the volume of gas delivered by Seller during the preceding month and

33 Buyer's calculation of the amounts due under this Contract for the preceding month's deliveries. Buyer

34 will make payment to Seller on or before the last Day of each month for all gas delivered during the

35 preceding month. As between the parties, late payments by Buyer and recoupments/refunds from Seller

36 will carry simple interest at the lower of 6% per annum or the maximum lawful interest rate; provided

37 that no interest will accrue as to monthly principal amounts of less than $1,000 due for less than one

38 year when paid. The parties waive any rights to differing interest rates. Except as limited in Section G.2

39 below, Buyer may recover any overpayments or collect any amounts due from Seller to Buyer for any

40 reason at any time under this or other transactions by deducting them from proceeds payable to Seller.

41 **G.2**   **Audit Rights; Time Limit to Assert Claims.**

42 (a)   Each party will have the right during reasonable business hours to examine the books, records

43 and charts of the other party to the extent necessary to verify performance of this Contract and the

44 accuracy of any payment, statement, charge or computation upon execution of a reasonable

45 confidentiality agreement. If any audit examination or review of the party's own records reveals an

46 inaccuracy in any payment, Buyer will promptly make the appropriate adjustment.

(b)   No adjustment for any billing or payment shall be made, and payments shall be final after the lapse of two years from their due date except as to matters that either party has noted in a specific written objection to the other party in writing during the two year period, unless within the two year period Buyer has made the appropriate correction. However, Seller's responsibilities for severance taxes and third party liabilities and related interest are not affected by this subsection. (c) No party will have any right to recoup or recover prior overpayments or underpayments that result from errors that occur in spite of good faith performance if the amounts involved do not exceed $10/month/meter. Either party may require prospective correction of such errors.

G.3   Metering Records Availability. Buyer will not be required to furnish gas volume records relating to electronic recording devices for gas meters other than daily volume information unless there are indications the meter was not operating properly.

H. FORCE MAJEURE

H.1   Suspension of Performance. If either party is rendered unable, wholly or in part, by Force Majeure to carry out its obligations under this Contract, other than to make payments due, the obligations of that party, so far as they are affected by Force Majeure, will be suspended during the continuance of any inability so caused, but for no longer period.

H.2   Force Majeure Definition. "Force Majeure" means acts of God, strikes, lockouts or other industrial disturbances, acts of the public enemy, wars, blockades, insurrections, riots, epidemics, landslides, lightning, earthquakes, storms, floods, washouts, arrests and restraints of governments and people, civil disturbances, fires, explosions, breakage or accidents to machinery or lines of pipe, freezing of wells or lines of pipe, partial or entire failure of wells or sources of supply of gas, inability to obtain at reasonable cost servitudes, right of way grants, permits, governmental approvals or licenses, inability to obtain at reasonable cost materials or supplies for constructing or maintaining facilities, and other causes, whether of the kind listed above or otherwise, not within the control of the party claiming suspension and which by the exercise of reasonable diligence the party is unable to prevent or overcome.

H.3   Labor Matters Exception. The settlement of strikes or lockouts will be entirely within the discretion of the party having the difficulty, and settlement of strikes, lockouts, or other labor disturbances when that course is considered inadvisable is not required.

I. WARRANTY OF TITLE

Seller warrants that it has good title and processing rights to the gas delivered, free and clear of any and all liens, encumbrances, and claims, and that Seller has good right and lawful authority to sell the same. Seller grants to Buyer the right to process Seller's gas for extraction of NGLs and other valuable components. If Seller's title or right to receive any payment is questioned or involved in litigation, Buyer will have the right to withhold the contested payments without interest until title information is received, during the litigation, until the title or right to receive the questioned payments is freed from question, or until Seller furnishes security for repayment acceptable to Buyer. Without impairment of Seller's warranty of title to gas and gas processing rights, if Seller owns or controls less than full title to the gas delivered, payments will be made only in the proportion that Seller's interest bears to the entire title to the gas.

J. ROYALTY AND OTHER INTERESTS

Seller is responsible for all payments to the owners of all working interests, mineral interests, royalties, overriding royalties, bonus payments, production payments and the like. Buyer assumes no liability to Seller's working or mineral interest, royalty, or other interest owners under this Contract.

K. SEVERANCE AND SIMILAR TAXES

K.1 __Included in Price.__ Reimbursement to Seller for Seller's full liability for severance and similar taxes levied upon Seller's gas production is included in the prices payable under this Contract, regardless of whether some included interests may be exempt from taxation.

K.2 __Tax Responsibilities and Disbursements.__ Seller shall bear, and unless otherwise required by law, will pay to taxing authorities all severance, production, excise, sales, gross receipts, occupation, and other taxes imposed upon Seller with respect to the gas on or prior to delivery to Buyer. Buyer will bear and pay all taxes imposed upon Buyer with respect to the gas after delivery to Buyer.

L. INDEMNIFICATION AND RESPONSIBILITY FOR
INJURY OR DAMAGE

L.1 __Title, Royalty, and Severance Taxes.__ SELLER RELEASES AND AGREES TO DEFEND, INDEMNIFY, AND SAVE BUYER, ITS AFFILIATES, AND THEIR OFFICERS, EMPLOYEES, AND AGENTS HARMLESS FROM AND AGAINST ALL CLAIMS, CAUSES OF ACTION, LIABILITIES, AND COSTS (INCLUDING REASONABLE ATTORNEYS' FEES AND COSTS OF INVESTIGATION AND DEFENSE) RELATING TO (a) SELLER'S TITLE TO GAS AND GAS PROCESSING RIGHTS, (b) PAYMENTS FOR WORKING, MINERAL, ROYALTY AND OVERRIDING ROYALTY AND OTHER INTERESTS, AND (c) SALES, SEVERANCE, AND SIMILAR TAXES, THAT ARE THE RESPONSIBILITY OF SELLER UNDER SECTIONS I, J, AND K ABOVE.

L.2 __Responsibility for Injury or Damage.__ **As between the parties, Seller will be in control and possession of the gas deliverable hereunder and responsible for any injury or damage relating to handling or delivery of gas until the gas has been delivered to Buyer at the Delivery Points; after delivery, Buyer will be deemed to be in exclusive control and possession and responsible for any injury or damage relating to handling or gathering of gas. THE PARTY HAVING RESPONSIBILITY UNDER THE PRECEDING SENTENCE SHALL RELEASE, DEFEND, INDEMNIFY, AND HOLD THE OTHER PARTY, ITS AFFILIATES, AND THEIR OFFICERS, EMPLOYEES, AND AGENTS HARMLESS FROM AND AGAINST ALL CLAIMS, CAUSES OF ACTION, LIABILITIES, AND COSTS (INCLUDING REASONABLE ATTORNEYS' FEES AND COSTS OF INVESTIGATION AND DEFENSE) ARISING FROM ACTUAL AND ALLEGED LOSS OF GAS, PERSONAL INJURY, DEATH, AND DAMAGE FOR WHICH THE PARTY IS RESPONSIBLE UNDER THIS SECTION; PROVIDED THAT NEITHER PARTY WILL BE INDEMNIFIED FOR ITS OWN NEGLIGENCE OR THAT OF ITS AGENTS, SERVANTS, OR EMPLOYEES.**

M. RIGHT OF WAY

Insofar as Seller's lease or leases permit and insofar as Seller or its lease operator may have any rights however derived (whether pursuant to oil and gas lease, easement, governmental agency order, regulation, statute, or otherwise), Seller grants to Buyer and Buyer's gas gathering contractor, if any, and their assignees the right of free entry and the right to lay and maintain pipelines, meters, and any equipment on the lands or leases subject to this Contract as reasonably necessary in connection with the purchase or handling of Seller's gas. Upon written request from Buyer to Seller, Seller shall grant, in writing, to Buyer or Buyer's designee, recordable rights of ingress and egress as necessary or appropriate for the purposes of complying with the terms of this Contract. All pipelines, meters, and other equipment placed by Buyer or Buyer's contractors on the lands and leases will remain the property of the owner and may be removed by the owner at any time. Without limitation, Buyer or its gathering contractor may disconnect and remove measurement and other facilities from any Delivery Point due to low volume, quality, term expiration, or other cause.

N. ASSIGNMENT

N.1 __Binding on Assignees.__ Either party may assign this Contract. This Contract is binding upon and inures to the benefit of the successors, assigns, and representatives in bankruptcy of the parties, and, subject to any prior dedications by the assignee, shall be binding upon any purchaser of Buyer's Facilities and upon any purchaser of the properties of Seller subject to this Contract. Nothing contained in this Section will prevent either party from mortgaging its rights as security for its indebtedness, but security is subordinate to the parties' rights and obligations under this Contract.

N.2 __Notice of Assignment.__ Any assignment or sublease by Seller of any oil and gas properties or any gas rights contracted to Buyer will be made expressly subject to the provisions of this Contract. No transfer of or succession to the interest of Seller, however made, will bind Buyer unless and until the original instrument or other proper proof that the claimant is legally entitled to an interest has been furnished to Buyer at its Division Order address noted in the Notices Section or subsequent address.

O. MISCELLANEOUS PROVISIONS

O.1 __Governing Law.__ THIS CONTRACT SHALL BE GOVERNED BY AND CONSTRUED IN ACCORDANCE WITH THE LAWS OF THE STATE OF _____, without reference to those that might refer to the laws of another jurisdiction.

O.2 __Default and Nonwaiver.__ A waiver by a party of any one or more defaults by the other in the performance of any provisions of this Contract will not operate as a waiver of any future default or defaults, whether of a like or different character.

O.3 __Counterparts.__ This Contract may be executed in any number of counterparts, all of which will be considered together as one instrument, and this Contract will be binding upon all parties executing it, whether or not executed by all parties owning an interest in the producing sources affected by this Contract. Signed copies of this Contract and facsimiles of it shall have the same force and effect as originals.

O.4 __Negotiations; Entire Agreement; Amendment; No Third Party Beneficiaries.__ The language of this Contract shall not be construed in favor of or against either Buyer or Seller, but shall be construed as if the language were drafted mutually by both parties. This Contract constitutes the final and complete agreement between the parties. There are no oral promises, prior agreements, understandings, obligations, warranties, or representations between the parties relating to this Contract other than those set forth herein. All waivers, modifications, amendments, and changes to this Contract shall be in writing and signed by the authorized representatives of the parties. The relations between the parties are those of independent contractors; this Contract creates no joint venture, partnership, association, other special relationship, or fiduciary obligations. There are no third party beneficiaries of Buyer's sales contracts or of this Contract.

O.5 __Ratification and Third Party Gas.__ Notwithstanding anything contained herein to the contrary, Buyer has no duty under this Contract to purchase or handle gas attributable to production from interests of third parties that has been purchased by Seller for resale, except that Buyer will purchase Other WI Gas. "Other WI Gas" means gas attributable to working and mineral interests owned by third parties in wells operated by Seller that are subject to this Contract that Seller has the right to market under an operating agreement. If Buyer requests in writing that Seller obtain ratification of this Contract from owners of Other WI Gas, Seller will use reasonable commercial efforts to cause those Other WI Gas owners to execute and deliver to Buyer an instrument prepared by Buyer for the purpose of ratifying and adopting this Contract with respect to the owner's Other WI Gas, and the ratifying owner will become a party to this Contract with like force and effect as though the Other WI owner had executed this Contract as amended as of the time of the ratification, and all of the terms and provisions of this Contract as then amended will become binding upon Buyer and the ratifying owner.

1 **O.6** **Compliance with Laws and Regulations.** This Contract is subject to all valid statutes and rules
2 and regulations of any duly constituted federal or state authority or regulatory body having jurisdiction.
3 Neither party will be in default as a result of compliance with laws and regulations.
4 **O.7** **Fees and Costs; Damages.** If a breach occurs, the parties are entitled to recover as their sole
5 and exclusive damages for breach of the price and quantity obligations under this Contract the price for
6 gas taken by Buyer in the case of Seller and the lost margin less avoided costs in the case of Buyer. If
7 mediation or arbitration is necessary to resolve a dispute other than one arising under the
8 indemnification obligations of this Contract, each party agrees to bear its own attorneys' fees and costs
9 of investigation and defense, and each party waives any right to recover those fees and costs from the
10 other party or parties.
11 **O.8** **Mutual Waiver of Certain Remedies.** Except as to the parties' indemnification obligations,
12 NEITHER PARTY SHALL BE LIABLE OR OTHERWISE RESPONSIBLE TO THE OTHER FOR
13 CONSEQUENTIAL OR INCIDENTAL DAMAGES, FOR LOST PRODUCTION, OR FOR
14 PUNITIVE DAMAGES AS TO ANY ACTION OR OMISSION, WHETHER CHARACTERIZED AS
15 A CONTRACT BREACH OR TORT, THAT ARISES OUT OF OR RELATES TO THIS CONTRACT
16 OR ITS PERFORMANCE OR NONPERFORMANCE.
17 **O.9** **Arbitration.** The parties desire to resolve any disputes that may arise informally, if possible.
18 All disputes arising out of or relating to this Contract that are not resolved by agreement of the parties
19 must be resolved using the provisions of this Section. To that end, if a dispute or disputes arise out of or
20 relating to this Contract, a party shall give written notice of the disputes to the other involved parties,
21 and each party will appoint an employee to negotiate with the other party concerning the disputes. If the
22 disputes have not been resolved by negotiation within 30 Days of the initial dispute notice, the disputes
23 shall be resolved by arbitration in accordance with the then current International Institute for Conflict
24 Prevention and Resolution Rules for Non-Administered Arbitration and related commentary ("Rules")
25 and this Section. The arbitration shall be governed by the Federal Arbitration Act, 9 U.S.C. §§ 1, et
26 seq., and the Rules, to the exclusion of any provision of state law inconsistent with them. The
27 arbitration shall be initiated by a party seeking arbitration by written notice sent to the other party or
28 parties to be involved. The parties shall select one disinterested arbitrator with at least ten years'
29 experience in the natural gas industry or ten years' experience with natural gas law, and not previously
30 employed by either party or its Affiliates, and, if possible, shall be selected by agreement between the
31 parties. If the parties cannot select an arbitrator by agreement within 15 Days of the date of the notice of
32 arbitration, a qualified arbitrator will be selected in accordance with the Rules. If the disputes involve
33 an amount greater than $100,000, they will be decided by a panel of three arbitrators with the above
34 qualifications, one selected by each party, and the third selected by the party-appointed arbitrators, or in
35 the absence of their agreement, pursuant to the Rules. The arbitrator(s) shall resolve the disputes and
36 render a final award in accordance with the substantive law of the state referenced in Section O.1 above,
37 "Governing Law." The arbitration award will be limited by the provisions set forth in Sections O.7,
38 "Fees and Costs; Damages" and O.8 above, "Mutual Waiver of Certain Remedies." The parties intend
39 case specific dispute resolution; either party may opt out of any attempted class action for all claims of
40 any party related to this Contract. The arbitrator(s) shall set forth the reasons for the award in writing,
41 and judgment on the arbitration award may be entered in any court having jurisdiction.

EXHIBIT B to GAS PURCHASE AND PROCESSING CONTRACT
Between _____ as Seller and
DCP MIDSTREAM, LP as Buyer

Dated as of _____, 20__

COMMITTED LEASES AND WELLS

_____ COUNTY, _____

No.	Buyer's Meter No.	WELL/LEASE NAME	LOCATION
1.			
2			

1.   This is an example of a longer-term gas purchase contract where the seller is dedicating gas from a geographic area to the purchaser. As part of the transaction the purchaser is providing transportation to its gas processing facility where natural-gas liquids (NGLs) are removed from the gas stream. The agreement compensates the seller with a percentage of the revenues from the sale of the liquid hydrocarbons extracted from the gas stream plus a percentage of the residue gas sales revenues.

2.   The editors thank Richard J. Gognat, who prepared the introductory comments and helped develop this form, and his employer, DCP Midstream, LP, for granting permission to use this form. For information regarding the natural-gas midstream services offered by DCP Midstream, LP, visit its web site at http://www.dcpmidstream.com.

3.   After natural gas has been discovered, the common transactions at and downstream of the wellhead for natural gas (and the entrained NGLs that fall out of the gas stream) are as follows:

Regulation: gathering of natural gas (as opposed to purchase, sale, transportation and storage) is generally non-regulated by the U.S. Federal Regulatory Commission (FERC) and state public utility commissions (PUCs), but some states (notably Texas and Oklahoma) do have legislation governing gathering. NGL interstate transportation is subject to the Interstate Commerce Act, and is generally considered to be lighter handed regulation than for natural gas. Pipelines may also be subject to safety regulations of the U.S. Department of Transportation.

Gathering: raw natural gas is gathered from the wellhead or a central delivery point and redelivered to another point (such as a processing plant, treater, or intrastate or interstate transportation pipeline).

Processing and Treating: generally raw natural gas from the wellhead must be processed, treated, or both to meet pipelines quality specifications.

Processing: generally refers to the process whereby NGLs are removed from the natural gas. This lowers the heating content (usually measured in Btus or dekatherms) of the natural gas. This may be done through several types of processes (including, simple refrigeration plants, cryogenic plants, or lean oil plants). These types of processes have different degrees of efficiencies in recovering the entrained NGLs. Many times the gas is treated at plant complexes to remove impurities such as nitrogen, carbon dioxide and hydrogen sulfide. The NGLs are marketed separately from the residue gas stream. Some NGLs (such as ethane) may only be transported in liquid form via pipeline, while most others (e.g., propane) may also be trucked.

Treating: generally refers to the process whereby gas or NGLs are treated at plant complexes to remove impurities such as nitrogen, carbon dioxide and hydrogen sulfide. Types of processes used to treat gas may include cryogenic plant, lean oil plant, molecular sieve or amine.

Dehydration: the process of removal of water from the gas stream, which typically occurs at or near the wellhead prior to the delivery into a gathering and processing system.

Fractionation: refers to the refining process whereby NGLs are separated into components, including propane, isobutane, natural gasoline and ethane. These refined products have a variety of uses, including heating, crude oil refining, and petrochemicals.

Compression: natural gas in its vaporous form may be compressed up to the maximum allowable operating pressures of the facilities through which it is transported or stored.

Transportation: Transportation is usually associated with regulated interstate or intrastate transportation pipelines and generally of burner tip quality gas. Natural gas may be sold to an end user or local distribution company directly from the gas plant, or from a transportation pipeline. In interstate transportation, the transporting pipeline company is solely a service provider. FERC regulations prohibit the transporting pipeline company form holding title to the gas. Gas on intrastate pipeline may also provide Section 311 service, which is FERC regulated. PUCs generally regulate the purchase, sale and transportation on intrastate pipeline.

Storage: Natural gas (generally of burner tip quality) and NGLs may be may be stored for later use in periods of high demand. Natural gas is commonly stored in underground reservoirs. These facilities are generally regulated by the FERC. NGLs may also be stored in above ground tanks.

Charge for Services: gathering, processing, treating and compression might be for a fee per MMBtu or Mcf or it might be included as part of a purchase agreement. FERC regulated storage and transportation is done for a fee, generally an amount per MMBtu.

Purchase: gas may be purchased in raw from at the wellhead or a central delivery point (where a producer has aggregated gas to deliver to a first purchaser). Residue gas may be purchased at the tailgate of a gas plant or as it enters an interstate or intrastate transportation pipeline.

    a.   For purchases and sales of burner tip quality gas at or downstream of the tailgate of gas plants or on transportation pipelines, the NAESB (North American Energy Standards Board) forms are now customary. NAESB was formerly known as the Gas Industry Standards Board or GISB, and changed its name to NAESB because NAESB began also handling wholesale and retail electric transactions.

    b.   For hedging natural gas, it is customary to used forms from the International Swaps and Derivatives Association, Inc. or ISDA.

    c.   Gas purchase and sales transactions may be structured in many different ways, including:

    (i)   Percentage of index, fixed price per MMBtu or Mcf, and keep-whole transactions -- the gas is purchased at a wellhead or central delivery point at a fixed price or price equal to all or a percentage of a referenced index price per MMBtu or Mcf. A keep-whole transaction is where a gatherer agrees to redeliver to the producer an equivalent amount of Btus of residue gas at the tailgate of a gas plant (and the gatherer keeps some or all of the NGLs recovered) In these types of transactions, the purchaser or gatherer is considered to be taking the risk that the value of any entrained NGLs that will be removed will be of greater value per Btu than the residue gas, and that such excess will cover the cost and provide a profit on the ownership and operation of a gas plant. This difference in value is referred to as the "frac spread." NGL prices generally follow crude oil prices.

(ii) Percentage of proceeds -- the gas and/or NGLs are purchased based on a percentage of either or a combination of (1) what the buyer receives (referred to as weighted average sales price or WASP) for the sale of residue gas and/or NGLs or (2) referenced index prices for residue gas, such as Gas Daily and NGLs, such as Oil Price Information Services or OPIS).

(a) For processed gas, efficiencies of the gas plant can either be fixed or based on actual recoveries.

(b) If prices are based on an index, the processor has greater risk or reward (because the price received may be more or less than the index), but there is less likelihood of accounting or audit disputes.

(c) If efficiencies are fixed, the processor has greater risk or reward (because the amount of NGLs recovered may be more or less favorable than the amount calculated by the fixed efficiencies), but there is less likelihood in of accounting or audit disputes.

(iii) Residue gas sales – generally sold at a referenced index price, plus or minus a basis. Basis differential is meant to encompass time, location or quality differences.

(iv) NGL sales – may be sold at an index price plus or minus a transportation and fractionation fee or T&F Fee. NGLs might be based on an index (like OPIS) and residue might be based on a WASP or vice versa.

GAS GATHERING CONTRACT
Between _____ as Shipper and
DCP MIDSTREAM, LP as Gatherer
Dated as of _____, 20___

* * *

GAS GATHERING CONTRACT

This Gas Gathering Contract ("Contract") is entered as of _____ __, 20___, between _____ ("Shipper") and **DCP MIDSTREAM, LP** ("Gatherer").

For and in consideration of the mutual covenants contained herein, the parties agree as follows:

1. **COMMITMENT.** Shipper commits to Gatherer for gathering under this Contract Shipper's gas produced from all leases and wells now or later located on all oil and gas interests now or later owned or controlled by Shipper on or allocated to the following lands in _____ County, State:

[Describe, or state: See Exhibit C-1.]

Definitions and General Terms and Conditions included in this Contract are attached as Exhibit A. All Exhibits referenced herein are attached and incorporated by reference.

2. **DELIVERY AND REDELIVERY POINTS.** The Delivery Points for gas to be delivered by Shipper to Gatherer will be at or near the inlet flange of the meter station at or near the wells or other points described in Exhibit C-1. The Delivery Points for future sources of production committed under this Contract will be established under Section B.2 of Exhibit A. The Redelivery Points will be as described in Exhibit C-2.

3. **DELIVERY PRESSURE.** Shipper will deliver the gas at the Delivery Points at a pressure sufficient to enable it to enter Gatherer's Facilities against the working pressure at reasonably uniform rates of delivery, not to exceed the maximum allowable operating pressure established by Gatherer or pressures that prevent others from producing ratably. Gatherer in its discretion may require that Shipper install and operate a pressure relief or reduction device upstream of any Delivery Point, set at the pressure designated by Gatherer to limit the pressure at which Shipper delivers gas, where Shipper's deliveries might interfere with ratable deliveries from others, or to enhance safety.

4. **QUANTITY.**

    (a)   Subject to the operating conditions and capacity of Gatherer's Facilities, Gatherer agrees to receive and gather for Shipper and Shipper agrees to deliver the gas volumes nominated by and owned or controlled by Shipper at the Delivery Points. Gatherer will redeliver and Shipper or its designee will receive at the Redelivery Points MMBtu quantities of gas equivalent to those received from Shipper by Gatherer at each Delivery Point, less the applicable fuel and losses percentage of the gas shown on Exhibit C-1 of the MMBtus received by Gatherer at each Delivery Point. If Gatherer installs or operates additional field compression downstream from any of Shipper's Delivery Points or changes gas flows so that Shipper's gas flows through additional field compression, Gatherer may adjust Shipper's applicable fuel and losses percentage for the affected Delivery Points upward by the percentage of fuel/throughout required to accomplish the additional compression. Shipper and Gatherer will receive and redeliver gas as nearly as practicable at uniform hourly and daily rates of flow. Gatherer and Shipper will, through the Nomination process and other procedures consistent with Exhibit B, reduce or increase receipts or redeliveries as necessary to maintain them in balance.

    (b)   Gatherer's gathering service will be on a reasonable efforts basis. Gatherer will use commercially reasonable efforts to operate its Facilities in an effort to maintain consistent takes of all available quantities. Gatherer may at any time for any reason, including without limitation Gatherer's obligations to take gas ratably, inadequate capacity, Force Majeure, threat to system integrity, maintenance, construction, or other operational causes, interrupt or reduce its receipt, gathering, and redelivery of Shipper's Gas. In these events, Gatherer will use reasonable efforts to restore service as quickly as feasible.

(c) If Gatherer takes less than the full quantities tendered, within the capabilities of its Facilities Gatherer will take gas from the lands covered by this Contract consistently with its takes of similar gas subject to similar legal and contractual take commitments in each common gathering system or area in compliance with contractual commitments and applicable laws and regulations, including consistent purchases or takes from Gatherer's Affiliates. Gatherer will have no obligation to provide back-up or standby gas supplies or service to Shipper or to Shipper's gas suppliers, customers, or end users regardless of whether service is interrupted or reduced.

(d) Shipper may dispose of any gas not taken by Gatherer for any reason, including events of Force Majeure, subject to Gatherer's right to resume takes at any subsequent time. If Gatherer does not take gas for ____ consecutive Days and Shipper secures a different temporary outlet, Gatherer may resume takes only upon ____ Days' advance written notice as of the beginning of a month unless otherwise agreed.

(e) Shipper will use commercially reasonable efforts to deliver gas meeting the quality requirements and to avoid delivery of Inferior Liquids as defined in Exhibit A, Section A. If the gas at any Delivery Point becomes insufficient in volume, quality, or pressure, Gatherer may cease gas takes from the Delivery Point for so long as the condition exists. If Gatherer ceases taking gas under this Section for ____ consecutive Days for reasons other than quality [Exhibit A Section E] or Force Majeure [Exhibit A Section G], Shipper may terminate this Contract with respect to the affected Delivery Points as to the then productive zones upon ____ Days' advance written notice to Gatherer; provided that during the notice period Gatherer may resume consistent takes and purchases, and thereby avoid termination under Shipper's notice.

5. **GATHERING FEES.**

5.1 **Gathering and Compression Fees.** In addition to the in kind fuel/loss volumes discussed in Section 4(a) above and in Exhibit C-1, for services rendered hereunder Shipper shall pay Gatherer each month the fee per MMBtu delivered by Shipper at each Delivery Point shown for the Delivery Point in Exhibit C-1.

5.2 **Fee Adjustment.** The gathering and compression fees referenced in Section 5.1 will be adjusted as follows, but will never be less than their initial amounts. As of April 1 of each year beginning with ____, Gatherer will adjust the current year's cash gathering fees upward or downward in proportion to the percentage increase or decrease in the simple average of the (a) Oil & Gas Extraction Index and (b) Professional & Technical Services Index for the last calendar year compared to the previous calendar year for both, as published by the U.S. Department of Labor Bureau of Labor Statistics, rounded to the nearest 100th cent, or in its absence, a similar successor adjustment factor designated by Gatherer.

5.3 **Conditioning Fee.** If gas processing becomes uneconomic and Gatherer performs a processing, treating, or conditioning service to satisfy downstream pipeline requirements, Gatherer may charge a conditioning fee. The fee will be the gas or equivalent value of the plant fuel plus the positive difference between (a) the gas or equivalent value of the MMBtu reduction for extracted NGLs and (b) Gatherer's liquids value for the NGLs at the plant net of TF&S deductions from market center price quotations. An example of this calculation is shown in Exhibit D, which also defines the methods of establishing the gas or equivalent values and NGL values to be used.

5.4 **Taxes and Assessments.** Gatherer may increase its fees as necessary to recover the cost of any tax, assessment, or other charge imposed by a governing authority on Gatherer relating to the

- 2 -

handling of Shipper's gas or to the ownership or operation of Gatherer's Facilities, other than ad valorem taxes and taxes based on Gatherer's income or right to do business.

    5.5   **Low Volume Delivery Points.** If the volume delivered to Gatherer at any Delivery Point has averaged less than _____ Mcf per month for _____ consecutive months, Shipper will pay Gatherer an additional low volume fee of $_____ per month per affected Delivery Pont, escalated annually as stated in Section 5.2 above. The low volume fee will be effective the first Day of the month following the _____ month period and will remain in effect until the quantity delivered from the Delivery Point again averages at least _____ Mcf per month for _____ consecutive months, effective as of the first Day of the following month.

    6.   **GAS PROCESSING RIGHTS.** Shipper grants to Gatherer the right to process Shipper's gas for extraction of NGLs and other valuable components, subject to Gatherer's redelivery obligations stated herein. Gatherer may retain in kind without any duty to pay to Shipper any value for extracted NGLs and any other raw gas components from which Gatherer might derive revenue, including helium, sulfur, CO_2, and other non-hydrocarbons; no payment to Shipper or value calculation for those components is required, again subject to Gatherer's gas MMBtu redelivery obligations stated herein.

    7.   **TERM.**   This Contract shall be in force for a primary term through _____, 20__, and from year to year thereafter until canceled by either party as of the end of the primary term or as of any anniversary thereafter by giving the other party at least _____ Days' but no more than _____ Days' advance written notice of termination.

    8.   **ADDRESSES AND NOTICES.** Either party may give notices to the other party by first class mail postage prepaid, by overnight delivery service, or by facsimile with receipt confirmed at the following addresses or other addresses furnished by a party by written notice. Unless Shipper objects in writing, Gatherer may also use Shipper's current invoicing address for notice purposes. Shipper's payments shall be to Gatherer's bank and account stated below. Any telephone numbers below are solely for information and are not for Contract notices. The parties opt out of electronic delivery of notices and amendments under this Contract, except that notices and hand-signed amendments may be delivered by facsimile with receipt confirmed as stated above.

Notices to Shipper:

                                    Attn: _____

                                      _____

                                      _____

                                    Phone: _____

                                    Fax: _____

Notices to Gatherer - General: DCP Midstream, LP
(Gas Acquisitions and Accounting)   Attn: Commercial

                                      _____

                                    Phone: _____

                                    Fax: _____

Division Orders, Ownership changes: DCP Midstream, LP
                                  Attn: Division Orders

                                      _____

                                    _____

                                    Phone: _____

                                    Fax: _____

- 3 -

Gas control, imbalances, nominations   DCP Midstream, LP
and revisions: Attn: Commercial Operations

                                              _____

                                              Phone: _____
                                              Fax: _____

Payments to Gatherer via wire transfer: _____

                                              _____
                                              For credit to:
                                              DCP Midstream, LP,
                                              Account No. _____

Payments to Gatherer via check: DCP Midstream, LP

                                              _____
                                              _____

Instructions from any third parties, including brokers, marketers, or other intermediaries will not represent proper notice, and Gatherer will not be obligated to take any action as a result.

      9.   **TERMINATION OF PRIOR CONTRACTS AND RELEASE.**

      9.1   **Termination and Release.**   This Contract terminates and supersedes any prior contracts for the sale or handling of gas between the parties or their predecessors in interest that apply or applied to any gas produced from any sources covered by this Contract effective as of its date. In negotiating the terms of this Contract, the parties have compromised and settled any and all price, fee, payment, and other disputes relating to or under the superseded contract(s). In consideration of the covenants contained herein, each party hereby releases the other party, its Affiliates, and its predecessors in interest under the prior contracts from any causes of action, claims, and liabilities (i) that they failed to pay the full prices or fees under the prior contracts, including interest, (ii) that they failed to perform any other obligation under the prior contracts, and (iii) arising from their relationship as parties to the prior contracts.

      9.2   **Exceptions.**   This termination and release does not include, and the parties expressly retain, the right to receive payments under the prior contract(s) relating to gas imbalances and relating to current gas production for which payment is not yet due and for which a party has not yet made payment in the ordinary course of business. This mutual release also does not include matters relating to title to gas and gas processing rights, Shipper's obligations for payment of third parties and severance taxes, related interest and penalties, or to gas imbalances under prior gathering or take in kind agreements.

      The parties have signed this Contract by their duly authorized representatives as of the date first set forth above.

SHIPPER   **DCP MIDSTREAM, LP**

[signatures and dates]

EXHIBIT A

To GAS GATHERING CONTRACT
Between _____ as Shipper and
DCP MIDSTREAM, LP as Gatherer
Dated as of _____, 20__

GENERAL TERMS AND CONDITIONS

A. DEFINITIONS

Except where the context indicates a different meaning or intent, and whether or not capitalized, the following terms will have meanings as follows:

a.　Affiliate – a company (i) in which a party owns directly or indirectly 50% or more of the issued and outstanding voting stock or other equity interests; (ii) which owns directly or indirectly 50% or more of the issued and outstanding voting stock or equity interests of the party; and (iii) in which a company described in (ii) owns, directly or indirectly, 50% or more of the issued and outstanding voting stock or other equity interests.

b.　Btu – British thermal unit. MMBtu – one million Btus.

c.　Day – a period of 24 consecutive hours beginning and ending at _____ local time, or other 24 hour period designated by Gatherer and a downstream pipeline.

d.　Delivery Points – whether one or more, see Sections 2, and Exhibit A Sections B.1 and B.2.

e.　Facilities – the gas delivered by Shipper will be gathered in gathering systems and may be redelivered to a gas processing plant or plants for the removal of NGLs together with gas produced from other properties. The gathering systems and plant or plants, or successor facilities, are Gatherer's "Facilities" whether owned by Gatherer, an Affiliate of Gatherer, or an unaffiliated third party. No facilities downstream of the processing plant or plants other than short connecting lines to transmission lines are included in Gatherer's "Facilities."

f.　Force Majeure – see Section G.2 below.

g.　Gas or gas – all natural gas that arrives at the surface in the gaseous phase, including all hydrocarbon and non-hydrocarbon components, casinghead gas produced from oil wells, gas well gas, and stock tank vapors.

h.　Inferior Liquids – Mixed crude oil, slop oil, salt water, nuisance liquids, and other liquids recovered by Gatherer in its gathering system or at plant inlet receivers. Revenues from Inferior Liquids, drips, and other gathering system liquids will be retained by Gatherer to defray costs of treating and handling; Gatherer will not allocate or pay for those liquids.

i.　Mcf – 1,000 cubic feet of gas at standard base conditions of 60°F and _____ psia.

j.　MMcf – 1,000 Mcf.

k.　Month or month – a calendar month beginning on the first Day of a Month.

l.　NGL or NGLs – natural gas liquids, or ethane and heavier liquefiable hydrocarbons separated from gas and any incidental methane in NGL after processing.

m.　psi – pounds per square inch; psia – psi absolute; psig – psi gauge.

n.　Redelivery Points – See Section 2 and Exhibit C-2.

o.　TF&S – NGL transportation, fractionation, and storage.

B. DELIVERY DATE; COMPRESSION

B.1　Connected Sources Delivery Date. As to committed sources of production already connected to Gatherer's Facilities, deliveries under this Contract will commence as of _____, 20__.

B.2　Additional Sources. As to sources not yet connected, Shipper will commence and complete with due diligence the construction of the facilities necessary to enable Shipper to deliver the committed gas at the Delivery Points and Gatherer will cause prompt commencement and complete with due diligence the construction of the Facilities necessary and economically feasible to enable Gatherer or its gas gathering contractor to receive deliveries of gas at the Delivery Points. If Gatherer determines it is not profitable to construct the Facilities, Shipper will have the option to construct facilities necessary to deliver gas into Gatherer's then existing Facilities. If neither Gatherer nor Shipper elect to construct the necessary facilities, either party may cancel this Contract as to the affected gas upon ____ Days advance written notice to the other.

B.3 **Delivery Rates.** Under normal conditions, Shipper and Gatherer will deliver and receive gas at reasonably uniform rates of delivery. Shipper will have agents or employees available at all reasonable times to receive advice and directions from Gatherer for changes in the rates of delivery of gas as required from time to time.

B.4 **Options to Compress.** If Shipper's wells become incapable of delivering gas into Gatherer's Facilities, neither party will be obligated to compress, but either party will have the option to do so. If neither party elects to compress within a reasonable time after the need for compression appears, Gatherer upon written request of Shipper will either arrange promptly to provide compression or, as Shipper's sole remedy, release the affected gas as to the then-producing formations from commitment under this Contract. If Gatherer provides additional compression, the gathering fee to be paid to Gatherer shall be increased by a reasonable compression fee that allows recovery of the related fuel and provides Gatherer a reasonable return on investment.

C. METERING AND MEASUREMENT

C.1 **Gatherer to Install Meters.** Gatherer will install, maintain and operate orifice meters or other measuring devices of standard make at or near the Delivery Points. Except as otherwise specifically provided to the contrary in this Section C, orifice meters or other measurement devices will be installed and volumes computed in accordance with accepted industry practice. Gatherer may re-use metering equipment not meeting current standards but meeting 1985 or later published standards for gas sources not expected to deliver in excess of 100 Mcf per Day. A party providing compression facilities will also provide sufficient pulsation dampening equipment to prevent pulsation from affecting measurement at the Delivery Points. Electronic recording devices may be used. Shipper will have access to Gatherer's metering equipment at reasonable hours, but only Gatherer will calibrate, adjust, operate, and maintain it.

C.2 **Unit of Volume.** The unit of volume will be one cubic foot of gas at a base temperature of 60°F and at a pressure base of ____ psia. Computations of volumes will follow industry accepted practice.

C.3 **Pressure, Temperature.** Gatherer may measure the atmospheric pressure or may assume the atmospheric pressure to be ____ psia. Gatherer may determine gas temperature by using a recording thermometer; otherwise, the temperature will be assumed to be 60°F.

C.4 **Check Meters.** Shipper may install, maintain, and operate in accordance with accepted industry practice at its own expense pressure regulators and check measuring equipment of standard make using separate taps. Check meters shall not interfere with operation of Gatherer's equipment. Gatherer will have access to Shipper's check measuring equipment at all reasonable hours, but only Shipper will calibrate, adjust, operate, and maintain it.

C.5 **Meter Tests.** At least annually, Gatherer will verify the accuracy of Gatherer's measuring equipment, and Shipper or its lease operator will verify the accuracy of any check measuring equipment. If Shipper's lease operator or Gatherer notifies the other that it desires a special test of any measuring equipment, they will cooperate to secure a prompt verification of the accuracy of the equipment. If either at any time observes a variation between the delivery meter and the check meter, it will promptly notify the other, and both will then cooperate to secure an immediate verification of the accuracy of the equipment. Only if so requested in advance by Shipper in writing, Gatherer will give Shipper's lease operator reasonable advance notice of the time of all special tests and calibrations of meters and of sampling for determinations of gas composition and quality, so that the lease operator may have representatives present to witness tests and sampling or make joint tests and obtain samples with its own equipment. Shipper will give or cause its lease operator to give reasonable advance notice to Gatherer of the time of tests and calibrations of any check meters and of any sampling by Shipper for determination of gas composition and quality.

C.6 **Correction of Errors.** If at any time any of the measuring or testing equipment is found to be out of service or registering inaccurately in any percentage, it will be adjusted promptly to read accurately within the limits prescribed by the manufacturer. If any measuring equipment is found to be inaccurate or out of service by an amount exceeding the greater of (i) 2.0 percent at a recording corresponding to the average hourly rate of flow for the period since the last test, or (ii) 100 Mcf per month, previous readings will be corrected to zero error for any known or agreed period. The volume of gas delivered during that period will be estimated by the first feasible of the following methods:

(i)   Using the data recorded by any check measuring equipment if registering accurately;

(ii) Correcting the error if the percentage of error is ascertainable by calibration, test, or mathematical calculation; or

(iii) Using deliveries under similar conditions during a period when the equipment was registering accurately.

No adjustment will be made for inaccuracies unless they exceed the greater of (i) 2.0 percent of affected volumes, or (ii) 100 Mcf per month.

C.7 **Meter Records.** The parties will preserve for a period of at least two years all test data, charts and similar measurement records. The parties will raise metering questions as soon as practicable after the time of production. No party will have any obligation to preserve metering records for more than two years except to the extent that a metering question has been raised in writing and remains unresolved.

D. DETERMINATION OF GAS COMPOSITION, GRAVITY, AND HEATING VALUE

At least annually, Gatherer will obtain a representative sample of Shipper's gas delivered at each Delivery Point; Gatherer may use spot sampling, continuous samplers or on-line chromatography. By chromatography or other accepted method in the industry, Gatherer will determine the composition, gravity, and gross heating value of the hydrocarbon components of Shipper's gas in Btu per cubic foot on a dry basis at standard conditions, then adjust the result for the water vapor content of the gas (by either the volume or Btu content method) using an industry accepted practice. No heating value will be credited for Btus in H_2S or other non-hydrocarbon components. The first determination of Btu content for Shipper's deliveries will be made within a reasonable time after deliveries of gas begin. If a continuous sampler or on-line chromatography is used, the determinations will apply to the gas delivered while the sampler was installed. If not, the determination will apply until the first Day of the month following the next determination.

E. QUALITY OF GAS

E.1 **Quality Specifications.** The gas shall be merchantable natural gas, at all times complying with the following quality requirements. The gas shall be commercially free of crude oil, water in the liquid phase, brine, air, dust, gums, gum-forming constituents, bacteria, and other objectionable liquids and solids, and not contain more than:

a.   ____ grain of H_2S per 100 cubic feet.

b.   ____ grains of total sulfur nor more than ___ grain of mercaptan per 100 cubic feet.

c.   ____ mole percent of carbon dioxide.

d.   ____ mole percent of nitrogen.

e.   ___ parts per million by volume of oxygen, and not have been subjected to any treatment or process that permits or causes the admission of oxygen, that dilutes the gas, or otherwise causes it to fail to meet these quality specifications.

f.   ____ mole percent of combined carbon dioxide, nitrogen, and oxygen.

The gas shall:

    g. Not exceed ____ F in temperature at the Delivery Point.

    h. Have a total heating value of at least ____ Btus per cubic foot.

    i. Otherwise meet the specifications required by the transporting pipelines at the Redelivery Points.

E.2   **Quality Tests.** Gatherer will make determinations of conformity of the gas with the above specifications using procedures generally accepted in the gas industry as often as Gatherer reasonably deems necessary. If in the lease operator's judgment the result of any test or determination is inaccurate, Gatherer upon request will again conduct the questioned test or determination. The costs of the additional test or determination will be borne by Shipper unless it shows the original test or determination to have been materially inaccurate.

E.3   **Separation Equipment.** Shipper will employ only conventional mechanical separation equipment at all production sites covered by this Contract. Low temperature, absorption, and similar separation facilities are not considered conventional mechanical separation equipment. Except for liquids removed through operation of conventional mechanical separators and except for removal of substances as required to enable Shipper to comply with this Section E, Shipper will remove no components of the gas prior to delivery to Gatherer.

E.4   **Rights as to Off Specification Gas.**

(a)   If any of the gas delivered by Shipper fails to meet the quality specifications stated in this Section, Gatherer may at its option accept delivery of and pay for the gas or discontinue or curtail taking of gas at any Delivery Point whenever its quality does not conform to the quality specifications. If Gatherer accepts delivery of off specification gas from Shipper or incurs costs relating to inferior gas quality in its gathering system, Gatherer may deduct from the proceeds otherwise payable a reasonable fee for monitoring the gas quality and treating and handling the gas. Gatherer typically adjusts gas quality deduction levels annually, but may do so more often if needed.

(b)   If Gatherer is declining to take off quality gas, Shipper may by written notice to Gatherer request a release of the affected gas from commitment under this Contract. In response, Gatherer will within ____ Days either (i) waive its right to refuse to take the affected off quality gas (subject to its right to charge treating fees under this Section E) and again take gas from the affected sources, or (ii) release the affected gas from commitment under this Contract.

F. BILLING AND PAYMENT

F.1   **Statement and Payment Date.** Gatherer will render to Shipper on or before the last Day of each month a statement for the preceding month showing the MMBtus of gas delivered by Shipper, the MMBtus of gas redelivered by Gatherer, the Exhibit B Imbalance status and Monthly Cash Out amount due or payable, any conditioning fee due, and the amount due to Gatherer for services. Shipper shall pay Gatherer the amount shown as due by the billing in immediately available funds within 10 Days of issuance of the billing. Any overdue payments shall bear interest from the due date to the date of payment at the lower of (a) the prime rate posted at noon on the first Day of the month in which the delinquency occurs by J.P. Morgan Chase & Co., New York, New York, plus ___%, per annum or (b) the maximum lawful interest rate; provided that no interest will accrue as to monthly principal amounts of less than $1,000 due for less than one year when paid. The parties waive any rights to differing interest rates.

F.2   **Lack of Payment; Creditworthiness.**

(a)   If Shipper is in arrears in its payments, or is otherwise in breach of this Contract, upon ten Days advance written notice Gatherer may suspend services under this Contract unless payment is forthcoming within the notice period. If Shipper remains in default after notice to pay or otherwise perform as to any fee or imbalance, or if Gatherer is insecure of Shipper's performance, without prejudice to other remedies Gatherer may (i) refuse to receive or deliver gas, (ii) suspend performance pending adequate assurance of payments, (iii) demand an irrevocable letter of credit, surety bond, or other reasonable security for payment, (iv) require advance payment in cash or payment on a more frequent billing cycle than monthly, (v) collect any amounts due from Shipper to Gatherer or its Affiliates for any reason at any time under this or other transactions by deducting them from any proceeds payable to Shipper or Affiliates of Shipper, or (vi) take other action as Gatherer deems reasonable under the circumstances to protect its interests.

(b)   Gatherer may also require Shipper at any time to supply Gatherer credit information, including but not limited to bank references, financial statements, and names of persons with whom Gatherer may make reasonable inquiry into Shipper's creditworthiness and obtain adequate assurance of Shipper's solvency and ability to perform.

(c)   Shipper hereby grants Gatherer a security interest in gas owned or controlled by Shipper in Gatherer's possession to secure payment of all fees and other amounts due under this Contract, and following a Shipper default. Gatherer may foreclose this possessory security interest in any reasonable manner.   Upon request Shipper will execute a UCC-1 or similar Financing Statement suitable for recording describing this security interest and lien.

(d)   If Shipper in good faith disputes the amount of any billing, Shipper shall nevertheless pay to Gatherer the amounts it concedes to be correct and provide Gatherer an explanation and documentation supporting Shipper's position regarding the disputed billing. Gatherer may then continue service for a reasonable time pending resolution of the dispute.

F.3   Audit Rights; Time Limit to Assert Claims.

(a)   Each party will have the right during reasonable business hours to examine the books, records and charts of the other party to the extent necessary to verify performance of this Contract and the accuracy of any statement, charge, or computation upon execution of a reasonable confidentiality agreement. If any audit examination or review of the party's own records reveals an inaccuracy in any payment, Gatherer will promptly make the appropriate adjustment.

(b)   No adjustment for any billing or payment shall be made, and payments shall be final after the lapse of two years from their due date except as to matters that either party has noted in a specific written objection to the other party in writing during the two year period, unless within the two year period Gatherer has made the appropriate correction. However, Shipper's responsibilities for severance taxes and third party liabilities and related interest are not affected by this subsection.

(c)   No party will have any right to recoup or recover prior overpayments or underpayments that result from errors that occur in spite of good faith performance if the amounts involved do not exceed $10/month/meter. Either party may require prospective correction of such errors.

F.4   Metering Records Availability. Gatherer is not required to furnish gas volume records relating to electronic recording devices other than daily volume information except to the extent that there are indications the meter was not operating properly.

G. FORCE MAJEURE

G.1   Suspension of Performance. If either party is rendered unable, wholly or in part, by Force Majeure to carry out its obligations under this Contract, other than to make payments due, the obligations of that party, so far as they are affected by Force Majeure, will be suspended during the continuance of any inability so caused, but for no longer period.

G.2   Force Majeure Definition. "Force Majeure" means acts of God, strikes, lockouts or other industrial disturbances, acts of the public enemy, wars, blockades, insurrections, riots, epidemics, landslides, lightning, earthquakes, storms, floods, washouts, arrests and restraints of governments and people, civil disturbances, fires, explosions, breakage or accidents to machinery or lines of pipe, freezing of wells or lines of pipe, partial or entire failure of wells or sources of supply of gas, inability to obtain at reasonable cost servitudes, right of way grants, permits, governmental approvals or licenses, inability to obtain at reasonable cost materials or supplies for constructing or maintaining facilities, and other causes, whether of the kind listed above or otherwise, not within the control of the party claiming suspension and which by the exercise of reasonable diligence the party is unable to prevent or overcome.

G.3   Labor Matters Exception. The settlement of strikes or lockouts will be entirely within the discretion of the party having the difficulty, and settlement of strikes, lockouts, or other labor disturbances when that course is considered inadvisable is not required.

H. WARRANTY OF TITLE

Shipper warrants that it has good title and processing rights to the gas delivered, free and clear of any and all liens, encumbrances, and claims, and that Shipper has good right and lawful authority to sell the same. Shipper grants to Gatherer the right to process Shipper's gas for extraction of NGLs and other valuable components. If Shipper's title or right to receive any payment is questioned or involved in litigation, Gatherer will have the right to withhold the contested payments without interest until title information is received, during the litigation, until the title or right to receive the questioned payments is freed from question, or until Shipper furnishes security for repayment acceptable to Gatherer. Without impairment of Shipper's warranty of title to gas and gas processing rights, if Shipper owns or controls less than full title to the gas delivered, payments will be made only in the proportion that Shipper's interest bears to the entire title to the gas.

I. ROYALTY AND OTHER INTERESTS

Shipper is responsible for all payments to the owners of all working interests, mineral interests, royalties, overriding royalties, bonus payments, production payments and the like. Gatherer assumes no liability to Shipper's working or mineral interest, royalty, or other interest owners under this Contract.

J. TAX AND PAYMENT RESPONSIBILITIES

J.1   Gatherer Taxes. Gatherer will render and pay taxes and assessments imposed upon or attributable to its Facilities and operations, including ad valorem, franchise, sales and use, and income taxes, without prejudice to its right to recover taxes and assessments imposed on its services for Shipper under Section 5.4 above.

J.2   Shipper Taxes. Shipper shall bear and pay to taxing authorities all severance, production, excise, sales, gross receipts, occupation, and other taxes imposed upon Shipper with respect to the gas on or prior to delivery to Gatherer and other taxes imposed on Shipper's facilities and operations.

K. INDEMNIFICATION AND
RESPONSIBILITY FOR
INJURY OR DAMAGE

K.1   Title, Royalty, and Severance Taxes. SHIPPER RELEASES AND AGREES TO DEFEND, INDEMNIFY, AND SAVE GATHERER, ITS AFFILIATES, AND THEIR OFFICERS, EMPLOYEES, AND AGENTS HARMLESS FROM AND AGAINST ALL CLAIMS, CAUSES OF ACTION, LIABILITIES, AND COSTS (INCLUDING REASONABLE ATTORNEYS' FEES AND COSTS OF INVESTIGATION AND DEFENSE) RELATING TO (a) SHIPPER'S TITLE TO GAS AND GAS PROCESSING RIGHTS, (b) PAYMENTS FOR WORKING, MINERAL, ROYALTY AND OVERRIDING ROYALTY AND OTHER INTERESTS, AND (c) SALES, SEVERANCE, AND SIMILAR TAXES, THAT ARE THE RESPONSIBILITY OF SHIPPER UNDER SECTIONS H, I, AND J ABOVE.

K.2   Responsibility for Injury or Damage. As between the parties, Shipper will be in control and possession of the gas deliverable hereunder and responsible for any injury or damage relating to handling or delivery of gas until the gas has been delivered to Gatherer at the Delivery Points; after delivery, Gatherer will be deemed to be in exclusive control and possession and responsible for any injury or damage relating to handling or gathering of gas. THE PARTY HAVING RESPONSIBILITY UNDER THE PRECEDING SENTENCE SHALL RELEASE, DEFEND, INDEMNIFY, AND HOLD THE OTHER PARTY, ITS AFFILIATES, AND THEIR OFFICERS, EMPLOYEES, AND AGENTS HARMLESS FROM AND AGAINST ALL CLAIMS, CAUSES OF ACTION, LIABILITIES, AND COSTS (INCLUDING REASONABLE ATTORNEYS' FEES AND COSTS OF INVESTIGATION AND DEFENSE) ARISING FROM ACTUAL AND ALLEGED LOSS OF GAS, PERSONAL INJURY, DEATH, AND DAMAGE FOR WHICH THE

PARTY IS RESPONSIBLE UNDER THIS SECTION; PROVIDED THAT NEITHER PARTY WILL BE INDEMNIFIED FOR ITS OWN NEGLIGENCE OR THAT OF ITS AGENTS, SERVANTS, OR EMPLOYEES.

L. RIGHT OF WAY

Insofar as Shipper's lease or leases permit and insofar as Shipper or its lease operator may have any rights however derived (whether pursuant to oil and gas lease, easement, governmental agency order, regulation, statute, or otherwise), Shipper grants to Gatherer and Gatherer's gas gathering contractor, if any, and their assignees the right of free entry and the right to lay and maintain pipelines, meters, and any equipment on the lands or leases subject to this Contract as reasonably necessary in connection with the purchase or handling of Shipper's gas. Upon written request from Gatherer to Shipper, Shipper shall grant, in writing, to Gatherer or Gatherer's designee, recordable rights of ingress and egress as necessary or appropriate for the purposes of complying with the terms of this Contract. All pipelines, meters, and other equipment placed by Gatherer or Gatherer's contractors on the lands and leases will remain the property of the owner and may be removed by the owner at any time. Without limitation, Gatherer or its gathering contractor may disconnect and remove measurement and other Facilities from any Delivery Point due to low volume, quality, term expiration, or other cause.

M. ASSIGNMENT

M.1 <u>Binding on Assignees.</u> Either party may assign this Contract. This Contract is binding upon and inures to the benefit of the successors, assigns, and representatives in bankruptcy of the parties, and, subject to any prior dedications by the assignee, shall be binding upon any purchaser of Gatherer's Facilities and upon any purchaser of the properties of Shipper subject to this Contract. Nothing contained in this Section will prevent either party from mortgaging its rights as security for its indebtedness, but security is subordinate to the parties' rights and obligations under this Contract.

M.2 <u>Notice of Assignment.</u> Any assignment or sublease by Shipper of any oil and gas properties or any gas rights contracted to Gatherer will be made expressly subject to the provisions of this Contract. No transfer of or succession to the interest of Shipper, however made, will bind Gatherer unless and until the original instrument or other proper proof that the claimant is legally entitled to an interest has been furnished to Gatherer at its Division Order address noted in the Notices Section or subsequent address.

N. MISCELLANEOUS PROVISIONS

N.1 <u>Gatherer's Facilities.</u> Gatherer's service using its Facilities hereunder is and will be considered gas gathering service, and the Gatherer Facilities used to perform this Contract will be classified as non-utility exempt gas gathering facilities.

N.2 <u>Governing Law.</u> THIS CONTRACT SHALL BE GOVERNED BY AND CONSTRUED IN ACCORDANCE WITH THE LAWS OF THE STATE OF _____, without reference to those that might refer to the laws of another jurisdiction.

N.3 <u>Default and Nonwaiver.</u> A waiver by a party of any one or more defaults by the other in the performance of any provisions of this Contract will not operate as a waiver of any future default or defaults, whether of a like or different character.

N.4 <u>Counterparts.</u> This Contract may be executed in any number of counterparts, all of which will be considered together as one instrument, and this Contract will be binding upon all parties executing it, whether or not executed by all parties owning an interest in the producing sources affected by this Contract. Signed copies of this Contract and facsimiles of it shall have the same force and effect as originals.

N.5 <u>Negotiations; Entire Agreement; Amendment; No Third Party Beneficiaries.</u> The language of this Contract shall not be construed in favor of or against either Gatherer or Shipper, but shall be construed as if the language were drafted mutually by both parties. This Contract constitutes the final and complete agreement between the parties. There are no oral promises, prior agreements, understandings, obligations, warranties, or representations between the parties relating to this Contract other than those set forth herein. All waivers, modifications, amendments, and changes to this Contract shall be in writing and executed by the authorized representatives of the parties. The relations between the parties are those of independent contractors; this Contract creates no joint venture, partnership, association, other special relationship, or fiduciary obligations. There are no third party beneficiaries of this Contract.

N.6   Ratification and Third Party Gas. Notwithstanding anything contained herein to the contrary, Gatherer has no duty under this Contract to receive or handle gas attributable to production from interests of third parties that has been purchased by Shipper for resale, except that Gatherer will handle Other WI Gas. "Other WI Gas" means gas attributable to working and mineral interests owned by third parties in wells operated by Shipper that are subject to this Contract that Shipper has the right to market under an operating agreement. If Gatherer requests in writing that Shipper obtain ratification of this contract from owners of Other WI Gas, Shipper shall use all reasonable commercial efforts to cause those Other WI Gas owners to execute and deliver to Gatherer an instrument prepared by Gatherer for this purpose of ratifying and adopting this Contract with respect to the owner's Other WI Gas, and the ratifying owner will become a party to this Contract with like force and effect as though the Other WI Gas owner had executed this Contract as amended as of the time of the ratification, and all of the terms and provisions of this Contract as then amended will become binding upon Gatherer and the ratifying owner.

N.7   Compliance with Laws and Regulations. This Contract is subject to all valid statutes and rules and regulations of any duly constituted federal or state authority or regulatory body having jurisdiction. Neither party will be in default as a result of compliance with laws and regulations.

N.8   Fees and Costs. Except as to matters covered by the parties' indemnification obligations in Section J above, if mediation or arbitration is necessary to resolve a dispute other than one arising under the indemnification obligations of this Contract, each party agrees to bear its own attorneys' fees and costs of investigation and defense, and each party waives any right to recover those fees and costs from the other party or parties.

N.9   Mutual Waiver of Certain Remedies. Except as to the parties' indemnification obligations, NEITHER PARTY SHALL BE LIABLE OR OTHERWISE RESPONSIBLE TO THE OTHER FOR CONSEQUENTIAL OR INCIDENTAL DAMAGES, FOR LOST PRODUCTION, OR FOR PUNITIVE DAMAGES AS TO ANY ACTION OR OMISSION, WHETHER CHARACTERIZED AS A CONTRACT BREACH OR TORT, THAT ARISES OUT OF OR RELATES TO THIS CONTRACT OR ITS PERFORMANCE OR NONPERFORMANCE.

N.10   Waiver of Trade Practices Acts. The parties intend that Shipper's rights and remedies with respect to this Contract and all related practices of the parties shall be governed by legal principles other than the Texas Deceptive Trade Practices--Consumer Protection Act, Tex. Bus. & Com. Code Ann. §17.41 et seq. ("DTPA"). THE PARTIES HEREBY WAIVE APPLICABILITY OF THE DTPA TO THIS CONTRACT AND TO ANY AND ALL DUTIES, RIGHTS, OR REMEDIES THAT MIGHT BE IMPOSED BY THE DTPA, WHETHER THEY ARE APPLIED DIRECTLY BY THE DTPA ITSELF OR INDIRECTLY IN CONNECTION WITH OTHER STATUTES; PROVIDED THAT THE PARTIES DO NOT WAIVE §17.555 OF THE DTPA. EACH PARTY WARRANTS THAT IT IS A "BUSINESS CONSUMER" FOR PURPOSES OF THE DTPA, THAT IT HAS ASSETS OF $5 MILLION OR MORE AS SHOWN IN ITS MOST RECENT FINANCIAL STATEMENTS, THAT IT HAS KNOWLEDGE AND EXPERIENCE IN FINANCIAL AND BUSINESS MATTERS THAT ENABLES IT TO EVALUATE THE MERITS AND RISKS OF THE TRANSACTIONS CONTEMPLATED IN THIS CONTRACT, THAT IT HAS BEEN REPRESENTED BY LEGAL COUNSEL OF ITS OWN CHOICE IN ENTERING INTO THIS CONTRACT AND THE TRANSACTIONS CONTEMPLATED IN IT; AND THAT IT IS NOT IN A SIGNIFICANTLY DISPARATE BARGAINING POSITION WITH THE OTHER PARTY. Each party recognizes that the consideration for which the other party has agreed to perform under this Contract has been predicated upon the inapplicability of the DTPA and this waiver of

1 the DTPA. Each party further recognizes that the other party, in determining to proceed with entering into
2 this Contract, has expressly relied upon this waiver and the inapplicability of the DTPA.
3 **N.11   Arbitration.** The parties desire to resolve any disputes that may arise informally, if possible.
4 All disputes arising out of or relating to this Contract that are not resolved by agreement of the parties
5 must be resolved using the provisions of this Section. To that end, if a dispute or disputes arise out of or
6 relating to this Contract, a party shall give written notice of the disputes to the other involved parties,
7 and each party will appoint an employee to negotiate with the other party concerning the disputes. If the
8 disputes have not been resolved by negotiation within 30 Days of the initial dispute notice, the disputes
9 shall be resolved by arbitration in accordance with the then current International Institute for Conflict
10 Prevention and Resolution Rules for Non-Administered Arbitration and related commentary ("Rules")
11 and this Section. The arbitration shall be governed by the Federal Arbitration Act, 9 U.S.C. §§ 1, et
12 seq., and the Rules, to the exclusion of any provision of state law inconsistent with them. The
13 arbitration shall be initiated by a party seeking arbitration by written notice sent to the other party or
14 parties to be involved. The parties shall select one disinterested arbitrator with at least ten years'
15 experience in the natural gas industry or ten years' experience with natural gas law, and not previously
16 employed by either party or its Affiliates, and, if possible, shall be selected by agreement between the
17 parties. If the parties cannot select an arbitrator by agreement within 15 Days of the date of the notice of
18 arbitration, a qualified arbitrator will be selected in accordance with the Rules. If the disputes involve
19 an amount greater than $100,000, they will be decided by a panel of three arbitrators with the above
20 qualifications, one selected by each party, and the third selected by the party-appointed arbitrators, or in
21 the absence of their agreement, pursuant to the Rules. The arbitrator(s) shall resolve the disputes and
22 render a final award in accordance with the substantive law of the state referenced in Section N.2 above,
23 "Governing Law." The arbitration award will be limited by the provisions set forth in Section N.8, N.9,
24 and N.10 above, "Fees and Costs," "Mutual Waiver of Certain Remedies," and "Waiver of Trade
25 Practices Acts." The parties intend case specific dispute resolution; either party may opt out of any
26 attempted class action for all claims of any party related to this Contract. The arbitrator(s) shall set forth
27 the reasons for the award in writing, and judgment on the arbitration award may be entered in any court
28 having jurisdiction.
29 **N.12   Recording Memorandum.** Upon request by either party, the parties shall execute and place of
30 record a reasonable short form recording memorandum of this Contract and any amendments.

EXHIBIT B
To GAS GATHERING CONTRACT
Between _____ as Shipper and
DCP MIDSTREAM, LP as Gatherer
Dated as of _____, 20__

NOMINATION, SCHEDULING, AND IMBALANCE PROCEDURES

1. REDELIVERY POINTS

(a)   **Existing Points.** Subject to the downstream pipelines' capacity allocation rules, and to the extent pipeline capacity is available, the Redelivery Points for Shipper's redelivered gas shall be the existing pipeline interconnects listed on Exhibit C-2. Gatherer will use reasonable efforts to deliver at the required pipeline inlet pressure and quality specifications of the applicable pipelines that may be used as Redelivery Points.   Gatherer shall not be required to install any additional Facilities to accommodate Shipper's redelivered Gas disposition. Redelivery Points will be from the same gathering system where the gas was received unless otherwise agreed in writing.

(b)   **Transportation on Others' Facilities.** If any Redelivery Point listed in Exhibit C-2 is located beyond the inlet of gas transmission facilities, Shipper hereby appoints Gatherer as Shipper's exclusive agent during the term of this Contract to arrange for interruptible transportation in Gatherer's or Shipper's name on those transmission facilities as Gatherer deems necessary to effect redeliveries hereunder at those Redelivery Points.   Shipper also grants to Gatherer the right to obtain title to Shipper's gas delivered under this Contract as Gatherer deems necessary to aid in gathering and any transportation to the Redelivery Points. If title to Shipper's gas is transferred to Gatherer under this Section, Gatherer will again transfer title to Shipper to the MMBtus of gas to be redelivered hereunder at the Redelivery Points. No additional fee will be payable by Shipper for transportation to the Redelivery Points requiring transportation unless the applicable additional fee or fee basis for transportation to a particular Redelivery Point is stated in Exhibit C-2.

2. NOMINATION PROCESS

(a)   **Definition; Information.** "Nominations" means Shipper's notifications to Gatherer of the relevant details of Shipper's gathering service requests and related gas transportation and sales, including but not limited to:

> Contract number
> Beginning date
> Ending Date
> Delivery Points,
> Redelivery Points,
> Delivery and redelivery quantities,
> Downstream transportation Contract number

and all other details required for proper and timely Nominations and confirmations in accordance with customary industry practice. Shipper will provide timely Nominations to Gatherer. Shipper or its sales customer will be responsible for all Nomination and other transportation arrangements at and beyond the Redelivery Points. Shipper shall make or cause its sales customer to make all arrangements with the downstream pipeline and shall ensure that its desired Nominations for downstream pipeline transportation are properly and timely placed with the downstream pipeline in accordance with that pipeline's Nomination and confirmation procedures.

(b)   **Initial Estimate.** For initial deliveries at each Delivery Point, Shipper and Gatherer will agree on an estimated daily quantity reasonably in advance of the Nomination deadlines preceding the commencement of deliveries.

(c)   **Nomination Deadlines.**

1   (i)   If Shipper desires service under this Contract on any Day, Shipper shall give written
2 notice of Shipper's Nomination to Gatherer specifying the quantity of gas Shipper requests under this
3 Contract for each Day of the month. The Nomination should reflect the service for each Delivery Point
4 and each Redelivery Point, any imbalance correction quantities, and any scheduled daily variations.
5 Shipper's Nominations shall be based in good faith upon the producing ability of Shipper's wells for the
6 upcoming month, adjusted as necessary to bring cumulative receipts into line with cumulative
7 redeliveries, and adjusted to cover in kind fuel and losses. Shipper shall furnish its Nominations to
8 Gatherer by facsimile or other electronic means. Nominations shall also specify the information
9 Gatherer determines is necessary in order to perform the service requested by Shipper.
10   (ii)   For a Shipper's initial Delivery Point Nomination to be accepted for the _____ (__) Day
11 of the month, Shipper's Delivery Point Nomination must be received by Gatherer by _____ _.m.
12 _____ on the _____ (__) business Day prior to the last Day of the preceding month, or sooner if
13 required by the confirming interconnect pipeline.
14   (iii)   Shipper may, on or after the first Day of the month submit a new Nomination or revise its
15 existing Nomination for any Day during the month, provided the Nomination is received by Gatherer
16 prior to _____ _.m. _____ on the business Day prior to the Day the new or revised service is
17 requested to commence. The new or revised Nomination shall specify Shipper's anticipated service
18 requirements for the remainder of the month. New or revised Nominations shall be scheduled and
19 implemented by Gatherer on a prospective basis and only to the extent the Gatherer is able to confirm
20 the receipt and delivery of gas with the operator of the Delivery Points and Redelivery Points.
21 **(d)**   **Late Nominations.** Gatherer may in its sole reasonable discretion accept Shipper's new or
22 revised Nominations if received by Gatherer after 11:30 a.m. Central Clock Time on the business Day
23 prior to the Day new or revised service is requested to commence. These new or revised Nominations
24 shall also specify Shipper's anticipated quantities for the remainder of the month. These late revised
25 Nominations will not "bump" any previously scheduled service.
26 **(e)**   **Confirmation of Nominations.** Shipper shall cause the operator of the Delivery Point and each
27 Redelivery Point designated in any Nomination or revised Nomination to confirm the Nominations or
28 changes to them in writing prior to scheduling of the nominated volumes by Gatherer. If a conflict
29 arises between Shipper's new or revised Nominations and the operators' confirmations, or if the
30 operator at the Delivery Point or Redelivery Point does not provide a confirmation to Gatherer, Gatherer
31 may elect to use either the lower of Shipper's Nominations or the previously scheduled and confirmed
32 quantities, or may proceed under Section 3(a) below.
33 **(f)**   **Gatherer Nomination Changes.** Shipper and Gatherer will assist each other in adjusting
34 Nominations to reflect actual flows, adjustments required by downstream pipeline recipients of the gas,
35 and the efficient operations of Gatherer's Facilities. Gatherer may at any time adjust Shipper's
36 Nominations quantity as necessary to conform to the above requirements and to maintain balance.
37 Gatherer will endeavor to timely notify Shipper of these adjustments. Gatherer has no obligation to
38 accommodate any imbalances caused by Shipper's inability or failure to match actual performance with
39 Nominations.
40 **(g)**   **Balancing.** Shipper will adjust Nominations to conform to all significant production changes to
41 minimize imbalances and to meet the delivery tolerances of the downstream pipeline at each active
42 Redelivery Point.
43 **(h)**   **Deadline Changes.** Gatherer reserves the right to adjust Nomination deadlines reasonably in
44 response to Gatherer's needs and changes in the practices of the downstream pipelines at the Redelivery
45 Points.
46 **(i)**   **Volume Verification.** Gatherer is not obligated to assist Shipper in resolving payment or
47 transportation disputes with downstream pipelines or Shipper's customers other than to confirm the
48 volumes delivered at the Redelivery Points for Shipper's account.

(j) **Delivery Rates.** Shipper shall have agents or employees available at all times to receive advice and requests from Gatherer for changes in rates of delivery of gas or Nomination changes as required by Gatherer from time to time, and Shipper will modify its deliveries accordingly. Gatherer shall have the right but not the obligation to require shut-in or curtailment of deliveries at any Delivery Point when the pressure at that Delivery Point prevents or limits the flow of other gas.

(k) **Notification of Interruptions.** Each party will endeavor to provide the other party prompt notice of scheduled maintenance, construction, and other material operational events (other than weather) that will affect Shipper's Nominations, including but not limited to Facility outages and operational changes.

(l) **Hazardous Situations.** Nothing in this Contract limits any party's right to take any action whatsoever to correct or remedy any potentially hazardous situation or condition on the party's facilities. That party shall promptly give notice of the action to the other.

3. ALLOCATIONS

(a) **Delivery Point Volume Allocations.** Within its abilities Shipper will cause the operator of the Delivery Point making deliveries to Gatherer to establish, observe, and communicate to Gatherer an appropriate predetermined allocation ("PDA") method, entitlement, or continuing Nomination/Confirmation, which may be based on the guidelines of COPAS Bulletin No. 28 or the North American Energy Standards Board ("NAESB") Standards adopted in FERC Order No. 587, as revised from time to time. When Gatherer receives a PDA that has not been revoked, Gatherer will use commercially reasonable efforts to allocate the nominated MMBtus at the affected Delivery Points among suppliers based on the PDA information. If Shipper's operator fails to provide current Nomination or PDA information, Gatherer may make allocations on a pro rata basis based on scheduled Nominations and PDA information at the Delivery Point that was received, or Gatherer may elect to proceed under Section 2(e) above.

(b) **Redelivery Point Volume Allocations.** Within its abilities, Gatherer will establish an appropriate PDA or Operational Balancing Agreement with the downstream pipelines at the Redelivery Points and will communicate the relevant PDA information to all affected Shippers prior to the flow of gas.

4. IMBALANCES

(a) **Continuous Balancing.** Gatherer will make all reasonable efforts to deliver to or for the account of Shipper each Day at the Redelivery Points a volume of Gas equal to Shipper's Nominated Gas Quantity, as adjusted hereunder, less the applicable in kind fuel and loss reduction, so long as Shipper's deliveries remain reasonably in balance with Nominations. Shipper will make all reasonable efforts to balance delivery quantities daily with its current Nominated Gas Quantity at each Delivery Point plus Shipper's applicable in kind fuel and loss reduction quantity. Shipper will separately state and Nominate any imbalance makeup quantities.

(b) **Changes in Procedures.** Gatherer reserves the right to change Nominations, allocations, and imbalance penalties and procedures from time to time upon notice to Shipper as Gatherer's policies change or in response to changes in the practices or requirements of the downstream pipelines at the Redelivery Points.

(c) **Gatherer's Right To Purchase and Sell Imbalance Gas.** Gatherer is authorized to purchase and sell gas at Delivery Points and Redelivery Points to manage imbalance quantities.

(d) **Monthly Imbalance Quantity.** Gatherer will account for any imbalances between Shipper's deliveries to Gatherer at the Delivery Points and Gatherer's redeliveries to Shipper at the Redelivery Points, less the applicable in kind fuel and loss reduction. Gatherer will calculate Shipper's Monthly Imbalance Quantity in MMBtus as follows:

Total Monthly Redelivery Point MMBtus

Less (total Monthly Delivery Point MMBtus less applicable in kind fee, NGL, fuel, and loss reduction MMBtus).

1 **(e)** **Monthly Imbalance Percentage.** Gatherer will calculate Shipper's Monthly Imbalance
2 Percentage as the Monthly Imbalance Quantity divided by Shipper's total actual Redelivery Point
3 MMBtus.
4 **(f)** **Mandatory Cash Out of Monthly Imbalances.** Each month Shipper's Monthly Imbalance
5 must be cashed out using the following principles.
6   (i) **Cash Out Price.** The price used to cash out imbalances will be based on the daily prices
7 per MMBtu for the delivery month as reported for the Houston Ship Channel in the Midpoint column of
8 the Daily Pricing Survey in Platts ***Gas Daily*** (now published by The McGraw-Hill Companies). The
9 month's average of these daily price quotations is the "Cash Out Price." If a range of prices is shown
10 for any particular Day, the midpoint of the range will be that Day's price. If for any reason *Gas Daily*
11 ceases to be available for any month, the Cash Out Price for that month will be determined by Gatherer
12 based on price quotations for the general location indicated above as reported by any other generally
13 accepted industry publication chosen by Gatherer.
14   (ii) **Monthly Cash Out Valuation.** The Month's Cash Out Price will be used when the
15 Shipper's Monthly Imbalance Percentage is 5% or less. For valuation of negative Shipper's Monthly
16 Imbalance Quantities payable to Shipper, the Cash Out Price will be adjusted by the applicable Monthly
17 Imbalance Percentages as shown in the table in (iii) below. For valuation of positive Shipper's Monthly
18 Imbalance Quantities payable to Gatherer, the Cash Out Price will be adjusted similarly as shown in the
19 table in (iv) below.
20   (iii) **Monthly Imbalance Quantity Due To Shipper.** If Shipper's Monthly Imbalance
21 Quantity is negative (i.e. due Shipper, or receipts exceeding redeliveries), Gatherer will calculate Cash
22 Value Percentages according to the table below. Gatherer will value the portion of Shipper's Monthly
23 Imbalance Quantity that falls within each range below as the product of the Monthly Imbalance Quantity
24 that falls within the range multiplied by the corresponding Cash Value Percentage below multiplied by
25 the lowest price included in the month's Cash Out Price calculation.

Monthly Imbalance Percentage	Cash Value Percentage
-0% to -5%	100%
greater of -5% or 1000 MMBtu to < -10%	___%
- 10% to < -15%	___%
- 15% to < -20%	___%
- 20% to < -25%	___%
- 25% or over	___%

35   (iv) **Imbalances Due To Gatherer.** If Shipper's Monthly Imbalance Quantity is positive (i.e.
36 due Gatherer or redeliveries exceeding receipts), Gatherer will calculate Cash Value Percentages
37 according to the table below. Gatherer will value the portion of Shipper's Monthly Imbalance Quantity
38 that falls within each range below as the product of the Monthly Imbalance Quantity that falls within the
39 range multiplied by the corresponding Cash Value Percentage below multiplied by the highest price
40 included in the month's Cash Out Price calculation.

Monthly Imbalance Percentage	Cash Value Percentage
0% to 5%	100%
greater of 5% or 1000 MMBtu to < 10%	___%
10% to < 15%	___%
15% to < 20%	___%
20% to < 25%	___%
25% or over	___%

1   **(g)**   <u>Pipeline Penalties.</u> Any imbalance penalties, interest, and related costs imposed upon Gatherer
2   by pipelines attributable to Shipper's over or under deliveries or other actions or omissions shall be paid
3   by Shipper.

4   **(h)**   <u>Unauthorized Gas.</u> "Unauthorized Gas" is any quantity of gas, either received or delivered by
5   Gatherer, that cannot be identified as being received or delivered pursuant to a confirmed Nomination on
6   behalf of a Shipper, and is not otherwise identified to another contract. When Unauthorized Gas is
7   delivered to Gatherer and is identified to Shipper, Gatherer will purchase the Unauthorized Gas at a
8   price of 50% of the average Monthly Cash Out Price for the month in which the Unauthorized Gas is
9   delivered to Gatherer. When Unauthorized Gas is taken from Gatherer and the unauthorized overtake is
10   identified to Shipper, Gatherer will sell the Unauthorized Gas to Shipper at 150% of the average
11   Monthly Cash Out Price for the month in which the Unauthorized Gas was taken. Gatherer is not
12   required to pay interest for these purchases or sales if statements are delayed due to difficulties in
13   tracking of sources.

5. FORCE MAJEURE

15   If Gatherer experiences a loss of supply or inability to deliver gas due to weather, equipment
16   failure, or other Force Majeure conditions as defined in this Contract, Shipper's gas volume will be
17   reduced by a percentage equal to the overall system reduction for gas in each priority category, with
18   preference being given to the extent feasible to casinghead gas. Gatherer will use reasonable efforts to
19   notify Shipper promptly of any reduction and to restore gas volumes equitably to Shipper as soon as the
20   Force Majeure situation is corrected. Gatherer will not impose imbalance penalties for a circumstance
21   resulting from Force Majeure on its Facilities or those of others so long as notification of an event of
22   Force Majeure on the facilities of others is provided to Gatherer within 48 hours after its occurrence.

EXHIBIT C-1
To GAS GATHERING CONTRACT
Between _____ as Shipper and
DCP MIDSTREAM, LP as Gatherer
Dated as of _____, 20__

DELIVERY POINTS
AND COMMITTED LEASES AND WELLS

_____ County, [State]

No	Operator	Lease/Well Description	Delivery Point Meter #	Fuel & Loss % Reduction (X Delivery Point MMBtus)	Gathering Fee (X Delivery Point MMBtus)
1.				__ %	$0.__
2.					
3.					

EXHIBIT C-2
To GAS GATHERING CONTRACT
Between _____ as Shipper and
DCP MIDSTREAM, LP as Gatherer
Dated as of _____, 20__

REDELIVERY POINTS

_____ County, [State]

No.	Pipeline	Location	County, State	Meter #
1.				

EXHIBIT D
To GAS GATHERING CONTRACT
Between _____ as Shipper and
DCP MIDSTREAM, LP as Gatherer
Dated as of _____, 20__

SAMPLE CONDITIONING FEE CALCULATION

Plant Extraction	(A)	(B)	(C)	(D)
NGL Component	Theoretical Delivery Point Gallons Per Mcf	Plant Extraction	Gallons Extracted per Mcf	MMBtus of Extracted NGL Gallons
Ethane	1.254	3%	0.037	0.0024
Propane	0.536	19%	0.103	0.0094
Iso-Butane	0.120	42%	0.050	0.0050
Normal Butane	0.261	51%	0.133	0.0138
Pentanes+	0.324	83%	0.269	0.0305
Plant fuel MMBtu			(E)	0.018
Total shrinkage and fuel (MMBtu)				0.0792

Pricing Information
Value of Recovered NGLs

	(F)	(C)	(G)		
	Value ($/gallon)	Gallons Extracted	NGL Values		
Ethane	0.555417	0.037	0.0204		
Propane	0.830268	0.103	0.0854		
Iso-Butane	0.918512	0.050	0.0460		
Normal Butane	0.806726	0.133	0.1071		
Pentanes+	0.838661	0.269	0.2258		
Total NGL Value, $/Gal.			(G)	$	0.4848

Value of shrink & fuel

Delivery Point Btu/cf	(O)		1.150
Index Price – PEPL	(H)		$9.92
Shrink & fuel MMBtus	(J)		0.079
Shrink & fuel value	(K)	$	0.7852
Conditioning loss	(L)	$	(0.3004) per Mcf
Conditioning loss	(M)	$	(0.2612) per MMBtu
Conditioning fee		$	(0.2612) per MMBtu

Formulas:

	Plant Extraction	(A) * (B) = (C)
	Total Shrink and Fuel	Sum of (D) + (E) = (J)
	Value of NGLs	(F) * (C) = (G)
	Value of Shrink and Fuel	(J) * (H) = (K)
(L)	Processing Loss Mcf	(K) - (G) = (L)
(M)	Processing Loss MMBtu	(L) / (O) = (M)

Where:

(A):	Wellhead GPM
(B):	Plant Extraction
(C):	NGL Gallons Extracted
(D):	Total MMBtu of NGL Gallons Extracted

(E):	Plant Fuel Use Percent
(F):	NGL Price – Monthly Average *OPIS* Mont Belvieu posting, less Plant's T&FS
(H):	Gas Price – imbalance Cash Out Price
(J):	Total Shrink and Fuel
(K):	Shrink and Fuel Value

NOTES

1.   Instead of selling gas at the wellhead, the producer may prefer to seek markets beyond the leased premises or the field of production. Typically the first major link of transportation away from the wellhead is provided by a gathering system. This form illustrates the terms required to measure, receive, transport, and deliver gas for a per MMBtu fee.

2.   The editors thank Richard J. Gognat, who prepared the introductory comments and helped develop this form, and his employer, DCP Midstream, LP, for granting permission to use this form. For information regarding the natural-gas midstream services offered by DCP Midstream, LP, visit its web site at http://www.dcpmidstream.com.

GAS TRANSPORTATION AGREEMENT
EFFECTIVE DATE:

TRANSPORTER CONTRACT NO.	**SHIPPER CONTRACT NO.**
TRANSPORTER:	**SHIPPER:**

OVERLAND TRAIL TRANSMISSION, L.L.C.
370 17TH STREET, SUITE 900
DENVER, CO 80202

ATTN: CONTRACT ADMINISTRATION	**ATTN:**
TELEPHONE: (303) 595-3331	TELEPHONE:
FACSIMILE: (303) 595-0480	FACSIMILE:

THIS AGREEMENT FOR TRANSPORTATION SERVICE IS ENTERED INTO EFFECTIVE AS OF 9:00 AM CENTRAL CLOCK TIME ON _____ AND SHALL CONTINUE IN FULL FORCE AND EFFECT FOR A PRIMARY TERM UNTIL _____ AND MONTH TO MONTH THEREAFTER UNTIL TERMINATED BY EITHER PARTY UPON (1) DAY'S PRIOR WRITTEN NOTICE.

THIS AGREEMENT INCORPORATES AND IS SUBJECT TO ALL OF THE TERMS AND CONDITIONS SET OUT HEREIN; ON EXHIBITS A THROUGH C TO THIS AGREEMENT; AND IN APPENDIX "A", TRANSPORTER'S STATEMENT OF OPERATING CONDITIONS APPLICABLE TO TRANSPORTATION SERVICE UNDER NGPA SECTION 311(A)(2), AS FILED WITH FERC AND AS MAY BE AMENDED FROM TIME TO TIME; AND ANY SPECIAL PROVISIONS SPECIFIED BELOW.

ACCEPTED AND AGREED TO THIS _____ DAY OF

_____,_____	_____,
TRANSPORTER:	**SHIPPER:**
OVERLAND TRAIL TRANSMISSION, LLC	
BY:	BY:
NAME:	NAME:
TITLE:	TITLE:

FORWARD TWO EXECUTED COPIES OF THIS DOCUMENT TO OVERLAND TRAIL TRANSMISSION, LLC FOR PROCESSING

1. **Exhibit "A" <u>Interruptible 311</u>**: The Transportation rate, Fuel rate, Point(s) of Receipt, Point(s) of Delivery and quantities set forth on Exhibit "A" shall be in effect for the term of this Agreement and may be modified, added to, or deleted by a replacement Exhibit "A" with each party's written agreement to such amendment. Each replacement Exhibit "A" shall be numbered in consecutive order from "A-1" through "A-n" and shall supersede the previous Exhibit "A-n". Herein, Exhibit "A" refers collectively to Exhibit "A-1" through Exhibit "A-n".

2. **Exhibit "B" <u>Firm 311</u>**: The Transportation rate, Fuel rate, Point(s) of Receipt, Point(s) of Delivery and quantities set forth on Exhibit "B" shall be in effect for the term of this Agreement and may be modified, added to, or deleted by a replacement Exhibit "B" with each party's written agreement to such amendment. Each replacement Exhibit "B" shall be numbered in consecutive order from "B-1" through "B-n" and shall supersede the previous Exhibit "D-n". Herein, Exhibit "D" refers collectively to Exhibit "D-1" through Exhibit "D-n".

3. **Quantity**: Subject to all of the terms and conditions of this Agreement and the attached Statement of Operating Conditions, Appendix "A", Transporter agrees to receive into its Pipeline System for the account of Shipper up to the maximum daily quantity of gas, plus applicable fuel, at the Point(s) of Receipt specified in Exhibits A through C for delivery by Transporter to Shipper at the Point(s) of Delivery specified in Exhibits A through C, less applicable fuel, subject to interruption or curtailment as set forth in the Statement of Operating Conditions attached hereto as Appendix "A".

4. **Rate**: Shipper agrees to pay Transporter a transportation fee for each MMBtu of gas delivered at the Point(s) of Delivery, as specified on Exhibits "A" through "B", attached to this Agreement. Transporter shall retain a percentage of the MMBtu received at the Point(s) of Receipt for fuel and line loss as denoted on Exhibits A through B.

5. **Term**: The term of this Agreement shall be the term specified on the front page of this Agreement, except that, in the event the quantities of gas received and delivered hereunder are not equal at the end of the term of the Agreement, the term will be extended for the receipt or delivery of gas until such balance is achieved in accordance with the Statement of Operating Conditions, attached hereto as Appendix "A".

6. **Regulatory Status of Gas:**

(a) Whenever Shipper's gas is delivered from a receipt point or to a delivery point that is not interconnected with the facilities of an interstate pipeline company, Shipper shall be deemed to have represented and warranted to Transporter that all of the gas so delivered to Transporter or received from Transporter shall (i) have been produced in the State of Wyoming from reserves not dedicated or committed to interstate commerce, (ii) not be or have not been received from or transported through any interstate pipeline company or any intrastate pipeline company which claims exemption from the provisions of the Natural Gas Act of 1938 pursuant to Section 1(c) thereof, and (iii) not have been or be commingled at any point with gas which is received from or transported through any interstate pipeline company or any intrastate pipeline company which claims exemption from the provisions of the Natural Gas Act of 1938 pursuant to Section 1(c) thereof, or with Gas which is or may be sold, consumed, transported, or otherwise utilized in interstate commerce, in such a manner which will subject the gas delivered by or to Shipper hereunder or any of Transporter's or its affiliate's pipeline, transmission, storage or related facilities, or any portions thereof, to the jurisdiction of the FERC or any successor authority incident to the provisions of Section 1(b) or Section 1(c) of the Natural Gas Act of 1938 (the "NGA").

(b) When Shipper's gas that is delivered to or from Transporter's pipeline is also transported by an interstate pipeline company, Shipper shall be deemed to have represented and warranted to Transporter that the transportation of gas hereunder is "on behalf of" an interstate pipeline company or a local distribution company served by an interstate pipeline company and otherwise qualifies as transportation pursuant to Section 311(a)(2) of the NGPA and FERC's rules, regulations and orders thereunder. If requested by Transporter, Shipper shall provide evidence satisfactory to Transporter that the service provided hereunder is "on behalf of" an interstate pipeline company or a local distribution company served by an interstate pipeline company, and that such service otherwise qualifies as transportation pursuant to Section 311(a)(2) of the NGPA and FERC's rules, regulations and orders thereunder.

(c) Transporter shall have no obligation under this Agreement if Transporter, in its sole discretion determines at any time that Shipper has breached any applicable representation or warranty referenced above or that the transportation to be provided hereunder does not so qualify. Shipper agrees to indemnify and hold Transporter harmless from and against any and all such, actions, damages, costs, losses and expenses sustained by Transporter relative to any breach by Shipper of any representation or warranty herein expressed.

(D) THE RULES AND REGULATION OF THE APPLICABLE JURISDICTIONAL AGENCY (WYOMING PUBLIC SERVICE COMMISSION, IN THE CASE OF INTRASTATE SERVICE AND FERC, IN THE CASE OF 311 SERVICE) GOVERN TRANSPORTER'S PROVISION OF SERVICE UNDER THIS AGREEMENT, AND IN THE EVENT ANY CONTRACT TERM OF PROVISION IS INCONSISTENT WITH THESE RULES AND REGULATIONS, OR, IN THE CASE OF 311 SERVICE, WITH THE STATEMENT OF OPERATING CONDITIONS THAT TRANSPORTER HAS ADOPTED AND IS REQUIRED TO KEEP ON FILE WITH FERC, SUCH RULES AND REGULATIONS OR THE STATEMENT OF OPERATING CONDITIONS WILL CONTROL AND THIS AGREEMENT WILL BE MODIFIED

7. **Notices**: Unless otherwise provided in this Agreement, any notice, request or demand which either party desires to serve upon the other respecting this Agreement, shall be in writing and shall be considered as delivered when hand delivered or, if mailed by United States certified mail, postage prepaid, three (3) days after mailing or, if sent by facsimile transmission, when receipt is confirmed by the equipment of the transmitting party; provided, if receipt of a facsimile transmission is confirmed after normal business hours, receipt shall be deemed to be the next business day. Such notice shall be given to the other party at the following address:

TRANSPORTER:
FOR ACCOUNTING MATTERS:
OVERLAND TRAIL TRANSMISSION, LLC
ATTN: REVENUE ACCOUNTING
370 17TH STREET, SUITE 2500
DENVER, COLORADO 80202
Telephone: (303) 595-3331
Facsimile: (303) 595-0480

FOR REMITTANCE:
AT ADDRESS SHOWN ON INVOICE
X___ By Wire Transfer
____ By Check
____ ACH Transfer
____ Other

FOR SCHEDULING:
OVERLAND TRAIL TRANSMISSION, LLC
ATTN: MARKETING OPERATIONS – OTTCO
370 17TH STREET, SUITE 2500
DENVER, COLORADO 80202
Telephone: (303) 595-3331
Facsimile: (303) 595-0480

FOR DISPATCHING EMERGENCY:
OVERLAND TRAIL TRANSMISSION, LLC
ATTN: GAS CONTROL
370 17TH STREET, SUITE 2500
DENVER, COLORADO 80202
Telephone: (303) 595-331
Facsimile: (303) 595-0480

SHIPPER:
FOR ACCOUNTING MATTERS: FOR CONTRACT NOTICES:FOR SCHEDULING:

Telephone: Telephone: Telephone:
Facsimile: Facsimile: Facsimile:

or to such other address as either party shall designate by notice in the manner provided above. Operating communications by telephone or other mutually agreeable means shall be considered as duly delivered without subsequent written confirmation, unless written confirmation is requested by either party or is required by this Agreement.

Appendix "A"
OVERLAND TRAIL TRANSMISSION, LLC
Statement of Operating Conditions

NOTES

1.   Once gas is gathered at or near the field of production, or processed in a processing facility, the producer may desire to purchase additional transportation services to move the gas to other available markets. The above form is representative of a transportation contract on an intrastate pipeline system. Often there may be subsequent deliveries of the gas, with the need for additional transportation contracts, on other intrastate or interstate pipelines as the commodity is moved further away from its production situs.

2.   The editors thank Richard J. Gognat, who prepared the introductory comments and helped develop this form, and his employer, DCP Midstream, LP, for granting permission to use this form. For information regarding the natural gas midstream services offered by DCP Midstream, LP, visit its web site at http://www.dcpmidstream.com.

Chapter 6

FEDERAL, STATE AND
INDIAN LANDS

Form 3100-11
(July 2006)

UNITED STATES
DEPARTMENT OF THE INTERIOR
BUREAU OF LAND MANAGEMENT

Serial Number

OFFER TO LEASE AND LEASE FOR OIL AND GAS

The undersigned (page 2) offers to lease all or any of the lands in Item 2 that are available for lease pursuant to the Mineral Lands Leasing Act of 1920. as amended and supplemented (30 U.S.C. 181 et seq.). the Mineral Leasing Act for Acquired Lands of 1947. as amended (30 U.S.C. 351-359), or _____ (other).

READ INSTRUCTIONS BEFORE COMPLETING

1. Name

   Street

   City, State. Zip Code

2. This application/offer/lease is for: *(Check Only One)* ☐ PUBLIC DOMAIN LANDS ☐ ACQUIRED LANDS (percent U.S. interest _____)

   Surface managing agency if other than Bureau of Land Management (BLM): _____ Unit/Project _____

   Legal description of land requested: *Parcel No.: _____ *Sale Date (mm/dd/yyyy): _____

   *See Item 2 in Instructions below prior to completing Parcel Number and Sale Date.

T.	R.	Meridian	State	County

Total acres applied for _____

Amount remitted: Filing fee $ _____ Rental fee $ _____ Total $ _____

DO NOT WRITE BELOW THIS LINE

3. Land included in lease:

T.	R.	Meridian	State	County

Total acres in lease _____

Rental retained $ _____

This lease is issued granting the exclusive right to drill for, mine, extract, remove and dispose of all the oil and gas (except helium) in the lands described in Item 3 together with the right to build and maintain necessary improvements thereupon for the term indicated below, subject to renewal or extension in accordance with the appropriate leasing authority. Rights granted are subject to applicable laws, the terms, conditions, and attached stipulations of this lease, the Secretary of the Interior's regulations and formal orders in effect as of lease issuance, and to regulations and formal orders hereafter promulgated when not inconsistent with lease rights granted or specific provisions of this lease.

NOTE: This lease is issued to the high bidder pursuant to his/her duly executed bid or nomination form submitted under 43 CFR 3120 and is subject to the provisions of that bid or nomination and those specified on this form.

Type and primary term:

☐ Noncompetitive lease (ten years)

☐ Competitive lease (ten years)

☐ Other _____

THE UNITED STATES OF AMERICA

by _____
                        (BLM)

_____
        (Title)   (Date)

_____ EFFECTIVE DATE OF LEASE _____

(Continued on page 2)

410

4. (a) Undersigned certifies that (1) offeror is a citizen of the United States; an association of such citizens; a municipality; or a corporation organized under the laws of the United States or of any State or Territory thereof. (2) all parties holding an interest in the offer are in compliance with 43 CFR 3100 and the leasing authorities; (3) offeror's chargeable interests, direct and indirect, in each public domain and acquired lands separately in the same State, do not exceed 246,080 acres in oil and gas leases (of which up to 200,000 acres may be in oil and gas options or 300,000 acres in leases in each leasing District in Alaska of which up to 200,000 acres may be in options, (4) offeror is not considered a minor under the laws of the State in which the lands covered by this offer are located; (5) offeror is in compliance with qualifications concerning Federal coal lease holdings provided in sec. 2(a)2(A) of the Mineral Leasing Act; (6) offeror is in compliance with reclamation requirements for all Federal oil and gas lease holdings as required by sec. 17(g) of the Mineral Leasing Act; and (7) offeror is not in violation of sec. 41 of the Act. (b) Undersigned agrees that signature to this offer constitutes acceptance of this lease, including all terms conditions, and stipulations of which offeror has been given notice, and any amendment or separate lease that may include any land described in this offer open to leasing at the time this offer was filed but omitted for any reason from this lease. The offeror further agrees that this offer cannot be withdrawn, either in whole or in part unless the withdrawal is received by the proper BLM State Office before this lease, an amendment to this lease, or a separate lease, whichever covers the land described in the withdrawal, has been signed on behalf of the United States.

This offer will be rejected and will afford offeror no priority if it is not properly completed and executed in accordance with the regulations, or if it is not accompanied by the required payments.

Duly executed this _____ day of _____ _____ , 20 ____   _____

(Signature of Lessee or Attorney-in-fact)

Title 18 U.S.C. Section 1001 and Title 43 U.S.C. Section 1212 make it a crime for any person knowingly and willfully to make to any department or Agency of the United States any false, fictitious, or fraudulent statements or representations as to any matter within its jurisdiction.

LEASE TERMS

Sec. 1. Rentals--Rentals must be paid to proper office of lessor in advance of each lease year. Annual rental rates per acre or fraction thereof are:

(a) Noncompetitive lease. $1.50 for the first 5 years; thereafter $2.00;

(b) Competitive lease, $1.50; for the first 5 years; thereafter $2.00;

(c) Other, see attachment, or

as specified in regulations at the time this lease is issued.

If this lease or a portion thereof is committed to an approved cooperative or unit plan which includes a well capable of producing leased resources, and the plan contains a provision for allocation of production, royalties must be paid on the production allocated to this lease. However, annual rentals must continue to be due at the rate specified in (a), (b), or (c) rentals for those lands not within a participating area.

Failure to pay annual rental, if due, on or before the anniversary date of this lease (or next official working day if office is closed) must automatically terminate this lease by operation of law. Rentals may be waived, reduced, or suspended by the Secretary upon a sufficient showing by lessee.

Sec. 2. Royalties--Royalties must be paid to proper office of lessor. Royalties must be computed in accordance with regulations on production removed or sold. Royalty rates are:

(a) Noncompetitive lease, 12 1/2%;

(b) Competitive lease, 12 1/2 %;

(c) Other, see attachment; or

as specified in regulations at the time this lease is issued.

Lessor reserves the right to specify whether royalty is to be paid in value or in kind, and the right to establish reasonable minimum values on products after giving lessee notice and an opportunity to be heard. When paid in value, royalties must be due and payable on the last day of the month following the month in which production occurred. When paid in kind, production must be delivered, unless otherwise agreed to by lessor, in merchantable condition on the premises where produced without cost to lessor. Lessee must not be required to hold such production in storage beyond the last day of the month following the month in which production occurred, nor must lessee be held liable for loss or destruction of royalty oil or other products in storage from causes beyond the reasonable control of lessee.

Minimum royalty in lieu of rental of not less than the rental which otherwise would be required for that lease year must be payable at the end of each lease year beginning on or after a discovery in paying quantities. This minimum royalty may be waived, suspended, or reduced, and the above royalty rates may be reduced, for all or portions of this lease if the Secretary determines that such action is necessary to encourage the greatest ultimate recovery of the leased resources, or is otherwise justified.

An interest charge will be assessed on late royalty payments or underpayments in accordance with the Federal Oil and Gas Royalty Management Act of 1982 (FOGRMA) (30 U.S.C. 1701). Lessee must be liable for royalty payments on oil and gas lost or wasted from a lease site when such loss or waste is due to negligence on the part of the operator, or due to the failure to comply with any rule, regulation, order, or citation issued under FOGRMA or the leasing authority.

(Continued on page 3)   (Form 3100-11, page 2)

Sec. 3. Bonds - A bond must be filed and maintained for lease operations as required under regulations.

Sec. 4. Diligence, rate of development, unitization, and drainage - Lessee must exercise reasonable diligence in developing and producing, and must prevent unnecessary damage to, loss of, or waste of leased resources. Lessor reserves right to specify rates of development and production in the public interest and to require lessee to subscribe to a cooperative or unit plan, within 30 days of notice, if deemed necessary for proper development and operation of area, field, or pool embracing these leased lands. Lessee must drill and produce wells necessary to protect leased lands from drainage or pay compensatory royalty for drainage in amount determined by lessor.

Sec. 5. Documents, evidence, and inspection - Lessee must file with proper office of lessor, not later than 30 days after effective date thereof, any contract or evidence of other arrangement for sale or disposal of production. At such times and in such form as lessor may prescribe, lessee must furnish detailed statements showing amounts and quality of all products removed and sold, proceeds therefrom, and amount used for production purposes or unavoidably lost. Lessee may be required to provide plats and schematic diagrams showing development work and improvements, and reports with respect to parties in interest, expenditures, and depreciation costs. In the form prescribed by lessor, lessee must keep a daily drilling record, a log, information on well surveys and tests, and a record of subsurface investigations and furnish copies to lessor when required. Lessee must keep open at all reasonable times for inspection by any representative of lessor, the leased premises and all wells, improvements, machinery, and fixtures thereon, and all books, accounts, maps, and records relative to operations, surveys, or investigations on or in the leased lands. Lessee must maintain copies of all contracts, sales agreements, accounting records, and documentation such as billings, invoices, or similar documentation that supports costs claimed as manufacturing, preparation, and/or transportation costs. All such records must be maintained in lessee's accounting offices for future audit by lessor. Lessee must maintain required records for 6 years after they are generated or, if an audit or investigation is underway, until released of the obligation to maintain such records by lessor.

During existence of this lease, information obtained under this section will be closed to inspection by the public in accordance with the Freedom of Information Act (5 U.S.C. 552).

Sec. 6. Conduct of operations - Lessee must conduct operations in a manner that minimizes adverse impacts to the land, air, and water, to cultural, biological, visual, and other resources, and to other land uses or users. Lessee must take reasonable measures deemed necessary by lessor to accomplish the intent of this section. To the extent consistent with lease rights granted, such measures may include, but are not limited to, modification to siting or design of facilities, timing of operations, and specification of interim and final reclamation measures. Lessor reserves the right to continue existing uses and to authorize future uses upon or in the leased lands, including the approval of easements or rights-of-way. Such uses must be conditioned so as to prevent unnecessary or unreasonable interference with rights of lessee.

Prior to disturbing the surface of the leased lands, lessee must contact lessor to be apprised of procedures to be followed and modifications or reclamation measures that may be necessary. Areas to be disturbed may require inventories or special studies to determine the extent of impacts to other resources. Lessee may be required to complete minor inventories or short term special studies under guidelines provided by lessor. If in the conduct of operations, threatened or endangered species, objects of historic or scientific interest, or substantial unanticipated environmental effects are observed, lessee must immediately contact lessor. Lessee must cease any operations that would result in the destruction of such species or objects.

Sec. 7. Mining operations - To the extent that impacts from mining operations would be substantially different or greater than those associated with normal drilling operations, lessor reserves the right to deny approval of such operations.

Sec. 8. Extraction of helium - Lessor reserves the option of extracting or having extracted helium from gas production in a manner specified and by means provided by lessor at no expense or loss to lessee or owner of the gas. Lessee must include in any contract of sale of gas the provisions of this section.

Sec. 9. Damages to property - Lessee must pay lessor for damage to lessor's improvements, and must save and hold lessor harmless from all claims for damage or harm to persons or property as a result of lease operations.

Sec. 10. Protection of diverse interests and equal opportunity - Lessee must pay, when due, all taxes legally assessed and levied under laws of the State or the United States; accord all employees complete freedom of purchase; pay all wages at least twice each month in lawful money of the United States; maintain a safe working environment in accordance with standard industry practices; and take measures necessary to protect the health and safety of the public.

Lessor reserves the right to ensure that production is sold at reasonable prices and to prevent monopoly. If lessee operates a pipeline, or owns controlling interest in a pipeline or a company operating a pipeline, which may be operated accessible to oil derived from these leased lands, lessee must comply with section 28 of the Mineral Leasing Act of 1920.

Lessee must comply with Executive Order No. 11246 of September 24, 1965, as amended, and regulations and relevant orders of the Secretary of Labor issued pursuant thereto. Neither lessee nor lessee's subcontractors must maintain segregated facilities.

Sec. 11. Transfer of lease interests and relinquishment of lease - As required by regulations, lessee must file with lessor any assignment or other transfer of an interest in this lease. Lessee may relinquish this lease or any legal subdivision by filing in the proper office a written relinquishment, which will be effective as of the date of filing, subject to the continued obligation of the lessee and surety to pay all accrued rentals and royalties.

Sec. 12. Delivery of premises - At such time as all or portions of this lease are returned to lessor, lessee must place affected wells in condition for suspension or abandonment, reclaim the land as specified by lessor and, within a reasonable period of time, remove equipment and improvements not deemed necessary by lessor for preservation of producible wells.

Sec. 13. Proceedings in case of default - If lessee fails to comply with any provisions of this lease, and the noncompliance continues for 30 days after written notice thereof, this lease will be subject to cancellation unless or until the leasehold contains a well capable of production of oil or gas in paying quantities, or the lease is committed to an approved cooperative or unit plan or communitization agreement which contains a well capable of production of unitized substances in paying quantities. This provision will not be construed to prevent the exercise by lessor of any other legal and equitable remedy, including waiver of the default. Any such remedy or waiver will not prevent later cancellation for the same default occurring at any other time. Lessee will be subject to applicable provisions and penalties of FOGRMA (30 U.S.C. 1701).

Sec. 14. Heirs and successors-in-interest - Each obligation of this lease will extend to and be binding upon, and every benefit hereof will inure to the heirs, executors, administrators, successors, beneficiaries, or assignees of the respective parties hereto.

(Continued on page 4)   (Form 3100-11, page 3)

412

A. General:

    1. Page 1 of this form is to be completed only by parties filing for a noncompetitive lease. The BLM will complete page 1 of the form for all other types of leases.

    2. Entries must be typed or printed plainly in ink. Offeror must sign Item 4 in ink.

    3. An original and two copies of this offer must be prepared and filed in the proper BLM State Office. See regulations at 43 CFR 1821.2-1 for office locations.

    4. If more space is needed, additional sheets must be attached to each copy of the form submitted.

B. Special:

    Item 1 - Enter offeror's name and billing address.

    Item 2 - Identify the mineral status and, if acquired lands, percentage of Federal ownership of applied for minerals. Indicate the agency controlling the surface of the land and the name of the unit or project which the land is a part. The same offer may not include both Public Domain and Acquired lands. Offeror also may provide other information that will assist in establishing title for minerals. The description of land must conform to 43 CFR 3110. A single parcel number and Sale Date will be the only acceptable description during the period from the first day following the end of a competitive process until the end of that same month, using the parcel number on the List of Lands Available for Competitive Nominations or the Notice of Competitive Lease Sale, whichever is appropriate.

Payments: The amount remitted must include the filing fee and the first year's rental at the rate of $1.50 per acre or fraction thereof. The full rental based on the total acreage applied for must accompany an offer even if the mineral interest of the United States is less than 100 percent. The filing fee will be retained as a service charge even if the offer is completely rejected or withdrawn. To protect priority, it is important that the rental submitted be sufficient to cover all the land requested. If the land requested includes lots or irregular quarter-quarter sections, the exact area of which is not known to the offeror, rental should be submitted on the basis of each such lot or quarter-quarter section containing 40 acres. If the offer is withdrawn or rejected in whole or in part before a lease issues, the rental remitted for the parts withdrawn or rejected will be returned.

Item 3 - This space will be completed by the United States.

NOTICES

NOTES

1.   The federal leasing process is dominated by statute and administrative regulation. The relevant leasing regulations are found at 42 C.F.R. Part 3100. Information concerning onshore oil and gas leasing and development operations on federal lands can be obtained from the Bureau of Land Management (BLM). The BLM's web site can be found at http://www.blm.gov; this site also has links to the various BLM state offices.

2.   Note that the first page of the Offer to Lease for Oil and Gas provides that the "Rights granted are subject to … regulations and formal orders hereafter promulgated when not inconsistent with the lease rights granted or specific provisions of this lease." Section 2 of the Offer to Lease and Lease for Oil and Gas Form states: "Royalties must be computed in accordance with regulations on production removed or sold." Another portion of section 2 provides: "Lessor reserves the right to specify whether royalty is to be paid in value or in kind, and the right to establish reasonable minimum values on products after giving lessee notice and an opportunity to be heard." Royalty-valuation regulations are found at 30 C.F.R. Part 206 and are administered by the Minerals Management Service (MMS). The MMS is the agency tasked with collecting, auditing, and distributing oil and gas revenues from federal and Indian lands. Information concerning the MMS and its programs can be found at http://www.mms.gov. In addition to its royalty management programs, the MMS also administers offshore oil and gas leasing and development activities.

Office	Serial number
Cash bonus	Rental rate per acre, hectare or fraction thereof
Minimum royalty rate per acre, hectare or fraction thereof	Royalty rate
	Profit share rate

UNITED STATES
DEPARTMENT OF THE INTERIOR
MINERALS MANAGEMENT SERVICE

OIL AND GAS LEASE OF SUBMERGED LANDS
UNDER THE OUTER CONTINENTAL SHELF LANDS ACT

This form does not constitute an information collection as defined by 44 U.S.C. 3502 and therefore does not require approval by the Office of Management and Budget.

This lease is effective as of _____ (hereinafter called the "Effective Date") and shall continue for an initial period of _____ years (hereinafter called the "Initial Period") by and between the United States of America (hereinafter called the "Lessor"), by the Minerals Management Service, its authorized officer, and

(hereinafter called the "Lessee"). In consideration of any cash payment heretofore made by the Lessee to the Lessor and in consideration of the promises, terms, conditions, and covenants contained herein, including the Stipulation(s) numbered _____ attached hereto, the Lessee and Lessor agree as follows:

Sec. 1. Statutes and Regulations. This lease is issued pursuant to the Outer Continental Shelf Lands Act of August 7, 1953, 67 Stat. 462; 43 U.S.C. 1331 et seq., as amended (92 Stat. 629), (hereinafter called the "Act"). The lease is issued subject to the Act; all regulations issued pursuant to the Act and in existence upon the Effective Date of this lease; all regulations issued pursuant to the statute in the future which provide for the prevention of waste and conservation of the natural resources of the Outer Continental Shelf and the protection of correlative rights therein; and all other applicable statutes and regulations.

Sec. 2. Rights of Lessee. The Lessor hereby grants and leases to the Lessee the exclusive right and privilege to drill for, develop, and produce oil and gas resources, except helium gas, in the submerged lands of the Outer Continental Shelf containing approximately _____ acres or _____ hectares (hereinafter referred to as the "leased area"), described as follows:

Form MMS-2005 (March 1986)
(Supersedes MMS-2005 August 1982)

415

These rights include:

(a) the nonexclusive right to conduct within the leased area geological and geophysical explorations in accordance with applicable regulations;

(b) the nonexclusive right to drill water wells within the leased area, unless the water is part of geopressured-geothermal and associated resources, and to use the water produced therefrom for operations pursuant to the Act free of cost, on the condition that the drilling is conducted in accordance with procedures approved by the Director of the Minerals Management Service or the Director's delegate (hereinafter called the "Director"); and

(c) the right to construct or erect and to maintain within the leased area artificial islands, installations, and other devices permanently or temporarily attached to the seabed and other works and structures necessary to the full enjoyment of the lease, subject to compliance with applicable laws and regulations.

Sec. 3. Term. This lease shall continue from the Effective Date of the lease for the Initial Period and so long thereafter as oil or gas is produced from the leased area in paying quantities, or drilling or well reworking operations, as approved by the Lessor, are conducted thereon, or as otherwise provided by regulation.

Sec. 4. Rentals. The Lessee shall pay the Lessor, on or before the first day of each lease year which commences prior to a discovery in paying quantities of oil or gas on the leased area, a rental as shown on the face hereof.

Sec. 5. Minimum Royalty. The Lessee shall pay the Lessor, at the expiration of each lease year which commences after a discovery of oil and gas in paying quantities, a minimum royalty as shown on the face hereof or, if there is production, the difference between the actual royalty required to be paid with respect to such lease year and the prescribed minimum royalty if the actual royalty paid is less than the minimum royalty.

Sec. 6. Royalty on Production.

(a) The Lessee shall pay a fixed royalty as shown on the face hereof in amount or value of production saved, removed, or sold from the leased area. Gas (except helium) and oil of all kinds are subject to royalty. Any Lessee is liable for royalty payments on oil or gas lost or wasted from a lease site when such loss or waste is due to negligence on the part of the operator of the lease, or due to the failure to comply with any rule or regulation, order, or citation issued under the Federal Oil and Gas Royalty Management Act of 1982 or the Act. The Lessor shall determine whether production royalty shall be paid in amount or value.

(b) The value of production for purposes of computing royalty on production from this lease shall never be less than the fair market value of the production. The value of production shall be the estimated reasonable value of the production as determined by the Lessor, due consideration being given to the highest price paid for a part or for a majority of production of like quality in the same field or area, to the price received by the Lessee, to posted prices, to regulated prices, and to other relevant matters. Except when the Lessor, in its discretion, determines not to consider special pricing relief from otherwise applicable Federal regulatory requirements, the value of production for the purposes of computing royalty shall not be deemed to be less than the gross proceeds accruing to the Lessee from the sale thereof. In the absence of good reason to the contrary, value

Page 2

computed on the basis of the highest price paid or offered at the time of production in a fair and open market for the major portion of like-quality products produced and sold from the field or area where the leased area is situated will be considered to be a reasonable value.

(c) When paid in value, royalties on production shall be due and payable monthly on the last day of the month next following the month in which the production is obtained, unless the Lessor designates a later time. When paid in amount, such royalties shall be delivered at pipeline connections or in tanks provided by the Lessee. Such deliveries shall be made at reasonable times and intervals and, at the Lessor's option, shall be effected either (i) on or immediately adjacent to the leased area, without cost to the Lessor, or (ii) at a more convenient point closer to shore or on shore, in which event the Lessee shall be entitled to reimbursement for the reasonable cost of transporting the royalty substance to such delivery point.

Sec. 7. Payments. The Lessee shall make all payments (rentals, royalties and any other payments required by this lease) to the Lessor by electronic transfer of funds, check, draft on a solvent bank, or money order unless otherwise provided by regulations or by direction of the Lessor. Rentals, royalties, and any other payments required by this lease shall be made payable to the Minerals Management Service and tendered to the Director. Determinations made by the Lessor as to the amount of payment due shall be presumed to be correct and paid as due.

Sec. 8. Bonds. The Lessee shall maintain at all times the bond(s) required by regulation prior to the issuance of the lease and shall furnish such additional security as may be required by the Lessor if, after operations have begun, the Lessor deems such additional security to be necessary.

Sec. 9. Plans. The Lessee shall conduct all operations on the leased area in accordance with approved exploration plans and approved development and production plans as are required by regulations. The Lessee may depart from an approved plan only as provided by applicable regulations.

Sec. 10. Performance. The Lessee shall comply with all regulations and Orders. After due notice in writing, the Lessee shall drill such wells and produce at such rates as the Lessor may require in order that the leased area or any part thereof may be properly and timely developed and produced in accordance with sound operating principles.

Sec. 11. Directional Drilling. A directional well drilled under the leased area from a surface location on nearby land not covered by this lease shall be deemed to have the same effect for all purposes of the lease as a well drilled from a surface location on the leased area. In those circumstances, drilling shall be considered to have been commenced on the leased area when drilling is commenced on the nearby land for the purpose of directionally drilling under the leased area, and production of oil or gas from the leased area through any directional well surfaced on nearby land or drilling or reworking of any such directional well shall be considered production or drilling or reworking operations on the leased area for all purposes of the lease. Nothing contained in this Section shall be construed as granting to the Lessee any interest, license, easement, or other right in any nearby land.

Sec. 12. Safety Requirements. The Lessee shall:

(a) maintain all places of employment within the leased area in compliance with occupational safety and health standards and, in addition, free from recognized hazards to employees of the Lessee or of any contractor or subcontractor operating within the lease area;

(b) maintain all operations within the leased area in compliance with regulations or orders intended to protect persons, property, and the environment on the Outer Continental Shelf; and

(c) allow prompt access, at the site of any operation subject to safety regulations, to any authorized Federal inspector and shall provide any documents and records which are pertinent to occupational or public health, safety, or environmental protection as may be requested.

Sec. 13. Suspension and Cancellation.

(a) The Lessor may suspend or cancel this lease pursuant to section 5 of the Act, and compensation shall be paid when provided by the Act.

(b) The Lessor may, upon recommendation of the Secretary of Defense, during a state of war or national emergency declared by Congress or the President of the United States, suspend operations under the lease, as provided in section 12(c) of the Act, and just compensation shall be paid to the Lessee for such suspension.

Sec. 14. Indemnification. The Lessee shall indemnify the Lessor for, and hold it harmless from, any claim, including claims for loss or damage to property or injury to persons caused by or resulting from any operation on the leased area conducted by or on behalf of the Lessee. However, the Lessee shall not be held responsible to the Lessor under this section for any loss, damage, or injury caused by or resulting from:

(a) negligence of the Lessor other than the commission or omission of a discretionary function or duty on the part of a Federal Agency whether or not the discretion involved is abused; or

(b) the Lessee's compliance with an order or directive of the Lessor against which an administrative appeal by the Lessee is filed before the cause of action for the claim arises and is pursued diligently thereafter.

Sec. 15. Disposition of Production.

(a) As provided in section 27(a)(2) of the Act, the Lessor shall have the right to purchase not more than 16 2/3 percent by volume of the oil and gas produced pursuant to the lease at the regulated price or, if no regulated price applies, at the fair market value at the wellhead of the oil and gas saved, removed, or sold, except that any oil or gas obtained by the Lessor as royalty or net profit share shall be credited against the amount that may be purchased under this subsection.

(b) Pursuant to section 27(b) and (c) of the Act, the Lessor may offer and sell certain oil and gas obtained or purchased pursuant to a lease. As provided in section 27(d) of the Act, the Lessee shall take any Federal oil or gas for which no acceptable bids are received, as determined by the Lessor, and which is not transferred to a Federal Agency pursuant to section 27(a)(3) of the Act, and shall pay to the Lessor a cash amount equal to the regulated price or, if no regulated price applies, the fair market value of the oil or gas so obtained.

(c) As provided in section 8(b)(7) of the Act, the Lessee shall offer 20 percent of the crude oil, condensate, and natural gas liquids produced on the lease, at the market value and point of delivery as provided by regulations applicable to Federal royalty oil, to small or independent refiners as defined in the Emergency Petroleum Allocation Act of 1973.

(d) In time of war or when the president of the United States shall so prescribe, the Lessor shall have the right of first refusal to purchase at the market price all or any portion of the oil or gas produced from the leased area, as provided in section 12(b) of the Act.

Sec. 16. Unitization, Pooling, and Drilling Agreements. Within such time as the Lessor may prescribe, the Lessee shall subscribe to and operate under a unit, pooling, or drilling agreement embracing all or part of the lands subject to this lease as the Lessor may determine to be appropriate or necessary. Where any provision of a unit, pooling, or drilling agreement, approved by the Lessor, is inconsistent with a provision of this lease, the provision of the agreement shall govern.

Sec. 17. Equal Opportunity Clause. During the performance of this lease, the Lessee shall fully comply with paragraphs (1) through (7) of section 202 of Executive Order 11246, as amended (reprinted in 41 CFR 60-1.4(a)), and the implementing regulations which are for the purpose of preventing employment discrimination against persons on the basis of race, color, religion, sex, or national origin. Paragraphs (1) through (7) of section 202 of Executive Order 11246, as amended, are incorporated in this lease by reference.

Sec. 18. Certification of Nonsegregated Facilities. By entering into this lease, the Lessee certifies, as specified in 41 CFR 60-1.8, that it does not and will not maintain or provide for its employees any segregated facilities at any of its establishments and that it does not and will not permit its employees to perform their services at any location under its control where segregated facilities are maintained. As used in this certification, the term "segregated facilities" means, but is not limited to, any waiting rooms, work areas, restrooms and washrooms, restaurants and other eating areas, timeclocks, locker rooms and other storage or dressing areas, parking lots, drinking fountains, recreation or entertainment areas, transportation, and housing facilities provided for employees which are segregated by explicit directive or are in fact segregated on the basis of race, color, religion, or national origin, because of habit, local custom, or otherwise. The Lessee further agrees that it will obtain identical certifications from proposed contractors and subcontractors prior to award of contracts or subcontracts unless they are exempt under 41 CFR 60-1.5.

Sec. 19. Reservations to Lessor. All rights in the leased area not expressly granted to the Lessee by the Act, the regulations, or this lease are hereby reserved to the Lessor. Without limiting the generality of the foregoing, reserved rights included:

(a) the right to authorize geological and geophysical exploration in the lease area which does not unreasonably interfere with or endanger actual operations under the lease, and the right to grant such easements or rights-of-way upon, through, or in the leased area as may be necessary or appropriate to the working of other lands or to the treatment and shipment of products thereof by or under authority of the Lessor;

(b) the right to grant leases for any minerals other than oil and gas within the leased area, except that operations under such leases shall not unreasonably interfere with or endanger operations under this lease;

(c) the right, as provided in section 12(d) of the Act, to restrict operations in the leased area or any part thereof which may be designated by the Secretary of Defense, with approval of the President, as being within an area needed for national defense and, so long as such designation remains in effect, no operations may be conducted on the surface of the leased area or the part thereof included within the designation except with the concurrence of the Secretary of Defense. If operations or production under this lease within any designated area are suspended pursuant to this paragraph, any payments of rentals and royalty prescribed by this lease likewise shall be suspended during such period of suspension of operations and production, the term of this lease shall be extended by adding thereto any such suspension period, and the Lessor shall be liable to the Lessee for such compensation as is required to be paid under the Constitution of the United States.

Sec. 20. Transfer of Lease. The Lessee shall file for approval with the appropriate field office of the Minerals Management Service any instrument of assignment or other transfer of this lease, or any interest therein, in accordance with applicable regulations.

Sec. 21. Surrender of Lease. The Lessee may surrender this entire lease or any officially designated subdivision of the leased area by filing with the appropriate field office of the Minerals Management Service a written relinquishment, in triplicate, which shall be effective as of the date of filing. No surrender of this lease or of any portion of the leased area shall relieve the Lessee or its surety of the obligation to pay all accrued rentals, royalties, and other financial obligations or to abandon all wells on the area to be surrendered in a manner satisfactory to the Director.

(Continued on reverse)

Page 3

417

Sec. 22. Removal of Property on Termination of Lease. Within a period of 1 year after termination of this lease in whole or in part, the Lessee shall remove all devices, works, and structures from the premises no longer subject to the lease in accordance with applicable regulations and Orders of the Director. However, the Lessee may, with the approval of the Director, continue to maintain devices, works, and structures on the leased area for drilling or producing on other leases.

Sec. 23. Remedies in Case of Default.

(a) Whenever the Lessee fails to comply with any of the provisions of the Act, the regulations issued pursuant to the Act, or the terms of this lease, the lease shall be subject to cancellation in accordance with the provisions of section 5(c) and (d) of the Act and the Lessor may exercise any other remedies which the Lessor may have, including the penalty provisions of section 24 of the Act. Furthermore, pursuant to section 8(o) of the Act, the Lessor may cancel the lease if it is obtained by fraud or misrepresentation.

(b) Nonenforcement by the Lessor of a remedy for any particular violation of the provisions of the Act, the regulations issued pursuant to the Act, or the terms of this lease shall not prevent the cancellation of this lease or the exercise of any other remedies under paragraph (a) of this section for any other violation or for the same violation occurring at any other time.

Sec. 24. Unlawful Interest. No member of, or Delegate to, Congress, or Resident Commissioner, after election or appointment, or either before or after they have qualified and during their continuance in office, and no officer, agent, or employee of the Department of the Interior, except as provided in 43 CFR Part 20, shall be admitted to any share or part in this lease or derive any benefit that may arise therefrom. The provisions of Section 3741 of the Revised Statutes, as amended, 41 U.S.C. 22, and the Act of June 25, 1948, 62 Stat. 702, as amended, 18 U.S.C. 431-433, relating to contracts made or entered into, or accepted by or on behalf of the United States, form a part of this lease insofar as they may be applicable.

(Lessee)

THE UNITED STATES OF AMERICA, Lessor

(Signature of Authorized Officer)

(Signature of Authorized Officer)

(Name of Signatory)

(Name of Signatory)

(Title)

(Title)

(Date)

(Date)

(Address of Lessee)

If this lease is executed by a corporation, it must bear the corporate seal.

Page 4

418

NOTES

1.   The oil and gas lease form currently used by the Minerals Management Service on off-shore federal lands is limited to oil and gas and expressly excludes helium. Separate forms are used for leasing other substances, such as sulphur and salt. Information concerning the MMS and its programs can be found at http://www.mms.gov.

2.   Although its format is generally similar to private leases, the federal lease contains several types of clauses that are unlikely to be found in private leases. Some, such as sections 12, 17, and 18, effectuate specific federal statutes or policies. Others, such as sections 10 and 16, give the Lessor special rights or powers.

THIS AGREEMENT, entered into as of the date shown in Section 10 hereof by and between the parties subscribing, ratifying, or consenting hereto, such parties being hereinafter referred to as "parties hereto."

W I T N E S S E T H:

WHEREAS, the Act of March 3, 1909, (35 Stat. 783) as amended by the Act of August 9, 1955, (69 Stat. 540) and the Act of May 11, 1938, (52 Stat. 347) require that all operations under oil and gas leases on tribal and/or allotted Indian lands shall be subject to the rules and regulations of the Secretary of the Interior, and the regulations issued pursuant to said statutes provide that in exercise of his judgment, the Secretary of the Interior may take into consideration among other things, the Federal laws, State laws, regulations by competent Federal or State authorities, or lawful agreements among operators regulating either drilling or production or both (25 CFR Secs. 211.28, 212.28; and

WHEREAS, it is deemed necessary in the interest of conservation of natural resources and in the interest of tribal and/or allotted lessors to communitize or pool lands covered by an Indian oil and gas lease, or any portion thereof, with other lands, whether or not included in another Indian lease, when separate tracts under such Indian lease cannot be independently developed and operated in conformity with an established well-spacing program or pattern for the field or area; and

WHEREAS, the parties hereto own working, royalty or other leasehold interests, or operating rights under the oil and gas leases and lands subject to this Agreement which cannot be independently developed and operated in conformity with the well-spacing program established for the field or area in which said lands are located; and

WHEREAS, the parties hereto desire to communitize and pool their respective mineral interests in lands subject to this Agreement for the purpose of developing and producing communitized substances in accordance with the terms and conditions of this Agreement:

NOW, THEREFORE, in consideration of the premises and the mutual advantages to the parties hereto, it is mutually covenanted and agreed by and between the parties hereto as follows:

1.   The lands covered by this agreement (hereinafter referred to as "communitized area") are described as follows:

containing _____acres, and this agreement shall include only the _____Formation(s) underlying said lands and the_____, hereinafter, referred to as "communitized substances, producible from such formation(s).

2.   Attached hereto, and made a part of this agreement for all purposes, is Exhibit B, designating the operator of the communitized area and showing the acreage, percentage and ownership of oil and gas interests in all lands within the communitized area, and the authorization, if any, for communitizing or pooling any patented or fee lands within the communitized area.

3.   All matters of operation shall be governed by the operator under and pursuant to

the terms and provisions of this agreement. A successor operator may be designated by the owners of the working interest in the communitized area, and four (4) executed copies of a designation of successor operator shall be filed with the Authorized Officer.

4. Operator shall furnish the Secretary of the Interior, or his authorized representative, with a log and history of any well drilled on the communitized area, monthly reports of operations, statements of oil and gas sales and royalties and such other reports as are deemed necessary to compute monthly the royalty due the United States, as specified in the applicable oil and gas regulations.

5. The communitized area shall be developed and operated as an entirety, with the understanding and agreement between the parties hereto that all communitized substances produced therefrom shall be allocated among the leaseholds comprising said area in the proportion that the acreage interest of each leasehold bears to the entire acreage interest committed to this agreement.

6. The royalties payable on communitized substances allocated to the individual leases comprising the communitized area and the rentals provided for in said leases shall be determined and paid on the basis prescribed in each of the individual leases. Payments of rentals under the terms of leases subject to this agreement shall not be affected by this agreement except as provided for under the terms and provisions of said leases or as may herein be otherwise provided. Except as herein modified and changed, the oil and gas leases subject to this agreement shall remain in full force and effect as originally made and issued.

7. There shall be no obligation on the lessees to offset any well or wells completed in the same formation as covered by this agreement on separate component tracts into which the communitized area is now or may hereafter be divided, nor shall any lessee be required to measure separately communitized substances by reason of the diverse ownership thereof, but the lessees hereto shall not be released from their obligation to protect said communitized area from drainage of communitized substances by a well or wells which may be drilled offsetting said area.

8. The commencement, completion, continued operation, or production of a well or wells for communitized substances on the communitized area shall be construed and considered as the commencement, completion, continued operation, or production on each and all of the lands within and comprising said communitized area, and operations or production pursuant to this agreement shall be deemed to be operations or production as to each lease committed hereto.

9. Production of communitized substances and disposal thereof shall be in conformity with allocation, allotments, and quotas made or fixed by any duly authorized person or regulatory body under applicable Federal or State statutes. This agreement shall be subject to all applicable Federal and State laws or executive orders, rules and regulations, and no party hereto shall suffer a forfeiture or be liable in damages for failure to comply with any of the provisions of this agreement if such compliance is prevented by, or if such failure results from, compliance with any such laws, orders rules or regulations.

10. This Agreement shall be effective as of _____, upon execution by the necessary parties, notwithstanding the date of execution, and upon approval by the Secretary of the Interior or by his duly authorized representative, and shall remain in force and effect for a period of two (2) years so long thereafter as communitized substances are produced from the communitized area in paying quantities, provided, that prior to production in paying quantities

from the communitized area and upon fulfillment of all requirements of the Secretary of the Interior, or his duly authorized representatives, with respect to any dry hole or abandoned well, this Agreement may be terminated at any time by mutual agreement of the parties hereto.

11. The covenants herein shall be construed to be covenants running with the land with respect to the communitized interests of the parties hereto and their successors in interests until this agreement terminates and any grant, transfer, or conveyance of any such land or interest subject hereto, whether voluntary or not, shall be and hereby is conditioned upon the assumption of all obligations hereunder by the grantee, transferee, or other successor in interest, and as to restricted Indian land shall be subject to approval by the Secretary of the Interior, or his duly authorized representative.

12. It is agreed between the parties hereto that the Secretary of the Interior, or his duly authorized representative, shall have the right of supervision over all operations within the communitized area to the same extent and degree as provided in the oil and gas leases in which owners of restricted Indian lands are the lessor and in the applicable oil and gas regulations of the Department of the Interior.

13. This agreement shall be binding upon the parties hereto and shall extend to and be binding upon their respective heirs, executors, administrators, successors, and assigns.

14. This agreement may be executed in any number of counterparts, no one of which needs to be executed by all parties, or may be ratified or consented to by separate instrument, in writing, specifically referring hereto, and shall be binding upon all parties who have executed such a counterpart, ratification or consent hereto with the same force and effect as if all parties had signed the same document.

15. Insofar as concerns the undersigned parties who hold interests in the restricted Indian land which is described as Tract __ in Exhibit "B" hereto, this Agreement shall be subject to the approval of the Secretary of the Interior or his duly authorized representative.

16. In the performance of work under this Agreement, the operator and working interest owners hereunder agree to comply with the nondiscrimination provisions of Executive Order 11246 (30 F.R. 12319), as amended, except as this Agreement may be exempt from the provision of Executive Order 11246 by-law or by reason of the provision of any lease committed hereto, granting preference rights of employment to Indians.

IN WITNESS WHEREOF, the parties hereto have executed this Agreement as of the day and year first above written and have set opposite their respective names the date of execution.

(date, signatures, and acknowledgments)

Plat of communitized area covering ___NE 1/4___ sec. __22__ , T. _31 N._ ,
R. __47 E.__ , _M.P.M.,_ _Benrud, East_ field, _Roosevelt_ County, _Montana_.

ABC Oil Company 100% Tr. No <u>1</u> 80.00 ac. 14-20-0256-1234	Harry Smith 50% Needmore Oil Co. 50% Tr. No. <u>2</u> 80.00 ac. Fee Well No. 14-22 ●

22

NOTE: Show well location and tract numbers, in addition to ownership and
      tract acreage.

To Communitization Agreement dated _____ ,embracing NE¼, Sec. 22,
T. 31 N., R. 47 E., M.P.M., Benrud, East field, Roosevelt County, Montana.

Operator of Communitized Area: BC Oil Company

<u>DESCRIPTION OF LEASES COMMITTED</u>
<u>Tract No. 1</u>

Lease Serial No.: 14-20-0256-1234
Lease Date: October 1, 1970
Lease Term: 10 years
Lessor: John Two Bears Walking Estate
Lessee: ABC Oil Company 100%
Description of Land Committed:

<u>Township 31 North, Range 47 East, M.P.M.</u>
Section 22: W½NE¼

Number of Acres: 80.00
Royalty Rate: 16-2/3 percent
Name and Percent ORRI Owners: John Doe 3%
Name and Percent WI Owners: ABC Oil Company 100%

<u>Tract No. 2</u>

Lease Serial No.: Fee
Lease Date: November 1, 1972
Lease Term: 10 years
Lessor(s): Jack Smith
Lessee on effective date of agreement if different from present lessee: Same
Present Lessee: Harry Smith 50%
                 Needmore Oil Company 50%
Description of Land Committed:

<u>Township 31 North, Range 47 East, M.P.M.</u>
Section 22: E½NE¼

Number of Acres: 80.00
Pooling Clause: Not Applicable
Basic Royalty Rate: 12-½ percent
Name and Percent ORRI Owners: None
Name and Percent WI Owners: Needmore Oil Company 100%

<u>R E C A P I T U L A T I O N</u>

Tract No.		No. of Acres Committed	Percentage of Interest in Communitized Area
1		80.00	50.0000%
2		80.00	50.0000%
	Total	160.00	100.0000%

NOTES

1.   Communitizing (pooling) blocks of acreage to satisfy the minimum-acreage requirements of state well-spacing and well-density regulations is more involved when federal or Indian mineral lands are within the pooling block. As states have no authority to pool federal or Indian lands, to effectively pool such lands, the developer must obtain the consent of the Secretary of Interior. The Communitization Agreement is used to obtain the required consent and to set out the essential pooling terms. The above form proposes to communitize an Indian lease.

2.   The regulations governing communitization are found at 43 C.F.R. § 3105.2 (federal non-Indian lands) and 25 C.F.R. § 211.28 (Indian lands). Also a portion of the BLM Manual, § 3160.9, addresses communitization. To obtain information concerning the Department of Interior s mineral programs, visit the Bureau of Land Management's website at http://www.blm.gov and the Mineral Management Service's website at http://www.mms.gov.

43 C.F.R. Subpart 3186—Model Forms
(current through February 12, 2008)
3   **§ 3186.1   Model onshore unit agreement for unproven areas.**
4   Introductory Section
5   1 Enabling Act and Regulations.
6   2 Unit Area.
7   3 Unitized Land and Unitized Substances.
8   4 Unit Operator.
9   5 Resignation or Removal of Unit Operator.
10   6 Successor Unit Operator.
11   7 Accounting Provisions and Unit Operating Agreement.
12   8 Rights and Obligations of Unit Operator.
13   9 Drilling to Discovery.
14   10 Plan of Further Development and Operation.
15   11 Participation After Discovery.
16   12 Allocation of Production.
17   13 Development or Operation of Nonparticipating Land or Formations.
18   14 Royalty Settlement.
19   15 Rental Settlement.
20   16 Conservation.
21   17 Drainage.
22   18 Leases and Contracts Conformed and Extended.
23   19 Convenants Run with Land.
24   20 Effective Date and Term.
25   21 Rate of Prospecting, Development, and Production.
26   22 Appearances.
27   23 Notices.
28   24 No Waiver of Certain Rights.
29   25 Unavoidable Delay.
30   26 Nondiscrimination.
31   27 Loss of Title.
32   28 Nonjoinder and Subsequent Joinder.
33   29 Counterparts.
34   30 Surrender.[1]
35   31 Taxes.[1]
36   32 No Partnership.[1]
37   Concluding Section IN WITNESS WHEREOF.
38   General Guidelines.
39   Certification—Determination.
40

UNIT AGREEMENT FOR THE DEVELOPMENT AND OPERATION
OF THE _____ UNIT AREA

County of

State of

No.

    This agreement, entered into as of the _____ day of _____, 19__ by and between the parties subscribing, ratifying, or consenting hereto, and herein referred to as the "parties hereto,"

    WITNESSETH:

    WHEREAS, the parties hereto are the owners of working, royalty, or other oil and gas interests in the unit area subject to this agreement; and

    WHEREAS, the Mineral Leasing Act of February 25, 1920, 41 Stat. 437, as amended, 30 U.S.C. Sec. 181 *et seq.,* authorizes Federal lessees and their representatives to unite with each other, or jointly or separately with others, in collectively adopting and operating under a unit plan of development or operations of any oil and gas pool, field, or like area, or any part thereof for the purpose of more properly conserving the natural resources thereof whenever determined and certified by the Secretary of the Interior to be necessary or advisable in the public interest; and

    WHEREAS, the parties hereto hold sufficient interests in the _____ Unit Area covering the land hereinafter described to give reasonably effective control of operations therein; and

    WHEREAS, it is the purpose of the parties hereto to conserve natural resources, prevent waste, and secure other benefits obtainable through development and operation of the area subject to this agreement under the terms, conditions, and limitations herein set forth;

    NOW, THEREFORE, in consideration of the premises and the promises herein contained, the parties hereto commit to this agreement their respective interests in the below-defined unit area, and agree severally among themselves as follows:

    1. ENABLING ACT AND REGULATIONS. The Mineral Leasing Act of February 25, 1920, as amended, supra, and all valid pertinent regulations including operating and unit plan regulations, heretofore issued thereunder or valid, pertinent, and reasonable regulations hereafter issued thereunder are accepted and made a part of this agreement as to Federal lands, provided such regulations are not inconsistent with the terms of this agreement; and as to non-Federal lands, the oil and gas operating regulations in effect as of the effective date hereof governing drilling and producing operations, not inconsistent with the terms hereof or the laws of the State in which the non-Federal land is located, are hereby accepted and made a part of this agreement.

    2. UNIT AREA. The area specified on the map attached hereto marked Exhibit A is hereby designated and recognized as constituting the unit area, containing ___ acres, more or less.

    Exhibit A shows, in addition to the boundary of the unit area, the boundaries and identity of tracts and leases in said area to the extent known to the Unit Operator. Exhibit B attached hereto is a schedule showing to the extent known to the Unit Operator, the acreage, percentage, and kind of ownership of oil and gas interests in all lands in the unit area. However, nothing herein or in Exhibits A or B shall be construed as a representation by any party hereto as to the ownership of any interest other than such interest or interests as are shown in the Exhibits as owned by such party. Exhibits A and B shall be revised by the Unit Operator whenever changes in the unit area or in the ownership interests in the individual tracts render such revision necessary, or when requested by the Authorized Officer, hereinafter referred to as AO and not less than four copies of the revised Exhibits shall be filed with the proper BLM office.

1   The above-described unit area shall when practicable be expanded to include therein any
2   additional lands or shall be contracted to exclude lands whenever such expansion or contraction
3   is deemed to be necessary or advisable to conform with the purposes of this agreement. Such
4   expansion or contraction shall be effected in the following manner:
5   (a) Unit Operator, on its own motion (after preliminary concurrence by the AO), or on
6   demand of the AO, shall prepare a notice of proposed expansion or contraction describing the
7   contemplated changes in the boundaries of the unit area, the reasons therefor, any plans for
8   additional drilling, and the proposed effective date of the expansion or contraction, preferably the
9   first day of a month subsequent to the date of notice.
10 (b) Said notice shall be delivered to the proper BLM office, and copies thereof mailed to the
11 last known address of each working interest owner, lessee and lessor whose interests are
12 affected, advising that 30 days will be allowed for submission to the Unit Operator of any
13 objections.
14 (c) Upon expiration of the 30-day period provided in the preceding item (b) hereof, Unit
15 Operator shall file with the AO evidence of mailing of the notice of expansion or contraction and
16 a copy of any objections thereto which have been filed with Unit Operator, together with an
17 application in triplicate, for approval of such expansion or contraction and with appropriate
18 joinders.
19 (d) After due consideration of all pertinent information, the expansion or contraction shall,
20 upon approval by the AO, become effective as of the date prescribed in the notice thereof or such
21 other appropriate date.
22 (e) All legal subdivisions of lands (i.e., 40 acres by Government survey or its nearest lot or
23 tract equivalent; in instances of irregular surveys, unusually large lots or tracts shall be
24 considered in multiples of 40 acres or the nearest aliquot equivalent thereof), no parts of which
25 are in or entitled to be in a participating area on or before the fifth anniversary of the effective
26 date of the first initial participating area established under this unit agreement, shall be
27 eliminated automatically from this agreement, effective as of said fifth anniversary, and such
28 lands shall no longer be a part of the unit area and shall no longer be subject to this agreement,
29 unless diligent drilling operations are in progress on unitized lands not entitled to participation on
30 said fifth anniversary, in which event all such lands shall remain subject hereto for so long as
31 such drilling operations are continued diligently, with not more than 90-days time elapsing
32 between the completion of one such well and the commencement of the next such well. All legal
33 subdivisions of lands not entitled to be in a participating area within 10 years after the effective
34 date of the first initial participating area approved under this agreement shall be automatically
35 eliminated from this agreement as of said tenth anniversary. The Unit Operator shall, within 90
36 days after the effective date of any elimination hereunder, describe the area so eliminated to the
37 satisfaction of the AO and promptly notify all parties in interest. All lands reasonably proved
38 productive of unitized substances in paying quantities by diligent drilling operations after the
39 aforesaid 5-year period shall become participating in the same manner as during said first 5-year
40 period. However, when such diligent drilling operations cease, all nonparticipating lands not then
41 entitled to be in a participating area shall be automatically eliminated effective as the 91st day
42 thereafter.
43 Any expansion of the unit area pursuant to this section which embraces lands theretofore
44 eliminated pursuant to this subsection 2(e) shall not be considered automatic commitment or
45 recommitment of such lands. If conditions warrant extension of the 10-year period specified in
46 this subsection, a single extension of not to exceed 2 years may be accomplished by consent of

1 the owners of 90 percent of the working interest in the current nonparticipating unitized lands
2 and the owners of 60 percent of the basic royalty interests (exclusive of the basic royalty interests
3 of the United States) in nonparticipating unitized lands with approval of the AO, provided such
4 extension application is submitted not later than 60 days prior to the expiration of said 10-year
5 period.

6   3. UNITIZED LAND AND UNITIZED SUBSTANCES. All land now or hereafter
7 committed to this agreement shall constitute land referred to herein as "unitized land" or "land
8 subject to this agreement." All oil and gas in any and all formations of the unitized land are
9 unitized under the terms of this agreement and herein are called "unitized substances."

10   4. UNIT OPERATOR. _____ is hereby designated as Unit Operator and by signature hereto
11 as Unit Operator agrees and consents to accept the duties and obligations of Unit Operator for the
12 discovery, development, and production of unitized substances as herein provided. Whenever
13 reference is made herein to the Unit Operator, such reference means the Unit Operator acting in
14 that capacity and not as an owner of interest in unitized substances, and the term "working
15 interest owner" when used herein shall include or refer to Unit Operator as the owner of a
16 working interest only when such an interest is owned by it.

17   5. RESIGNATION OR REMOVAL OF UNIT OPERATOR. Unit Operator shall have the
18 right to resign at any time prior to the establishment of a participating area or areas hereunder,
19 but such resignation shall not become effective so as to release Unit Operator from the duties and
20 obligations of Unit Operator and terminate Unit Operator's rights as such for a period of 6
21 months after notice of intention to resign has been served by Unit Operator on all working
22 interest owners and the AO and until all wells then drilled hereunder are placed in a satisfactory
23 condition for suspension or abandonment, whichever is required by the AO, unless a new Unit
24 Operator shall have been selected and approved and shall have taken over and assumed the
25 duties and obligations of Unit Operator prior to the expiration of said period.

26   Unit Operator shall have the right to resign in like manner and subject to like limitations as
27 above provided at any time after a participating area established hereunder is in existence, but in
28 all instances of resignation or removal, until a successor Unit Operator is selected and approved
29 as hereinafter provided, the working interest owners shall be jointly responsible for performance
30 of the duties of Unit Operator, and shall not later than 30 days before such resignation or removal
31 becomes effective appoint a common agent to represent them in any action to be taken
32 hereunder.

33   The resignation of Unit Operator shall not release Unit Operator from any liability for any
34 default by it hereunder occurring prior to the effective date of its resignation.

35   The Unit Operator may, upon default or failure in the performance of its duties or
36 obligations hereunder, be subject to removal by the same percentage vote of the owners of
37 working interests as herein provided for the selection of a new Unit Operator. Such removal shall
38 be effective upon notice thereof to the AO.

39   The resignation or removal of Unit Operator under this agreement shall not terminate its
40 right, title, or interest as the owner of working interest or other interest in unitized substances,
41 but upon the resignation or removal of Unit Operator becoming effective, such Unit Operator
42 shall deliver possession of all wells, equipment, materials, and appurtenances used in conducting
43 the unit operations to the new duly qualified successor Unit Operator or to the common agent, if
44 no such new Unit Operator is selected to be used for the purpose of conducting unit operations
45 hereunder. Nothing herein shall be construed as authorizing removal of any material, equipment,
46 or appurtenances needed for the preservation of any wells.

1 6. SUCCESSOR UNIT OPERATOR. Whenever the Unit Operator shall tender his or its
2 resignation as Unit Operator or shall be removed as hereinabove provided, or a change of Unit
3 Operator is negotiated by the working interest owners, the owners of the working interests
4 according to their respective acreage interests in all unitized land shall, pursuant to the Approval
5 of the Parties requirements of the unit operating agreement, select a successor Unit Operator.
6 Such selection shall not become effective until:
7   (a) a Unit Operator so selected shall accept in writing the duties and responsibilities of Unit
8 Operator, and
9   (b) the selection shall have been approved by the AO.
10   If no successor Unit Operator is selected and qualified as herein provided, the AO at his
11 election may declare this unit agreement terminated.
12   7. ACCOUNTING PROVISIONS AND UNIT OPERATING AGREEMENT. If the Unit
13 Operator is not the sole owner of working interests, costs and expenses incurred by Unit
14 Operator in conducting unit operations hereunder shall be paid and apportioned among and borne
15 by the owners of working interests, all in accordance with the agreement or agreements entered
16 into by and between the Unit Operator and the owners of working interests, whether one or more,
17 separately or collectively. Any agreement or agreements entered into between the working
18 interest owners and the Unit Operator as provided in this section, whether one or more, are
19 herein referred to as the "unit operating agreement." Such unit operating agreement shall also
20 provide the manner in which the working interest owners shall be entitled to receive their
21 respective proportionate and allocated share of the benefits accruing hereto in conformity with
22 their underlying operating agreements, leases, or other independent contracts, and such other
23 rights and obligations as between Unit Operator and the working interest owners as may be
24 agreed upon by Unit Operator and the working interest owners; however, no such unit operating
25 agreement shall be deemed either to modify any of the terms and conditions of this unit
26 agreement or to relieve the Unit Operator of any right or obligation established under this unit
27 agreement, and in case of any inconsistency or conflict between this agreement and the unit
28 operating agreement, this agreement shall govern. Two copies of any unit operating agreement
29 executed pursuant to this section shall be filed in the proper BLM office prior to approval of this
30 unit agreement.
31   8. RIGHTS AND OBLIGATIONS OF UNIT OPERATOR. Except as otherwise
32 specifically provided herein, the exclusive right, privilege, and duty of exercising any and all
33 rights of the parties hereto which are necessary or convenient for prospecting for, producing,
34 storing, allocating, and distributing the unitized substances are hereby delegated to and shall be
35 exercised by the Unit Operator as herein provided. Acceptable evidence of title to said rights
36 shall be deposited with Unit Operator and, together with this agreement, shall constitute and
37 define the rights, privileges, and obligations of Unit Operator. Nothing herein, however, shall be
38 construed to transfer title to any land or to any lease or operating agreement, it being understood
39 that under this agreement the Unit Operator, in its capacity as Unit Operator, shall exercise the
40 rights of possession and use vested in the parties hereto only for the purposes herein specified.
41   9. DRILLING TO DISCOVERY. Within 6 months after the effective date hereof, the Unit
42 Operator shall commence to drill an adequate test well at a location approved by the AO, unless
43 on such effective date a well is being drilled in conformity with the terms hereof, and thereafter
44 continue such drilling diligently until the ___ formation has been tested or until at a lesser depth
45 unitized substances shall be discovered which can be produced in paying quantities (to wit:
46 quantities sufficient to repay the costs of drilling, completing, and producing operations, with a

1 reasonable profit) or the Unit Operator shall at any time establish to the satisfaction of the AO
2 that further drilling of said well would be unwarranted or impracticable, provided, however, that
3 Unit Operator shall not in any event be required to drill said well to a depth in excess of __ feet.
4 Until the discovery of unitized substances capable of being produced in paying quantities, the
5 Unit Operator shall continue drilling one well at a time, allowing not more than 6 months
6 between the completion of one well and the commencement of drilling operations for the next
7 well, until a well capable of producing unitized substances in paying quantities is completed to
8 the satisfaction of the AO or until it is reasonably proved that the unitized land is incapable of
9 producing unitized substances in paying quantities in the formations drilled hereunder. Nothing
10 in this section shall be deemed to limit the right of the Unit Operator to resign as provided in
11 Section 5, hereof, or as requiring Unit Operator to commence or continue any drilling during the
12 period pending such resignation becoming effective in order to comply with the requirements of
13 this section.

14   The AO may modify any of the drilling requirements of this section by granting reasonable
15 extensions of time when, in his opinion, such action is warranted.
16   [2] 9a. Multiple well requirements. Notwithstanding anything in this unit agreement to the
17 contrary, except Section 25, UNAVOIDABLE DELAY, __ wells shall be drilled with not more
18 than 6-months time elapsing between the completion of the first well and commencement of
19 drilling operations for the second well and with not more than 6-months time elapsing between
20 completion of the second well and the commencement of drilling operations for the third well, . .
21 . regardless of whether a discovery has been made in any well drilled under this provision. Both
22 the initial well and the second well must be drilled in compliance with the above specified
23 formation or depth requirements in order to meet the dictates of this section; and the second well
24 must be located a minimum of __ miles from the initial well in order to be accepted by the AO as
25 the second unit test well, within the meaning of this section. The third test well shall be diligently
26 drilled, at a location approved by the AO, to test the ___ formation or to a depth of __ feet,
27 whichever is the lesser, and must be located a minimum of __ miles from both the initial and the
28 second test wells. Nevertheless, in the event of the discovery of unitized substances in paying
29 quantities by any well, this unit agreement shall not terminate for failure to complete the ___
30 well program, but the unit area shall be contracted automatically, effective the first day of the
31 month following the default, to eliminate by subdivisions (as defined in Section 2(e) hereof) all
32 lands not then entitled to be in a participating area.[2]

33   Until the establishment of a participating area, the failure to commence a well subsequent to
34 the drilling of the initial obligation well, or in the case of multiple well requirements, if specified,
35 subsequent to the drilling of those multiple wells, as provided for in this (these) section(s), within
36 the time allowed including any extension of time granted by the AO, shall cause this agreement
37 to terminate automatically. Upon failure to continue drilling diligently any well other than the
38 obligation well(s) commenced hereunder, the AO may, after 15 days notice to the Unit Operator,
39 declare this unit agreement terminated. Failure to commence drilling the initial obligation well,
40 or the first of multiple obligation wells, on time and to drill it diligently shall result in the unit
41 agreement approval being declared invalid *ab initio* by the AO. In the case of multiple well
42 requirements, failure to commence drilling the required multiple wells beyond the first well, and
43 to drill them diligently, may result in the unit agreement approval being declared invalid *ab initio*
44 by the AO;

45   10. PLAN OF FURTHER DEVELOPMENT AND OPERATION. Within 6 months after
46 completion of a well capable of producing unitized substances in paying quantities, the Unit

1 Operator shall submit for the approval of the AO an acceptable plan of development and
2 operation for the unitized land which, when approved by the authorized officer, shall constitute
3 the further drilling and development obligations of the Unit Operator under this agreement for
4 the period specified therein. Thereafter, from time to time before the expiration of any existing
5 plan, the Unit Operator shall submit for the approval of the AO a plan for an additional specified
6 period for the development and operation of the unitized land. Subsequent plans should normally
7 be filed on a calendar year basis not later than March 1 each year. Any proposed modification or
8 addition to the existing plan should be filed as a supplement to the plan.

9   Any plan submitted pursuant to this section shall provide for the timely exploration of the
10 unitized area, and for the diligent drilling necessary for determination of the area or areas capable
11 of producing unitized substances in paying quantities in each and every productive formation.
12 This plan shall be as complete and adequate as the AO may determine to be necessary for timely
13 development and proper conservation of the oil and gas resources in the unitized area and shall:

14   (a) Specify the number and locations of any wells to be drilled and the proposed order and
15 time for such drilling; and

16   (b) Provide a summary of operations and production for the previous year.

17   Plans shall be modified or supplemented when necessary to meet changed conditions or to
18 protect the interests of all parties to this agreement. Reasonable diligence shall be exercised in
19 complying with the obligations of the approved plan of development and operation. The AO is
20 authorized to grant a reasonable extension of the 6-month period herein prescribed for
21 submission of an initial plan of development and operation where such action is justified because
22 of unusual conditions or circumstances.

23   After completion of a well capable of producing unitized substances in paying quantities, no
24 further wells, except such as may be necessary to afford protection against operations not under
25 this agreement and such as may be specifically approved by the AO, shall be drilled except in
26 accordance with an approved plan of development and operation.

27   11. PARTICIPATION AFTER DISCOVERY. Upon completion of a well capable of
28 producing unitized substances in paying quantities, or as soon thereafter as required by the AO,
29 the Unit Operator shall submit for approval by the AO, a schedule, based on subdivisions of the
30 public-land survey or aliquot parts thereof, of all land then regarded as reasonably proved to be
31 productive of unitized substances in paying quantities. These lands shall constitute a
32 participating area on approval of the AO, effective as of the date of completion of such well or
33 the effective date of this unit agreement, whichever is later. The acreages of both Federal and
34 non-Federal lands shall be based upon appropriate computations from the courses and distances
35 shown on the last approved public-land survey as of the effective date of each initial
36 participating area. The schedule shall also set forth the percentage of unitized substances to be
37 allocated, as provided in Section 12, to each committed tract in the participating area so
38 established, and shall govern the allocation of production commencing with the effective date of
39 the participating area. A different participating area shall be established for each separate pool or
40 deposit of unitized substances or for any group thereof which is produced as a single pool or
41 zone, and any two or more participating areas so established may be combined into one, on
42 approval of the AO. When production from two or more participating areas is subsequently
43 found to be from a common pool or deposit, the participating areas shall be combined into one,
44 effective as of such appropriate date as may be approved or prescribed by the AO. The
45 participating area or areas so established shall be revised from time to time, subject to the
46 approval of the AO, to include additional lands then regarded as reasonably proved to be

1   productive of unitized substances in paying quantities or which are necessary for unit operations,
2   or to exclude lands then regarded as reasonably proved not to be productive of unitized
3   substances in paying quantities, and the schedule of allocation percentages shall be revised
4   accordingly. The effective date of any revision shall be the first of the month in which the
5   knowledge or information is obtained on which such revision is predicated; provided, however,
6   that a more appropriate effective date may be used if justified by Unit Operator and approved by
7   the AO. No land shall be excluded from a participating area on account of depletion of its
8   unitized substances, except that any participating area established under the provisions of this
9   unit agreement shall terminate automatically whenever all completions in the formation on which
10   the participating area is based are abandoned.
11   It is the intent of this section that a participating area shall represent the area known or
12   reasonably proved to be productive of unitized substances in paying quantities or which are
13   necessary for unit operations; but, regardless of any revision of the participating area, nothing
14   herein contained shall be construed as requiring any retroactive adjustment for production
15   obtained prior to the effective date of the revision of the participating area.
16   In the absence of agreement at any time between the Unit Operator and the AO as to the
17   proper definition or redefinition of a participating area, or until a participating area has, or areas
18   have, been established, the portion of all payments affected thereby shall, except royalty due the
19   United States, be impounded in a manner mutually acceptable to the owners of committed
20   working interests. Royalties due the United States shall be determined by the AO and the amount
21   thereof shall be deposited, as directed by the AO, until a participating area is finally approved
22   and then adjusted in accordance with a determination of the sum due as Federal royalty on the
23   basis of such approved participating area.
24   Whenever it is determined, subject to the approval of the AO, that a well drilled under this
25   agreement is not capable of production of unitized substances in paying quantities and inclusion
26   in a participating area of the land on which it is situated is unwarranted, production from such
27   well shall, for the purposes of settlement among all parties other than working interest owners,
28   be allocated to the land on which the well is located, unless such land is already within the
29   participating area established for the pool or deposit from which such production is obtained.
30   Settlement for working interest benefits from such a nonpaying unit well shall be made as
31   provided in the unit operating agreement.
32   12. ALLOCATION OF PRODUCTION. All unitized substances produced from a
33   participating area established under this agreement, except any part thereof used in conformity
34   with good operating practices within the unitized area for drilling, operating, and other
35   production or development purposes, or for repressuring or recycling in accordance with a plan
36   of development and operations that has been approved by the AO, or unavoidably lost, shall be
37   deemed to be produced equally on an acreage basis from the several tracts of unitized land and
38   unleased Federal land, if any, included in the participating area established for such production.
39   Each such tract shall have allocated to it such percentage of said production as the number of
40   acres of such tract included in said participating area bears to the total acres of unitized land and
41   unleased Federal land, if any, included in said participating area. There shall be allocated to the
42   working interest owner(s) of each tract of unitized land in said participating area, in addition,
43   such percentage of the production attributable to the unleased Federal land within the
44   participating area as the number of acres of such unitized tract included in said participating area
45   bears to the total acres of unitized land in said participating area, for the payment of the
46   compensatory royalty specified in section 17 of this agreement. Allocation of production

433

hereunder for purposes other than for settlement of the royalty, overriding royalty, or payment out of production obligations of the respective working interest owners, including compensatory royalty obligations under section 17, shall be prescribed as set forth in the unit operating agreement or as otherwise mutually agreed by the affected parties. It is hereby agreed that production of unitized substances from a participating area shall be allocated as provided herein, regardless or whether any wells are drilled on any particular part or tract of the participating area. If any gas produced from one participating area is used for repressuring or recycling purposes in another participating area, the first gas withdrawn from the latter participating area for sale during the life of this agreement shall be considered to be the gas so transferred, until an amount equal to that transferred shall be so produced for sale and such gas shall be allocated to the participating area from which initially produced as such area was defined at the time that such transferred gas was finally produced and sold.

13. DEVELOPMENT OR OPERATION OF NONPARTICIPATING LAND OR FORMATIONS. Any operator may with the approval of the AO, at such party's sole risk, costs, and expense, drill a well on the unitized land to test any formation provided the well is outside any participating area established for that formation, unless within 90 days of receipt of notice from said party of his intention to drill the well, the Unit Operator elects and commences to drill the well in a like manner as other wells are drilled by the Unit Operator under this agreement.

If any well drilled under this section by a non-unit operator results in production of unitized substances in paying quantities such that the land upon which it is situated may properly be included in a participating area, such participating area shall be established or enlarged as provided in this agreement and the well shall thereafter be operated by the Unit Operator in accordance with the terms of this agreement and the unit operating agreement.

If any well drilled under this section by a non-unit operator that obtains production in quantities insufficient to justify the inclusion of the land upon which such well is situated in a participating area, such well may be operated and produced by the party drilling the same, subject to the conservation requirements of this agreement. The royalties in amount or value of production from any such well shall be paid as specified in the underlying lease and agreements affected.

14. ROYALTY SETTLEMENT. The United States and any State and any royalty owner who is entitled to take in kind a share of the substances now unitized hereunder shall be hereafter be entitled to the right to take in kind its share of the unitized substances, and Unit Operator, or the non-unit operator in the case of the operation of a well by a non-unit operator as herein provided for in special cases, shall make deliveries of such royalty share taken in kind in conformity with the applicable contracts, laws, and regulations. Settlement for royalty interest not taken in kind shall be made by an operator responsible therefor under existing contracts, laws and regulations, or by the Unit Operator on or before the last day of each month for unitized substances produced during the preceding calendar month; provided, however, that nothing in this section shall operate to relieve the responsible parties of any land from their respective lease obligations for the payment of any royalties due under their leases.

If gas obtained from lands not subject to this agreement is introduced into any participating area hereunder, for use in repressuring, stimulation of production, or increasing ultimate recovery, in conformity with a plan of development and operation approved by the AO, a like amount of gas, after settlement as herein provided for any gas transferred from any other participating area and with appropriate deduction for loss from any cause, may be withdrawn from the formation into which the gas is introduced, royalty free as to dry gas, but not as to any

1　products which may be extracted therefrom; provided that such withdrawal shall be at such time
2　as may be provided in the approved plan of development and operation or as may otherwise be
3　consented to by the AO as conforming to good petroleum engineering practice; and provided
4　further, that such right of withdrawal shall terminate on the termination of this unit agreement.
5　　Royalty due the United States shall be computed as provided in 30 CFR Group 200 and paid
6　in value or delivered in kind as to all unitized substances on the basis of the amounts thereof
7　allocated to unitized Federal land as provided in Section 12 at the rates specified in the respective
8　Federal leases, or at such other rate or rates as may be authorized by law or regulation and
9　approved by the AO; provided, that for leases on which the royalty rate depends on the daily
10　average production per well, said average production shall be determined in accordance with the
11　operating regulations as though each participating area were a single consolidated lease.
12　　15. RENTAL SETTLEMENT. Rental or minimum royalties due on leases committed
13　hereto shall be paid by the appropriate parties under existing contracts, laws, and regulations,
14　provided that nothing herein contained shall operate to relieve the responsible parties of the land
15　from their respective obligations for the payment of any rental or minimum royalty due under
16　their leases. Rental or minimum royalty for lands of the United States subject to this agreement
17　shall be paid at the rate specified in the respective leases from the United States unless such
18　rental or minimum royalty is waived, suspended, or reduced by law or by approval of the
19　Secretary or his duly authorized representative.
20　　With respect to any lease on non-Federal land containing provisions which would terminate
21　such lease unless drilling operations are commenced upon the land covered thereby within the
22　time therein specified or rentals are paid for the privilege of deferring such drilling operations,
23　the rentals required thereby shall, notwithstanding any other provision of this agreement, be
24　deemed to accrue and become payable during the term thereof as extended by this agreement and
25　until the required drilling operations are commenced upon the land covered thereby, or until
26　some portion of such land is included within a participating area.
27　　16. CONSERVATION. Operations hereunder and production of unitized substances shall
28　be conducted to provide for the most economical and efficient recovery of said substances
29　without waste, as defined by or pursuant to State or Federal law or regulation.
30　　17. DRAINAGE. (a) The Unit Operator shall take such measures as the AO deems
31　appropriate and adequate to prevent drainage of unitized substances from unitized land by wells
32　on land not subject to this agreement, which shall include the drilling of protective wells and
33　which may include the payment of a fair and reasonable compensatory royalty, as determined by
34　the AO.
35　　(b) Whenever a participating area approved under section 11 of this agreement contains
36　unleased Federal lands, the value of 121/2percent of the production that would be allocated to
37　such Federal lands under section 12 of this agreement, if such lands were leased, committed, and
38　entitled to participation, shall be payable as compensatory royalties to the Federal Government.
39　Parties to this agreement holding working interests in committed leases within the applicable
40　participating area shall be responsible for such compensatory royalty payment on the volume of
41　production reallocated from the unleased Federal lands to their unitized tracts under section 12.
42　The value of such production subject to the payment of said royalties shall be determined
43　pursuant to 30 CFR part 206. Payment of compensatory royalties on the production reallocated
44　from unleased Federal land to the committed tracts within the participating area shall fulfill the
45　Federal royalty obligation for such production, and said production shall be subject to no further
46　royalty assessment under section 14 of this agreement. Payment of compensatory royalties as

provided herein shall accrue from the date the committed tracts in the participating area that includes unleased Federal lands receive a production allocation, and shall be due and payable monthly by the last day of the calendar month next following the calendar month of actual production. If leased Federal lands receiving a production allocation from the participating area become unleased, compensatory royalties shall accrue from the date the Federal lands become unleased. Payment due under this provision shall end when the unleased Federal tract is leased or when production of unitized substances ceases within the participating area and the participating area is terminated, whichever occurs first.

18. LEASES AND CONTRACTS CONFORMED AND EXTENDED. The terms, conditions, and provisions of all leases, subleases, and other contracts relating to exploration, drilling, development or operation for oil or gas on lands committed to this agreement are hereby expressly modified and amended to the extent necessary to make the same conform to the provisions hereof, but otherwise to remain in full force and effect; and the parties hereto hereby consent that the Secretary shall and by his approval hereof, or by the approval hereof by his duly authorized representative, does hereby establish, alter, change, or revoke the drilling, producing, rental, minimum royalty, and royalty requirements of Federal leases committed hereto and the regulations in respect thereto to conform said requirements to the provisions of this agreement, and, without limiting the generality of the foregoing, all leases, subleases, and contracts are particularly modified in accordance with the following:

(a) The development and operation of lands subject to this agreement under the terms hereof shall be deemed full performance of all obligations for development and operation with respect to each and every separately owned tract subject to this agreement, regardless of whether there is any development of any particular tract of this unit area.

(b) Drilling and producing operations performed hereunder upon any tract of unitized lands will be accepted and deemed to be performed upon and for the benefit of each and every tract of unitized land, and no lease shall be deemed to expire by reason of failure to drill or produce wells situated on the land therein embraced.

(c) Suspension of drilling or producing operations on all unitized lands pursuant to direction or consent of the AO shall be deemed to constitute such suspension pursuant to such direction or consent as to each and every tract of unitized land. A suspension of drilling or producing operations limited to specified lands shall be applicable only to such lands.

(d) Each lease, sublease, or contract relating to the exploration, drilling, development, or operation for oil or gas of lands other than those of the United States committed to this agreement which, by its terms might expire prior to the termination of this agreement, is hereby extended beyond any such term so provided therein so that it shall be continued in full force and effect for and during the term of this agreement.

(e) Any Federal lease committed hereto shall continue in force beyond the term so provided therein or by law as to the land committed so long as such lease remains subject hereto, provided that production of unitized substances in paying quantities is established under this unit agreement prior to the expiration date of the term of such lease, or in the event actual drilling operations are commenced on unitized land, in accordance with provisions of this agreement, prior to the end of the primary term of such lease and are being diligently prosecuted at that time, such lease shall be extended for 2 years, and so long thereafter as oil or gas is produced in paying quantities in accordance with the provisions of the Mineral Leasing Act, as amended.

(f) Each sublease or contract relating to the operation and development of unitized substances from lands of the United States committed to this agreement, which by its terms

436

1 would expire prior to the time at which the underlying lease, as extended by the immediately
2 preceding paragraph, will expire is hereby extended beyond any such term so provided therein so
3 that it shall be continued in full force and effect for and during the term of the underlying lease
4 as such term is herein extended.

5 (g) The segregation of any Federal lease committed to this agreement is governed by the
6 following provision in the fourth paragraph of sec. 17(m) of the Mineral Leasing Act, as
7 amended by the Act of September 2, 1960 (74 Stat. 781–784) (30 U.S.C. 226(m)):

8 "Any [Federal] lease heretofore or hereafter committed to any such [unit] plan embracing
9 lands that are in part within and in part outside of the area covered by any such plan shall be
10 segregated into separate leases as to the lands committed and the lands not committed as of the
11 effective date of unitization: *Provided, however,* That any such lease as to the nonunitized
12 portion shall continue in force and effect for the term thereof but for not less than two years from
13 the date of such segregation and so long thereafter as oil or gas is produced in paying quantities."

14 If the public interest requirement is not satisfied, the segregation of a lease and/or extension
15 of a lease pursuant to 43 CFR 3107.3–2 and 43 CFR 3107.4, respectively, shall not be effective.

16 ³ (h) Any lease, other than a Federal lease, having only a portion of its lands committed
17 hereto shall be segregated as to the portion committed and the portion not committed, and the
18 provisions of such lease shall apply separately to such segregated portions commencing as of the
19 effective date hereof. In the event any such lease provides for a lump-sum rental payment, such
20 payment shall be prorated between the portions so segregated in proportion to the acreage of the
21 respective tracts.

22 19. CONVENANTS RUN WITH LAND. The covenants herein shall be construed to be
23 covenants running with the land with respect to the interests of the parties hereto and their
24 successors in interest until this agreement terminates, and any grant, transfer or conveyance of
25 interest in land or leases subject hereto shall be and hereby is conditioned upon the assumption of
26 all privileges and obligations hereunder by the grantee, transferee, or other successor in interest.
27 No assignment or transfer of any working interest, royalty, or other interest subject hereto shall
28 be binding upon Unit Operator until the first day of the calendar month after Unit Operator is
29 furnished with the original, photostatic, or certified copy of the instrument of transfer.

30 20. EFFECTIVE DATE AND TERM. This agreement shall become effective upon
31 approval by the AO and shall automatically terminate 5 years from said effective date unless:

32 (a) Upon application by the Unit Operator such date of expiration is extended by the AO, or

33 (b) It is reasonably determined prior to the expiration of the fixed term or any extension
34 thereof that the unitized land is incapable of production of unitized substances in paying
35 quantities in the formations tested hereunder, and after notice of intention to terminate this
36 agreement on such ground is given by the Unit Operator to all parties in interest at their last
37 known addresses, this agreement is terminated with the approval of the AO, or

38 (c) A valuable discovery of unitized substances in paying quantities has been made or
39 accepted on unitized land during said initial term or any extension thereof, in which event this
40 agreement shall remain in effect for such term and so long thereafter as unitized substances can
41 be produced in quantities sufficient to pay for the cost of producing same from wells on unitized
42 land within any participating area established hereunder. Should production cease and diligent
43 drilling or reworking operations to restore production or new production are not in progress
44 within 60 days and production is not restored or should new production not be obtained in paying
45 quantities on committed lands within this unit area, this agreement will automatically terminate
46 effective the last day of the month in which the last unitized production occurred, or

(d) It is voluntarily terminated as provided in this agreement. Except as noted herein, this agreement may be terminated at any time prior to the discovery of unitized substances which can be produced in paying quantities by not less than 75 per centum, on an acreage basis, of the working interest owners signatory hereto, with the approval of the AO. The Unit Operator shall give notice of any such approval to all parties hereto. If the public interest requirement is not satisfied, the approval of this unit by the AO shall be invalid.

21. RATE OF PROSPECTING, DEVELOPMENT, AND PRODUCTION. The AO is hereby vested with authority to alter or modify from time to time, in his discretion, the quantity and rate of production under this agreement when such quantity and rate are not fixed pursuant to Federal or State law, or do not conform to any Statewide voluntary conservation or allocation program which is established, recognized, and generally adhered to by the majority of operators in such State. The above authority is hereby limited to alteration or modifications which are in the public interest. The public interest to be served and the purpose thereof, must be stated in the order of alteration or modification. Without regard to the foregoing, the AO is also hereby vested with authority to alter or modify from time to time, in his discretion, the rate of prospecting and development and the quantity and rate of production under this agreement when such alteration or modification is in the interest of attaining the conservation objectives stated in this agreement and is not in violation of any applicable Federal or State law.

Powers is the section vested in the AO shall only be exercised after notice to Unit Operator and opportunity for hearing to be held not less than 15 days from notice.

22. APPEARANCES. The Unit Operator shall, after notice to other parties affected, have the right to appear for and on behalf of any and all interests affected hereby before the Department of the Interior and to appeal from orders issued under the regulations of said Department, or to apply for relief from any of said regulations, or in any proceedings relative to operations before the Department, or any other legally constituted authority; provided, however, that any other interested party shall also have the right at its own expense to be heard in any such proceeding.

23. NOTICES. All notices, demands, or statements required hereunder to be given or rendered to the parties hereto shall be in writing and shall be personally delivered to the party or parties, or sent by postpaid registered or certified mail, to the last-known address of the party or parties.

24. NO WAIVER OF CERTAIN RIGHTS. Nothing contained in this agreement shall be construed as a waiver by any party hereto of the right to assert any legal or constitutional right or defense as to the validity or invalidity of any law of the State where the unitized lands are located, or of the United States, or regulations issued thereunder in any way affecting such party, or as a waiver by any such party of any right beyond his or its authority to waive.

25. UNAVOIDABLE DELAY. All obligations under this agreement requiring the Unit Operator to commence or continue drilling, or to operate on, or produce unitized substances from any of the lands covered by this agreement, shall be suspended while the Unit Operator, despite the exercise of due care and diligence, is prevented from complying with such obligations, in whole or in part, by strikes, acts of God, Federal, State, or municipal law or agencies, unavoidable accidents, uncontrollable delays in transportation, inability to obtain necessary materials or equipment in the open market, or other matters beyond the reasonable control of the Unit Operator, whether similar to matters herein enumerated or not.

26. NONDISCRIMINATION. In connection with the performance of work under this agreement, the Unit Operator agrees to comply with all the provisions of section 202 (1) to (7)

1 inclusive, of Executive Order 11246 (30 FR 12319), as amended, which are hereby incorporated
2 by reference in this agreement.

3   27. LOSS OF TITLE. In the event title to any tract of unitized land shall fail and the true
4 owner cannot be induced to join in this unit agreement, such tract shall be automatically regarded
5 as not committed hereto, and there shall be such readjustment of future costs and benefits as may
6 be required on account of the loss of such title. In the event of a dispute as to title to any royalty,
7 working interest, or other interests subject thereto, payment or delivery on account thereof may
8 be withheld without liability for interest until the dispute is finally settled; provided, that, as to
9 Federal lands or leases, no payments of funds due the United States shall be withheld, but such
10 funds shall be deposited as directed by the AO, to be held as unearned money pending final
11 settlement of the title dispute, and then applied as earned or returned in accordance with such
12 final settlement.

13   Unit Operator as such is relieved from any responsibility for any defect or failure of any
14 title hereunder.

15   28. NONJOINDER AND SUBSEQUENT JOINDER. If the owner of any substantial
16 interest in a tract within the unit area fails or refuses to subscribe or consent to this agreement,
17 the owner of the working interest in that tract may withdraw the tract from this agreement by
18 written notice delivered to the proper BLM office and the Unit Operator prior to the approval of
19 this agreement by the AO. Any oil or gas interests in lands within the unit area not committed
20 hereto prior to final approval may thereafter be committed hereto by the owner or owners thereof
21 subscribing or consenting to this agreement, and, if the interest is a working interest, by the
22 owner of such interest also subscribing to the unit operating agreement. After operations are
23 commenced hereunder, the right of subsequent joinder, as provided in this section, by a working
24 interest owner is subject to such requirements or approval(s), if any, pertaining to such joinder,
25 as may be provided for in the unit operating agreement. After final approval hereof, joinder by a
26 nonworking interest owner must be consented to in writing by the working interest owner
27 committed hereto and responsible for the payment of any benefits that may accrue hereunder in
28 behalf of such nonworking interest. A nonworking interest may not be committed to this unit
29 agreement unless the corresponding working interest is committed hereto. Joinder to the unit
30 agreement by a working interest owner, at any time, must be accompanied by appropriate joinder
31 to the unit operating agreement, in order for the interest to be regarded as committed to this
32 agreement. Except as may otherwise herein be provided, subsequent joinders to this agreement
33 shall be effective as of the date of the filing with the AO of duly executed counterparts of all or
34 any papers necessary to establish effective commitment of any interest and/or tract to this
35 agreement.

36   29. COUNTERPARTS. This agreement may be executed in any number of counterparts, no
37 one of which needs to be executed by all parties, or may be ratified or consented to by separate
38 instrument in writing specifically referring hereto and shall be binding upon all those parties who
39 have executed such a counterpart, ratification, or consent hereto with the same force and effect as
40 if all such parties had signed the same document, and regardless of whether or not it is executed
41 by all other parties owning or claiming an interest in the lands within the above-described unit
42 area.

43   [4] 30. SURRENDER. Nothing in this agreement shall prohibit the exercise by any working
44 interest owner of the right to surrender vested in such party by any lease, sublease, or operating
45 agreement as to all or any part of the lands covered thereby, provided that each party who will or

might acquire such working interest by such surrender or by forfeiture as hereafter set forth, is bound by the terms of this agreement.

If as a result of any such surrender, the working interest rights as to such lands become vested in any party other than the fee owner of the unitized substances, said party may forfeit such rights and further benefits from operations hereunder as to said land to the party next in the chain of title who shall be and become the owner of such working interest.

If as the result of any such surrender or forfeiture working interest rights become vested in the fee owner of the unitized substances, such owner may:

(a) Accept those working interest rights subject to this agreement and the unit operating agreement; or

(b) Lease the portion of such land as is included in a participating area established hereunder subject to this agreement and the unit operating agreement; or

(c) Provide for the independent operation of any part of such land that is not then included within a participating area established hereunder.

If the fee owner of the unitized substances does not accept the working interest rights subject to this agreement and the unit operating agreement or lease such lands as above provided within 6 months after the surrendered or forfeited, working interest rights become vested in the fee owner; the benefits and obligations of operations accruing to such lands under this agreement and the unit operating agreement shall be shared by the remaining owners of unitized working interests in accordance with their respective working interest ownerships, and such owners of working interests shall compensate the fee owner of unitized substances in such lands by paying sums equal to the rentals, minimum royalties, and royalties applicable to such lands under the lease in effect when the lands were unitized.

An appropriate accounting and settlement shall be made for all benefits accruing to or payments and expenditures made or incurred on behalf of such surrendered or forfeited working interests subsequent to the date of surrender or forfeiture, and payment of any moneys found to be owing by such an accounting shall be made as between the parties within 30 days.

The exercise of any right vested in a working interest owner to reassign such working interest to the party from whom obtained shall be subject to the same conditions as set forth in this section in regard to the exercise of a right to surrender.

[4] 31. TAXES. The working interest owners shall render and pay for their account and the account of the royalty owners all valid taxes on or measured by the unitized substances in and under or that may be produced, gathered and sold from the land covered by this agreement after its effective date, or upon the proceeds derived therefrom. The working interest owners on each tract shall and may charge the proper proportion of said taxes to royalty owners having interests in said-tract, and may currently retain and deduct a sufficient amount of the unitized substances or derivative products, or net proceeds thereof, from the allocated share of each royalty owner to secure reimbursement for the taxes so paid. No such taxes shall be charged to the United States or the State of __ or to any lessor who has a contract with his lessee which requires the lessee to pay such taxes.

[4] 32. NO PARTNERSHIP. It is expressly agreed that the relation of the parties hereto is that of independent contractors and nothing contained in this agreement, expressed or implied, nor any operations conducted hereunder, shall create or be deemed to have created a partnership or association between the parties hereto or any of them.

IN WITNESS WHEREOF, the parties hereto have caused this agreement to be executed and have set opposite their respective names the date of execution.

_____

Unit Operator

_____

Working Interest Owners

_____

Other Interest Owners

General Guidelines

1. Executed agreement to be legally complete.

2. Agreement submitted for approval must contain Exhibit A and B in accordance with models shown in §§3186.1–1 and 3186.1–2 of this title.

3. Consents should be identified (in pencil) by tract numbers as listed in Exhibit B and assembled in that order as far as practical. Unit agreements submitted for approval shall include a list of the overriding royalty interest owners who have executed ratifications of the unit agreement. Subsequent joinders by overriding royalty interest owners shall be submitted in the same manner, except each must include or be accompanied by a statement that the corresponding working interest owner has consented in writing to such joinder. Original ratifications of overriding royalty owners will be kept on file by the Unit Operator or his designated agent.

4. All leases held by option should be noted on Exhibit B with an explanation as to the type of option, i.e., whether for operating rights only, for full leasehold record title, or for certain interests to be earned by performance. In all instances, optionee committing such interests is expected to exercise option promptly.

5. All owners of oil and gas interests must be invited to join the unit agreement, and statement to that effect must accompany executed agreement, together with summary of results of such invitations. A written reason for all interest owners who have not joined shall be furnished by the unit operator.

6. In the event fish and wildlife lands are included, add the following as a separate section:

"Wildlife Stipulation. Nothing in this unit agreement shall modify the special Federal lease stipulations applicable to lands under the jurisdiction of the United States Fish and Wildlife Service."

7. In the event National Forest System lands are included within the unit area, add the following as a separate section:

"Forest Land Stipulation. Notwithstanding any other terms and conditions contained in this agreement, all of the stipulations and conditions of the individual leases between the United States and its lessees or their successors or assigns embracing lands within the unit area included for the protection of lands or functions under the jurisdiction of the Secretary of Agriculture shall remain in full force and effect the same as though this agreement had not been entered into, and no modification thereof is authorized except with the prior consent in writing of the Regional Forester, United States Forest Service, _____ , _____

8. In the event National Forest System lands within the Jackson Hole Area of Wyoming are included within the unit area, additional "special" stipulations may be required to be included in the unit agreement by the U.S. Forest Service, including the Jackson Hole Special Stipulation.

9. In the event reclamation lands are included, add the following as a new separate section:

"Reclamation Lands. Nothing in this agreement shall modify the special, Federal lease stipulations applicable to lands under the jurisdiction of the Bureau of Reclamation."

10. In the event a power site is embraced in the proposed unit area, the following section should be added:

"Power site. Nothing in this agreement shall modify the special, Federal lease stipulations applicable to lands under the jurisdiction of the Federal Energy Regulatory Commission."

11. In the event special surface stipulations have been attached to any of the Federal oil and gas leases to be included, add the following as a separate section:

"Special surface stipulations. Nothing in this agreement shall modify the special Federal lease stipulations attached to the individual Federal oil leases."

12. In the event State lands are included in the proposed unit area, add the appropriate State Lands Section as separate section.

(See §3181.4(a) of this title).

13. In the event restricted Indian lands are involved, consult the AO regarding appropriate requirements under §3181.4(b) of this title.

Certification—Determination

Pursuant to the authority vested in the Secretary of the Interior, under the Act approved February 25, 1920, 41 Stat. 437, as amended, 30 U.S.C. sec. 181, *et seq.,* and delegated to (the appropriate Name and Title of the authorized officer, BLM) under the authority of 43 CFR part 3180, I do hereby:

A. Approve the attached agreement for the development and operation of the __, Unit Area, State of ___. This approval shall be invalid *ab initio* if the public interest requirement under §3183.4(b) of this title is not met.

B. Certify and determine that the unit plan of development and operation contemplated in the attached agreement is necessary and advisable in the public interest for the purpose of more properly conserving the natural resources.

C. Certify and determine that the drilling, producing, rental, minimum royalty, and royalty requirements of all Federal leases committed to said agreement are hereby established altered, changed, or revoked to conform with the terms and conditions of this agreement.

Dated ____.

_____

(Name and Title of authorized officer of the Bureau of Land Management)

[1] Optional sections (in addition the penultimate paragraph of Section 9 is to be included only when more than one obligation well is required and paragraph (h) of section 18 is to be used only when applicable).

[2] Provisions to be included only when a multiple well obligation is required.

[3] Optional paragraph to be used only when applicable.

[4] Optional sections and subsection. (Agreements submitted for final approval should not identify section or provision as "optional.")

R. 59 W.

DEER 6-30-88 16 (7) 78-620	FROST 6-30-81 15 (1) W-8470	FROST 6-30-81 14 (1) W-8470	DOE 5-31-82 13 (8) J.C. Smith
FROST 6-30-85 21 (3) W-41345	SMITH 5-31-82 22 (9) T.J. Cook	FROST 6-30-81 23 (1) W-8470	HOLDER 2-28-86 24 (6) W-53970
FROST 6-30-85 28 (3) W-41345	DEER et al. 27 (4) W-41679	DEER 12-31-85 26 (5) W-52780	HOLDER 2-28-86 (6) 25 DEER 12-31-85 (5) W-52780
DEER et al. 6-30-85 33 (4) W-41679	DEER 6-30-82 34 (10) Swan, et al	DEER 7-31-81 35 (2) W-9123	DEER 6-30-88 (7) 36 78-620

T. 54 N.

(1) Means tract number as listed on Exhibit B

☐ Public Land

Public Land

State Land

Patented Land

Scale - Generally 2" = 1 mile.

Include acreage for all irregular sections and lots.

§ 3186.1-2 Model Exhibit "B".
Swan Unit Area, Campbell County, Wyoming

Tract No.	Description of land	No. of acres	Serial No. and expiration date of lease	Basic royalty and ownership percentage	Lessee of record	Overriding royalty and percentage	Working interest and percentage
	All in the area of T54N–R59W, 6th P.M.						
	Federal Land						
1	Sec. 14: All	1,920.00	W–8470, 6–30–81	U.S.: All	T.J. Cook 100%	T.J. Cook 2%	Frost Oil Co. 100%.
	Sec. 15: All						
	Sec. 23: All						
2	Sec. 35: All	640.00	W–9123, 7–	U.S.: All	O.M.	O.M. Odom	Deer Oil Co.

			31–81		Odom 100%	1%	100%.
3	Sec. 21: All	1,280.00	W–41345, 6–30–85	U.S.: All	Max Pen 50%	Max Pen 1%	Frost Oil Co. 100%.
	Sec. 28: All				Sam Small 50%	Sam Small 1%	
4	Sec. 27: All	1,280.00	W–41679, 6–30–85	U.S.: All	Al Preen 100%	Al Preen 2%	Deer Oil Co. 50%.
							Doe Oil Co.,30%
							Able Drilling Co. 20%.
	Sec. 33: All						Deer Oil Co. 50%.
							Doe Oil Co., 30%
							Able Drilling Co. 20%.
5	Sec. 26: All	961.50	W–52780,12–31–85	U.S.: All	Deer Oil Co. 100%	J.G. Goodin 2%	Deer Oil Co. 100%.
	Sec. 25: Lots 3,4, SW 1/4, W 1/2SE 1/4						
6	Sec. 24: Lots 1,2,3,4,W 1/2, W 1/2E 1/2 (All)	965.80	W–53970, 2–28–86	U.S.: All	T.H. Holder 100%		T.H. Holder 100%.
	Sec. 25: Lots 1,2,NW 1/4, W 1/2NE/4						
	6 Federal tracts totalling 7,047.30 acres or 68.76018% of unit area						

	State Land						
7	Sec. 16: All	1,280.60	78620, 6–30–88	State: All	Deer Oil Co. 100%	T.T. Timo 2%	Deer Oil Co. 100%.
	Sec. 36: Lots 1, 2, 3, 4, W 1/2, W 1/2E 1/2 (All)						
	1 State tract totalling 1,280.60 acres or 12.49476% of unit area.						
	Patented Land						
8	Sec. 13: Lots 1, 2, 3, 4, W 1/2, W 1/2E 1/2 (All)	641.20	5–31–82	J.C. Smith: 100%	Doe Oil Co. 100%		Doe Oil Co. 100%.
9	Sec. 22: All	640.00	5–31–82	T.J. Cook: 100%	W.W. Smith 100%	Sam Spade 1%	W.W. Smith 100%.
10	Sec. 34: All	640.00	6–30–82	A.A. Aben: 75%, L.P. Carr: 25%	Deer Oil Co. 100%		Deer Oil Co. 100%.
	3 Patented tracts totalling 1,921.20 acres or 18.74506% of unit area						
Total: 10 tracts 10,249.10 acres in entire unit area.							

NOTES

1.   Unlike private leases, which are usually unitized only when secondary or enhanced recovery operations are undertaken, federal leases are often unitized for exploratory and primary development purposes. The special attributes of federal exploratory units are detailed at pages 991-998 of the casebook.

2.   The federal form for unit operations on unproven land, which is set out above, is taken from 43 C.F.R. Subpart 3186. Additional related forms can also be found in this subpart. See http://ecfr.gpoaccess.gov/cgi/t/text/text-idx?c=ecfr&tpl=%2Findex.tpl

Chapter 7

ENVIRONMENTAL REGULATION OF
THE OIL & GAS INDUSTRY

Lessor's Lease Addendum
Environmental and Indemnity Clauses

1. Land Use Restrictions. To the maximum extent feasible, LESSEE will minimize the use of surface pits and hazardous materials in drilling operations on the Leased Land. Any pits, ponds, or other surface impoundments used in connection with the development or operation of the Leased Land shall comply with all applicable local, state, and federal standards and in any case shall meet or exceed the standards for such structures located within a wellhead protection or critical aquifer protection area as defined by the federal Safe Drinking Water Act or any state law counterpart. Any pit or other surface disruption associated with drilling operations on the Leased Land will be fully reclaimed and restored to its natural condition immediately following the completion of drilling operations. All substances brought onto the Leased Land, and wastes generated as part of the exploration, development, or production process, will be removed from the Leased Land immediately following the completion of drilling operations. All equipment designed to separate, dehydrate, treat, compress, process, or otherwise condition Leased Substances will be located off of the Leased Land. Any tanks used to collect and store a Leased Substance prior to marketing will be located off of the Leased Land. No injection or disposal well will be placed on the area encompassed by the Leased Land. No pipe, chemicals, or other material or equipment will be placed on the Leased Land except items that are on-site for immediate use in operations. Equipment or material placed on site and not actively used for ten consecutive days will be deemed not to be for immediate use in operations. Within five days after a development or production operation is completed, all the associated development structures, equipment, and any other material brought to or generated at the site will be removed from the site. If any topsoil has been disturbed by the operation, the area will be graded to its original contour, and the topsoil replaced, properly seeded, fertilized, and maintained until the original cover in the affected area is reestablished.

2. Assumption of Liability. LESSEE assumes the following liabilities associated with the Leased Land: LESSEE acknowledges that it is entering into this Lease without relying on any representations by LESSOR concerning the condition, environmental or otherwise, of the Leased Land. Instead, LESSEE is relying solely upon its independent investigation to determine the status of the Leased Land. As partial consideration for this Lease, LESSEE agrees to assume all liabilities it may incur as an owner or operator of the Leased Land, including any environmental cleanup obligations that may be imposed under any local, state, or federal law, including the common law. LESSEE further agrees to hold LESSOR harmless from any claim LESSEE may have or acquire, in contribution or otherwise, associated with the condition of the property or LESSEE's liability as an owner or operator. This includes, without limitation, any claim or cause of action LESSEE may have at common law or under any local, state, or federal statute such as the Comprehensive Environmental Response, Compensation and Liability Act (CERCLA) or a state or local counterpart. LESSEE agrees to assume all liabilities associated with any activity conducted on the Leased Land, by LESSEE, its contractors, and any other person or entity exercising or purporting to exercise rights through LESSEE or on LESSEE's behalf.

3. Agreement to Remedy Environmental Problems. LESSEE agrees to remedy any Environmental Problem resulting from, arising out of, or in any manner associated with any activity by LESSEE, its contractors, and any other person or entity exercising or purporting to exercise rights through LESSEE or on LESSEE's behalf, that presently impacts, or is likely to impact, the Leased Land. In the event an Environmental Problem is identified, LESSOR will give LESSEE notice of the Environmental Problem and LESSEE will, at its sole risk and expense, take the necessary action to define and remedy the Environmental Problem. For purposes of this section, "Environmental Problem" means any situation which: violates any local, state, or federal requirement, is reportable under any environmental law, gives rise to a cleanup, sampling, testing, monitoring, assessment, or similar obligation under any common law, statutory, or regulatory theory, concerns conditions, structures, or substances that require special environmental handling for their proper renovation, demolition, or disposal, or exposes LESSOR to a substantial threat of liability associated with the health, safety, and welfare of the public, workers, or the environment.

4. Agreement to Indemnify. LESSEE will protect, indemnify, hold harmless, and defend LESSOR against any claim, demand, cost, liability, loss, or damage suffered by LESSOR (including LESSOR's reasonable attorney fees and litigation costs) resulting from, arising out of, or associated with one or more of the following events: LESSEE's breach of any covenant, obligation, or duty created by the terms of this Lease. LESSEE's failure to comply with the LESSOR's retained rights under this Lease. Any matter encompassed by LESSEE's assumption of liabilities, including environmental liabilities, under the terms of this Lease. Any activity expressly or impliedly authorized or required by this Lease. Any matter associated with producing wells, nonproducing wells, existing wellbores, unplugged wells, or previously plugged wellbores. Any matter associated with the management, use, and disposal of produced water and wastes or substances associated with the development or operation of the Leased Land. Any matter associated with this Lease relating to the generation, processing, handling, transportation, storage, treatment, recycling, marketing, use, disposal, release or discharge, or threatened release or discharge, of oil, natural gas, natural gas liquids, all other petroleum substances, any waste material, or any "hazardous substance" or "pollutant or contaminant" as those terms are defined (now or in the future) under CERCLA and its state counterpart. Any matter relating to LESSEE's ownership, use, or occupancy of the Leased Land or any area impacting the Leased Land. LESSEE's obligations created by this Section are continuing obligations which will remain in effect, and be enforceable by LESSOR, even after the Lease terminates or otherwise ceases to burden the Leased Land. In the event LESSOR conveys or assigns all or any part of its interest in the Leased Land, LESSOR will nevertheless continue to be covered by LESSEE's indemnity. However, LESSOR's grantees or assignees will also be covered by LESSEE's indemnity to the extent of the interest they receive in the Leased Land. LESSEE's indemnity obligation will apply even though the basis for LESSOR's liability arises out of LESSOR's statutory or common law strict liability, sole or concurrent negligence, or any other statutory, tort, or contract theory.

NOTES

1.   This form attempts to provide the Lessor with broad protection against environmental claims that may be raised by their lessee and also leverages the Lessor's third-party environmental risk associated with the lessee's development activities. The "Environmental Problem" provisions in paragraph c. are designed to protect the Lessor from situations where the property may be contaminated but it is not being pursued by a regulatory agency or a third party. Absent such a provision a lessee may balk at conducting a cleanup until the problem becomes the subject of a regulatory proceeding or a third-party action.

2.   In the next-to-the-last sentence in paragraph 4 the lessee's indemnity is made assignable and divisible. If the lessee is financially sound, such a provision becomes a sort of environmental insurance which passes with the property and should make it more valuable—or at least displace some of the devaluation associated with the environmental risks of historical mineral development on the property.

* * *

3.   RESTRICTIVE COVENANTS. Grantee promises to comply with the following restrictions concerning the rights it is receiving in the Land by this Conveyance (the "Conveyed Property"), which shall be deemed covenants that run with the Conveyed Property:

a.   Pits.   No pits, ponds, or other surface impoundments will be used in developing or operating the Conveyed Property.

b.   Production-Related Equipment and Storage Tanks. No above ground or underground storage tanks will be placed on the area encompassed by the Conveyed Property. No equipment designed to separate, treat, dehydrate, compress, or process the Conveyed Property will be placed on the area encompassed by the Conveyed Property.

c.   Injection and Waste Disposal. No injection or disposal well will be placed on the area encompassed by the Conveyed Property. No solid, liquid, or gaseous waste will be stored or disposed of on the area encompassed by the Conveyed Property.

d.   Hazardous Substances. No substance, defined as a "hazardous substance" (now or in the future) under the federal Comprehensive Environmental Response, Compensation and Liability Act ("CERCLA"), the Kansas statutory counterpart to CERCLA, and any amendments or substitutions for CERCLA and its Kansas counterpart, will be brought onto the area encompassed by the Conveyed Property.

e.   Storage of Equipment or Material. No pipe, chemicals, or other material or equipment will be placed on the area encompassed by the Conveyed Property except items that are on-site for immediate use in operations. Equipment or material placed on site for longer than five consecutive days will be deemed not to be for immediate use in operations.

f.   Restore Development and Production Areas. Within five days after a development or production operation is completed, all the associated development structures, equipment, and any other material brought to or generated at the site will be removed from the site. If any topsoil has been disturbed by the operation, the area will be graded to its original contour, and the topsoil replaced, properly seeded, fertilized, and maintained until the original cover in the affected area is reestablished.

g.   Set-Back Requirements. No equipment, material, or operation site will be located within 300 feet of any house, garage, barn, stream, creek, pond, lake, or other structure, improvement, or water source located on the area encompassed by the Conveyed Property.

4.   LEGAL AND EQUITABLE RELIEF. Grantee acknowledges that Grantor may, in addition to damages and any other remedy at law or equity, obtain injunctive relief to enforce the covenants specified in this conveyance.

5.   GRANTEE'S ASSUMPTION OF LIABILITY. Grantee assumes the following liabilities associated with the Conveyed Property:

a.   Condition of the Area Encompassed by the Conveyed property. Grantee acknowledges that it is purchasing the Conveyed Property without relying on any representations by Grantor concerning the condition, environmental or otherwise, of the conveyed Property or the area encompassed by the Conveyed Property. Instead, Grantee is relying solely upon its independent investigation to determine the status of the Conveyed Property and the area encompassed by the conveyed Property. As partial consideration for this conveyance, Grantee agrees to assume all liabilities it may incur as an owner or operator of the Conveyed Property and the area encompassed by the Conveyed Property, including any environmental cleanup obligations that may be imposed under any local, state, or federal law, including the common law. Grantee further agrees to hold Grantor harmless from any claim Grantee may have or acquire, in contribution or otherwise, associated with the condition of the property or Acme's liability as an owner or operator. This includes, without limitation, any claim or cause of action Grantee may have at common law or under any local, state, or federal statute such as CERCLA or a state or local counterpart.

b. **Activities on the Area Encompassed by the Conveyed Property.** Grantee agrees to assume all liabilities associated with any activity conducted on the conveyed Property or the area encompassed by the Conveyed Property, by Grantee, its lessees, contractors, and any other person or entity exercising or purporting to exercise rights through Grantee or on Grantee's behalf. In addition to such liabilities, Grantee will be strictly liable for any damage to: cultivated land, growing crops, pasture land, unimproved land, livestock, fences, roads, ditches, culverts, trees, turf, terraces, springs, water wells, groundwater, personal property, fixtures, and improvements located now or in the future on the area encompassed by the conveyed Property.

6. **GRANTEE'S INDEMNITY OF GRANTOR.** Grantee will protect, indemnify, hold harmless, and defend Grantor against any claim, demand, cost, liability, loss, or damage suffered by Grantor, including Grantor's reasonable attorney fees and litigation costs, associated with or arising out of one or more of the following events:

a. **Breach of Covenant.** A breach of any restrictive covenant contained in paragraph numbered 3 of this conveyance.

b. **Assumption of Liability.** Any matter encompassed by Acme's assumption of liabilities, including environmental liabilities, under paragraph numbered 4 of this conveyance.

c. **Specific operations.**

   (1) Any activity expressly or impliedly authorized or required by this Conveyance.

   (2) Plugging and abandonment of producing wells nonproducing wells, existing wellbores, or previously plugged wellbores.

   (3) Management, use, and disposal of produced water and wastes or substances associated with the development or operation of the Conveyed Property.

   (4) Grantee's generation, processing, handling, transportation, storage, treatment, recycling, marketing, use, disposal, release or discharge, or threatened release or discharge, of oil, natural gas, natural gas liquids, all other petroleum substances, any waste material, or any "hazardous substance" or "pollutant or contaminant" as those terms are defined (now or in the future) under the federal Comprehensive Environmental Response, Compensation and Liability Act ("CERCLA"), the Kansas statutory counterpart to CERCLA, and any amendments or substitutions for CERCLA and its Kansas counterpart.

d. Other Matters. Any matter relating to Grantee's ownership, use, or occupancy of the Conveyed Property or the area encompassed by the Conveyed Property.

* * *

NOTES

1. By granting a mineral interest to a third party, the landowner creates the opportunity for an outside party to enter the property and do things, such as drilling oil and gas wells or authorizing others to drill wells, that can increase the landowner's environmental risk. Therefore, if the grantor is going to retain an interest in the property from which the mineral interest is being conveyed, the conveyance document should contain the necessary provisions to protect the grantor.

2. The form provisions seek to protect the grantor first by imposing restrictive covenants on the grantee to limit how development can be pursued on the property. Second, paragraph 5 seeks to protect the grantor from claims that might be raised by the grantee and third parties. Third, paragraph 6 provides the grantor with indemnity for grantee-related activities on the land. However, an agreement to indemnify does not shift the legal liability of the indemnified party— it merely shifts the ultimate economic burden of liability and then, of course, only to the extent the indemnifying party is able to perform its indemnity obligations.